History and Human Nature

Previous books by the author:

From Rationalism to Existentialism

The Passions

Introducing Philosophy

Books edited by the author:

Phenomenology and Existentialism

Nietzsche

Existentialism

History and Human Nature

*A Philosophical Review
of European Philosophy
and Culture, 1750–1850*

Robert C. Solomon

Harcourt Brace Jovanovich, New York and London

Requests for permission to make copies of
any part of the work should be mailed to:
Permissions, Harcourt Brace Jovanovich, Inc.
757 Third Avenue, New York, N.Y. 10017

Excerpts from Voltaire, *Philosophical Letters*, translated by Ernest Dilworth,
reprinted by permission of Bobbs-Merrill Co.

Excerpts from Jean-Jacques Rousseau, *The Social Contract*, translated by
Charles M. Sherover, reprinted by permission of New American Library.

Excerpts from Jean-Jacques Rousseau, *Discourse on the Origins of Inequality
among Men*, translated by Cole, reprinted by permission of E. P. Dutton
and J. M. Dent, Ltd.

Excerpts from Goethe's *Faust*, translation copyright © 1961 by Walter
Kaufmann, reprinted by permission of Doubleday & Company, Inc.

Excerpts from Hegel's early manuscripts and from the *Introduction* to the
Critique of Hegel's Theory of the State are from *Karl Marx: Early Writings*,
translated by T. Bottomore, copyright © 1964. Used with permission of
McGraw-Hill Book Company.

Excerpts from *Mill* and the text of Marx's *Critique of Hegel's Theory of
the State* are from *Early Writings* by Karl Marx, edited by Quentin Hoare,
translated by Gregor Benton and Rodney Livingstone, with an introduction
by Lucio Coletti, translation copyright © 1974 by Rodney Livingstone;
selection and notes copyright © 1974 by *New Left Review*. Reprinted by
permission of Random House, Inc., and Penguin Books Ltd.

Printed in the United States of America

Library of Congress Cataloging in Publication Data

Solomon, Robert C
History and human nature.

Includes bibliographical references and index.
1. Philosophy, Modern—18th century. 2. Philos-
ophy, Modern—19th century. 3. Europe—Civilization.
I. Title.
B802.S66   001.4'094   79–1846
ISBN 0–15–140547–6

First edition

B C D E

For Katy Marshall, Paris, the summer of '72

*And to Kristine Hanson, for Spring
and springs to come*

Contents

Preface

> One more word about giving instructions as to what the world ought to be. Philosophy in any case comes on the scene too late to give it. As the thought of the world, it appears only when actuality is already there, cut and dried, after its process of formation has been completed. . . . When philosophy paints its grey on grey . . . it cannot be rejuvenated but only understood. The owl of Minerva spreads its wings only with the falling of dusk.
>
> G. W. F. Hegel

My aim in this book is twofold: first, I want to offer the general reader a cross-disciplinary portrait of a particularly fascinating period in modern European history and culture, 1750–1850. My focus is philosophy in France and Germany (Britain requires another book, a different period of time). Second, I want to argue a philosophically contentious thesis about the nature of history—or rather, about our own peculiar history and ideas about history, human nature, and "humanity." This argument contends that these ideas are profoundly pretentious and have reached their twilight, as Hegel suggested over 150 years ago in his birdbrain image of Western wisdom: "The owl of Minerva spreads its wings only with the falling of dusk."

Several years ago I taught a course called "The Philosophy of History." Its function was to debate—endlessly, it seemed—whether human history has progressed in a straight line or not at all, or in circles, spirals, or sine curves; whether it has a purpose or a pattern or is just, in the words of the poet John Masefield, "one damn thing after another." But if Lewis Carroll's Alice found that history was "the driest thing in the world," my students and I were soon desiccated by a subject still drier, as we tried to condense four thousand years of historical trauma and accomplishment into simple Voltairean, Hegelian, Marxian, and Toynbeean platitudes. "I'm tempted to say that over-simplification is the philosopher's professional hazard," commented the late J. L. Austin of Oxford, "except that I'm also tempted to say that it is his profession." The problem, however, turned out to be much more than mere "oversimplification." The very idea of the "purpose of history"—"universal history," as it was so quaintly entitled in the last century—was an outrageous presumption that I call "the transcendental pretense." This was the self-congratulatory pretense that we—the white middle classes of European descent—were the representatives of all humanity, and as human nature is one, so its history must be one as well. This transcendental pretense was—and still is—the premise of our thinking about history, "humanity," and human nature.

There was a time—the period of our concern in this book—when European philosophers turned to history with fascination and enthusiasm, looking for the key to their own purpose and destiny. Whatever the geometry of the path, they really did believe that history was moving toward some desirable end—universal freedom or the classless society, the general availability of happiness, or the realization of God's will on earth. Today we are more subdued—disappointed, in fact—because history has not lived up to our extravagant hopes and expectations. In contrast to the enthusiastic prognoses of Hegel and Marx, for example, consider the sarcastic ending of H. A. L. Fisher's more recent *History of Europe* (1936):

Men wiser and more learned than I have discerned in history a plot, a rhythm, a predetermined pattern. These harmonies are concealed from me. I can see only one emergency following another, as wave follows wave.

In other words, "just one damn thing after another." We have been raised on the wisdom of George Santayana—"those who do not learn from history are condemned to repeat it"—which is another short lesson in cynicism. And in the 1960s a popular slogan declared that "nothing happens until it happens"—which was no mere tautology, but the total rejection of history. There is our philosophy of history: wholesale cynicism. But one feature remains intact—the transcendental pretense: this, in the words of Marx and Engels, is the need to give our ideas—whether optimistic or cynical—"the form of universality, and represent them as the only rational, universally valid ones."[1]

Minerva's bird has taken a beating, from philosophers who think that history has nothing to do with philosophy, from historians who think that philosophy has nothing to do with history, and from all who believe that philosophy has nothing to do with anything—with history least of all. But modern European history (which is ours, too) does have a logic, a peculiarly philosophical logic of grand abstractions—in other words, an *ideology*—which developed most dramatically and articulately from the Enlightenment in England and France to its culmination in German philosophy, only to end in disillusionment throughout Europe by 1850. Historically, this was the ideology expressed by the personalities and the movements of the "middle" classes of Europe, the bourgeoisie.[2] The major currents of modern European thought—the Enlightenment, romanticism, German idealism, Marxism, and existentialism, as well as their analogues in the arts, sciences, and politics—were all expressions of this same bourgeois ideology. Whatever the conflicts among them, they belonged to a tight-knit if quarreling family of concepts, hopes, and demands. Philosophically, this book is a diagnosis as well as an appreciation of the invention, development, and first signs of disintegration of the grand abstractions which constitute this bourgeois family of ideas. And these ideas, in turn, define modern European history and culture.

An abstraction can be a piece or a part, wrenched out of context and treated as if an integral whole. Or an abstraction can be an extravagant projection, the presumption of a unified whole when all one knows are a few particulars. Bourgeois ideology is constructed out of both kinds of abstractions. The first includes the familiar idea of "the individual," and individual freedom, rights, and happiness, as if these in no way derived from or depended upon the nature of particular cultures, concepts, and societies. The concept of the individual soul, of course, had long been a tenet of Christianity; bourgeois ideology adds to this a secular individuality and a new sense of psychological privacy ("subjectivity"). The second kind of abstraction seems at first to be in direct contrast to these, but on reflection turns out to be necessary for their ideological support; these are the grand abstractions Humanity, Morality, the ideas of Reason, and the ideal of Rationality, and the notion that we are all endowed by Nature, if not by our Creator, with certain fundamental and common feelings; our "human nature." The philosopher David Hume, for example, expressed the self-evident truth of the age in 1738 when he wrote:

It is universally acknowledged, that there is a great uniformity among the actions of men, in all nations and ages, and that human nature remains still the same, in its principles and operations. The same motives always produce the same actions: . . . Mankind are so much the same, in all times and places, that history informs us of nothing new or strange in this particular. Its chief use is only to discover the constant and universal principles of human nature, by showing men in all varieties of circumstances and situations.[3]

These two abstractions together—the primary existence of an autonomous, "natural," individual human being with his or her own private, subjective consciousness, and the thesis that this consciousness is everywhere the same ("*the* Human Mind")—form the central dogma of that most successful of modern religions, *humanism*. At one time humanism had been a rebellion, a defense of "human" interests against the domination of religion and cosmology; but by the end of the eighteenth century, it had itself become the dominant religion and cosmology. With glances back to the ancients and the Renaissance, the philosophers of the Enlightenment turned it into a powerful ideological weapon. The bourgeoisie identified itself with humanity, and humanity was now absolute. It alone was the measure of value. And since the same ideas and ideals must apply to everyone, bourgeois ideas and ideals, as products of universal Reason, human nature, and common sense, could be applied without exception to all humanity. Applied to kings, clergy, aristocrats, and the old feudal societies, this new ideology succeeded in changing the world in less than a century. But with its success, this ideology became arrogant: it developed into the transcendental pretense—the idea that humanity conforms to oneself writ large, and that all ideals are bourgeois ideals. The idea of humanity as a singular entity is the foremost expression of this same pretense. (In Hume's term "Mankind" or simply "Man," one prominent bias of the pretense is made explicit.)

In retrospect, the motivation and strategy of the new ideology become obvious. The history of bourgeois ideology was a struggle for recognition and power by isolated individuals (like Jean-Jacques Rousseau), by ambitious groups (like the French middle class in 1750), and by underdeveloped societies (like Germany in 1800), all of whom lacked a distinguished past and distinct identities. Their philosophical tactic was to compensate for their impotence and insecurities by appealing to universal humanity, which they claimed to represent; to universal reason, on whose behalf they spoke; and to human nature, whose interests they served. It was an extravagant and self-serving strategy, adapted from Greek philosophy, Christian theology, and Luther's Reformation. It was eminently successful. The arrogant pretensions of the new humanism undermined the legitimacy of governments, exposed the "artificiality" and "corruption" of societies, and underscored the contingency of families and communities in contrast to those two new abstractions, the integrity of the individual and the unity of humanity. It carved out a new dimension of existence, the primacy of the human mind, and expanded this into a universal principle.

The development of the new ideology began only with its success, for it was then that the inadequacy of its simple slogans, grand abstractions, and transcendental pretense started to become evident. The seemingly simple ideal of "humanity" turned out to be a simpleminded gloss over irreconcilable differences between people, and a denial of real historical change. The apparently undeniable existence of "the individual" became a problem, and between the poles of humanism and individualism a glaring omission started to become obvious: the new ideology lacked a satisfactory conception of human relationships, families, communities, and cultures. The spokesmen for humanity were typically isolated, defensive, and often in exile and embittered. Rootlessness and self-contempt were the unspoken dimension of the new ideology, and the terms "universal" and "individual" were its philosophical symptoms.

But even if these mostly bachelor and embittered philosophers, artists, and poets were exceptional in both their alienation and their talents, they obviously touched a common chord and voiced a widespread need for bourgeois individualism and self-importance. Families and cultural origins came to be viewed more as hindrances than as shelters and security; universal humanism and aggressive individualism swept away these primal sources of identity and replaced them with a solipsistic celebration of individual conscience, duty, and achievement.[4] The ideals of universal reason and scientific objectivity made detachment a virtue; attachments, commitments, rituals, and relationships all came to appear unnecessary. True humanity was to be found in the cosmopolitan individual and in universal human nature, not in mere customs and contingencies. A new psychological awareness ennobled the individual, identified him with all humanity, but separated him from everyone. The terrible price and the arrogance of the pretense became evident only with time.

In logical terms, the development of this new ideology was a *dialectic,* which means that it was not so much a sequence of deductions and implications as a series of often desperate and conflicting attempts to work out a noble but inherently inadequate idea. No one could willfully be against "humanity," but neither could anyone say what it meant. Accordingly, the period 1750–1850 displayed all the adolescent signs of conceptual obscurity and transcendental pretentiousness—inconsistency, pompousness, self-contempt, excessive emotionalism, empty rationalism, withdrawal and despair, self-righteousness, and above all, hypocrisy. For there was no way to be "faithful" to an impossible ideal.

It is not my intention to add to the thoughtless and self-destructive attack on all things "bourgeois" that has been so fashionable since the term came into existence—an attack launched first by the aristocrats above the bourgeoisie, then by the self-declared geniuses among them, and finally by the disgruntled and deprived below or by their bourgeois representatives. Whatever might be said against it, the bourgeois ideology has been the source of precisely those ideals and tools, as well as the confidence, which are presupposed in attacking it; if I too am critical, it will be only in order to move beyond, not reject, an impressive but now dated and dangerous way of thinking. This book is an appreciation as well as a diagnosis of the ideology that has made our present lives possible.

In the following pages I have formulated a case-by-case account of the development of "humanity" and the transcendental pretense, beginning with the Enlightenment in France and in particular the *philosophes* Voltaire and Rousseau, and culminating in the French Revolution of 1789–95. The scene then shifts to Germany, where the new ideology and its pretense received their most profound philosophical expression in the work of Immanuel Kant and his followers, including G. W. F. Hegel, who took these themes to their ultimate conclusion, and in doing so anticipated their breakdown. Along the way, the consequences of the new pretense emerged in a new authoritarianism—of which Robespierre and Napoleon are but the most obvious examples—under which old abuses (imperialism, fascism, puritanical moralism, resentment, and greed) were given new labels and excuses in the name of "the people," "humanity," or "liberation." The pretense emerged in the arts, where humanism as well as the new authoritarianism proved as successful and as absolute as in politics and morals. Finally, the bourgeois ideology turned against itself in the reaction of the romantics; in Karl Marx, who used the no-longer-new ideology *against* the now prosperous middle class that had created it; and in Søren Kierkegaard, who reduced the isolated individualism of the Enlightenment to its devastating conclusion, turning some of the main themes of the Enlightenment—individualism, freedom, subjectivity, and the inner worth of each human being—into an ominous *rejection* of the Enlightenment in favor of the faith-full securities of the unenlightened Middle Ages and dogmatic Christianity.

This case-by-case account, preoccupied as it is with the importance of ideas, requires a curious bias toward history. For example, we shall find ourselves spending far more time in Immanuel Kant's Spartan study in the far reaches of East Prussia than in the courts of the great Prussian monarchs who thought themselves the living examples of the principles of the age. We shall spend as much time trying to understand two eccentric thinkers of the French Enlightenment as discussing the great Revolution they inspired. And we shall spend less time discussing Napoleon's decisive victory at Jena than pondering a single sentence or two of the obscurities of Hegel's dialectic, which was formulated, so the story goes, on the very eve and within earshot of that great battle. Against this, of course, there will be those who insist that history can be understood only in terms of economics and disasters, endless catalogues of treaties, tariffs, taxes, Tories, and tithes, the means of production, the promise of profit, and of course battles.[5] The fate of the nineteenth century is often said to have been determined by the "definitive" battles of the Napoleonic Wars—for instance, Austerlitz, Leipzig, and Waterloo. But in the midst of those grand confrontations, I always picture some once bold eighteen-year-old like Stendhal's Fabrizio or Tolstoy's Nikolushka, filled with ideas as he quivers from one mudhole to the next. That is where our history is to be understood—in those adolescent ideas and in individuals as their examples. If battles are the stuff of history, then history is indeed meaningless—or worse. And economics fares little better. If philosophy has anything to do with history, it is to reject this blood-and-greed cynicism and to transcend what Hegel called the "slaughter bench" of history, to make our past more than "one damn thing after another" spiced with romantic gossip, like one of those badly abridged editions of *War and Peace*. But philosophy must also attempt to undermine the self-righteous ideology of "universal history," to see what is peculiar—and this means ideologically peculiar—to our own history and concept of human nature. That is what I have tried to do in the following pages.

This is not a scholarly book. There are no new sources or details or theories here, no new archaeological finds in an already thoroughly tweezered and pricked-over period. I have come to believe, as Edgar Allan Poe wrote in his "Murders in the Rue Morgue," that "truth is not always in a well. In fact, as regards the more important knowledge, I do believe that she is invariably superficial." "Depth" has become the euphemism, as well as the excuse, for a possibly fatal intellectual irresponsibility that has brought into ill repute and nearly eliminated "accessible" (worse still, "popular") interdisciplinary studies aimed at a general audience, while favoring instead the secure insularity of technical specialization. Even in the best Liberal Arts programs, a university student will get but a taste of art, "exposure" to great music, one or two isolated periods of exclusively political history, and a scattering of literature that is too often wrenched from context as mere "text" to stand alone on its own. If one is particularly lucky or clever, one may come upon the exceptional insight that these departmentalized experiences actually have something to do with one another. But academic efficiency is equipped to process culture, not cultivate it. ("Interdisciplinary" studies are those that inconveniently refuse to fit in the standard-size cans.) We are left with a smorgasbord of warmed-over fragments. And since philosophy is, first of all, a *synthetic* discipline, it will be the first to be misunderstood—a certain sign of a more general malaise. ("The decline of speculative philosophy is one of the diseases of our culture," diagnosed Alfred North Whitehead.)

My intention, then, is not only to argue a contentious thesis about the transcendental pretense, but to provide a readable introduction to the organic unity of "speculative" philosophy, history, art, and poetry during our formative years—those innocent decades when we could still pretend, in good conscience, that there were such things as "universal history" and "human nature."

In a project ranging over so many well-cultivated fields, I have come to owe an enormous debt of gratitude to a number of friends, colleagues, and other scholars whom I have acknowledged wherever possible in appropriate notes. More immediately, I am thankful for the knowledge, encouragement, and criticism of Kathryn Pyne Parsons, Elke Solomon, Michael Kwartler, Peninah Petruck, Robert Rosenblum, Lynda Obst, Frankie Denton, Christopher Middleton, Dore Ashton, Douglas Kellner, Dina Sherzer, Caroline Marshall, Gabriele Röger, Nick Partridge, James Anderson, Clifford Browder, Sam Mitnick, and Tom Stewart, my editor at Harcourt Brace Jovanovich. Harry O'Hara devoted an exceptional amount of time and energy to this project, for which he deserves a very special acknowledgment. Trisha Ingman, Ellie Thomas, and Carolyn Appleton helped me through many harried moments with the manuscript. The University of Texas provided me with a leave of absence in 1977, and the Centre Universitaire International generously allowed me the use of their facilities in Paris. The National Endowment for the Humanities supported my research in 1976. Janet Hamilton helped me through the final revisions and notes. Kathryn Marshall first inspired, then shared, supported, and later saved the book; so it is to her that it is dedicated.

History and Human Nature

Introduction

> . . . history is written by learned men and so it is natural and agreeable for them to think that the activity of their class is the basis for the movement of all humanity, just as it would be natural and agreeable for merchants, agriculturalists and soldiers to entertain such a belief (if they do not express it, it is only because merchants and soldiers do not write history).
>
> Tolstoy, *War and Peace*

Modern Europe is rich in philosophers and other self-appointed spokesmen for human history. (It has even been said that the nineteenth century *invented* history.) These various spokesmen, as theorists, artists, and personalities, will be our eyes and ears to the past. But since the structure of our study is a sequence of case studies, I want to use this introduction to explain some of the concepts already mentioned in the Preface. Most important is the concept of *ideology*, and in particular the concept of *bourgeois* ideology. But I also want to say something more about "transcendental pretense" and try to provide a nontechnical account of what it means to insist that the following chapters form a *dialectic*. To approach our history without being wary of these concepts makes it all too easy to fall into the transcendental trap they set for us.

The Concept of Ideology

> The kind of philosophy a man chooses depends upon the kind of man he is. For a philosophical system is no piece of dead furniture one can acquire and discard at will.
>
> Johann Gottlieb Fichte

Ideas do not exist off in a world of their own ("the history of ideas"), occasionally (and usually through misinterpretation) inspiring revolutions, "movements," and catastrophes. Ideas are the conceptual structures of history, often before they become articulated and popularized by philosophers. Philosophers in turn have no privileged access to them; they are rather their curators, or perhaps janitors.[1] They have no rights of owner-

3

ship, no special license to ideological privacy at professional meetings, and no authority to lend them out to historians to fill the gaps between the battles in their books. An idea can be shared by any number of people and expressed in many ways, only one of which is articulation in philosophy. History, with or without the help of philosophy, is another expression. Often the philosophical articulation comes only after an idea has already infiltrated and converted an entire generation. Occasionally an eccentric ("untimely") philosopher gets there first, but not usually. Artists have painted it, musicians have scored it, pop culture has platitudinized it, and politicians have appealed to it—all before a philosopher "sees" the idea in its abstract, articulate form. The philosophical formulation is never the idea. Philosophy too is an expression of something far more basic than itself: it is that system of ideas, desires, images, and symbols—and more —that I call an *ideology.*

It is said—for example, by copyright lawyers—that "an idea belongs to no one." This is also true of ideologies. Like the kindred concepts of Rousseau's General Will, Hegel's *Zeitgeist,* and Marx's "class consciousness," "ideology" refers to a set of ideas that are necessarily general, never the property of one or two people alone.[2] If we talk about "the indignation of the working class," we are not talking about the attitudes of any particular persons (not every worker is indignant), nor about a detachable attitude that can be described apart from the people who hold it. A detached philosopher's *theory,* no matter how indignant, may not be an expression but rather a professional fashion, for example. A simple gesture may "say it all." An ideology may be articulated by a single philosopher who may be credited with its invention, as for instance "Marxist ideology." But the ideology is never just its philosophical expression, and the philosopher in question is—for all his insight and creativity—merely its representative. With mixed humility and arrogance, Hegel insisted that his ideas were never "his" but the ideas of "humanity"—in fact, the ideas of the universe itself ("the Absolute")—and he only their spokesman. Similarly, what Rousseau and Marx articulated were not just their own ideas but the brooding, half-baked, inarticulate dissatisfaction of their times; accordingly, they earned their reputations as the architects of modern Europe.[3]

The word "ideology" was itself a product and a symbol of the period we are studying. The term was innocently introduced by Antoine Destutt de Tracy, an Enlightenment philosopher who came just after the French Revolution.[4] He used it to refer to "the science of ideas," which in turn expressed the new confidence in reason and the pursuit of knowledge, but was also an explicit attack on faith and metaphysics, "superstition" and "prejudice." Ideology was the spirit of criticism which had undermined traditional France. It turned out to be the weapon of a single class, the bourgeoisie, and so the concept of ideology has itself been described as an inherently bourgeois conception, a half truth at best.[5] Because it began as an *-ology,* as an explicit study and articulation of ideas, ideology has often been confused—even by some of the best theorists[6]—with its "conscious" verbalization; but behind the words is a fundamental set of concepts in terms of which people define their reality and their lives. And because "ideologues" have so often exaggerated their claims, abused the facts, and gotten carried away by their hopes and resentments, ideology has been contrasted with science and truth and dismissed as "unrealistic," "impractical," and worst of all, "mere wishful thinking."[7] Only a few years after Tracy's invention of the term, Napoleon turned it into a word of abuse, for he soon saw that the Enlightenment interfered with his own purely pragmatic politics. On December 20, 1812 (just after the Russian debacle), he declared: "It is to ideology, that sinister metaphysics, . . . that we must attribute all the misfortunes of our beloved France."

Ideology has been ideologized to such an extent that it is now this term of contempt rather than a fundamental cultural-philosophical category. It is abused by conservatives to dismiss with opprobrium impractical leftist intellectuals and their whimsical and dangerous ideas; it is flung in contempt by Marxists as part of their attack on the oppressive rationalizations of the "ruling class."[8] Underlying both abuses is the idea, to be found in almost every use of the term since the eighteenth century, that an ideology is essentially a *distortion,* an illusion and rationalization for either revolutionary ambition or established dominance ("hegemony").[9] It is a philosophically dubious assumption (what philosophers call "naive realism") to believe that Reality is as it is, whatever we think of it; but at least where human society, culture, and symbols are concerned, it is clear that what we think of "it" makes all the difference: that Reality ("human reality") is *defined* by the ideology through which we conceive it. The assumption that ideology is a superficial intellectual embellishment—what Marx famously called the "superstructure" on top of an economic "base"—is utter nonsense. Not even Marx suggested that the "superstructure" was superfluous. Before we can even begin, therefore, it is necessary to defend a neutral or rather *positive* sense of "ideology" which is inherently neither revolutionary nor conservative, which defines rather than distorts Reality, which precedes verbalization and is anything but superficial.[10]

An ideology, as we shall understand it here, is a blueprint for a form of life, a form of consciousness. Where the emphasis is on theory and knowledge, it appears as a "conceptual framework," a systematic way of interpreting our experiences and fashioning a coherent world view. But an ideology is not just concerned with more or less passive observation and understanding; it also involves evaluation and action ("praxis"). With this emphasis, an ideology defines what could be called a "life style"—a set of attitudes and programs for behavior. Where the emphasis is cultural and sociological, an ideology is what Hegel called "the spirit of the times" or *Zeitgeist,* and what Carl Becker has more recently called "the climate of opinion." (The shift from "active spirit" to meteorological metaphor is itself significant.) Given that, among other things, an ideology is a set of ideas about human life and culture, in most cases it will have something to say about forms of government and codes of justice, but this does not mean that an ideology is primarily political. Politics may be tangential and can be shunned altogether, as in some forms of anarchism or aestheticism; but most ideologies do require some theoretical, behavioral, cultural, and personal structure for their politics.

An ideology is a system—though not necessarily a coherent one—of concepts, theories, interests, images, desires, values, fears, superstitions, maxims, moods, prejudices, platitudes, symbols, emotions, key words, and intrinsic confusions—in short, "ideas"—through which people define their existence. Expressed in common behavior and rituals (such as the philosophical arguments of the Enlightenment and Byronic adventures to the Orient), an ideology defines a culture.[11] Expressed in words, an ideology assumes the articulate form by which it is usually identified, and becomes a philosophy. Whether it is articulated or not, however, and whether it is articulated as philosophy or not, are very significant and even definitive aspects of an ideology. Bourgeois ideology is defined, in part, by the very high premium it places on articulation.[12]

Articulation is a preliminary to rational criticism; articulation in universal terms is the first step in a philosophical defense. These universal concerns are peculiarly our own. Some of our most prominent rituals, in fact, consist in ideological articulation and justification, regardless of accompanying actions. (Thus Catherine the Great of Russia was considered part of the Enlightenment, even by the philosophers Diderot and Voltaire, because she could talk its rituals.) Not every ideology emerges as philosophy, for not every ideology involves universals. That our ideology and our concept of ideology are obsessed with universals is a curiosity of history which it is our purpose here to understand.[13]

If ideologies are necessarily general, and if our ideology actually prides itself on its universality, then our concern with so many individuals (Voltaire, Rousseau, Kant, etc.) needs explanation. I see the individuals discussed in the following chapters as representatives of an ideology, and in this respect biography and personal anecdotes are of secondary importance. However, I have also suggested that *personality* is not a matter of ideological indifference. A personality is not just a pattern of traits and tendencies that distinguishes one person from another; it is also what makes them an instantiation of a particular *kind* of person—French, German, or Italian; cynical or idealistic; jovial or morbid; classical or romantic; medieval or enlightened; personable or paranoid. The personalities of Voltaire and Rousseau, for example, are even better illustrations of the ideological structures of the Enlightenment than their respective philosophies. Napoleon and Beethoven, who had no "philosophies" as such, exemplify the ideologies of their worlds as well as any philospher including Hegel, their self-appointed spokesman. Sometimes what seems most personal turns out to be what is most profoundly general as well. The artist or philosopher who "goes deepest inside," perhaps even withdrawing from the world, may nevertheless emerge with the widest and most durable appeal.

Ideology is too often discussed as if it were something wholly distinct and distinguishable from a person or a culture, an intellectual façade which can be worn to a political meeting or a cocktail party. But an ideology is nothing less than a blueprint for living, in the spirit of which Fichte insisted that a philosophy—more basically an ideology—"is no piece of dead furniture that one can acquire and discard at will." The kind of ideology we live determines the kind of people we are.

Bourgeois Ideology and the Transcendental Pretense

> It is only a society which possesses the greatest liberty, and which consequently involves a thorough antagonism of its members, that the highest purpose of nature, which is the development of all her capacities, can be attained in the case of mankind.
>
> Immanuel Kant, *The Idea of a Universal History*

Like most historical terms, "bourgeois" and "bourgeoisie" do not fit into rigid definitions; they rather refer to a family of concepts linked through their shared development.[14] In fact, many "bourgeois" attributes —for example, the familiar emphasis on material goods, comfort, and security[15]—are applicable to other classes, cultures, and ideologies as well, and bourgeois ideas are often opposed to each other, as for instance hard-headed materialism and soft-hearted romanticism. But bourgeois ideology, despite its vicissitudes and long-standing abuse, constitutes a recognizable and respectable form of life, defined as much by its transformations and internal oppositions as by its more durable properties. The base of those transformations is that period of ideological adolescence called "the Enlightenment," and until the twentieth century those ideological factions most strongly opposed to the Enlightenment were themselves thoroughly bourgeois. These last include romanticism, Marxism, and existentialism, for all of which "bourgeois" was a term of derogation.[16]

Three centuries ago the bourgeoisie were a varied, scattered group of people in societies that did not know how to classify them. As the name implies, they lived in the cities of Europe,[17] where there was the need for people in the "middle": merchants, between farmers and consumers; civil servants, between rulers and citizens; lawyers, between the law and the citizen; managers, between workers and owners; teachers, between knowledge and students. They were more than "hands" and more specialized than "labor," but lacked natural means—the inheritance, power, and status that could be had by birth alone. In the cities they became detached from nature. (Later this would be called "alienation"; in the eighteenth century, it was freedom from rural hardships.) They acquired a new sense of dependency on other people, and on the sophistication, social complexities, and rapid changes (particularly technological) that made them so needed in the interstices of post-feudal society. They survived through their individual talents, thrived on competition, and took pride in their dependability as "solid citizens." They did their jobs and they prospered. In the seventeenth century they did not yet form a class, for they did not have a sense of themselves *as* a class, and were just becoming more than a scattered minority that was without political bonds and of necessity politically timid. But beginning in the eighteenth century with the Enlightenment, they became aware of their growing numbers as well as of their indispensability.[18] They began to make demands and formulate ideals appropriate to their talents, ambitions, efficiency, and competitive individualism—ideals formulated in the language of "humanity" and "human rights," thus discounting a priori those "decadents" who did not agree with them.

This a priori (or in plain English, dogmatic) dismissal of anyone holding views different from one's own—different, that is, in the most basic ideological concepts—is what I call "the transcendental pretense." Even if there is no explicit theme that spans and defines bourgeois ideology from the Enlightenment to its own mid-nineteenth-century decadence, the transcendental pretense is its characteristic if not definitive trait. This is not to say that every bourgeois theorist declared his commitment to it in so many words (though many did—Hume and Kant, for example). But virtually every person and movement in our story used it as a foundation, as a constant source of support, even when their discussions turned to human and cultural differences.[19] It is the nature of the pretense, in fact, that it retains a certain vagueness when pressed for precision about its universal claims, precisely in order to leave room for superficial differences and to avoid falsification of a pretension that is only as convincing as it is abstract. If we are to understand the transcendental pretense and the ideology it defines, we must appreciate its evasions and obscurities as well as its superficially attractive humanism.

In terms of substance, neither humanism nor individualism is a continuous theme in bourgeois ideology, despite the fact that together they are the key to the Enlightenment. (Some romantics, for example, rejected both, while Marx rejected individualism and Kierkegaard, humanism.) And certainly such specific doctrines as materialism and rationalism, so often cited by critics as the key to bourgeois ideology, are not even plausible candidates for its definition. (In fact, they were not even essential or generally accepted in the Enlightenment.) When I try to say what ties together the figures discussed in this book, therefore, I find it impossible to cite a single doctrine or theme that concerns them all; however, I do believe that, without squeezing them into philosophical preconceptions, they all demonstrate this transcendental pretense which, better than any of the standard suggestions, characterizes that modern period in European history of which we are direct descendants.

The transcendental pretense is more than the claim that people are basically the same. It is also a method of abstraction which employs those peculiar concepts that we have referred to as universals. A universal is a concept which postulates an indefinitely large class and ascribes some essential property to all its members.[20] The concept of "humanity," for example, is the postulation, by no means established by observation, that there are unique and essential properties which all humans—whether in Paris, Berlin, Peking, or the far reaches of the Andromeda galaxy—must share.

This is something more than the common tribal equation—for example, "to be human is to be Javanese"—which gives conceptual privilege to a more or less determinate group.[21] The concept of "humanity," however, is not an attempt to delineate one group from another but, to the contrary, an attempt to deny all such groupings. As such, it is a conception that was invented only recently, whatever its precedents in the ancient world, the medieval church, and the Renaissance; and only now is it beginning to run aground on the inescapable fact of cultural differences.[22]

Humanity (mankind) is but the patriarch of the family of universals which structure bourgeois ideology. What all of these have in common is the appearance of descriptive terms as if simply pointing out something, when in fact they are a priori (dogmatic) postulations—distinctively moral categories of a peculiarly powerful kind.[23] "Humanity," for example, would seem to be an innocent categorial term designating all beings belonging to a certain species. But to be of the species is not yet to be human, and it was more than mere hypocrisy that allowed some of the most adamant humanists in early America to own slaves.[24] "Human" was, for bourgeois ideologues as for the Greeks, an *evaluative* term. "Humanity" does not so much describe a class as provide an obscure source of appeal, not all that different from the court in Kafka's *Trial,* in the light of which all thoughts and acts can be justified. So too the concept of "human nature" surely looks like a descriptive term, denoting all those characteristics that every being of the species must share. But what an incredible assumption it is to suppose that there are such shared characteristics, particularly when assumed by provincial Frenchmen and Germans, some of whom have perhaps never even crossed their own borders, much less spoken to the Orientals or Persians whom they credit with their own sense of "humanity." It is easy enough to point out the biological similarities of

all *homo* infants—ten fingers, four-chambered hearts, inability to manufacture vitamin C, apelike characteristics, and so on—but no thinking
humanist has ever believed that every *homo sapiens* is "human." When
people talk about "human nature," what is at stake are not these obvious
features, but the subtle debates of moral philosophers: whether everyone is
essentially selfish (Hobbes) or essentially virtuous (Rousseau), whether
compassion is natural or envy inevitable, etc. The debate continues today:
whether people are innately aggressive (Lorenz) or instinctively cooperative (Leakey); whether the structures of language are biologically determined (Chomsky) or only the general capacity to learn a language
(Goodman et al.); whether kinship structures and other symbolic systems
have a substantial biological basis (Lévi-Strauss) or do not (Leach et al.).
But cutting beneath these familiar, sometimes fascinating, and seemingly
endless debates, it is necessary to ask how such questions become intelligible
in the first place. Why do we assume that there must be a fundamental
answer to these questions, an answer which is true for all people in all
cultures? In fact, why do we even ask such questions?

The answer begins with the long history of dubious attempts to build a
morality—what people *ought* to do—on a biological foundation of what
they naturally *want* to do.[25] But the word "naturally" is suspicious. The
plasticity of human development makes it possible for people to learn to
want almost anything; and even if there are natural instincts (for example,
Freud's suggestions that male children naturally want to kill their fathers),
it does not follow that anyone *ought* to obey them. The word "natural"
itself is such that it can serve any end, answer any appeal—just like
"humanity." The word "natural" plays not a biological but a moral role.
This is also true of "human nature," which is only rarely the object of
anthropological curiosity and almost always a moral weapon, the pretense
of a universal justification for a prejudice perhaps just our own.

"Natural" often means "rational." The concept of Reason plays an
enormous role in bourgeois ideology. Certainly the ability to reason is
distinctively and admirably a part of human nature; but rational arguments
would have no force without the presumption of agreed-upon rules of
inference and shared ("self-evident") axioms and postulates, if not premises as well. And so Reason is "natural" not only in the innocent sense but
in a transcendental sense, too, with a pretense of universal agreement even
in the face of direct evidence to the contrary. (Chinese logic could be
dismissed because it lacked modes of inference common to European
logic; "primitive" thought was said to be "prelogical" and "magical";
those who did not share the European logical apparatus were simply not
"rational" and consequently something less than human, too.) But this
transcendental pretense did not stop with the mere rules and axioms of
logic. It also presumed—on evidence that was scanty and often contradicting—that all human beings shared substantial beliefs and principles as

a matter of "human nature," that is, as a matter of their simply being *rational*. Thus for Voltaire belief in justice, efficiency, and religious tolerance were matters of Reason applying to every human being, and if the great majority failed to agree, that simply showed their "irrationality." For Kant, rationality guaranteed agreement "by all rational creatures" of just those moral principles that he, as a bourgeois Protestant, had happened to be taught in provincial Germany. "Reason" and "rationality," like "humanity" and "human nature," seemed at first to be innocent descriptions of a human facility, but in fact functioned as the most pretentious moral imperialism.

It is almost always supposed that this concept of reason characterized only the early phase of bourgeois ideology and only one aspect of the Enlightenment.[26] For example, it is taken for granted by most historians of the period that romanticism was directly opposed to the Enlightenment primarily in its *rejection* of reason. But where reason was rejected, most often it was because it *failed* to satisfy the transcendental pretense; the pretense itself was not rejected. Thus Rousseau, whose alleged rejection of reason is equivocal at best, stressed the importance of sentiment just because he believed that certain sentiments could be defended as natural and universal. The German romantics, who followed Rousseau more than any other theorist, shared this idea that passion, not reason, was the essence of human nature. And many of the romantic philosophers (Schelling and even Schopenhauer) continued to glorify *Reason* as a metaphysical absolute. Goethe, who is impossible to classify in these terms, held on to the notion but with an Aristotelean twist, and he was followed by Hegel, for whom Reason was the soul as well as the substance of the grandest universal of all, the Absolute. In other words, the universal function of reason survived the dialectic of bourgeois ideology safely intact, in function if not in name. And that function was (and still is) the transcendental pretense. Even Kierkegaard continued the pretense—against reason, perhaps—but if one single presumption underlies Kierkegaard's attack on the Enlightenment, it is not the falseness of reason but its emptiness, its inapplicability to the individual case, which is again a limitation of reason and not a rejection of it. What is required is a still more universal term; ironically, Kierkegaard's universal is "the Individual." No other author in our study will present as strong a moral sense of human existence and the way one *ought* to live.

The pretense is found elsewhere, too. Where could the universals governing social interaction be better expressed than in laws, which differ from customs, mores, shared expectations, and mutual trust in exactly this universality? Laws maintain an abstract existence regardless of individuals and groups; they are applicable to everyone in a society, including those not yet born. One of the most prideful slogans of the American Enlightenment was "a government of laws, not men." It is the first step to the now vehemently resented "government of the lawyers, by the lawyers and for the lawyers."[27]

The pretense is found too in the concept of "experience," which was so central to the Enlightenment and after. Every student of philosophy learns about that grand dispute of the seventeenth and eighteenth centuries between the champions of Reason ("the rationalists") and the champions of experience ("the empiricists"), but that age is far better characterized by their shared pretension. The appeal to experience, like the appeal to Reason, could have no force without the assumption that everyone's experience was essentially the same, that the same observation or experiment was repeatable in London or Zanzibar, and that distortions and illusions could be found out and corrected. Eccentric experiences like color blindness or mysticism could of course be properly dismissed.[28] The claim that all truth could be found in experience, however, was not a principle that could be defended *through* experience, and the assumption that everyone's experience was essentially the same was in fact contradicted *by* experience. John Locke claimed to attack Reason in the name of experience, but appealed to Reason whenever he had a nonempirical principle to defend— for example, the existence of God. Voltaire praised Locke's empiricism and damned Descartes's rationalism, but never made the slightest attempt to understand their differences even while using them indiscriminately. David Hume demonstrated the frailties of Reason by using the most rational arguments, meanwhile presupposing with Rousseau the universality of the moral sentiments and of experience as well. The transcendental pretense remained alive and well even in Reason's most vigorous opponents, for Reason too was only a tool of the pretense, and not wholly indispensable.[29]

How did the pretense survive? It was supported and seemingly justified by the one domain in which it seemed unquestionable: science. In science, the ideal of universality appeared unshakable; what was true now must have been true in Babylon (whatever those sorcerers believed), and in Joseph's Egypt, too. Either objects accelerated at thirty-two feet per second per second or they did not, and the answer was repeatedly testable, its criteria clear and unarguable. If religion had once laid claim to The Truth, that claim had been shattered by the fragmentation of authority, by the Enlightenment attack on authority, by the untestability if not the unintelligibility of religious doctrine.[30] But science, taking religion as its antithesis, began to claim for itself the highest achievements of humanity, the one endeavor where "progress" seemed undeniable, and where established authority was not only challenged but tested. Science was not just a means (to move things, mash things, make things), but the ultimate demonstration of human rationality, the proof that a single individual could discover the workings of the universe itself. Accordingly, it could function as a model for morality and society as well, a display of universality which they too might soon attain. Only a few years later, John Locke and then David Hume claimed to do precisely this.

If we do not talk much about science in the following chapters, that is because, as the finest product of the pretense, it is the one human endeavor which is rarely questioned. This is true even of the romantics, who attacked neither science nor the pretense but only a certain kind of science—Newton's physics. Goethe preferred biology to physics, but never rejected science as the ultimate model, even for human psychology and literature. Kant defended Newton as the foundation of human experience; Hegel could praise his own work no more than by calling it "science"; and so too Marx. Even Kierkegaard exclaimed, "I always say, all power to the sciences . . ." and exempted them from criticism except to emphasize (against the Enlightenment) what they could not do. To be sure, there were vigorous disputes about the proper methods of science; paradigms were at war (especially biology and physics), and the unity of science was by no means as obvious as its Enlightenment defenders supposed. But the general claims for science as being objective, detached from provincial prejudices, free from established authority, methodically universal, and immanently successful were beyond dispute, and with this example in mind, thinkers had only to see if the pretense could be extended to every other facet of human life.[31]

The transcendental pretense, then, was and is the heart of the bourgeois ideology, in method if not also in substance—the postulation of an indefinitely large and largely unknown class, humanity, based upon the uncritical identification of a biological species, and upon the arrogant assumption that one's own virtues defined the nature of that species itself. Socially, the pretense became "cosmopolitan"—the projection of one's own urban virtues on the "cosmic" (i.e., universal) city. Politically it soon became the weapon of every oppressed or underappreciated group; by denying all differences, they could destroy any reason why "we shouldn't have this, too." Or, failing in this, they could glorify the differences, declare *themselves* the representatives of humanity, and denounce those above them as "decadent," "inhuman," or "bourgeois." (The ideology of the German romantics is a particularly fascinating example of these two moves.) Now it may well be that the battle for power and status is common to almost all societies (and not just "human" ones); it may even be a "natural" fact. But the bourgeois ideology adds to this battle its transcendental principles, justifying victories and rationalizing defeats; it provides universal moral excuses for personal interests and prejudices, not transcending these (as the Enlightenment claimed) but further indulging in them. Even (and especially) in defeat, the transcendental pretense allows one the luxury of felt superiority in *resentment*—an emotion particularly rich in pretense, and virtually unimaginable except in psychologically and philosophically sophisticated societies.[32]

In our interest in the transcendental pretense, however, we must not neglect individualism. The claim that everyone is essentially the same and endowed with universal reason meant that a given individual—perhaps anyone with suitable education—could go "into" him or herself and find truths applicable to everyone, just as Isaac Newton, using his own intelligence, had discovered the laws of the universe. Using this model, Rousseau claimed that, by looking into his own tortured, eccentric soul, he had discovered the intrinsic "natural" goodness in all humanity, while Kant, armed with his "enlightened" confidence that everyone was naturally rational, defended the autonomy of every individual to discover independently the universal principles of morality and human rights. The new ideology opened up a totally new vista unimagined by the ancient humanists and only dimly anticipated by Christian theology; the "inner" person, the life of the mind, the human soul viewed no longer as an indescribable metaphysical nugget but as the domain of psychology, as a private, personal world, the world of *subjectivity*.[33] And in this domain a new meaning and new emphasis could be found for the words "freedom," "dignity," and "happiness."[34] The individual was his own little world, and whatever the battles in the bigger, public world, freedom, dignity, and happiness must first be found within. This "inner" world of subjectivity played as large a role in the Enlightenment as it would for the romantics and Kierkegaard, who made the term "subjective truth" philosophically famous. It provided a basis for the most radical ideological imagination, an Archimedean point from which the whole weight of traditional society could be toppled.

The excesses of individualism—laissez-faire capitalism, anarchism, lack of respect for authority, loss of community, histrionic romanticism—all these must be weighed against the fact that, in the Enlightenment and after, individualism was supported by the assumptions of universal reason and the natural goodness of human nature. For example, historians and economists have wondered how Adam Smith could have written both *Wealth of Nations* and the *Theory of the Moral Sentiments*—the first the bible of "hands-off" capitalism, and the second a little-known work on "natural" moral emotions very much in the spirit of his contemporaries Rousseau and Hume. But these two books complemented each other, and it was the use of the first without the underlying moral confidence of the second that inspired horror. (I have tried to defend a similar claim for Marx's philosophy in Chapter 15.) Individualism required humanism for its very conceivability. Thus it is more than a curiosity that the most individualistic terms of the Enlightenment are not only supported by, but even turn into, universals. For example, the concept of "subjectivity" itself (mainly inspired by Kant), and the earlier concepts of "thought" and "experience" (championed by Descartes and Locke respectively), came to be defined in terms of their link to objectivity and the transcendental pretense. Kant's argument summarized the general move: subjectivity alone makes objectivity possible, but there can be no subjectivity without the possibility of objectivity. The concept of "freedom"—an inherently individual notion during the Enlightenment—became instead a property of whole societies, one in which individuals *participated* (thus Rousseau, Hegel, and Marx), before it was returned to individual status by Kierkegaard. Similarly, the concept of human dignity shifted between the universal pride in being human and the dignity of the individual, but the latter was predicated on the former (as in Kant). Human dignity depended on being human more than on any individual traits or achievements. And even the all-important concepts of Self, self-esteem, and self-consciousness emerged in Hegel and the romantics, not as individual terms, but as properties of the Absolute, the identity of humanity writ large. The individual and the universal were mutually dependent, in other words, and when they were actually opposed it was in the manner of a tug-o'-war, with the tension between them restraining both. Sometimes, it was even hard to tell them apart.

Before leaving this friendly tug-o'-war between individualism and the transcendental pretense, let us return briefly to an omission in the bourgeois ideology which was a primary force in its development. Between the pull of the individual and the appeal to the universal ("humanity"), the status of interpersonal and community relations was terribly confused. Some philosophers simply took the social order for granted and accepted it as the basis of their ideology, but saw no need to talk about it except to reform it and make it more "rational"—for example Voltaire. Others like Rousseau recognized its necessity and tried to *construct* society by agreement among individuals on the basis of universal principles, thus making society *derivative* rather than primary, and a matter of *convention* (if no longer a "corruption," as he had argued earlier). But like some other "spokesmen for humanity," Rousseau despised other men even as he was enthralled by Man; he never understood and could not accept the intimacy of personal relationships, and he clumsily tried to manufacture them in the brilliant web he created between the secure poles of individual existence and universal abstractions. Finally there were philosophers who, though recognizing the "natural" family, were willing to reject it in the name of their ideology. Kierkegaard, for example, did not even attempt to provide the appearance of philanthropy, and wholly rejected the community life which was the bedrock of Danish bourgeois society.

The family, accordingly, was often neglected in philosophy. Although it was an excellent candidate for the "natural" unit of humanity—far more "natural" than the individual, it could be argued—the family received too little explicit attention in bourgeois ideology, and suffered severe changes in ideological status. During the initial phases of bourgeois development, the image of the "solid citizen," the demand for privacy and private residential property, and the central tenets of "bourgeois morality" were all on the side of the intimate if truncated nuclear family (see Lukacs, pp. 625 ff.). One of the most common bourgeois criticisms of both aristocrats and peasants was their lack of family unity (that is, of nuclear family unity); it is revealing that even Marie Antoinette yielded to this bourgeois attack at least long enough to have her portrait painted with her children in 1787. But since bourgeois ambition was highly competitive and individualistic, and since the development of bourgeois talents was thwarted by the old emphasis on birth and family origins, the family foundered. Sexism took on a new form of efficiency—and of eliminating half the competition. But if sexism would sometimes become a matter of principle, it was equally a matter of ideological neglect. Bourgeois ideology expended so much of its attention on abstract universals that it virtually forgot about the social and sexual bases of everyday life. If there is a single omission that should shock us in its persistence, it is the almost total absence of explicit awareness of the family and the local community in an ideology self-consciously concerned with everyday human life and happiness. In Kant, for example, the entire fabric of human morality and practical reason could be described without a single analysis of interpersonal relationships.

A very different kind of example is the still dominant Enlightenment attitude toward what we call "natural character." Because of its twin beliefs in the primacy of the individual and the homogeneity of humanity, the Enlightenment displayed belligerent contempt for generalizations about "the German mind" or "the French temperament," thus denying on principle what every casual tourist, seasoned traveler, and anthropologist knows beyond question. Though the reason often given is that such generalizations gloss over individual exceptions, the deeper principle is the opposite; that such generalizations are not general enough, limited as they are to a single arbitrarily designated subgroup of humanity. Consider the enormous difference between the Enlightenment attitude toward language and that of the ancient Greeks; the Greeks assumed that ignorance of Greek alone was sufficient to determine all-important differences, while in the modern age the assumption has been that all languages say the same thing, therefore can be translated without loss of meaning and ultimately replaced by a single universal language (a suggestion that Leibniz made in the seventeenth century).

The rejection of national (racial, religious, ethnic, and neighborhood) character is part of a general rejection of character itself. This is why I insist that personalities are ideologically significant, and that personal identity is far more a matter of origins and community (family) roles than of either bare particular existence or participation in the great abstraction of humanity. Talk as we will about "just being a good person" and "being treated as an individual human being," these vacuous demands leave us nowhere, either taking for granted our sociocultural positions or disastrously rejecting them. No wonder one of the most predictable reactions against such "enlightened" thinking is ethnic backlash—a reaffirmation of local autonomy, family integrity, cultural differences, and romantic appeals to the "mysterious" (even "mystical") ties between people, which seem so only because the Enlightenment neglected or denied them altogether. Even in the eighteenth century this backlash was evident, as in the German philosophers Lessing and Herder. Tired of the dominance of French internationalism, they insisted—as the French did not—on the integrity of different cultures and the legitimacy of local mores. Both philosophers held on to the transcendental pretense, however, unwilling to take their belief in the cultural *Volkgeist* (the "folk spirit" of a particular people) to its anti-universalist conclusion. But they at least anticipate a grave ideological flaw in bourgeois thinking. Even the most articulate ideology is capable of missing the obvious.

If there is one last trait that is familiar to almost every reader of these bourgeois authors, artists, poets, and politicians, it is the enormous *ego* that is part and parcel of the bourgeois ideology; a sense of self-importance which manifests itself both in individual self-glorification like the romantic cult of genius, and in the transcendental pretense whereby one sees in oneself the whole of humanity. But balanced against this arrogance is always the insecurity and the sometimes pathetic impotence it hides. Voltaire never once doubted his own rationality, but for most of his life he felt that no one was taking him seriously, as if he were a mere bourgeois entertainer at an aristocratic gathering, a witty jester, a buffoon. Rousseau never once doubted his own inner integrity, even as he blamed the whole of society for corrupting him and making him into a liar and a libertine—but what a pathetic human being requires such a defense! Immanuel Kant, sitting stiffly in his bachelor flat in remote East Prussia, compensated for his isolation by ensnaring the whole of the universe in his philosophical critiques. And if Hegel identified himself with the Absolute and absorbed all history into a single idea, his arrogance must be viewed against the impotence of an unarmed German philosopher caught in the middle of the Napoleonic Wars at a time when Germany (including even mighty Prussia) had no effective power.

A Few Words on Dialectic

> It seems to be an unfailing law of nature that every action is opposed by a negation.
>
> Goethe

Along with humanity and history, the bourgeois ideology believed in *progress*. Whatever their differences, Voltaire, Goethe, Kant, Hegel, Marx, and even Kierkegaard—though he would have nothing to do with it— believed in it. Only Schopenhauer rejected it, but he thought progress so important that its absence signified the meaninglessness of life as well. The philosophical variant of this emphasis on conflict and growth is called *dialectic*. It is a logic that grows and expands and alters its concepts, and in this respect differs from classical logic, which insists on constant meaning, strict implication, obliviousness to context, and abhorrence of contradiction. If the model of classical logic is mathematics, the model for dialectic is biology and its themes of development and growth. Beginning with a simple and perhaps naive idea—for example, the idea of humanity —dialectic attempts to develop that idea by changing the concept as necessary to make it fit the facts of the world and cohere with other ideas, working it out in such a way that it is no longer an adolescent slogan (as during the early Enlightenment), but a substantial ideological system. Used thus, dialectic is a technique for rooting out not only inconsistencies within the system (for example, the delicate balance between individualism and authoritarianism that emerges from bourgeois political theories), but inconsistencies from without as well (for example, the failure of bourgeois ideology to develop an adequate account of interpersonal, family, and communal relationships). Ideally, perhaps, the end of dialectic is a system that accounts for everything, but as Marx and Kierkegaard show so clearly in regard to Hegel, this ideal end is more likely to involve self-deception than completeness. That is why the transcendental pretense is indeed a pretense: dialectic has no end. There is no guarantee of agreement, no end to the possibilities. "Human" life—that is, *life*—will always be a confrontation of differences.

In discussing dialectic as a "logic," however, I do not mean that a philosopher sits down and charts out a sequence of steps. The logic we are tracing is the logic of an ideology, one which develops through history, not at the whim of philosophers but according to its own needs and limitations. A system of ideas might sit unchanged in a book for centuries, but in history ideas are subject to the reality of their own consequences. Rousseau's *Social Contract* might survive a senior tutorial at Oxford, but there was no way it could survive the French Revolution, which it inspired and in which it was used almost as a bible by Robespierre and others. Its ideas could not stand unchallenged when used again by Napoleon, nor could the myth of the "intrinsically good individual" withstand the horrors of 1794. Hegel's path of history neatly drawn in 1806 was already out of date by 1820, and the Marx of 1844, writing in a vacuum of social consciousness, could hardly be the same Marx who drafted plans for real-life experimental communes a few decades later. Dialectic, in other words, is the development of ideas through their realization in history. One might call this "progress," but then again, any sophomore pessimist can point out that every moment of growth is also a further step toward death. But neither does this make it regress, nor reduce it to "one damn thing after another."

The twisting and changing of ideas has one consequence in particular that is always embarrassing to the defenders of classical logic: the frequency of—and even the need for—internal contradictions. But we all know young socialists who turn without pause to Ayn Rand, orthodox believers who embrace a vigorous atheism, and so on, and it is a matter of logic that the most obvious alternative to any idea is its opposite. In the dialectic of history, then, the turn of revolutionary France from uncontrollable populism bordering on anarchy to the absolute dictatorship of Napoleon with full popular support should come as no surprise, nor should Marx's early switch from romantic versifying to revolutionary proselytizing embarrass any but the most antidialectical Marxists (of whom there are many). It is often said that dialectic means conflict, but this entirely neglects the nature of that conflict, in which the alternatives share a common base and a common goal—for example, Enlightenment and romanticism, so often treated as mere antagonists. Still, this does not mean that for every "thesis-antithesis" there is some "synthesis," any more than it means that dialectic is inevitably "going somewhere." It is often the painful revelation of our own limitations and pretensions.

It is with dialectic in mind that I have structured this book around figures and movements, rather than allowing myself the luxury of an extended philosophical essay. Philosophy too easily tends to the transcendental and universal; case histories are intrinsically limiting. If as I claim, the transcendental pretense is to emerge as the characteristic attitude of an exceedingly diverse family of figures, then they will have to show this themselves. I have tried to present each personality and each movement in its context, including many details that would otherwise seem wholly irrelevant to a philosophical theme, so as to display the ideology of the pretense—the isolation and eccentricity of its defenders, as well as the universalist faith in humanity they share. Even so, this book too is admittedly an abstraction, a clumsy gloss over a century of discontinuities and eccentricities, and as such, a part of the pretension it is trying to examine.

1 The Enlightenment in France and the Rise of the Bourgeoisie

> It is not difficult to see that our epoch is a birth time, a period of transition. The spirit of man has broken with the old order of things, and with the old ways of thinking. . . . The spirit of the times, growing slowly and quietly ripe for the new form it is to assume, disintegrates one piece after another of the structure of the previous world. That it is tottering to its fall is now indicated only by symptoms here and there . . . but something else is approaching. This gradual crumbling to pieces will be interrupted by the sunrise, which in a flash and at a single stroke brings to view the form and structure of the new world.
>
> "Enlightenment." By this simple means pure insight will resolve the confusion of the world.
>
> G. W. F. Hegel, Phenomenology of Spirit

Our European adolescence began as a timid demand for individual autonomy and reason. It was, or seemed to be, our emancipation from the paternalism of the Middle Ages, a step out into a new world, a bigger world, *our* world. People asked little for themselves. They wanted respect, the freedom to think and explore, and the right to trust their own experience. They did not think of overthrowing the long-established order of things; they were too comfortable and too dependent. They only wanted what was reasonable—that people should be reasonable, that government should be reasonable, that the world should be reasonable. They subjected old ideas and institutions to respectful scrutiny, hoping thereby to defend them and accept them on the grounds of reason. They wanted some improvements, but just those improvements which they had been taught to expect by the very society they wanted to improve. It was our coming of age, our "Enlightenment"—a burst of sunlight. It seemed so reasonable, this demand for reasonableness. But it was full of latent inconsistencies that would one day explode into bloody contradictions.

The Enlightenment began as an idea, a childlike dream of self-styled "philosophers" under the stern paternity of the great kings of Europe.[1] It was not unlike a personal adolescence still submerged in bourgeois comfort, but inspired by a restless urge to experience "life as it really is." That meant taking risks. It meant being rebels, but always within limits. It was an effort to see for oneself, with the right to reject the authorities without being rejected by them. Nourished by the social aspirations of a young and enthusiastic middle class, this simple demand for reasonableness became an aggressive way of life. It spread beyond a few philosophers to become a general climate of opinion, the spirit of the new times. It became, in other words, an ideology. In France, by 1750 what had begun as the idea of reasonableness had become a demand for power and the revolutionary ideology of an increasingly prosperous and ambitious bourgeoisie. But the original idea had been corrupted. It had become an uncomfortable alliance of differing interpretations and interests. The simple idea of reason had become a convoluted tale told by a hundred squabbling philosophers, full of sound and fury and signifying too many things.

If enlightenment is adolescence, we should expect *the* Enlightenment to involve a spirit of rebellion, mixed with timidity and respect, based on an arrogant, newly discovered self-righteousness. It was an uncomfortable synthesis of sophisticated rhetoric and defensive boisterousness. And for all the talk about *reason,* the Enlightenment was nothing if not *impassioned.* Not a time of calm deliberations, it was filled with noise—shouted arguments, cries of indignation, rallies of solidarity, sarcasm, and relentless moral lecturing. "Overbearing and fanatic: they preach incessantly," complained Horace Walpole after meeting the French philosophers. The Western "Enlightenment," despite the name, had virtually nothing in common with the peaceful, selfless revelations of Buddhism; it was all frenzy and egotistical commotion. The forbidden topics of politics and religion invaded the once tactful drawing rooms of Paris. Controversy was relished rather than avoided; the most passionate disagreements became the mark of true friendship.[2]

The Enlightenment spirit extended to the world of the flesh, as well as to ideas and debate. The newfound sense of liberation manifested itself also in a new sensuousness and in a biting attack—in the name of what is "natural"—on the prevailing sexual mores of the time. In the 1750s as in the 1960s, this so-called "new morality" was hardly new. It was the same old assertion of the "natural" pleasures and passions of the body against the frigid authority of the Church and the inhibitions of the middle class itself. (The aristocracy, on the other hand, openly enjoyed its sexual scandals, while adultery as much as marriage had become the bedrock of royal society.) This sexual revolution was as much a part of liberation as the exchange of ideas; one cannot fully grasp the Enlightenment without taking into account Diderot's passionate love for his mistress, Voltaire's long-running affair with his niece, Rousseau's painfully neurotic romances and sporadic whoring, and even the fabled lechery of the American Ambassador in Paris, the honorable Ben Franklin. Thus Diderot, one of the champions of the new morality, circulated (but dared not publish) an ironic and almost pornographic supplement to the then recently released reports of Tahiti. Capitalizing on the already extravagant sexual fantasies that the exotic islands of the South Pacific inspired, Diderot forced an embarrassing contrast between the natural delights of Tahiti with the neurotic inhibitions of Christian Europe. "A little while ago," his Tahitan chieftain complains to a Christian missionary,

the young Tahitian girl blissfully abandoned herself to the embraces of a Tahitian youth and awaited impatiently the day when her mother, authorized to do so by her having reached the age of puberty, would remove her veil and uncover her breasts. She was proud of her ability to excite men's desires, to attract the amorous looks of strangers, of her own relatives, of her own brothers. In our presence, without shame, in the center of a throng of innocent Tahitians who danced and played the flute, she accepted the caresses of the young man whom her young heart and the secret promptings of her senses had marked out for her. The notion of crime and the fear of disease have come among us only with your coming. Now our enjoyments, formerly so sweet, are attended with guilt and terror. That man in black, who stands near to you and listens to me, has spoken to our young men, and I know not what he has said to our young girls, but our youths are hesitant and our girls blush. Creep away into the dark forest, if you wish with the perverse companion of your pleasures, but allow the good, simple Tahitians to reproduce themselves without shame under the open sky and in broad daylight.[3]

Every inhibition was as suspect and as subject to critical scrutiny as every institution. The Enlightenment's rebellion was an effort at personal and not just intellectual liberation. It was an expression of one's whole being—of body and desire, as well as one's ideas about the State. Enlightenment meant a whole way of life, and nothing less.[4]

Philosophy and Power

The Enlightenment was the ideology of the middle class. This is not to say that every bourgeois was a rebellious philosopher and libertine, or that their philosophies were mere rationalizations of the Protestant work ethic, laissez-faire economics, the "new" morality, and resentment of the privileges of the aristocracy and clergy. The rise of the bourgeoisie was not just the product of Enlightenment philosophy, any more than that philosophy constituted mere rationalization of this new class. They grew together, an adolescent and his self-image, mocked by fears of social inferiority and political impotence, urged on to fanaticism by self-generating pressures not then understood. If the word "bourgeoisie" today connotes the established class, one must not forget that the bourgeoisie of the eighteenth century was a class in the midst of struggle, and that no class struggle in history has generated such furor, enthusiasm, and success. If today the middle class appears to share many of those faults once criticized in the aristocracy—vulgarity and indifference, conservatism and rigidity—that is because it has become the new ruling class. Even the most vicious critiques of the entrenched bourgeoisie of the mid-nineteenth century—for example, those of Marx and Kierkegaard—are themselves advanced from a position that is wholly bourgeois. The nineteenth century was indeed the century of the middle class, a century filled with the battles, conflicts, and jealousies that raged within that class and its ideologies. In Britain and America the spirit of calm if heated debate, and the delight in uncritical exchange of basic platitudes, has kept the lid on the explosive contradictions of the Enlightenment until this day. But in France, Germany, and elsewhere in Europe these contradictions were allowed to enter into full battle with each other, not in the realm of the intellect alone, but throughout the theater of human experience.

If the Enlightenment was the ideology of lawyers and bankers, intellectuals and libertines, we should not be surprised to find *utility* as the dominant social value, *freedom* as the dominant political concept, *science* as the most valued human endeavor, *naturalism* as the accepted metaphysics, and the pagan *harmony of nature* as its philosophical ideal. It was a rejection of inefficiency and inequity, an appeal to competition and egalitarianism. But reason, progress, utility, and liberty could no longer tolerate despotism, or an inefficient monarchy characterized by unequal distribution of wealth and a system of privileges without regard to merit. The "harmony of nature" could not be extended to human society unless the old institutions and authorities were replaced by human reason and universal law. Some enlightened philosophers looked forward to a utopian advance for humanity. Others looked far back to the early Greeks and Romans and to more "primitive" times for their ideals.[5] But whether the Enlightenment was very new or very old, the Old Regime would necessarily be its victim.

The French aristocracy had been seriously weakened by that powerful autocrat, Louis XIV, the "Sun King." Louis had crippled the power of the aristocracy by favoring the bourgeoisie in their place, playing the one group against the other while providing the bourgeoisie with rich contracts and powerful government positions. (The King's minister Colbert, for example, was of bourgeois origins.) The Bourbon hereditary line had then passed to Louis XV, a twit of a king more interested in hunting and court intrigue at Versailles than in his government. The monarchy endured, but it no longer controlled the quarreling between the defensive aristocracy and the increasingly powerful and resentful middle class. In 1774, Louis XV's indecisive and ineffectual twenty-year-old grandson mounted the throne of France, married to a spoiled, domineering, and goading princess of Austria. Louis XVI attempted long-sought reforms, and in fact improved the lot of the French workers and peasants considerably. But he could not influence, much less control, either the aristocracy who were plotting against him, or the bourgeoisie who were beginning to influence the country and even the court through their "enlightened" ideas and, soon, through their commercial ambitions. Given Louis XIV's war on the aristocracy and his patronage of the bourgeoisie, and the weakening of the monarchy itself through two successive reigns, the victory of the middle class appears in retrospect to have been inevitable.

"The Spirit of Criticism"

The intellectual manifestation of this middle-class ideology of rebellion has been called "the spirit of criticism."[6] This spirit was most obvious in the debates and quarrels, in the pamphlets and political battles, and in the deliberate provocation of Church and civil authorities. But beneath the noise and antagonism lay a firm and righteous ideology supported by strong traditions of Christianity,[7] the Reformation, and the Renaissance, and a renewed appreciation for Greek and Roman philosophy.[8] The Enlightenment was above all an appeal to Reason, and the spirit of criticism was a demand to be rational. The Enlightenment was concerned not only with conclusions but with arguments.

The rationality of criticism presupposed a set of solid and unquestioned ideals, according to which all criticism could proceed. The ultimate ideal, however, was individual autonomy—the right, ability, and need for every person to think and speak for him or herself; the right, ability, and need to criticize, and to take nothing—except perhaps autonomy itself—for granted.

Regardless whether one ultimately retained faith in orthodox religion or defended the new heresies, or became a political liberal or a conservative, the point was always to be critical, to accept whatever one believed only after exhaustive argument and full consideration of all possible objections. Voltaire, for example, personally rejected atheism, but insisted that he would prefer a world of critical atheists to a world of pious, unthinking Christians.[9] Yet in point of fact, after such scrutiny the Enlightenment philosophers accepted a surprisingly large proportion of traditional institutions and beliefs. David Hume was a staunch conservative, for example. Rousseau left the moral claims of religion unchallenged. Voltaire endorsed the necessity of monarchy, and Kant insisted, "Argue as much as you like, but obey."

The philosophical father of the Enlightenment was René Descartes.[10] Though his intellectual heirs would later attack him as part of the problem, Descartes had in fact been a true revolutionary. In a subtle but subversive set of philosophical *Meditations* (1637), he forced himself to cast off all prejudice and authority with the extreme and simple purgative of total doubt. He doubted everything he had ever been taught to believe, even to the extent of doubting his own experience and the very existence of the world. Depending solely on his own reason, he insisted on grasping the truth for himself and proving it, by himself and to himself, beyond all possible doubt. There could be no appeal to authority or tradition, no retreat to "common sense" or the assertion that "we've always known that." It was a revolution in philosophical method, and ultimately a revolution in human thought. The key to his method was the idea of *autonomy*, a new confidence in one's individual ability to seek out and find the truth by "the natural light of reason." This concept was itself medieval,[11] but its employment in the name of personal autonomy was new and radical, even though Descartes's conclusions to his bold experiment were anything but revolutionary; in the end, he believed just what he had been taught to believe, and even took it as one of his "rules for the direction of the mind" to obey the laws and customs of society. Nevertheless, he ended up fleeing France because of a minor heresy, proving once again that the step toward autonomy, however cautious, was never a safe one.

It took nearly a century before Descartes's method, outlined in his *Discourse on Method* (1641), was used to its full potential in Enlightenment ideology in France. (Nurtured in more progressive England, that same ideology had meanwhile provoked the Glorious Revolution of 1688 and produced the powerful new metaphysics of Isaac Newton and John Locke.) It was ironic that Descartes's method came to be looked upon as part of the oppressive past, rather than the presupposition of the Enlightenment itself. Given proper credit or not, however, that method—once adopted by the newly powerful, literate, and increasingly restless middle class—would make possible the most astounding revolution in temperament since the Renaissance and the Reformation.

This revolution was first of all a revolution on paper, and *of* paper—reams and reams of it, distributed in the streets and read aloud, very loud, almost everywhere. Without lapsing into McLuhan-esque overstatement, one can and must say that without the medium of print and the increased literacy of the time, the Enlightenment would not have been possible.[12] The materials of the Enlightenment were neither the specific traumas of war and starvation nor the tangible ideologies of warring religious factions. Its substance was largely abstraction: abstractions of considerable personal significance, to be sure, but abstractions nonetheless, requiring print and argument for their very existence. The materials of the Enlightenment were treatises on metaphysics, books on human nature, studies of the heavens and the elements of earth, and sermons on Reason, morality, and utopian societies. Its vehicles were plays and parodies, editorials on religion, attacks on superstition, and mockeries of human frailty and foolishness of all kinds. Passionate notes and letters—never meant to be published, though they often were—crossed paths in every direction. Never before had there been such confidence in the power of the printed word—or at least in the secular word.

Perhaps the most exemplary effort of the entire Enlightenment was the twenty-eight-volume *Encyclopédie* edited by Diderot and D'Alembert and published over twenty-one years.[13] Its explicit purpose, according to Diderot, was "to assemble the knowledge scattered over the face of the earth . . . so that the labors of past centuries may not be useless to future times; so that our descendents, by becoming better informed, may in consequence be happier and more virtuous." This is the summary statement of the Enlightenment ideology—that knowledge leads to happiness. The enormous effort of engaging, encouraging, encapsulating, and editing other people's ideas earned Diderot the title *"the* philosopher." Philosophical speculation and investigation were not for him. His virtues were his rebelliousness and a ravenous desire to know. Consequently, he at one time found himself in prison for "conspiring to destroy royal authority, establish the spirit of independence and revolt." His dedication and enthusiasm provided the rallying point for the Enlightenment, and made possible its conversion from isolated defensiveness to an ideology that would soon govern France.

The *Encyclopédie* became the ideological forum of the Enlightenment. Political critiques were hidden between essays on the making of rouge and the foraging of a cannon. Touchier subjects were necessarily cloaked in anonymity or disguised in satire. The writing was both clear-headed and passionate, but where passion obscured clarity, the obscurity was compensated by style. In France, criticism *was* style; first of all a style of living to be characterized not in terms of its arguments (often fallacious and frequently absent), but in terms of its self-consciously clever displays of irony and its sense of moral superiority. With reason their weapon, the philosophers declared open season on all superstition, tradition, and stupidity. "What is justice?" asked Diderot, as if it were an entirely new question. "Justify yourselves to us!" demanded the philosophers, aiming at every doctrine and dogma, every law and legality, every authority, every article of faith, and every institution. If Jericho had been destroyed by mere sound, the Old Regimes of Europe would soon be shouted down by the sarcasm of philosophers.[14]

Later, critics of the Enlightenment would say that it only replaced one set of superstitions with another.[15] True, some of the worst features of the twentieth century can be traced back to the Enlightenment, but they can also be traced back to Abraham or ancient Rome. It is a cynical perversion to describe human growth as nothing but a series of errors. Surely the "error" of the Enlightenment—bloated self-confidence and pride—was a welcome substitute for the outgrown error of uncritical subservience to authority. As a matter of fact, the philosophers of the Enlightenment were often the first to recognize their colleagues' errors and to point them out to each other—as tactlessly as possible. *Self*-criticism, however, was not one of the virtues of the age.

The New World of Humanity

> Our hopes for the future condition of the human race can be subsumed under three important heads: The abolition of inequality between nations, the progress of equality within each nation, and the true perfection of mankind.
>
> Condorcet, Sketch for a Historical Picture
of the Progress of the Human Mind[16]

On the American continent a new world was already being built according to Enlightenment principles. But in Europe the same principles had first to be used to destroy the old world. In America there was the luxury of open, seemingly endless space; in Europe the battle was defined by time.

The old world was the traditions of the Middle Ages, the world of authority and faith, and "the divine right of kings."[17] It was a world too of security and stability, and since people were treated as children, it was not altogether disagreeable. The concepts of responsibility, choice, and freedom, so important today, played a relatively small part in human affairs. The battle for the Enlightenment, accordingly, was first a battle against childlike timidity in favor of self-assertion. The children of the past would ask the philosophers, "Once we begin to criticize, where will it stop?" The philosophers' answer, here summarized in the words of Condorcet, was as vague as any medieval promise of salvation:

The time will therefore come when the sun will shine only on free men who know no other master but their reason; when tyrants and slaves, priests and their stupid or hypocritical instruments will exist only in works of history and on the stage; and when we shall think of them only . . . to learn how to recognize and so to destroy by force of reason, the first seeds of tyranny and superstition, should they ever dare to reappear amongst us. (Jones, p. 2)

The children of the past would ask, "Once we question our faith, what will we have left?" And the philosophers answered, "Freedom!" But freedom for what? Again, the answers were as vague as they were dazzling:

How consoling for the philosopher who laments the errors, the crimes, the injustices which still pollute the earth and of which he is often the victim, is this view of the human race, emancipated from its shackles, released from the empire of fate and from that of the enemies of its progress, advancing with a firm and sure step along the path of truth, virtue and happiness. (p. 3)

And if the new righteousness was as dogmatic and naive as the old, nevertheless the first step had been made. Once discovered, self-consciousness does not move backward.

Because the old world of the Middle Ages had to be portrayed as an evil to be rejected (just as an adolescent has to see his domineering parents as "unreasonable"), the Enlightenment view of its traditions and institutions was anything but fair. In fact, the differences between the warring parties were often no more than shifts of emphasis. Small flaws in the old world became targets of relentless criticism and revulsion. Innocent superstitions became objects of merciless ridicule. Routine corruption was attacked as a perversion of the natural order. Traditions were viewed as conspiracies, and mere inefficiency provoked moral outrage. Yet beneath the noisy rebellion and self-righteous criticism, a full-blooded ideology was developing, powerful enough to require a shift in the very dimensions of the universe.

The Ideology of Enlightenment

Any understanding of the ideology of the Enlightenment must begin with its *humanism,* its insistence on seeing the universe as primarily a *human* stage. Whether or not the philosophers believed in a God behind the scenes (some did, some did not), they believed in the primary importance of human happiness and in reasonable secular laws and institutions, including the Church, to assure that happiness. Human suffering and political injustice could no longer be excused by divine rights or established traditions, or dismissed as fleeting moments in eternity. Humanism introduced a new emphasis on the free individual, as the source of autonomy and the bearer of happiness. Democracy as such was far too radical for the philosophers of Europe, but they shared with their more radical American peers a renewed belief in individual responsibility, in the significance of personal opinions, and in the ultimate importance of individual happiness. Together with the equally slippery but all-important conception of individual freedom, these became the platitudes upon which we have built our lives. The demand for "liberty," which in particular cases of oppression seemed so clear, would become the confusion through which all else would fall apart.

The presupposition of humanism was a belief in *human nature,* the idea that people differ essentially from animals, and more important, that all people share basically the same characteristics. The old world accepted the idea of a human *soul,* to be found in each and every individual, but had little faith in the community of humanity, the "brotherhood of man."[18] The English hated the French; both despised the Prussians. The Prussians thought the Russians primitive, and the Russians—like everyone else—

hated the Turks. One's neighbors were always either primitive or decadent, illiterate or overeducated, too rich or too poor, not religious enough or fanatical, immoral or inhibited, provincial or snobbish. Xenophobia was the accepted mentality, and with small allowances for Christian humanitarianism (the very opposite of Enlightenment humanism), one believed everyone else to be decidedly inferior.

Because the Enlightenment philosophers believed in human nature, even despite their own sense of superiority they were decidedly tolerant of differences. They believed that all human beings were similar not just in some intangible, divine essence and basic biological similarities, but in terms of reason, emotions, desires, interests, and values. The differences between nations and races, therefore, were superficial and negligible— mere matters of expression and local customs. *Reason* was the same for all. The philosophers may have been distinctively of the middle class and embroiled in a bitter class struggle, but they saw themselves as representatives of a universal class of humanity. In fact, humanity—or in the sexist parlance of the age, *mankind*—was a new discovery of sorts, a grand abstraction without geographical or anthropological limits. This universal category reached beyond the limited personal experiences of a bourgeois arrondissement in Paris, and cut across provincial differences in language and customs everywhere. Philosophers envisioned a universal language, universal customs, universal canons of Reason. Differences between people could be ignored, because ultimately people were all the same uniform products of nature; thus Hume declared: "In all nations and ages, human nature remains still the same."[19]

Ideologically, the Enlightenment philosophers were xenophiles—in the name of their newfound universal humanism, and strategically, too, as a way of finding an Archimedean point from which to overturn their own societies. The best books of the period—and the most subversive—used foreign visitors or exotic settings to make a satirical point, to look at one's own society through fresh and critical eyes—Montesquieu's *Persian Letters*,[20] for example, Voltaire's many exotic tales from the East, and Diderot's Tahitian dialogues. Literary characters were dressed in foreign costume, spoke in strange dialects, defended outlandish customs, but they spoke the views of the Enlightenment. Some philosophers knew only their own corner of Paris and perhaps the provincial town of their childhood, yet they spoke confidently of the customs in America and Russia, and made up convincing tales of Persia, China, and the South Pacific, confident that they spoke for "humanity."[21] And when differences did indeed exist, this new genre of exotic literature always made it clear that the error lay in the traditions and institutions of France. (Do not adolescents always find their neighbors superior and their parents at fault?)

In the name of Enlightenment humanism, the middle-class philosophers could declare their interests to be universal interests, and their human interests to be the dictates of Reason. And since Reason was the very heart of human nature, one's own enlightened self-interest was never merely one's own, but in the interest of everyone. To emphasize the universality of such interests, therefore, they could be turned into universal laws, and it is extremely significant that the Enlightenment philosophers insisted on "government of laws, not men."[22] One can defend a law impersonally, objectively, and without a hint of personal interest, especially if that law already has built into it the projection of one's own interests for the whole of society. With Reason and this new, secular conception of natural law, the philosophers could defend an ideology just as absolute in its values as the old world's theology. With Reason they could hold together the fragile agreement between the ideal of universality and their individual pursuits of life, liberty, property, and happiness. And when the Enlightenment collapsed, it was above all because this illusion of common interest exploded. The unspoken presupposition of those aspiring middle-class philosophers was that the opportunities they sought were in some sense plentiful, that there would be enough land, jobs, and community involvement to provide everyone with the investment in enlightened society that they themselves had. When philosophers found themselves shut out of those investments— Rousseau by virtue of his personality, for example, or young Marx because of his (hardly radical) reform politics—those same Enlightenment ideals would turn against the Enlightenment, even against Reason.

The emphasis upon Reason in the Enlightenment necessarily raises the question of the role properly assigned to the passions in human affairs. It is often thought, but wrongly, that the Enlightenment in general, with the sole exception of Rousseau, defended Reason and attacked the passions as "irrational." But both Voltaire and Diderot maintained persistently that the passions provide us with pleasures as well as pains, and that without passion there would be no meaning to human life. In England, of course, the role of the passions as a motivating force in human nature was generally accepted, and it was not only David Hume who believed that "reason is, and ought to be, the slave of the passions." The key to the Enlightenment is therefore not Reason as opposed to passion, but rather a recognition or perhaps a rationalization *of* the passions. The "natural" and wholly rational emotions of sympathy and compassion, for example, were respected by all the philosophers. And Rousseau, who more than anyone recognized the dangers and even the criminality of "unbridled" passion, insisted throughout on the need for rational constraint and guidance of the emotions. When Reason is overly praised at the expense of the passions, as in Kant, for example, Enlightenment thinking betrays a schizoid disharmony which typically leads to a rejection of Reason—but still in accordance with overall Enlightenment ideals—as for example in the romanticism which follows Kant and is intellectually even derived from him.

As suggested in our introduction, society plays an ambiguous and clearly derivative role in the bourgeois polarity of universal humanism and enlightened self-interest. The philosophers of course recognized the existence of society; Voltaire loved it, Rousseau hated it. But the general view of the Enlightenment was that society was a compromise of individual interests through universal reason, through conventions and mutual contracts, not a "natural" entity in its own right. This dangerously perverted view was strategic: it let the philosophers use the leverage of Reason against their societies, to their individual advantage as well as to the advantage of their class (in the name of "humanity"). On the other hand, to have made society primary, and individual rights and even Reason itself derivative, would have encouraged a view as hateful to the Enlightenment philosophers, for all their talk about tolerance, as it was to their authoritarian forebears: *relativism,* the idea that different cultures might be radically, essentially different, so that there are no "right" answers in either science or morals. The emphasis on "laws, not men" betrays radical distrust of anything less than universal. So the Enlightenment philosophers held firmly to the primacy of Reason and Human Nature, these absolutes being their best weapon against another system whose absolutes were crumbling. But this left the Enlightenment with perhaps an impossible task, which we are still trying to carry on today: to develop a theory of society without first taking the concept of society seriously.[23]

The word "nature" played a huge role in Enlightenment ideology, and that alone should make us suspect that it too, like "Reason," was as much a weapon as a concept. Sometimes, "nature" meant the cosmic order, within which human affairs were governed by "natural laws" just like the stars and the planets. It was this concept that philosophers used when they spoke of "human nature" and "natural laws," their message being that human societies should be run as smoothly and efficiently as the heavens. (Some Enlightenment thinkers retained the belief that God was behind both kinds of laws—Isaac Newton and René Descartes, for example.) But humans also had a distinctive "nature," and this was above all to be *rational.* Thus "natural" would also mean "rational" (as it had in the "natural law" of the medieval theologians), and an appeal to nature was tantamount to an appeal to universal reason—an appeal which, in Enlightenment ideology, could not be challenged.

Besides this use of "nature," however, the Enlightenment also marked a dramatic change in the concept of the natural world. For all recorded time, and certainly before, nature had been a tyrant, a source of danger, and an unpredictable source of food and shelter. Mountains were natural fortresses or obstacles; plants were edible or poisonous; animals domestic or dangerous; rivers provided irrigation or had to be crossed; stars controlled human destiny; and weather alone could dictate the survival of nations. But in recent years humanity had begun to conquer nature. There were still fearful reversals—famines and earthquakes, for example—and much was still to be conquered, but the role of humanity in the universe had changed.[24] People were no longer just *in* or *part of* nature, nor did they "rise above" it only in a religious sense. And with its domestication, nature could also become an aesthetic object, to be appreciated in a safe and contemplative way—not as the work of God or as the master of man, but as a sublime and benign piece of art. The world was becoming a human world; nature served human purposes, not the other way around. As Condorcet observed:

Organic perfectibility or deterioration amongst the various strains in the vegetable and animal kingdom can be regarded as one of the general laws of nature. This law also applies to the human race. No one can doubt that, as preventative medicine improves and food and housing become healthier . . . the average length of human life will be increased. . . . It is reasonable to hope that all other diseases may likewise disappear as their distant causes are discovered. Would it be absurd then to suppose that this perfection of the human species might be capable of indefinite progress; that the day will come when death will be due only to extraordinary accidents . . . and that ultimately the average span between birth and decay will have no assignable value?[25]

Two abused Enlightenment concepts were *progress* and *optimism*.[26] It was progress that the Enlightenment offered as an alternative to the old world—longer life, less suffering, more wealth and happiness. But to understand the Enlightenment, one must grasp how completely self-serving that notion of progress was: progress in the distribution of rights and wealth, from the aristocracy to the middle class; progress in morality and virtue, whereby the virtues of the middle class are duly recognized and rewarded; progress in the arts, so that middle-class taste and moralism reign supreme; progress in science, the new technology for business; progress in philosophy, canonizing the Enlightenment in the same sort of metaphysical system that the philosophers so despised. It might be, as the philosophers insisted, that such progress would indeed benefit humanity. But it is clear who would be the most obvious benefactors. And there is no form of "progress" that cannot, with a slight shift in vantage point, be termed "decadence" and "degeneration."[27]

A few glossy pamphlets aside, one will not find much optimism in the Enlightenment. Voltaire was wholly concerned with human stupidity; Rousseau, with human corruption. Even Condorcet, whose rosy projections we have quoted, had his doubts—and was guillotined during the French Revolution. What they believed in and had to offer were *possibilities*. For all their disappointment and sarcasm, they held on to the dream that it might be possible—in America, or in some small country village or some monstrously authoritarian court—to start afresh with a new social arrangement and a more rational (that is, more bourgeois) way of living.

But as for optimism, one recalls how Voltaire's delightful *Candide* exposes it—whether divine or human—as absolutely idiotic. The philosophers of the Enlightenment were far too beleaguered to be optimistic.

The Dark Side of Enlightenment

To understand the ideology of the Enlightenment simply as a set of ideas, rather than as a polemic and a weapon, is not to understand it. Its grand schemes of humanism and progress are arrogant precisely because they are defensive. The philosophers indeed believed that knowledge is power, but mainly because they did not as yet have any power. They preached reason, but found themselves surrounded by stupidity. They told the world that it was unreasonable, but the world changed far too slowly. Confident of the righteousness of their cause, the philosophers kept up the battle, too blinded by their bitterness and insecurity to see the dangerous consequences of their own ideas.

The philosophers saw themselves as defending principles and attacking stupidity and injustice. As their ideas became more popular, they attributed this to the power of Reason, but it was in fact the power of self-interest. What was defended in the name of reason turned out to benefit most people in France—enough, certainly, to support the contention that the bourgeoisie was indeed the "universal class." The bourgeois philosophers became the spokesmen for the Third Estate, which consisted of all of France except the nobility and clergy. (That meant 23 million merchants, bankers, shopkeepers, lawyers, ministers, clerks, housewives, workers, peasants, and general riffraff, versus 400,000 in the first two Estates.)[28] But as the bourgeoisie demanded equality of power and privilege with the nobility (many of the bourgeoisie were already equal in wealth, even to the point of *buying* titles of nobility), a second set of inequities lay hidden in the ideological rhetoric. The rest of the Third Estate, by appealing to the same principles, would have a legitimate set of demands against their bourgeois spokesmen in the name of "liberty and equality." But so long as the bourgeoisie was a struggling class, fighting in the name of the entire Third Estate ("the People"), the lack of clear distinctions within that Estate rendered possible a common and soon overwhelming popular front.

The *nouveaux riches* could join forces with peasants and menial workers, the former demanding the money, respect, and position the government owed them, while the latter fought for fewer taxes and more jobs. Once victory was achieved, however, it became obvious that the Enlightenment ideology was inconsistent, obscure, and sometimes blatantly hypocritical. So long as the myth of *égalité* could be sustained, the illusion of unity assured relative peace if not harmony. But as the threads of ideology unraveled, separating the "universal class" into its subclasses, antagonisms resulted: liberty against duty, civil rights against the State, reason against experience, science against religion, naturalism against humanism, national security against international ambitions, progress against happiness, and politically, workers and peasants against the bourgeoisie. Thus the Enlightenment gave birth to demons that its seemingly simple confidence in Reason would never have recognized as its own.

2 The Double-Edged Sword: Voltaire

> I am tired of hearing how only twelve men established the Christian church; I want to show that only one can destroy it.
>
> Voltaire

> I consider him a saint . . . not a humorist but a fanatic. Did Voltaire laugh? No—he gnashed his teeth.
>
> Gustave Flaubert

One figure, more than any other, inspired the French Enlightenment; he called himself "Voltaire" (1694–1778). His *Philosophical Letters* brought many of the philosophers their first encounter with the new spirit of criticism. He was the first of the new generation of spiritual rebels—old enough to have known the days of Louis XIV, but young enough to almost see the Revolution. The span of his long life was, appropriately, the span of the Enlightenment in France. He reached the peak of his powers just as the middle class was attaining its own sense of potential power and its first real political successes. He turned from criticism to activism just as it too was readying itself for some great battle.[1]

Voltaire used reason as a weapon, warming its cold steel blade with passion, wit, and sociability. It was a period of pretentiousness, and Voltaire performed brilliantly. Commenting on the philosophers, Peter Gay notes that they were both witty and humorless: "The wit was demanded by their profession, the humorlessness imposed upon them by their belligerent status."[2] It is an apt description of Voltaire. As Flaubert observed, Voltaire did not laugh, he gnashed his teeth. He was the bark, if not the bite, of the French Enlightenment.

Even his name was a mark of his ambition and rebellion. He was born François-Marie Arouet, a Paris bourgeois; his father was a minor official in the massive bureaucracy of the Sun King, full of higher ambitions for both himself and his son. Young Arouet was sent to school to become a friend of the children of the nobility, and for the rest of his life drew his friends mainly from the elite classes. The name "Voltaire"—originally Arouet de Voltaire, the signature he adopted for his first play—was itself an aspiration to pseudo-nobility, an ambition which would have him quarreling and fighting for status all his life. He would not spend much time around bourgeois dinner tables; he preferred courts and châteaus. And in those luxurious surroundings the ambiguity of the Enlightenment was already obvious. Voltaire was willing to criticize the Old Regime and denounce its stupidities; while in exile later in life, he was a dedicated defender of human rights and demanded justice for all classes. But in his tastes and his friends, in his conception of himself and society, he was— like Locke, whom he often followed—an unabashed elitist. He could refer to the people as "the rabble," and his social attitudes are as well summarized by his friendship with the autocratic Frederick the Great of Prussia as by his contributions to the Revolution's *Declaration of the Rights of Man.*[3]

Voltaire was never the revolutionary. He believed in slow and painful progress, at best. His activism, Peter Gay remarks ironically, was merely "thoughtful resignation to reality."[4] Compared to his contemporaries, he was always conservative, no friend of new ideas not his own, nor of the many young artists and thinkers who were attracting attention and notoriety in Paris during his own long periods of exile. His were the elitist ambitions and the restrained conservatism of an *haute bourgeoisie* that wanted recognition by an already established, albeit reactionary, society. He was always the tolerated outsider, his career curiously checkered by respect and rebellion, by official recognition and at the same time the constant threat of arrest. His *History* was confiscated and condemned, but he was made historiographer of France in 1745. He attacked French intellectual life and letters and was attacked in return, yet in 1746 was elected a member of the esteemed French Academy. His books were banned, but he was the best-selling author in France. Forbidden to appear at court, he remained under the protection of the King's own mistress. Like Socrates, Voltaire was always the gadfly, never the revolutionary. A man of reason, he was often unreasonable—at the same time a dogmatic enemy of prejudice and a critic who could not take criticism, a rebel and a staunch defender of the established order.

Even as a schoolboy Voltaire had been a rebel and a "rogue," using his quick, sarcastic wit to intellectually skewer his father, teachers, and friends, and later to offend powerful nobles and acquire enviable mistresses. His rapier tongue, coupled with an arrogant ego and a bad temper, landed him twice in the Bastille, once for nearly a year, and often forced him into exile from his beloved Paris for indiscreet comments against powerful government figures, including the Regent himself, who governed France during the youth of Louis XV. Voltaire's family pressed him into law as a practical and potentially powerful profession, but he refused to take it seriously, insisting that he would be a man of letters and nothing else. Voltaire choked on the force-fed theology that he learned from his Jesuit teachers, and rebelled against it violently from his adolescence on.

Yet Voltaire never forgot the rigorous training that they had imposed upon him, nor would he ever, like so many of the younger philosophers, abandon religion entirely. Though he said that he preferred a world of atheists like D'Holbach to a world of Christians, he always added that atheism was a "dangerous" position, and one which he found personally intolerable. Christianity, however, was another matter; he would dedicate most of his life to its destruction, "cutting this rotten tree at its very roots."

By the age of thirty, Voltaire was considered the best playwright in France, Racine's successor, and the wit of Paris. He had already attained a status at court far superior to any he might have expected along the bureaucratic road plotted by his father. However, he was still a bourgeois —much to his chagrin, since he saw no reason why his genius and charm should not be socially rewarded with an appropriate boost in status. He lived and dined with aristocrats, feuded and fought with them, yet they treated him with a patronizing toleration that he resented. On one occasion he offended the powerful Chevalier de Rohan-Chabot. Had he been a peer, a duel would have followed. But as an inferior, a mere bourgeois philosopher, Voltaire was beaten by the Chevalier's lackeys, and for the second time in his life unceremoniously whisked off to the Bastille. After two unhappy weeks in prison, he was exiled from France—an inconvenience which proved to be the turning point of his life.[5]

The Philosophical Letters

In the spring of 1726 Voltaire arrived in England, where the Enlightenment had already triumphed. London was filled with émigrés; not the aristocratic refugees who would frequent St. James in the 1790s, but modest families and a great many outspoken thinkers who had escaped religious persecution in France. The contrast between England and France was dramatic, and Voltaire would make the most of it in his future political polemics. His first great work, the *Philosophical Letters,* are properly also called his *English Letters.*[6] Returning to France after two and a half years in London, he wrote them in haste and published them in the face of considerable danger. The work was condemned and burned by the Parlement of Paris as "likely to inspire a license of thought most dangerous to religion and civil order." Later it would be said that the *Letters* were "the first bomb thrown at the old regime."

Superficially, the *Letters* read like a travelogue of London. But the comparisons with France, and with Paris in particular, are rarely far below the surface and often explicit, always to the disadvantage of the French. The differences between enlightened England and semifeudal France were considerable, but the power of Voltaire's polemics must be understood not just in terms of rival ideologies, but in terms of chauvinism as well.

Throughout centuries of war and diplomacy, the two countries had wavered between mutual respect and hostility. The French viewed the English as a sophisticated but perverted and dangerous people, while the English thought the same of the French. (It is worth noting that syphilis was called "the English disease" in France and "the French disease" in England.) To play the two countries one against the other, therefore, was a stroke of perverse ingenuity.

While Voltaire's delicious irony attacks both nations, it shows a marked respect and friendly humor toward the English, and an obvious bitterness toward the French:

Clergymen here [in England] are all reserved, by temperament, and almost all pedantic. When they learn that in France young men, who are known for their debauchery and who have been raised to the prelacy by the plots of women, make love in public, divert themselves with the composing of sentimental songs, entertain daily with long and exquisite supper parties, and go from there to beseech the light of the Holy Spirit and boldly call themselves the successors of the Apostles—then the English thank God they are Protestants. (p. 5)

Again:

With regard to morals, the Anglican clergy are better ordered than those of France, and this is the reason: all clergymen are brought up in Oxford University, or in Cambridge, far from the corruption of the capital . . . the priests are almost all married; the awkwardness they pick up in the university, and the fact that, socially, Englishmen have little to do with women, result in a bishop's ordinarily being forced to content himself with his own wife. (p. 5)

The first seven letters are concerned with English religions, particularly the Quakers, whom Voltaire uses to paint a striking portrait of rational religion, as opposed to French Catholicism. Despite its political power, even the Church of England fares far better than his native religion, for at least "an Englishman, as a free man, goes to Heaven by whatever road he pleases," and "everyone here may serve God in his own fashion" (p. 5). Of the Presbyterians, he ironically comments that they make "the grave airs and severe expressions all the fashion in this country, and sanctify the Sabbath, doing nothing on Sunday but go to church, to the tavern, and to the brothel" (p. 6). In praise of this diversity, Voltaire concludes: "If there were only one religion in England, there would be danger of tyranny; if there were two, they would cut each other's throats; but there are thirty, and they live happily together in peace" (p. 6). The English, unlike the French, are beyond the era of religious warfare: "I see in them no longer any inclination to cut one another's throats over syllogisms" (p. 8).

Most important is the English government. Though Voltaire prudently limits himself to comparing England with ancient Rome, the message is clearly addressed to contemporary France.

In Rome the fruit of civil wars was slavery, in England it is freedom. The English are the only people on earth who have managed to prescribe limits to the power of kings by resisting them, and who by long endeavor have at last established that wise form of government in which the prince, all-powerful to do good, is restrained from doing evil; in which the nobles are great without insolence or feudal power, and the people take part in the government without disorder. (p. 8)

The English had weathered their revolution over a quarter of a century before, but the concept of the "middle class" had yet to gain currency in England; not until the French Revolution and its internecine rivalries would it become ideologically explicit. (During the Enlightenment, one can say in retrospect, this concept was the basis of the reigning ideologies without yet being made explicit in them.) Yet Voltaire was keenly sensitive to the importance of the English House of Commons and the "free men" who were so clearly distinct from the aristocrats. Regarding justice, he comments, "You hear no talk in this country of high, middle, and low justice" (p. 9). Concerning taxation—a matter of vital importance in France's impending financial disasters—he writes: "A man is not exempt here from paying certain taxes because he is a nobleman or priest. All taxes are levied by the House of Commons, which, though second in rank, is first in importance" (p. 9). Finally: "Nobody is downtrodden and nobody complains. The feet of the peasant are not tortured by wooden shoes, he eats white bread, he is well-clothed . . . they own property and . . . they live free" (p. 9). The implied contrast with the French peasantry may have been exaggerated, but it would be extremely effective by the end of the century.

The *Letters* include high praise of English commerce, again with a slap at the inefficiency and vanity of the French aristocracy:

I don't know which is the more useful to a state, a well-powdered lord who knows precisely what time the king gets up in the morning and what time he goes to bed, and who gives himself airs of grandeur while playing the role of slave in a minister's antechamber, or a great merchant who enriches his country, sends orders from his office to Surat and to Cairo, and contributes to the well-being of the world. (p. 10)

Only a small number of the *Philosophical Letters* deal with philosophy as such. There is a chapter on John Locke, with extravagant praise of the great British empiricist to the detriment of the masters of French rationalism.

Perhaps there has never been a wiser, more orderly mind, or a logician more exact, than Mr. Locke; and yet he was no mathematician. [A reference to the deductive proofs of Descartes and his contemporaries in France, especially Pascal.] He never could submit to the drudgery of calculations, nor to the dryness of mathematical truths, which in themselves offer nothing concrete to the understanding. (p. 13)

Voltaire wholly approves of Locke's empiricism, and treats him as if he were the last word in philosophy and the direct antithesis of French rationalism:

Locke has unfolded to man the nature of human reason as a fine anatomist explains the powers of the body. He dares sometimes to affirm, but he also dares to doubt. Instead of defining at once what we know nothing about, he examines, bit by bit, that which we want to understand. He takes a child at the moment of birth, he follows step by step the growth of its understanding, he marks what it has in common with the animals, and in what ways it is superior to them. Above all, he consults his own experience, the consciousness of his own thoughts. (p. 13)

In contrast, Voltaire says of his own intellectual master, Descartes:

Our Descartes, born to bring to light the errors of antiquity and to put his own in their place, being led astray by that spirit of system which blinds the greatest of men, imagined he had demonstrated that soul is the same thing as thought. ... He maintained that we are perpetually thinking, and that the soul makes its arrival in the body already provided with every possible metaphysical notion, knowing God, space and infinity, as well as the whole range of abstract ideas, and filled in other words, with splendid knowledge all of which it unfortunately forgets as it leaves its mother's womb. (p. 13)

This is surely unfair to Descartes, but the battle lines are sharply if not fairly drawn. Voltaire sides decisively with Locke's attack on the very idea of "soul" and with his rejection of all "innate ideas," which, as he and Locke understood that term, meant any concepts whatever which were not drawn from experience.[7] In point of fact, both Locke and Voltaire would have been sorely embarrassed, had they known the absurd consequences which their mutual supporter David Hume would draw from these seemingly reasonable doctrines. In the context of the *Letters*, however, Locke was an excellent antidote for the lethargy of French scholasticism, and empiricism a welcome appeal to the senses and the common sense of the rebellious young Enlightenment philosophers.[8]

One of Voltaire's most important intellectual gifts to France was his celebration in the *Letters* of the physics of Isaac Newton. Later on, in 1738, he would write the first popular exposition of Newton's system for the French reading public; here he confines himself to a comparison of Newton and Descartes—much in favor of the former, needless to say. He makes some small concessions to Descartes's bold experiments, but with a measure of bitter and usually unwarranted sarcasm. Yet despite the irony and polemic, Voltaire ends up in a celebration of Descartes that is rarely appreciated; he praises Descartes as a hero searching for the truth, as the man who got rid of the absurd chimeras with which we had infatuated our youth for two thousand years. He taught the men of his time how to reason, and how to fight him with his own weapons. I do not think one can truly compare his philosophy in any way with that of Newton; the first is an experimental sketch, the second a finished masterpiece. But he who has set us on the road to truth is perhaps as worthy as he who since then has gone on to the end of it. (p. 14)

Three letters on Newton's theories follow. What Voltaire and his readers found inspiring in these theories was not simply the mechanical view of the universe (Descartes had developed such a viewpoint a half century earlier), but the inherent rationality of Newton's scheme, the rational order of the universe, and also the rational ability of human genius to understand it. The concept of an orderly universe was among the oldest of ideas, but Newton's physics established the new sense of this order that would define the Enlightenment. (Newton himself, like Voltaire, never accepted the atheistic and materialistic interpretations of his theories; throughout his life he remained a devout believer of sorts.) But most dramatically, it was this new confidence in human understanding that provided the bedrock of Voltaire's confidence in Reason.

After several letters on theater, poetry, and literature comes the twenty-fifth and final letter, added sometime after the original twenty-four were completed—a sometimes brutal attack on another of his genius countrymen, Blaise Pascal. Voltaire assails Pascal's "gloomy pessimism," using the empiricism of Locke as his philosophical weapon against the Christian tradition of "despair." The ultimate message is clear: "What makes us hate our nature? Our existence is not so unhappy as they try to make us think" (p. 25).[9]

It is said that Voltaire went to England a poet and returned a philosopher. One might say that he became the first French empiricist, following the English tradition of Bacon and Locke. He added little to this philosophy, often misunderstood it, and misused his new method as a deceptive façade for his incurably Cartesian urge to rationalize. But by using this method, Voltaire could turn his personal resentment into a political attack on the arbitrariness, oppressiveness, and inequalities of the French regime. He left England as a philosopher, but arrived on the shores of France an angry ideologist.

Reason as a Weapon

No matter how much Voltaire explicitly celebrated the Lockean "testimony of the senses" and the British virtue of dialogue, he remained a stubborn rationalist and very much a monologuist. His "empiricism" was limited to the little scientific experiments that he conducted with his mistress, the learned Mme du Châtelet. His ultimate appeal was always to

Reason. And for Voltaire as for Descartes before him, Reason above all meant autonomous thinking, a willingness to question *all* the rules. Voltaire had few qualms about borrowing an argument straight from Descartes's *Discourse on Method,* even while polemicizing against Cartesianism and the abstract proofs and principles which he himself employed most successfully. The concept of *self-evident truth,* for example, which played such a dominant role in the Enlightenment—and in the various declarations, constitutions, and revolutions that would follow it—was a product of the European rationalist tradition and of Descartes in particular; only later was it borrowed by the British empiricists. The notion of self-evidence is the mark of Descartes's first principles—those which cannot be intelligibly doubted. Here is the central strategy of Voltaire's tireless attacks: the presupposition of principles which *cannot be intelligibly doubted,* principles of Reason which stand at the foundation of every dispute but themselves stand beyond dispute. Here is the Archimedean standpoint from which the philosophers toppled centuries of established tradition, power, and prejudice.

The concept of Reason, though it has had many different senses throughout the long history of Western rationalism, almost always carries with it an aura of nonnegotiability. The presumption is that certain principles are obviously right to any reasonable man; they are not worth discussing, and anyone who does not accept them is to be dismissed—and despised—as an "irrational" and therefore inferior being. In medieval thinking, the nonnegotiability of Reason was assured by the belief that Reason was—as the ancients had also argued—the "divine spark" given to us by God (or the gods). Voltaire repeats this ancient formula, giving to Reason a sanctity as well as an authority which could not possibly be questioned or challenged. Even when the later Enlightenment would deny the scholastic equation of God and Reason, the sanctity of Reason would remain. Here was the invincible weapon—an appeal to human reasonableness that would penetrate deep within the guarded circles of the elite. For who would want to be "unreasonable," whatever power he held? But despite its acceptance by the despots of Europe, including Frederick the Great of Prussia and Catherine the Great of Russia, Reason was advantageous to the bourgeoisie, presenting itself as universal but in fact proving most favorable to a singular class of aspiring young men.[10] Given this absolute confidence in Reason, any belief, custom, institution, or power could be criticized.

Curiously, the one idea that was above criticism was the notion of Reason itself; it received remarkably little critical attention. Even Locke, who had made his philosophical reputation by apparently finding an alternative to it, rarely criticized reason and often appealed to it to solve his problems. And Kant, who would also make his reputation with his *Critiques* of Reason, ultimately left it unassailable, criticizing only its more flagrant philosophical abuses (see Chapter 6, pp. 114–27). But then, it is difficult if not unwise to examine a tool while using it—particularly a weapon wielded in the midst of battle. It was enough that Reason *worked:* it forced conclusions upon the world that the world had no resources to deny. Every argument could be premised upon "self-evident truths" which no reasonable man could possibly doubt. If King George had questioned the "self-evident truths" of the American Declaration of Independence, that would only have been further proof of his tyrannical incompetence, and not a point of argument at all.

The power of Reason lies in its absolute universality and necessity. Its claims are not limited to a particular context or a particular set of conditions. They apply equally to all men and at all times—"even to the Turks," as Descartes remarked in a comment about the universal appeal of his philosophy. Its claims are unconditional and independent of the whims of power and authority—"inalienable" was the word of the times. And as no one wants to appear "unreasonable," everyone will feel compelled to accept the new principles. On the presumption that Reason is universal, it can be used to criticize anything—and anyone. And it must be accepted by everyone. In 1774, when Voltaire was already a very old man, a very young king would ascend the throne of France who was steeped in the new philosophy, in the ideals of rationality and the principles it apparently entailed. Unfortunately, he lacked the will to make it work, and the dominant theology, which he himself accepted, would express itself against him at his considerable expense.

What Voltaire admired most in the English was their "reasonableness," their emphasis upon discussion and debate, their insistence upon tolerance and efficiency; but such reasonableness was of little use in a society still dominated by the Church, tradition, hereditary privileges, and religious intolerance.[11] In a contest in which rational discussion was honored only as display of wit and learning, reason could not be used as in a duel, but rather as a disruption. It could be used to challenge and disturb—used as Socrates used it, puncturing the pretensions of established but unearned rights and the questionable legitimacy of traditional authorities. Criticism, not dialogue, was the role of Reason in prerevolutionary France, and it had to be employed surreptitiously, sneaked into conversation in parables and wisecracks, disguised as humor and entertainment. Voltaire, who gained entrance to the inner circles of the most powerful courts of Europe by virtue of his wit and charm, was the ideal personality to lead such guerrilla attacks. From within the elite circles of the nobility—though he would never be accepted as one of them—he would read his compositions and entertain with his brilliance. But though he may have appeared as an "entertaining" bourgeois in the midst of the aristocracy, he easily turned his role into that of the man of reason among the unenlightened. Of course they wanted to be "enlightened," too—and soon they would be. Louis

XV—perhaps wisely—forbade Voltaire's appearance at his court, but his favorite mistress, Mme de Pompadour, gladly became the upstart's protector, and the next King Louis would soon perish according to the Enlightenment's unseen contradictions.

The Nature of "Natural Rights"

The demands of the Enlightenment philosophers and later of the Revolution—demands for liberty, equality, power, and the pursuit of happiness; for food, health, and decent shelter for the less fortunate; for religious toleration and freedom of speech and press—these demands were not seen as mere matters of self-interest. They were matters of Reason, of "natural rights," and like all things rational, were nonnegotiable, self-evident truths. They were demands that needed no defense, the premises of arguments that allowed no refutation.

Like the notion of "Reason" itself, the concept of "Nature" had its origin in scholastic metaphysics, in a divine conception of human nature endowed by God with certain inalienable rights as compensation for the dangers and inconveniences of Reason. In fact, in this context, the notions of Reason and Nature were virtually synonymous, designating laws and rights sanctioned by God and created as part of human nature. In their arguments for natural law, the Enlightenment philosophers—and, needless to say, the scholastics—did not have in mind any proto-Darwinian theory of biological selection, but rather universal, *rational* law. And when the Enlightenment philosophers spoke of "natural religion," they did not mean anything like Santayana's "animal faith" or the romantic "feeling" view of Christianity, but a universal *rational* religion, not one rooted in mystery, miracle, and authority but based upon, and compatible with, the secular intelligence and scientific learning of the most educated men. (And when the philosophers argued about "natural sex," they did not have in mind copulation in the forest, but rather sexuality freed from the *unreasonable* fetters of Christian prohibitions.) Demands made in the name of Nature were always to be defended in the name of Reason. And that meant that they too were nonnegotiable, to be accepted at face value as valid currency anywhere in the world, including the estates of France's most powerful aristocrats.

The concept of natural rights was the cutting edge of revolutionary Reason. It allowed the bourgeoisie to make the most radical demands, never in their own name and always irrefutably. Armed with the concept of natural rights, an individual could force those in power, through their alleged obligations *to him,* to recognize his demand and right to speak his mind, worship as he pleased, and not pay excessive taxes or have his land or property taken from him. Again, the notion of rights—"natural rights" in particular—was not itself subject to the critical scrutiny of Voltaire and the philosophers; it remained as their presupposition, the basis upon which their demands and fine speeches rested. A "natural" right is one which need not be argued.

Like all such self-evident truths, the concept of natural rights is dangerously equivocal. As a weapon it served the bourgeoisie well because, as they employed it, it was an expression of bourgeois rights—namely, those middle-class desires and aspirations which defined the Enlightenment. Through the universality of Reason these aspirations were presented to the aristocrats as a set of demands for equal privileges and advantages, and to the "lower" classes of workers, peasants, and the poor as a set of implicit promises. The right to food, shelter, and freedom from torture were thus applicable to the lower classes, whereas the right to interfere with bourgeois business through strikes or concerted "mob" action was quite another matter. The conception of natural rights, in other words, had no content of its own; it was only a claim of logical status, of axiomatic irrefutability. To call a claim a "natural right" was to give it "trump" status above all other claims and expectations. The aristocrats had previously employed the similar conception of "divine right" to defend their privileges and self-indulgences, and the monarchy would still employ it for several decades to defend its own right to govern, however incompetently. The lower classes, and workers in particular, would later learn to use it from their own perspective, to make on their wealthy bourgeois employers the same powerful and irrefutable—but not therefore undeniable— demands. But in the middle of the eighteenth century, the bourgeoisie was the struggling class, and therefore needed the concept of natural rights to defend their positions and give them a power of persuasion that they did not yet have politically. But there was nothing inherent in the concept to automatically justify the bourgeois content presupposed in their arguments.[12]

This problem of content emerges in another more philosophically profound dilemma. Even if the concept of natural rights is granted its privileged logical status, it might be argued that such status cannot be merely a matter of logical privilege. The priority of natural rights, it can be claimed, is supported by certain extralogical *utilitarian* considerations; certain rights are justifiable because they best serve the overall welfare or efficiency of the society and its populace. This utilitarian conception of natural rights has the philosophical advantage of explaining the privileged status of such rights, but the political disadvantage of thereby becoming context-bound to sociological contingencies. According to this view, violations of individual rights are allowable in cases in which social utility overrides the rights of an individual—for example, sending to prison or into exile a brilliant but trouble-brewing young philosopher.

By way of contrast, the "pure" view of natural rights defends individual rights against such violations *no matter what the consequences,* and the dispute between these two views has formed the primary source of disagreement in political philosophy ever since the Enlightenment. But this is not simply a philosophical problem of logical justifications: the entire notion of the rights of the individual against society and the State, and consequently the notion one has of the State, depend upon it. By increasing the strength of a man's claim to natural rights, one is bound to anarchy as an ultimate position, since this is the only view that categorically rejects the right of states and societies to violate the rights of individuals. (Of course the content of those rights, as always, is yet to be determined.) As one moves away from emphasis on the rights that the individual may demand from society and toward the duties that society may demand from him, the origins of the totalitarian State begin to come into philosophical focus. As one moves further from the "pure" view of rights toward the utilitarian viewpoint, the question of "utility" naturally comes to the fore —*whose* utility? How to measure the welfare of one individual against the welfare of groups? How to measure the welfare of one class against another's?

These queries have defined the question of legitimacy—seemingly a philosopher's problem—as intimately linked with ideological problems of power; the *content* of the various claims to natural rights differs according to the classes favored by that content. The natural rights of the aristocracy and the monarchy were variously defended as "pure" (divine) or—for example, by English conservatives—as utilitarian, depending on the challenges encountered. The rights in question were those which benefited their continuing privileges. The natural rights of the working class, which would emerge as the industrial revolution came more and more to define the life of Europe, were defended in terms both of "pure" rights (the right of a man to keep what he had produced) and of utility (to motivate greater productivity, to give the worker a sense of meaningfulness and control over his labors)—again, depending on the struggle involved. But in any case the rights demanded were directed toward giving the workers a greater share in the products of their labor, and toward material recognition of the now essential role that they played in society.

The natural rights of the bourgeoisie were also defined by their own interests at the time, however couched in the universal language of Reason and "humanity." Their content, accordingly, was directed at their own opportunities in power and privilege, and against the special powers and privileges of the estates above them. The lower classes would, to some extent, benefit from these aspiring demands as well. But the natural rights to freedom of speech and the press, to private property and freedom to conduct business without government interference, and to be philosophers and atheists and make incendiary comments against the nobility and the

Church—these were not rights which the often tragically poor, sometimes starving, brutally exploited, and hopelessly needy lower classes found particularly interesting. The middle classes were already well off; they wanted something more than the material necessities. They wanted power and freedom—luxuries in the eyes of the poor.

If the content of middle-class natural rights remained more or less constant, the strategy of their Enlightenment demands changed in a dramatic and philosophically illuminating way. In the first half of the century, when the demand for rights was an uphill and ill-supported struggle, the conception of natural rights remained "pure," safe from the contingencies of upper-class conceptions of social utility, and from conservative arguments that the realization of such rights would undermine the established order of society. But after 1750, when the Enlightenment had acquired a significant following, the justifications were no longer "pure": the familiar arguments became strictly utilitarian. (After the Revolution, when the aspirations of the bourgeoisie had become realities, the language of "natural rights" would drop out altogether; by that time, such arguments could only be used *against* them.)

The main conflict and inconsistencies of the Enlightenment—and later of the Revolution—can be understood ideologically through these important philosophical conceptions of rights and their justification. If the mode of justification changes in accordance with the power of its advocates, then the style of argument—purist versus utilitarian—can be used as a diagnostic tool, in order to understand the ideology of its advocates and, in particular, their sense of their own status and power. Furthermore, the *content* of the rights demanded will be the major ideological force in determining material needs and political expediency, in separating one class from another and playing them against each other. For example, consider the supposed rights to free medical care, unemployment compensation, and minimal material necessities for the poor: are these natural rights, and if so, are they to be defended as "pure" rights or only by arguments from utility and social welfare? From the vantage point of the sick, the unemployed, the poor, and their advocates, these will certainly be defended as rights—*pure* rights requiring no further demonstration about the advantages or disadvantages to the rest of society. To the political leader with a multiple constituency, some of whom must pay for the welfare demanded by the others, the argument will be couched in terms of overall utility (decrease in crime rates, etc.), with a modest if not limp appeal to "human rights." To the libertarian and privileged members of that society who resent being coerced to pay for others' welfare—whether they invoke a new version of aristocratic privilege or more contemporary Protestant-ethic arguments about work and rewards—these will not be matters of "rights" at all, but at most, questions of charity and political policy. Following John Locke, Voltaire in particular embraced this libertarian policy where such rights were involved. His conception of natural rights was a weapon to be used by the bourgeoisie against their superiors; insofar as the lower classes could also benefit, so much the better. But he had no intention of allowing the same rights to be used against him.

The best example of this Voltairean double edge is to be found in the concept of private property. Locke had argued that the right to "own the soil with which one had mixed his own labour" was a natural right; so too was the right to pass on such property to one's heirs through "legitimate" channels. Voltaire followed him in this, arguing vehemently that private property was an "inalienable right," unabridgeable by royal decree. (He owned several extensive properties in nearby Switzerland.) But why should private property be a natural right? Because of the utility of encouraging people to develop land by allowing them to "own" it? Or is it, as Locke and Voltaire attempted to argue, purely a natural right? Rousseau, taking the contrary view, argued not only that such a right was not a right at all, but that it was the source of inequality among men and the basis of any number of other social ills. Significantly, this was a right advocated by those who already owned land, in order that it not be taken from them or be unduly taxed or controlled. But what of those who had no land at all, the migrant farmers and workers, the unlanded peasants and the urban poor? Did they too have a natural right to private property, and if so, to *what* property—that already owned by others? To the unlanded, such conceptions were a cruel joke—the right to own property which they could not possess because of the same rights of others. And what of any particular piece of property, earned or inherited "legitimately"? Where is the property that was not, at some point in history, stolen from its "natural" inhabitants by some invading army or powerful lord? To what extent was this right historically a question of might—of already established power of possession? As a matter of general principle, Voltaire would be the first to distinguish "right" from "might." (It was on this topic that he would later quarrel with Frederick the Great, rupturing their friendship.) But in the case of private property, he unwittingly found himself an implicit advocate of the contrary. Accordingly, there was always a strong touch of libertarianism in his liberalism—a reactionary anchor that tied his ideology to the established interests of the past in spite of his aspirations toward the future.

The Faith of a Misanthrope

> And when the hour arrives, it becomes clear that we have lived to no purpose. All reflections are vain, all reasoning on necessity and human wretchedness are only wasted words.
>
> Voltaire[13]

Voltaire was, above all, bitterly passionate and cantankerous. He was not a man of compassion as much as a compulsive combatant. His humanism was a hatred of stupidity; his hope for the future was begotten of disgust with the present. He was not in any real sense a philosopher: contradictions never bothered him; he used whatever premises he needed to win an argument, always in the nonnegotiable terms of Reason. On all the major issues of philosophy and metaphysics—about which he pretended not to care—he held dogmatic and inconsistent opinions. His hero Newton had spent his life trying to reconcile his physical discoveries with his belief in God and human freedom—a problem that never bothered Voltaire. The hero *philosophe* of Reason could not or would not grapple with abstract ideas, preferring the intellectual safety of polemics and parables.[14]

After 1750 Voltaire's ideological work was essentially done. With the weakening of the monarchy and aristocracy, the growth of the philosophers' middle-class audience, the publication of the *Encyclopédie,* and the adoption of the Enlightenment ideology throughout much of Europe (even in the courts of despots), Voltaire's weapon of reason was already victorious. The notion of natural rights had done its job and could now be bronzed in platitudes, like an old cannon. Accordingly, Voltaire himself changed—from the defensive polemicist to the indignant activist. He entered the political arena as a public defender, trying to protect the underdog against the prejudices of the past.[15] But again, what motivated Voltaire was not compassion so much as disgust. His personal life had become a series of misfortunes: Mme du Châtelet died in childbirth in 1749, he was again running from the law, he was being eclipsed by younger philosophers in Paris, and was unable to defend himself. The champion of humanity was still attacking a world that seemed to him irredeemably stupid.

It is often said that naive optimism was the outstanding feature of the Enlightenment, yet Voltaire was anything but optimistic. He believed that "man is a very wretched being who has a few hours of relief, a few minutes of satisfaction, and a long series of sorrows in his short life." His best-known work, *Candide,* is a philosophical satire which reduces optimism to utter nonsense: "Optimism is only a doctrine of despair under a consoling name." But pessimism was no better; long before, in his *Philosophical Letters,* he had rejected it in Pascal, whom he called "all gloominess and unreason." Accordingly, he attacked both views, and trying to classify him as either pessimist or optimist is impossible. Likewise it is said that the Enlightenment was essentially atheistic and against religion, but Voltaire again proves this wrong: one of his contributions to the new ideology was a cautious demonstration of the extent to which the concepts of "God" and "religion" could be stretched and made free of superstition and the authority of the Church, so as to encourage rather than belittle the human pursuit of happiness and become "natural"—in other words, a *rational* religion.

The link between Enlightenment optimism and pre-Enlightenment religious faith was never quite broken, and the distinction between them is not easily discernible. Voltaire rejected totally the Christian conception of a God who paid special attention to man and his welfare, insisting for example that "it is as absurd to call God just or unjust as it is to say that he is blue or square." Yet Voltaire never gave up his belief in God or in the idea of an orderly and rational universe. But both beliefs were derived as much from Newton as from Christianity. God was the first principle of physics, the ultimate cause which set the great Newtonian mechanism in motion. This view, which was and still is referred to as *deism,* was far removed from the traditional Judaeo-Christian view of God as a just Father and Judge. Voltaire's God was pure hypothesis, necessary to explain the existence and order of the universe. He might allow that God created human intelligence as part of the mechanism, but never that God had any special designs on men. Against the Christian viewpoint, Voltaire insisted that humanity had no special place in the universe. But by denying it a special place in God's universe, he elevated humanity in its own eyes, making it its own protector and judge—which amounted to an adolescent declaration of independence from God "the father" and the family of the Church.[16] For two thousand years, humanity had felt superior to nature but inferior to God; now God was no longer superior.

In a nominal sense, deism is still a theism, still constitutes belief in God. But it is not a God to whom it makes any sense to appeal through prayer or good works; not a God who provides or invokes moral laws for men to obey; not a God who will judge and praise or condemn. Deism inspires no fear of God, nor even respect or awe. There is no appeal to God's "mysterious ways" as a rationalization for human suffering, for God does not care about human fortune, nor does he have any "mysterious ways" other than the elegant and absolutely predictable machinery of the Newtonian laws of motion. Deism, in other words, is only nominally a "belief in God"; it is like the religion of an adolescent who has torn himself away from his parents' belief but who, being timid and dependent, still speaks with residual respect of some "Force" behind the world, a "Creator" no longer endowed with judicial powers. Looking back from an ideological milieu in which belief in God is wholly on the defensive, it is easy for us today to perceive the uneasy timidity with which most of the Enlightenment philosophers—and Voltaire in particular—denied, but could not quite reject, the traditional Christian God.[17]

Yet the God of deism did not lord it over any particular church. He did not have a "chosen people," or any interest in saving some souls rather than others. Deism allowed all men to share the same set of minimal religious beliefs. There were no privileged religions, no reason to battle one against the other. Deism was simply a rational belief in the order of the universe. As such, it was an apt synthesis of the Newtonian vision of the world, the Cartesian insistence upon autonomous Reason, and Voltaire's own demand for religious toleration. And if there was no need for Church authority, no need for superstitions and eccentric practices to prove one's "privileged" status in the eyes of God, then the persecution and intolerance of the Church made no sense whatever.

In 1755 Voltaire's personal despair was heightened by a calamitous earthquake in Lisbon, which set him—and virtually every other philosopher in the Western world—to rethink the question of human suffering. Were humanism and faith in human progress enough? Could one live without religion? And if one did believe, was the Christian belief in divine justice even plausible in the face of such a catastrophe? The old way of thinking had been simple: it is God's will, his ways are mysterious. But the new philosophers no longer believed in "mysterious ways"; they held faith that the universe was rational. In England, accordingly, Alexander Pope had argued in verse that so it must be, for "whatever is, is right." And in Germany the philosopher Leibniz had systematically defended the view that, contrary to appearances, this was indeed "the best of all possible worlds," and that "evil cannot be excluded from a world in which man is free." But this cruel conclusion—rather than the dubiousness of the arguments—enraged Voltaire, again not so much out of compassion as hatred of stupidity. Of course, Leibniz was anything but stupid, but his ideas are made to appear so and be remembered thus through the character of Dr. Pangloss in *Candide*.[18]

Candide displays, better than any other of Voltaire's writings, his impatience with abstract philosophy and metaphysics, his preference for satire over argument, and despite his use of "Reason," his distrust of "pure" reason.[19] Such was the double edge of Voltaire's philosophical method: Reason was his ideal and his weapon, but he was aware of its abuses. The life of Reason, once removed from daily experience and common sense, was as foolish as the worst superstitions. This is his argument against Leibniz via Pangloss—ultimately, an argument against the Enlightenment as well. For underlying these satirical double twists is Voltaire's recognition that we in fact have but a tenuous grasp on reality, and the very Reason and philosophy which he is so instrumental in promoting may be just the force that loosens our hold altogether. Ultimately, the Enlightenment must throw itself into particular deeds and projects, as Voltaire himself insisted after finishing this short novel. In fact it did so—but only until the consequences of a more abstract and violently radical ideology reduced all such good deeds and projects to nothing.

The recurrent theme of *Candide*, with both Candide and Dr. Pangloss as its spokesmen, is the defense of Leibniz's "best of all possible worlds" doctrine in the face of every conceivable atrocity. The novel is a masterpiece in ridiculous rationalization. When Pangloss catches syphilis from one of the servants in the Baron's castle ("the best of all possible castles"), he accepts the necessity of this, since if Columbus had not brought syphilis back from America, we would not now have chocolate. In this modern odyssey no one is spared Voltaire's irony. Rousseau's primitive state of nature receives special ridicule: Candide proclaims it good because the savages of South America, "instead of eating me, offered me a thousand civilities as soon as they knew I was not a Jesuit."[20] And even Eldorado, the Enlightenment Utopia of Voltaire's own fancy, is cast in sarcasm. Based on Pure Reason, Eldorado is a state that has all comforts, natural religion and general toleration, and no wars or crimes; science and literature are highly honored there, and "reasonable discussion" is the constant activity. But Candide misses his mistress, and greed is a more powerful motive than happiness: if he and his friends remain in Eldorado, Candide says, they will only be like everyone else—happy; but if they return to their own world with some of the gold and gems that are worthless in Eldorado, they will be "richer than all the kings put together." So much for Utopia.

In the course of the novel, Candide, Cunegonde, and Pangloss are subjected to the spectrum of human cruelties, being variously tortured, beaten, hanged, dissected, raped, disemboweled, and intolerably degraded, while Pangloss reflects, "I am a philosopher, and it would be unbecoming for me to recant, since Leibniz . . ."—a refrain inevitably ending with the phrase, "best of all possible worlds" (p. 107). By the end of the novel, this small band of philosophical heroes has endured and recovered from tortures and humiliations that would have killed fifty nonfictional characters. Exhausted and poor, they settle on a small plot of land to grow and sell vegetables. Pangloss, naturally, rationalizes endlessly to maintain the "bestness" of this ridiculous world. Finally Candide, who had always been the faithful disciple, dismisses these now tiresome explanations: "That's all very well, but we must cultivate our garden" (p. 115). An apt metaphor for Voltaire's philosophy: hard work, a minimum of abstract argument, and above all "cultivation" of our own potential, of our Reason, and the active attempt, however humble, to better the circumstances in which we involuntarily find ourselves.[21]

Reason's Hero

The inconsistencies in Voltaire's philosophy can be easily understood as soon as one moves from the explicit philosophical level to the not always articulated ideological level. Voltaire was not interested in defending the empiricism of John Locke, but in undermining the intolerance and stupidities of the French aristocracy. He was less interested in rejecting Descartes or Leibniz than in deflating the pretensions of an abstract rationalism that neglected the realities of everyday life. He was not as concerned to develop a new religion as to destroy the abusive established one, and less interested in analyzing Reason than in using it to gain his advantage. His inconsistencies in metaphysics and method were of little consequence—either to his own thinking or to the thought of those who followed him. (In fact, two of the greatest German philosophers, Kant and Hegel, were to argue that such inconsistencies or "antinomies" of Reason were unavoidable.) What would be of great consequence, however, were the inconsistencies in his own ideology: the personal aspirations of a member of the *haute bourgeoisie,* as opposed to the universal demand for natural rights in which these aspirations were expressed; the emphasis upon "reasonableness," combined with a distrust of Reason; the ideal of human progress, contrasted with an extreme lack of confidence in human intelligence. These inconsistencies were not fully philosophical, but neither were they merely personal. They were marks of a general ideology which, once it had accomplished its purposes in France, would explode in contradictions that we are still trying to work out today.

After *Candide,* Voltaire turned even further from philosophy and, in accordance with his own conclusions in the novel, directed his attention to the particular misfortunes and injustices of the real world. Now in continuous exile, he spent his last years in quarreling bitterly with friends and battling in the law courts, even while he proved himself to still be the champion of humanity. But his deism was too timid and his monarchism too strong for the new age. The struggle against the superstitions and abuses of the Old Regime and the absolute authority of the Church was coming to an end: his defensive ideology of Reason and natural rights had triumphed, even to the point of now being taken for granted as the basis of the new ideology. A few months before his death in 1778, he returned to Paris for the first time in many years and received a hero's welcome.

3 Paranoia to Politics: Rousseau

> Nature made man happy and good, and society depraves him and makes him miserable.
>
> Rousseau, *Emile*

> As Newton was the first to discern order and regularity in nature, Rousseau was the first to discover beneath the varying forms human nature assumes, the deeply concealed essence of man and the hidden law in accordance with which providence is justified.
>
> Immanuel Kant

As long as the Enlightenment limited itself to concrete reforms and criticisms or particular stupidities and abuses, it could pretend to be a single ideology, representing the whole of the bourgeoisie and therefore the whole of humanity. But once the ideology of the Enlightenment was fashioned into an explicit philosophy—something beyond useful slogans and catchwords like "humanity," "reason," "natural," and "liberty"—it became obvious that there was no single system. Violent disagreements and dangerous ambiguities were tenuously united. They were all thoroughly bourgeois, but now one had to talk about bourgeois ideologies in the plural, all of them equally faithful to their original ideas.[1]

Jean-Jacques Rousseau was not really one of the philosophers. He came to Paris a provincial musician from Geneva, with none of the sophistication and urbanity of Voltaire and the Encyclopedists. In personality he did not fit in, either: he lacked their sense of camaraderie and mutual protection, was quarrelsome even beyond their generous tolerance for argument, and was suspicious to the point of paranoia, notwithstanding the very real threats of censorship and arrest against all of them. In his own words, he was "dishonest and untrustworthy"—to such an extent that he was finally excluded and disowned by his best philosopher friends—his *only* friends—including Voltaire, Diderot, and David Hume, who considered him a traitor to their cause.[2] He even had the audacity to say that "the man who thinks is a depraved animal." In *Emile* he would chide his colleagues: "I do not wish to philosophize with you. . . . If all the philosophers in the

54

world should prove that I am wrong, and you feel that I am right, that is all I ask."[3]

Consequently, it has often been argued that Rousseau was not part of the Enlightenment, but rather one of its first critics. But this presumes a falsely simplistic idea of Enlightenment ideology, as if Voltaire's sarcasm alone could define an immensely complex set of ideas. Whatever their disagreements, Rousseau and the philosophers shared essential concepts of humanity, human nature, natural law and natural rights, a sense of "progress," and qualified optimism regarding the perfectibility of humanity.[4] Despite Rousseau's overcelebrated talk about "sentiment" and "the heart," he shared the Enlightenment's conviction in the importance of reason and rational society: "Our natural sentiments shall guide reason to know the good, our conscience then to love it." Like the philosophers, Rousseau attacked institutional religion. Unlike most of them, he had been raised a Protestant, and so found appeals to individual conscience and the rejection of Church authority even more congenial than they did. He too was a spokesman and a martyr for freedom, and though he preached a view that would eventually beget the anti-Enlightenment, he was as much a part of the Enlightenment as any of the philosophers. Ironically, he would prove to be the only one among them with a developed theory to support the platitudes they shared. And if that theory was, in Voltaire's words, "peppered with paradoxes," it was mainly because Rousseau delved deeply into ambiguities that the others glossed over. Voltaire, for example, limited his concern for "liberty" to a narrow set of concrete issues—freedom of speech and the press, religious toleration, the right to own property; but Rousseau tried to get a grip on the concept of freedom itself. And in that concept he uncovered not only a blueprint for future society, a way of rebuilding from the foundations, but a paradoxical horror that would eventually split the Enlightenment—and Europe—asunder.[5]

The Problem of Jean-Jacques Rousseau

> So my birth was the first of my misfortunes.
>
> Rousseau, *Confessions*

If personality reflects ideology (or vice versa), then Rousseau is a very special case: "I am unlike anyone I have ever met; I will even venture to say that I am like no one in the whole world."[6] Introspective, antisocial, and paranoid, Rousseau projected a sense of self-righteousness and philosophical resentment that would inspire half the world. He saw in himself the whole of humanity, and on that basis promised others a kind of happiness, virtuousness, and sense of belonging that he himself never knew. In his bitterness he created a vision of life which went so much further than the limited reforms of the other philosophers that it became a motive for revolution first in France and then throughout the world.

Unlike Voltaire and the other philosophers, Rousseau lacked the advantages of good schooling, a comfortable middle-class upbringing, and the love, if not support, of his family. He was born into a very different middle class, a "lumpen bourgeoisie" in provincial Geneva. His mother died in childbirth, and one need not be a Freudian to trace the origins of his unhappiness in the autobiographical *Confessions:*

A poor, sickly child, and I cost my mother her life. . . . I never knew how my father stood up to his loss, but I know that he never got over it. He seemed to see her again in me, but could never forget that I had robbed him of her; he never kissed me that I did not know by his sighs and his convulsive embrace that there was a bitter grief mingled with his affection, a grief which nevertheless intensified his affection for me. (p. 19)

His father proved somewhat of a scoundrel, and when fleeing the law abandoned his children when Rousseau was ten. Without schooling, Rousseau had little regard for the classics, having in his own words been a youth "hating books, idle, bored and restless, dishonest and untrustworthy" (p. 16). While Voltaire was entertaining the French court, Rousseau held a job as a lackey. While Voltaire carried on with the learned Mme du Châtelet in luxurious châteaus, Rousseau married a maid in his run-down hotel. He fathered five children by her, but when she died he unsentimentally sent them away to orphanages. By contrast, Voltaire adopted children not his own, to assure them a proper upbringing. Yet it is Rousseau who emerged as the defender of intrinsic human goodness and the proponent of education.

While Voltaire developed the charm and wit which made him a celebrity in the most powerful salons of Europe, his younger Swiss colleague found little satisfaction or comfort in any sophisticated or—as he would put it—hypocritical and frivolous society. Yet it was Rousseau, by his own admission and by the evidence of his acquaintances, who wanted companionship and devoted friendship most desperately.

My reader has already guessed, if he has paid the least attention to my progress so far. The impossibility of attaining the real persons precipitated me into the land of chimeras; and seeing nothing that existed worthy of my exalted feelings, I fostered them in an ideal world which my creative imagination soon peopled with beings after my own heart. (*Confessions*, p. 27)

While Voltaire found himself at home everywhere in Europe, Rousseau belonged nowhere. He was always the outsider, wanting to be where he was not. He had a nostalgia for Geneva that was close to worship, yet he did not return until he had to, and then was run out of town. While Voltaire had his happy and sustaining relationships with women, Rousseau found every affair a disaster—often more of an incestuous mother-son relationship than love (he called his mistress "maman"). Again, the Freudian psychohistorian will find more material than he could hope for:

> If the fire in my blood demands women, the emotion in my heart cries more loudly for love. Women who could be bought would lose all their charm for me. I doubt whether I could even take advantage of the situation. It is the same with all pleasures within my reach. If they are not to be had for nothing, they have no attraction for me. The only things I like are things that belong to no one but the first person who knows how to enjoy them. (p. 28)

Just as Voltaire celebrated the elitism in which he fit so well, Rousseau damned the society that made him feel so uncomfortable. As he approached middle age, he began to make increasingly explicit a self-righteous suspicion that his own inherent goodness and virtue could breathe in the stagnant airs of high society. In his well-known *Second Discourse (On the Origins of Inequality among Men,* 1754), he would complain of the contrast between the "natural" goodness and easy contentment that he imagined in himself, and the corruption and maliciousness of society:

> Savage man, when he has dined, is at peace with all nature, and the friend of all his fellow-creatures. If a dispute arises about a meal, he rarely comes to blows, without having first compared the difficulty of conquering his antagonist with the trouble of finding subsistence elsewhere: and, as pride does not come in, it all ends in a few blows; the victor eats, and the vanquished seeks provision somewhere else, and all is at peace. The case is quite different with man in the state of society, for whom first necessaries have to be provided, and then superfluities; delicacies follow next, then immense wealth, then subjects, and then slaves. He enjoys not a moment's relaxation; and what is yet stranger, the less natural and pressing his wants, the more headstrong are his passions, and, still worse, the more he has it in his power to gratify them; so that after a long course of prosperity, after having swallowed up treasures and ruined multitudes the hero ends up by cutting every throat till he finds himself, at last, sole master of the world. Such is in miniature the moral picture, if not of human life, at least of the secret aspirations in the heart of every civilized man.[7]

His *Confessions* pursue this theme relentlessly: Jean-Jacques Rousseau, the naturally good, poor, misunderstood innocent versus the corruption and viciousness of society. Accordingly, nothing that he did was his own fault. In his affairs, his mistresses always "seduced" him. When he slept with whores in Venice, it was "because society would have called him a fool if he didn't." When he slept with a twelve-year-old, "she was corrupted anyway." The entire *Confessions* are a paradox, not a "confession" but a justification and system of excuses. In this supposed presentation of Rousseau's "innermost secrets," the real "secrets"—his feelings about his father's abandoning him, his sense of impotence, of defensiveness, of worthlessness—are barely touched. There is not a single instance of an attempt to understand another person. Is this the "indifference" he projects back into primitive man? What always emerges is Rousseau the victim—paranoia that he projects into the nature of society as such.

The secret of Rousseau's brilliance was his imagination, an imagination that had the ability to escape the unhappy reality of his everyday existence:

It is a very strange thing that my imagination never works more delightfully than when my situation is the reverse of delightful, and that, on the other hand, it is never less cheerful than when all is cheerful around me. My poor head can never submit itself to the facts. It cannot beautify; it must create. . . . If I want to describe the spring it must be in winter; if I want to describe a fine landscape I must be within doors; and as I have said a hundred times, if ever I were confined to the Bastille, there I would draw the picture of liberty.[8]

His imagination in turn invented the marvelous myth of primal innocence —the notion that, deep inside, a person could be wholly good despite the most wicked and unhappy life.[9]

I drew this great maxim of morality, perhaps the only one of practical use, to avoid situations which put our duties in opposition with our interests and which show us our good in the hurts of others, sure that in such situations, however sincere our love of virtue, we weaken sooner or later without realizing it, and become unjust and wicked in our actions, without having stopped being just and good at heart. (*Confessions*, p. 8)

"Wicked in our actions, without having stopped being just and good at heart"—here is the key to Rousseau's lifelong dilemma. He continues: "Let us penetrate to . . . the bottom of our hearts, and let us reflect on what state of things must be in which all men are forced to caress each other and to destroy each other, and in which they are born enemies out of duty and crooks out of self-interest" (p. 8).

Walking through the public forests of St. Germain, virtuously alone in a deep and almost mystical contemplation, Rousseau had visions of natural harmony and of men living together in a rational society, free of possessiveness and greed, like the large family he often dreamed about but never had. Here his childish vision was replaced by a powerful argument against the authority of kings; his loneliness became a utopian vision of belonging, and his self-righteousness a moral theory—far more radical than those of the philosophers—about the intrinsic goodness of the human heart. His former hatred of books seemed not to interfere with his becoming the most articulate philosopher of the French Enlightenment, as he forged his visions into a philosophy, and replaced his psychopathic nostalgia for the peace of those forests with an articulate ideology that would soon change humanity.

Two Discourses on Human Nature and Corruption

In 1749, while visiting his one friend, Diderot, who was in prison in Vincennes, Rousseau came across an advertisement for an essay contest in Dijon on the topic, "Has the restoration of the sciences and arts tended to purify morals?" In a great "revelation," Rousseau mustered all his literary abilities and wrote an inspired essay—his *First Discourse*—arguing that the sciences and arts have corrupted if not maimed morality. The essay was not satisfactory to Rousseau, who later judged it mediocre, but it won the contest nonetheless. Its central theme, the corruption of man's natural goodness by the conventions of society, provided the postulate from which all Rousseau's subsequent writings evolved. It was a philosophy well suited to his misfit personality: a strange celebration of the estranged individual, combined with a dreamlike appeal to the perfectibility of man in society. Defending "natural inclinations" against the artificiality of "customs, politeness and propriety," it declared that "one no longer dares to appear as he is." While defending Voltaire Rousseau accused the arts of using these conventions to stifle original and "natural" reason. He inveighed against politeness and public success in favor of the "heart's disposition" and "self-esteem" (*amour-propre*). He was writing, he said, "not so much against science but for virtue," and as much as any post-Newtonian English philosopher, he used science and history to establish his thesis of the corruption of morals by science. The *First Discourse* was also an attack on academic philosophy and sophisticated reason by a "common man," as he called himself, though he appealed not to the public, whom he despised as ignorant, but to "a few wise men"—his audience throughout his career. His "populism" combined an abstract love of man with hatred and distrust of individual men: "Man is good, men are perverse."

The main sources of evil, Rousseau argued, were inequality, then wealth, then luxury, from which the fine arts come, and idleness, which begets science. In his *Philosophical Dictionary* Voltaire had said:

What does a dog owe a dog, a horse owe a horse? Nothing. No animal depends upon his fellow beast; but as man has received the ray of divinity we call *reason*, what has been the result? To be enslaved almost the whole world over.[10]

Such was Rousseau's opinion as well, but his reaction was not to glorify reason, which made possible the institution of property and consequently the evils of luxury, idleness, and inequality, but to look beyond or behind it: "One cannot reflect on morals without delighting in the recollection of the simplicity of the earliest times," he says in the *First Discourse*. "Virtue is not incompatible with ignorance"; man is "depraved" by reason. In this first essay the single problem that would obsess Rousseau all his life was explicit: how to realize man's natural goodness in a corrupt society. Though he was never the revolutionary, revolution always appeared as a very real and perhaps necessary possibility: "There is no longer a remedy, except for some great revolution almost as greatly to be feared as the evil that it could cure, and that it is blameworthy to desire and impossible to foresee." (Yet Rousseau turned down an invitation to join the revolution in his native Geneva.)

Voltaire was by far the more clever and learned polemicist, but his wit proved too sharp, and his brilliance too restless, to allow him that necessary intellectual discipline which makes for definitive philosophical thinking. And so Rousseau, though neither learned nor particularly clever, reveals the more subtle and disciplined mind, and his philosophy, unlike that of Voltaire, can be viewed, as he viewed it himself in his *Confessions,* as the development of a single idea: "the natural goodness and potential virtue of humanity."

In his *Second Discourse,* entitled *On the Origins of Inequality among Men,* Rousseau developed these themes far more radically and completely than he had a few years earlier. He submitted this second essay as an entry in the 1754 contest at Dijon, confident of winning again. He did not, but clearly it was this essay that established the legacy of Rousseau's "primitivism," providing the enlightened world with its popular model of the "noble savage," of man in the state of nature.[11] In a lengthy series of speculations Rousseau suggests that primeval man was strong and self-loving, absolutely independent and without the need for society or speech. He was, basically, a "stupid and dull-witted animal." Though a vegetarian, he ate meat when he needed it, and was capable of surviving and defending himself alone. The role of the family was minimal—biological but not social, like a "family" of cats or mice. (It is worth remembering that Rousseau had been abandoned by his father, and abandoned his own children in turn, "since society would corrupt them anyway.") Sexuality was a matter of chance coupling, without the need for speech, between males and females who "left each other with the same ease." Thus the family was not essential to the state of nature or to sexuality and childbirth —a view that contradicted Locke and has offended English commentators ever since. Because it is also true that Rousseau's state of nature is decidedly male-dominated, one can interpret "the independence of each man" as applying solely to *men,* as opposed to women and children. But what is important is that there was no society, little or no communicative speech, and little or no dependence of one man upon another.

Yet this life was not, as Hobbes had suggested, "nasty, brutish and short"; it was not a "war of all against all," nor was primitive man ruled by selfishness.[12] War and violence were foreign to these primitive people, who had no conception of "mine" and "thine," of property or jealousy, and therefore left each other alone. And where there was no property, there could be no selfishness. Primitive man took care of himself first, but this did not entail taking care of himself to the exclusion of another. The relation of man to man was one of indifference, not mutual hostility. Moreover, Rousseau argues, man's natural sentiment of self-esteem was coupled with another: *pity,* or the dislike of seeing fellow creatures in pain. Here is the source of man's natural goodness—not a rational principle such as "Do unto others as you would have them do unto you," but rather a law of instinct, a sentiment that says, "Do what is good for you without doing harm to others." It is a law of the strong and independent, and from it emerges Rousseau's problematic and radical conception of freedom as *independence from other men:*

Savage man and civilized man differ so much at the bottom of their hearts and in their inclinations, that what constitutes the supreme happiness of the one would reduce the other to despair. The first sighs for nothing but repose and liberty; he desires only to live, and to be exempt from labor; . . . Civilized man, on the other hand, is always in motion, perpetually sweating and toiling, and racking his brains to find out occupations still more laborious: he continues a drudge to his last minute; nay, he courts death to be able to live, or renounces life to acquire immortality. He pays court to men in power whom he hates, and to rich men whom he depises; . . . proud of his slavery, he speaks with disdain of those who have not the honor of sharing it. . . . The savage lives within himself, whereas social man, constantly outside himself, knows only how to live in the opinion of others; and it is, if I may say so, merely from their judgment of him that he derives the consciousness of his own existence.

Or as he puts it more bluntly elsewhere: "The man who stands in dependence on another is no longer a man."[13]

Rousseau's tendency to romanticize the state of nature should not mislead us into thinking that it is a utopian ideal for him, and cause us to conjure up visions of a primitive paradise as depicted by another Rousseau —Henri Rousseau, the artist—a century and a half later. The state of nature functions for Jean-Jacques as a test, as a radical standard against which one can measure the conventions and dictates of society. The "stupid and dull-witted animal" was no ideal, but liberation from the niceties of social intercourse (including the unnecessary courtesies of presexual discourse) has appealed to generations of misanthropes from Rousseau's time down to the present.

It was in response to the *Second Discourse* that Voltaire wrote Rousseau (while the two were still speaking):

I have received, sir, your new book against the human race; I thank you for it. You will please men, to whom you frankly tell their faults, but you will not correct them. . . . the reading of your book makes us want to creep on all fours. However, as it is now more than sixty years since I lost that habit, I feel unfortunately that it is impossible for me to take it up again. . . . I agree with you that the letters and sciences have sometimes caused a great deal of harm [but] confess truly sir, that . . . the thorns attached to literature and to a reputation however small are only flowers in comparison with other evils which in every age have inundated the earth.[14]

But Rousseau's "primitivism" is not at all what it is usually taken to be; the so-called noble savage plays no role in it.[15] In the *Second Discourse* Rousseau carefully outlines four distinct presocietal stages of human development. The first is the beastly savage state mocked by Voltaire; but Rousseau no more admires or longs for that state than Voltaire. He too considers it subhuman—"natural" only in the sense that it happened once in nature. But what is "natural" also refers to *potentiality,* to what humanity inherently can and will become. The potentiality that distinguishes man from the beasts, according to Rousseau, is precisely his intellect and reason. So much for the legend of Rousseau's attack on reason and the Enlightenment. He is as Aristotelean[16] and rationalist as Voltaire; if anything, he distrusts the passions—so violent and destructive in himself—even more than his avowedly empiricist contemporary: "My passions are extremely strong, and while I am under their sway nothing can equal my impetuosity" (*Confessions*, p. 29). The "state of nature" in which humanity first existed is neither enviable nor imitable; it is in the development of human reason, with all its flaws and stupidities, that Rousseau sees the promise of human perfectibility: "I do not want to make modern man a savage and send him back to the woods, rather teach him, in the whirl of social life, not to be carried away by passions and prejudices of men" (*Emile*). Just as he does not insist on sending man back into the woods as a savage and finds the loss of the state of nature "irretrievable," so Rousseau has no desire to sacrifice reason to the passions, to send man back to innocent stupidity. Rather, it is in the later stages of human development—but still before society—that he finds ideals that are worth resurrecting and developing in the present.

Yet as always, a qualification is in order, for Rousseau's hatred of contemporary society was such that he could not help but feel a certain nostalgia and "delight" in contemplating even the stupid life of the brute. At least that animal was happy, healthy, and relatively harmless. People in contemporary society—not the least of them Jean-Jacques Rousseau—were comparatively sickly, dangerous, and unhappy, all at once: "Such is the melancholy evidence that we might have avoided almost all the ills we suffer from, if we had kept to the simple, uniform, and solitary existence prescribed to us by nature. If she intended us to be healthy, I venture almost to affirm that the state of reflection is a state contrary to nature, and the man who thinks is a depraved animal" (*Second Discourse*). Moreover, this ignoble but at least happy savage had a primitive sort of fellow feeling or "sympathy" that modern sophisticates have lost. Despite their isolation and lack of community in any sense, the first people hated to see one another suffer, unlike the comparative sadists of contemporary life. Those primitives were selfish, to be sure, but their rare attacks on one another were always the result of real necessity, not the ego and status needs of societal vanity.

Rousseau's concern is humanity's development from this primitive state to perfection. He does not believe that man has suffered a long and unhappy decline from primitive perfection; to the contrary, humanity has endured "a slow and painful ascent from animality to the life of a rational and social being" (Lovejoy, p. 42). The first step beyond the state of nature, and the second stage of human development, is the appearance of self-consciousness and with it self-esteem, vanity, and a strong concern for other human beings. If this is the origin of most of the evils that Rousseau deplores in contemporary society, it is also, according to him, the definitive step that lifts humanity *above* the animals and starts it on the road to human perfection. And for Rousseau as for Aristotle, "human" perfection means perfection in accordance with man's intrinsically human nature as a social and a rational animal. Then comes the third stage of development, the stage which Rousseau explicitly does take as his model and source of political ideals: the stage of primitive community, still presocietal, prepolitical in the grand sense, still less than the full development of humanity, but filled with a fellow feeling much more sophisticated than the simple "sympathy" of the savage, and far more powerful and satisfying than any of the "sentiments" of contemporary society. The paradigm of this simple community is the human family, which will become the initial model for Rousseau's theory of the modern state in his great political work, *The Social Contract*, where he asserts that "the most ancient of all societies, and the only one that is natural, is the family."[17]

Rousseau's use of the family as a paradigm requires a word of caution, however. It is important to note that the family is not "natural" in the state of nature of stage one, and must therefore be in some sense conventional even though it precedes the social contract. And no sooner does Rousseau introduce this paradigm than he proceeds immediately to its extended manifestation in tribes and communities. We can only conclude that Rousseau takes his family paradigm much less seriously than he claims. In the context of his theory as a whole, with its emphasis on the primacy of the individual and on society and its universal laws, the family in fact drops out of the discussion. The most obvious features of society according to Rousseau—namely, its contractual nature and the right of the governed to replace the governing—cannot plausibly be thought of as "natural" to the family in any state whatever.

This third stage too might be said to represent a "state of nature," but this ambiguity has its obvious dangers. A community without written or contractual laws—a primitive tribe, for example—is still an advanced system of symbolic rituals, gestures, and dependencies, and therefore far removed from what Rousseau calls "natural" in other contexts. But when Rousseau talks about his longing for a return to the state of nature, it must be kept perfectly clear that it is this relatively advanced state of nature that he has in mind: "Though men now had less endurance, and though natural sympathy had suffered some diminution, this period of the development of human faculties, holding a just mean between the indolence of the primitive state and the petulant activity of our self-esteem, must have been the happiest and most lasting epoch." Rousseau adds that all subsequent advances have been, in fact, "steps towards the decrepitude of the species." Yet this is not a cry of despair, but a source of Enlightenment hope: "Far from thinking that there is no longer any virtue or happiness attainable by us, and that Heaven has abandoned us without resource to the depravation of the species, let us endeavor to draw from the very evil from which we suffer the remedy which shall cure it."

The Social Contract

Living in Paris, Rousseau was uncomfortable in the plush surroundings of society and the witty intellectual life. He remembered provincial Geneva and idolized its small-town sophistication. (Ironically, Voltaire was then in exile in Geneva, longing desperately for Paris.) As Rousseau developed his image of the ideal legitimate society during the 1750s, it is not surprising that it bore a resemblance to Geneva: "Having been born a citizen of a free State and a member of the sovereign, . . . I feel happy, whenever I meditate on governments, always to discover in my researches new reasons for loving that of my own country" (*Social Contract,* p. 5). During this period of his life, punctuated by political and personal problems that included his complete and final break with Voltaire, Rousseau worked feverishly on a pair of manuscripts. The first was *Emile,* his most eloquent plea for natural man and a theory of education to regain the happiness and moral qualities of a simpler epoch. It is a rather philosophical work based on the principle that man is naturally good but is made wicked by society. The second book, a treatise on government called *The Social Contract,* would become the ideological bible of many revolutions. (While Fidel Castro was fighting in the mountains of Cuba, *The Social Contract* was his constant companion.) "Man is born free," Rousseau declared, setting the premise for the next two centuries; yet "everywhere he is in chains. One thinks himself the master of others, and still remains a greater slave than they" (p. 5). Even masters are slaves—in this inversion we can already see the thought of the whole of the nineteenth century, and much of our own.

In 1762 Rousseau published both books. As his prize for *Emile,* a warrant was issued for his arrest in Paris. Once again he returned to Switzerland, but he was soon threatened there with arrest for both books, and his house was stoned by the very citizens whom he had honored in the *Social Contract*'s flattering dedication. So much for the reality of his model and his nostalgia for his "home." He fled to Prussia, then to England and David Hume, but that friendship too exploded in ill feeling and paranoia. He returned to France under an assumed name, friendless and utterly desperate.

In contrast to his personal situation, both *Emile* and *The Social Contract* paint man as a potentially happy, harmonious creature, at peace with his fellow men and himself. The theme of *The Social Contract* (and of *Emile*) is the *legitimacy* of the communal state, as opposed to the arbitrary and oppressive governments of Europe, and the innocent and "natural" communities of the days before Society: "I wish to inquire whether, taking men as they are and laws as they can be made, it is possible to establish some just and certain rule of administration in civil affairs" (p. 5). Here is the great change from the earlier *Discourses* to the theory of *The Social Contract:* the corruption of nature by society is no longer the problem; rather it is how can man live well in society and, conversely, what kind of society is justified, in that it allows people to live as closely as possible to the happiness and moral harmlessness of their more "natural" state.

The passage from the state of nature to the civil state produces in man a very remarkable change, by substituting in his conduct justice for instinct, and by giving his actions a moral quality that they previously lacked. It is only when the voice of duty succeeds physical impulse, and law succeeds appetite, that man, who till then had regarded only himself, sees that he is obliged to act on other principles, and to consult his reason before listening to his inclinations. Although, in this state, he is deprived of many advantages that he derives from nature, he acquires equally great ones in return. . . . He is transformed from a stupid and ignorant animal into an intelligent being and a man. (p. 31)

The question of *legitimacy* is the most radical of political questions. It does not accept established political structures just because they exist, nor even because they are obeyed and respected (p. 7). It does not simply look at the particular injustices and inequalities that had been attacked by Voltaire and the other philosophers. It requires an investigation into the very nature of society, one possible consequence of which might well be the call to a total overthrow of the society. Thus Rousseau calls into question an institution which the other philosophers, following Locke, had considered sacred: private property. In his first essay, *On the Origins of Inequality*, Rousseau had traced the inequities of modern society to insatiable demands for power and wealth. It is indeed as Locke had argued, that property is the basis of civil society. But far from being a natural right, Rousseau now argues, it has become the unnatural seed of corruption, the degradation of humanity, and the origin of such perverse human relationships as slavery.

The first man who enclosed a plot of ground and bethought himself of saying "this is mine" and found others foolish enough to believe him, was the true founder of civil society. How many crimes, how many wars, how many murders, how many misfortunes and horrors, would that man have saved the human species, who pulling up the stakes or filling up the ditches should have cried to his fellows: Beware of listening to this impostor; you are lost, if you forget that the fruits of the earth belong equally to us all, and the earth itself to nobody! (p. 212)

Most important of all, Rousseau shifts the basis of legitimacy from governments, their origins, and their actions, to a revolutionary political entity, *the People,* or what he calls the *sovereign.* "The sovereign" is not a king or a minister or a government of any form, but the people themselves. Governments of any kind, according to Rousseau, are mere intermediaries between individuals and the people as a whole, nothing more and nothing less. When they cease to function as intermediaries, they must be replaced (the theory that will justify the traumatic events of the 1790s in Paris). But when Rousseau insists that the basis of legitimacy lies in the people, he is saying something much more powerful than the familiar requirement that governments must serve the people and take account of their interests and well-being. Any enlightened philosopher or politician would have accepted that. What Rousseau is arguing is that the government is an instrument of the people, that power itself belongs to the people, and that the power of the people is the only possible legitimate power. This is the meaning of his social contract. The contract is a mutual agreement, of everyone with everyone, to form the social bond we call "society."[18] It is a bond that is absolute, which creates citizens out of isolated and indifferent men and women, which creates moral beings with mutual obligations and duties in the place of amoral creatures given to self-interest and simple contentment. As he had already said in an essay on "Political Economy" in Diderot's *Encyclopedia* (1775): "There can be no patriotism without liberty, no liberty without virtue, no virtue without citizens; create citizens and you have everything you need."[19]

Thus the problem is no longer simply to defend human nature against corruption, or natural man against societal man, but to "create citizens" to enable us to "resist the passions and prejudices of men." But against those who take Rousseau's interest to be a defense of either individualism or the State, it is necessary to emphasize that at the heart of both *Emile* and *The Social Contract,* and of all his work, is his concern with virtue and morality. The problem is how to make people *good,* and his concern with both individual freedom and citizenship are means to this end. In *Emile,* the theme is once again "natural goodness":

Let us lay it down as an incontrovertible rule that the first impulses of nature are always right; there is no original sin in the human heart, the how and why of the entrance of every vice can be traced. The only natural passion is self-love or selfishness taken in a wider sense. . . . yet we find our consolation in our sufferings in the charms of friendship and humanity, and even in our pleasures we should be too lonely and miserable if we had no one to share them with us. If there is no such thing as morality in man's heart, what is the source of his rapturous admiration of noble deeds, his passionate devotion to great men? . . . Not only do we wish to be happy ourselves, we wish others to be happy too, and if this happiness does not interfere with our happiness, it increases it. In conclusion, whether we will or not, we pity the unfortunate; when we see their suffering we suffer too. (*Emile,* p. 56)

But the sentiment of pity or sympathy, spontaneous in the state of nature, must now be rationalized and enforced against the corruptions of possessiveness and social vanity. The image of innocence must be given up, but in the name of virtue. Where "natural goodness" consisted largely in a virtue of omission, in not harming others needlessly, this new and powerful concept of virtue requires the rational conquest of the violent passions— the strength of which Rousseau avowed in himself—and the recognition of one's duties as a citizen. This is what Kant and the romantic philosophers will later identify as "positive freedom"—not simply freedom from re-straint, but freedom to act in accord with duty, conscience, and virtue— the freedom to obey. Agreeing to the social contract is equivalent to prescribing the law to oneself, which in turn makes people independent of one another, but at the same time binds them to society. "In nature, man lives for himself; he is the unit, the whole, dependent only upon himself. . . . The citizen is but the numerator of a fraction, whose value depends on its denominator; his value depends on the whole, that is, on the commun-ity" (p. 97).

It has often been argued that in this bad reasoning lie the seeds of fascism, the primacy of the State *against* individuals. But Rousseau would counter that the *mutual* nature of the contract makes this antagonism impossible: "The engagements which bind us to the social body are obliga-tory only because they are mutual; and their nature is such that in fulfilling them we cannot work for others without also working for ourselves" (p. 25). To bring about this situation is to "create citizens," to make man unnatural, to exchange his independence for dependence, to merge the unity in the group, so that he no longer regards himself as one, but as part of the whole, and is only conscious of the common life.

This common, as opposed to individual, life gives birth to a common or General Will, to be distinguished from individual desires and demands.

Society is based upon the General Will, which is more than a consensus of individuals, being an entity in itself. In his earlier essay on "Political Economy," Rousseau had written:

The body politic, taken individually, may be considered as an organized living body, resembling that of man. The sovereign power represents the head, the laws and customs are the brain, the public income is the blood, the citizens are the body which make the machine live, move and work. . . . The body politic, therefore, is also a moral being possessed of a will, and this general will, which tends always to the preservation and welfare of the whole and of every part, is the source of the laws.[20]

The model of the natural goodness of man now extends to a kind of natural goodness of society, so long as it is embodied in the General Will. In fact, the goodness of particular wills comes to be measured by the General Will. In the same early essay Rousseau comments: "If you would have the general will accomplished, bring all the particular wills into conformity with it; in other words, as virtue is nothing more than this conformity of the particular wills with the general will, this will establish the reign of virtue."

In *The Social Contract,* the theory of the General Will becomes the basis of the social contract:

The problem is to find a form of association which will defend and protect with the whole common force the person and goods of each associate, and in which each, while uniting himself with all, may still obey himself alone, and remain as free as before. This is the fundamental problem of which the Social Contract provides the solution. . . . Each man, in giving himself to all, gives himself to nobody; and as there is no associate over which he does not acquire the same right as he yields others over himself, he gains an equivalent for everything he loses, and an increase of force for the preservation of what he has.

If then we discard from the social compact what is not of its essence, we shall find that it reduces itself to the following terms: Each of us puts his person and all his power in common under the supreme direction of the general will, and, in our corporate capacity, we receive each member as an indivisible part of the whole. (pp. 23–25)

Despite the strong and radical emphasis on the General Will, Rousseau is not advocating democracy or a republic; he insists that the General Will cannot be represented: "If there were a nation of gods, it would be governed democratically. So perfect a government is unsuited to men" (p. 113). His political model is compatible with a number of governmental forms, so long as the expression of the General Will is "sovereign." There may or may not be a king. Rousseau suggests that a monarchy would be "the most perfectly united," but the king would not be "absolute," just another "particular will" with obligations to the General Will. Sovereignty always resides in the people, but this is not yet a commitment to the republicanism of the French Revolution or to the democratic thinking of the extreme radicals or the Americans. In fact, Rousseau even suggests that sovereignty might be centered in "a few wise men" like Plato's philosopher-kings—that small number of select peers who have been Rousseau's intended audience since his first *Discourses.*

In his earlier essay on "Political Economy" Rousseau had enthusiastically commented that the voice of the people is the voice of God. In *The Social Contract* he is somewhat more restrained, but not much. Though he personally hated or at least distrusted almost everyone, Rousseau defends the most strongly "populist" theory of government that had ever been formulated in Europe. (In England, of course, the social contract had long been an accepted axiom of both philosophy and politics.) Suddenly, the traditional respect owed to kings, royal and noble families, and established laws and customs became open to radical questioning: "Do they conform to the will of the people?" In place of traditional authorities over the people, the people themselves were elevated to the rank of sovereign, even to the role of a divine power.

The concept of "the people," however, leaves open the place of individuals. On the one hand, "no one has the right to demand that another should do what he will not do himself." But then, what of the individual who does not agree with the majority and the General Will?

But it will be asked how a man can be free and yet forced to conform to wills which are not his own. How are opponents free and yet subject to laws they have not consented to? . . . When the opinion opposed to my own prevails, that simply shows that I was mistaken, and that what I considered to be the general will was not so. . . . The only law to require unanimous consent is the social contract itself. (p. 113)

In a much-quoted passage, Rousseau insists that the individual is not permitted his own way, and that freedom must not be confused with individuality. Freedom is obedience. Thus, paradoxically, "whoever refuses to obey the general will shall be constrained to do so by the whole body; which means nothing else than that he shall be forced to be free" (p. 31). Furthermore, the individual's "life is no longer a gift of nature, but a conditional gift of the State" (p. 36).

The greatest good and end of every system of legislation, according to Rousseau, should be liberty and equality—"liberty because all particular dependences mean so much force taken from the body of the state, and equality, because liberty cannot exist without it." But notice that the justification of liberty and equality has subtly shifted to the service of the State; no longer is it only the purpose of the State to serve liberty and equality. Here is the source of that dangerous shift that will determine so much of subsequent history: from the State serving individual liberty to the individual serving the State; from the State ill serving individual liberty as a justification for revolution, to the individual ill serving the State as a justification for oppression. In one sentence, here is the history of the French Revolution—and of many others, too.

This same duality appears in Rousseau's conception of freedom. If freedom means freedom to obey the laws of society, one may paradoxically be "forced to be free, for this is the condition which, by giving a citizen to his country, secures him against all personal dependence." Thus one sees again the fragile combination of individual liberty, or freedom from other men, and collective obligation, or duty, which pervades Rousseau's philosophy. Consequently, it has long been debated whether Rousseau is really a libertarian or a protototalitarian. Evidently he can be read as either, and the interpretation will depend—as always in abstract political theory—on the contingencies of particular situations and the nuances of needs and opinions. It is not uncommon to see Rousseau either as inconsistent or as having shifted from individualism to authoritarianism.[21] What makes him significant, however, is precisely that his ideas, however ambiguous, are not just inconsistent, and that throughout his career he pursues a single "grand principle," a concept of "virtue" that lies at the base of both his individual and his political concerns. This primitive virtue is best expressed in a small, communal rural society—a small and independent New England or Swiss town in the early nineteenth century, for example. But in a large anonymous city or in a country in the turbulence of revolution, the simple exercise of virtue becomes impossible, and the principles of the social contract become rationalizations for tyranny; "the more a social bond is extended, the more it is weakened."

This dangerous shift occurs again in Rousseau's attitude toward religion. Although he switched faiths twice in his lifetime, Rousseau was always a devout Christian. Like Voltaire, he was repulsed rather than enlightened by the atheism of Diderot and the Encyclopedists. He considered religion to be as essential to his ideal society as law, and even suggested capital punishment for atheism. What he ultimately preached was a simple "natural religion," much like that of Voltaire. But instead of reason, Rousseau followed "his heart"—like Voltaire's old enemy, Pascal. Thus in 1756 he replied to Voltaire's poem about the Lisbon earthquake: "All the subtleties of metaphysics would not lead me to doubt for a moment the immortality of my soul or a spiritual Providence; I feel it, I believe in it, I desire it, I hope for it and will defend it." And in the *Confessions:* "Since [my childhood], I have never again doubted my salvation" (p. 27). He rejected the Church as "against nature" but accepted on faith, as absolutely necessary for morality, a few simple doctrines: "the existence of a mighty intelligent beneficent divinity, possessed with foresight and providence, the life to come, the happiness of the just, the punishment of the wicked, the sanctity of the social contract, and the laws" (*Social Contract,* p. 237). Indeed, "it is very important for the State that every citizen should have a religion which may make him delight in his duties . . . a purely civil profession of faith, . . . not exactly as dogmas of religion, but as sentiments of sociability, without which it is impossible to be a good citizen or a faithful subject" (p. 145). He could tolerate any religion that accepted these doctrines, but had brutal thoughts about those who believed anything less. A similar attitude, however, was entertained toward him by the good citizens of Geneva, who thought his heresy far more hateful than his political radicalism. Luckily, Rousseau never had the chance to have his way. In his place, however, Robespierre did.

Personally, Rousseau was a malcontent, but hardly a revolutionary. (He refused to take part in a rebellion in Geneva, when solicited on the basis of his own theories.) But once his theory had shifted the attention of reformers from particular questions of justice within a state to the *legitimacy* of the State itself, revolution became an obvious possibility wherever governments were corrupt and unpopular. In his earlier writings Rousseau had argued that all society was corruption. In his later works he distinguished between legitimate and illegitimate government, at least indicating that society, if not corruption, is something we have to live with. But the notions of legitimacy and illegitimacy, coupled with their interpretations regarding the relationship between sovereignty and the General Will, once again raised the awesome specter of revolution. *The Social Contract* states that "such changes are always dangerous, and the established government must never be touched except when it becomes incompatible with the public good" (p. 171). But in *Emile,* addressing the aristocracy, Rousseau declares:

You have faith in the present order of society without thinking that this order is subject to inevitable revolutions, and that it is impossible for you to foresee or to forestall that which can affect your children. The great becomes little, the rich becomes poor, the monarch becomes subject; are the blows of chance so rare that you can count on being exempt? We approach the state of crises and the century of revolutions. Who can tell you what will become of you then?

Conclusion: The Outsider

Rousseau's task was to reconcile, for all humanity as well as himself, the dual demands of independence and belonging. One might easily explain this in strictly *ad hominem* terms—his incipient paranoia and the fact that he himself never "belonged" anywhere—but the impact and significance of Rousseau's task is that, together with the more conservative and reformist Voltairean ideology, it virtually defines the Enlightenment. Rousseau's dual demands have often been called contradictory, but we will understand far more if we see them as expressing on the one hand our desire for individual autonomy and independence, and on the other our

equally strong, equally natural (or unnatural) desire for a coherent, harmonious community. And if Rousseau's ideology emerges with a dangerously ambiguous tension between individualism and authoritarianism, this
does not mean that he has formulated his thesis badly and therefore merits
dismissal, but rather that we should become concerned—as the other
philosophers of the Enlightenment were not—about the very meaning of
the word "freedom," and the possibility of the utopian reconciliation
promised by reason. Of course Rousseau himself was impossibly unhappy,
without hope of happiness for himself in his lifetime. He placed his hope in
his faith in an afterlife, and in the "few wise men" who might eventually
implement his ideas. But given the latter's dialectical tensions, one must
question whether—Jean-Jacques's fantasies aside—this happy world
would ever come to pass as a world of human beings.

When Rousseau died in July of 1778, about a month after Voltaire, he
was impoverished, a refugee, and nearly psychotic. Eleven years later, in
one of the grand festivals of the French Revolution, he and Voltaire would
be reinterred together in Paris.

4 Warning Signs: Hume and Sade

It is not irrational for me to prefer the destruction of half the world to the pricking of my finger.

David Hume, *An Enquiry Concerning Human Morals*

Let the criminal not constrain himself; let him blindly, unthinkingly deliver himself up to causing every pain the idea for which may be born in him, it is only Nature's voice that suggests this idea; such is the only fashion in which she makes us her laws' executors. When her secret inspirations dispose us to evil, it is evil she wishes, it is evil she requires.

Marquis de Sade, *Justine*

Philosophy, according to Hegel, comes on the scene at the end of the struggle, recognizing inconsistencies in retrospect. But this is not always the case, and sometimes the writings of philosophers provide early warning of contradictions which have not yet exploded into violence. The Enlightenment, unlike many ideological movements, would come to an end in France not because it was crushed by superior forces or because it had become tired and familiar, but because it was completely successful; victorious, it had to face up to the contradictions and inconsistencies that had once been united in common battle. These contradictions were anticipated before the Revolution by two exceptional philosophers of the most different personalities and persuasions imaginable: David Hume, a friend of Rousseau and the French philosophers, and the most important British follower of John Locke; and the marquis Donatien-Alphonse-François de Sade, who, though not usually taken for a philosopher, was, to say the least, an enthusiastic follower of Rousseau. For both, subversion began by taking seriously—perhaps too seriously—the concept of human nature.

The inconsistencies of the Enlightenment existed not only *between* the ideologies of Voltaire and Rousseau, but also *within* them. We have seen, for example, how the political ideals of both philosophers have dangerous ambiguities: in Voltaire, the selective use of the principle of natural rights, and in Rousseau, the tenuous synthesis of individual autonomy and authoritarianism. But the inconsistencies can be found at a more profound ideological level as well, in the very concepts of "reason" and "nature" which form the basis of both theories. The Enlightenment philosophers had too glibly assumed that reason and human nature were one and the same. Hume and Sade separated them and played them *against* each other.

David Hume pursued the Enlightenment epistemology of John Locke to its logical conclusions, whereas Voltaire had contented himself with uncritical acceptance of a few superficial methodological rules. And where Voltaire had assumed that the consequences of Locke's method would be an enlightened society and a final assault on ignorance, Hume showed that the results of Locke's method would be pure nihilism and inevitable ignorance. Hume was sufficiently popular among the French philosophers—they called him their "favorite uncle"—that they failed to see how damaging his skepticism would be. And he himself viewed philosophizing as "a harmless pleasure," hardly the undermining of the critical spirit he enthusiastically defended. But what he did, in effect, was to destroy the pretenses of "reason." Our "natural" dispositions, he demonstrated, are not defensible by reason, and since our natural dispositions turn out to be our *established* dispositions, the project of rational criticism is indeed undermined.

But in France the marquis de Sade developed his own ideas about these natural dispositions, quoting Rousseau at every juncture, but turning them into the very opposite of natural goodness. Needless to say, he personally revolted the puritanical Rousseauans around him as he became involved in one sexual scandal after another. Yet he was one of them—their evil shadow, displaying the same pretensions and the same self-righteousness, the same appeals to nature and the same diatribes against the hypocrisy and corruption of society. He too looked for the natural foundations of human existence, and found them not in the human soul or even the human mind, but in the brute if not brutal fact of universal copulation. What could be more "natural"?

Convivial Nihilism: David Hume

David Hume was a Scottish version of Voltaire, an aristocratic wit of seductive charm, with an ambitious "love of literary fame" fueled by a genius for "scientific" if abstract philosophy. Hume was also a historian, and his literary success was first due to his monumental *History of England*. He too was a reform liberal—a conservative by later standards— and a gadfly to those in power. But where Voltaire was sarcastic, Hume tended to be humorous, and where Voltaire would become indignant, Hume was merely skeptical. It was a difference not only of personality but of national temperament. Like Voltaire, Hume had an ambiguous reputation: he was known as both "le bon David" and "the great infidel." In already enlightened England, Hume was not subject to the severe penalties and persecution which constantly threatened Voltaire. Yet he was accused of atheism and heresy, and on that account was refused university posts in Edinburgh, Glasgow, and London. His most heretical work, the *Dialogues on Natural Religion,* were withheld from publication until after his death.[1]

Hume spent several years in Paris (while Voltaire was in exile), and like Voltaire in London, immediately drew the most exceptional talent around him by virtue of his own brilliance and charm. He befriended the beleaguered Rousseau and gave him refuge in England following the publications of *Emile* and *The Social Contract.* But Rousseau's paranoia, fully developed during that difficult period, turned him against his benefactor, whom he accused of plotting against him. The break was ugly, and Hume felt compelled to publish their correspondence to exonerate himself from the wild charges leveled against him. It was a familiar episode for Rousseau, but he was probably the only friend that Hume ever lost.

David Hume was perhaps the brightest philosopher that Britain ever produced, at least until this century. He was a student of John Locke, whose empirical methods he pursued with greater rigor and insight than Locke had ever dared. His starting point in philosophy was, both temperamentally and methodologically, identical to the starting point of Voltaire. But while Voltaire used Locke's philosophy to give a new respectability to physics and the natural sciences, to the ideal of natural and social harmony, and to the deist conception of God, Hume used the same methods to reduce these central themes of the Enlightenment to empty sounds and indefensible slogans. For what emerges from Hume's inquiries is not a more persuasive or more justifiable version of empiricism, but a reduction to absurdity of every premise and conclusion of the Voltairean Enlightenment.

Hume was only twenty-six when he completed his *Treatise of Human Nature.*[2] It was a devastating and ominous attack on the new ideas of the Enlightenment, but from *within* (just as Voltaire's *Letters* had attacked the Old Regime from within). His method was the Enlightenment spirit of criticism, and his goal, the establishment of a science of man and a solution—or dissolution—of the problems of philosophy. The book was not published for two years, and then in 1739 "fell still-born from the press." It took his *History of England* to establish his literary fame, in order that the two main themes of the *Treatise,* regarding knowledge and ethics respectively, could be recast in two more popular *Enquiries: Concerning Human Understanding* (1748) and *Concerning the Principles of Morals* (1751).[3] The books became immensely popular in France as well as England, but the full force of their arguments would not be felt for several years, and then not in England or France but in Germany.

Like Locke and Voltaire, in *Concerning Human Understanding* Hume begins his inquiry with the empiricist premise that "all knowledge comes from experience" (or "impressions"). He too rejects metaphysics yet defends reason. Reason, however, must not be the "abstruse speculations" of the past, but the careful thinking of the Enlightenment.

Accurate and just reasoning is the only catholic remedy, fitted for all persons and all dispositions; and is alone able to subvert that abstruse philosophy and metaphysical jargon, which, being mixed up with popular superstition, renders it in a manner impenetrable to careless reasoners, and gives it the air of science and wisdom.

Anything else, he argues, must be rejected.

Let us ask, Does it contain any abstract reasoning concerning quantity and number? No. Does it contain any experimental reasoning concerning matter of fact and existence? No. Then commit it to the flames, for it can contain nothing but sophistry and illusion.

All claims to knowledge must be subjected to critical scrutiny, and all ideas must be traced to the senses, to original "impressions," and never allowed to be free-floating thoughts alone, for "the most lively thought is still inferior to the dullest sensation."

Nothing, at first view, may seem more unbounded than the thought of man, which not only escapes all human power and authority, but is not even restrained within the limits of nature and reality. To form monsters, and join incongruous shapes and appearances, costs the imagination no more trouble than to conceive the most natural and familiar objects.

But though our thought seems to possess this unbounded liberty, we shall find, upon a nearer examination, that it is really confined within very narrow limits, and that all this creative power of the mind amounts to no more than the faculty of compounding, transposing, augmenting, or diminishing the materials afforded us by the senses and experience. In short, all the materials of thinking are derived either from our outward or inward sentiment: the mixture and composition of these belongs alone to the mind and will. Or, to express myself in philosophical language, all our ideas or more feeble perceptions are copies of our impressions or more lively ones.

A healthy dose of skepticism—which Hume had inherited from Locke as well as Descartes, and which he shared with Voltaire—was supposed to place our scientific, moral, and religious beliefs on new and sounder foundations than the authority and dogma of the past. But in Descartes, Locke, and Voltaire this skeptical attitude was only a methodological stance adopted to clear the ground of unwarranted authority, so that the "natural" laws of truth, morality, and justice could be reestablished on firmer ground. As a conclusion, however, skepticism was for them intolerable. There could be no doubting the validity of Newton's picture of a rational and harmonious universe comprehensible to man. Nor could there be any question of the objectivity of the laws of morality and justice, upon which the demands for legislative and social reform were based. And it was beyond the realm of intelligible doubt that God existed, and that his existence could be proved by appeal to the design of the universe. But David Hume employs the empirical-skeptical method to show that skepticism must emerge as the *conclusion* of any adequate philosophical investigation.

Beginning with Locke's method and pursuing the idea that all knowledge must be based upon our experience, Hume proved, through a series of lightninglike arguments, that our experience could not even support the most basic and seemingly unquestionable beliefs, as for instance that there is an "external world" apart from our experience: "The mind has never anything present to it but the perceptions, and cannot possibly reach any experience of their connexion with objects. The supposition of such a connexion . . . is, therefore, without any foundation in reasoning." Nor can reason justify even the most elementary beliefs—for example, that the future will be like the past, or that the sun will rise tomorrow.

The contrary of every matter of fact is still possible; . . . *That the sun will not rise to-morrow* is no less intelligible a proposition, and implies no more contradiction than the affirmation, *that it will rise*. We should in vain, therefore, attempt to demonstrate its falsehood.

According to Hume, we cannot justify our conception of causality, the idea that one event in the world "causes" another.

. . . after a repetition of similar instances, the mind is carried by habit, upon the appearance of one event, to expect its usual attendant, and to believe that it will exist. This connexion, therefore, which we *feel* in the mind, this customary transition of the imagination from one object to its usual attendant, is the sentiment or impression from which we form the idea of power or necessary connexion. . . . The first time a man saw the communication of motion by impulse, as by the shock of two billiard balls, he could not pronounce that one event was *connected:* but only that it was *conjoined* with the other. After he has observed several instances of this nature, he then pronounces them to be connected. What alteration has happened to give rise to this new idea of *connexion?* Nothing but that he now *feels* these events to be *connected* in his imagination.

All that we can "know" are our own present ideas and memories, and the associations we form "by habit," which cannot be justified. The basis of Hume's argument is deceptively simple and extremely difficult to refute, given the Enlightenment methodology. All knowledge, he insists, is either mere manipulation of symbols, "truths of reason" such as arithmetic and logic ("if every *a* is *b* and every *b* is *c* then every *a* is *c*") or "matters of fact," ascertainable only through experience. But our basic beliefs, he demonstrates, are neither "truths of reason" nor "matters of fact," and therefore cannot be knowledge at all.

May I not clearly and distinctly conceive that a body, falling from the clouds, and which, in all other respects, resembles snow, has yet the taste of salt or feeling of fire? Is there any more intelligible proposition than to affirm, that all the trees will flourish in December and January, and decay in May and June? Now whatever is intelligible, and can be distinctly conceived, implies no contradiction, and can never be proved false by any demonstrative argument or abstract reasoning *a priori*. . . . We have said that all arguments concerning existence are founded on the relation of cause and effect; that our knowledge of that relation is derived entirely from experience; and that all our experimental conclusions proceed upon the supposition that the future will be conformable to the past. To endeavour, therefore, the proof of this last supposition by probable arguments, or arguments regarding existence, must be evidently going in a circle, and taking that for granted, which is the very point in question.

Hume's conclusion is that we can have no knowledge of the world, for all knowledge rests on these basic foundation principles concerning the existence of the external world: the future resembling the past and the existence of causal connections. This means that Newton's picture of an orderly and causally determined universe—which Hume himself accepted enthusiastically—could not be demonstrated by reason or experience, and therefore could not be known. In place of Voltaire's enlightened confidence in reason and experience, Hume substitutes mere habit, and here ends the confidence of the Enlightenment. In the *Treatise on Human Nature* he asks:

Where am I, or what? From what causes do I derive my existence, and to what condition shall I return? Whose favour shall I court, and whose anger must I dread? What beings surround me? and on whom have I any influence, or who have any influence on me? I am confounded with all these questions, and begin to fancy myself in the most deplorable condition imaginable, inviron'd with the deepest darkness, and utterly depriv'd of the use of every member and faculty.

I am ready to throw all my books and papers into the fire, and resolve never more to renounce the pleasures of life for the sake of reasoning and philosophy. [Nevertheless] I cannot forbear having a curiosity to be acquainted with the principles of moral good and evil, the nature and foundation of government, and the cause of those several passions and inclinations, which actuate and govern me. I am uneasy to think I approve of one object, and disapprove of another; call one thing beautiful, and another deform'd; decide concerning truth and falsehood, reason and folly, without knowing upon what principles I proceed.

In the realm of morality, Hume argued similarly that there are no "objective" or "rational" defenses of our moral attitudes. These are only based upon our "sentiments," he argues (much like Rousseau) in *Concerning the Principles of Morals;* "reason is and ought to be the slave of the passions."

It appears evident that the ultimate ends of human actions can never, in any case, be accounted for by *reason,* but recommend themselves entirely to the sentiments and affections of mankind, without any dependence on the intellectual faculties.

There are no natural laws of justice and fairness, but again, only our passions and habits. "Whatever is valuable in any kind, so naturally classes itself under the *useful* or *agreeable*." Again like Rousseau (whom he no doubt influenced in these matters), he asserts that our sentiments of self-preservation and utility are augmented by the sentiment of sympathy: "To the most careless observer there appear to be such dispositions as benevolence and generosity; such affections as love, friendship, compassion, gratitude." But if morality and justice are based only upon sentiment, that is not sufficient as a justification of them, any more than a prejudice is justifiable simply because it is strongly felt by many. Justification, in fact, is not possible. Morality and politics, like Newtonian science, are reduced to the status of habits and prejudices—*universal* habits, perhaps, but unjustifiable nonetheless.

Hume's reliance on established habits and beliefs betrays an inescapable conservative bias, a reluctance to change as well as a devastating skepticism regarding the justification of change. In this, despite their agreement on the importance of the "natural" sentiments, Hume could not have been more at odds with Rousseau. The most destructive arguments to emerge from Hume's philosophy are those concerning religion, particularly Voltaire's treasured deism. Against the argument from design, Hume argues that the universe shows no trace of any design, or if it was indeed designed, it shows its designer to be incompetent. The universe appears to be "faulty and imperfect . . . only the first rude essay of some infant deity . . . or the production of old age and dotage in some superannuated deity." The idea of God as Creator is just an "empty hypothesis."

But were this world ever so perfect a production, it must still remain uncertain, whether all the excellences of the work can justly be ascribed to the workman. If we survey a ship, what an exalted idea must we form of the ingenuity of the carpenter, who framed so complicated, useful, and beautiful a machine? And what surprise must we feel, when we find him a stupid mechanic, who imitated others, and copied an art, which, through a long succession of ages, after multiplied trials, mistakes, corrections, deliberations, and controversies, had been gradually improving? Many worlds might have been botched and bungled, throughout an eternity, ere this system was struck out: Much labor lost: Many fruitless trials made: And a slow, but continued improvement carried on during infinite ages in the art of world-making. In such subjects, who can determine, where the truth; nay, who can conjecture where the probability lies; amidst a great number of hypotheses which may be proposed, and a still greater number which may be imagined? (*Dialogues Concerning Natural Religion*)

With regard to the problem of evil that tormented Voltaire, Hume simply remarks that, if there is a God, he is either naive or evil:

Look round this universe. What an immense profusion of beings, animated and organized, sensible and active! You admire this prodigious variety and fecundity. But inspect a little more narrowly these living existences, the only beings worth regarding. How hostile and destructive to each other! How insufficient all of them for their own happiness! How contemptible or odious to the spectator! The whole presents nothing but the idea of a blind nature, impregnated by a great vivifying principle, and pouring forth from her lap, without discernment or parental care, her maimed and abortive children.

Moreover, there is nothing "natural" about theism; in a primitive anthropological survey, Hume demonstrates that there have been many religions without a God, and that the only common element in all religions has been terror. Like Voltaire, Hume is a radical against religion, but a relative conservative in politics. With him, the enlightened universality and objectivity of Voltaire turn to skepticism and find themselves reduced to a psychological zoo of habits, associations, and passions—no longer "enlightened" at all.

Curiously, these drastic conclusions seem not to have affected Hume's life and happiness in the least:

Most fortunately it happens, that since reason is incapable of dispelling these clouds, nature herself suffices to that purpose, and cures me of this philosophical melancholy and delirium, either by relaxing this bent of mind, or by some avocation, and lively impression of my senses, which obliterate all these chimeras. I dine, I play a game of back-gammon, I converse, and am merry with my friends; and when after three or four hours' amusement, I wou'd return to these speculations, they appear so cold, and strain'd, and ridiculous, that I cannot find in my heart to enter into them any farther.

His refutation of the laws of causality did not interfere with his billiards game. He gained a reputation as a devoted sensualist as well as an empiricist, but his sensuality always remained urbane and charming. His rejection of the rationality of morality still left him a dependable friend and a trustworthy citizen. His rejection of God and religion did not prevent him from living and finally dying with a sense of satisfaction and tranquillity which neither Voltaire nor Rousseau would ever know.[4] Hume was a true exponent of the Enlightenment in both his criticism and his urbane charm. More important, however, the basis and support for his attack on reason, as well as his solution to it, is more than anything else the *transcendental pretense*, the assumption that "nature" assures each and every individual of the validity of experience, the unity of mankind, and the dependability of human nature. Nevertheless, in a most important sense Hume had already destroyed the philosophy of the Enlightenment, and reduced it to absurdity in its own terms.

Nature Perverted: Sade

> De Sade got to the bottom of both God and man.
>
> Algernon Swinburne

The notorious marquis de Sade was also a sensualist, but his sensualism, while paraded in an elegant literary style, was hardly urbane or charming.[5] This "monster author" was an unabashed Rousseauan, but with a bizarre and perverse twist. He too believed that freedom existed in individuality, in our independency of others: " 'The first principle of my philosophy,' Mme. Delbene explains to Juliette, 'is to defy public opinion. . . . Our happiness should depend only on ourselves, on our conscience.' "[6] Sade too believed in the dictates of nature and human nature: "I only report of not having sufficiently recognized her [Nature's] omnipotency and my sole regrets are only of the indifferent use I made of the faculties—criminal in your eyes, but natural in mine—she endowed me with to serve her."[7] And he too accepted the radical dichotomy between nature and society. About the time that Rousseau was completing *Emile* and *The Social Contract*, the marquis was involved in a series of scandals; engaged to two girls at once, he was also accused of "excesses committed in a brothel" and commited to prison for a month. Rousseau had a rather full, albeit unsatisfactory, sex life, but he never sentimentalized sexuality or raised it to preeminence among the "sentiments" he celebrated. But Sade, following Rousseau, found that one's "natural" sentiments are essentially physical and preeminently sexual, that self-esteem and virility are identical, and that pity serves only to excite sexual desire, which is fundamentally a desire to dominate.

Nature should be the sole guide of our life.
    Can the isolated individual fight against everyone? Can he flatter himself he is happy and tranquil if, refusing to submit to the social contract, he does not consent to give up a little of his happiness to insure the rest? Virtue is necessary even in a criminal society.
    Is not the state of nature the only state to which we are really adapted? All men are born isolated, envious, cruel and despotic; wishing to have everything and surrender nothing, incessantly struggling to maintain either their rights or achieve their ambition, the legislator comes up and says to them: Cease to fight; if each were to retreat a little, calm would be restored. I find no fault with the position that is implicit in this agreement. But I maintain that two species of individuals cannot and ought not be confused, the strong and the weak.[8]

Sade's childhood resembled that of Voltaire more than that of Rousseau. He was born into newly emergent Paris nobility and educated at the finest Jesuit college. He served in the army against Prussia as an officer, and except for the many servants of both sexes with whom he typically shared his exploits, his acquaintances were aristocrats. But it is also arguable that Sade's personality—rebellious and philosophical, curiously blending misanthropy and the need of companionship—was remarkably similar to that of Rousseau. While he acted out many of his perverse desires—particularly that penchant for shared cruelty which has been named in his honor—his actions were but a shadow of his fantasies, and according to him, were wholly based on rational principles. Sade's attack on the enlightened society in which he was raised, like Rousseau's attack on the unenlightened society that similarly made him suffer, was predominantly literary, expressed in essays and addresses, arguments and analogies that found their way into his many volumes of writings (most of which were later destroyed by his family, by officials, and by the looters of the Revolution). But where Rousseau was only forced into exile by the condemnation of his books, the marquis was committed to prison and asylums where he spent over twenty-five years of his life.[9] In 1768 he was forced to flee Paris to escape arrest for flogging an unemployed cook in a series of sexual excesses in one of his cottage retreats. In 1772 he and his servant Latour were arrested for various "acts of sodomy and perversion" (including suspected poisoning) during an all-night orgy with four young prostitutes. They were condemned to death *in absentia,* since they both had gone into hiding. The marquis was finally caught and imprisoned under the marquis de Launay (of whom more in Chapter 5), who described his prisoner as "unreliable and impulsive, and capable of desperate action." Sade and Latour then escaped and disappeared until 1775, when Sade was arrested in Lyons for sexual abuses with several young servants, mostly girls of fifteen. Thereafter he spent most of his remaining years in prison, reading the works of the Enlightenment and writing his own contributions to the thoughts of Rousseau and Voltaire, who—to their own misfortune, perhaps—stand at the foundation of even the most pornographic of his works.

Until recently, Sade's works have been considered unpublishable, although they were underground best sellers both before the Revolution and after. But although his reputation continues to be that of "a writer of dirty books" (in the words of one British encyclopedist), and therefore a tourist commodity in the Left Bank bookstalls, Sade appeared to his contemporaries as a philosopher, and after his release from prison in 1789 was hailed as one of the fathers of the Revolution. Baudelaire later celebrated him as a "poet of evil" to whom he would return "again and again," and Apollinaire called him "the freest spirit that ever lived." Sade's *Philosophy in the Bedroom* and *Justine,* although far more bedroom than philosophy, contain within their pages a reduction to absurdity of the key themes of the Enlightenment of Rousseau. If Hume exposed the inconsistencies of the Enlightenment of Voltaire by pursuing its method to its limits, Sade exploded the romantic mythology of Rousseau by pursuing its source to its extremes. Who can say, after all, what "natural man" must be like? Sade, a self-acknowledged Rousseauan, took the heart of the Enlightenment to be its appeal to nature.

Unlike Rousseau, Sade did not find in nature the innocence of a pure conscience, a set of moral sentiments available in the state of nature but distorted by civilization.

. . . the most extraordinary, the most bizarre acts, those which most arrantly seem to conflict with every law, every human institution (as for Heaven, I have nothing to say), well Eugenie, even those are not frightful, and there is not one amongst them all that cannot be demonstrated within the boundaries of Nature.[10]

Furthermore, as he states in the same work, "Destruction, like creation, is one of Nature's mandates" (p. 275). But if nature commands everything, she commands nothing: "The relations of man to nature are nothing; nature cannot bind any man by law. . . . They owe nothing to each other, neither can offend the other. Once he is launched, man is free from nature" (*Juliette*, p. 168). This precociously existentialist conclusion (anticipating Camus and Sartre) destroys the claims of the Enlightenment philosophers to find a natural law or morality. Sade draws the conclusion from this that all morality is strictly relative and not worthy of concern:

I ask you now, if, after these reflections, I can still retain any feeling of guilt for having committed, either for the sake of pleasure or of self-interest, a crime in France which is nothing but a virtue in China? Or if I ought to make myself very miserable or be prodigiously troubled about practicing actions in France which would have me burned in Siam? (*Justine*, p. 696)

Or, put otherwise: "Moral science is simply geography misconstrued" (p. 696). But cosmic rebellion is not easily contained; while Rousseau succeeds in retaining his respect for man and nature at the expense of men, Sade turns even against nature, resenting the fact that she condones and endures everything:

In everything we do there are nothing but idols offended and creatures insulted, but Nature is not amongst them, and it is she I should like to outrage. I should like to upset her plans, thwart her progress, arrest the wheeling courses of the stars, throw the spheres floating in space into mighty confusion, destroy what serves Nature and protect what is harmful to her; in a word, to insult her in her works—and this I am unable to do.[11]

In early July of 1789 Sade was reported to be hurling messages inciting to revolution from his window on the Bastille. He was transferred to Charenton and so missed the festivities of the fourteenth, when his books and possessions, including most of his writings up to that time, were destroyed in the looting. Then in March of 1790 the new Assembly released all political prisoners, and Sade was let loose on the world after thirteen years of imprisonment. He was full of complaints, not the least of which was that he had lost three-quarters of the fifteen volumes of his writings over the past years. He published those that were left as quickly as possible; *Justine,* appearing in 1791, was a great success. Sade became a respected participant in the Revolution, and immediately took up residence with a young actress in Paris.

It is a matter of controversy whether Sade actually believed the loftier principles of Rousseau then prescribed in revolutionary Paris, or only played the role necessary to allow him to remain there. He did endorse Rousseau in the abstract, and he believed in the vital distinction between "legitimate" and "illegitimate" governments. His speeches were typically in tune with the period, and the revolutionary philosophy found its way into his novels, as for instance in *Philosophy in the Bedroom:* "Frenchmen, I repeat to you: Europe awaits her deliverance from both scepter and censer [the monarchy and the Church]" (p. 298); and: "One of Christianity's key dogmas was to render unto Caesar what is Caesar's. However, we have dethroned Caesar, we are no longer disposed to render him anything" (p. 296). He claimed, with his usual gallows humor, that he was into the Revolution "up to his neck," and was one of the more popular but less political orators of the Terror, until his quasi-aristocratic background began to interfere. His politics aside, however, his pleasures and their descriptions—whether real or fictional—could not have appealed to the prudish morality of the new Rousseauans, least of all to Robespierre. More than once Sade was arrested and condemned to the guillotine, but then released. In the following years he penned his most caustic and intentionally offensive works. They were underground best sellers, but Sade was evidently always in desperate financial straits. Never free from troubles with the law, he managed to keep out of prison at least until 1803, when under the new puritanism of Napoleon he was committed—on the basis of a relatively minor scandal—to the asylum at Charenton, where he would spend the rest of his life as an "incorrigible" and "incurable" inmate.

Sade's perversity, and the sex and cruelty in his fiction, may easily distract both the prurient reader and the morally indignant one from recognizing the strong and continuous appeal to Enlightenment themes that dominate his work. He was, whatever else besides, a philosopher, even if an often incoherent one—an Enlightenment radical who borrowed much from Rousseau and was never unaffected by the complementary teachings of Voltaire. But Sade's Enlightenment carried the arrogance and rebellion of Rousseau and Voltaire to intolerable extremes. Rousseau's appeal to nature had been an innocent but effective defense against what he perceived as a serious degrading of morality and virtue in high society. Sade adopted this same appeal to nature and twisted it into a justification of his own cruel tastes. But what served as a method for undermining the customs and mores of society in the one instance served equally well in the other, for society was unnatural in both cases. Similarly, Rousseau had formulated his abstract standard of legitimate and justifiable authority with the intention of bringing about the same reforms and promoting the same ends—general human welfare and happiness—that provoked Voltaire to use very different methods. But for Sade, these abstract standards become inoperative both for the man of strength, who can get away with his crimes, and for the weakling, who cannot enforce them on his own. And all of us, he argues, are either weak or strong. Thus Sade's political thought, much like that of Nietzsche a century later, is essentially antipolitical. Revolution becomes another opportunity for the advantages of the strong.

Sade's revolutionary attacks on authority and the Church were sincere, but his aim was not reform or general happiness. For Sade, Rousseau's social contract involved the sovereignty and liberty of the individual, a bargain to be accepted—or broken—as necessary and when dictated. He was a minor aristocrat. Under threat of death, he was forced to obey those who intended that the individual should serve the virtues of the State. But what he really believed in was only his own survival and his perverse needs.[12] So what began in Rousseau as an innocent appeal to Nature ended with the recognition that Nature is indifferent to morality, and that in the fact of this cosmic indifference, man must invent his morality. Thus the Revolution of Rousseau, turned to terror by Robespierre and his chief theoretician, Jean Paul Marat, would slaughter whole populations so as to consolidate its own power in the name of the sovereignty of the people. The dramatist Peter Weiss has imagined a conversation:

Sade: Nature herself would watch unmoved
        If we destroyed the entire human race

        I hate nature,
        this passionless spectator, this unbreakable ice-berg face
        that can bear everything
        this goads us to greater and greater acts

Marat: . . . what you call the indifference of nature is your own lack of
        compassion

Sade: Compassion is the property of the privileged classes. . . . For you just
        as for me
        only the most extreme actions matter

Marat: If I am extreme I am not extreme in the same way as you
        Against nature's indifference I invent a meaning. . . . The important
        thing
        is to pull yourself up by your own hair
        to turn yourself inside out
        and see the whole world with fresh eyes.[13]

Rousseau appealed to nature as Voltaire had appealed to reason and experience, in order to provide an objective, solid foundation for his defense of morality and justice, natural religion, and faith in human perfectibility. But Sade—and later the Revolution—reduced the dictates of Rousseau's nature, as Hume had reduced Voltaire's appeals to reason and experience, to their very opposites, to subjective and unjustifiable prejudices which, Sade asserts, may be just as "natural" as our "goodness."

5 In the Name of Humanity: The French Revolution

It was the best of times, it was the worst of times, it was the age of wisdom, it was the age of foolishness, it was the epoch of belief, it was the epoch of incredulity, it was the season of Light, it was the season of Darkness, it was the spring of hope, it was the winter of despair, we had everything going for us, we had nothing before us, we were all going direct to Heaven, we were all going direct the other way.

Dickens, *A Tale of Two Cities*

If Voltaire once, in splenetic humor, asked his countrymen: "But you *Gualches*, what have you invented?" they can now answer: "The Art of Insurrection." It was an art needed in these last singular times; an art for which the French nature, so full of vehemence, so free from depth, was perhaps of all others the fittest.

Carlyle, *The French Revolution*

The success of the Enlightenment could be measured by the wide acceptance of its ideas as well as the increasing domination of society in social and financial matters by the bourgeoisie. By 1780, it was all but obvious that the antiquated political structures and social strata no longer enjoyed either ideological or social support. As early as 1755, Lord Chesterfield in England had written his son, "All the symptoms which I have ever met with in history, previous to great changes and revolutions in government, now exist, and daily increase, in France." To employ a worn geological analogy still useful in politics, an upheaval was under way: a long, slow shifting of weight and balance leading to a sudden, unexpected quake, as the elements quickly found their new level, and only then a horrible period of violence and confusion while everyone tried to adjust to the change, helping or betraying one another depending on the panic of the moment. So it was in France. The slow shifting of weight toward the bourgeoisie, and consequently to "the people," had taken most of the eighteenth century.[1] The cataclysm, when it came, would be so fast and simple that history hesitates to call it "the Revolution," preferring to extend that term to the entire aftermath, to the panic and adjustments. The

Revolution—the actual exchange of power—took only a few bloodless hours; the panic and adjustments took six bloody years.[2]

The basic facts of the Revolution are familiar. In this short review one consideration must preside—the way that ideology gives shape and direction to events, and the extent to which ideology is capable of bringing about those events.[3] If the French Revolution was the political manifestation of the bourgeois ideology of the Enlightenment, then it must also be true that the conflicts and contradictions in that ideology—or rather, in those ideologies—will become overt political conflicts and contradictions, too. From a philosophical perspective, one can see the Revolution falling into two well-defined periods. First came the Voltairean period of moderate reform, involving the transfer of power within the monarchy; the rise of the bourgeoisie to full legislative and judicial power; and the political expression of Enlightenment ideology in the drafting of the first documents of the new order. Then followed the Rousseauan period of radical republicanism, the dangerous experiment with Rousseau's "social contract," for which the French were without both experience and authority; the attempt to extend the advantages of the Revolution throughout the rest of the Third Estate; and the protracted violence of anarchy. It was discovered that "the general will" was not so tangible as it sounded. Humanity was an elusive entity, even in relatively homogeneous France. The logic and confusion of the Enlightenment were repeated in the logic and confusion of the Revolution, fueled by hysteria, war, and starvation. Simple Voltairean reforms—undermined by opposing self-interests, vague and excessive promises, and public paranoia—turned into radical demands and an impossible idealism.[4] And the confrontation of ideas in the streets was not the same as the civilized exchange of philosophical opinions.[5]

The problem for any ideology, particularly an ideology of universals, is how to apply it to everyday life, how to translate its universal terms into concrete feelings, thoughts, and actions. The abstract ideals of humanity, human nature, and Reason, because they were capable of supporting so many courses of action, dictated none. One can lionize Voltaire and master the arguments of Rousseau's *Social Contract,* but once these philosophies leave the drawing rooms and enter the streets, more specific concepts are needed, with tangible imperatives. Thus while the slogans of the Revolution were the grand concepts of the Enlightenment, its conceptual driving force was the idea of "liberation," derived from abstract "freedom" but geared in every case to some more or less specific grievance that was designated "oppression." Material crises—taxation, crime, famine, war—though not ideological in themselves, became matters of ideology as soon as someone or something could be *blamed* for them. Whether they were the real causes or not mattered little. What was essential was the need to blame, to direct one's resentment, to be able to *do* something while believing at least that the attack on oppression, whether effective or not in treating the original grievance, was a matter of pride. It was a form of self-expression supported by the whole of Enlightenment thinking, and fueled by resentment inspired by an ideology that promised too much too vaguely. Sometimes the grievance and the blame were clearly justified; often the blame was manufactured, and the grievance itself but a faulty inference from the obscure promises of freedom, equality, and happiness. Yet often both cases held, for it is the nature of resentment that its victories tend to increase demand rather than satisfaction, and the conquest of one oppressor inevitably uncovers another. However directed, liberation is as abstract as the concepts behind it, as unlimited as the Enlightenment rejection of authority, and as obsessive as the resentful emotions behind it. Once the Revolution began, it would be driven by the logic of an ideology which, whatever its successes, had never yet been required to reveal itself or recognize its limitations. The Revolution would demonstrate, not the dangers of ideology, but the dangers of an ideology of universals in a revolution that consequently had no end until, as Carlyle said, "all the fuel is done."

A Model for Liberation

> Thus we destroy even the shadow of that king who refused to reign over a free people.
> President of the Committee of Safety, on burning a portrait of George III in Dover, Maryland, on July 2, 1776

The political manifestation of the Enlightenment demand for liberation did not first appear in France. In a sense, it had already been responsible for the Glorious Revolution in England and, more ominously, for a "war of independence" in North America. The American Revolution was the first demonstration for enlightened Europe that the people could organize themselves into a successful fighting force against professional armies, and organize themselves as well into an effective constitutional government based upon Enlightenment ideals: "self-evident truths," "the equality of man," "inalienable rights" including "life, liberty, and the pursuit of happiness," the right to private property, freedom of speech and religion, and the right to rebel against despotism. The war itself was hardly the people's revolution against tyranny that Enlightenment mythology made it out to be: the American forces consisted mainly of bourgeois lawyers, merchants, shopkeepers, and landowners; the "revolution" effected little if any change in life style or social conditions.[6] The "tyranny" consisted of an ineffectual and disoriented king, and a troubled British Parliament that was attempting to find a mutually agreeable tax in order to come to terms with an overwhelming national debt. At the time of the insurrection, the current debate in the colonies between the abstractions of freedom and a concrete prosperity did not lead to overwhelming support for the Revolution. Moreover, when the American struggle is placed in the context of continuing global warfare between the French and the British, the disturbances in the American colonies of 1776 appear as insignificant as the trouble in Vietnam appeared to Americans in the early days of 1964. The American war was a single scene in a worldwide conflict.

Nevertheless, America became the model for "the people's revolution," much like the Chinese revolution today. The realities were not as important as the ideas. America appeared to be the first emergence of Rousseauan philosophy as a workable government by "social contract," governed by the General Will of the people in a small agrarian society, set in a rich and expansive land free from the inhibiting traditions of feudalism and aristocracy. Thus Goethe could declare, "America thou hast it better/Than our continent, the old one."

However exercised its armies were elsewhere, during the war Europe sent its "advisers" by the dozen to America, ostensibly to help the colonies, but ultimately to help smash England's worldwide colonial power. From France came Lafayette, Jourdan, and Berthier; from Prussia, Gneisenau; and from Poland, Pulaski. All wanted a hand in the launching of the new society—a timely and convenient assistance that promised rich returns in the future. But their support for the American war, together with the devastating costs in the European theater, brought economic collapse to many European nations, particularly France. The financial crisis brought the immediate benefit of peace through exhaustion, but the resulting insolvency of the French monarchy caused its final loss of legitimacy in the eyes of the French middle class. For the rich businessmen to whom the government owed vast sums of money, "illegitimacy" was not so much a Rousseauan matter of agreement with the General Will as a Voltairean concern for good business. Financial collapse and famine were the crises that would kindle the Revolution; Enlightenment ideals and the mythology of the American war would direct it.

Hunger and Hope

> Rebellions of the belly are the worst.
>
> Francis Bacon

> Twenty years before, nothing was hoped from the future; in 1780, nothing was feared.
>
> Tocqueville

The financial crisis caused by the war, added to the years of war and extravagance under the two preceding reigns, left the France of Louis XVI in a state of near bankruptcy and chaos. Meanwhile, feudal laws exempted those who could pay taxes most easily—the aristocracy and the clergy—while passing the burden to those who could least pay: workers and shop-keepers, the so-called *sans-culottes* and peasants. To make matters worse, these poor people were expected to support not only the failing government, but the Church and the aristocracy as well. And to make things utterly impossible, this crisis was aggravated by an emergency—the dry, cold spring of 1788, which destroyed the crops. People starved; business-men complained; the government made promises.[7]

The predictable food riots and government confusion followed, but there was not yet the forum for a revolution. That forum was provided by the King and the aristocracy. France could no longer afford its traditional privileges: even the aristocracy agreed, as did the clergy. The only question was, how were the new taxes to be distributed? In a mood that savored more of timidity and confusion than enlightenment, the King made a public request for advice by calling a meeting of the States-General, the old assembly of the nobility, clergy, and commons that had not met since 1614. The arrangement of the meeting itself, with the three Estates sitting together, signified a tacit recognition of Enlightenment principles of popular representation—a step that would trigger the Revolution.[8] Ironically, it was by a move for reform that the government undermined itself.

The Queen probably never said, "Let them eat cake," but the financier Foulon, one of the greedy speculators who was making a fortune from the famine, probably did say, "Let them eat grass, like my horses." (He would not live through the summer.) The desperate murmuring that circulated such rumors replaced the learned treatises of the philosophers as the voice of the people. As hope for reform and relief from above proved futile, the idea of action from below gained prominence. The first attacks were against the "monopolists," the speculators who held what grain could be harvested for higher prices. Then a "monopolist" became anyone who had more than he needed and soon anyone who had what he needed. (The same logic would later be used with the word "aristocrat.") Famine created furor, and the resentment that had been brewing for decades expressed itself as best it could.

In the two months preceding the celebrated attack on the Bastille in mid-July, there were over three hundred major riots throughout France. Châteaus were burned and church graineries raided. "Monopolists" were beaten, or hanged and beheaded. "Justice" was quick, brutal, careless, but by no means arbitrary. The same spirit rose up all over France, fed by the fast but dramatically distorting channels of communication that stretched from Paris to the provinces and back. Whatever the injustices, the grievances were real and very old.

No one could control the new power of "the people," but everyone began to court it. They would ride with it, careful that they not fall from the crest of the wave under its murderous tide of resentment. France was in a state of anarchy. Power was in the streets, and while no one would hold on to it for long, it would remain there for another five years. Meanwhile, the intellectuals could plan the reformulation of the world.

The Summer of '89

> Man has natural and imprescriptable rights. These rights are liberty, property, personal security and resistance to oppression.
> Lafayette, in the *Declaration of the Rights of Man and Citizen*

The States-General convened in May of 1789. It bred confusion and resentment from the first. The almost exclusively bourgeois representation of the Third Estate excluded the peasants and the working class. The nobles and clergy had the advantage of two-to-one odds on every decision, since tradition dictated voting by Estates. But given those odds, it was possible to view the Third Estate as a unified front, led by the bourgeoisie. Ironically, it was the nobility who had the most systematic plan for reform, for they distrusted the Bourbon monarchy far more than they feared the disorganized bourgeoisie. And since the King in turn feared the nobility, like Louis XIV he used the Third Estate against them, declaring that the States-General should meet as a single body with double representation for the Third Estate. The great body became deadlocked, exchanged threats and insults for five frustrating weeks. Then, accompanied by great celebration, a few lower clergy shifted their allegiance to the Third Estate. The balance tipped: the Third Estate could now act as a concerted body. On June 17 they declared themselves the National Assembly, following which a majority of nobles and clergy resigned. By simple *fiat* the Enlightenment ideology of popular sovereignty had become a political reality. As a popular pamphlet announced at the time, the Third Estate *was France*.[9]

These few hours two months before the fall of the Bastille and the bloody events that have come to be called "the French Revolution" might have been the whole revolution—if France had been more like America, if there had been no famine, no mobs, no centuries of privileges and tradition, and most of all, had it not been for the stupidity of the King and the obstinacy of the Queen. The King did not understand that his using the people as pawns against the aristocracy had misfired. He did not understand that the action of the Third Estate was a revolutionary act with the whole of the Enlightenment behind it. Rather he saw the new declarations as momentary arrogance, another moblike "civil disturbance," and so declared the Assembly dispersed and ordered his soldiers to close the meeting hall. The indignant representatives and their even more vocal representees stormed over to the nearest open building, a tennis court (now the Impressionist Museum by the Tuileries), and vowed not to disperse until they had drafted a satisfactory constitution after the American model. This Tennis Court Oath would later be viewed as one of the pivotal points of the Revolution, but the King saw it only as disrespect for his authority. Egged on by his derisive wife, he asserted his authority again with soldiers, who only joined the Assembly, too. Embarrassed, the King accepted what he could not alter, acknowledging the National Assembly as the legitimate deliberative body of France.

Within the Assembly, however, deliberation was not forthcoming. Speakers screamed in faint hope of making themselves heard, overwhelmed by the noise and commotion. A few great orators emerged—Danton, for example, whose greatest rhetorical virtue was his booming voice. Robespierre, the future dictator, found his weak and scratchy moralizing suited only to a small captive audience, and so confined most of his comments to the Jacobin Club. Deputies who voted against the popular will were sometimes hanged and beheaded, which bypassed the more time-consuming ordeal of voting them out of office. The Assembly existed by virtue of its recognition by the King, but mobs in fact ruled the Assembly and Paris as well. There were public lynchings and beatings; Foulon, who had suggested that the people eat grass, was one of the first victims. Assaults and robberies now carried the stamp of ideological legitimacy, being committed in the name of "the people." Wealthy men were accosted and beaten, handsome houses were burgled and ransacked, and women were raped, all in the name of the people. Conservatives observing from a distance, like Burke and Taine, have called it "anarchy."[10] So it was. But behind the chaos were very real needs—for food and for justice. What happened in Paris during the summer of '89 cannot be understood from the lists of crimes or from the records of the National Assembly. It must be understood in terms of very personal hopes and fears, the keen sense that something momentous was happening, coupled with an intolerable fear for one's safety and the security of one's family and possessions, no matter how modest. The streets were filled with expectation, and those who saw only the fears and not the hopes failed to perceive that crucial difference between the ideological miracle then being realized and the mere anarchy of a popular riot.[11]

On July 11 the King dismissed his popular finance minister, Jacques Necker, who had urged him once too often to ignore his frivolous and too proud Queen and compromise with the Assembly. Riots began immediately in Paris.

On July 12 radicals openly advocated armed insurrection and organized attacks on the King's own troops, composed of Swiss and German mercenaries.

By July 13 the French troops announced their sympathies with the people and made it quite clear to their superiors that, if ordered to fire on their compatriots, they would turn their rifles on the officers instead.

The poor scavenged for food, looting homes and alarming the wealthy. The gap within the Third Estate was already apparent. The poor gathered in gangs; the wealthy formed their own militia. And in one of the most confused nights in history, crowds of armed bourgeoisie, sympathetic French troops, shouting mobs, looters, muggers, and rapists, plus thousands of curious observers, crowded the streets. Today one can see a direction to this confusion, but at the time people knew what was happening only in the sense that one knows the tides while being rocked in a small, fragile boat at sea.

Then, July 14:

An early-morning raid on the virtually unguarded Invalides provided the crowd with arms. A search began for gunpowder, which reportedly was stored in that nearly deserted fourteenth-century fortress, the Bastille. One might say that "the rest is history," but it was not. It was myth, a "media event," what Norman Mailer would call a "factoid," a turning point in history created from almost nothing. The Revolution had taken place in June, with a small transfer of votes and the declaration of the National Assembly. But that is hardly the stuff of commemorations and heroics, so the "storming of the Bastille"—a medieval fortress crumbling from neglect, manned by a hundred retired and incompetent soldiers, and containing just seven prisoners, none of them political—became the locus of the most celebrated myth in modern history. The Bastille was not a symbol of oppression (it was more the *absence* of government that bothered most people by this time), but a source of supplies, a public shopping spree watched by crowds of fine ladies and friendly troops, with local shopkeepers and vagrants drifting in and out. De Launay, the garrison commander of the day, began to negotiate, opened the front gate, and had his soldiers lower their arms. Then he hesitated. Carlyle would comment later:

Woe to thee, De Launay, in such an hour, if thou canst not, taking some one firm decision, *rule* circumstances! Soft speeches will not serve; hard grapeshot is questionable; but hovering between the two is *un*questionable. (I, 164)

Pushed from the rear by impatience, the crowd surged forward. De Launay gave the order to fire—too late to save himself, too bloody to be forgiven. Ninety-eight citizens fell dead, and the garrison's quick surrender provoked a massacre. De Launay was beheaded by a butcher with a pocketknife who later claimed he had just come to watch. Bearing the commander's head on a pike, the mob paraded through Paris.

Such was the "storming" of the Bastille on July 14, 1789. By no account could it be considered a political, ideological, or military victory of any kind. In perspective, it was but one of several hundred similar storms that raged in Paris and the rest of France during those chaotic months. But in retrospect it was immediately raised to the level of symbol—a symbol of the People's victory. It persuaded the King to recall Jacques Necker to power, and His Majesty even adopted a new robe of revolutionary colors, combining the red and blue of Paris with white, the symbol of the purity of the Bourbon monarchy. (In a French revolution, fashion is of great importance.) The story has been told how Louis, going to bed that evening, wrote in his diary that "nothing" had happened that day, only to be awakened at two in the morning by the duc de la Rochefoucauld-Liancourt. "It is a revolt, then?" asked the King. "Sire," replied the Duke, "it is a revolution!" The profound and long-coming victory of the Enlightenment had found its superficial visible symbol.

In the provinces, meanwhile, all action was suspended awaiting word from Paris, the brain of the nervous system of France. When news did arrive, it was far more dramatic than the events themselves, and by the time it reached the peasants, there were rumors of civil war and armies of nobility on the march. As in Paris, the provincial poor armed themselves and, not finding the civil war they heard rumored, turned to creating one. Typically attacking in the name of the King, they raided and often razed the châteaus and manors of the nobility and rich bourgeoisie alike. Again expanded and exaggerated, news of these raids traveled back to Paris, where the bourgeois leaders saw the need to absorb the peasant revolt into the Revolution. On August 4 the Assembly decreed what it could not prevent, abolishing feudalism in France. It was a nominal gesture to the peasants, but it made the Revolution in Paris a national movement. (Feudalism had been all but dead in France since Louis XIV; the peasants were as well off as any in Europe, owned 40 percent of the land in France outright, and had relatively free access to most of the rest of it.)[12] But the token acknowledgment of the peasant revolt had another implication as well: it underscored, in the country as well as in the cities, that the Revolution was an incoherent amalgam of two contradictory ideologies, one conservative and elitist after Voltaire, and the other revolutionary and egalitarian after Rousseau. Already the illusion of "the Third Estate" was no more, and "the people" were divided between those who were already satisfied with the Revolution's achievements and those for whom it had scarcely begun.

On August 27 the Assembly presented its *Declaration of the Rights of Man and Citizen,* modeled after the same Enlightenment principles that had already created the American Declaration of Independence and Constitution. The main author was the marquis de Lafayette, an aristocrat and a friend of Thomas Jefferson (who was with him in Paris at the time). Here at last was the Enlightenment ideology finally realized in full political dress—no longer as mere hopes and possible programs, but as the governing document of the new nation, its constitution. All members of the

Third Estate were now guaranteed full citizenship, and the nobles and clergy were denied anything more than that. Taxation was to be shared. Government posts were now open to everyone on the basis of character and talent alone. Everyone was declared equal before the law, and no one could be accused, arrested, or imprisoned except through the law. Everyone was to be considered innocent until proven guilty. Free expression of thought and opinion were to be guarded as "the most precious rights of man." And lastly, property was "an inviolable and sacred right." The *Declaration* was a loose but agreeable amalgam of all that had been learned from the Enlightenment, ignoring its contradictions and problems. Locke, Voltaire, and Rousseau could be quoted side by side, and aristocrats, businessmen, and peasants all appeared to get their due. The Enlightenment seemed fulfilled.[13]

Edmund Burke, watching from a safe distance in England, condemned the revolution in France as a "conspiracy." But with a more or less common ideology, there is no need for conspiracy: the Revolution was the inevitable realization of "an idea whose time had come." And it was already a success: the mere drafting of the *Declaration* had proved that. The rest could proceed almost haphazardly through six years of rumors and miscalculations; through paranoia and overreaction, and indecision on the part of the Assembly as well as the King; through constant anarchy in the streets and rampant crime at night; through selfishness and piggishness, as well as high-flown slogans. By the end of the summer of 1789, most Parisians were saying that the Revolution was over, and in one sense they were right. Thomas Jefferson, an eyewitness, declared:

It is impossible to conceive of a greater fermentation than has worked in Paris, nor do I believe that so great a fermentation ever produced so little injury in any other place. I have been through it daily, have observed the mobs with my own eyes, and declare to you that I saw so plainly the legitimacy of them that I have slept in my house as quietly through the whole as I ever did in the most peaceful moments. The National Assembly have now as clean a canvas to work on here as we had in America. . . . I will agree to be stoned as a false prophet if all does not end well in this country. Nor will it end with this country. Here is but the first chapter of the history of European liberty.[14]

Interlude: The Personalities of the Revolution

Politically, the situation in France by 1791 can only be described as popular anarchy. But philosophically, it was not the absence of Law that accounted for the confusion, but rather a conflict of laws, a conflict of expectations, and a conflict of laws and expectations with each other. The alliance called the Third Estate was already as out of date as its name. The struggle was on for a new unity, and spokesmen competed for the impossible privilege of speaking in one voice for "the People." The Assembly split into political clubs, and these clubs supplanted the Assembly itself as the center of political activity. In a club an advocate could speak his mind to the like-minded, and a strong speaker could emerge not only as spokesman but as director, and so perhaps become a major force in the Revolution. It is worth noting that all the clubs were exclusively bourgeois—even the Jacobins, who never opened their ranks to the working class they claimed to represent. The point was made earlier that the history of the French Revolution can be traced through the vicissitudes of the ideas of Voltaire and Rousseau, and the conflicts between and within them. In the clubs these debates were explicit.

The spectrum of opinion was wide. Inspired by Voltaire were clubs like the Patriots, an elitist conservative organization intent on protecting the monarchy as well as business, and upon consolidating the Revolution and returning to "business as usual" as soon as possible. Among its distinguished and exclusive membership was the marquis de Lafayette, a hero of the American Revolution. On the left, meanwhile, the philosophy of Rousseau had already begun to manifest its internal inconsistencies. On the far left were the devotees of the General Will and "the People," the Jacobins —the Society of Friends of the Constitution—whose leader from 1790 on was Maximilien de Robespierre, a brilliant lawyer and advocate of the poor, a scholar who knew *The Social Contract* as a fundamentalist knows the Bible, an immaculate dresser and snob, a moral prig who was called the "incorruptible." Ruthless and determined, he knew the fears if not the hopes of the French people. By 1793, he would be virtually the dictator of France. Somewhat more conservative, following the libertarian and republican Rousseau, were the Girondists. While the Jacobins presented themselves as democrats and friends of the people, the Girondists were the radical republicans, defenders of the bourgeoisie and the monarchy, moderates and rationalists who desired a middle way between popular anarchy and a "return to normalcy." But as always, the middle way would be caught in the middle as the blandest of alternatives, without the uncompromising radicalism of a Robespierre or the heroic reputation of a Lafayette.[15]

Five personalities emerged; between them, they would define the ideologies of the Revolution, but only one would survive it.

Mirabeau (1749–1791)

Of Honoré Gabriel Riqueti, comte de Mirabeau, H. G. Wells has drawn an irreverent portrait, showing him sneaking down the back stairs of the Queen's apartment to join the Assembly—which was probably not a fact, but true in a certain sense anyway. Mirabeau was the genius liaison between the royal family, the aristocracy, and the revolutionary Assembly, where he was by far the most eloquent speaker. He was a thorough aristocrat, but "enlightened" by the new principles as well. He epitomized the Enlightenment of Voltaire, being elegant, witty, and sarcastic: a prolific writer with a sense of power, connections, a desire for justice, and a flair for reform, as well as a conservative awareness of the limits of popular freedom. "I tremble for the royal authority, which was never so necessary as at a moment when it is on the verge of ruin," he declared.[16] He believed that royal authority should rest on the interests and sovereignty of the French people, but he believed in that authority nonetheless. (He once described the Queen, however, as "the only real *man* in court.") Until he died in 1791, he was the driving force behind the chaotic and confused Assembly, but also, according to a contemporary, a "man without moral scruples" who, to make himself the most powerful person in France, planned to restore the King's old powers. As president of the Assembly and confidant of the Queen, Mirabeau found himself abused both by the other aristocrats (Lafayette included) and by the radical republicans whose ideas he abhorred. He retorted:

All sensible people are on my side, and even part of the rabble. I am suspected, I know. I am accused of being in the pay of the Court. Little I care! No one will believe that I have sold my country's liberty, or that I am plotting to enslave it. You have seen me fighting against tyranny, and it is against tyranny that I am fighting now. But I have always maintained that it was my right and my duty to defend the authority of the laws, the constitutional monarchy, and the king's claim to be the champion of the people. And don't forget that I am the only one in this mob of patriots who can speak so without inconsistency. I have never shared their romantic ideas, their philosophy, or their useless crimes.[17]

Lafayette (1757–1834)

Marie Joseph Paul Yves Roch Gilbert du Motier, marquis de Lafayette, was the precocious son of an ancient family of nobility, orphaned as a child. He married at sixteen and in 1777, at the age of nineteen, became a major general in the American army. "On loan" from the French army, he had no command and little initial support. But he became a friend of George Washington, and in 1781, as commander of the Continental Army in Virginia, was largely responsible for the surrender of the British at Yorktown. A hero of both countries, and a citizen of both countries as well, he returned to France the symbol of the French-American alliance and—more important—of revolution. Although an aristocrat, Lafayette was outspoken on behalf of social reform—an enlightened Voltairean who had made exemplary changes in the administration of his own estates, and who argued publicly for a constitution, religious tolerance, an end to slavery, and the creation of a National Assembly. Ironically, since he attended the States-General of 1789 as a representative of the nobility, he could not vote for the formation of the National Assembly that he so fervently advocated. Once the revolutionary move had been made, Lafayette became one of its leaders, supported enthusiastically by the common people as well as the bourgeoisie. He was appointed the head of the bourgeois militia in Paris by the King, who also trusted him. Those who despised Mirabeau loved Lafayette. Mirabeau was a wit and a libertine, Lafayette a "noble" in the best sense of the word. He was devoted to both popular sovereignty and the King, a combination which subsequent events would make impossible. But at the outset this dual loyalty endeared him to radicals and loyalists alike. As an advocate of egalitarianism and "law and order" (a position which would soon become senseless), he was—for a while—the second most powerful man in France, the first being the King—or the Queen.

By 1791, Lafayette's universal popularity had given way to attacks from all sides—so much so that he planned to retire from politics, until the threat of war with Austria brought him back into military service. He was among the first to urge the military "liberation" of Europe. But the war went badly and Lafayette shared the blame. Then, having attempted to save the life of the King, he was proscribed by the Jacobins. Having once known the universal love of his countrymen, he now found himself almost daily condemned by the left and by the popular papers. Attempting to emigrate to America, he was captured by the Austrians and was kept prisoner for five years. Finally he made it to America, where he was still a hero. When he returned to France under Napoleon, he did not get along with the Emperor, whose abdication he helped bring about in 1814. But then he once again found himself an undesirable in the reactionary monarchy that followed, and once again sought refuge in America, returning to France with the revolution of 1830. This pattern of constant popularity and escape, of constancy to liberal principles in the face of varying and at times bewildering opposition, reminds one of Voltaire. Whatever the vicissitudes of revolution, the ideology of Lafayette remained firm. French liberalism would return to him again and again, even as he at times found himself overwhelmed and shouted down by radicals on the left and by reactionaries on the right.[18]

Danton (1759–1794)

Mirabeau and Lafayette were established figures in Paris before the Revolution. Great upheavals break the surface of established recognition, however, allowing a breed of "new men" to emerge from the activities of revolution itself. Thus in France in 1788 there were certain men virtually unknown even in their own corners of France, who by 1792, through the auspices of the political clubs and the popular underground journals, would take control of France, sweeping away established reputations. They had no long titles or lineages, were often poor, not always well educated, and to the unsympathetic and conservative observer might well have appeared as part of the "rabble" (a term used often by Mirabeau and Lafayette), coughed up from the depths of the mob in order to lead France to ruin.

Georges-Jacques Danton was one of these men. He himself has given an account of his background:

The old regime made a great mistake. It brought me up on a scholarship in Plessis College. I was brought up with nobles, who were my comrades, and with whom I lived on familiar terms. On completing my studies, I had nothing; I was poor, and tried to get a place. The Paris bar was unapproachable, and it required an effort to get accepted. I could not get into the army, without either rank or a patron. There was no opening for me in the church. I could purchase no employment, for I hadn't a cent. My old companions turned their backs on me. I remained without a situation, and only after many long years did I succeed in buying the post of advocate in the Royal Council. The revolution came, when I, and all like me, threw themselves into it. The ancient regime forced us to do so, by providing a good education for us, without providing an opening for our talents.[19]

Danton was no aristocrat who could coast his way through the Revolution, riding comfortably—or so one might have thought—on its crest. He was one of those who had to fight his way up to power against overwhelming opposition. He was a bourgeois, but (as Taine so unfairly objects) not a wealthy one. Despite his success, he was not a politician, and had many interests that he enjoyed far more—among them the pleasures of life, which the wealth he gained through power allowed him to indulge in more and more. In contrast to Robespierre, the Incorruptible, Danton was known as "the corruptible." He didn't care.[20]

Danton's great gift was oratory. He spoke—or rather roared—like a lion. He had a voice that would carry over the hysteria of the National Assembly, and the wiles if not wisdom to sense the direction that Assembly was about to take. He was truly a man of the people, and even his critics admitted that he had a heart. His lack of principle often acted as a humanitarian corrective to Robespierre's dogmatism.

Danton, however, had not been much of a club member—the requisite for power in the late days of the Revolution; he had wavered between the Girondists and the Jacobins. But he had endeared himself to the Jacobins as the constant enemy of Lafayette, whom he censured for the King's intrigues and flight, and for the failure of the war effort. At first Danton joined Robespierre in denouncing the war, but when it became inevitable he became an enthusiastic patriot, re-creating the concept of France's "natural boundaries," the rallying cry for the next ten years of battle. He cared little about the fate of the King, arguing first for mercy, then voting for execution. He played politics as it had to be played, forming alliances when necessary. He became a solid Jacobin at the point when the Girondists were about to lose their power and their heads. His resistance to Robespierre was one of his few impolitic moves during those treacherous years, but it can be argued that two such different creatures could hardly share the same ground for long. The two have often been treated as polar opposites, which they were in personality but not in politics, where they remained allies until near the end. Danton's lack of ambition allowed him to stay with Robespierre, until the latter's ceaseless guillotining prompted him to a humanitarian complaint. Danton was guillotined on April 5, 1794.

Marat (1743–1793)

In any ideological account of the Revolution, its dark side—the paranoia as well as the politics of Rousseau, the resentment and lust for vengeance as well as the practical demands for stability and security—emerges in the person of Jean-Paul Marat. Not a political leader or spokesman as such, he was a social critic, a journalist, a mere "friend of the people" who had the genius to see tragedies before they occurred, but rarely stopped them. He rather used tragedy to instigate more vindictiveness, further excesses. His aim was total revolution, not mere reform or restructuring. Accordingly, it was he who goaded the Revolution through its worst days. From his ideological sideline, he could afford to make demands and look further ahead than the vulnerable members of the Assembly.[21]

Marat had once been a scientist of some reputation. Benjamin Franklin took an active interest in certain of his experiments, and Marat was generally recognized as a young doctor of considerable ability. But he was first of all a rebel and a cynic, with a keen sense of injustice—particularly to himself—and a violent hatred of authority. He spent several years in London, talking about revolution, then returned to Paris to promulgate it. His bible was Rousseau's *Social Contract,* to which all his pamphlets and demands would appeal, just as it is to Rousseau's personality that his own can best be compared. His underground newspaper, *The Friend of the People,* was launched—with the Revolution—in the summer of 1789. It was always extreme, suspicious of everyone, vengeful and violent. At first it was merely an extremist paper, urging the execution of the King and the proclamation of a people's republic long before events had taken such a turn; when they did, Marat became not only the prophet but in many ways the intellectual fuel of the Revolution. Robespierre used him, and without

Marat's passionate prose in circulation before his own speeches, it is doubtful that the frail and not very articulate lawyer could have made those violent points by himself.

It was Marat's role in the Revolution—and his genius—to constantly remind the people how far the Revolution had to go to realize their most basic demands. Mirabeau had said from the start, with a smirking cynicism, that all that was required for the people—but required absolutely— was "more money in their pockets, living more easily, more work and better wages." But for Marat the demands were ideological, abstract, and elusive, and he would spare nothing to have them achieved.[22] To consolidate the Revolution, he announced publicly that he was in favor of cutting off at least 300,000 more heads. He openly planned some of the worst massacres of the Revolution, and regretted only that they never touched the more prominent politicians, whom he denounced as a new breed of tyrants.

Marat's painful skin affliction and his most unglamorous death at the hands of Charlotte Corday are well known: she avenged her losses in the Terror and rid the country of a villain by stabbing him in his bath on July 13, 1793. The result, however, was to turn him into a martyr. He was eulogized in the Assembly and buried in the glorious Pantheon—in the place of Mirabeau, who was "depantheonized"—as one of the giants of the Revolution. (Not surprisingly, Marat too was depantheonized soon after the end of the Terror—as were eventually all those once buried there as heroes of the Revolution, with two exceptions who by virtue of their ideas remained: Voltaire and Rousseau.)

Robespierre (1758–1794)

The first dictator of France, encouraged directly by Marat but fundamentally by Rousseau, was Maximilien François Marie Isidore de Robespierre. It is worth noting, to be sure, that even a few short years before, nothing would have repulsed this prototype of Napoleon more than the idea of a dictatorship. He was like the hero of Anatole France's excellent novel of the Revolution, *The Gods Are Thirsty,* in which a sensitive young boy, moral and kind to obsessiveness, is turned into a tyrant by the Revolution's tension and violence.

Robespierre accepted as holy dogma Rousseau's doctrines about the General Will, popular sovereignty, and the natural goodness of humanity. He was not a cynic like Marat, nor an opportunist like Danton. He was the incorruptible, beyond personal ambition and above the simple things that obsessed other revolutionaries. He demanded purity above all, condemned profanity, and was revolted by the sexual license that the Revolution had inevitably let loose. Among other things, he criticized Danton even for his sloppy dress. He was a provincial moralist, a precocious orphan who, like Rousseau, expressed his bitterness at his misfortunes in generalized philosophical phrases giving no hint of the personal impotence that provoked them.[23]

Trained as an attorney, Robespierre had used his profession to pursue justice and consequently remained poor. An intense opponent of capital punishment, he resigned from one position because it entailed endorsing the same. The bloodthirstiness of Marat was completely foreign to Robespierre, and forced upon him by circumstances. He abhorred fanaticism and loved the study of history and what we would now call sociology, which gave him the knowledge he needed to follow the Revolution so closely, and to defend his self-appointed constituency, the poor and the oppressed. He shared Rousseau's mixed love of companionship and his fear of society. Despite his lofty position, he would often disappear for long periods, giving his enemies the opportunity to raise suspicions against him. His appearance, though impeccably neat, was always unimpressive; he was scrawny, weak-voiced, stuttering, nervous, and had a "sea-green complexion." He was a moral prig, cold as ice, seemingly without true sentiment, and, as events proved, capable of committing the most inhumane acts in the name of his humanitarian principles.[24] (As Rousseau too would have done, no doubt, had he also been catapulted to such a dizzying and tenuous position of power.) Thus he declared: "If we have to choose between an excess of patriotic zeal and the empty shell of bad citizenship, or the morass of moderatism, we will not hesitate."

The Head of a King

> The kings of Europe would challenge us. We throw them the head of a king!
>
> Danton

The Assembly, and France with it, muddled on through the relatively calm years of 1790 and 1791. Frightened aristocrats and conservative bourgeoisie quietly left the country. Intimidated deputies just as quietly resigned their troublesome posts. Mirabeau had died in 1791. The Assembly shifted to the left—a trend that the Voltaireans termed dangerous and the Rousseauan republicans hopeful. The pressing problems of 1788–89 were at least partially solved. Food was expensive, but there was no famine. There was peace, even if there were threats from the East. France was now a "limited monarchy," with the King and Queen virtually prisoners in Paris. The King was an undependable figurehead whose mere existence served to keep the Rousseauans in check. So far, the idea of a kingless republic appealed to only the extremists. But if the majority of the

French people were still monarchists at heart, they did not trust the person who happened to be their King.

Then in June 1791 Louis XVI and his family made a desperate attempt to flee Paris—the so-called "Flight to Varennes" that, like most of Louis's efforts, ended in pathos. The King was recognized and the party stopped before the border, whereupon the King surrendered without a fight, spent the night in a local village, insisted on a large dinner, and complimented his hosts on the wine, as if he had stopped by on vacation.[25] The Flight to Varennes was not surprising, nor did it show the King to be any less foolish or less competent than his subjects already believed. But Louis XVI was first of all a symbol of France and its unity. As a result of his treachery, the French Revolution became a war of universals which transcended national boundaries and would soon engulf all Europe. The French bourgeoisie had already come to see itself as the "universal" class (like the struggling workers a few decades later). But what now had become painfully evident was the reactionary brotherhood of monarchs.[26]

The family bonds of international nobility required some sword-rattling, at the least. To appease his nagging sister as well as the émigré nobles, in August 1791 Leopold called together a convention at Pillnitz and issued a hypothetical and weakly worded declaration suggesting a united intervention in the affairs of France if the royal family were threatened further. But Leopold did not desire a war with France, and except for the safety of his sister, saw little reason to intervene in that country's affairs. Like most of the royalty of Europe, he in fact took a certain sly delight in the collapse of the once haughty and competitive Bourbon monarchy.

That same August the Assembly produced the long-awaited constitution, establishing essentially a businessman's monarchy with emphasis on free enterprise, free access to power and privilege through financial gain, and increased freedom of competition. First and foremost stood "the sacred and inviolable right to private property." The emphasis on universal rights in the *Declaration* of 1789 was gone; in its place was a condemnation of "licentiousness." The revolt against privilege had now become a rejection of *unearned* privilege in the name of efficiency. Skeptics said that it defended "the freedom to get richer."

In September the Assembly dissolved, its job completed. On the twenty-eighth of that month the King announced, "The Revolution is over." A year later he was arrested, and on January 21, 1793, he was guillotined.

The Second Revolution and the Reign of Terror

Revolutions always appear to succeed with amazing ease in their initial stage, and the reason is that the men who make them first only pick up the power of a regime in plain disintegration; they are the consequences but never the causes of the downfall of political authority.

Hannah Arendt, *Revolution*

In August 1792 the Revolution was over three years old, and the urban workers and the sans-culottes began to see that they had gained nothing from their enthusiastic support of it. Unemployment was as bad as ever; food was still scarce and very expensive. The new constitution of 1791 said nothing about the poor, the unemployed, or high prices. Dissatisfaction exploded in riots, but popular anarchy no longer served the interests of the ruling bourgeoisie. The disturbances were greeted by martial law, censorship of the press, and a law against unions. Once again conditions in France were intolerable.

The second revolution was the rebellion of the people against the bourgeoisie, and a struggle for power within the bourgeoisie. The Revolution of 1789 had taken place within the established framework of the traditions, classes, and monarchy of France; the new revolution had no traditions, no framework, and no limits ("until the fuel is done," said Carlyle). A comment by Rousseau in his *Confessions* might serve as the autobiography of the Revolution as well: "If the revolution had only restored me to myself, all would have been well; but unfortunately it went further, and carried me quickly to the other extreme." The "other extreme" was not expected by any but the extremists, and perhaps not even by them. The royalists and aristocrats saw a choice simply between the moderate revolutionary state of affairs of 1791 and the old life. In the words of H. G. Wells:

They wanted to be back in their lost paradise of privilege, haughtiness, and limitless expenditure, and it seemed to them that if only they could make the government of the National Assembly impossible, then by a sort of miracle the dry bones of the ancient regime would live again. They had no sense of the other possibility, the gulf of the republican extremists, that yawned at their feet. (p. 896)

The second revolution, unlike the first, attempted to uproot French life, even going so far as to change the calendar, the length of the week, and every aspect of the citizens' daily life.[27] Meanwhile the royalists and aristocrats exerted pressure on the young regime through continuous attempts to undermine it from within and without. From within, there was the threat of counterrevolution, plotted even by those who professed to be devoted revolutionaries. And given the continued food shortages, civil discontent, internecine ideological battles within the Revolution, and the discovery periodically of plots in the highest places, anyone might be suspect at any time.[28] From without, the émigré nobles were conspiring with foreign armies for the invasion of France. Whatever the real threat of the Pillnitz declaration, the French people now had a concrete object for their fears, and the bourgeoisie saw a strategy to ease domestic pressures and unite the factions of the Revolution against a common enemy. Even those who had remained aloof from the politics of vengeance had good reason to fear the repercussions if the enraged exiles should return home in full power.[29] On April 20, 1792, France declared war on Austria. And within France, chaos was met with legitimized terror—the reigning monarch, "Madame Guillotine."

The Terror can be understood only if we dislodge from our imaginations the mythology learned from *A Tale of Two Cities, The Scarlet Pimpernel, Orphans of the Storm,* and other conservative commentaries. It is true that the two-and-a-half-year Reign of Terror was largely imposed by popular anarchy, public riots, and a radical push to the left; but it is also true that the victims were more often the very people responsible for the Terror than the infamous "aristo's." And over 80 percent of the victims of the Terror were peasants, workers, and radicals who had come out on the losing end of local power struggles. It is easy to be horrified by the statistics (some forty thousand—modest enough by twentieth-century standards), but it is more important to appreciate the urgency of these extreme measures. The threat of counterrevolution and its accompanying vengeance was very real, and to them seemed imminent; the war was going badly. There was still unemployment and a food shortage, and consequently riots, looting, and violence, particularly in the workers' districts and the provinces. The official Terror reduced this enormously, and in balance was probably a humanitarian move. In that period of paranoia and continuous violence, the systematic if not always rational murders by the State were preferable to the much more irrational murders in the street. And one must not forget, in the midst of that visible violence, the routine violence of the Old Regime, and the far greater and purely vindictive reactionary violence that followed the Terror, encouraged by the reigning bourgeoisie but without even the stamp of legitimacy.

By 1793, France had become something of a Hobbesian (not Rousseauan) "state of nature," in which everyone seemed to be at war with everyone. The Jacobins and Girondists purged the remaining conservatives; then the Jacobins wiped out the Girondists, supposedly supported by the people, the shock troops of the Revolution. But now the Jacobins found they could no longer control the violent resentment and anger they had released. Robespierre, the man supposedly in power, found it necessary to compromise his thoroughgoing Rousseauism to bring a semblance of order into mob-controlled Paris. The new constitution of 1793 said less of revolution and rights, and more of duties and respect of property. In October the Queen was led to the scaffold. In April 1794 Danton and the chief terrorist, Hébert, were executed. Marat was already dead. The Jacobins had turned on one another, and the party of democracy found itself with a single remaining leader in a society in total chaos. Robespierre once again retreated into the safe and comfortable confines of the Jacobin Club.

The Fall of Robespierre

From the first, the war had gone very badly. The peasants and workers had temporarily united with the conservatives in defense of France, but it soon became evident that the war was also an excuse for austerity at home, a cover-up as well as a cause for increased inflation and hardship. The disasters of war had turned the favors of the people and power to the Jacobins; Lafayette and the spirit of Voltaire had been exiled from the Assembly. As the war continued to go badly, paranoia increased. Robespierre, the arch-Rousseauan of the extreme left, emerged in control of the newly established state. As one of the few Paris leaders who had opposed the war, he benefited from its daily setbacks, each of which confirmed his wisdom. Using this unique position to feed his own power, he turned the people's growing desperation into indignation against their own ineffectual government. As a member of the powerful Committee of Public Safety, he had functioned as the architect of the Terror. By early 1794 he had used his behind-the-scenes manipulation to become, in effect, the first modern dictator of Europe.

Even if Robespierre had gained his power through opposition to the war, once in power he used his ideological resources to win it. The ideology of Rousseau and the General Will were responsible for molding France into a popular and effective fighting force, the likes of which had never been seen in Europe. The Austrian, Prussian, Russian, and other armies were professional, whereas France developed a people's army superior at least in numbers and enthusiasm. Fighting an indifferent and mutually jealous alliance of the great powers, it finally began to score impressive victories. The people's army turned back the Prussians at Valmy—a small battle which Goethe would call "the beginning of a new era"—then overran Belgium and pushed as far as the Rhine in Germany. Whatever the troubles within the Revolution, it had now become a military as well as an ideological power that was beginning to force its way across Europe.

International victories no longer diverted attention from the Terror at home, however. Unlike fear, victory does not distract from dissatisfaction, but fuels it. Not only the Terror, but continued food shortages and financial disasters were cause for complaint—and for the rejection of Robespierre. Ironically, the charge against him was not his use of fear and injustice, which might well have been considered a breach of faith with the people he claimed to protect; rather it was his pure allegiance to Rousseau.

One of the key themes of the Enlightenment, in both Voltaire and

Rousseau, was the attack on the Catholic Church. Accordingly, one of the themes of the Revolution—motivated by the privileges that the clergy had shared with the nobility—was a prolonged attack on the political institution of the Church. From the early days of the Revolution, there had been confiscation of church property and disruption of the institutional Church. But the Revolution had made the mistake, also from its earliest days, of attacking Christianity as well as the Christian Church. Such an attack had not been part of the doctrines of either Voltaire or Rousseau, each of whom had clung to the "natural" religion of Reason or sentiment. Irreligion was clearly not part of the French revolutionary spirit. In revolutionary France there developed two churches, one official and negligible, the other clandestine and popular. In its attack on the Church, the Revolution had already undermined itself by separation from the spiritual base of French Catholicism. In the future this was also to prove a major source of power to the Catholic Church and to the Pope in Rome. Where the French Church had prided itself on its autonomy before the Revolution, the counterrevolutionary French Church now looked for support to Rome. The more the Church was repressed, the more effective it became as a counterrevolutionary force.

In desperation, the Revolution then attempted to replace the all-too-popular faith with a Voltairean Cult of Reason. This met with lack of enthusiasm not only among the people in general but from Robespierre himself, still a Rousseauan, who countered with a Cult of the Supreme Being. Like Rousseau, Robespierre thought God necessary to any moral order.[30] This apparently counterrevolutionary act was of great convenience to Robespierre's many enemies, who at last succeeded in having him tried and guillotined in late July of 1794. He became a historical convenience, accused, now that he was dead, of both tyranny and conservatism, wholly to blame for the Terror and the crises of the young republic. With his death the Terror ended, and also the Revolution. "The death of Robespierre," says Carlyle, "was a signal at which great multitudes of men, struck dumb with terror heretofore, rose out of their hiding places" (II, 343).

Aftermath: The Directory

From the summer of 1794 on, Voltaire once again dominated French ideology. The power of France returned to the bourgeoisie without democratic pretensions and without excessive zeal or appeal to "the People." The Assembly was once again a body of hardheaded businessmen, many of whom had gained enormously from the Revolution, but whose interests now required domestic stability and increased international trade. In 1795 a five-man Directory was installed as the head of government, republican and business-oriented in temperament. Emigrés returned, and bitter bourgeois youths and sons of the victims of the Terror began a counter-reign of terror (the White Terror) against Jacobins and workers. The Directory did little to control such incidents, which were not a threat to its power or stability.

The Directory was in as much confusion as the early Assembly, but its stability was more or less maintained by bourgeois business interests and by the ongoing wars against Europe and England. In early 1795 food shortages and intolerable conditions in the cities led to riots and demonstrations, but leaders were lacking who could use this anger as a political weapon. Police measures and repressions followed, Robespierre in retrospect gained the stature of a folk martyr, and there were several calls to armed insurrection. The most that happened was a four-day invasion of the Assembly by irate housewives. Without bourgeois leaders, the people lacked direction and strategy, so their efforts came to nothing, and the new Directory signaled a complete return to bourgeois republican rule. Encouraged by the new conservatism, royalists and counterrevolutionaries started agitating and threatened to reinstate themselves. But on October 5, 1795, a "whiff of grape shot" delivered by a young general, Napoleon Bonaparte, stopped that once and for all. With the end of the Revolution, Enlightenment ideology was wholly victorious. But the Enlightenment itself, which had always been a struggle rather than a coherent position, was dead in France.[31]

6 The Enlightenment in Germany: Kant's Transcendental Revolution

> Enlightenment is the emergence of man from the immaturity for which he is himself responsible. Immaturity is the inability to use one's understanding without the guidance of another. Man is responsible for his own immaturity, when it is caused, by lack not of understanding, but of the resolution and courage to use it without the guidance of another. Have courage! *Sapere aude!* Have the courage to use your own reason! is the slogan of the Enlightenment.
>
> Immanuel Kant, "What Is Enlightenment?"

> I have found it necessary to deny *knowledge,* in order to make room for *faith.*
>
> <div align="right">Immanuel Kant, <i>Critique of Pure Reason</i></div>

In France, the Enlightenment evolved into political force, protected and polemicized by a quarreling family of self-styled "philosophers." In Germany, however, the Enlightenment had to develop in a political vacuum —in the "realm of the spirit"—and its champions were philosophy professors writing in isolation, but formulating the bourgeois concepts of "humanity" and "reason" with a profound elegance and grandeur unimagined in France. The greatest of these isolated spokesmen for humanity was Immanuel Kant, a solitary bachelor professor in the outer reaches of Eastern Europe, as far removed as possible from the enlightened courts and cities of the West and the excitement of the French Revolution. Unlike Rousseau, who was in many ways his philosophical prototype, and unlike Robespierre, who was in some ways his political alter ego, Kant remained a faithful servant of the Old Regime, never plotting to overthrow society and never risking arrest or the guillotine. He preferred to sit alone in his study, where he articulated bourgeois prejudices and the doctrines of the Enlightenment as a grand and systematic philosophy of unprecedented ambition. He was no mere member of a "movement," but—as he himself announced—a revolution unto himself. He did not just assume the Enlightenment doctrines, but proved them. He did not take the existence of humanity for granted, but developed and demonstrated it. He did not just use the transcendental pretense, but explicitly formulated it, defended it, and made it into the main theme of his entire philosophy. He was the first philosophical giant of the bourgeoisie—not merely an illustrious example, like Voltaire, or a brilliant ideological polemicist, like Rousseau, but a true warrior, a conqueror, a hero. And because philosophical heroes are so much less costly than their political counterparts (even in an indecisive battle, thousands die), Kant taught the bourgeoisie to fully appreciate its primal source of power: not its politics but its ideas, its unmatchable intellectual arrogance. The transcendental pretense was proving to be the most devastating weapon ever employed in the decisive battles of peace-time.

The German Middle Class

In the mid-eighteenth century Germany, like France, had a growing middle class. But unlike France, Germany was not a unified nation, and its middle class had little political potential and still less self-esteem. What is now called Germany then consisted of several hundred small states, principalities, "free cities," and imperial domains, ruled by various princes, bishops, and knights. In some nominal sense, these were united as the "Holy Roman Empire." But the decay of all political and social ties between the Emperor and his states, and between the states themselves, had been so great following the Thirty Years War (1618–1648) as to prompt Voltaire's justified and well-known wisecrack that this entity was "neither Holy nor Roman, nor an Empire." Many of these independent and sometimes isolated states and cities maintained a medieval social and political structure of prince, nobility, and serfs, with the bourgeoisie or *Bürgers* occupying the gray middle as local bureaucrats, lawyers, doctors, teachers, musicians, clergy, and merchants. Capitalism and commerce were not advanced in the German states, many of which were still economically crippled from the wars of the previous century. And so, despite the size of the middle class, the unity, coalitions, pressures, and self-confidence that exploded in France were not present in Germany.[1]

The largest single state in Germany, and the only European power to speak of (excluding the Austrian Empire), was Prussia, located in northern Germany and stretching east along the Baltic Sea. Prussia was ruled by one of the most "enlightened" monarchs of Europe, Frederick II or the Great, a friend of Voltaire, an accomplished musician, philosopher, and literary figure, as well as the most powerful military and political leader of eighteenth-century Europe. Frederick had made Prussia one of the great European powers, had brought serfdom virtually to an end, and had instituted many important legal and financial reforms of great benefit to his people. His "primary occupation," he once wrote to Voltaire, was "to fight ignorance and prejudice in this country. . . . to enlighten its people, cultivate their manners and morals, and make them as happy as human beings can be." But the enlightened freedom and pursuit of happiness in the Prussia of "Old Fritz" left grounds for complaint. The author and critic Gotthold Lessing, after spending some time in Berlin, remarked that such freedom consisted of "the freedom to advertise as many anti-religious imbecilities as you wish. . . . But let someone stand up who wants to raise his voice for the rights of subjects and against exploitation and despotism."

Lessing's complaint betrayed a deep-rooted flaw in the German Enlightenment or *Aufklärung*,[2] of which he would be one of the founders. The cries for "liberty" that had sparked the French Revolution were first of all cries for political freedom; French Enlightenment philosophers were men of the law, practical men as well as ideologists and theoreticians. But in Germany "freedom" was a conception shorn of political meaning; there, Enlightenment philosophers upheld a profound split between philosophy and politics, between their idealism and political ideology. They lacked the sense of a distinguished history, which the French philosophers could take for granted in their attacks. Their growing sense of nationalism was frustrated by provincialism. In desperation, they proclaimed themselves "citizens of the world," since they did not yet have a country. Without a strong bourgeoisie to forge an ideology and a political front out of political philosophy, German thought turned increasingly to problems of knowledge and personal morality, aesthetics and self-realization. Without self-confidence as a class, the bourgeois intellectuals and poets turned to themselves, and instead of supporting that class attacked its infirmity. While the French Revolution would have considerable impact on the German middle class, the Prussians retained full confidence in their own monarchy and saw no need for revolution. There were local Jacobin clubs, but their desire for "a revolution without tears" expressed less than total willingness to make the sacrifices of extreme political action. As R. R. Palmer wryly comments, the German bourgeoisie "favored the rights of man, they wished well to humanity."[3] But Karl Marx was less polite:

While the French bourgeoisie, by means of the most colossal revolution that history has ever known, was achieving domination and conquering the Continent of Europe, while the already politically emancipated English bourgeoisie was revolutionizing industry and subjugating India politically, and all the rest of the world commercially, the impotent German burghers did not get any farther than "good will." . . . Kant's good will fully corresponds to the impotence, depression and wretchedness of the German burghers, whose petty interests were never capable of developing into the common national interests of a class [but] had their counterpart, their cosmopolitan swollen-headedness.[4]

If, as we have argued, the Enlightenment was the ideology of an increasingly powerful middle class, one would expect that the Enlightenment would never achieve its full impact in Germany, and this was certainly the case. Much of the energy that might have supported the Enlightenment bypassed it and went directly into romanticism, particularly the Storm and Stress *(Sturm und Drang)* movement in poetry. In such states as Prussia, one reason for this is worth special mention: with an enlightened monarch ruling over them (and *Aufklärung* was popular with many German princes), the sense of rebellion felt by men of letters often manifested itself *against* the Enlightenment as an ideology of despotism. In France, on the other hand, the Enlightenment had been exclusively the weapon of the bourgeoisie, even when adopted by the aristocracy and lower classes. In Germany the Enlightenment was as much a threat to the middle class as an inspiration or promise. So it is in Germany, far more than in France or elsewhere, that the Enlightenment becomes the *nemesis* of the middle class, estranging them from themselves and giving birth to vitriolic anti-bourgeois prophets even within their own ranks—to Schiller and Lessing in the Enlightenment's milder beginning, and to Marx and Nietzsche in the years to come.

Voltaire and Rousseau were both well known throughout the German states in the late 1760s. Yet the intellectual scene there was still based on theology and dogmatic metaphysics, particularly the philosophy of Leibniz, one of the early Enlightenment geniuses.[5] German art was still in the rococo style of pre-Enlightenment France, and music was largely baroque. As the French Enlightenment of Voltaire became popular among the provincial ruling class, the German middle class grew more enthusiastic about German nationalism and culture. It was at this time that Lessing and Schiller determined to establish a German theater to challenge the dominant French influences, and that Herder and Hamann began to argue for folk tradition and nationalism in manners and literature. It was then too that the Storm and Stress movement, including Herder and Schiller, began its celebration of individual genius, poetry, striving and struggle, folkways and emotion, and moral and aesthetic enthusiasm (see Chapter 7). While the middle-class German intellectuals did not share Rousseau's critique of culture and the State, and ignored the revolutionary message that inspired the French Revolution, in Rousseau they did find much to their liking, not the least his inspirations concerning individual goodness and his insight into the moral law. Thus threads that were still intertwined in France became separated in Germany: while Voltaire determined the Enlightenment of Frederick the Great and other German princes, Rousseau governed both the Enlightenment and the Storm and Stress romanticism of the German bourgeoisie.

Despite all the confusion of ideologies, the philosophy of the *Aufklärung* is almost entirely of a single type: idealism.[6] Herbert Marcuse, following Marx, has rightly commented that "German idealism is the theory of the French Revolution."[7] Yet "idealism" need not mean (as it so often does) political hopefulness perhaps tinged with a willful naiveté. German idealism involves minimal concern with political ideals as such. Where it does include such ideals, they are rarely applied concretely, almost never locally, and remain cautiously conservative in spirit. The French ideals of liberty, equality, and fraternity are indeed spelled out theoretically by the German idealists, but in metaphysical and personal conceptions. Most important, idealism involves a dramatic emphasis on the metaphysical and personal importance of *ideas* and their expression. Crudely stated, idealism is the theory that the world is composed of ideas. (Even more crudely, German idealism is the theory that the world is composed of German ideas.) Freedom, accordingly, is the recognition of a certain idea, rather than the realization of a certain political situation.[8]

Kant

If there is one point of agreement among virtually all students of German idealism, it is that its definitive source is the philosophy of Immanuel Kant. Kant was a devotee of Isaac Newton and an accomplished scientific theorist himself. Of Kant the man, the provincial professor of Königsberg, there is little to say. (The poet Heine complained that Kant "had neither a life nor a history.")[9] He was born in the tiny town of Königsberg, in remote East Prussia, where news of the cataclysmic events of his time reached him only through newspapers and with considerable delay. There he lived all his life, never having even considered any of the far more exciting positions offered him once his fame had spread. Sexually he was a virgin until he died—a philosophical record of sorts. His three-o'clock walks were legendary, giving rise to the familiar comment that his neighbors set their clocks by them. (Heine: "I do not believe that the great clock of the cathedral there did its daily work more dispassionately and regularly than its compatriot Immanuel Kant.")

Writing far from Paris, the bourgeois professor could afford to be an armchair revolutionary, and in fact enthusiastically supported the French Revolution even through the Reign of Terror, when most of his companions recoiled in horror. Yet with regard to his own existence he could say, "All change frightens me." His pamphlet *Perpetual Peace* sought to encourage Prussian neutrality in 1795, so as to allow the struggling Republic of France to consolidate itself. Yet he taught for over forty years in the ultraconservative state university, whose authority he never challenged. "With regard to the State," said Nietzsche, "Kant was not great."[10]

Despite his staggering brilliance and his vast influence, Kant the professor inspired no heroic image; he was one of millions of middle-class Germans lost amid the great political events of the times. But in the privacy of his study, and at the already advanced age of fifty-five, this obscure bachelor professor exploded the world and began to replace it with a new one. Heine compares Kant to Robespierre, rightly commenting that the former went far beyond the latter in his terrorism.

First, we find in both the same inexorable cutting prosaic sober sense of honor and integrity. Then we find in them the same talent for mistrust, which the one showed as regards thoughts and called it criticism, while the other applied it to men and entitled it republican virtue. But there was manifested in both, to the very highest degree, the type of *bourgeoisie*, of the common citizen. Nature meant them to weigh out coffee and sugar but destiny determined that they should weigh other things; so one placed a king, and the other a god in the scales—and they both gave exact weight. (*Works*, V, 137)

Kant's great revolution was a revolution in *method*. His philosophical principles might easily be characterized as the same middle-class moral and Christian prejudices that he had grown up with, plus the already well-known results of Newton's physics. What was important was not *what* he defended, but *how*. In philosophy courses he is most often presented as the man who reconciled the antagonistic methods of the Continental rationalists (Descartes, Spinoza, Leibniz) and the British empiricists (Locke, Berkeley, Hume). The rationalists shared confidence in the powers of human reason to ascertain basic truths about the world, while the empiricists insisted that knowledge of the world could come only from experience itself. Complicating this battle was the fact that both methods now seemed to result in skepticism: Hume had shown that neither reason nor experience could justify the most basic principles of human knowledge.

Kant credited Hume with "waking him from his dogmatic slumbers"—that is, with showing him that his Leibnizian confidence in reason was not sufficient to defend either the foundations of science or the principles of morality and Christianity. But Kant found Hume's skeptical conclusions intolerable. Newton's science was not just a convenience, it was *true*. Morality was not just a matter of utility and sentiment; moral principles were absolutely *right*. And religion was not, as Hume had argued, a matter of fear and superstition; faith in God was utterly rational, despite the failure of traditional arguments and attempted "proofs" of God's existence.

Kant's purpose, simply stated, was to develop a method for defending the foundations of science, the principles of morality, and the central doctrines of Christianity against the skeptical arguments of Hume and others. The reconciliation of the rationalists and the empiricists was a by-product of this attempt. What Kant really wanted was a way of defending principles that he refused to give up—"prejudices," if you like—and in this he resembled not so much Hume or even Leibniz, but the often neglected influence whom Kant himself considered his single most important model: Jean-Jacques Rousseau.[11] Like Rousseau, Kant was obsessed with the idea of humanity's intrinsic goodness and perfectibility, and it is this idea, more than any other, that provides the living core of his philosophy. Kant's defense of science was the familiar French defense of human progress. His defense of morality was an attempt to undercut the rampant subjectivism and excessive social secularism that he, like Rousseau, believed was corrupting the new generations. And his defense of Christianity was an attempt—again like Rousseau—to defend what he considered the only absolutely dependable moral sanction he knew. Ironically, despite their vast differences in personality and temperament, it was through chaste, superrational Immanuel Kant that the ideology of the paranoid libertine Jean-Jacques Rousseau made its most powerful impact in newly enlightened Germany.

As the great synthesizer, Kant had to reconcile a large number of apparently inconsistent doctrines and methods. Above all, the foundations of science and the principles of morality and religion—all of which Kant was intent on justifying—were not evidently compatible. Since the Renaissance, science and religion had battled each other. For years, science had been on the defensive, but now, in the Enlightenment, it could claim to be the dominant authority. The empirical methods of science seemed to rule out any possibility of knowing a God who could not be experienced. The Christian belief in the immortality of the human soul was empirically untestable—which was why Hume had insisted that all such doctrines were nothing but "sophistry and illusion" and should be "committed to the flames." Newtonian belief in strict causal determination of all events seemed to undermine the notion that human beings at least sometimes act freely and choose their courses of action. But if there were no such freedom, then the concept of moral responsibility would collapse, and with it the concept of morality itself. If one accepted the new Enlightenment doctrines, what room was left for faith? If science really could explain everything, what was left for morality and religion? Kant's task was to find not only a method to defend science, morality, and religion, but also a way of making them compatible. Given the conflicts and arguments of the past several centuries, this could not be easy.

The Need for Necessity

The key to Kant's philosophy is his idea of *universal necessity*. Hume had argued that the basic principles of human understanding were mere habits not justifiable by either experience or reason. In confronting Hume, Kant had to show that these principles were much more than this: that they were applicable to every experience of every conscious creature; that they were presuppositions without which our experience would not be possible; that they were justifiable, if not on the basis of reason or experience, then on the basis of the very existence and nature of human consciousness. Kant's formidable terminology expresses these ideas in a variety of ways. The simplest and most common formulation is that these basic principles must be both "universal and necessary"—that is, they must apply to *all* conscious creatures ("universal"), and apply necessarily.[12] Hume had argued that our belief in the causal necessity of certain connections between events was not a function of the way the world is, but rather a matter of our own habits and expectations. Kant, in rejoinder, must therefore argue that causal necessity is *real* necessity, that anyone who experiences the world at all *must* experience it in causal terms. Just as the key claim of Hume's skeptical philosophy had been the unjustifiability of our knowledge of causal connections, so the key claim of Kant's philosophy will be that such connections are universal and necessary—that they *must* be the basis of experience for any person or creature whatever.

In Kant's writings, the phrase "universal and necessary" is often replaced by the technical term "a priori." *A priori knowledge* is knowledge that is possessed by everyone everywhere at all times (universal), and that they could not conceivably lack (necessary). Kant also refers to principles which are known a priori as *transcendental principles*, principles that are presupposed and lie at the basis of every experience.[13] It should be evident that this characterization of "universal and necessary" or a priori principles captures much of what the French Enlightenment philosophers tried to include in their concept of *Reason*. This is, of course, exactly what Kant intends to do, but his concept of reason will prove to be much more concise than theirs.

The idea that all events have causes—obviously, one of the basic principles of all science—is, according to Kant, universal and necessary a priori knowledge of a transcendental principle. So too will the other basic principles of science be shown to be universal and necessary, including our ideas about space and time. All such principles will be shown to be not mere functions of human understanding, Humean habits, or whatever, but necessary truths about the way the world must be. If causality were simply the way we happen to interpret sequences of events, then we should be able to conceive of and apply alternative interpretations. But according to Kant we cannot even conceive of, much less understand, such interpretations. This inconceivability turns out to be characteristic of universal and necessary principles. In fact, it is their most important test.[14]

The idea of universal necessity applies equally to the realm of morality and religion. The problem with the Enlightenment equation of morality and utility, according to Kant, was that it left out what he saw as the central ingredient of any principle that deserved to be called a *moral* principle: namely, that it should hold true of everyone at all times, regardless of personal or social circumstances. For example, if lying is truly immoral, and not just counterproductive or socially unacceptable in one particular society, it must be wrong *on principle.* If what is moral is simply what is useful, lying might be moral or immoral, depending wholly on what is useful at the time, and on the customs of that particular society. This way of thinking is common enough now, but for Kant it was intolerable. The Ten Commandments did not specify a way of behaving for a single group of "chosen" people under a particular set of circumstances; they said simply, for instance, "do not kill." No qualifications; no extenuating circumstances; no social advice. Kant wanted to show that the justification of morality could not be social utility or anything else that might vary from person to person, from situation to situation, or from society to society. Nor could morality be based on feelings, since feelings too might easily vary with circumstances. Morality consisted of a priori principles; anything less was not worth the name of "moral."[15]

The same held for Christianity, if it was to be viewed as anything more than European folk religion, as anything more than one set of peculiar beliefs and superstitions among others. The existence of the Christian God, and of divine punishment and reward, must be shown to be universal and necessary principles—matters of reason, as the Enlightenment insisted, rather than matters of personal faith. (Some confusion results from Kant's use of the word "faith"; it must be emphasized that for him faith is a rational and not at all an emotional attitude.) The idea that Christianity should be universal and necessary clearly implies the inferiority or error of alternative religions. The French idea of all religions being ultimately one is nonsense, from this point of view. Kant does not shrink from this conclusion; he is explicitly intolerant of Jews, heretical Christians, and any religion that does not include the Christian conception of God and his moral sanctions. The Enlightenment ideal of tolerance never did find much of a home in Germany.[16]

The French Enlightenment had defended the concepts of reason and experience without carefully distinguishing or identifying them. Voltaire is the most illustrious example: he defended both Reason and the empiricist methods of Locke, never appreciating the considerable extent to which Locke's empiricism was an attack on that same idea of Reason. Of course Voltaire adopted the proper empiricist stance of contemptuousness toward metaphysics as an abstruse and useless study, but he never appreciated the complexity of metaphysical issues built into the empiricist doctrine. For example, if knowledge comes only through experience, does this mean that nothing exists except what we can see, touch, hear, smell, and taste? Not even Locke was satisfied with that consequence of his theory, and therefore struggled to defend commonsense realism—the notion that things in the world are real, and not just products of our experience—without compromising his theory. Bishop George Berkeley easily showed how idealism—the belief that things are just ideas—and not realism, followed from empiricism, and finally Hume showed that empiricism made it impossible to justify the notion of "things in the world" at all.

Voltaire remained oblivious of such problems, which he found tedious, but what is at stake is nothing less than the efforts of the entire Enlightenment. If so basic and inescapable a belief as our notion that a world exists outside of us cannot be justified through experience, then how indeed can it be justified? The traditional rationalist would say, "through reason," but Hume's arguments had already refuted him. Different rational arguments, equally valid, had yielded opposite pictures of the world, including pictures compatible with Humean skepticism's assertion that all that existed was our own experience. Far from being the ultimate court of appeal, Reason itself was thrown on the defensive. Yet there could be no retreat from the new advances of Reason and the Enlightenment; one could not deny the virtues of empiricism, despite its skeptical consequences à la Hume. Certainly one could not go back to the dogmatic metaphysics of the Church, which would be an admission of total defeat. Nor could one comfortably rely on common sense, since it was the superstition, unthinking dogma, and ignorance built into so-called "common sense" that had inspired much of the Enlightenment in the first place. This was Kant's challenge; in meeting it, his conception of universal necessity and a priori knowledge turned into one of the most radical ideas of all time.

Kant's Copernican Revolution: The Critique of Pure Reason

> The understanding does not derive its laws from, but prescribes them to, nature.
>
> Kant, *Prolegomena to Any Future Metaphysics*

Kant's monumental *Critique of Pure Reason* is presented as a study in "the possibility or impossibility of metaphysics." But it quickly becomes clear that very different kinds of concerns are included under this title. There are those abstruse exercises rejected by Voltaire (more through contempt than argument), which Kant shows to be undecidable and therefore—in agreement with Voltaire and recent positivists—meaningless to talk about. With regard to these "pseudoproblems" in particular, Kant complains that metaphysics, once the queen of the sciences, "has rather to be regarded as a battle-ground for those who desire to exercise themselves in mock combats, and in which no participant has ever yet succeeded in gaining even so much as an inch of territory, not at least in such manner as to secure him in its permanent possession."[17] But metaphysics is more than this, and Kant does not reject it as such: "That the human mind will ever give up metaphysical researches is as little to be expected as that we,

to avoid inhaling impure air, should prefer to give up breathing altogether."[18] Some of these problems, he says, are the basic problems of
human existence, as for instance, "God, Freedom and Immortality"—the
existence of God, the possibility of seeing ourselves and others as free
moral agents, and the immortality of the human soul (*CPR* B 7). These
are what Kant calls *practical* problems, and their solutions must wait for
the second of Kant's three mighty *Critiques: The Critique of Practical
Reason.* The main concern of *The Critique of Pure Reason* is a third set of
problems which are "metaphysical" in the sense that they are basic to the
foundations of all human knowledge.[19] That every event has a cause is
one such principle, as are the idea that the laws of nature will be the same
in the future as in the past, and the notion that a world exists outside of us.
In other words, the bulk of Kant's first *Critique* is a theory about a priori
knowledge. It is his attempt to overcome Hume's skepticism and make
good the promises of the Enlightenment.

But though all our knowledge begins with experience, it does not follow that it
arises out of experience. For it may well be that even our empirical knowledge
is made up of what we receive through impressions and of what our own
faculty of knowledge (sensible impressions serving merely as the occasion)
supplies from itself. If our faculty of knowledge makes any such addition, it
may be that we are not in a position to distinguish it from the raw material,
until with long practice of attention we have become skilled in separating it.
  This, then, is a question which at least calls for closer examination, and does
not allow of any offhand answer:—whether there is any knowledge that is thus
independent of experience and even of all impressions of the senses. Such
knowledge is entitled *a priori,* and distinguished from the *empirical,* which has
its sources *a posteriori,* that is, in experience. (*CPR* B 1)

Throughout the Enlightenment—as even through the Middle Ages—
Reason referred to our (God-given) ability to know and calculate necessary truths. But reason, as used by different philosophers, had provided
very different answers to philosophical questions, so that the confidence of
Voltaire had turned into the confusion facing Kant. Given, as Hume had
argued, that experience alone could not provide us with an adequate account of the foundations of knowledge, to what extent was appeal to
reason necessary and justified? What were the *limits* of Reason? When
would one answer be as good as any other? Kant's critique directed the
spirit of criticism of the Enlightenment to the key concepts of the Enlightenment itself.[20]
  Two kinds of necessary principles must be distinguished, according to
Kant. First, there are the basic principles of experience—the notions, for
instance, that the objects of our experience are "outside of us," and that
the different events of our experience are causally related one to another.
These Kant calls the *principles of the understanding*—that is, principles

which say something about what any human experience *must* be like. Second, there are necessary principles which have nothing to do with experience as such, but simply define the way our language works. For example, a statement like "horses are animals" is not so much information about horses as a lesson in English, a covert definition of the word "horse." Another example would be the statement, "If Sally is a cowgirl and all cowgirls wear spurs, then Sally wears spurs." Even if one has just learned something about Sally and cowgirls, the form of the statement is a matter of pure logic, and need not refer to any experience whatever to be known to be valid. These logical or linguistic principles—what we might call the rules of logic, grammar, and semantics—are *principles of reason*—more precisely, Kant would say, "pure theoretical reason."

Regarding these principles of pure reason—logical principles—neither Kant nor any of the other philosophers had serious reservations. Hume, for example, accepted the idea that some statements are true just because of Reason. The problematic principles were those of the understanding. Unlike the logical principles, these were not true because of language or Reason, and since they were the basis of all experience, one could not appeal to experience to justify them either. (That would be like asking a hostile witness in court whether or not he was trustworthy.) Which brought one back to Hume's test: these principles could not be justified by either reason or experience. Should they therefore be "committed to the flames"? Certainly not. So what Kant had to do was to show a new way of justifying principles which are basic to experience and necessary (that is, a priori), but not logical truths or truths of reason. Kant called all nonlogical truths "synthetic." These crucial principles, therefore, he termed *synthetic a priori principles*.[21] In his *Critique of Pure Reason* he asked a single central question: "How is synthetic a priori knowledge possible?" That is, how does one justify these basic and necessary principles of experience? Notice that the question is "How?" and not, "Are they possible?" Kant, like Hume, was sure that we do use such principles, and unlike Hume believed that there must be a way of defending them. So what is Kant's way?

So far, we have only seen Kant reclassify some of the concepts and statements of traditional philosophy. But with this reclassification—and reclassification implies rethinking—the revolutionary method of Kant's philosophy is ready to begin. The strategy of his defense of synthetic a priori knowledge—that is, the basic principles of our experience—lies in his theory of *concepts*. A concept is a rule for interpreting experience. The concept of "tree," for example, lets one pick out trees when one encounters them. More important still, having the concept "tree" makes it possible for one to see trees as trees, for it is through the concept that one interprets raw experience (which Kant calls "the manifold of intuition") as a particular kind of object. *Understanding* is the application of concepts to sensations, so as to give us experience of particular objects and events.

Knowledge, according to Kant, always requires both sensations ("intuitions") and concepts. As he elegantly insists: "Thoughts without content are empty; intuitions without concepts are blind" (*CPR* B 75).

In addition to particular concepts like "tree," which are learned through experience and are therefore empirical concepts, there are certain other concepts basic to *all* experience. For example, the concepts of "something," of "cause of," of "at the same time as." These are a priori concepts, necessary for every experience; Kant calls them *categories*. Kant's position now begins to be clear: these categories are the basic rules by which we interpret our experience. Through these a priori concepts we actually construct—Kant uses the words "constitute" and "synthesize"—the world of our experience. They are necessary, therefore, in the same sense that the basic rules of a game are necessary for that game. Furthermore, Kant will argue, they are necessary because they are the *only* set of rules in town, the only possible rules for the game of human experience.

Philosophers before Kant had asked, "How can we know what the world is really like?" Some had replied, "Through God-given reason." Others had said, "Only through experience." A few skeptics had said, "We can't!" But what had not been questioned was the question itself. What all parties had presumed was the actual existence of a world "outside of us," independent of our experience of it. The question then became, "How do we know that our (supposed) knowledge corresponds to the world?" With Kant, however, the question is rejected, and its inverse is raised instead: if we compose the objects of our experience through the use of our concepts, then *what must these objects be like?* In other words, what *are* these concepts? The question of the truth of our beliefs in corresponding to "external" reality is no longer intelligible. The world is what is constituted by us—constituted necessarily as a world outside of us, but not therefore outside of our experience.

Hitherto it has been assumed that our knowledge must conform to objects. But all attempts to extend our knowledge of objects by establishing something in regard to them *a priori,* by means of concepts, have, on this assumption, ended in failure. We must therefore make trial whether we may not have more success in the tasks of metaphysics, if we suppose that objects must conform to our knowledge. This would agree better with what is desired, namely, that it should be possible to have knowledge of objects *a priori,* determining something in regard to them prior to their being given. (*CPR* B 75)

Here, then, is Kant's "Copernican revolution":

We should then be proceeding precisely on the lines of Copernicus' primary hypothesis. Failing of satisfactory progress in explaining the movements of the heavenly bodies on the supposition that they all revolved round the spectator, he tried whether he might not have better success if he made the spectator to revolve and the stars to remain at rest. A similar experiment can be tried in metaphysics, as regards the *intuition* of objects. If intuition must conform to the constitution of the objects, I do not see how we could know anything of the latter *a priori;* but if the object (as object of the senses) must conform to the constitution of our faculty of intuition, I have no difficulty in conceiving such a possibility. Since I cannot rest in these intuitions if they are to become known, but must relate them as representations to something as their object, and determine this latter through them, either I must assume that the *concepts,* by means of which I obtain this determination, conform to the object, or else I assume that the objects, or what is the same thing, that the *experience* in which alone, as given objects, they can be known, conform to the concepts. In the former case, I am again in the same perplexity as to how I can know anything *a priori* in regard to the objects. In the latter case the outlook is more hopeful. For experience is itself a species of knowledge which involves understanding; and understanding has rules which I must presuppose as being in me prior to objects being given to me, and therefore as being *a priori.* They find expression in *a priori* concepts to which all objects of experience necessarily conform, and with which they must agree. . . . We can know *a priori* of things only what we ourselves put into them. (*CPR* B 75)

Now we can see what is wrong with Hume's skepticism and, more important, what is so earth-shattering in Kant's revolutionary conception of knowledge. Suppose one were to attack a move in a football game as either stupid or illegitimate. One appeals to the rules and strategies of football. But now suppose that someone were to attack the football rules themselves as "illegitimate." That would not make any sense, since the rules of legitimacy are *defined* by the rules of football. What Hume had done, in effect, was to wrongly view the *rules of the game*—in this case, experiencing the world—as *moves in the game,* neglecting their *defining* role in that game. What Kant said, in effect, was that we ourselves supply the rules of the game; it makes no sense to say that our rules might be wrong, for there is nothing whatsoever for us to compare them to.

Kant's "Copernican revolution" was the ultimate step in the development of anthropocentric humanism, which had begun with Socrates and come to fruition in the Enlightenment. It was indeed "Copernican": Contrary to common sense, the world was not simply "out there," waiting for us to understand it; the world was there by the act of our own understanding. With Kant, even science became thoroughly humanized, a product of human concepts and projections. After Kant, philosophers would lose their fears of impotence against skepticism, and for the following generations in Germany and France, Hume's arguments would be dead issues. Instead, philosophers would attempt to give systematic descriptions of what the world *must* be like, according to the categories we supply. Philosophy became the search for ultimate categories. The humble distinction between our ideas and the world, between experience and reality, had been destroyed. For Kant and German idealism in general, the world was nothing other than the world of our experience.

What Must Be, Must Be

> All necessity, without exception, is grounded in a transcendental condition.
>
> Kant, *Critique of Pure Reason*

It is one thing to identify the a priori concepts or categories that are basic to our experience. It is something more to prove that these categories are not just provincial structures, common to modern European man but possibly different from the categories of an ancient Persian or a contemporary Hopi Indian. It might be argued that all Kant has done is to show that, *for us,* talking about a world different from the one we experience is utter nonsense. But could not other people use different categories and so see the world differently? Perhaps their seeming necessities would be different from ours. If so, given Kant's view, would they not in fact experience a different world?

To achieve his ambition of demonstrating the universal necessity of the principles of our understanding—that is, their necessity for *any* conscious creature—Kant has to show that such alternative sets of categories are impossible. Once he has identified the various categories of the understanding, he must therefore prove that they are basic not just to our own, but to any possible experience. Such categories are *transcendental* in the sense that they are necessarily the basis of every experience on the part of anyone and anything anywhere. The structure of Kant's first *Critique,* therefore, is a series of *transcendental arguments*—arguments which show a concept or a principle to be transcendental. (It is important to distinguish "transcendental" from the world "transcendent," which Kant also uses. A thing is transcendent if it is outside of experience; but transcendental if it is basic to experience.)

The structure of the *Critique* is a simple tripartite form. Psychologists of Kant's time divided the faculties of the human mind into (1) *sensibility,* or receiving sensations; (2) *understanding,* or applying concepts to experience; and (3) *reason,* or manipulating concepts and calculating. Accordingly, Kant divides the *Critique* into three corresponding parts: (1) the Transcendental Aesthetic, which deals with sensibility; (2) the Transcendental Analytic, which deals with the concepts and principles of the understanding; and (3) the Transcendental Dialectic, which deals with the uses and abuses of pure reason. All three sections have the same function: to identify and prove, through transcendental arguments, that the categories we use in our experience are the only possible ones.[22]

In the Transcendental Aesthetic Kant identifies two a priori forms of intuition. (Technically speaking, he says these are not true concepts, but this need not concern us here.) These two forms are space and time. He argues that these are the forms of any possible experience and that no person or creature, however constructed, could experience true timelessness or five-dimensional space. (Modern science has raised serious questions on this point, but they need not detain us.) Corresponding to space and time are the a priori principles of Euclidean geometry and arithmetic. According to Kant, the reason why 2 plus 5 must equal 7, and why parallel lines never meet, is that these involve descriptions of some of the a priori structures of all possible experience.

In the Transcendental Analytic Kant discusses the twelve categories without which no object can be thought. The principles which correspond to each of these categories are precisely those foundation principles which Hume had challenged. For example, one of these categories is the a priori concept of *cause*, an "objective order of appearances according to a rule." Hume had argued that our experience itself never includes necessary connections, which are added by us. Kant agrees: "We cannot represent to ourselves anything as combined in an object which we have not ourselves previously combined" (*CPR* B 130). But according to Kant, such combinations are shown to be necessary by the very nature of human consciousness. This is his final reply to Hume.

The Transcendental Dialectic: Criticizing Poor Reason

The third part of the *Critique* is very different from the first two. The first two parts are devoted to defending certain principles as universal and necessary through transcendental arguments. The third part is primarily an attempt to show that certain metaphysical principles *cannot* be adequately defended, however hard philosophers have tried to do so. Kant calls the dialectic "a logic of illusion," and sets out to destroy much of what has passed for metaphysics and theology in Western history.

We quoted Kant as saying, "Thoughts without content are empty; intuitions without concepts are blind." Much of metaphysics consists of "thoughts without content." As a matter of fact, Kant has defined reason as the manipulation of concepts *not* applied to experience. This does not mean that all of reason is "illusion" or empty. Logic is a function of reason, but has a perfectly defensible role in human knowledge. But when someone starts talking about the world beyond all possible human experience—in other words, a transcendent world—there is no way to distinguish "sound knowledge from mere shallow talk." Theological discussions about the existence of God, for example, involve talk about matters that are not possible objects of human experience. Talking about the immortality of the soul and life after death is, for all secular purposes, talking about something —a soul—which cannot be experienced. Such discussions, according to Kant, are pointless. Metaphysics of this kind cannot give us knowledge, no matter how wise its arguments or how firm our belief in its principles.

The Transcendental Dialectic is itself divided into three parts. The first is dedicated to refuting traditional metaphysical doctrines about the human soul. The second is concerned with traditional attempts to prove that God exists. Kant argues that all such arguments arrive at their conclusion through fallacious reasoning, and that no possible argument could ever let us know that God exists. But these first two "debunking" sections are not intended to lead us to atheism or even agnosticism. What Kant intends is to destroy a family of wrong-headed arguments, in order to make room for other arguments that he believes will stand the test of criticism. What he says is that we can know nothing about God or the soul. He never says we should not *believe*. He denies knowledge in order to make room for faith.

The third section of the Dialectic is a demonstration of a most remarkable property of reasoning which is free from the constraints of experience. We have already remarked on how different philosophers presenting equally valid arguments often reach opposite conclusions. (For example, Spinoza said the world is a unity, whereas Leibniz said that it consists of many many individual parts called "monads.") Kant shows this capacity to generate opposite conclusions from equally sound arguments is a property of reason itself. To prove this, he offers us four pairs of such equally compelling contradictions, called "antinomies." For example, the first:

Thesis: The world has a beginning in time and space.
Antithesis: The world has no beginning in time and space. (*CPR* B 454)

Kant then proves *both* conclusions, which is tantamount to showing that there is something fatally wrong with the problem itself. The second antinomy is:

Thesis: Everything consists of ultimately simple elements.
Antithesis: Everything is composite; there are no simple elements. (*CPR* B 462)

The third:

Thesis: Human actions are free.
Antithesis: There is no freedom, only natural causes. (*CPR* B 472)

Here is the basic conflict between science and moral responsibility, defended as a pair of theses each of which, according to Kant, can be equally justified. But here too, as in the case of God and immortality, Kant is not willing to give up freedom to science. Instead, as we have anticipated, freedom must be taken out of the realm of things *known* and placed in the realm of things *practiced;* God, freedom, and immortality are not matters of knowledge, though they remain inescapable human concerns even so. Finally, the fourth antinomy returns to the idea of God, and shows once again that, given certain familiar arguments of his existence, one could actually prove anything:

Thesis: There is a necessary being.
Antithesis: No being is necessary. (*CPR* B 480)

The arguments all boil down to what Kant calls "the ontological argument," the argument that the very idea we have of God entails his existence. Kant argues that this argument, in all its forms, is invalid.

The Return of the "Thing-in-itself"

The key to Kant's revolution, and the starting point of nineteenth-century German idealism, is the rejection of the long-standing idea of a world independent of our experience. The Copernican revolution is Kant's insistence that the objects of our experience, as we experience them, are the *only* objects that it makes any sense to talk about. It is with some dismay, therefore, that Kant's idealistic followers read back into the *Critique* and found that Kant himself did not pursue this view with consistency, but found it necessary to introduce a new distinction that, for some, seemed to undermine what he had done so elegantly. Kant was not particularly troubled by differences in perception due to differences in sensory apparatus (for example, bees see ultraviolet, we do not; dogs do not see colors, but we do). Nor was he troubled by differences due to variance in empirical concepts (for example, Eskimos see many different things for what we simplistically call "snow"). However, Kant asked himself how an all-knowing being, who had no need of sense organs or understanding as such—namely God—would know the world. God, he reasoned, must simply know the world by intellectual intuition, without being conditioned by sense organs and the concepts of a finite understanding. And so, Kant concluded, God knows the world as it is *in itself,* whereas we know it just as it is *for us.* The latter—the world as we experience it—he calls the *phenomenal* world, and the world in itself he terms the *noumenal* world. The world outside our experience thus reappears in Kant's philosophy as *noumenon.*

This does not mean that Kant retreats to the traditional dichotomy of our ideas of the world versus the world as it really is. In fact, the word "really" becomes highly problematic, for the world as it appears to us, according to Kant, is the only reality that makes any sense. In the old view, ideas were merely "subjective" and the world "objective" or "real"; but in Kant's view the world as we experience it is necessarily objective, since objectivity is defined by the categories. Yet obviously, as soon as the concept of the world "in itself" is introduced, Kant can be pushed dangerously close to the old traditions, for as long as the world of our experience is in any sense different from the world as it is "in itself," the skeptic has a space in which to apply his wedge and soon convince us, despite the categories, that what we think we know may not *really*—for example, in God's view—be the case.

It would be a mistake to think, along with some of Kant's most enthusiastic followers, that the introduction of the noumenon-phenomenon distinction was simply a lapse on Kant's part, an unwillingness to leave the old tradition behind altogether. Kant does indeed say that the concept of noumenon is a "limiting concept"; that is, there is nothing to be said about it except in the negative sense that we cannot know what a thing would be in itself, once our experiences of it were subtracted. ("X, the unknown," he sometimes calls this result of subtraction.) But in Kant's philosophy the distinction also has a positive function that is central to his entire enterprise: namely, to find a way of defending both Newtonian science and religion/morality. The requirements of science are such that the laws of causality can allow no exceptions, neither for miracles nor for free human choices. We have already indicated that Kant denies knowledge in order to make room for faith by distinguishing knowledge from *practice,* but this by itself would not warrant the limitations of science. So what he does is to distinguish, in effect, two different worlds of human involvement: first, the world of science and nature, or the phenomenal world, which is constituted through the categories of the understanding so as to yield knowledge; and second, the world of action and faith, or the noumenal world, which lies *outside the categories and therefore beyond the realm of knowledge.*

Kant hesitates to say that these are actually two worlds—that is, situated in different space-time coordinates—because the very notions of space and time lie *within* the phenomenal world. But even as a metaphor, the "two worlds" view is so pervasive in his writings that it is impossible not to take it as philosophical doctrine:

As regards mere perception and the capacity for perceiving sensations, [a person] must count himself as belonging to the sensible world, but as regards whatever there may be in him of pure activity (whatever comes into consciousness. . . . immediately), he must count himself as belonging to the intelligible world.[23]

So in an important sense, it does seem that there are two worlds of human involvement: the world of sensory experience and knowledge ("the sensible world"), and the world of action and immediate consciousness ("the intelligible world"). But one should not move on to the obvious problems in such an account before trying to understand how this strange two-worlds view allows Kant to solve the central problem of philosophy.

Morality and Religion

> Two things have always filled me with ever new and increasing admiration and awe: the starry heavens above and the moral law within.
> Kant, *Critique of Practical Reason*

Oh Duty,
Why hast thou not the visage
Of a sweety or a cuty.

Ogden Nash, "Kind of an Ode to Duty"[24]

So far, we have been concerned with human knowledge, which is the focus of Kant's first *Critique, The Critique of Pure Reason.* Among the most important conclusions of that book are these: that the realm of knowledge extends only as far as the application of our concepts to possible experience; that the world in itself is beyond our concepts and experience, therefore cannot be known. Furthermore, Kant has shown that all attempts to know God's existence must end in failure. The same is true of attempts to know the human soul and its hoped-for immortality, and likewise human freedom of action, the subject of the third antinomy of pure reason. Consequently, the whole of the subject matter of the second *Critique, The Critique of Practical Reason,* has little to do with knowledge. This does not mean that such matters as God, morality, freedom, and immortality are in any sense irrational. But they are rational according to a different *kind* of reason—practical reason, which does not *know* but *acts.*

The point of the second *Critique* is to show that the doctrines of Christianity and contemporary middle-class morality are as firmly justifiable, as universal and necessary, as a priori as the basic principles of knowledge. The strategy is similar to the first *Critique:* to identify the basic a priori principles of practical reason, then to justify them with transcendental arguments. In this case, however, it is not to be shown that these principles are necessary presuppositions of any possible experience, but rather that they are necessary presuppositions of any *rational life.* The key to practical reason—in fact, it is almost its synonym—is *morality.* The book therefore analyzes and defends the basic principles of morality, then identifies and defends what Kant claims to be the presuppositions of morality: the postulates of God, freedom, and the immortality of the human soul.[26]

It is important to see that what Kant is doing is inspired by, and analogous to, the work of Rousseau. What Rousseau described psychologically as the "inner self," Kant characterizes metaphysically in terms of his noumenon-phenomenon distinction. Rousseau's inner self thus becomes a metaphysical noumenal self (a self-in-itself), and the laws which Rousseau ascribed to "the heart" Kant ascribes instead to the intelligible world of practical reason: "Rousseau proceeds synthetically and begins with natural man: I proceed analytically and begin with civilized man."[25] Rousseau had announced to the world that he had discovered within himself the intrinsic worth of humanity. Kant, without a trace of self-aggrandizement, takes as the basis of his moral philosophy this same idea that each person is autonomous and capable of discovering what is right for him or herself, so that human *dignity*—the ultimate goal of the Enlightenment—is both possible and necessary.

Kant, like Rousseau, is obsessed with the pure idea of *right*. Although Rousseau established this pure righteousness through an imaginative anthropological myth of the "state of nature," Kant pursues the idea with the added demand that, to be a necessary principle, it must be established through reflection. This *necessity* of the moral law, like the necessity of the principles of knowledge, lies at the heart of Kant's philosophy. Many philosophers had attempted, and been satisfied with, an analysis of the moral law that viewed moral principles as expressions either of desire, or of a peculiarly moral sentiment, or of a generally agreed-upon utility. Such analyses were common in Enlightenment thinking about ethics. To claim that morality is based upon natural law meant for them that human desires, properly enlightened to take into account the whole of society, would provide the only necessary foundation for morality. But cynics like the marquis de Sade had undermined such optimism. Kant's second *Critique* was published just before the widely circulated editions of *Justine* and *Philosophy in the Bedroom,* but one can be absolutely certain that Kant would not have read Sade even if he could. Yet Kant saw more clearly than anyone else that the moral law could not be based upon human passion, motivation, sentiment, or utility. The moral law, if it was to be claimed as law at all, must be rational, applicable to every human moral agent without regard to personal feelings, desires, or circumstances.

For this reason, Kant begins his ethics with an enormous stress on the concept of a "good will," which has nothing to do with the advantages or abilities of individuals.

Nothing can possibly be conceived in the world, or even out of it, which can be called good, without qualification, except a Good Will. Intelligence, wit, judgment, and the other *talents* of the mind, however they may be named, or courage, resolution, perseverance, as qualities of temperament, are undoubtedly good and desirable in many respects; but these gifts of nature may also become extremely bad and mischievous if the will which is to make use of them, and which, therefore, constitutes what is called *character,* is not good. It is the same with the *gifts of fortune.* Power, riches, honour, even health, and the general well-being and contentment with one's condition which is called *happiness,* inspire pride, and often presumption, if there is not a good will to correct the influence of these on the mind, and with this also to rectify the whole principle of acting, and adapt it to its end. The sight of a being who is not adorned with a single feature of a pure and good will, enjoying unbroken prosperity, can never give pleasure to an impartial rational spectator. Thus a good will appears to constitute the indispensable condition even of being worthy of happiness. (*Foundations*, p. 9)

A "good will," he argues, is good in itself, whatever consequences result. "A good will is good not because of what it performs or effects, not by its aptness for the attainment of some proposed end, but simply by virtue of the volition, that is, it is good in itself, and considered by itself is to be esteemed much higher than all that can be brought about by it in favour of any inclination, nay, even of the sum-total of all inclinations" (*Foundations*, p. 10). Accordingly, the central concept of his moral philosophy becomes the concept of *duty*, which is the application of this good will with respect for moral law.

> *Duty is the necessity of an action executed from respect for the law.* . . . Now an act done from duty wholly excludes the influence of inclination, and therewith every object of the will, nothing remains which can determine the will objectively except the *law*, and subjectively except *pure respect* for this practical law. This subjective element is the maxim that I ought to follow such a law even if it thwarts all my inclinations. (*Foundations*, pp. 16–17)

Duty is indifferent to situation and personal inclination. Duty might require that one act counter to one's every whim and desire. Duty might be awkward or embarrassing or dangerous in many situations. But in accordance with the bourgeois morality which alone Kant thought worth the name of "morality," only such impersonal principles of duty could satisfy the demands of universality and necessity. In reply to the challenge, "Why should I be moral?" Kant had a ready answer: "To be moral is simply to be rational." As to the further query, "Why should I be rational?" Kant knew that there could be no rational reply. If knowledge of universal causality was a necessary condition for any knowing consciousness, recognition of impersonal duty and the moral law was a necessary condition for any rational will, the consciousness of a moral agent. We may grant that there are tensions in Kant's attempt to bring the universal status of the moral law in line with the universal status of Newtonian science. But his analysis focuses on an often neglected feature of morality that will henceforth be a major point of controversy: any *moral* imperative (as opposed to a merely prudential principle) must be *categorical*—that is, universally applicable without personal privilege, and necessary without personal excuse. In this, Kant's morality is the perfection of Enlightenment moral thinking. With Rousseau, the moral law is "pure"; with Voltaire, it is a product of reason. But with Kant, it is "pure practical reason":

> Man and generally any rational being *exists* as an end in himself, *not merely as a means* to be arbitrarily used by this or that will, but in all his actions, whether they concern himself or other rational beings, must be always regarded at the same time as an end. . . .
>
> If then there is a supreme practical principle or, in respect of the human will, a categorical imperative, it must be one which, being drawn from the conception of that which is necessarily an end for everyone because it is *an end in itself,* constitutes an *objective* principle of will, and can therefore serve as a universal practical law. The foundation of this principle is: *rational nature exists as an end in itself.* (*Foundations*, p. 47)

Such a lawbound view of morality has its gloomy side. The appeal of the Enlightenment utilitarian moral theory had been its guarantee that all virtue was ultimately harmonious with general happiness. With Kant, virtue and happiness part company with the separation of freedom/duty and (human) nature. But the necessity of applying and obeying the moral law becomes intolerable without the promise of universal justice. Since clearly there was no such justice even in Frederick the Great's Prussia, Kant saw a strategy for defending on rational ground his belief in Christianity. *If* the moral law is necessary, and *if* the moral law presupposes justice, and *if* there is no justice in this life, then belief in the existence of an omniscient and eternal Judge, and in justice and the immortality of the human soul to await such judgment and justice, would follow necessarily. Of course there is a resounding flaw in the argument hidden in those several *ifs*: just because the moral law presupposes belief in such principles, it does not follow that any such principles—or the moral law itself—are necessary or true. Hegel would make this objection several years later. But meanwhile the spirit of Kant's philosophy introduced a new notion of morality into European thought, destroyed the well-established discipline of "rational theology," and forced all defenses of religion onto new ground. Like Rousseau, his theology was purely "ethical" and devoid of metaphysics or pseudoscience. But, Kant hastened to add, this made it no less rational, no less justified, and no less important than Newton's science.[27]

In the same logical manner, Kant proves the postulate of freedom by arguing that there could be no moral responsibility, unless man were free to act or not to act in accordance with the moral law. *If* the duties commanded by the moral law and practical reason are necessary and universally valid, then freedom of action must be presupposed in order to make such commands intelligible. Otherwise, expecting a man to do his duty would be no more rational than to expect of a tree that it might act in accordance with duty. With regard to our own actions, Kant argues, "a man cannot but think of himself as free." Furthermore: "I assert that every being who cannot act except under the idea of freedom is by this alone—from a practical point of view—really free" (*Foundations*, p. 100). But "freedom" for Kant means far more than the "negative" freedom from causal constraints; it signifies the "positive" freedom to obey the moral law. For Kant, freedom is always more than an escape from the Newtonian viewpoint and the strictures of causality. As for Rousseau, it is always freedom to do one's duties as a good citizen.

The *will* is a kind of causality belonging to living beings in so far as they are rational, and *freedom* would be this property of such causality that it can be efficient, independently on foreign causes *determining* it; . . .

The preceding definition of freedom is *negative*, and therefore unfruitful for the discovery of its essence; but it leads to a *positive* conception which is so much the more full and fruitful. Since the conception of causality involves that of laws, according to which, by something that we call cause, something else, namely, the effect, must be produced; . . . hence, although freedom is not a property of the will depending on physical laws, yet it is not for that reason lawless; on the contrary, it must be a causality acting according to immutable laws, but of a peculiar kind; otherwise a free will would be an absurdity. . . . What else then can freedom of the will be but autonomy, that is the property of the will to be a law to itself? . . . Now this is precisely the formula of the categorical imperative and is the principle of morality, so that a free will and a will subject to moral laws are one and the same. (*Foundations*, p. 64)

Here again is that dangerous ambiguity between freedom from something and freedom to obey, which will allow the original Enlightenment demand for autonomy to be subverted into an ideological defense of authoritarianism.

Nature, Freedom, and Purpose

> The idea of freedom is the only concept of the supersensible which . . . proves its objective reality in nature.
>
> Kant, *Critique of Judgment*

Kant's philosophy is strangely dualistic. On the one hand, it establishes that the realm of nature is such that every event is naturally and sufficiently caused by other events. But it also holds that some events—human actions —cannot be considered as caused except as effects of the human will, which cannot be determined by anything but itself. If we consider this pair of claims out of context, they would appear flatly contradictory. But within the Kantian framework these two propositions come to us from very different standpoints: man as an object of nature, and man as a willing subject acting under rational laws of freedom. This "two-standpoints view" is not a straightforward contradiction, but neither does it give the unified portrait of man that is the persistent demand of philosophy. Accordingly, it will be a new point of departure and provide a new form of philosophical conflict that will dominate the nineteenth century. The idea that Newtonian science and religion/morality are each necessary and universally valid within their own mutually exclusive realms will split philosophers once again into opposed movements. For some—Fichte and Hegel —the concept of human freedom will be made central, and they will advance German idealism far beyond the boundaries established by Kant. For others—Feuerbach and Marx—human autonomy will be sacrificed to a more Newtonian model of nature, and their materialism and determinism will create new sciences of man and a new political ideology.

Kant himself was not satisfied with the split between nature and freedom in this extreme form. At the time of the French Revolution he sat down to write a third *Critique,* the *Critique of Judgment* (1790),[28] in which he suggested a synthesis of his two earlier *Critiques* and a compromise in his extreme two-standpoints view. The tension between nature and freedom is least tolerable at two points of contact: first, in the account of individual human actions in which nature explains them as effects of other events (motives and needs, for example), while freedom accounts for them in terms of a free will acting in accordance with moral law; and second, in the need to reconcile virtue and happiness in accordance with our demand for justice. To ease the tension of the first contact, Kant must find an account which will satisfy both the principle that every event has its cause, and the demand that the will is free to act morally. He finds it in the concept of *teleology* or "design." A teleological view of the universe, or of systems of events, does not see Newtonian mechanisms of cause and effect, but instead a harmonious and organized whole in which each part plays its assigned role. This view is not Newtonian, but neither is it incompatible with the Newtonian view. Thus Voltaire could accept both Newton and his own "argument from design" without a conflict. But one must insist, as Kant does, that the teleological view is to be applied only in those cases in which the Newtonian mechanical view becomes too complex. Kant asserts that such a case occurs in any attempt to account for the life processes or behavior of an organism. Accordingly, human behavior would be accountable in teleological or purposive terms, and not in mechanical terms, yet such an account would not be inconsistent with the universality of Newtonian mechanics. To deny that we can explain the life processes and behavior of organisms according to Newton is not yet to insist that there could be no such account. To complete this compromise, Kant found it necessary to insist that such a teleological conception did not presuppose the existence of a conscious intention or a purposive agent behind it. Thus one could describe the functioning of an organ in an animal as serving a given purpose, without implying that either the organ, the animal, or some "designer" *had a purpose* in this functioning.[29]

The conception of a teleological view of the universe was also a partial answer to the second point of tension between nature and freedom, in the search for ultimate justice and agreement of virtue and happiness. This tension had been rendered explicit in Voltaire's parody of Leibniz's optimism in *Candide.* (It was a tension that Rousseau evidently did not feel, since he replaced Leibniz's reason with his own sentimental faith.)[30] The attempt to defend the goodness of God's ways ("theodicy") would become a strenuous concern for the philosophers of the nineteenth century also. Kant had once sided with Leibniz and Rousseau, but in his later work saw increasingly that pure optimism is naive, whether defended by pure reason or blind faith. With a teleological conception of the universe, Kant could defend the idea of a growing, developing, organic universe, but without appeal to ultimate purposes or the well-refuted "argument by design." Accordingly, the demand that virtue and happiness should be in agreement could be made a matter of rational hope. In the later philosophers of the nineteenth century, particularly the German idealists after Kant, teleology became central, it being one of their main concerns to explore this hitherto neglected conception of history and the universe. With it, the traditional dispute between optimism and pessimism lost its present-oriented view and turned instead to the development of history and the promises of the future.[31]

Despite the revolutionary changes in method and perspective that Kant introduced, his conclusions were ultimately conservative—not politically, but personally—which was an understandable outcome for a man who "found all change frightening." For Kant, small-town bourgeois morality and duty received universal justification; the Christian faith whose millennium-old foundations he had utterly destroyed he nevertheless defended as rationally necessary and universally valid. No other philosopher has ever defended bourgeois ideals so profoundly—or, as Marx once said, "whitewashed" them so thoroughly. In the preface to his first *Critique,* which established absolute confidence in the mechanistic science which was beginning to revolutionize industry, Kant tells us that "it is bad management if we blindly pay out what comes in, and are not able, when the income falls into arrears, to distinguish which part of it can justify expenditure, and in which line we must make reductions" (*CPR* B x). In the second *Critique* Kant gave absolute authority to the freedom of the human moral will, and provided the most secure Enlightenment defense against the interfering authority of monarchs and clergy. But underlying the moral law was always a regard for the primary source of bourgeois power. In *Perpetual Peace* Kant argues:

The spirit of commerce, which is incompatible with war, sooner or later gains the upper hand in every state. As the power of money is perhaps the most dependable of all the powers included under state power, states see themselves forced, without any moral urge, to promote honorable peace.[32]

Because Kant is so important in the history of philosophy, and also because he is so difficult in his terminology and expression, it is all too easy to forget that he, like all philosophers, is an expression of attitudes which themselves are not openly philosophical. Perhaps Kant is most important in his relationship to the empiricists and rationalists before him, and the idealists and scientists after him. But he is also the foremost philosophical manifestation of that point in German consciousness when the bourgeoisie turned from their mutual timidity to a period of unmatched arrogance. This arrogance, so evident in post-Kantian philosophy, did not receive its political expression for another half century. But that is, perhaps, the minimal period of growth from idea to ideology and political power.[33]

7 The Poetry of Self-Realization: Goethe and His *Faust*

A mind like yours realizes how far it has progressed and how little reason there is for it to borrow from philosophy, which can only learn from you. Philosophy can take apart only what is given to it. The giving itself is not the business of the analyst but of the genius . . . under the occult but assured influence of pure reason.
Friedrich Schiller to Goethe, August 23, 1794

There is a man!
Napoleon, on meeting Goethe in 1806

Goethe once commented, "When I was eighteen years old, Germany was only eighteen herself." That would have been 1767, a half century after Leibniz's death and three years before Kant would announce the first hints of his philosophical revolution. But Leibniz had written in Latin for a universal audience, and Kant insisted that his work was not only cosmopolitan and international but "for every rational being." There was nothing self-consciously German about either of them. It was Johann Wolfgang von Goethe (1749–1832) who would establish a distinctively German ideology, still humanist and international, but with some decidedly Teutonic and "unenlightened" twists. He rejected the egalitarianism of French Enlightenment autonomy, and in its place restored the role of the exceptional individual—the genius—as the essential expression of universal humanity. In place of the proud adolescence and presumptuous adulthood of the French Enlightenment, he would express the timid gropings and confused if boisterous struggles of a culture still in its childhood. He exchanged the "enlightenment" metaphor of illumination for gothic metaphors of the "daemonic" and "the Unconscious," and in place of eternal Reason offered a very different image—modeled on biology instead of Newton's cosmology—of Reason as change, growth, and development.[1] The Enlightenment of Kant and the French represented an ideology of clarification; Goethe's ideology would represent a dark but inspired struggle.

Goethe knew his limitations too well to declare himself, as Kant did, the spokesman for eternal reason. He was a spokesman for life, and life, with all its contradictions and changes, is never available for single-blade dissection. ("For analysis, one must have a corpse," wrote D'Annunzio.) But the life that Goethe represented—whatever his praise for his own genius and whatever his aristocratic pretensions—was unabashedly bourgeois. He still believed in Reason and he still believed in universal humanity, even if he gave himself, as Kant did not, a very privileged role in not only its expression but its realization.[2]

Goethe embraced, at one time or another, virtually every bourgeois tendency of the age. He was, as much as Kant, the disciple of Rousseau. He insisted on the restrained discipline as well as the aristocratic internationalism of Voltaire, and like the latter loved the company of the nobility, disdained the common people whom he "represented," and wholly lacked the discipline of a systematic philosopher. (He confessed that he could not even read Kant's already mandatory *Critique of Pure Reason*.) Goethe's first published work was in fact a translation of Voltaire, and at the end of his life he would identify his three greatest literary influences as Voltaire, Rousseau, and Shakespeare. But he was not only a poet; Goethe was also a botanist of considerable reputation, and introduced the concept of *genesis* not only as a model of plant growth, but as an alternative model of humanity—very different from the static categories of Kant's conception of Reason and understanding.[3] Individuals, cultures, and humanity itself were constantly striving, growing, and changing. Reason, for Goethe, was the silent wisdom of all living things, the logic of life, rather than Kant's reflective awe concerning the starry skies above and the eternal moral law within. He never gave up the childish enthusiasm of the Storm and Stress poets, of whom he was the most distinguished in his youth. He fathered the romantic movement, but called it "sickly." He said he was a classicist, but later termed classicism "empty." He admired the philosophers—Friedrich Schiller, Kant's student, was his best friend—but he paid careful attention, as Kant did not, to the inspirational and occultist tendencies of his German contemporaries. He shared with Kant's forgettable Königsberg colleague Johann Hamann (1730–1788)[4] the gothic side of the German spirit—the demons, passions, and mysteries that would eventually emerge in Germany's greatest single piece of literature: *Faust*.

The Logic of Life

> I hold that whatever genius does as genius is done unconsciously. The man of genius can act according to reason when convinced by reflection, but all that is incidental. No work of genius can be improved or freed from its faults by reflection. . . .
>
> Goethe, letter to Schiller, 1801[5]

Goethe's life defies the simple summary that was possible for Kant ("neither life nor history," as Heine wrote). While Kant's entire career can be summed up by the phrase "the transcendental pretense," Goethe's life, like his ideas—if that is what one calls the thousands of scattered comments in his *Journals* and *Conversations*—is impossible to categorize. While Kant is epitomized by his sixty-year tenure at Königsberg University and his punctual three-o'clock walks, Goethe's life was a sequence of varied stages upon which he played the most divergent roles. Not inappropriately, Heine compared Kant to the Königsberg clockworks; Goethe's life should rather be compared to the metamorphoses of one of the plants he studied, sometimes flowering and fertile, sometimes broadcasting his seed around Europe, but other times dormant and almost unnoticeable. He was in turn a prankish student, a respectable lawyer, a sentimental novelist enjoying international success, an established poet refusing to publish, and a literary has-been at the age of thirty. He was the model civil servant, the "solid citizen," the good bourgeois bureaucrat, and a local institution. Also, a bohemian artist, a passionate libertine with a taste for scandal, an offense to public propriety in very proper Weimar. Also, an incurable romantic who forced his poetry into the most restrictive classical forms, and a self-styled classicist who enjoyed scribbling obscene lyrics in ancient styles, and used his classical fantasies as an excuse for fornicating his way across Europe. He displayed "Olympian" haughtiness, but considered himself a defender of the common man.[6] A bourgeois humanist, he despised the petty bourgeoisie around him, preferring the company of dukes and princes. Seeming to wholly lack warmth and humor, he displayed a taste for pranks and puns rivaled only by Shakespeare. (In fact, one wonders how Shakespeare might have fared in that gothic world of German letters and timid, haughty seriousness, saddled with such a language. What would have happened to that Elizabethan levity? And could a German Hamlet have limited himself to a simple disjunction of choices?) Equally revealing, however, were the roles that Goethe did *not* play; he was never a soldier or statesman, never a worker, farmer, or peasant, never a political activist or aristocratic man of leisure. He was not Protean but the variable bourgeois—politically conservative, socially ambitious, artistically driven, self-congratulatory, impersonal, bureaucratic, brilliant. As such, his life mirrored well the confused life of Germany: insecure, humorless, talented, passionate, timid, ambitious, unappreciated, demonic, conservative, and newly, painfully, self-conscious. As he wrote the philosopher Jacobi in 1813, "One single way of thinking cannot be enough for me with the many sides of my personality."

Goethe is generally considered the greatest German poet, and some would say the greatest German of all times.[7] It is the controlled chaos of his life and works that have made him so, and the contrast with the French Enlightenment passion for clarity and order should be extremely revealing.

Goethe's often quoted phrase, "freedom within limitation," would summarize German ideology for years to come; a self-indulgent compromise between political and social conservatism and the increasingly desperate drive for self-expression.[8] Kant and the French believed in the transcendental existence of an already formed and finished system of universal ideals, waiting only to be institutionalized at whatever cost. Goethe and most Germans, however, believed in a humanity not yet formed, and in ideals in the making. The German ideology was an implicit logic of growth and development, unconsciously driven by forces it did not pretend to understand. It believed humanity to be part of nature—the nature not of Newton's physics but of Goethe's botany, defined by its rapid changes and contrasting stages. When Goethe rejected Kant's static categories, it was to replace them with a universalism of his own, the logic of change, the logic of life, a philosophy not so much thought as lived, an unconscious law of urgency toward no end in particular.

Every action and so every talent needs some inborn faculty which acts naturally, and unconsciously carries with it the necessary aptitude, and which, therefore, continues to act in such a way that though its law is implicit in it, its course in the end may be aimless and purposeless. (letter to Humboldt, 1832)

Goethe's work, like his life, was a long journey of sometimes brilliant but often banal rambling.[9] His works fill 150 volumes that contain spectacular scenes, lines, and aphorisms interrupted by stretches of unredeemable mediocrity and blatant imitation. Like Voltaire, Goethe was an irrepressible, obsessive writer, a craftsman of genius who, no matter how extensively he reworked his creations (*Faust* took sixty years), lacked the humility necessary for critical self-editing. Even *Faust* often seems to be without a coherent theme, without the single-mindedness of Voltaire and Rousseau, and the systematic thinking that makes even Kant comprehensible. But life is like that, too (whether or not the one imitates the other)—a "free" association, a hidden logic, rambling from brilliance to boredom. Yet it is difficult to withhold the hyperbole that is axiomatic in German letters. Even T. S. Eliot, who once dismissed Goethe as "not a poet, not a philosopher," later ranked him with only Dante and Shakespeare.[10]

Goethe had no system; in a life of varied experience and expression, no permanent or "transcendental" base was possible for such a system. Instead of solid, definitive masterpieces like Kant's three *Critiques,* which were in preparation fifty-five years before emerging fully formed to redefine the intellectual world, Goethe poured forth novels, plays, poems, essays (literally "attempts"), criticism, aphorisms, limericks, and quasi-autobiographical "confessions" for two-thirds of a century. A fragment of *Faust* appeared in his youth; he was still working at it in his eighties. And that varied and uneven poetic drama contains not only the occult tribulations of a semifictional character and a quasi-autobiographical chronicle of its self-styled genius author, but an epic portrait of the self-realization of the German spirit from senility (the last days of the Holy Roman Empire) through a reincarnation tutored by the devil, whereby it reattains childhood, adolescence, and adulthood.

For more than sixty years the conception of *Faust* has lain here before my mind with the clearness of youth, though the sequence with less precision. I have let the idea go quietly along with me through life. (letter to Humboldt, 1832)

Faust is Germany's *Odyssey*. The fact that an old metaphysician plays the titular role, lusting after but losing ancient Helen, tells us far more about German ideology than a hundred volumes of German history and philosophy.

If Kant spurred the German intellect, Goethe stirred her soul. Yet his long life was curiously unheroic, perhaps even uneventful. He was no Lord Byron (an admirer of his, incidentally), scandalizing his way across Europe in search of glorious causes. Nor was he a Napoleon (another admirer), conquering the world and controlling it utterly. Goethe was aloof, unfriendly, stuffy. After his brief period of international fame in his twenties, he went into retirement for many years. He was not, as other authors would insist of themselves, "ahead of his time," but rather too far "above" that provincial world of amateur bourgeois poets, dull aristocrats, and civil administrators among whom he lived. He saw himself as a genius, whose duty it would be to express for all of humanity in distinctly German form the sense and spirit of his times. He saw himself, in the words of his best friend Schiller, as "a mirror in which the customs, the character and the full wisdom of the age are gathered in a purified and ennobled form."[11] But he also saw himself, beneath the tightly controlled public façade, as a "daemonically" driven individual, expressing the darker side of the modern age as well as the Enlightenment search for perfection. He recognized the chaos within him and the chaos of his times, quite in contrast with Enlightenment clarity, and he hoped to reveal through his images as well as his life (as after him Hegel would through philosophy) that fragile but inescapable necessity, that unconscious reason, that logic of life which formed his own conception, however unformulated, of the promised perfection of universal humanity.

The Sorrows of Young Goethe

The other day I chanced on a first edition of my *Werther*, and this tune that had so long been dead for me, began to play again. One wonders how a man can bear to live another forty years in a world that even when he was young seemed to him so devoid of meaning.
Goethe, letter to Zelter, 1816

As a student in Strasbourg, Goethe met Johann Herder (1744–1803), a proponent of the Storm and Stress movement, an ex-student of Kant who had turned against his teacher in favor of Shakespeare, German folk mythology, a touch of Hamann's mysticism, and Lessing's revolutionary conception of human history as educational development. Goethe himself may have referred to Voltaire and Rousseau, but his real spiritual parentage was not these exotic foreigners but those first self-consciously German thinkers from his own native soil, Gotthold Lessing and Herder. Goethe's humanism, though cosmopolitan in its appeal, was strictly cultural, a celebration of his own "folk spirit" as his way of approaching the abstractions of humanity. Though he may have shared the sufferings of Rousseau and admired the universal reason of Voltaire, the problems he had to work through were particularly German.

About the same time that Kant was discovering in Rousseau the inner realities of the moral law, Goethe was discovering for himself the almost mystical sentimentality for nature that Rousseau had once experienced in the forests of St. Germain: "I lie in the tall grass beside a rushing brook and become aware of the remarkable diversity of a thousand little growing things on the ground, with all their peculiarities . . . and can sense the presence of the Almighty" (*Werther,* pp. 24–25). But to protect this fragile Rousseauan heart, Goethe adopted a firmly Voltairean exterior. He returned to his hometown of Frankfurt with a degree in law, was outwardly urbane and charming, bright and excessively respectable. No one in provincial Frankfurt would have guessed that this young lawyer was a seething genius who was already laying the literary foundations for modern German culture. While practicing law in Frankfurt, he completed a fragment of *Faust* and published two books. The first of these, *Götz von Berlichingen* (1771, published 1773), was a romantic Storm and Stress drama, heroic and Shakespearean as well, that featured an elderly robber baron of noble but archaic character—a quixotic champion of freedom and honor in a world that no longer offers a place for such ideals. His next major work, *The Sorrows of Young Werther* (1774), was dashed off in a few weeks in an effort to purge its author of the pain of one of his own unhappy love affairs: "I had lived, loved, and suffered much; that's what it was" (p. 25). The novel was an almost instant success, not only in Germany but throughout Europe; Napoleon listed it among his favorites, and often carried it with him on his campaigns. *Werther* was the first piece of German "world literature" (a concept invented by Goethe)—a distinctively German work that appealed to everyone.[12] In fact, Goethe practically defined "genius" as this same *universal* appeal: "I paid little attention to criticism . . . all good people could digest it as they pleased."

The style of *Werther* is soppily sentimental, extremely simple, and embarrassingly serious. "Oh this void, this dreadful void in my breast! Often I think—if just once I could press her to my heart it would be filled" (pp. 62–63). The hero is a very bourgeois, very supersensitive young German. Goethe himself later summarized his novel:

. . . a young man, gifted with deep unspoiled sensitivity and penetrating insight, who loses himself in visionary dreams, undermines himself by empty speculations until finally, deranged by unhappy passions he experiences, especially an unending love, he puts a bullet through his head. (p. 63)

The novel was the first fragment of what Goethe later called "a great confession." In this early work as in all his works, he purged himself of personal emotional crises by "acting" them out. ("If I didn't write dramas, I would perish.") At the time of *Werther,* Goethe was in the agonies of one of his many unhappy love affairs. But his confession is not merely autobiography or romantic self-display.[13] However much he may have admired Rousseau's very personal and revealing *Confessions,* Goethe's writings always kept a certain "distance." They were always formal and idealized, an expression rather than a confession of a romantic and elitist soul with a strong sense of privacy and of what not to say about himself. Goethe, even more than young Werther, was very much a romantic, repeatedly falling in love with women with whom he would first have a Platonic relationship, then an intense and passionate affair. "Passion, Inebriation, Madness," he called it (*Werther,* p. 58). Ultimately he would give in to his dominating fear of marriage and commitment, and discover passively that the relationship had painfully ended.

Werther shares with the young Goethe the Rousseauan worship of nature and sentiment, and there is no doubt that Goethe considers his alterego hero as an admirable and lovable human being (his name is a pun on "worthy"). Yet it is equally clear that Goethe finds Werther less of an ideal than an expression of his own youthful confusion: "A young man soon becomes aware . . . that moral epochs change just as the seasons do" ("Reflections," p. 141). Like Werther, Goethe is trying to throw off the bourgeois obstacles to his feelings and talent. Werther agrees with the Storm-and-Stressers, Rousseau, and the marquis de Sade that rules are "unnatural," that "taking pleasure in oneself" is most important: "I laugh at my heart and do whatever it wants." He has an abstract admiration for the lower classes, being convinced that "the man who plants his potatoes and drives his wagon to town" is doing more than he is (p. 72), and feels hatred for his own bourgeois society: ". . . the glittering misery, the boredom of the perfectly horrible people I meet here! Their social aspirations! . . . I cannot understand how people can be so insensitive as to prostitute themselves in such vulgar fashion" (pp. 72–73). Werther is a pure middle-class hero who turns on both the bourgeoisie and the aristocracy in order to search for a harmonious personality. His finest thoughts come from feeling, not reason. He wants to "live, not learn." He values his freedom as much as his love, but cannot reconcile either with his sense of duty. Werther, like Goethe, is looking for an ideal which he has not yet found.

"A man is a man," Goethe has Werther say, "and the little bit of sense he may have plays little or no part at all when passion rages in him, and the limitations of humankind oppress him" (p. 61). Goethe is not yet a classicist, has not at all broken away from the bourgeoisie that raised him. Werther is torn between Voltaire and Rousseau, a need for rational ideals and a need for natural harmony. Having placed himself as well in an impossible love triangle (parallel to one in which Goethe had found himself), young Werther commits suicide—a dramatic and romantic ending to the failure of his quest. ("One of us three must go and I wish to be the one.") But his hero's suicide was good enough for Goethe, who made no such attempt himself: "I owned a costly sharp dagger . . . I would try to see if I could sink the sharp point into my breast. But I never could and finally laughed at myself . . . and decided to live" ("Reflections," p. 146). The success of his novel was already allowing him an opportunity for entirely new forms of self-realization—as a representative, spokesman, and example for humanity at large: "Yes, I am a wanderer on this earth— a pilgrim," Werther had said. "Are you anything more than that?" (p. 83).

A Pagan Vacation

> One thing is certain—nothing justifies a man's existence like being loved.
>
> Goethe, *Werther*

As a celebrity, Goethe moved to Weimar, a prominent cultural center, and found himself immediately welcomed into the elite enlightened circle surrounding the reigning Duke. Within a few short weeks, he had established himself as the resident poet of Weimar, an instant cultural institution and a powerful public official as well. As a result his creativity waned and his Storm and Stress romanticism dissolved. Saddled with dozens of inane responsibilities—for example, running the local fire department—he did well to keep his mind alive at all. Outwardly, he maintained his usual charm and respectability. But a poet of spiritual self-realization could hardly be expected to find fulfillment while keeping tabs on fire-fighting equipment in a provincial duchy of six thousand people. He had already vented his romantic histrionics in *Werther,* and the split between interior and exterior, between genius and respectability, had by now become unbearable. By the end of the summer of 1786, the tedium of his duties so oppressed Goethe that he fled Weimar. Nearly middle-aged, he had exhausted the forms of his earlier life and required a very different atmosphere—one that encouraged genius instead of admiring it at a distance while burying it alive, one that appealed to simplicity and nobility without bourgeois embellishments and façades. But where to go? No respectable German could take seriously Rousseau's appeal to simple and noble nature. But a new myth was emerging at that time, one which had already received scholarly popularization in the work of Johann Winckelmann, and literary and artistic resurrection in Paris. This was the myth of the ancients, whom Winckelmann had described in terms of "noble simplicity and quiet grandeur."[14] It was a myth that Goethe would cherish for twenty years:

Too much altruism, discipline, devotion to the "demands of the day"—and too much "Platonic" love?—threatened to alienate him from his real self. In September, 1786, he left for Rome, telling no one of his goal. It was a flight, but Goethe's real aim was freedom *for* something, even more than liberation *from* something; it was self-realization.[15]

In Rome Goethe masqueraded as a German painter in order to avoid his reputation as the author of *Werther*. For two years he romanticized the Italy of the ancients and the sun and brightness of modern Rome: "Everything arbitrary, merely imaginary falls away; there is necessity, there is God." The "necessity" was pure Enlightenment, for quite far from God and Christianity, Goethe educated himself as a neo-pagan, explicitly taking the ancient and "eternal" idea of simple balance and noble harmony as his single goal, integrating his individual genius and his romanticism into a disciplined framework based upon millennia-old ideas and rules of necessity, including pure foolishness:

At the Carnival: All that is given here is a simple sign that each man is at liberty to go fooling to the top of his bent, and that all license is permissible short of blows and stabs. . . . the mutual license and wantonness is kept in balance only by the universal good humor. . . . everyone should be reminded . . . of the importance of every momentary, and often apparently trivial, enjoyment of life.[16]

He began to see that a life of discipline and a life of passion were possible together, if one could only escape the rigid morality and vulgarity of bourgeois society, and the artificial sophistication of the decadent German aristocracy, so as to return, à la Rousseau, to a more "natural" and ideal life. During his first two-year stay in Rome, Goethe formulated the classical canons which would rule classical literature—and influence the other arts as well—and enjoyed a rebirth of creative energy.

> Happy now I can feel the classical climate inspire me
> Past and present at last clearly, more vividly speak.[17]

Within a few years he had replaced—at least in his own mind—the Storm and Stress excesses of *Werther* with its opposite, or its antidote. His *Tasso*

(1790) is an "intensified *Werther*," but the work itself is totally different in style, being formal, limited, and unsentimental. In the mid-1790s Goethe published his *Roman Elegies* and *Venetian Epigrams,* and as the French Revolution was beginning to spill across the borders of Germany, he wrote *Hermann and Dorothea* (1797), defending in classical verse the solid if dull virtues of German domesticity against the new revolutionary enthusiasm. Unlike many of his contemporaries, Goethe was not enthused about the new turns of world events; they interfered with his life style, and any enthusiasm which did not arise spontaneously from his own artistic genius he considered unworthy of him. It was poetry that expressed the soul of humanity, not this nonsense in Paris.

When he returned to Weimar, Goethe struggled to maintain his new attitudes and classical ideals. Consequently, he alienated most of his friends with his so-called "Olympian" attitudes and in general made himself aloofly obnoxious. In fact, Goethe was the very opposite of an aloof Olympian, and his new paganism made him far more earthy and passionate than his estranged and envious friends. The Olympian manner, we can surmise, was rather a cool façade of protection. Following surprise with scandal, Goethe began living with a simple and probably illiterate working girl—perhaps the prototype for Gretchen in *Faust*—and had a child by her in the notable year 1789. They did not marry until 1806, and in the meantime the former institution of respectability became a source of scandal in conservative Weimar, remaining conscientiously indifferent to a life that seemed to him "unnatural":

> But throughout the nights by Amor I'm differently busied,
>   If only half improved, doubly delighted instead.
> Also, am I not learning when at the shape of her bosom,
>   Graceful lines I can glance, guide a light hand down her hips?[18]

Bildung and Self-Realization

> Art is long, life short; judgment is difficult, opportunity fleeting. . . . the heights attract us, not the steppes; but with the summit in view we gladly wander on the plain.
>
> Goethe, *Conversations*

The key to Goethe's writings is the concept of *Bildung,* which means "education" or "development." Those who find *Faust* without a theme, or Goethe without a unifying idea, have failed to see the *Wald* for the trees. Though a familiar notion now, in Goethe's time the idea of describing human life and history in quasi-biological and evolutionary terms was a conceptual revolution, equal in scope to Kant's "Copernican revolution": given its affinities with Aristotelean metaphysics, one might call it a "counterrevolution" of sorts, waged in the midst of the static universals of Kant's transcendental revolution and the eternal Reason of the French Enlightenment.

It is this sense of development, or *Bildung,* that distinguishes the German ideology from its French counterparts, not only in the time of Enlightenment, but throughout the nineteenth and even into the twentieth century. Voltaire may have been a distinguished historian, and Hume, too. And Rousseau may have built his eighteenth-century reputation largely on such "educational tracts" as *Emile* and *The New Heloise* (*The Social Contract* became his most popular work only with the Revolution, and in Germany remained second to *Emile*). But the French and English Enlightenments were largely ahistorical: they lacked a sense of real historical change and growth. They believed in progress, but saw progress as presupposing an already recognized goal, whether universal justice, welfare, reasonableness, or whatever. In German ideology, on the other hand, development includes the evolution of goals, the recognition of genuine differences, the importance of different cultures and ways of thinking. Kant, here as elsewhere, straddles the French and German sensibilities; as its title suggests, his *History from a Cosmopolitan Point of View* is teleological in the strong sense, presupposing a universal principle of progress for all humanity.[19] But the real father of the German sense of history was Gotthold Lessing (1729–1781), who at considerable cost to himself was the first major author to reject the dominant French influence in German courts and culture, and to insist on a genuine German sensibility, on a German sense of history as well as "universal history," and on a sense of history that is itself historical. It was Lessing who issued the call to German genius to reinterpret the chaos and contingency of history as divine necessity, "to convert the useless treasures of memory into food for the soul." He himself suggested such a history in his *Education of Mankind* (1780). Years later Hegel would realize Lessing's project in the most ambitious historical system ever imagined. But prior to that, Goethe would translate Lessing's call into epic literature.

Goethe's biology provided him with his model of necessity. After all, what is the "logic" in the development of a multilegged worm into a butterfly, or a fishlike creature into a frog? This is hardly the Enlightenment notion of progress, and one would have to stretch the imagination considerably to find a rational reason for these changes. (Indeed, it was this sense of purposive reason that Voltaire had lampooned in *Candide.*) Yet these changes are necessities of nature governed by laws, and thus have internal and eternal "reasons" of their own. This is the source of Goethe's concept of universal law—not in the reflections of philosophy but in the changes of life. "All life," he writes, "is a firmly stamped form, developing as it lives." So too for humanity: each individual seems to develop in his or her own way, but in fact is following the natural laws of development, aided or hindered by society,[20] but necessarily growing—or dying—in distinctly human ways. And humanity as a whole is also developing in much the same way, according to internal and eternal laws which, contrary to the Enlightenment, we may never, and perhaps never should, understand: "Altogether man is a darkened being; he knows not whence he comes, nor whither he goes; he knows little of the world, and least of all himself. I do not know myself, and God forbid I should" (*Conversations,* 1829).[21]

What is universal to humanity, according to Goethe, is not a set of faculties or principles (as in Kant and the French Enlightenment), but the *striving* itself, the various changes and experiences whose purpose is often dubious and whose nature may be unknown. This leaves room, as the universals of the Enlightenment did not, for cultural and individual differences, since the growth of a particular society (for instance, Germany) or a given personality (for instance, Goethe) follows a natural course of development of its own, facing its peculiar contingencies, times, and necessities—even if, ultimately, all societies and personalities develop according to the same internal principles. A simple example is one of Goethe's own youthful exploits: while a student in Strasbourg, he climbed the high tower of the famous cathedral on a dare. From an "adult" point of view, one might say that such pranks are stupid and pointless, and involve totally unnecessary risks. But life too is risky and pointless, and what must be "proved" by one person one day may be as necessary for his development as its first leap out of the water for a tadpole. Would a Goethe who had not climbed the spire have been inspired to write *Faust?*

We each have something peculiarly our own that we mean to develop by letting it take its course. This strange thing cheats us day by day, and so we grow old without knowing how or why. When I look at it clearly, I realize it is only talent in me that helps me through all the predicaments in which I see false steps, chance, and the complications of fate involving me. (letter to Zeller, 1816)

This emphasis on individual and cultural variations, however, in no way undermines the general humanist thesis. Goethe says, "Every man has his own truth. Yet truth is one." And he fully agreed with his friend Schiller, who insisted that "every individual human being carries within himself, as his potential and destination, the pure ideal image of man." This is indeed a most important modification of the transcendental pretense, which is perhaps not even "transcendental" at all if by that term we mean, following Kant, a set of changeless categories that are in some sense *already realized* in every human being. But the spirit of the pretense surely remains intact, and Goethe himself insists repeatedly—perhaps confusedly—that human ideals are *eternal* ideals, holding for all people at all times. The difference is that these ideals which define humanity are there to be striven for and achieved, if only rarely, in those few great geniuses among whom

Goethe and Schiller numbered themselves. Furthermore, what these geniuses express is never just themselves but all humanity, most of whom have not the good fortune to be capable of either expressing or realizing themselves. The transcendental pretense takes on an extra elitist twist: to be fully human is not only to be European, male, and bourgeois; one should be a German poet of genius as well.

The concept of the "daemonic" that so obsesses Goethe is also part of his transformed humanism, even if it parades itself in the fashionable occultism of his times. What Goethe is celebrating is the inspiration of genius, which Kant had discussed in a far less murky manner as the freewheeling voice of creativity. It is, in other words, the spirit of humanity pushing itself ahead through particularly talented or articulate individuals, and it is "dark" or "daemonic" only in contrast to the imagined clarity of Enlightenment Reason: "The daemonic is that which cannot be explained by Reason or Understanding; it lies not in my nature, but I am subject to it" (*Conversations*, 1831). Needless to say, this posture of passivity has its dramatic self-congratulatory effect: "The demon throws itself willingly into figures of great importance. . . . It would scarcely find occasion to manifest itself in a clear, prosaic city like Berlin" (*Conversations*, 1831). Like Kant, Goethe could turn his provincialism into a universal virtue. And like Kant, he had a mission to perform for humanity.

Every extraordinary man has a certain mission to accomplish. If he has fulfilled it, he is no longer needed upon this earth in the same form, and Providence uses him for something else. But as everything here below happens in a natural way, the demons keep tripping him up until he falls at last. Thus it was with Napoleon and many others. Mozart died in his thirty-sixth year. Raphael was dead at the same age. Byron only a little older. But these had all perfectly fulfilled their missions; and it was time for them to depart, that other people might still have something to do in a world made to last a long while. (*Conversations*, 1831)

Goethe's concept of *Bildung* found an exactly appropriate form of expression in a new kind of novel, the *Bildungsroman*. In a *Bildungsroman* the theme is the education and development of a character, rather than the adventures of an already fully formed character or a morality lesson in which the fixed ideal is already formulated from the beginning. *Wilhelm Meister*, Goethe's most famous *Bildungsroman*, depicts the development of a thoroughly bourgeois young man not unlike Goethe whose adventures, as in most novels of the genre, are far more cerebral than exciting. (Hermann Hesse and Thomas Mann are two of the better-known recent practitioners.) But the definitive *Bildungs* epic is of course *Faust*, which presents not only the education of a lone lecherous scholar but the spiritual development of a people.

There is more than a touch of Christian salvation in this philosophy of striving for perfection graced by the demon, and we should not be surprised that the ending of *Faust* involves a curious metaphor of salvation, even though Goethe remained an atheist and an anti-Christian all his life. The life of striving is its own salvation, and the only cause for damnation would be to give up the struggle for perfection. But then again, could a tadpole "give up" its struggle to become a frog? Goethe's ambivalent attitude toward the dull bourgeoisie surrounding him was rooted—or rationalized—in a basic philosophical uncertainty. We are all necessarily "saved," it seems, but some are more worthy of salvation than others.

Although Goethe often talked as if the end of the struggle was unknown and unknowable, he did have an ancient and eternal ideal which in his own mind was the universal ideal for humanity. This was the classical Greek conception of "the harmonious soul," in which reason and passion, duty and inclination, personal interest and community welfare, are all in accord. During his pagan vacation Goethe adopted this ideal explicitly in the name of classical humanism and the ideals of the ancient Greeks. Yet Goethe's classicism was but one expression of this basic ideal—the ideological form of his insecurity about his own seemingly volatile passions, and his place in that dull, petty aristocratic and bourgeois world to the north. It was an ideal which again derived from his Aristotelean biology, but an ethical ideal which was by no means limited to the ancient Greeks. Like the Enlightenment ideal of universal reason, Goethe's ideal of harmony was a weapon of self-defense—in his Storm and Stress days an inspiration, à la Rousseau, and in later years a source of discipline and an antidote to the too static and divided Enlightenment portrait of man so evident in his colleague Kant. The concept of harmony was the idealistic capstone of his all-important concept of *Bildung*—at once a personal justification for his own long and varied life, and an expression of the equally chaotic spiritual history of the German nation then in formation. It was Goethe who, in poetic form, realized Lessing's call to turn history into soul-food, and Herder's demand for a uniquely German folk epic. But if Goethe's *Bildung* expressed the German ideology in a fashion dramatically opposed to Kant, it is not worth debating whether Goethe's ideology counts against the German Enlightenment or for it (the same empty debate that has often surrounded Rousseau). Goethe complemented Kant as well as opposed him, and *Bildung* was not so much an attack on Kant as a re-emphasis of themes to which Kant had given only belated attention. For Goethe and for the future German ideology, humanity would be a goal, not a fact, and Reason would not be so much a faculty of reflection as a process of growth.

Goethe and Schiller

> But how does the artist secure himself against the corruptions of his time, which everywhere encircle him? By disdaining its opinion. Let him look upwards to his own dignity and to Law, not downwards to fortune and to everyday needs. . . . let him resign the sphere of the actual to the intellect, whose home it is; but let him strive, through the union of the possible with the necessary, to produce the Ideal.
>
> Schiller, *On the Aesthetic Education of Man*, Letter IX

In 1789 Goethe met Friedrich Schiller (1759–1805). Schiller had arrived in Weimar during Goethe's stay in Italy, but had found "traces of Goethe's genius everywhere." Schiller was ten years younger than Goethe and of very different background, being from a military and therefore itinerant family providing harsh discipline, but no encouragement whatsoever for the arts. Yet Schiller's literary itinerary paralleled Goethe's with a ten-year lag. His first novel, *The Robbers,* employed the same subject matter as Goethe's *Götz,* and served the same personal purpose as Goethe's *Werther*—an emotional catharsis and a reaction to vulgar and anti-aesthetic surroundings. *The Robbers,* again like *Werther,* was an immediate international success, confirming Schiller's own youthful conception of himself as a genius. By the time he arrived in Weimar, he was an internationally famous and as uncompromisingly arrogant as Goethe. But unlike Goethe he was also a philosopher, a serious student of Kant, and thus between them they represented both sides of the German ideology under a single roof and in a single friendship.

The Robbers was a Storm and Stress drama that had come to Goethe's attention just when he was most vehemently rejecting romanticism and the Storm and Stress movement he had helped establish. Consequently, he had expressed little desire to meet his eventual alter ego, who reminded him too much of his own youthful sentimentalism. A chilly distance separated them for years, the younger author fuming with mixed admiration and frustration, the older poet apparently indifferent or silently uneasy. Even when they finally became inseparable friends, the distance remained. After several years of mutual support and inspiration, they had not gotten beyond calling each other "sir." This personal distance reflected a deeper ideological difference, however, between Goethe the self-consciously "naive" poet with his biological *Bildung,* and Schiller the "sentimental" philosopher—"a poet when I ought to have philosophized, philosophical when I wanted to be a poet"—who was ever a victim of the Kantian divorce of Nature and Reason even as he struggled to unite them.[22] As Goethe observed, "Neither of us could claim victory, both thought their position to be impregnable."

Once he had turned away from the Storm and Stress movement under Goethe's influence, Schiller remained the champion of Enlightenment, armed with Kant's three *Critiques.* But—also like Goethe—he preferred the *Critique of Judgment,* thus shifting the emphasis of his Enlightenment ideology toward art and aesthetics.[23] His virtually obsessive concern—despite (or because of) his commitment to Kant's dualism of Nature and freedom—was his own version of Goethe's ideal of "harmony": "the whole man," in place of the fragmented bourgeois specialist who was becoming so common in Germany. This "whole man" would be reached neither through morality and "natural virtue" (as Rousseau had urged) nor through freedom (as Kant had suggested). (The Terror in France had taken its toll on Schiller, once an advocate of the Revolution, as well as on Goethe and so many other German intellectuals.) The "whole man" would be reached through art and an appreciation of beauty. Like Rousseau, Schiller saw his project of "aesthetic education" as a way of restoring man to his "natural" self, which in turn would restore that lost virtue bemoaned by Rousseau. In his earlier writings he even suggested that such a restoration would make all external constraints unnecessary; coining a phrase that would have many repercussions in later German ideology, he predicted that as a result the State would "wither away."

Before meeting Goethe, Schiller had been a professor of history at Jena and, following Kant, had developed his own version of "universal history" as "the struggle for human freedom" (a conception which would powerfully influence Hegel a few years later). In this universal history he defended an unabashed humanism which Goethe, though not disapproving, thought far too speculative and neglectful of the biological determinism that defined his own concept of development. Schiller's transcendental pretense, however, did not emphasize the universal categories of Kant's first *Critique* or the universal moral law of the second, so much as the aesthetic universality of the third: "It is art that unifies; the law is beauty, whose sisters are morality and science."[24] Accordingly, the teleology of Kant's *Critique of Judgment* brings him closer to Goethe in his belief that it is Nature herself who is responsible for the internal and eternal ideals implanted in every human being.

> Everything human must slowly arise, must unfold, and must ripen;
> Ever from phase to phase plastic time leads it on.
> But neither beauty nor fortune are ever born into being:
> Perfect ere time began, perfect they face us today.[25]

Even in his Storm and Stress lyricism Schiller had worshipped Nature, as for example in his "Ode to Joy" of 1785 (Beethoven's text in the Ninth Symphony):

> All drink joy from Mother Nature
> All she suckled at her breast

> Good or evil, every creature
> Follows where her foot is pressed.[26]

But by the end of the century he had subordinated Nature to beauty, freedom to art:

> Now at this century's impressive close
> As actuality itself is turned
> To art, as we see mighty natures locked
> In struggle for a goal of lofty import
> As conflict rages for the mighty ends
> Of man, for masterdom, for freedom, now
> Art is allowed assay of higher flight
> Upon its shadow-stage; indeed it must be,
> Lest it be put to shame by life's own stage.[27]

Virtually paraphrasing Goethe, he insisted that "truth is the same for us all, though to each it appears as he sees it," and with Goethe came to base his entire philosophy on the realization of human perfection in and through Nature:

> Nature begins with man no better than with the rest of her works. She acts for him where he cannot yet act for himself as a free intelligence. But it is just this that makes him a man, the fact that he does not stop with what Nature made him, but possesses the capacity to retrace with his reason the steps which she anticipated for him, to transform the work of necessity into a work of his free choice and to elevate physical necessity to moral necessity.[28]

Schiller's appeal to Nature, however, was as confused and ambiguous as Goethe's appeal to ideals in Nature; sometimes Schiller's "Nature" refers to Kant and at other times to the Enlightenment notion of Reason, so that the philosophy itself is incoherently ambiguous.[29] Thus his blend of Kant's Enlightenment and Goethe's *Bildung* was as much a smear as a synthesis, and he failed to appreciate, or at least to demonstrate, the joint ideological power of the two positions (which would have to wait for Hegel). But Goethe acknowledged the value of Schiller's attempt, and their mutual inspiration alone served as proof of the complementary strength of their positions. Even Hegel paid tribute to Schiller for his emphasis on the whole man and his poetic synthesis of Kant—for "having broken through the Kantian subjectivity and abstractness of thought, daring to transcend them by intellectually apprehending the principles of unity and reconciliation as the truth, and realizing them as art." And when Schiller died in the spring of 1805, Goethe was crushed. "I lose half my existence," he lamented, and became seriously ill for several months. Soon afterward Goethe's wife died, Napoleon invaded Germany, and life as he had known it for over fifty years came to an end. But his greatest work was yet to appear, eclipsing all that had come before.

Faust

Goethe's *Faust* spans his entire productive period from the 1770s until 1831, the year before his death. A fragment (*Urfaust*) was completed while he was still in his Storm and Stress days. This is the core of the "Gretchen tragedy" that many readers still find the most admirable part of the drama. There are contributions from his classical period, from the period of his friendship with Schiller, and from the later days when his paganism began to wane and he turned to a mystical naturalism. It is the epic *Bildungs* poem. Of a long life that defies summary, one could hardly expect a full-grown expression of that life to appear as a unity, a linear sequence, or a series of episodes with a central thread. To his secretary Goethe remarked sarcastically: "As if I wanted to string such a rich, varied, and extremely versatile life, as I represented in *Faust,* on the slim thread of one central idea!" *Faust* is not a philosophical treatise, but a long, brilliant series of spiritual "impressions." It is not, like the historical *Faust* legends, a morality play. Nor is it a tragedy in any obvious sense— far more a "divine comedy." One gets the impression that the ending—like so many apparently inessential scenes in the play—is just another "impression," not to be taken as more definitive than any other. Faust is finally "saved," as Gretchen is "saved" at the end of Part I. But to think that salvation is the subject of the play is to adopt a simple moral attitude that is blind to the brilliance of Goethe's intentions.

The *Faust* legend goes back centuries. The historical Faust was a contemporary of Luther who studied science, magic, theology, law, and medicine—all standard topics for a learned man in those days. He practiced magic, was a lecher with his students, and claimed to have a contract with the devil, for which he was run out of town. Inevitably, such stories tend to become exaggerated and made the object of fantasy, horror, and moral indignation by the righteous, as did this one in particular. Marlowe wrote a magnificent *Faust* in which the protagonist becomes more a tragic hero than one of the wicked; Lessing made another attempt several years before Goethe.

The historical legend, however, is not essential: it is a vehicle for Goethe's genius. Its traditional theme of the old and cynical scholar who seeks radical change and growth is convenient for his purposes. If viewed as a development of the traditional story, Goethe's play will appear, as many critics have found it, overstuffed with irrelevant material, confusing and ambiguous, and not always serious enough for the subject matter. (Thomas Mann's comment at one point—"but the autobiographical temporarily triumphed over the legend"—might better be applied to its entirety.) But *Faust,* like *Wilhelm Meister,* is the story of an idealized development, not an autobiography, even if it is also the major "fragment of a great confession." Faust is not Goethe, for as Nietzsche said, "A Homer would have created no Achilles, a Goethe no Faust, had Homer been an Achilles or Goethe a Faust."[30] Yet the reader who is not obsessed with the need for a simple story will come to know Goethe through every scene of the play. It is impossible not to be reminded constantly, for example, that Goethe referred to his own genius as his "daemon" (and Mephistopheles has the best lines in the play).

In *Wilhelm Meister* the education of the hero progressed through a sequence of experiences. In Faust the development is anything but linear —perhaps not even a development at all, but rather a pure and continuous *striving.* The recurrent theme of *Faust* is Kantian dualism, though not of course by name. If one wants a historical protagonist for Faust, Schiller or a romantic Kantian would perhaps be as appropriate as the historical Faust or Goethe himself. Part I launches a protracted attack against pure reason and scholarship:

> Grey are all theories
> And green the tree of life.[31]

Unlike Marlowe's Faust, Goethe's hero does not primarily seek *knowledge*; it is the pathetic pedant Wagner, his assistant, and not Faust, who insists, "I know much, but I want to know it all." Goethe's hero also seeks "experience," but neither is this his primary goal, particularly if interpreted in the usual way as adventure or pleasure. What Faust seeks above all else is *harmony,* that harmony represented by the sublime and intentionally boring Lord of Hosts of the Prologue ("this whole is made only for God"). This harmony is the same ideal that we have traced throughout Goethe's development, a calm unity of reason and passion, desire and satisfaction, happiness and virtue.

But for Faust as for mankind, such harmony is impossible—an inescapable ideal, an unrealizable but necessary goal. Human life is an irresolvable Kantian disharmony which Faust shares with a very human Mephistopheles. If we interpret Mephistopheles as one aspect of Faust—in other words, of man—that aspect will not be an "evil" side (Goethe, like Schiller, is not particularly concerned with evil), but rather the most human or perhaps Humean aspect. Mephistopheles is the man of passion and sentiment for whom reason is necessary, but necessary only as "the slave of the passions." Thus Mephistopheles, like Faust, is subject to desires without the cleansing insight of pure reason, so that such desires become interminable. (Goethe complained, "From desire I rush to satisfaction, and from satisfaction I rush to desire.") In the Prologue, Mephistopheles complains to the Lord in words worthy of Rousseau:

> man's life might be a little better
> had you not given him that spark of divine light;

> he calls it reason and only uses it
> to be more brutish than every brute.

Rushing to the defense, God insists that "a good man in his dark quest/ knows the right road well," and that "if he now serves me only in confusion/so I shall lead him soon into clarity." The Lord knows that "as long as he is alive, man . . . will err as long as he will strive." Even Mephistopheles, however, does not attack reason as such, for he recognizes, as Goethe repeatedly tells us, that reason is the greatest enemy of disharmony: "Just you despise reason and knowledge—man's supreme strength."

Faust's pact with the devil is not the traditional sale of a soul, and Mephistopheles's Job-like wager with the Lord is not aimed at Faust's renunciation of God. Quite to the contrary, the conflict of both the pact and the wager is a conflict between striving and satisfaction. The bet of the devil is that Faust can be satisfied, can be made to "beg for the fair moment to remain." Life is striving, is Kant's aesthetic "purposeless purposiveness" (see Chapter 6, pp. 134–35). So long as Faust is striving, the devil is losing. At the end of all striving, however, lies the divine promise of ultimate unity. But such unity is impossible in life, and the devil's victory—Faust's defeat—can come only with premature satisfaction, with false contentment that pretends the struggles of life have been resolved. Life is struggle; it is stagnation that is hell: "We have asked for eternal truths, but the gods will not allow it."

At one point Mephistopheles addresses Faust as "Herr Mikrocosmos." It is as if Faust were a Leibnizian monad, in whom the whole of humanity is reflected and for whom, according to Leibniz, "happiness can never consist in complete enjoyment, only in continual progress of delights and new perfections." But the model of the Leibnizian monad must always be balanced with the dualism of Kant and the threat of a schizoid world. The Faustian monad is an unhappy monad, always on the brink of flying into pieces:

> two souls there dwell, alas, within my breast
> and one would put itself away from the other;
> one clutches with lustful senses at the world it loves
> the other rises powerfully from the dust
> to reach the fields of lofty ancestors.

Again:

> that I may learn the secret chain,
> that saves this world from bursting into twain.

The goal of harmonious unity remains the unattainable but inescapable ideal—unattainable, that is, except through divine grace: the "mysticism" that comes with old age. God's gift of salvation comes abruptly with impending death, and not at the end of a carefully scheduled development.

Faust is the epic poem of the German Enlightenment. Its theme is taken from Leibniz, its central problem from Kant. Henry Hatfield even suggests that "if Mephistopheles reflects the Voltairean wit and brilliance of the Enlightenment, Wagner reflects its duller side."[32] Reason is the abstract hero, together with striving, progress, and morality. Yet feeling and romantic sentimentality get their full due also:

> Call it what you will, then. Call it Bliss! Heart!
> Love! God! I have no name for it! Feeling is everything.

There are remnants of *Werther,* too, and of Rousseau: "You gave me glorious nature."[33] *Faust* has often been praised as a modern *Divine Comedy,* but just as Dante summarizes and poeticizes centuries of Christian thought before him, Goethe gives us a literary synthesis and reply to Kant's three *Critiques* and the eighteenth-century Germany romantic spirit.

A detailed analysis of *Faust* cannot be given here, but a quick summary may be in order. The play is divided into two parts, variously distinguished as "the small world" and "the great world," the life of the North and the life of the South, the modern and the classical, the literal and the allegorical. Part I (published in 1808) is a simple sequence of events which just barely add up to tragedy—the tragedy of Gretchen, not Faust. Faust finds himself "too old to play with passion/Too young to be without desire." Accordingly, Mephistopheles has an old witch give Faust an aphrodisiac, following which he has an erotic fantasy and wanders into the street "ready to see a Helen in every woman." He meets an innocent young maiden named Margaret (Gretchen), and with the nagging help of Mephistopheles, seduces her. She becomes pregnant. Faust duels with and kills her unlikable brother. To occupy the reader during Gretchen's pregnancy, Mephistopheles takes Faust off to the perversities of Walpurgis Night, an orgy of witches and creatures. Mephistopheles thoroughly enjoys himself, but Faust's conscience cannot be distracted from guilty thoughts of Gretchen. They return to find her in prison: she has murdered her child and is condemned. Mephistopheles concludes, "She is judged." A divine voice resounds from offstage: "Saved!"

Faust I is a simple play taken in itself. Its brilliance lies not in the story, which is incomplete and smacks of soap opera. Sentimental readers have traditionally tended to oversympathize with Gretchen, but her tragedy is clearly not that of an Antigone or a Medea; as Mephistopheles comments, "She's not the first one." More memorable are the story's interruptions, including the brilliant satirical tour through the vulgarity of a German beer cellar, a number of pointed satires on academic life, and the Walpurgis Night, which does nothing for the Gretchen tragedy but distract us from it. The genius of *Faust I* lies in the poetry, the insights, and often the wit of these isolated scenes, which collectively give a portrait—and not a flattering one—of the German bourgeois spirit, and an allegorical portrait of Faust. Goethe always stressed that "the poet translates life into a picture, an image," and that "the individual always appears as image and symbol of the universal." Accordingly, the entire *Faust* cast is symbolic, not so much of particular types as of human life itself. *Faust* is at one and the same time a portrait of imagined individuals and an image of us all.

In Part I this imagery lies close to the surface and is obvious, but in Part II it becomes far more sophisticated, for the character of Faust himself is now constituted more by the characters around him than through his own words and deeds. Not just Faust, but man as a whole is paraded through an allegory of the whole of human spirit and history, much as in Hegel's systematic philosophy. Part II offers a "loftier, brighter world." (Goethe once suggested that he would have liked Mozart to score *Faust* with music like that of *Don Giovanni*—light yet resolute.) Faust's remorse from the Gretchen Tragedy is gone already. There is no transition from Part I, but rather the appearance of a fresh start. In many ways Part II is more a parallel to Part I than a continuation of it. There is more poking fun at the impotence and pedantry of the Academy; another Walpurgis Night; an obvious parallel between Gretchen and Helen, both of whom lose their children and perish; and a final act of divine salvation. But in Part I Faust was an uncomprehending German tourist being led through the "little world" by his devil-guide, whereas in Part II Faust and Mephistopheles are traveling companions until Faust's final blindness, when he finally comes to "see the bright light within" and go at life alone.

Early in Part II, Faust and Mephistopheles arrive in the medieval court of a buffoonish Emperor who "has all possible qualities for losing his throne." (Louis XVI? The Holy Roman Emperor? Napoleon?) Through Mephistopheles's magic, Faust becomes powerful in the court, but after his first vision of Helen, leaves the court for the classical Walpurgis Night, returning after the classical period of the play has been completed. The biographical parallel with Goethe's success in Weimar, flight to Italy, and subsequent return is evident enough. The second Walpurgis Night is not under the guidance of Mephistopheles, however, whose Northern lust and obscene perversity are inappropriate to the mythical purity of classical sensuality and love. Their guide is rather the curious *Homunculus*, a form of disembodied life created by Wagner (who is now a professor, of course) without the "filthy" sexual "pranks" of procreation. Consequently, Homunculus is pure intellect (it can be argued that he represents this aspect of Faust), and his search in classical Walpurgis Night, like that of Faust, is for a whole life.

Faust meets Helen, who has an identity problem—how to cope with her legendary image and her classical role as mere sex object, "shape of shapes." Faust and Helen have a son, Euphorion, who ignores the warning, "Beware of flying, unrestricted flight is forbidden you," takes off to fight for Greek independence against the Turks, and perishes. Goethe identified Euphorion with the spirit of romantic poetry, and with Byron in particular. It has been suggested that reference could be made to Napoleon as well, though ultimately the romantic offspring of Northern Faust and classical Helen is another bit of Goethe biography. Helen joins her son in the underworld, and Faust is left alone with his devil.

As a reward for helping the Emperor in battle, Faust receives an enormous gift of land by the sea. Out of greed he covets the additional small plot owned by a gentle old couple, and sends Mephistopheles to secure it for him; the older people are murdered as a result. Here Faust appears in the most unfavorable light of the entire play. (A comment on the greed of the German princes who benefited from Napoleon? Or on growing bourgeois greed?) At this point Want, Guilt, Care, and Need attack him as the Furies attacked Orestes. (The Treaty of Vienna and the end of the German Confederation?) When Care attempts to seduce the old Faust with its unhappy gift of dread and anxiety, and Faust refuses, Care spitefully blinds him. It is then that Faust, like Oedipus, "sees the light." The mysticism of Goethe's old age becomes a final clarity, a vision of social concern (he sees his land converted into a home of "free people on free land"), and an awareness of the ultimate equivalence of life, freedom, and striving: "Only he deserves freedom and life who daily has to conquer them." As Faust is dying, Mephistopheles—following the Marlowe conclusion in which Faust is torn apart—orders his lackeys to "tear the wings from his soul, leaving a nasty worm." But there is last-minute divine intervention, and a chorus of angels "bear off Faust's divine part" away from a cursing Mephistopheles.

Early in Part II, Mephistopheles abuses the members of the court: "The way desert and fortune blend/The fools will never comprehend." These lines might have come from the end of Kant's second *Critique*, for Kant, like Goethe, sees the ultimate harmony—the resolution of "desert and fortune," virtue and happiness, striving and satisfaction—as an unfathomable human mystery. Yet it is also a universal and necessary human ideal. Thus Goethe ends his life's work, as Kant was forced to end his, rounding off the transcendental pretense with a touch of inexplicable mysticism: "Life is incomprehensible, but we cannot remove the desire to apprehend it."

8 "The Finest Man since Caesar": Napoleon and Revolutionary Despotism

One never climbs so high as when he knows not where he is going.
Napoleon

Only two virtues are basic. Would they were always united—Always
the Good also great, always the Great also good.
Schiller

The perennial arguments about the "great man" have never been so exhaustively presented as in the nineteenth century, and for one good reason: Napoleon. Voltaire and Rousseau expressed the ideology of the Enlightenment, and Danton and Robespierre rode the crest of its popular waves. But they did not guide it and drive it, or impose their will upon it and use it as if it were their personal destiny. It was Napoleon who rescued the revolutionary fervor from its decadent confusion during the Directory, turned it into an international force, and carried its ideology to Italy and Spain, to Russia and even Africa and the Middle East. The Napoleonic Code was the Enlightenment as international law, and the catchwords of Napoleonic imperialism were "liberation" and "self-realization." These same ideas that several years later would be turned against him—in Spain, in Germany, in Russia—had been used by the young commander in 1800 to gain control of virtually all of Europe (which in Enlightenment thinking meant virtually all the world).[1] Napoleon exemplified a new ideological danger in the world, beyond the ancient threat of ruthless personal ambition: a new despotism that cultivated the oldest abuses (greed, resentment, fascism, imperialism), but in the name of "enlightenment," "liberation," and "self-realization."[2] In defense of his planned invasion of England, for example, Napoleon insisted, "We would have offered as our credentials the magic words, 'liberty and equality.' "[3]

Carlyle believed in heroes; Tolstoy did not. But even Tolstoy could not treat Napoleon as a mere anonymity, whatever his theories and prejudices. Tolstoy deceptively argued that, as Napoleon never fired a cannon, never

160

shot a Russian soldier himself, it was not he who caused the wars but, most immediately, the men who did the fighting, ultimately the intangible "spirit of the people."[4] That upstart Napoleon, Tolstoy argued, was—like all commanders—but coincidentally connected to the events he supposedly commanded: "Our erroneous idea that an event is caused by the command that precedes it is due to the fact that when the event has taken place, and out of thousands of commands those few that were consistent with the event have been executed, we forget that others were not executed because they could not be" (*War and Peace*, p. 1432). But what Tolstoy mystically renders as "the spirit of the people" is what we have been calling an ideology—intangible perhaps, but hardly mysterious; and whether or not Tolstoy is correct about the *causal* ineffectiveness of Napoleon (perhaps plausible at Borodino, hardly so at Austerlitz or Marengo), he misses or dismisses the crucial point: namely, that Napoleon represented not only himself but the ambitions, greed, pride, chauvinism, Enlightenment ideology, and General Will of several million Frenchmen and a million more Europeans. In this representation lay both his power and his genius.

Stendhal, who considered Napoleon "the finest man since Caesar," called him a "nineteenth-century tyrant," but with this qualification: "Whoever says tyrant says superior mind, and it is impossible for an outstanding genius not to absorb, almost unwittingly, the good sense that fills the air."[5] The "good sense," of course, was Enlightenment common sense. Leaving aside Stendhal's dubious definition of tyranny, one must agree that Napoleon's genius, whatever else it may have entailed, lay first of all in his ability to capture both the spirit and the imagination of an ideology already in full force with its transcendental pretensions. Transcendentalism, translated into political terms, means nothing less than imperialism. Contrary to some historians' retrospective indignation at the seemingly sudden shift from Enlightenment to dictatorship, the bourgeois ideology was from its first conception authoritarian, and self-righteously so.[6] In Napoleon's own words, "A revolution is an opinion that has acquired some bayonets."

It is true that the Emperor Napoleon emerged from Lieutenant Buonaparte by virtue of "that feverish agitation which follows revolutions," and the comparative clumsiness and mutual jealousies of the old regimes. But this does not mean that he was simply the instrument of his times, bound to follow the one inevitable course, nor can we suppose that, without him, history would have been the same.[7] His strategic genius, charisma, and restless ambition were essential ingredients in an ideology of the practical which had not yet learned to be practical, in the cult of egalitarianism that needed a vulgar hero. The hardened materialist or cynic can always come back with a new reason why "it had to be," but mindless determinism pales quickly before the force of personality. Robespierre remained dictator of revolutionary France only so long as the current of public hysteria flowed in the narrow direction he faced as "the citizen of virtue." Napoleon, little troubled by virtue and free from the ideological compulsion that limits lesser men to a "direction," used the varying currents of hope and despair, fear and pride, to give the flagging Revolution his own direction, albeit one that, as one sees in historical retrospect, it wanted to take anyway. He had a genius for pragmatism—"opportunism," if one wants to be nasty, "open-mindedness" if one chooses to be kind—but these were cardinal virtues of the new ideology itself. He was ready for every change, seemed always to have the appearance of control—which in politics may be the same as having it.[8] He spoke ironically of his "Destiny"; he knew—and did not need Hegel or Tolstoy to tell him—that his ambitions depended on the forces he represented, which were not themselves in his control. But despite the fact that every Napoleonic battle would leave behind more dead than the guillotine through three full years of Terror—the cause of the endless damnation of Robespierre—Napoleon never lost the support of his constituency, even in the years of his defeat. This was because he never stopped representing their dreams, but never lost sight of his own cynicism. He knew he represented the vanity of the Enlightenment as much as its ideals. Stendhal's *Life* approvingly quotes him as saying:

The French . . . are indifferent to liberty. They neither understand it nor like it. Vanity is their ruling passion and political equality, which enables them to feel that any position is open to them, is the only political right they care about. (p. 42)

During this period the concept of "representation" has a complex but inconclusive history. It is often assumed, using the American democrats as a model, that the dominant sentiment of the revolutionary period was the right of each individual to represent himself since each bore the universal stamp of human nature, Reason. But this view was defended by neither Voltaire nor Rousseau, who argued that such representation was dangerous nonsense. Kant may have believed it in the realm of morality, but not in his politics. Goethe explicitly repudiated it even in the realm of the arts. Humanity would be represented, then, not by every human being, but by exceptional human beings by virtue of their intelligence (Voltaire), their integrity (Rousseau), their creative genius (Goethe), or their political acumen (Napoleon). All men may be equally represented, we might say, but some people are more representative than others. In this sense, Napoleon was not breaking faith with the Enlightenment but realizing it. He himself was the most visible representative of humanity, aided in no small part by his own relatively vulgar origins. He spoke for the Enlightenment at a time when only one man could have had the power to do so.

From his first victories in Italy in 1796, Napoleon was followed by the Napoleonic legend, which he took pains to cultivate. It was the legend, as much as the power and genius of the man, that determined the course of events in Europe, the inspiration of the people he represented and conquered, and the remarkable stamina and energy of his troops. But this is exactly what we would expect of an ideological representative. Not only was the legend inseparable from the facts, but it had come to replace them. Stendhal quite rightly insisted that there would have to be a new history of Napoleon every year, in the light of not just new facts but new needs as well. Only a few years after Napoleon's death, when the young romantics of Paris were already nostalgic for the exciting days they had never known, it was clear that the legend was very much alive and growing with the times. Like Jesus and Achilles, Napoleon became an idea. He knew well why Aristotle had praised Thucydides—not for his accurate portrayal of the Peloponnesian Wars (which it surely was not), but for his universal fictions, his insights into human nature. Regarding his legend, Napoleon was no fatalist: he spent his last years as he had spent his first, cultivating the legend that would come to define him. It was, as one commentator has suggested, "his most successful campaign."[9]

"Too Ambitious"

> There is still one country in Europe capable of legislation, the island of Corsica. . . . I have some presentiment that this small island will one day astonish Europe.
>
> Rousseau, 1762

Napoleon Buonaparte was born in 1769, the same year that his native Corsica was acquired by the French. ("I was born as my country was dying.") His father had fought bitterly against the occupation, but once the French were established, he shrewdly switched sides—a tactic that Napoleon would employ on a far grander scale. Like his father, Napoleon remained anti-French even until he was the First Consul of France. The strongest of thirteen children, he became the head of the family when his father died. He never let his European success overshadow his Italian family pride: he gave away more crowns to more siblings than any king of France, and at the height of his powers declared, "My success, and everything good I have done, I owe to my mother." By 1807 the political life of Europe would be determined by the family life of the Buonapartes, and their sibling rivalry would be one of the dominant forces in the destinies of nations.

Napoleon was a sensitive and temperamental child. A childish arrogance would characterize him throughout his life of power. He endured colossal emotional tensions, masked in public by an insolent self-confidence. His self-doubts and weaknesses emerged in particular with his women, of whom there were many. In his youth he read and loved Rous-

seau, and he was captivated by Goethe's *Werther*. As a student he read
Voltaire and the new military strategists, and at the end of his life still
listed among his favorite authors Rousseau, Voltaire, and Machiavelli. Of
these three, Rousseau became his tool, Voltaire his ideologue, and
Machiavelli his teacher. Napoleon's attachment to the Revolution never
diminished his horror of "the People," and his dedication to the Enlightenment never developed beyond enlightened despotism. He despised the
French government even as they supported him through military school,
and he despised the "vile people" even as he used their enthusiasm and
their blood to conquer Europe. It was his skillful use of principles mixed
with deceit, Enlightenment ideals mixed with ambition, and tenderness
mixed with resentment that guided him even through his difficult adolescence in French schools. For like most geniuses, he had a difficult time in
school. He was humbly born and poor, and spoke French badly, in a class
of wealthy young French aristocrats. Even as a child, he channeled and
directed his burning ambition and resentment. He hated both school and
the military (in his first seven years of service, he accumulated over four
years of leaves and furloughs in Paris and Corsica), but used them to
achieve the most distinguished military career in the history of modern
Europe.

Napoleon was in Paris during the summer of 1792, the beginning of the
Terror, and witnessed the mob attacks on the Tuileries on June 20 and
August 10. After the first of these he wrote his brother, "The Jacobins are
lunatics." But he himself was already a Jacobin, became their president for
a brief period, and was an acquaintance of Robespierre and his brother.
Even as a loyal revolutionary, Napoleon had little faith in republicanism
and the people, with whom he had never had any significant contact. His
Goethean hatred of anarchy was balanced, however, by his disgust at the
weakness of Louis XVI. "If I were king, . . ." Napoleon said to one of his
friends at the time.

In 1793 there was civil war in Corsica, resulting in an English takeover.
The entire Buonaparte family was forced to flee to Marseilles, and Napoleon took his usual advantage of necessity to declare himself a French
republican. The new patriot received his first opportunity in December at
Toulon, where a strategic application of the new military tactics made
Napoleon a French hero at considerable cost to the British. Napoleon was
promoted to brigadier general, and won unusual praise from Augustin
Robespierre. But that praise nearly cost him his life, since in July of the
following year the Assembly guillotined both Robespierres. Napoleon was
fortunate not to have been in Paris. He was arrested in Antibes and jailed
for a short time as a Jacobin. Soon released, he was ordered to put down a
peasant rebellion in the west of France. Already picturing himself as a
potential hero of the people, and sensing that carrying out such an order

would do little for his future, he refused. Consequently, he was taken off duty; "I'm finished," he said.

Broke and frustrated, Napoleon became somewhat of a joke around the War Office, as he literally "banged on doors" looking for a commission. He was sustained during this difficult period by his first serious love affair (since made into a best seller and a Marlon Brando movie) with Désirée Clary, the daughter of a wealthy Marseilles businessman and sister of Joseph Buonaparte's wife. Judged by their surviving letters, Napoleon was a tender and enthusiastic lover. While in Paris, however, he began socializing in more fashionable circles, and became infatuated with a young Creole fashion queen, Josephine de Beauharnais. Though Désirée was unceremoniously dumped, Napoleon conscientiously sought a match for her (one of his favorite domestic pastimes was matchmaking). Soon after Napoleon's marriage to Josephine, Désirée married Bernadotte, also a young man on his way up. As Napoleon later crudely put it, "In exchange for Désirée's maidenhead, I made Bernadotte a marshall, a prince, and a king." (Désirée and Bernadotte would end up the King and Queen of Sweden and Norway—and kept their throne after Napoleon's exile and death.)

Napoleon was thought "too ambitious" for an important command, but the Directory that then ruled France was in serious trouble: royalists were plotting a mob overthrow of the unstable government and a restoration of the monarchy. Barras, the strong man of the Directory, needed fast military support, but all his generals were in the provinces or on foreign fronts. Napoleon, being unemployed, available, and a recognized genius with artillery, was called to help. In fact, his sympathies were as much with the royalists as with the Directory. His politics were nebulous, but the path of his ambitions was clear. With a "whiff of grapeshot"—the phrase is Carlyle's—the royalist rebellion collapsed, and Napoleon was a hero of France.

With this success, Napoleon became a suitable lover for Josephine, who had ambitions to match her charms. If the young Napoleon had been too much for a provincial girl like Désirée, in Josephine he surely met his match. Josephine's husband had been guillotined during the Terror, and she now had numerous lovers among the most powerful men in France. Six years older than Napoleon, she was seductive where he was naive; toying with his emotions, she fired his insecurities—who knows at what cost to history. He would write to her, "You are my one anxiety, my only pleasure in life, and my only torment." She would comment, "He's funny," and call him "puss-in-boots." Among Josephine's recent lovers had been Barras, the Director. When Napoleon married Josephine on March 9, 1796, Barras gave him the command in Italy as a wedding present.

The Face of Victory

> Glory has become stale. At 29, I have drunk life to the dregs. There
> is nothing left for me but to become a complete egoist.
>
> Napoleon

Two days after his wedding, General Bonaparte (who now Frenchified
his name) left for Italy, where he found a badly fed, badly equipped army,
lacking in morale and discipline. The new tactics that he now put into
practice included the principle that "war should pay for itself," which
freed him and his army from long supply trains and also from dependence
on the government. It was good Enlightenment efficiency, good politics,
and brilliant strategy. Once he began to score his lightning victories over
the Austrians and to seize northern Italy, the Directory needed him. In a
period when French armies were doing badly everywhere, it was Napoleon's victories alone that sustained French morale. And since, like
Goethe and so many Northern Europeans, he was thrilled by classical
Italian culture, the victorious young general shipped sculpture, antiques,
and monuments of all kinds back to France to feed the growing classicist
enthusiasms there. The image they produced was not that of an easy success over a clumsy Austrian army among the splintered little medieval
Italian principalities, but the grandeur of the Roman Empire—an image
which Napoleon would persistently exploit. The world would once again
be united under humanist ideals.

Taking control of the northern principalities, on his own authority Napoleon established an Italian republic, negotiated with the Austrians, and
conferred with the Pope. For the Directory, which had intended Napoleon's actions to be a kick from behind at the Austrians—a diversion to
remove them from the French borders—these actions and commitments
were a matter of horror. But Napoleon was, after all, an Italian by blood,
not French. The Directory needed him and his support, whereas he did not
need theirs; and given his popularity in Paris, they were just as glad to
have him in Italy. It was Italy, Napoleon later would say, "that made me
conceive the ambition of doing great things." This was Napoleon's first
"war of liberation" (excluding his political involvements in Corsica), and
the beginning of what was to be his French empire. The Directory could
not deny him. The Austrians made peace and England, already tired,
likewise dropped out of the fighting temporarily. Napoleon, the "Little
Corporal," ironically became a popular peace figure in Paris—a paradoxical role that he would play many times in the following years.[10]

In September 1797 France had her first free elections; the result was a
major victory for monarchists and conservatives. France was reacting to

the excesses of the Terror, but the powerful bourgeoisie, who ultimately controlled the government of France, saw their interests as dictating the continuation of the Directory. With the help of Napoleon's army, which by now had become the major political force in France, the Directory invalidated the results of the elections and continued its unstable rule over France.

At this point Napoleon was joined by one of the peculiar opportunists in history, Charles Maurice de Talleyrand, a former aristocrat and bishop who had spent the dangerous years of the Terror in the United States. Between them, they schemed a new campaign against England, one which they must have known could have no adverse effect on the English at all. But the plan was glorious, and "glory" was for both of them their first intention. The Directory, anxious as ever to get Napoleon out of Paris, gladly sponsored the glorious insanity. The plan was to attack Egypt and the eastern Mediterranean and block English shipping to and from the East (most of which in any event sailed around the Cape of Good Hope). The idea of challenging England's sea power with a land army is one which appears at several crucial moments in the Napoleonic Wars, but this time the aim was glory rather than defeating the English.

The Egyptian campaign was a military disaster. After a few easy victories at Malta and Alexandria, the entire French fleet was destroyed by Nelson in the Battle of the Nile, so that while Napoleon took control of Egypt, the British marooned him there. An attempted drive into Syria was repelled by the Turks, and Napoleon lost half his army within a few months. While he was there, his newly created Italian republic was destroyed by the Russians. Anyone else might have appeared defeated, but Napoleon's greatest genius resided in his ability to always appear self-confident and victorious. As he had used the grandeur of the Roman Empire to enhance his Italian campaign, so now he employed the romance of ancient Egypt to mythologize his Egyptian adventure. He paraded himself as Sultan, took advantage of the exotic Egyptian women, and sent out archaeological expeditions that among other treasures uncovered the Rosetta Stone, which allowed scholars to break the code of ancient Egyptian hieroglyphics. His engineers began plans for the Suez Canal, and his publicity agents spun tales of mystery and adventure. "Forty centuries look down upon you," he announced to his troops in the exotic setting of the great pyramids and the desert. "Universal history" had never seen a more dramatic example, and the ideals of the Enlightenment were now being realized—or imposed—even on the exotic shores of North Africa. Whatever the reality of the Egyptian invasion, its legend was a total success.

Meanwhile France—and Napoleon's marriage—was falling apart. Josephine had been running around Paris with a young and "more amusing" lover. As Castelot aptly comments, "The name Bonaparte was on everyone's lips but his wife's." Throughout the country chaos, inflation, and crime had destroyed the already delicate fabric of daily life, while military reverses on the borders raised the specter of foreign invasion. The people were tired of war, and the troops were dissatisfied and mutinous. There were threats of popular insurrection as well. France was ready for a savior.

In retrospect, the savior's "destiny" appears inevitable. Compared with the European military disasters, Napoleon's Egyptian adventure—in the wake of his Italian campaign—seemed the single source of Enlightenment confidence. To the populace, Napoleon looked like a man who could prevent invasion and bring victory. In the eyes of the bourgeoisie, he at least believed in strong central government and was not a royalist. The troops were already behind him. In August 1799 he left Egypt and slipped through the English blockade. Arriving in Paris on October 14, he immediately threw Josephine out of the house. She cried; he welcomed her back. His political moves were more durable. Together with the Abbé Sieyès—a pamphleteer who had helped initiate the Revolution, and who had managed to worm his way into power with his head still on his shoulders—Napoleon and a third man were sworn in by the Assembly as a consulate of three. Sieyès evidently thought to rule the government himself, using Napoleon as the military force behind him, but it was soon apparent who would be behind whom. Sieyès drew up a new constitution, but Napoleon knew well how much "freedom within limitation" was possible with French constitutions. With his charm and a military reputation, with Enlightenment slogans and bayonets, Napoleon soon reduced the triumvirate to a Caesarian consulate of one. Napoleon was now France, but one might have believed that he was Rome. A "plebiscite" ratified his position and the new constitution by a vote of over three million to fifteen hundred. "We have finished with the Romance of the revolution," Napoleon announced. "We must now begin its history."

The new Caesar unified the energy of France for the first time in decades. But the unification now embraced the entire populace, and the energy of France now included the enthusiasm and industry of all those people who had never before felt "responsible for France." The power of Napoleon's France was no longer confined to the wealth and whimsy of the aristocracy and the royal court; it derived from the workers and the peasants, the soldiers and the petty bourgeoisie. As for the rich bourgeoisie and intellectuals who had so long controlled the Revolution, they were never enthusiastic about Napoleon, and more than once they plotted to overthrow him. Napoleon saw that they were his gravest source of danger, because of their jealousy and business interests. But he maintained control of the people, and consolidated the bourgeois interests in the Revolution by way of legal and financial reform, while maintaining what was solid and realistic in Enlightenment and revolutionary thought, and holding in check the forces of disorder that had kept France in chaos for a decade. The

Enlightenment had not made good its promise to reconcile all interests. But in its name a new dictator would—temporarily—do just that.

Genius and Vulgarity

Who was this Napoleon—now First Consul of France, having just turned thirty? Except in his love affairs, which he typically warned himself against, Napoleon suppressed his childhood attachment to the sentimentality and libertarianism of Rousseau. His Enlightenment was strictly that of Voltaire and the authoritarian Rousseau, concerned with personal freedom, but only within the limits of strong authority and the interests of the State. He admired reason, but it was *his* reason that he admired—"calculation" we would call it. Napoleon was not a philosopher, and he viewed all ideology as a restriction of opportunity. He used Rousseau to consolidate his power with the people, and used Voltaire as a mask with the bourgeoisie around him and with the somewhat enlightened princes of Europe. But he was always a soldier, and whatever the philosophical ideas that maintained this policy or that, his only philosophy was efficiency, ambition, and glory. "My mistress is power, but it is as an artist that I love power—as a musician loves his violin."

Napoleon's energy is legendary. Butterfield says that he could not relax at all, "as though the springs inside him had been too tightly coiled" (pp. 33–34). He wrote to his brother in his youth, "The Southern blood in my veins runs as swiftly as the Rhine." He never stopped working or planning. During ceremonies and governmental gatherings he would be preparing a program, planning a campaign, weighing alternative strategies. He is said to have finished his meals in ten minutes and less, provoking the stomach trouble that persistently plagued him and ultimately killed him. He was extremely eloquent, not poetic but dynamic. He could say anything forcefully if not beautifully. He had the ability to retain large numbers of facts, to make quick and resolute decisions ("as if I had just remembered something"), and to pick out mistakes in long columns of statistics and calculations. His mind was always throbbing with alternative plans for every possible decision, from the charter for the comedy theater in Paris to a forthcoming campaign against Austria.

He had threatening charm but no sense of humor. He could not be entertained. With women and heads of state he would be menacing, then seductively charming, then brotherly, then sentimental. With deceit and his curiously relaxing smile, he could hoodwink the most sophisticated ministers in Europe. With childish playfulness he would seduce the most prominent women of France. Yet his attitude toward women was always childish: he would be loving and tender on one occasion, vulgar and discourteous on another. Stendhal relates:

Seated at a small table, his sword by his side, the Emperor would be busy signing decrees. The lady would enter the room. Without moving he would tell her to get into bed. Shortly after, carrying a candle he would show her out and would then return to reading his decrees, correcting and signing them. The essential part of the interview had lasted no more than three minutes. Sometimes Napoleon would ask the lady to take off her shift and then, without troubling to move, he would send her away. (Stendhal, pp. 116–17)

He wanted to think of himself as Caesar and Charlemagne, but never outgrew his common origins and inability to be elegant. "He could not rise from a chair, could not enter or leave a room, without betraying his origins" (Butterfield, p. 34). At court he was a *sans-culotte*, a shopkeeper. He always kept check on the price of coffee at the court, knew whether he was paying too much for his soldiers' shoes, and noticed when the beer they drank was watered down or of poor quality. His mother, too—always a cynic about the day "she would have to look after eight kings"—pinched pennies throughout her son's reign, consequently amassing a fortune which indeed served her and her sons well after the family's downfall. However great his power and his mind, Napoleon was capable of being mean and petty. He had a nasty temper and cheated at cards. His French was unforgivable—except that he was Emperor—and his manners and courtesy were often inexcusable. He was embarrassed by all of this, but his attempts to change were not directed at himself but at externals: a lavish court and marriage into one of the oldest of European royal families.

More than anything else, Napoleon had ambition. Not so much specific ambitions, however, since nothing could satisfy his lust for more. He was a political Faust, striving and insatiable. His rise was a Kantian purposiveness without purpose, and his downfall was as inevitable and dramatic as the finale of any Faust legend. As his eternal enemy, Mme de Staël, once said of him, "there is only one person, himself"; he saw the world as nothing other than an instrument of his destiny. He required absolute authority, had no patience for negotiations and balance of power, no tolerance for inefficiency, indecision, or intellectualization. Unlike his predecessor, Robespierre, he had no virtue; he used deceit as often as he used force, not only with his enemies, but with his friends and his people. Morality and virtue were for him tools, matters of policy. (To his brother Jerome, the new king of Westphalia, he wrote in 1807, "Be a constitutional king. Even if reason and the enlightenment of the age were not sufficient cause, it would be good policy for one in your position.") He ruled in the name of "the People," yet not for a moment did he believe in the General Will or popular sovereignty. ("If the people refuses its own happiness, the people is guilty of anarchy and deserves to be punished.") Yet there was the one exception: in matters of sexuality, Napoleon was as moralistic (though not incorruptible) as Robespierre. Thus he refused to allow mistresses of his officials into court, refused to meet Talleyrand's wife because they had slept together before they had married, and refused to allow a monument raised to Agnès Sorel because she had been the mistress of Charles VII.

Napoleon was a genius, but he was vulgar. He was sentimental, but he had ambition. He was strong, but he had fatal weaknesses. Napoleon was no longer simply the representative of Enlightenment; he was an ideological mutant who brought an end to one age by giving birth to another—a self-righteously terrifying world.

The New Empire

> Clever policy consists of making nations believe they are free.
>
> Napoleon

To excite and inspire France, Napoleon re-created the splendor of ancient Rome in Paris. He began the elegant buildings that still make Paris the most beautiful city in the world, some of which, like the Madeleine, were built after classical Roman models. The art of David, the aesthetic booty from Italy, the image of himself as Caesar, and a host of new institutions and laws based upon the Roman model allowed Napoleon to turn his personal fantasy into public policy. He won a lightning victory at Marengo over the Austrians and re-established the Republic of Italy. In the resultant Treaty of Luneville (1801) he secured peace with Austria, and early in 1802 the Treaty of Amiens secured peace with England. Europe experienced its first full year of peace since the outbreak of the French Revolution.

The soldiers were raised by official policy to the status of heroes, and became the best-paid and -equipped army in Europe. An effective secret police ended the gang and guerrilla warfare and kept domestic peace without excessive use of terror tactics. Taxation was made uniform, without exemption by birth or status. A new accounting system, the new Bank of France, and sound currency established fiscal responsibility for the first time in centuries. The confusing welter of local laws, together with thousands of sometimes absurd proclamations and mandates of the various revolutionary governments, were re-examined and boiled down to essentials, and made more liberal and uniform, as the Napoleonic Code. Whatever Napoleon's antirepublican, antipopular opinions might have been, he did prove himself the heir of the Revolution by consolidating and strengthening its most important demands.

Napoleon made his ally Talleyrand foreign minister, using the nostalgic old aristocrat and student of Voltaire to counterbalance his own sometimes wild ambitions. Furthermore, to end revolutionary bitterness and win support from the royalists, Napoleon invited back the émigré nobles, and to win popular and bourgeois support, he introduced a major campaign for "talent": government positions were no longer given on the basis of status or connections, but solely on the basis of merit. In so doing, Napoleon tapped the vital resources of France to create the most efficient and most powerful state in Europe.

In his attitude toward religion, Napoleon was a Voltairean deist at most. He sometimes said that he "was nothing," but in Egypt he had claimed allegiance to Islam, and in France he pretended to be a Catholic. He saw, as earlier revolutionary leaders had not, that religion was "the mystery of the social order." The Revolution's antagonism to religion had only driven the Church underground, alienated the people, and left Church power in the hands of the Pope and foreign influences. "The people must have a religion and that religion must be in the hands of the government." Accordingly, Napoleon began negotiations with the Pope and on July 15, 1801, signed the Concordat, which re-established the Catholic Church in France under government supervision. Although relations with the Church would soon sour again, Pope Pius VII would not forget Napoleon's important role in the restoration. Similarly, Napoleon would establish a Grand Sanhedrin for the Jews of Europe, signifying the end of their religious persecution in France—another goal of the Revolution. It was at this point in their history that "Jewish identity" emerged as a major dilemma, for only with their liberation did the possibility and temptations of assimilation become sufficiently great to challenge the endurance of Jewish traditions.

Having achieved peace and stability, the consolidation of the Revolution and the prosperity of France, the reconciliation with the Church and his own impressive image, Napoleon was adored by France as few leaders of any country ever. In August 1802 a new plebiscite overwhelmingly made Napoleon Consul for life. Although his power and his empire would grow enormously in coming years, one might well say that the zenith of Napoleon's leadership of France was this period of the consulship. For the first time in over a decade, there was trust in France.

Even at the height of his popularity as Consul, Napoleon was not without enemies. There were repeated threats and attempts on his life, including a notorious bomb attack on Christmas Eve of 1803. Cool as always, Napoleon used these attacks to consolidate his power. Regardless of the true source of the threat, he would publicly lay the blame wherever it was politically expedient. Jacobins were blamed for royalist plots, and when the royalists threatened him, an innocent noble was kidnapped outside of France and shot without trial as a conspirator. Eventually it was suggested to the more-than-willing Napoleon that such threats would be undermined, if the consulship were converted into a hereditary monarchy. In May 1804 another plebiscite overwhelmingly "entrusted the government of the republic to a hereditary emperor." The Pope was invited to perform the requisite ceremony, but Napoleon, in what even for him was an exceptional display of arrogance and political strategy, at the last minute managed to avoid the connotations of Papal authority. With the prior understanding of the Pope —he did not snatch it from him, as sometimes suggested—he placed the crown upon his own head. The world was thus forewarned that Napoleon's empire, while perhaps observed by God, was not "under God" in any practically limiting sense.

France was now an empire with an emperor. But she still called herself a "republic" and continued to inspire revolution throughout Europe. Leopold II of Austria's glib dismissal of the French Revolution now haunted his successor, as Napoleon continued to foment revolution in Italy and had himself declared "King of Italy." The small German states were whipped into their first nationalistic frenzy, and they too turned against Austrian domination. One of Napoleon's early strokes of political genius had been the provisions of the Treaty of Luneville that extended France's eastern boundary to the Rhine, causing the expulsion of a number of German princes. To them, Napoleon promised new territories across the Rhine in land once held by the clergy. The result was a land grab in which the greediest princes consolidated new German states which were wholly dependent upon Napoleon's protection and united in a "Confederation of the Rhine." The number of German states was reduced from its former confusion to fewer than forty. For them, nationalism and liberalism were new inspirations, incited and defended by Napoleon.

Austria was most unhappy with Napoleon's successes in Germany and Italy. Moreover, the British soon found that the terms at Amiens were no longer tolerable to British interests. Perhaps Napoleon had no desire for war, but his ambitions and policies made its avoidance impossible. Austria, England, and Russia joined together in a new coalition, and there would be war in Europe once again. Napoleon prepared his armies, planned an ambitious invasion of England, and sold Louisiana to the United States in order to free France of that liability and finance the new hostilities.

Playing Chess with "Destiny"

Napoleon's military success would appear overly brilliant, if we forgot about his equally brilliant diplomatic ruses and the chaotic state of the forces he faced. Until near the end of his power, Napoleon was never challenged by a united Europe. The coalitions against him—as Leopold had found when he organized the first—would not hold together. The mutual jealousies and fear of Austria, Prussia, and Russia, and their combined resentment of England, made military cooperation impossible. Accordingly, Napoleon won half his victories by playing off the enemy leaders one against another. ("I treat politics like war—I hoodwink one flank so as to trounce the other.") At the height of his power Napoleon gained all of Europe as an ally against the English, and more than once he allowed the mutual jealousies of others to win his battles for him.

Austria and Russia were marching from the East; England controlled the seas. Napoleon's bold plan was to strike suddenly and demolish the armies in the East, then to invade England immediately and "free the nation from a corrupt aristocracy." While his fleet was being built on the French coast, Napoleon led his troops to meet the Austro-Russian armies. In the battle of Austerlitz (December 2, 1805) he won his most stunning victory, "the most perfect battle in history." Austria sued for peace and the Russians withdrew into their own endless territory.

The second part of the plan was not similarly successful. England could be invaded only if the British fleet were destroyed or diverted. The combined French and Spanish fleets were still no match for the British under Admiral Nelson, who had already defeated the French during the early campaign in Egypt, so the only hope was to draw them away from their home base. Napoleon instructed his admirals to lead the British to the West Indies, then hurry back to the Channel, leaving a few crucial days for the troops to make the short crossing. But the British fleet caught the French and Spanish fleets and destroyed them in the Battle of Trafalgar (October 21, 1805). Nelson was killed, but he had assured England absolute domination over the seas for the remainder of the wars. The plans for invasion of England had to be canceled permanently.

Prussia had remained out of the wars for nearly ten years. She was, as Napoleon claimed, "my ally through fear," but she also saw advantage in the alliance for her interests in Poland and the East, as against Austria and Russia. Napoleon's stunning victory at Austerlitz frightened the Prussians, who unnecessarily and foolishly decided to march against France. As the Queen of Prussia would later admit to Napoleon, the Prussian armies "proudly acted as if they were still led by Frederick the Great." They attacked even without waiting for Russian support. Compared with Napoleon's fast modern army, the Prussian troops were clumsy and overburdened, badly led by generals not yet familiar with the new rules of warfare. As a result, they were soundly beaten at Jena in October 1806. The Prussian King had to flee to Kant's distant city of Königsberg, while Napoleon made a pilgrimage to the tomb and home of Frederick the Great. This victory was followed by another over the isolated Russians at Friedland (June 1807). Wiser than he would be later, Napoleon declined to push his troops into the vast expanses of Russia. Rather than continue the war, he and Czar Alexander agreed to negotiate. In July the two emperors met on a barge in the Niemen River at Tilsit, while the Prussian monarch, nervous and helpless, paced on the bank.[11]

In Alexander of Russia, Napoleon had at least one adversary who matched him, not in genius or strength, but in enlightened egoism and international ambition. Alexander saw himself as the savior of Europe, as Napoleon's personal equal, as the hope of the Enlightenment, and as the creator and leader of an international peace force. He combined rationalism with a dose of mysticism, ambition with a claim to destiny, international Europeanism with an enthusiastic knowledge of Voltaire and Rousseau. This was the world those philosophers created. At Tilsit the enlightened despot Alexander confronted the Emperor of the People, Napoleon—to share the world. They flattered each other, and from most reports, all but cast spells upon each other in pursuit of an agreement for which both were eager from the outset—the dividing of Europe between them. Already resentful of England for her control of the seas, her power in Austria and the Middle East, and her failure to help him when he needed it against Napoleon, Alexander gladly joined the Emperor in a united effort against England, whom they declared to be "the eternal enemy of the Continent." In their ambition, the English Enlightenment would conveniently be forgotten. International humanism is reasonable, it seems, only when it is in one's own control or image.

Through conquest or alliance, Napoleon now dominated most of Europe. It was easy, looking back, for both enthusiastic patriots in France and his enemies abroad to attribute this success to long-planned and carefully executed ambitions. But in fact, Napoleon was not Alexander the Great, whose aspirations of conquest were dominant even in childhood. Napoleon took the world as it presented itself; his ambitions arose with the opportunity, not before. It was his flexibility that brought him such incredible success. Not genius and strategy alone, but a healthy realism (aided by Talleyrand), a good mind for theory and planning, a talent for quick decisions, and the patience to wait for his opponent's first move—this is what allowed him to take Europe piece by piece. But once he had absolute power over Europe, his ambitions became rigid, his plans became compulsions, and his failures obsessions, while wild dreams clouded over the healthy realism. As in a classical tragedy, the virtues that had brought him success must now lead to his fall, his "Destiny."

England could not be invaded, could not be attacked outside the European continent. Yet she could be crippled economically, Napoleon thought, if the whole of Europe under his control were to shut out British goods. England, whose life rested on her international trade, could be destroyed from within through economic collapse, if Europe could be sealed against her. On the positive side, Napoleon's international ambitions had long included plans for a European economic community and international trade, in which all nations would help each other with low tariffs and uniform prices. Together, the destructive obsession and the constructive ambition gave birth to the "Continental System," whereby Napoleon attempted to force all European powers to break economic relations with Britain. From the first, the plan seemed unreasonable. A European economic community could have been a reality, but the attempt to destroy British trade, given Britain's command of the seas and her multiple alternative markets in the Americas and Asia, was foolish. From the first, the negative effects hurt the European countries—including France—more than England. There were "leaks" in the system every-where—not only individual merchants, but entire countries. The Continental System was the obsession that brought about Napoleon's downfall. Because of it, his unwilling allies suffered and turned against him. It can be argued that the Continental System in fact helped everyone in the long run, that the idea of a European economic community protected all of Europe against the English Industrial Revolution that was already well under way. But the immediate effects would be sufficient to bring the Napoleonic era to an end.

Rebellion and Disaster

If we judge Napoleon's success by the extent of his holdings, his empire continued to increase until 1811, when he either ruled or was in alliance with every country in Europe except the Balkans. Where he himself did not rule, he ruled through his family: Joseph in Naples and Spain, Jerome in the new German republic of Westphalia, Louis in Holland, his sister Caroline in Naples, his former mistress Désirée and her husband in Sweden—while his mother warned them all, "It's fine while it lasts." And wherever Bonapartes ruled went the Napoleonic Code, republicanism with a strong central government, tax reform, written constitutions, secularization of Church property, equality before the law (but rarely freedom), civil marriage, and male supremacy. But the old stability was breaking down, old allies were turning against him. Napoleon had encouraged nationalism and taught Europe a new kind of war—citizen wars for philosophy and justice, in the place of the Old Regime's heroic jousts for greed. But this same nationalism and sense of justice which had supported the French began to turn against them. In Germany, for example, nationalism had first signified consolidation and freedom from Austria and Prussia, but that same nationalism inevitably reacted against French domination as well. The consolidation of the "German spirit" was already under way; it now sought release from its French godfather. Prussia, taking advantage of the new German self-consciousness, presented herself as the center of pro-German feeling, the ideological father of the coming German wars of liberation. Employing Herder's popular concept of the *Volkgeist,* Prussia began to tap the same rich resources that had allowed the French to achieve such power.

Similarly, the Spanish turned on their former ally and began their own resistance to foreign domination. The French Enlightenment meant little to them. Spain had shared France's losses at Trafalgar and contributed to her armies in Europe, but now a new sense of nationalism and oppression turned against Napoleon. In his final exile at St. Helena, Napoleon would call the Spanish war a "running sore" and the "thorn in my side." Spain was the first dramatic instance of the corruption of Napoleon's power into arrogance and clumsiness. Despite the alliance, the Spanish people were not uniformly happy about the constant presence of French troops in Spain. In 1808, amid sporadic uprisings, Charles IV abdicated in favor of his son, Ferdinand, but then changed his mind, whereupon they both appealed to Napoleon for arbitration. But Napoleon, seeing only an opportunity for a further addition to the Empire, gave his brother Joseph (then King of Naples) the crown. Joseph had been in Madrid only a week and a half, when he was driven from the capital by peasant guerrilla bands, rebellious soldiers, and a general if disconnected uprising. Napoleon had made his first fatal mistake: Spain being not middle class but feudal in structure, the Spanish people were loyal to their decrepit royal family, and that loyalty was far more important than abstract Enlightenment ideals. The Catholic Church was antirevolutionary and anti-Enlightenment in sentiment, but did not oppose rebellion against foreign oppression. For the next five years peasants, nobles, clergy, and soldiers joined in a spectacular and bloody resistance against the French, supported by the English, who thus acquired their first solid foothold in Europe since the early days of the war. Napoleon's repression was ruthless and totally unsuccessful. The horrors of Spain, recorded by Goya, present a picture of the late Napoleonic Wars which would make their unqualified glorification a matter of poor taste.

If Spain had been the only problem facing Napoleon, no doubt he could have focused his attentions and armies there and imposed order. But Austria began her own war of liberation in 1809, and Prussia and Russia were restless under the restrictions of the Continental System. Meanwhile there were problems at home. Talleyrand had been replaced as foreign minister, for he had seen clearly how Napoleon's new arrogance and over-ambition endangered the Empire. He was still very much part of the political scene in Europe, but openly separated the Emperor and the interests of France. Already predicting the fall of Bonaparte, he was securing himself a place in post-Napoleonic Europe, advising Alexander of Russia in his dealings with Napoleon, and using his personal knowledge of Napoleon against him.

Napoleon was now forty years old, an Emperor without an heir. His relationship with Josephine had long been a matter more of pain than passion, so "in the interests of state" he decided to divorce her. He was obviously troubled by the decision, but as in all his decisions now, he remained firm in the face of Josephine's tears and an illness that predictably occurred just before the appropriate proceedings. The lack of an heir, Josephine could rightly point out, was hardly her fault alone, with two children by her former marriage. (Ironically, it was just at this time that Napoleon did father a child in his passionate affair with "his Polish wife," the Countess Marie Walewska; but the biological proof of fertility was not what Napoleon most needed for his empire.)

Over and above the political need for a son, Napoleon felt pride. He was still painfully conscious of his common background and personal lack of elegance, all the more evident in the splendor of one of the most elaborate courts in the world. The qualified egalitarianism of Enlightenment thinking had never altered the bourgeois envy for the old elitist pretensions. The mother of his son, therefore, would have to come from one of the oldest royal houses in Europe, which meant either the Hapsburgs of Austria or the Romanovs of Russia. After considerable negotiations with these two families and others, none of whom were delighted at the prospect of marrying off a princess to a lowborn antagonist, Napoleon won over Francis of Austria and his new minister, Clemens von Metternich, formerly ambassador to France. His new bride, Princess Marie Louise, had little to say about it. She was only eighteen, and very pretty and gracious. Impatient, Napoleon married her by proxy even before he met her, then married her properly and fathered a son, born in 1811, whom he designated "the King of Rome." The child with this pretentious title, and what appeared to be the most fortunate inheritance in history, would in fact reign as Napoleon II for a matter of hours, and die at the age of twenty-one as the Duke of Reichstadt in Germany, a virtual prisoner.

Napoleon's long marriage with Josephine, which had cost him so much in jealousy and feelings of inadequacy, had had its effects on his personality as well. Distrustful of women, he had often declared that "States are lost as soon as women interfere in public affairs," and added that "a woman's advice on a political matter was sufficient to decide upon the opposite course." Metternich observed that, regarding women, "Napoleon has more weaknesses than any other man." The Napoleonic Code, a great advance in many ways, unforgivably reflected Napoleon's own fears and prejudices about women, whom he thought should have beauty and charm, but be wholly subservient. Such opinions were legally expressed in the Code. Education for women was restricted. They were not allowed to make contracts, and in all social and legal matters were under the guardianship of their husbands.

Of this period of his life Napoleon later said, "It was an abyss hidden by flowers." While he enjoyed Marie Louise's charming company, the English were already in Spain, helping the guerrilla bands to make life intolerable for the French oppressors, whom on occasion they even beat in open battle. Russia was growing uneasy, and displayed unnecessary indignation at Napoleon's marriage to a daughter of Austria (although it was the Romanovs who had refused the alternative match). Czar Alexander, sensing Napoleon's new weakness but announcing his suspicions of the kinship of France and Austria, withdrew from the Continental System. Predictably furious, Napoleon decided on the course of action that would lose him his entire Grand Army and all that he had gained in ten brilliant years—the invasion of Russia.

As always, Napoleon planned on a quick confrontation and a lightning victory—the strategy that had won him so many brilliant battles in the past. Taking only three weeks' supplies, in June 1812 he moved into Russia the largest army that Europe had ever seen—over 600,000 men. But Alexander, who had learned something from history, avoided the desired confrontation and systematically retreated, burning all provisions along the way. The heat of summer, the lack of food, and frustration caused over 120,000 desertions even before the Russians had been confronted. In desperation Napoleon attacked the city of Smolensk in an attempt to win a victory, no matter how unstrategic, so as to keep up the morale of his soldiers. Even there, however, the Russians had withdrawn most of their forces. Napoleon became seriously ill, but his pride and his Destiny pushed him on to Moscow. Before Moscow, the Russians finally stood at Borodino and fought. Napoleon won a Pyrrhic victory, losing so many men that his army was exhausted when it finally entered Moscow on September 14—an entry without welcome ("Not even a pretty girl," Napoleon later complained). Still his own publicity agent, he sent word of victory back to France. But the victory had been a hollow one, and there was nothing to do but go home. The bitter Russian winter, the lack of food and supplies, and marauding Cossack bands reduced the Grand Army to a wretched battalion of 10,000 men who would finally make it back to Paris.

In Paris, Talleyrand and others had spread the rumor of Napoleon's death. To avoid the formation of a new government without him, Napoleon abandoned his men in the snow of Russia and hurried back to Paris and quashed the rumor. He succeeded in keeping his government, but he was rapidly losing the faith and enthusiasm of his people. With his usual haste and brilliance he raised a new army, but his opponents were no longer isolatable and mutually uncooperative. Napoleon had always said that any sign of weakness would bring out the open hostility of his enemies. Heartened by the destruction of the Grand Army in Russia, the Austrians turned on the French; the Prussians rallied the formerly friendly Germans as a new force for liberation; the Russians regrouped and joined their mutually distrustful allies in the East; and the British, led by Wellington, crossed into France from Spain. In the Battle of Nations at Leipzig, the largest coalition in the history of Europe decisively beat Napoleon's new and undertrained army, then marched into Paris and demanded Napoleon's abdication:

An incongruous alliance of British capitalism and east European agrarian feudalism, of the British navy and the Russian army, of Spanish clericalism and German nationalism, of divine right monarchies and newly aroused democrats and liberals, combined at last to bring the man of Destiny to the ground.[12]

Napoleon refused to abdicate and threatened to raise a new army. But France was exhausted: the army refused to fight, and the bourgeoisie were finished with Napoleon, and ready—at the urging of Talleyrand—for a return to a more "enlightened" monarchy. Alexander was pressing for the destruction of Paris in retaliation for the burning of Moscow, while the British wisely made it clear that their concern was directed not against the French people but Napoleon. On April 4, Napoleon abdicated. A few days later he attempted suicide by poisoning, but survived—which heartened him somewhat, since he took it as a sign that his Destiny had not yet been completed. Napoleon was given reign over the tiny island of Elba, and Louis XVIII was recalled to the throne with Talleyrand as his chief minister. But it was no longer the Old Regime, only the old royal family. The victories of the Revolution were intact, the Napoleonic Code remained the law of the land. France was again at peace, at least for a month or two.

Waterloo

With Napoleon out of the way, his conquerors' mutual distrust and antagonism developed into full-scale paranoia and greed. There were the usual tedious negotiations and claims and counterclaims in the name of "justice" and "natural right," motivated by selfishness and fear. And while the dignitaries of Europe were squabbling, the old Bourbon King proved as thick-skulled and aggravating as his predecessors, so that the French people became restless. The news reached Elba, where with his usual flair Napoleon sensed the time for his presence in Paris. On February 26 he escaped from his island prison-court with one thousand soldiers. Landing in France, he took the mountain roads north to Paris, gathering a small army of peasants on the way. When he reached Grenoble, he staged what may have been his greatest performance of all: confronting the King's troops who had orders to kill him, he bared his breast and gave them a chance to "kill their Emperor." They refused, and by the time he reached Lyons he had fourteen thousand men. There he secured the loyalty of his former generals and with them the entire French army. The Bourbons fled Paris, and once again the mythology of Caesar and Charlemagne ruled France. Gathering a new and more powerful army, the leaders of Europe met a less than confident Napoleon at Waterloo, the end of his Destiny (June 18, 1815). Forced to abdicate once again, he made a desperate attempt to seek refuge in England or the United States. But no one was willing to risk giving Napoleon further access to Europe. He was sent to the tiny island of St. Helena, thousands of miles away. "I asked for twenty years," he would reflect, "and destiny only gave me thirteen."

With Napoleon gone once again, the Holy Alliance shattered into a cacophony of quarreling diplomats who divided Europe among themselves and freely transferred people as well as land like chess pieces. They made bold proclamations against the possibility of any new Napoleon, but the turmoil and confusion in France which had given him his opportunities had subsided. His once clumsy enemies evolved new political wisdom and began to reap for themselves the same citizen energies that had fueled France. There was no time for heroes. It would take decades just to digest the sudden changes wrought by the French Revolution and Napoleon in a short twenty-five years. Europe was exhausted after a violent pregnancy. The post-Napoleonic era would give it the longest peace of modern times, until the arrogance of Napoleonic France would reappear in the nationalism and citizen energy of Germany.

Napoleon died on St. Helena in 1821, after using his last years to formulate a personal legend that would affect Europe for the next century. In the relative calm of the years that followed 1815, the Napoleonic legend could grow into a mythology without the dangers of a Napoleon.

dictator of the art world, as powerful in his domain—and as ruthless—as his friend Robespierre was in his. David served as a member of the National Assembly in 1792 and voted for the execution of his former patron, Louis XVI, who had paid for his artistic schooling. A member of the dreaded Committee on Public Safety during the Terror, he used his position to destroy the Royal Academy, which had given him his opportunity for fame. He used the Assembly and the Committee as forums for artistic declamations and denunciations of all "decadent"—that is, nonclassical—art. Some artists who would not conform were executed. When Robespierre was condemned by his own Revolution, David was sent to prison, narrowly escaping the guillotine. He denounced his friends, vowed to attach himself to "principles rather than men," and was set free. When Napoleon became First Consul, he saw in David's classical art an important instrument of propaganda, and David, seeing in Napoleon a new sponsor for his artistic dictatorship, gladly accepted the offer to be "the First Painter to the Consul of France." Elevated in 1804 to "First Painter of the Emperor," he retained this position until Waterloo, when he too was sent into exile in Belgium.

David's powerful, elegant, heroic classical painting was the visual expression of the Enlightenment in its days of near-total victory. His Greek and Roman subjects, as well as his paintings of contemporary martyrs and patrons, displayed universal human ideals, rather than just the likenesses of particular individuals, real or imagined. His luminous canvases, with their controlled coloration and precise linear drawing, signified the clarity of the new ideology. His moral lessons—unmistakable even to those who might not know the mythology or history of the subject matter—expressed the new aspirations of humanity, their appeal being addressed not just to the literate, to the bourgeoisie, or even to all Frenchmen, but to the world. And if his paintings were generally considered beautiful, that was because of their moral force; beauty was not an end in itself, even in art.

Not every genius of the Enlightenment had the passions of the Revolution to support his talent and further his ambitions. In Germany, Kant, Goethe, and Schiller found themselves facing a politically static culture in which their idealism had to be confined to the human "spirit" and kept free from politics and practical moralizing. In Spain, Francisco José de Goya y Lucientes (1746–1828) found himself facing an even bleaker situation in the most backward, reactionary, and corrupt country in Western Europe. He too was a genius and an opportunist, but there was little opportunity. He too was an enthusiast of Enlightenment ideology, but at the time of the French Revolution he was already expressing not its victory, but its despair and frustration. His paintings were not propaganda but protests, brutal displays of inhumanity, documentaries on current events and abuses, and public or private cries of disgust. If David was the painter of human ideals, then Goya was the diagnostician of human evil.[5] He painted the dark and demonic side of the Enlightenment, its failure rather than its success. His canvases are dark, even opaque, murky, dominated by shadows. And if David's ideals contributed to the beauty of his paintings, Goya's asses and demons gave a place in art to what Ingres would later call "the cult of the ugly," an art of private vengeance: "Divine Reason, let not one of them remain!"[6]

In the name of the Enlightenment, David beheaded his King; Goya could only continue to paint his monarch unflatteringly, as he deserved. David became a dictator, Goya a recluse. Where David's most revolutionary paintings were also his most successful, Goya's greatest works were private "diversions" and "caprices," only some of which were made public during his lifetime. The two artists were exact contemporaries: David was born in 1748, Goya in 1746; both lived long and died in exile, David in Brussels in 1825, Goya in southern France in 1828. Both were trained in a mix of baroque and classical styles.[7] Each has been called "the beginning of modern art,"[8] and both were the artistic culmination of the Enlightenment ideology. But in style, subject matter, and temperament, as well as in opportunity and public success, the two artists were emphatically different. Thus a contrast of their long careers presents us with a striking series of portraits of the spirit of the Enlightenment in the most advanced and the most backward country of Europe—a contrast in light and dark, the visual metaphors of the age.

Art and Ideology

> It is just in this that perfect style in any art reveals itself—that it is capable of removing the characteristic limitations of that art, without however removing the characteristic excellences, and of lending it a more universal character.
>
> Schiller[9]

David was born into a comfortable bourgeois family in Paris; Goya was thrown into a world of poverty near the medieval city of Saragossa in eastern Spain. No two settings in Europe could have been more different. And to judge by representative works, no two artists could seem more different. For example, walking into the grand hall of the Louvre, where David's large canvases are dwarfed by both the architecture and the mammoth paintings of his romantic successors, the viewer is struck by the vigor and the clarity of his *Oath of the Horatii* (1784; exhibited in 1785) —properties appropriate to the power and self-conscious rationality of the Enlightenment itself. Going closer, one is impressed by the "flawless" painting; by the luminous surfaces and the elegant, geometrical composition; by the perfect shapes and unbroken lines; the bright but restrained primary colors; the total absence of mystery and the minimal shadows—again, like the Enlightenment itself. One need not know the identity of these three warriors and the old man to whom they offer their oath (though the audience of David's time would know the story from the famous play by Corneille then being done in Paris). They are ideal figures, anonymous portraits of courage, perfect human beings—as we all would be, in the enlightened society to come.

How different one's impression upon approaching Goya's small, drab painting of the *Madhouse* (1794), with its near absence of primary color and its disordered, contorted figures, hidden in shadows and defined by their screams. The architecture is not a stage as in David's *Oath,* but an oppressive prison drawn without geometry, rather than the elegant simplicity of David's Roman columns. The painting is composed of shadows, not the clarity of lines; it is a painting of the ugly, and the message—though trite from overuse—is not lost: that this madhouse is a microcosm of humanity. If David's *Horatii* represent the Enlightenment ideal, Goya's madmen betray its impossibility.

And yet David and Goya share a common artistic heritage—the flamboyance of the baroque rococo, the austerity of the classicists. They were both Enlightenment liberals, and their paintings display a common sense of humanity, a common moral seriousness. It is true that these two paintings and their artists can be viewed as diametrical (or dialectical) opposites, but they also reveal affinities when compared to the eighteenth-century aristocratic art against which they were both rebelling.

The late baroque or rococo style that dominated the art world before David was extravagantly ornamental, self-consciously erotic, entertaining, and frivolous. Typically, the settings were the grounds of a château, and the subjects, lovers running through the manicured gardens. The colors were sensuous and the designs loose if discernible at all, while the background showed billowing trees and clouds pleasantly receding to infinity. Two artists illustrate the temperament of the rococo, with its emphasis on lavish visual entertainment, eroticism, and frivolity: François Boucher (1703–1770) and Jean Honoré Fragonard (1732–1806).[10] Their decorations were abundant and familiar, covering countless walls of stately mansions as colorful reminders of the pleasures of aristocratic life. Allegories of love—"courtly" love and adultery—were particularly popular, as were lovely young girls in flowing gowns on swings, or playing with puppies or nude, toying with cupids, admiring themselves in a mirror with sweet smiles and perfect skin, rounded breasts, and tantalizing poses. The endless luxury of their lives is reflected in the infinite space behind them, the baskets of spilled jewels at their feet. Flesh colors are the blushing pink of love just consummated, while all else swims in the warm flush of primary colors. However frivolous and teasing—and the off-canvas profession of the models is often implicit in the painting—the art itself is indisputably *charming,* fit to entertain even a king.[11]

Charm and sensuous entertainment, however, were not acceptable to the new critics—for example, Diderot—and the new audience of bourgeois "men of culture." With money to spend and a growing demand (if not always taste) for art, this new audience insisted on a more bourgeois art: scenes in the kitchen rather than the manor, more story and less eroticism, more of a moral and less ornamentation. As the new bourgeois market gained in influence, the aristocratic artists began to make concessions: Boucher learned to paint a family at breakfast as well as Venus grooming with cupids. Then the middle class began to produce its own artists with distinctive styles. The styles followed their ideology, and the concept of "good taste" came to have a moral, rather than a purely aesthetic, meaning.[12] Edification replaced entertainment as the acknowledged "purpose" of art. Subject matter and story began to take precedence over painting itself.[13] The painting was often mediocre and the subjects tedious, but it was in this atmosphere of moral seriousness and rejection of frivolity that David and Goya launched their careers.

Goya never adopted classicism. Like David, he made the compulsory artistic trip to Rome, but it seems to have affected him not at all.[14] For David, classicism became the vehicle for his moral seriousness; Goya returned from Rome to the old decadent style of the rococo, whose playfulness, open landscapes, and generous coloration remained evident in his early work. But when he turned away from the aristocratic style that he used as an employee of the court, it was to this bourgeois spirit of moral seriousness. David, of course, not only embraced classicism but came to define it. His early work too was rococo in style, and his first teacher was Boucher.[15] What defined David's mature style was not only his classical themes and compositions, however, but his moral seriousness both in execution and in unsubtle didactic allegories. To see the linkage between David and Goya, then, it is necessary to take a broader view of Enlightenment painting than the common identity of ideology and classicism. It is the Enlightenment as a whole, not just its appeal to the ancients, that defines the new styles—Goya's demonology as well as David's ideology.

Bourgeois art might best be illustrated by some of the more important mediocrities preceding David and Goya—for example, two artists specifically championed by Diderot: Greuze and Chardin. Jean Baptiste Greuze (1725–1805) seized on the new ideology to become one of the most successful artists in Paris in the 1760s. He was in many ways the artistic representative of Rousseau. Some of his clumsy moral allegories—for example, his return of the prodigal son—were borrowed in both theme and composition directly from Italian Renaissance artists, and especially Poussin. Other subjects were strictly contemporary, sentimental, and tediously moral, like his lesson on lost virginity in the sad-eyed girl with the broken milk pitcher (an apt contrast with the libertines of the manors and the lusty Venuses of Boucher).

Greuze depicted the idylls of Rousseau in a striking if not elegant celebration of country life and the natural virtues of the rural family. He elevated the middle class and even the peasantry to the level of classical heroism. He depicted the virtues of family life—a distinctively bourgeois virtue, such as the children of the aristocracy rarely saw in their parents. (When Marie Antoinette had herself painted with her children in 1787 by Mme Vigée-Lebrun, she was catering to the new bourgeois morality; it may have been the first occasion in months when she had spent so much time with them.) Significantly, because of these themes—and not because he painted rural scenes—Greuze was considered a painter of "nature."[16]

Greuze is exemplary because of his moralism, his "naturalism," and also because of his style (even if indifferently executed) and, most important, his Rousseauan *sensibilité*. Although retaining the influences of the rococo, he restrained his colors, restricted the number of figures in his paintings, condemned eroticism even as he exploited it,[17] and insisted on realistic, secular, and distinctly bourgeois or lower-class figures. Despite his public success, however, Greuze was officially judged by the aristocratic officials as "puny" and "mincing"[18]—opinions which are being reversed once again in the current Greuze revival. But his middle-class aspirations and accessibility made him a champion of the small-minded, winning him a significant place in the history of the bourgeoisie if not in the fine arts as well.[19]

A more domestic and less obviously moral bourgeois art developed in France under influences from Holland, where the bourgeoisie had been in full control for many years, and where baroque and bourgeois were the same. Jean Baptiste Siméon Chardin (1699–1779) borrowed from Hals, Rembrandt, Brouwer, and Steen to create a strictly middle-class kitchen art: still-lifes of the spoils of the day's hunting much like those that populate the Amsterdam Rijksmuseum, and ostentatious paintings of well-stocked pantries à la Brueghel, with more material arrogance than artistry. They may have been trivial, but they were not frivolous. They may have been tedious (as even Diderot admitted), but they were ideologically correct. Supported by the new critics, Chardin, like Greuze, made a respectable career in a new free-enterprise art market, no longer so dependent on the dictates of the government and the tastes of the nobility. The artist was now a spokesman, and his art a moral document. David's stark realism and restraint would be the ideal expression of these new conditions in one way, but there were other ways as well. Goya's protests derived from this moral seriousness as much as did David's propaganda, and the new secularism is visible in his earthly angels and demons as much as in David's ancient warriors.[20]

The overemphasis on David's classicism, to the exclusion of Goya's protoromantic paintings and etchings, gives rise to a serious but all-too-common misunderstanding, usually couched in the terminology of "the classic versus the romantic." This dichotomy is discussed in detail in Chapter 13, but it can be said even here that this distinction gives more trouble than understanding. One point to be emphasized is that David's "classicism" depended not only on his brilliant technique but just as much on his *passion*. (He has often been called—for example, by Dowd—a "romantic classicist," thus multiplying the confusion.)[21] Goya, on the other hand, has often been called an artist of the "irrational," along with Bosch, Brueghel, and the romantics who followed him. The distinction between the moral/rational and the emotional/irrational appears all too readily even in the best critics, for example Walter Friedlander, who uses this false dichotomy to summarize this entire artistic period.[22] But even in the eighteenth century Rousseau, Schiller, and Hume, to name but a few, were arguing that morality and proper sentiment were one and the same. If David rejected the sentimentality of Boucher and the rococo, it was a rejection of "false" sentiment and not of sentiment as such. In the language of the Enlightenment, of course, true sentiment was moral sentiment, as opposed to the "artificial" and "decadent" emotions of the aristocracy. And if Goya portrayed the "irrational" (whatever that means), it was always in the name of Reason and morality, which he defended passionately. He too rejected the "false" sentiments and hypocrisy of the rococo; his *Caprichos* are not nearly so much fantasy as moral criticism in the style of Voltaire, using etchings rather than the printed word. If he rejected beauty, it was because he saw that the world was not beautiful, just as Voltaire for the same reason had once rejected Leibniz (see pp. 49–52). Beneath Goya's horrors and David's ideals lay a common ideological foundation: the ideology of Rousseau and Voltaire, the morality of the true universal sentiments of humanity.

The Sword of the Revolution

> It is a great secret to touch the human heart, and by this means a great impulse might be given to the public energy and to the national character.
>
> David, *Catalogue*[23]

David completed *The Oath of the Horatii* in 1784, on a second trip to Rome. (Returning from his first trip as a student, he had declared, "A cataract has been removed from my eyes." Leaving for the second, he announced, "Only in Rome can I paint Romans.") It was indeed a Roman picture, and David, already an agréé of the Academy and a recognized genius, became the classicist painter par excellence. The painting was called "the most beautiful picture of the century." It was also a call to arms. "Philosophy," writes critic M. W. Brown, "was the fire in which art was forged as a sword of the revolution."[24] There is no more obvious symbol of the new ideological unity than this painting, which attracted so much enthusiastic attention in the Paris Salon of 1785.

The *Horatii* story—made popular through the play by Corneille—told of three Roman brothers who, according to the heroic customs of the period, were to fight against three enemies in a contest which would determine the outcome of the war. Two would be killed but the third, by separating his enemies, would emerge victorious. David's painting does not focus on the battle because action is not the subject, even if it is the theme, of his revolutionary paintings. The scene is the motionless moral preliminary: the three brothers joined together almost as one with arms outstretched in dedication toward their father, who holds their three swords before them.[25] The figures are stiff and frozen; they stand in a cold Roman setting, architecturally divided into three equal parts. There are no rococo billowing clouds, leafy trees, carpeted grass, or sensuous colors. The painting is, as David intended, like a piece of classical relief sculpture, without depth, and with figures that have none of the lightness and charm of recent painting. Each aspect—the space, the figures, even the light—is treated separately. To one side, the Horatii women fall against each other in contrast to the heroic stiffness of their men. The painting is sleek and brilliantly accurate, every line precise without extravagance or incidentals. There are no airy brushstrokes, and color is secondary—almost unimportant. The sharp, determined lines, and the lack of color and warmth, reinforce the starkness and strength of the theme.

Obviously, the *Horatii* is more than a brilliant painting. The sharp style and classical theme are not intended to entertain or amuse, but to inspire and strengthen the viewer. This is not merely a Roman fiction portrayed for contemporary enjoyment; it is a moral lesson in revolutionary loyalty and self-sacrifice.[26] Even in their coldness, the precisely drawn figures are flesh and blood, easily recognizable not as Romans but as personal ideals. David intended his painting to be comprehensible even to the illiterate. His painting is the visual portrayal of Voltaire and Rousseau, still united in an uncomfortable alliance of formalism and naturalism before the Revolution. Fifteen years later, David would summarize his revolutionary classicism:

The ancients are the source of beauty for the modern painter. We seek to imitate the ancients, in the genius of their conception, the purity of their design, the expressiveness of their features, and the grace of their forms. Could we not take a step further and imitate them also in the customs and institutions established by them to bring their arts to perfection? (David, *Catalogue*, p. 5)

Painting, unlike philosophy or poetry, cannot use the words "all" or "humanity"; its images are necessarily particular—a well-known person or story, a familiar landscape or a recognizable scene. But art too can represent the universal, albeit in concrete form, expressing eternal ideals or an illustration of humanity as such. The *Horatii* is such an illustration: not only its figures and its theme, but the painting itself is an example of a moral sense and a sense of beauty that are supposed to be universal, appealing to human nature and human dignity. The use of ancient themes and stories is, as David insisted, only a vehicle to make a contemporary point—to display those human virtues which have not changed in two thousand years, and to appeal to those human feelings, manifested here as beauty, that define itself.[27] Dowd has commented that David "imbued his canvases with the 'heroic morality' and the political and social reformist philosophy of the rising middle classes. . . . He brought neo-classicism to its technical perfection, established its artistic hegemony for two generations, gave it a new structure and a new vision, and endowed it with a new ideological content" (p. 6).

In 1787 David painted *The Death of Socrates*, another heroic story of the ancients, again portrayed in frozen poses in a stark and stony setting, without depth or color. As Socrates allows himself to be executed for the sake of the State, he sits stiffly upright, his arm raised in the cool gesture of a moral lesson. With the other hand he reaches for the fatal cup of poison, while the figures surrounding him droop and fall in despair. Socrates's pure, almost white body contrasts with his bleak surroundings. Another obvious moral message, another ancient example, another brilliant painting. But David was involved in frustrating struggles with Pierre, the first painter to the King, who saw to it that David was systematically denied the honors of the Academy. At the same time, the revolutionary preaching of his paintings had not escaped the admiring aristocracy. Consequently, in that same year of 1787 David was turned down—"because he is too young"—for the directorship of the Academy. Soon he would have his revenge.[28]

In 1789 David presented the Academy with another of his radical moral lessons drawn from antiquity. *Brutus and His Dead Sons* portrays the painful sacrifice of the Roman republican who has killed his sons for conspiring against the State—again, a topic popularized by a play (this one by Voltaire) then being performed in Paris. The bodies of the sons appear in the light of a background behind the heartbroken but resolute Brutus, who is in shadow except for his legs. His wife and daughters stand in the light on the opposite side—his daughters in the familiar pose of despairing collapse, his wife in a heroic pose, reaching stiffly toward her dead sons, yet resigned to the sacrifice. The painting is less impressive than his two previous successes, but its political message, appearing just at the outbreak of the Revolution (the Salon opened in late August), outraged the aristocrats who controlled the Academy, so that *Brutus* was refused a place in the exhibition. In reaction, the bourgeois revolutionary demanded that it be hung, and supplied a uniformed revolutionary guard to protect it. *Brutus* was celebrated as a manifesto of the Revolution, and the courage of Brutus was projected onto David himself. Classicism and David conformed ideally to the sentiments of the Revolution, and the artistic reputation and power that David had achieved under the Old Regime soon became a revolutionary authority far more powerful and dictatorial than any he had battled against. "Through his *Brutus* as through his *Horatii*," said a contemporary, "David talks to the people more directly and more clearly than all the inflammatory writers whom the regime has confiscated and burned."[29]

Goya and the Enlightenment in Spain

> Goya drew his inspiration from the hopes and struggles of his time. His art is linked by a thousand subtle threads with the daily life of his people. . . . by the genius of his art he made the concrete universal, and because he lived wholly and unreservedly in his time, Goya's name is immortal.
>
> Klingender[30]

Spain too had an Enlightenment, however brief and truncated, whose relative freedom of opportunity allowed Goya, who also displayed precocious talent for drawing, to pursue his career. He too was an Enlightenment liberal, but the nature of the Spanish Enlightenment defined a very different set of attitudes and ideals. This was not France, and the new liberalism in Spain more resembled the *Aufklärung* in Germany, where the impotence of the middle class and the local suspicion of "foreign" (French) ideas gave the Enlightenment a conservative inertia. Furthermore, Spain was also extremely poor, and its education and morals as well as its spiritual life were wholly in the hands of the Catholic Church. Feudalism still prevailed, and while nationalism in Germany was an aspiration for something new, in Spain it was a shadow of its former self. But as in France under Louis XIV, the Bourbon kings of Spain were competing with the nobles for power, so that the politics of the Enlightenment— particularly in the absence of a powerful middle class—depended largely on the efforts of the court to use the people as a tool against the nobility. Despite some success, even a "Golden Age" of sorts, the situation in liberal Spain might still be called "feudal anarchy."[31]

The most remarkable single difference between Goya's Spain and David's France, however—and Goethe's Germany as well—was the Spanish sense of "the common man." This did not strictly signify any particular class, peasant or bourgeois, but rather cut across all classes. It was not a political or even a social category so much as an aesthetic theatrical role, though it has been argued that it was primarily a *democratic* tradition (Klingender, p. 18). Where the manners and customs of the French were largely aristocratic (even those then being displayed so prominently by the bourgeoisie), the manners of the Spanish were largely folk customs, imitated even by the royal family. These customs centered around a character type, as different as imaginable from the philosopher heroes of Paris or the genius ideals of Germany: for men, the *majo* ("macho"); and for women, the *maja.* These ideal types were colorful, arrogant, indolent, passionate, dashing, and dramatic, and were imitated by almost everyone with greater and lesser success. This was the prevailing image when young Goya grew up, and it became the model of his liberalism. Whatever else the Enlightenment was in Spain—and there was for a time an unusual degree of freedom of speech, the press, and religion—it was first of all the *majo* and the *maja,* folk models of a colorful cultural freedom. After centuries of incompetent and corrupt government, authoritarian religion, and chronic poverty, life and ideology in Spain were based on a cynical realism, coupled with mystical escapism and a necessary indifference to the stupidities of political life. In this context of daily immediacy, there was little place for the fancy philosophical principles that structured the Enlightenment in France.

While France was forging ahead into an uncertain revolutionary future, Spain took an enormous step backward into the all-too-familiar excesses and corruptions of the Old Regime. In 1788 the King died. Charles III had been a competent if uninspired ruler in easy times. During his reign the country had been allowed to enjoy at least some fruits of the Enlightenment; it had been relatively prosperous, liberal within the bounds of the conservative Church, and free from war and internal strife. Goya had enjoyed these years as a *majo,* and his paintings reflect happiness, prosperity, and peace. But the new King Charles IV and his wife Maria Luisa embodied every objection and abuse that could be leveled against the Old Regime. Charles IV was weak and stupid. His responsibility and authority in Spain extended to his routinely asking his minister how the country was going, as if he had asked in passing, "How are you?" after which he walked on to breakfast without waiting for an answer. He was also excessively fat and quite ugly, as Goya's early portraits show with unflattering clarity. Maria Luisa, who flattered herself a *maja,* ruled Charles absolutely and the country irresponsibly. She preferred her own amusements to the tedium of politics, and among her fancies was a young palace guard, Manuel Godoy. As Maria Luisa's lover and "the King's best friend," within a few years Godoy became the most powerful and corrupt official in Spain.

When the French Revolution erupted in the summer of 1789, many Spanish liberals including Goya were enthusiastic. They too had been moved by the new philosophies. But the new Bourbon rulers of Spain were

properly horrified: the liberal leaders were exiled or executed, censorship
was strongly enforced, and all Enlightenment books, including those by
Voltaire and Rousseau, were banned. Although there was in fact virtually
no possibility that the events in France could have found fertile ground in
Spain, the Spanish court took no chances. The period of prosperity and
relative liberty came to an end, and the already oppressed and impoverished Spaniards experienced the worst repression and poverty in decades.
Amid the suffering of the Spanish people, Maria Luisa still carried on with
her minister Godoy, while the aristocracy in general imitated their cynical
contempt for moral conventions—the only form the perverted Enlightenment could still take in Spain.[32]

When Goya returned from his playboy visit to Rome, he married the
sister of his influential art teacher Bayen, obtained a job in the Royal
Tapestry Factory, and in 1786 became court painter to King Charles III.
Goya's paintings of the years 1786–88 were happy anecdotes of a relatively happy period, formally still resembling Fragonard, but depicting a
less aristocratic contentment. During this period Goya, like his work, was
sentimental, romantic, and gay. His self-portrait of 1787 displays none of
the anguish that would emerge from later works. But the artist in Spain,
unlike David and the young artists in France, had no middle class as
alternative patrons to the court and aristocracy. In Spain, to live as an
artist required obedience and submission. David could flaunt republican
virtue under the noses of the aristocracy in a France that was already
bourgeois and revolutionized. Goya could at best paint likenesses of his
ugly patrons without flattery, and the extent of his protest was his brilliant
psychological portraiture—smug ministers, stupid leaders, wretched victims.[33] In France the battle was between the "virtue" of the middle class
and the "corruption" of the nobility. In Spain there was no middle class,
and the antics of the court were offensive to everyone—to the nobility and
lower classes alike. While France even during the Terror lived through a
period of unmatched enthusiasm and hope, Spain entered its bleakest days.
In Goya's portraits terrified glances and compassionate looks betray the
colorful formalities of the dazzling uniforms. For David, Enlightenment
painting was the depiction of moral ideals; for Goya, it became the portrayal of universal fears and anxieties.

Robespierre of the Brush

> Each of us is accountable to the fatherland for talents which he has
> received from nature; if the form is different, the end ought to be the
> same for all. The true patriot ought to seize with avidity every means
> of enlightening his fellow citizens, and of presenting ceaselessly to
> their eyes the sublime traits of heroism and virtue.
>
> David, *Catalogue*

David was established and famous even before his *Oath of the Horatii;* by the time his *Brutus* was first censored and then hung under protest in the Salon of 1789, he was the most powerful artist in France and therefore in Europe. Yet the hostility of the aristocratic Academy still blocked his political ambitions; he had been refused its directorship in 1787, his *Socrates* was not mentioned on the royal honor roll that year, and his *Brutus* had been censored. But the Revolution destroyed the established hierarchy in the art world just as everywhere else, and by 1790 David was the official director of the arts in France.

During the Revolution itself, David's politics and his art were one; most of his artistic projects were not paintings but plans for pageants and settings for revolutionary celebrations. Of his three major paintings during the period, *The Tennis Court Oath* (1791) was never completed, although the finished drawings of it were reproduced and widely distributed; *The Death of Lepeletier* (1793), depicting a martyr of the Revolution assassinated for his vote against the King, was destroyed; while *The Death of Marat* (1793) has been acclaimed by many as his finest painting. In this last, the same stark, heroic classicism that had glorified the *Horatii, Socrates,* and *Brutus* is applied to a contemporary subject and a friend. The task of heroically portraying the murder of a naked journalist in a bathtub by a fully clothed woman had its obvious problems. David's solution was to avoid any portrayal of the event itself, as he had avoided the battle in the *Horatii.* Instead, he painted the dead Marat alone in his tub, with a small but prominent wound in his chest. The painting has no background whatever; the body of Marat is relaxed in death against a dark shadow behind him. Marat's face is peaceful, as if he were asleep (a similar technique was used in the *Lepeletier* painting). Marat's right hand has dropped to the floor, still holding the feather pen with which he was addressing the French people, while his message is clenched in his left. This genuinely nasty journalist would now become a secular martyr whose image was remembered along with the saints of earlier history. The painting brings to fruition all the elegant simplicity and stark realism that David's classical technique provided for heroic representation.

Most of David's time was spent in politics. Pageants and celebrations were staged almost continuously in the early years of the Republic, to keep up public spirits during the confusion and dangers of the Terror. There were festivals for martyrs, victories, and funerals; festivals to forget defeats; festivals for religion and unity. There was the festival of Voltaire in July 1791, when the Enlightenment hero was given the proper burial he had been denied over a decade before; the festival for the victory at Toulon, where the young artillery officer Buonaparte had won a stunning victory over the English; and a festival of the Supreme Being, Robespierre's personal counter to the atheism that the Revolution had encouraged. All these were planned and staged by David.

David had joined the Jacobins at the outbreak of the Revolution. He did not have to fight for power, since his friends Robespierre and Marat continuously won it for him. He became president of the Jacobin Club in 1793 and president of the Convention in 1794. A tumor on his lip made him a poor speaker, but when questions concerning the arts were on the floor, he could be eloquent enough. He used his power to support young artists and attack the Academy, which all but collapsed from his efforts. In September 1790 David founded a new Commune of the Arts, the Salon was opened up to young and unknown artists, and the museums were made public and accessible. In place of the Academy, David founded a new art school where the former stress on rococo and charm was replaced by studies of the human figure and classical representation. David protected some of the old artists—notably Fragonard and Vien—but he saw to it that all artists who used art for royalist propaganda received the death penalty. In the reaction against him after the Restoration, David was accused of using his power to eliminate all competition. This is extreme; David's genius had no competition in France, and there is no evidence that he used political power to overtly enforce classicism and classical styles. Yet it is indisputable that his support for young talent was determined by his own standards, and that his art school held unrivaled power not only in France but throughout Europe. The threat of the guillotine—even if abstract and unlikely—assured that painting styles in France followed David.

Voltaire had defended the fine arts as an instrument for making people enlightened. Rousseau had attacked art along with most of modern culture, but he did love festivals and endorsed them for their moral significance. For David, art and pageantry were the sword of the Revolution, far more effective than the meek speeches of Robespierre. But in 1794 Robespierre was condemned and executed by the Assembly, putting an end to the power behind the paintings and almost to the artist as well. When David was let out of prison a few months later, he had lost some of his artistic inspiration along with his political prestige. Friedlander comments:

Political interests had given life to his art. Once he had to renounce these, his principles could only be applied to purely artistic problems. Thus, the more rigorously he held to these principles the more aesthetic and empty they became. (p. 25)

To regain his full stature in the art world, David prepared his ambitious *Reconciliation of the Sabines* for exhibit in 1799. It was again a classical allegory with a contemporary message—a message of reconciliation.[34] As a painting, the *Sabines* represented David's most complex work, in that he tried to use his compositional principles to organize a battlefield strewn with figures, children crawling on the ground, horses rearing, distant battlements, and a thousand spears. The linear drawing is more refined than before, the surface even more controlled, and the painting in general, in

David's words, "more Greek" than his earlier works, which he now dismissed. The *Sabines* is virtually two-dimensional, the figures as geometrical as an archaic Greek vase. Where the *Horatii* displayed human flesh and muscle, the *Sabines* reflects a beautiful marble surface. The *Sabines* restored David's reputation across Europe, but the purely "aesthetic" enthusiasm it inspired betrayed the loss of a vital spark since the stunning *Horatii* of fifteen years before. What David had lost was that ideological enthusiasm and sense of abstract ideals which made his paintings expressions of universal humanity rendered concrete on a single canvas. And even if his technique had improved, and he had become even truer to his self-imposed "classical" rules, he had lost the sense of ideological expression which had defined his greatest works.[35] In the catalogue of the *Sabines* David commented that "it is a great secret to touch the human heart," but the comment was far more appropriate to his earlier work. Transcendental art—the art of the universal—needs more than beauty to make it live.

In the Service of the Emperor

Napoleon knew David's work. He had visited the artist's studio to look at the *Sabines,* and he had posed for a hasty oil portrait some years before. (Later he would order, "Paint my character, not my likeness.") Napoleon knew the value of David as a public relations assistant, while David recognized in Napoleon both the heroism portrayed in his paintings and the power required to retain his artistic position. David had long planned a glorifying portrait of Napoleon crossing the Alps during the Italian campaign. Napoleon rejected David's plan to portray him in battle, preferring instead a heroic pose on horseback (though in fact he had crossed the Alps by mule). The painting is a masterpiece of both portraiture and propaganda, showing Napoleon calm and reflective on a wild white stallion, as he directs his army. In case anyone should forget the importance of the occasion, David inscribes in the rock the name "Napoleon," just above the names of "Hannibal" and "Charlemagne."

Subsequently, David was the obvious choice to portray Napoleon's coronation in a politically and aesthetically appealing light for propagation all over France. In the absence of televised reporting, David's painting *Le Sacre* was the best means available to bring the visual excitement of the pomp of Paris to the rest of the country. Yet the assignment had more than its share of problems. Obviously, the monumental canvas (thirty by nineteen feet) would take years of preparation, even with the aid of many assistants. There were political problems, such as who in the painting would be doing what and when. David originally thought to paint Napoleon placing the crown on his own head, with the Pope standing by. But Napoleon, wiser than David in such matters, insisted that "the Pope did not come all the way to Paris to do nothing." Besides, the self-crowning gesture was perhaps a bit too pretentious for propaganda purposes. Instead, it was agreed that the moment should be Napoleon's crowning Josephine, with the Pope blessing the ceremony from behind. There were personal problems also. Napoleon's mother had missed the ceremony, but had to be prominently included. His brothers were dissatisfied with their position in the ceremony, so negotiations had to be carried on concerning placement, stimulating royal egotism and anger over many months. And Josephine, who was no longer a young princess of fashion but a badly preserved middle-aged Empress, had to be painted in a flattering light. Goya certainly would have been inappropriate here, but David was an expert at flattery in portraiture: the Josephine of the coronation is a slim yet elegant young woman. Finally, there were artistic problems. Since the light in Notre Dame was wholly inadequate, the lighting of the painting had to be wholly artificial. The work contained nearly two hundred separate portraits and took three years to complete. The detail is striking, but the color just barely agreeable. Though the confusion is disturbing, David, as always, succeeds in bringing forward the major protagonists, behind whom the huge crowd is no more obstrusive than the soldiers behind the Sabine and Roman leaders, or the walls behind Socrates and the Horatii.

Napoleon was highly pleased with the painting, which was followed by a further Napoleonic ceremonial portrait of grand proportions, *The Distribution of Eagles* (1810). But David, now in his sixties, found his powers waning; the two Napoleonic paintings had been completed only with a great deal of assistance from his students. Attempting to return to his classicism, David was not able to resume the style that he had developed from the *Horatii* to the *Sabines*. Although he continued to portray classical allegories in his precise technique until his death, the colossal part of his career was over. His portraits of the 1800s are beautiful, but with nothing of the moving spirit of *Marat* or *The Death of Socrates*. His exile in 1816, although a great personal misfortune, cannot be blamed for the interruption of his artistic efforts. His last classical allegories are easily forgettable, being habits of technique devoid of spirit. Like Napoleon, David spent his last years in exile and oblivion; and like Napoleon, his former conquests would continue to influence the future without any further contributions from the conqueror.

The Disasters of War

> The idea of Truth, in painting, is, to say the least, indistinct. . . .
> [Goya] asserts that he followed only three masters: nature, Velasquez and Rembrandt. By nature, did he mean truth? He cared very little

for the other kind; we have to ransack his etchings to find a tree.
Malraux

Goya was just beginning to discover his artistic abilities. They were nourished not by hope or heroism but by bitterness and resentment. Goya's wild days had ended, but his romantic life continued in a more serious and less flamboyant form. In 1795 he became a friend of the Duke and Duchess of Alba, whose portraits he had painted. The Duke died that same year. Goya fell desperately in love with the Duchess, and they supposedly carried on a long affair until her death in 1802. Goya painted her frequently, and they were almost constant companions. Though Goya kept most of his paintings of the Duchess, the rumors of their affair inevitably spread through the gossipy court. But in that particular court, a serious and discreet affair could not possibly hold continued attention, so Goya's position was not in jeopardy. It was during this affair that he produced his two famous *Majas,* one naked and one clothed, and the rumors inevitably suggested that the Duchess had posed for them. In fact the Duchess had not, but the scandal diverted attention from what serious viewers saw as a radical experiment in painting. The maja evince a feeling of weight, volume, and matter-of-fact sexuality that would not have been possible in the flighty rococo style or linear classical techniques. The opaque backgrounds appear to surround the monumental bodies, and the majas show none of the artificiality that current painting conventions seemed to require. The subject is, first of all, a naked woman. But the rarity of a female nude in Spanish painting (although Velasquez had gotten away with an equally matter-of-fact Venus one hundred years before) made the scandal more prominent than the brilliant paintings themselves.

In the particular can be seen the universal. But where David's faces and figures achieved this through idealization, Goya used the particularity itself as a means of universal expression. It is the psychology of his subjects, not their mythology, that marks his advocacy—the intentionally unflattering details and expressions of stupidity on the faces of the royalty he painted; the personal warmth and the anxiety or hesitation in the faces of his friends; and the happy scenes of peasant weddings, parties, fights, and games in his tapestry cartoons. The human condition can be described, though unconvincingly, in the abstractions of philosophy; but in art it can be touchingly or brutally depicted in a very particular face, or in a scene of gay prosperity or unspeakable brutality. Thus Goya's portraits, in their psychology and their disturbing isolation of the individual, become the representations of humanity. There is no background to these figures, no context, no individual story. Dresses and uniforms become inessentials, as social roles and position lose their significance. One might say that Goya was the first to depict the alienation of the individual, but it would be just as true to say that he displayed the whole of humanity, the universal significance of the individual, in each of his portraits. His frustrated ideology demanded no less of him.

Oppression and corruption ruled Spain during the years following the Revolution in France. Maria Luisa and Godoy had led their country into financial collapse. Spain was losing her American colonies to native revolutionaries, and her armies and navy in Europe to a questionable alliance with France. Charles's son was challenging the reign of his mother and her treacherous lover, and gaining a good deal of popular support in doing so. Goya found himself in the middle of all of this, for he was now a full-time court painter. The King, who despite his many faults was amiable and courteous, had long chats with his painter and occasionally would play his violin for Goya. Goya, however, was going deaf. The tragedy of Goya's life during this period was not the degrading society he was forced to keep, but the disease contracted during his extramarital escapades. In 1792 Goya very nearly died of syphilis, but he survived and luckily regained his eyesight, which had been taken from him by the dreadful disease. But his hearing was gone forever, the sounds of the court and children and Charles's violin being replaced by a cage of silence. The resulting distance between the artist and his world, which increased the trauma of his near-fatal confrontation with death, snatched Goya the court painter away from his unquestioning role as court artist and submissive servant, and robbed the adventurer of his loose faith in gallantry and benign human games. In his silent anguish, the ugliness of his patrons and human society in general emerged as brute facts. The monsters of human folly and hypocrisy appeared as real to him as the noses and capes of his earlier portrait subjects.

Soon after his recovery Goya "occupied [his] imagination" and "made room for observation, which is generally lacking from commissioned art, where one cannot develop one's fancy or one's invention." But far from being "fancy" and "invention," Goya's "black paintings" are more properly called realistic than imaginary. They display a humanity unflattered by the heroic conventions of David's classicism, by the charming poses of the rococo, or by the romantic heroism that Goya himself later influenced. In *The Burial* of 1793 there is an early appearance of the devilish and demonic masks that characterize so much of Goya's later work. In a similar vein are an *Incantation by Witches* of the same year, a *Flagellation* (1794), a *Madhouse* (1800), and a series of *Bullfights*.

It is in this same period that Goya begins his famous "inventions" in etching. A series of *Caprichos* finished in 1797 is annotated by Goya; "The artist dreaming. His only purpose to banish harmful vulgar beliefs, and to perpetuate in the work of caprice the solid testimony of truth."[36] But the truth is rarely flattering, least of all to the likes of the Spanish court. In these works Goya creates, in the words of Baudelaire, "a credible form of the monstrous," a "transcendental yet natural" art of "the absurd."[37] In the *Caprichos* the King is depicted as an ass, Godoy as a monkey. The references are unmistakable, as when the ass-king is seen looking up his genealogy in a book that shows only pictures of more asses, or when the monkey paints his portrait as a lion. There are equally bestial and brutal satires on prostitution and flirtation, corruption in government, and degradation in society. The series ends with a group of distorted monks announcing, "The hour has come." Most famously, there is the *Sleep of Reason Producing Monsters*. An Enlightenment plea—or a foreboding of insanity? Here is a very different moralism and realism from what one finds in David. Here is the beginning both of Goya's bitterness and of his genius. The *Caprichos,* needless to say, were too controversial to long remain on the Spanish art market when they appeared in 1799. They were publicly available for only a few days, then withdrawn. Goya avoided serious punishment only by wisely dedicating the series to the King, and taking advantage of his already favorable position at court. That same year he was appointed First Painter to the King, and would remain court painter for many years to come, producing his most memorable portraits of the ugly King and vile Queen on horseback in 1799, and the entire royal family—with the younger children resembling Godoy—in 1800. His official painting betrayed little of the stylistic revolution that Goya was creating in his private works. Indeed, after 1792 no single line of development characterized his work: set free at last, his genius experimented and changed style and content drastically and persistently until his death at the age of eighty-three.

The corruption of the Spanish court finally exceeded itself when Maria Luisa and Godoy attempted to tamper with the rights of succession. Godoy had spent a brief term out of office, but was back again in the midst of unprecedented poverty and oppression. The court had an alliance with Napoleon which had contributed little to the welfare of the country. It had not even kept out the French troops, for they regularly crossed the country on the way to Portugal, which was still allied with England. In 1808 there were sporadic uprisings in Spain, partly in protest against the court. Charles abdicated in favor of his popular son, Ferdinand, but then changed his mind. Both Ferdinand and Charles appealed to Napoleon for support, but Napoleon, who had plans of his own, and who was rightfully disgusted with the incompetence of the Spanish royal family, supplied his own unchallenged candidate for the Spanish throne—his brother Joseph. The Spanish were not revolutionary, but they resented these "foreign interlopers." Joseph was thrown out of Madrid in a matter of days by an alliance of peasants, workers, nobility, and clergy. Goya played at neutrality, although there can be little doubt that his sympathies were with Spain. He painted portraits of the French as well as of the Spanish, and even painted the English general Wellington's portrait while he was leading the English troops in Spain. Politics had virtually nothing to do with his art.[38]

In his private works, Goya portrayed the French occupation and the war in Spain in purely human terms. Even his demons are human. The series of paintings and etchings entitled *The Disasters of War* (1810–1814)[39] depict the other side of David's heroic glorifications of Napoleon. In Goya's *Disasters* there is no heroism, only horror and mutilation, monsters and victims. They carry captions like "I saw this myself" and "For that you were born." They are brutally realistic, but at the same time fantastic. Two paintings of the period, *The Second of May* (1814) and *The Executions of the Third of May* (1814), depict a popular uprising in Madrid in 1808 against the French troops, and its bloody aftermath. The first painting is as far as possible from David's portrayals of bourgeois nobility. There are no heroes, only savagery and murder. There are no noble frozen moments, only the confusion of battle and the distortions of death. There are no lines or precise shapes; the colors are disturbing; the masses are heavy volumes—bodies that bleed and collapse. For Goya, there is nothing classical or glorious about war.[40]

The Executions of the Third of May contains only one set of rigid figures à la David: the stiff, inhuman, uniform, and faceless French soldiers who are mechanically obeying orders to murder the defenseless and probably innocent Spaniards standing before them. The Spaniards, in contrast to the soldiers, are in wild disarray, each with his own gesture of prayer, defiance, despair, or appeal. The soldiers are dark and regimented, the Spaniards are painted brightly and expressively. One of the victims wears a bright white shirt of innocence and yellow pants, the bright spot of the painting, while beside him a priest, also in white, kneels in prayer. In the foreground the body of a victim lies sprawled and distorted in blood. The sky is almost black, and even the hills in the background are tinted red.

In the etchings of the *Disasters* series, French soldiers shoot, stab, butcher, rape, and dismember Spanish country people. A Spaniard in agony, being strangled and butchered by French soldiers, asks, "Why?" Another Spaniard is forced to watch as his wife is raped ("It is bitter to be present"). A pile of mutilated bodies is presided over by a final victim, who vomits blood as he falls ("For this you were born"). For Goya the human condition is not defined by its eternal ideals but rather by its stupidities and suffering. His concept of humanity is no less universal, only less flattering, like Voltaire's many tales of brutality. He does not reject the Enlightenment, but given its hopes and expectations, he shows how far we are from its achievement, and expresses the dark hopelessness that makes sense only in the light of those hopes. Goya is just as much the moralist as David, but Goya's moralism is a blanket condemnation of humanity, a uniform disgust with the unenlightened brutality which in this instance happens to find the Spanish as its victims.

In 1814 the war came to an end and the Bourbons returned to rule

Spain. Charles, Maria Luisa, and Godoy were gone, but Ferdinand VII, once the popular favorite, now proved the worst tyrant of them all. Under his rule Spain experienced the worst oppression since the terrible days of the Spanish Inquisition. Goya was pardoned for his services to the Bonapartes and reinstated as court painter, but being already over seventy, he retired. His last public portraits were completed in 1815, but his artistic skill was still blossoming. As an artist of human despair, he would not, like David, run out of inspiration. Under the oppression of Ferdinand, Goya produced a new series of etchings, *Los Proverbios* (1815–1820), which like the earlier *Caprichos* depict the follies of humanity in demonic and bestial imagery. But *Los Proverbios* are far more fantastic than the earlier works, far more concerned with witches, fate, insanity, satanism, and demons. During the same period he painted the walls of his house with symbolic and often bloody murals. His paintings and drawings of this time are the most realistic portrayals that we have, not of the demons of the imagination so much as the very real horrors of human anguish and despair. Goya saw in himself all the monsters he depicted; the symbols of his demons were personal revelations far more than mere nightmares. *Los Proverbios* are no mere playful satires of royalty and prostitutes in the form of animals; they are violent and bloody, shocking and terrifying. The images often imitate or resemble Bosch's horrors in *The Garden of Delights*. (In fact, one might well consider Goya's antithesis to the "healthy" classicism of David a modern parallel to Bosch and his classicist contemporary, Leonardo da Vinci.) Years later Baudelaire, the champion of romanticism in Paris, would look to Goya as the pioneer who "created a credible form of the monstrous," "those bestial faces . . . impregnated with *humanity.*"

In 1820 came the long-needed revolution in Spain. A constitution, which had been drawn up during the French occupation in 1812, was forced upon the King, who fought it every inch of the way. But the Spanish, fearing that their actions might follow the bloody course of the French Revolution, kept their demands mild and their forces reasonable, so much so that a provincial counterrevolution—encouraged by the King and supported by a Holy Alliance headed by Louis XVIII of France—returned Ferdinand to absolute power in 1823. As expected, the repression was worse than ever, with mass arrests and executions (the dreaded secret police arrested even those who had *received* subversive mail), organized mob violence, and murderous secret societies. Goya, still a quiet liberal, saw many of his friends imprisoned or killed. Almost eighty, he took his leave and went into voluntary exile in Bordeaux. Spending some time in Paris at the Salon of 1824, he saw the works of Delacroix and Géricault, who had learned a great deal from him. In his last years he experimented with the new art of lithography, producing a series of *Bullfights,* elegantly simple and moving, which influenced Picasso a century later. Finally, at the end of his life he seems to have found a peace that had been denied him for the past forty years. His last painting, *The Milkmaid of Bordeaux* (1828), is devoid of blood and demons. It shows a pensive and sentimental young woman clothed in softness, with radiant cheeks and a quiet joy. When Goya died in exile that year, he evidently felt some of that joy and innocence himself.

10 The Romance of Classicism: The Phantom of the Ancients

> Would you know the sentiments, inclinations and course of life of the Greeks and Romans? Study well the temper and actions of the French and English . . . Mankind are so much the same, in all times and places, that history informs us of nothing new or strange in this particular. Its chief use is only to discover the constant and universal principles of human nature.
>
> David Hume, *Enquiry Concerning Human Understanding*

We have all experienced that humbling romantic nostalgia which accompanies a confrontation with the ancient Greeks and Romans. Whether the stimulant is a series of marble fragments in a European museum or the bumbling Hollywood extravagance of *Demetrius and the Gladiators,*[1] that sense of brutal primitiveness, rendered elegant through philosophy, art, and cosmetics, strikes a chord of dissonance and dissatisfaction with the dull sophistication of our own lives. At the turn of the nineteenth century, ancient records were scarce and information undependable, but the contrast with modern life was therefore all the more exaggerated. The ancients —more often the Romans than the Greeks—became imaginary but "truly human" ideals, presented in theater, art, and philosophy clothed in modern fancy, much as Renaissance artists once dressed Hercules and Venus in Florentine costumes. The neoclassicists of 1800 celebrated the differences, but they presupposed a mutual identity. At the root of the classical revival was the transcendental pretense projected across the whole of history; these ancient peoples were the same as we, only more natural, more harmonious—somehow *better* at being human.

The romance varied, to be sure, with the needs and conceptions of particular people at particular times. In France, the ancient Romans represented courage, patriotism, and the civil virtues; in Germany, the archaic Greeks were exemplary of "nature," the real historical equivalent of Rousseau's imaginary state of nature. But just as Rousseau had begun his historical fantasy by dispensing with the facts, so the scholarly reconstructions of neoclassicism—like the commercial imaginations of Los Angeles producers—were far more fantasy than fact. In Germany the two mythologies—the classical and the Rousseauan—served essentially the same functions. Like the Enlightenment, classicism involved a rejection of the habits and traditions of Christian society in the name of the "eternal ideals" of the pagans.[2] The lack of knowledge was a great convenience; there was little to interfere with self-serving modern interpretations. Every classical revival was a re-creation, not of ancient life, but of the projected images of one's own ideals and fantasies.

The classicism that ruled Germany at the turn of the nineteenth century began as an imitation of the French classicism of the century before. In both cases classical structures were the timid expression of the literary bourgeoisie attempting to gain a sense of its own identity. In France, this identity was primarily a class identity; in Germany, it was as much a national identity. But the very idea of classical imitation—particularly as copied from French models—reveals the paradoxical nature and thus the inevitable failure of German classicism to achieve its purpose. It is a movement that, seeking autonomy and self-realization, proceeds by copying others. It is motivated by the German resentment of and reaction against French classicism and its hold over German culture (Frederick the Great spoke and wrote chiefly in French), yet at first it imitates the French. Even after Lessing's courageous break with the French theater, the concept of imitation of one's superiors ruled German culture. Of course the "superiors" turned out to be largely a product of the German imagination. Nevertheless, classicism in Germany was above all an *imitative* movement, a confused yet fantastic expression of both adolescent impotence and the demand for self-recognition. However, underlying its sometimes grotesque and schizophrenic fantasies, classicism is the necessary expression of a culture at a particular stage of growth. Once this adolescent dialectic of inferiority and autonomy is understood, these fantasies make perfectly good sense.[3]

From our point of view, perhaps no single philosophical naiveté is more striking in the Enlightenment and its immediate aftermath than the total lack of time sense—that sense of historical change and cultural difference which defines our present attitudes toward our world neighbors, other cultures, and even our own past. Voltaire virtually invented history, while Rousseau used it only to his own advantage. Inherent in both is the presupposition of the universality of human nature, the durability of a single "humanity" which might progress or corrupt itself, but which nevertheless remains the same. Kant could pretentiously write his philosophy "for all rational beings," because he never suspected that human consciousness might be essentially different from one culture or age to another. Both David and Goethe were classicists—at least at one point in their long careers—but neither really believed that the lives of ancient Greece and Rome could be resurrected in the modern age. In fact, neither David nor

Goya was overly concerned with the historical facts upon which their bold imagery and idealism were based. The Rome of David and the Greece of Goethe never existed. Yet it was sufficient for David and for his sponsor Napoleon that the stories and style based on ancient Rome had their desired emotional impact in Paris.

Had David looked beyond the quiet white ruins of Rome, however, to the Italians themselves, or to the coarse, neurotically driven Buonapartes, he might have suspected that the ancient Romans were anything but the statuesque heroes, colorless and stark, that he portrayed in his paintings. Had Goethe taken advantage of any of his several opportunities to travel to Greece, he might have seen that the jagged landscape and its monuments were evidence of civilizations in constant struggle against nature, against foreign enemies, and among themselves.[4] The worlds of David's Brutus and Goethe's Iphigenia were no more real than Rousseau's state of nature. Where truth is not at stake, the difference between analogy and mythology can be conveniently ignored. For the classicists of the early nineteenth century ancient Greece and Rome, and modern Germany and France, might all have been transtemporal identities. It is not surprising, therefore, that one fashion of dress in postrevolutionary Paris—weather permitting—was the Roman toga.

The Neoclassical Renaissance

Although it is typically treated as a unified conception, "classicism" embodies three very different themes, unified in general, but carved up and distorted during the battles of style that accompany decadent classicism. First, classicism is an appeal to an idealized ancient people, their lives, culture, artistic style, politics, and humanism. Second, it represents renewed emphasis upon, and a revitalized conception of, artistic *form,* usually rather narrowly defined from among the multitude of ancient styles in order to support a current prejudice. (Thus David defined classical style in terms of ancient relief sculpture, and Goethe redefined classical literature in terms of lyric meters.) Third, "classicism" becomes a term of praise used to exalt an arbitrarily chosen style as uniquely "correct." These three meanings often overlap and reinforce each other, but "classicism" sometimes tends to become nothing more than a prestigious name for "official" art, a verbal tool of artistic domination or stylistic one-upmanship.

Classicism is, in its superficial appearance, a form of romantic nostalgia, a longing for "better" days past. But this nostalgia may mask more revolutionary sympathies—a rejection of present realities in order to replace them. In the hands of Charlemagne, Louis XIV, and Napoleon, classicism was a political tool; in the minds of Goethe and Hölderlin, it became an instrument for wrenching oneself out of the tedious present. For classicism is not only a matter of historical appeal—the prestigious use of classical themes in Voltaire's plays, Goethe's poems, or David's paintings. It also provides the rigid consolidation, the structured formalism necessary to every radical movement. Classicism is the attempt to give theoretical and emotional solidarity to what is confused and in flux—to rationalize and simplify the complex demands of a world in change. David used the classics to inspire and solidify the Revolution. Napoleon used them to impress the populace and solidify his early Empire. Goethe used the classics to calm his wild and passionate temperament, his "chaotic daemon" within. So classicism is far more than it appears to be: it can be the expression of a radical will, the stern imposition of form and simplicity; but as an attempt to transform what is confused and complex, it uses its mythological appeal to the ancients only as a tool. The classicism of modern times, like the sublime forms of the ancient Greeks and Romans, is an attempt to live in the face of chaos.[5]

Classicism, like all stages of human development, has its internal periods of growth and decline, each with a cycle of a century or so. A classical revival begins in obedient service to power. Its first manifestations are often literary—a brilliant form of entertainment using classical themes as a subtle vehicle of implicit protest. Its simple idealism is an ideological alternative to the tired and chaotic values of the ruling class. Whether in Italy during the Renaissance, in France from the period of Louis XIV to the Revolution, or in Germany through the long and varied "age of Goethe," classicism begins with brilliant but less than wholly courageous or revolutionary intellectuals, poets, and artists who "entertain" and serve their princely hosts. As the struggling class gains power, the aspirations become demands and the struggle rises to revolution. In Italy the power of the Pope prevented this victorious phase of classicism from emerging: having spent itself in the brilliance of Leonardo, Michelangelo, and Raphael, classicism—after a brief prolongation in Venice—passed immediately into its third stage of decadence, of purely academic "mannerism" and its equally apolitical antagonists.

In France, however, the growth pattern ran its full course, with classicism dominant from the reign of the Sun King until the middle of the nineteenth century. As in Italy, it began as an intellectual and literary revival—the initial movements of the aspiring bourgeoisie. Still on the defensive, it controlled its moral messages through rigid conventions and often excessive sophistication. Then the classical drama of Corneille and Racine and the moral wit of Molière evolved into the Enlightenment of Voltaire, the difference between them being largely one of degree, Voltaire's universalist and rationalist claims having remained implicit in his predecessors. With the Enlightenment, classicism became explicitly contemporary, and also overtly undistinguished. After Voltaire there was no comparable literary genius in the classical tradition, and after Poussin

(1594–1665), who spent most of his career in Rome, there was no noteworthy classical artist until David, who quickly eclipsed his notably forgettable teacher Joseph-Marie Vien. With David, classicism became an open call first to revolt, then to courage and consolidation, and finally to unity and the glorification of the new Emperor. But David's later work—perhaps even his *Sabines* and celebrations, and certainly his classical work in exile—already displayed the symptoms of decadent classicism: a tight formal style uninspired by the moral and revolutionary fervor that gave life to the *Horatii* and nobility to *Marat;* an empty appeal to classical themes that implies mere disinterest in contemporary life. Decadence can survive far longer than a period of genius, even though it may spawn new geniuses. It surely did so in the painting of Ingres, David's most distinguished pupil, but at the cost of stifling hundreds of other talented and nonclassically inclined young artists, while encouraging and rewarding countless others with little talent but "correct" style.

While French classicism flourished through the Enlightenment of Voltaire and served as the vehicle for political revolution, German classicism was a variation on the Enlightenment of Rousseau and served as a medium for personal self-realization. Thus while David used the classics in the defense of moral rectitude and self-sacrifice, Goethe used the classics as an excuse for promiscuity and self-indulgence. As a source of discipline and authority, German classicism reacted against and corrected the romantic inspirationism of the Storm and Stress movement. In another sense, however, classicism and romanticism were two different forms of otherworldly longing and self-indulgent individualism. It is not surprising, therefore, that the Storm and Stress leaders—notably Goethe and Schiller—would also be the dominant figures of German classicism. (In France, on the other hand, classicism and romanticism were warring camps: Ingres and Delacroix would not speak to each other for decades.) German classicism began with provincial literary ambitions, not political but personal struggles, and won a victory of style but no power. As a result, where French classicism developed into something more, German classicism degenerated into something less. For while the classics in France gave the bourgeoisie in general a new handle on reality, the classics in Germany too easily provided fantasy and escape for a few intellectuals, a new mysticism to replace that which the Reformation had stolen from them. In France, the lives of the ancients were inspiration for the present; in Germany, the mythology of the ancient world was an escape from the gloom and vulgarity of the Teutonic North, a reaching after the sun of Homer (just as Goethe dragged Roman antiques back to Weimar and cluttered his house with them). It was one further attempt to reach an "absolute" of personal freedom in an oppressive society where relative freedoms were severely restricted (an attempt recently repeated in the courageous efforts of Solzhenitsyn in Russia). But where freedom cannot be political and universal, it tends to be reconceived as personal and exceptional, so in Germany the moral truths of France were reduced to a cult of aesthetic sensibility: not moral idealism and heroic action, but "noble simplicity and quiet grandeur."

Classicism in France: Before the Enlightenment

As an instrument of radicalism, giving form and support to revolutionary aspirations, classicism was an essential ingredient in the art of the rising bourgeois artisans and intellectuals in the service of Louis XIV. The Enlightenment was not yet ready: classicism prepared the way. The court of the Sun King was the stage for bourgeois classical drama, but uniquely French, even if Roman and Greek in costume and situation. (This same French style was popular with the German princes, so that Lessing's attempt to stage uniquely German bourgeois theater was initially a reaction against classicism as well.)[6] The plays of the classical tragedians Corneille (1606–1684) and Racine (1639–1699) were short on action but long on reflection, dialogue, and moral polemics. Their setting was ancient, but the situation contemporary. In Corneille, in particular, the classical themes were excuses for political sermons, disguised as entertainment to escape the attention of the censors (which sometimes they did not). They were tragedies, not in the Shakespearean style, where the drama ends with most of the characters dead or blinded, but in the sense that, as in Goethe's *Faust*, they revolve around existential conflict and insoluble moral dilemmas. There is little plot, little adventure, little interest in resolution for its own sake. Both Corneille and Racine, whose themes often found their way onto David's canvases, offered the court entertainment only as an invitation to a moral lesson. If some of these plays now seem formal and "cold" to us, it is only because they have lost their historical moment and their morally sensitive audience.

One might at first think that this emphasis on seriousness and morality at the expense of entertainment and wit broke down in the plays of Racine's contemporary Molière (1622–1673). His comedies teach us anything but admiration for their heroes and appear anything but serious. Molière even insisted that "enjoyment is more important than correctness." His protagonists, from his early *School for Wives* to *Tartuffe* and Alceste in *The Misanthrope,* were knaves and fools. The plot was often not only unprofound but downright silly. If in Racine all the heroes emerged as victims, in Molière they emerged as buffoons, or at least made buffoons of others. Yet Molière, like Racine, was a classical moralist, but with an inverted approach. Corneille gave us heroes to admire; Racine attempted to move us; Molière gave us fools to laugh at. Molière's plays also centered upon a single conflict or crisis, always of universal stature—piousness vs. hypocrisy, skepticism vs. faith, sincerity vs. cleverness, foolishness vs. wisdom, reason vs. nature. He too was interested in moral conflict and the foibles of the age. His plays were often banned for moral messages that did not escape the authorities of the period. The foolishness he portrayed was often more pointed than the explicit heroism of the classical French tragedies; in his words, "The ridiculous is the outward and visible form that nature's providence has fixed to all that is contrary to reason, in order to draw our attention to it and make us avoid it." Molière, like the tragedians, was a devotee of the new reason, the philosophy of Descartes, and the search for a unified personality that is free within the limitations of reason and nature.[7]

Classicism in Germany: Faust and Fantasy

Classicism in France was absorbed by the Enlightenment, which enlarged upon its conceptions and turned its ideals into demands. It was in Germany (and to a lesser extent in Italy) that the classical cycle would have its next performance. But German classicism—both an outgrowth and a forerunner of romanticism—would be reactionary instead of revolutionary, backward- instead of forward-looking; an impotent fantasy without a social or cultural reality to give it a basis in everyday life. From limited desire and striving, it grew into illusory conquest that grasped at phantoms and then declined into decadence. Such is the theme of *Faust:* the growth of the human imagination without apparent logic in the world of everyday appearance. Accordingly, perhaps the most suitable frame of reference for German classicism—itself a romantic fantasy from the first —is the most brilliant fantasy it produced: the classical Walpurgis Night of Part II of Goethe's *Faust.* While one cannot deny the very real human needs that gave rise to German classicism, neither can one deny the very obvious absurdities that populate the classical German spirit in its social isolation. Consequently, it is permissible to present its history in something less than serious form—as the phantasmagoria that it surely was.

Goethe's brilliant fantasy fills over three thousand lines of verse in two acts of *Faust II,* though many of these lines, in the words of one of his translators, are "untempting" to say the least.[8] The German classical fantasy lasts nearly a hundred years and is shared by two centuries, but most of its literature is surely "untempting." Goethe's Classical Walpurgis Night begins with a bizarre trio of tourists: Faust, who still longs after Gretchen; Mephistopheles, who agrees to leave his Northern haunts only with the promise of lusty new witches; and the Homunculus, an asexual creation of the pedant Wagner that is pure intellect in a bottle—the incomplete intelligence that characterizes so much scholarship then as now. To apply this fantasy to the three classical themes already mentioned, one might associate the perverse and lusty motivation for the ancients with Mephistopheles; the abstract and so easily lifeless classical formalism with Homunculus; and the idealistic aspirations for self-realization and inner harmony with Faust.

Moreover, one can easily find historical characters to play these roles. German classicism begins with the devilish figure of Johann Winckelmann (1717–1768), a disagreeable neurotic who was resentful of his poverty-stricken childhood and lustful to excess.[9] Winckelmann had all the seductive cleverness of Mephisto, but could not tie his fanciful conceptions to the chaotic realities of his own life. In the role of Homunculus one might cast the classical poet Johann Christoph Gottsched (1700–1766), who brought French classicism into Germany without salvaging even a spark of its original wit and vitality.[10] Or perhaps, less charitably, one could choose Lessing, who rejected this same French classicism for an intellectually pure classicism of his own.[11] In the title role stands Goethe himself. Whatever his celebration of pagan sexuality and however impressive his skill with classical forms, Goethe adopted classicism first and foremost as a means of self-realization, a vehicle for his struggle toward perfection. He used classical forms as his means of controlling his chaotic "daemon," but always to the advantage of his own genius. Like other German authors who followed him (for example, the Hess of *Steppenwolf*), Goethe was terrified of his sometimes cruel and extravagant fantasies, which in any case were expressed almost exclusively in his writing. His demon, one can surmise, was little more than a combination of his restless energy and his residual Rousseauan sentimentality, one so embarrassingly obvious in *Werther*. But by his own account, it was his mastery of form that allowed him to move past that brazenly confessional stage.

In Goethe's *Faust,* Mephistopheles, Faust, and Homunculus fly to the classical orgy of the second Walpurgis Night. In real life Winckelmann fled his unhappy present for a glorious past of "noble simplicity and quiet grandeur," first in books and then on foot to Rome. Just as Mephistopheles lusts after the most bizarre of "Southern shapes" and makes an absolute fool of himself with the nymphs, so Goethe becomes a pagan libertine and fornicates his way across Italy. Lastly, Homunculus searches for a body and a full life, then perishes, dashing himself against Galatea's chariot, while Winckelmann is brutally murdered in Trieste, upon returning from an abortive attempt to reach Greece. As in Goethe's dramatic poem, it becomes clear that these characters share a common role, as in the classical movement as a whole. Mephistopheles's lust, Homunculus's search for a full life, Faust's search for Helen—all these are ultimately one and the same, and the three characters are likewise in fact but one. So too Goethe picks up the threads of the German classical movement and integrates them wholly into his own personality.

It is clear that Mephistopheles, the devilish disharmony of the North, is out of place in the classical South; Homunculus says to him, "Only Romantic ghosts are known to you/A genuine phantom must be classic too," and also, "In gloom alone are you at home." Goethe too could not have been wholly at home in Rome, whatever his fantasies. Although the classical Greece of this second Walpurgis Night has none of the obscenity of the Northern witches' sabbath of Part I, neither is this Winckelmann's Greece of "noble simplicity and quiet grandeur." Rather it is a nightmare of sphinxes, griffins, centaurs, sirens, sylphs, dragons, and pre-Socratic philosophers (not wholly unlike the pedants of the North). Goethe, while retaining his sense of the classical ideal, can no longer pretend that the Greece of the ancients was all white marble and pure form. By 1824 he knows how much fantasy has been inextricably woven into so-called historical truth, how a Dionysian wildness was as much a part of Greek life as the noble Apollonian purity of ideals.

German classicism revolves almost wholly around Goethe. He is as essential to its inspiration and character as Faust and his demon are to *Faust*. Goethe's classicism is not a method or a set of ideals, however canonized his style might become, but a quest, a search for ideal beauty, for the reality of Schiller's cliché of the "beautiful soul." In *Faust* that "beautiful soul" is Helen. It is important that beauty is a woman, for the ideal that Goethe pursues throughout his long search for self-realization is strictly feminine. (Perhaps it is revealingly Freudian—an obvious falsification of male-dominated Greek warrior-society, and a marked departure from the traditionally male-focused mythology of Germany.) Thus Iphigenia leads Orestes, Gretchen attracts the early Faust, Dorothea guides the German bourgeois Hermann, and the Eternal Feminine saves Faust at the end of the play. The quest for Helen, for ideal beauty, is the goal of the eternal striving that is *Faust*'s central theme. But Goethe and his Faust find that ideal beauty, though perhaps Greek in origin, is not Greek in essence. It can be found anywhere, ultimately only on one's native ground. And Helen turns out to be much less—or rather much more—than an abstract ideal.

The first mention of Helen in *Faust I* casts her as just such an abstract ideal, a projection of the imagination (as Schiller had argued against Goethe). Mephistopheles, who has just watched Faust swallow the witch's aphrodisiac, advises him:

> Thou'lt find, this drink thy blood compelling,
> Each woman beautiful as Helen.[12]

Her next appearance is in the magic theater at the beginning of Part II. There she appears as a phantom, opposite an equally unreal Paris (both conjured up by Faust with the help of Mephistopheles and the Mothers—another feminine image). In the drafty gloom of the medieval castle, Helen appears as the seductive "shape of shapes," but still idealized, un-

real, and consequently unattainable. Goethe has his fun formulating the
petty jealousies of the audience, the men finding Paris foppish while the
ladies judge Helen's "head too small, feet too small, feet too big." The
Germans do not recognize ideal beauty even when it stands in front of
them. Even lustful Mephistopheles glibly dismisses her:

> *My* sleep she would not waste.
> She's pretty but she's not my taste.

Classical ideals and Northern vulgarity cannot be reconciled, but Faust
(Goethe) is affected dramatically. With the dramatic re-enactment of the
rape of Helen by Paris, Faust goes berserk, crying out, "Am I for nothing
here?" When he grabs at her ghostly body, an explosion renders him
unconscious, while Mephistopheles observes, "Whom Helena shall para-
lyze/Not soon his reason will recover." The message is evident: ideal
beauty cannot be vulgarly grabbed in a single moment of passionate inspiration; it must be struggled after and seduced slowly and discreetly.

When Helen finally appears in full flesh and with a voice in Act III, she
is no longer an abstract or phantomlike ideal. She is very much a woman,
tangible and sensuous, but suffering her own crisis of identity, being caught
between her abstract legend and her own sense of herself:

> I much admired and much reviled,
> Was I all that?—And am I now?

Faust wins her love—albeit through a curious process of teaching her how
to rhyme her speech: far more a vehicle for Goethe to display his command of Greek and Northern verse than an effective mode of seduction.
Or perhaps one should say that he wins her more or less, since Helen
clearly yields herself to Faust with the same casual indifference with which
she has given herself to any number of lusty suitors. The splendor of
Greece is available for condescending rape by any of us, but it cannot be
won. While Faust seduces Helen, Mephistopheles romps in disguise as an
ugly hag, Northern bad taste feasting on the bones of the classics.

The union of Faust and Helen produces progeny, the child Euphorion
or energy, "the spirit of modern poetry." It is generally agreed that
Euphorion represents romanticism and in particular Lord Byron, whom
Goethe considered a sort of personal hero. But Euphorion bears a far
more striking resemblance to one of the German classical poets, Friedrich
Hölderlin, the tragic offspring of medieval Germany and ancient Greece,
Storm and Stress and Goethe's classicism. Euphorion grows to adolescence
in less than a hundred lines and will not obey the classical warning against
"unrestricted flight," meaning freedom apart from limitation, imagination
without the categories of reality (like Kant's dove, which finds the light
atmosphere easier flying and imagines that it would be easier still with no
atmosphere at all). Euphorion, who is far more than phonetically akin to

Hölderlin's hero Hyperion, falls dead at the feet of his parents, while a classical Greek chorus cries, "Icarus! Icarus!" His body vanishes at once, leaving his cloak and lyre behind—the dress, but not the genius, for several generations of "classical" poets. Hölderlin, however, was not so fortunate: his nearly psychotic passion for times past destroyed his mind years before his body was abandoned. He was the last of the great German classicists.

After Euphorion's death Helen disappears as well, having embraced Faust once more:

> Also in me, alas! an old word proves its truth
> That bliss and Beauty never enduringly unite.
> Torn is the link of Life, no less than that of Love;
> So, both lamenting, painfully I say: farewell!

Helen also leaves her garment behind. (As in David's *Sabines,* the ancients do nothing of importance with their clothes on.) The garment acts as a magic carpet to transport Faust back to his own times and into the following act. With Helen's disappearance, the classical fantasy degenerates into an orgy, just as German poetry braced itself for years of mediocrity and undisciplined romantic lust. By 1840 Heinrich Heine had ridiculed the decadent classicism out of fashion. Yet its influence remained and a half century later Friedrich Nietzsche was still attempting to correct the false German images of the classical romance.[13]

Noble Simplicity and Quiet Grandeur?!

> There is but one way for the moderns to become great . . . by imitating the ancients.
>
> Winckelmann

It was Johann Winckelmann who formulated the oft-quoted image of the "noble simplicity and quiet grandeur" of the ancient Greeks. The new excavations at Pompeii and Herculaneum made his research possible, but his work was tied less to such evidence than to the need he felt—and so many Germans with him—for an ideal that would carry him beyond the gloom of the North and the confused and oppressed spirit of bourgeois Germany. Like Rousseau, Winckelmann satisfied that need by inventing the historical nobility of a simple past:

It is not only nature which the votaries of the Greeks find in their works, but still more something superior to nature: ideal beauty.[14]

With an almost mystical rapture, and as escape from an unhappy life of his own, Winckelmann created the dream for two generations. He watched his ideal slip into the past "like the image of a lover's face disappearing in the sails of a departing ship." In expressing his fantasy, Winckelmann virtually invented the discipline of art history—the attempt to see art as an expression of a historical people. More important still, he provided the magical image of Helen that would define German cultural adolescence and—two hundred years late—the German literary Renaissance.

Perhaps there is no better example of the victory of Winckelmann's fantasy over his scholarship than one of his own favorite examples of classical sculpture—one which would be taken by scholars as the paradigm of Greek art for decades following. This is the Laocoön, a graceful yet grotesque rendering of the violent death of a Trojan priest who dared threaten the Trojan horse plot with exposure, thus angering Poseidon, who sent a huge sea serpent to destroy the priest and his two sons. It is this piece, together with the smirkingly lascivious banality of the equally celebrated Apollo Belvedere, that inspired Winckelmann's worshipful interpretation of "noble simplicity and quiet grandeur." It is worth noting that the Laocoön was not in fact a product of the Greece that Winckelmann admired—the ancient Arcady preceding the Golden Age—but a very late and decadent Hellenistic work, produced when the Greeks, sundered into warring factions, were anything but a noble, simple, quiet people. It is also worth noting that Winckelmann did not see the original work, but inaccurate plaster copies. Yet these distortions mattered little to a scholar who based his theories of Greece on excavations of the less ancient Roman civilization, and who refused ever to visit the modern site of his ancient heroes.

Most important, however, is the piece itself, which displays anything but the qualities attributed to it by Winckelmann and later German admirers—nobility and grandeur, much less calm and simplicity. The sculpture depicts a nightmarish fable, based on the arbitrary injustice of a peevish and cruel deity. The human figures, trapped in the serpent's convolutions, are contorted in ignoble pain and terror. Although the work has a certain grace and balance (a serpent almost necessarily provides a certain graceful curvature), "simplicity" and "grandeur" hardly characterize it. Yet Winckelmann sees in it

an expression of so great a soul . . . beyond the force of mere nature . . . the depths of the sea are always calm, however wild and stormy the surface; and in the same way the expression in Greek figures reveals greatness and composure of soul in the throes of whatever passions.[15]

Hallucination? A fantasy-induced trance of preordained interpretation? The Laocoön is an extravagant baroque depiction of human suffering and horror, in which not a trace of composure can be found. Given such an example, one cannot doubt that the classical ideals "discovered" by the Germans were simply the projection of their own needs and demands.

Like so many unhappy souls of genius, Winckelmann complained bitterly that he had been born at the "wrong" time. In fact, he was born at precisely the right time, when the Faustian and Rousseauan nostalgia, and the pain of incompleteness of the Northern intellect, combined with the Northern devil to yearn for Winckelmann's Greece.

No one was more impressed by the image of "noble simplicity and quiet grandeur" than Goethe. Classicism provided the mythology of his youth, and when he arrived at Rome in 1786, he announced his "second birth." Like all Goethe's various phases, classicism provided him with a means of self-realization. Lessing had employed Winckelmann's classicism as a foil against the foreign and aristocratic domination of German culture; Goethe used this same classicism as a double-edged sword against bourgeois mediocrity and romantic overreactions to that mediocrity. Classical formalism allowed him the "freedom within limitation" that, in his literature and in his life, corrected the undisciplined sentimentality that had spawned *Werther* and his earlier unhappiness. Classicism, in other words, was a tool for self-discipline. Paradoxically, the same tool allowed Goethe the freedom of both his pagan promiscuity and the ever expanding resources of his imagination. Among the continuing themes of Goethe's lifelong "great confession" was his fear of himself, of his passions, his fantasies, his genius. His Tasso fears that his success and death must coincide; Faust will be damned wholly on the basis of his satisfaction with the moment. Goethe's classicism, like his "good citizenship" and services to the Duke, is an attempt to suppress Euphorion's unrestricted flight.

Goethe's classicism, like that of his predecessors, had very little to do with the realities of ancient Greece. Like Winckelmann, he never visited the country, and often his literary classicism seemed little more than imitation of ancient poetic meters. From his early Storm and Stress *Prometheus* and his later *Iphigenia* ("With my soul longing for the land of the Greeks") to his Italian poetry, Goethe's classical imagery and moralism is German Faustianism through and through. In every case, his classicism is simply an excuse for breaking through contemporary practices in an attempt to find both himself and the unique soul of German genius. Not only his *Iphigenia* but his own promiscuity was "very Christian" and "damnably humane." The Italians provided him with excuses for both self-control and the lack of it that he could not find in his "good citizen role" in Weimar. So too with the German spirit in general: classicism provided the projected image of its own fantasies that it needed, in order to gain self-confidence for further growth.[16]

It is symptomatic that Goethe's most memorable classical drama is set in modern Germany, its classicism virtually restricted to verse structure alone. *Hermann and Dorothea* (1797) is a reactionary Homeric epic lacking both Helen and Achilles. The war is the French Revolution, which is always kept at a safe distance offstage and plays no role whatever in the plot. The protagonists are Hermann, the dull son of a bourgeois farmer whose virtues are limited to cleanliness, modesty, and obedience; and Dorothea, a German refugee from the French invasions whose resemblance to Helen is limited to her Greek name. In place of Homer's heroic archetype, Goethe substitutes the eternal bourgeois; the classical harmony achieved in the marriage of the heroes is the victory of dullness. In achieving his ambition to become the latest "Homerid," Goethe reduced classicism to an empty bourgeois formula.

As Goethe's classical dramas become increasingly bourgeois and Teutonic, his younger colleague Hölderlin pursued his classical fantasies to disastrous lengths. Like Winckelmann, and unlike the always prudent Goethe (though he did say, "What time is this, that we envy the dead?"), Hölderlin thought that he had been born at the "wrong" time.

> Like the flat-footed goose, I am standing in a modern puddle,
> Impatiently flapping my wings towards the sky of ancient Greece.[17]

Where Goethe saw himself as a German seeking Greek ideals, Hölderlin viewed himself as a Greek (his hero Hyperion is a modern Greek) born in the wrong place and "searching for his world." He often spoke of himself as "one of the dead," and pursued his vanishing fantasy to the point of self-destruction: "I loved my heroes as a moth loves the light. I sought their dangerous proximity, and fled it and sought it again. . . . I became what I saw, and what I saw was God-like." By 1804 Hölderlin was hopelessly insane.

In 1805 Goethe delivered a eulogy on Winckelmann, praising the scholar for introducing the ancients to Germany. But already Goethe had moved beyond classicism. It had served his needs for a while, but now his poetic self-confidence had reached the point where it could shun external ideals. Schiller had just died, the Napoleonic Wars were tearing Germany apart, Goethe was old already. Now, relying upon the discipline and self-confidence that they had gained from classicism, Goethe and Germany alike could cut themselves free of foreign images and allow imagination and self-sustained ideals to elaborate themselves. For Goethe, the product of his newfound autonomy was the first part of *Faust*. For Germany, the self-confidence gave rise to nationalism and a sense of personal worth that would soon allow her to replace France as the center of European culture.

11 The Universal in Action: G. W. F. Hegel

Nature does nothing in vain. . . . with this I even believe I come close to Hegel's philosophy which, incidentally, attracts and repels me; may the genius be gracious unto all of us!

Goethe, *Conversations*

In his last book, written during the reactionary years following the fall of Napoleon, the great Professor Hegel compared his philosophy to the retrospective wisdom of Minerva's bird: "When philosophy paints its grey on grey, then it has a shape of life grown old. By philosophy's grey on grey it cannot be rejuvenated but only understood. The owl of Minerva spreads its wings only with the falling of dusk."[1] Well established as the official philosopher of Berlin, Hegel viewed philosophy conservatively, as understanding the present in terms of the past. He could contemplate the dangerous years of Napoleonic invasion and the German Wars of Liberation from the quiet of the Reaction and the security of his own success. But this popular image of Hegel, the crusty old professor, does not fit the dynamic, forward-looking enthusiast of 1800, who avidly applauded the approach of Napoleon as the "World Spirit on horseback," who brutally criticized all things German, Christian, petty bourgeois, and established, and like his good friend Hölderlin longed for other times and the sunny, erotic, pagan rites of the ancient Greeks. If Minerva and the owl of wisdom serve as a self-image for the established Professor Hegel, it is rather Apollo, connoting a poetry of hope and the illumination of the sun, who should represent the young Hegel. Anxious and excited, at the turn of the century his eyes and thoughts looked forward, and he saw understanding as a way of coping with the most radical changes in the history of the world. Hegel's universal humanity was a universal *in action,* a process of becoming. His *Phenomenology of Spirit,* completed—according to popular academic folklore—on the very eve of Napoleon's crushing victory at Jena (October 13, 1806), became a rejuvenating catalyst for synthesis:

. . . our epoch is a birth time, a period of transition. The spirit of man has broken with the old order of things, and with the old ways of thinking. . . . The spirit of the times, growing slowly and quietly ripe for the new form it is to assume, disintegrates one piece after another of the structure of the previous world. That it is tottering to its fall is now indicated only by symptoms here and there . . . but something else is approaching. This gradual crumbling to pieces will be interrupted by the sunrise, which in a flash and at a single stroke, brings to view the form and structure of the new world.[2]

The key to Hegel's philosophy—both the *Phenomenology* and his later work—is the organic image of *fusion,* of synthetic unity, of biological growth and development:

The bud disappears when the blossom breaks through, and we might say that the former is refuted by the latter; in the same way when the fruit comes, the blossom may be explained to be a false form of the plant's existence, for the fruit appears as its true nature in place of the blossom. (*Phenomenology*, p. 68)

This image, of course, he inherited directly from Goethe, and philosophically from Aristotle and Kant. Hegel's important addition to these earlier authors, however, was his acute sense of history, his sense of the development of universal humanity as what he calls World Spirit, growing through time. The familiar term *Zeitgeist* is most often used with reference to Hegel. Beneath the metaphysical complexities and the technicalities of his much-praised and much-damned system, Hegel's philosophy was first and foremost the bourgeois search for human *identity.* The gigantic forces reshaping the world in 1800 were viewed by Hegel with the new sense of history that had just been "discovered" in Germany, and in terms of the new ideals of "humanity" inherited from the French Enlightenment classicism and Kant. How to relate to the French Revolution and its ideals? How to relate to Napoleon and to Germany? How to relate to the new internationalism, to religion? How to recapture the long-lost life of the Greeks? How to realize and become part of the "perfection of humanity" that had become the watchword of the epoch?

The Concept of Spirit (Geist)

The significance of that "absolute" commandment, *Know thyself*— whether we look at it in itself or under the historical circumstances of its first utterance—is not to promote mere self-knowledge in respect of the *particular* capacities, character, propensities and foibles of the single self. The knowledge it commands means that of man's genuine reality—of what is essentially and ultimately true and real—of spirit as the true and essential being.

Hegel, *Encyclopedia of the Philosophical Sciences*[3]

The key word in Hegel's philosophy is *Geist,* or "Spirit."[4] It is a term that is familiar to us in a quasi-religious sense (as in "spiritual matters"), but the meaning here is more general, and secular as well, as in "the spirit of '76" or "team spirit." "Spirit" is more than a matter of agreement or a mere abstraction (like "the average American family"). It is essentially a *shared* sense of feelings and beliefs, a self-conscious awareness of mutuality and belonging. "Team spirit," to use the most trivial example, does not mean just that each member of the team wants to win; it means that they see their identities as intertwined and interdependent, that they share a sense of shared sense. The most important political antecedent of Hegel's Spirit is Rousseau's General Will; the most obvious religious antecedent, the Christian "Holy Spirit" and idea of "Communion." Morally, Hegel's spirit is the ideological heir of Voltaire's and Kant's concepts of "humanity." Evident in all these notions is the ideal of human unification, and of mutual respect not just between individuals, but between persons *by virtue* of their all being part of one great Being. In other words, *Geist* is Hegel's attempt to take the French slogan "brotherhood" seriously as shared identity, by the very fact of our mutual *human* origins.

This idea has become so familiar to us that we not only take it for granted but now react against it, accentuating individual differences as if to oppose this Enlightenment ideal of humanity with the other Enlightenment ideal of individuality. But what seems staid and even reactionary now was both radical and inventive in the early nineteenth century. We today may unceremoniously lump wealthy businessmen, peasants, talented artists, dictators, and street urchins all together in a single abstract notion of "humanity" and refer to their beliefs and behavior in terms of "the spirit of the times," but for the philosophers of 1800 the realization of similarities in interests and attitudes across national and religious boundaries— still more the recognition of some shared universal identity—was a great secular discovery. Nationalism, for example, which we now often view as the most reactionary of attitudes, was an expanding and synthesizing force in 1800 in Europe—as it is today in many "developing" countries. To the German patriots of that time, the ideal of a German nation meant a sense of personal identity, a linkage between people speaking the same language that for centuries had seemed impossible. Accordingly, nationalism seemed to be a step *toward* humanism, and not, as today, a step *away* from it. Hegel's Spirit expressed the new spirit of *inter*nationalism, while preserving local differences, too.[5]

So long as we look at the Enlightenment as an ideology rather than as a set of doctrines—or for that matter, as a temperament or mere set of attitudes—we should expect to find component concepts changing their status significantly as we move from one set of social circumstances to another. The concept of individuality, for example, which sometimes plays a leading role in Enlightenment thinking, is much less significant in times of war or crisis, when solidarity and unity are required far more than renewed attention to individual rights. Thus in Germany, where the primary obstacle to middle-class aspirations was a lack of intrastate unity, humanism and the urge to socialize took a very clear precedence over individualism. In Hegel's own words: "The share of any particular individual can only be very small. Because this is so, the individual must all the more forget himself" (*Phenomenology*, p. 130). Similarly, the concept of equality, which had played such a large role in the Enlightenment in America, played a far smaller role in Germany and even in France after 1800. As the bourgeoisie succeeded in achieving equality with the aristocracy, the lower strata of the Third Estate began in turn to demand equality with their bourgeois leaders. To protect its newly won interests, bourgeois ideology placed less stress on equality and more on citizenship. This shift was already evident in Rousseau's later works, *Emile* and the *Social Contract*, which exerted a heavy influence in Germany. Indeed, in Germany the concept of equality received little emphasis in political theory, the stress shifting rather to human dignity and moral participation. Even freedom, the most important single promise to the individual in England, America, and France, would become in Germany a property not of the individual but of society as a whole.

The most important and difficult idea in Hegel, accordingly, is this shift from the individual to the abstract group—what Marx would later call an "inversion" (other philosophers a "hypostatization") of relationship between concrete particular individuals and abstract classes or "universals." Hegel's "collectivism" is not, as many political writers have insisted, an isolated political theory, but rather a general ontological theory about the nature of reality. For Hegel, abstract classes are more real than individuals. Here is a simple example: consider a collection of sixty coins of different origins and denominations. One might say that the sixty individual coins together make up a collection; in other words, the collection is nothing but the sixty individual coins, which happen to be together. But instead, one could speak of the collection as an entity in itself, and of the individual coins simply as included in it. In this second description the abstraction "collection" is what is primary: the individual coins can be exchanged or replaced, but it will still be the same collection. The essential difference is between the individual significance of the coins in the first case, and their mere relative significance in the second. If we are talking about people instead of coins, however, it makes all the difference in the world whether we see individuals as primary, and relations between them —communities, states, and ultimately humanity—as secondary, and as merely a way of referring to increasingly large collections of individuals; or whether on the other hand we see the collections as primary, and individuals as being of importance chiefly insofar as they serve the collections.

In both the French and German Enlightenment, however, this important difference was often neglected, on the implicit rosy assumption that the good of the individuals and the good of the community or state or humanity were one and the same. In the philosophy of John Locke and other liberal thinkers, individualism usually received a distinctive edge. But in the age of turmoil at the turn of the new century, with Napoleon losing sometimes hundreds of thousands of soldiers in a single victorious campaign, the assumption of mutual benefit and the liberal edge had to be seriously challenged. In the wake of Napoleon's armies, the struggle to form a German state made it obvious that statehood had to take precedence over individuals, if it was going to become possible at all. Hegel's concept of Spirit was an instrument with which he sought to realize the ideal of the French Enlightenment and German unification, reconciling the seemingly opposed interests of individuals as a collection ("civil society") with the State, and conflicts of interest between states as well.[6] But this means that Spirit, or humanity, must be more than a mere abstraction, more than merely the collection of all existing human individuals. It is an entity in itself, even more real and important than the individuals who must serve it.

. . . at a time when the universal nature of spiritual life has become so very much emphasized and strengthened, and the mere individual aspect has become, as it should be, a matter of indifference . . . the share in the total work of spirit that falls to the activity of any particular individual can only be very small. Because this is so, the individual must all the more forget himself . . . all the less must be demanded of him, just as he can expect the less from himself, and may ask less for himself. (*Phenomenology*, p. 130)

The religious connotations of "spirit" are intentional; Hegel intends his philosophy to in effect *replace* religion. In fact, this Enlightenment ambition lies at the root of Hegel's philosophical efforts—even deeper than the German tendency toward the "spiritual." "Spiritual" in this context is not to be distinguished from "material." Conversely: "In my view . . . everything depends on grasping and expressing the ultimate truth not as Substance but as Subject as well. . . . True reality is the process of reinstating self-identity" (p. 80). Spirit includes all of nature as well as unified human consciousness. On occasion Hegel suggests that the material world as a whole is something like the superhuman body of the superhuman consciousness designated by Spirit. In other words, Spirit is *everything*, and it is partly for this reason that Hegel also refers to Spirit as "the Absolute" and as "Absolute Spirit"[7]: "Of the Absolute, it must be said that it is essentially a result, that only at the end is it what it is in truth; and just in that consists its nature, which is to be actual, subject, self-becoming, self-development" (*Phenomenology*, pp. 81–82). In Hegel's philosophy, to quote Hölderlin, "World's own spirit has condescended to mortals"; or rather humanity, as Spirit, has been elevated to that sense of universality formerly conceded only to God.

Reason, History, and Freedom

> But even as we contemplate history as this slaughter bench on which
> the happiness of peoples, the wisdom of states, and the virtue of in-
> dividuals have been sacrificed, our thoughts cannot avoid the question,
> *for whom, for what final aim* these monstrous sacrifices have been
> made.
>
> Hegel, *Philosophy of History*[8]

It is true that Spirit was a philosopher's idea; Hegel called it "The
Idea" in his *Logic*. It was the transcendental pretense of a unified humanity, the culmination of the humanism that had been developing throughout
the Enlightenment. But it was an idea that had been appearing on the stage
of human history—"universal history"—since ancient times. The French
Enlightenment had asserted that this world was an essentially human
world; and the French Revolution had proved it. No more would philosophers worry about earthquakes in Portugal: now they had to worry about
the guillotine and the Committee of Public Safety, the mobs in the streets,
and by 1800, Napoleon. Material nature provided the stage and the weapons for intrahuman struggle; nature was no longer an alien threat but an
instrument.[9] Beginning with Kant, the German idealists formulated this
humanistic change in the cosmos as a metaphysics in which the world of
nature itself was "constituted" by our categories. Hegel was the final step
in this progression: the world was nothing but a function of human Spirit.
And human history was nothing less than the dialectical key to the development of the universe itself.

Hegel said again and again that Spirit does not simply exist, but must be
realized: "it is essentially a result." The word "realize" is intentionally
ambiguous in this context: to realize something may mean (1) to *recognize* it, or (2) to *make* it so—just as a "result" may be (1) a conclusion
or (2) a product. But what constituted Spirit for Hegel was our mutual
recognition of our shared self-identity as Spirit, and so these two coincided
at least in one important sense: to recognize ourselves as Spirit, as one, is
to make ourselves Spirit. But this recognition is also what Hegel calls
"freedom." Spirit—that is, recognition of Spirit—is freedom: "Man as
man is free" (*Phenomenology*). But individuals are free only in a tenuous
sense, insofar as they recognize their subservience, their unimportance to
the whole. It is the State and humanity writ large—as Spirit—that are
really free, not the individual. Like Rousseau, Hegel argues that freedom
can be realized only within society, and in particular only within and as
part of a State. Unlike Rousseau, however, he gives no credence to the
proposition that "all men are born free." Individual freedom is not "natural," but depends upon the conventional but nonetheless necessary insti-

tutions of rational society. Hegel, following Kant, rejects the Enlightenment concept of freedom from restraint or "negative freedom," and instead emphasizes what Kant called "positive freedom": the freedom to participate and obey. Freedom, therefore, rather than distinguishing one individual from another, tends to bring individuals together, reducing their individual importance and binding them into a greater entity—ultimately, into humanity.

The idea that freedom is inherent in the whole of humanity is obscured by Hegel's insistence that the goal of human history and its present achievement (or at least the beginning of it) is the recognition that "all men are free." But here Hegel's transcendental pretense is most obvious, as he evaluates the whole of human history in terms of his contemporary Enlightenment ideals. Human history, he argues in some detail, can be divided into three stages, each to be characterized in terms of its recognition (and therefore realization) of universal freedom. First, there was the ancient Orient, where "only *one* was free, but for that very reason such freedom was only arbitrariness, savagery, dimness of passion . . . this *one* is therefore only a despot, not a free man, a human being." We cannot help but noticing that Hegel is insisting that these ancient beings, even including their one "free" ("negatively free") ruler, were not "human beings"; they did not even have a *word* for freedom.

Second, there were the Greeks:

Only in the *Greeks* did the consciousness of freedom arise, and therefore they were free; but they, as well as the Romans, knew only that *some* are free, not man as such. Plato and Aristotle did not know this; therefore the Greeks did not only have slaves . . . but their own freedom too was partly only an accidental, undeveloped, ephemeral and limited flower, partly at the same time the harsh servitude of man, of what is humane. (*Phenomenology*)

Even Hegel's early idols, the Greeks, therefore, were not wholly human, because they did not recognize the eighteenth-century concept of universal freedom. Of course Hegel knew Plato's *Republic* and Aristotle's *Politics*. Whether or not the concept of freedom played a significant role in their theories, Hegel knew that their descriptions of the ideal society shared many of the features he aspired to in modern Germany, not least of which was that spiritual sense of unity that formed the Greek *polis*. But they too had to be evaluated by Hegel's eternal modern standards, which he interpreted as the intrinsic criterion for everything human.

Finally, "only the Germanic nations attained the consciousness, in Christianity, that man as man is free. . . . This consciousness arose first in religion, in the inmost realm of the spirit; but to build this principle also into the affairs of this world, this was a further task whose solution and execution demands the long and hard work of education." Only in the present age,, Hegel concluded, were we beginning to build "governments

and constitutions . . . rationally, and founded on the principle of freedom."
The Greeks, in other words, were not wholly rational; they were not *like
us*. Has the transcendental pretense ever been clearer?

Freedom, then, is the goal of human history, "the long process which
constitutes history itself." But the recognition of this freedom is Reason,
and here, despite his loose but frequent references to God, Hegel shows
himself to be a true spirit of the Enlightenment. Combining Voltaire's
stress on Reason and Rousseau's emphasis on "free" participation in society, while borrowing openly from Kant's own synthesis of Freedom and
Reason (see pp. 128–36), Hegel argues that history, as the realization of
human freedom, has been nothing less than rational: "Reason governs the
world, and has consequently governed its history." But for Hegel Reason
is nothing but "purposive activity," a cosmic unrest which, he says, is "the
self," our own identity as humanity.

The formula linking freedom, reason, Spirit, and the goal of human
history is clearly the fruition of Enlightenment thinking, but how does it fit
into Hegel's own view of the "slaughter bench" of history and his experiences, most immediately, in the Napoleonic Wars? (Hegel lost his only
brother in those wars, so they were not, as critics have sometimes objected,
merely an abstraction for him.) The simple answer is that Hegel, sharing
the general confidence (if not exactly "optimism") of the Enlightenment,
but rejecting its general disgust with history, tried to show that *some* good
had come of it all (though not, as Goethe said, that "Nature does nothing
in vain"). He could not and would not deny the horrors of history, some
of which he had witnessed only a few miles from his study, but he could
argue, using the three-stage development of freedom discussed above, that
the slaughter had served some purpose, that there was a "cunning of
reason" behind the often brutal passions and ambitions of men: "This vast
congeries of volitions, interests and activities constitute the instruments
and means of the World Spirit for attaining its object, bringing it to consciousness, and realizing it" (*Phenomenology*, p. 2). Just as religious
people had once tried to resolve the "problem of evil" by accounting for
"God's mysterious ways on earth," so Hegel too attempted something like
a theodicy, but without appeal to a God behind the scenes or his "mysterious ways." It was a thesis that the world very much wanted and needed in
the early nineteenth century.

Hegel's philosophy, then, can be summarized in a simple phrase: the
realization of Spirit. But in this phrase we have to recognize the combined
forces of the Enlightenment and German mysticism, the visions of Goethe
and the hopes of the postrevolutionary era. Hegel's philosophy is an attempt to get us to identify with the turmoil of human history—to think of
world history as *our* history, to see the trials of humanity as something like
a cosmic family squabble with a "higher and broader purpose," a squabble
that has continued only because we have not yet appreciated the depth of

our mutual bonds of identity. So far, our recognition of Spirit has been too limited (confined, for example, to a single tribe or province), too competitive (as if Spirit required the existence of some great Being other than humanity, whether the Christian God, pagan deities, or just some mysterious "force"). The language and style in which Hegel works out this thesis is, to say the least, forbidding. But if one keeps in mind the context in which he wrote—the ideals of the Enlightenment, the ambitions of Germany, the waning of Christianity, and the promises and horrors of the Napoleonic Wars—the essential humanistic message should be clear enough.[10]

Young Hegel

> ... I think it would be interesting to disturb the theologians as much as possible in their ant-like industry as they amass Critical [i.e., Kantian] building materials to strengthen their Gothic temple; to make everything difficult for them, to whip them out of every nook and subterfuge till they found none any more and had to show their nakedness completely in the daylight.
>
> Hegel, letter to Schelling, January 1795[11]

With Hegel as with Kant, the philosopher takes a back seat to the philosophy, but Hegel's life history, unlike Kant's, is of interest. G. W. F. Hegel was born in Stuttgart in 1770, the son of a solid bourgeois family. As a theology student in Tübingen during the explosive years 1788–1793, he shared his enthusiasm for the French Revolution with his two best friends, Friedrich Hölderlin and Friedrich Schelling. He also shared Hölderlin's nostalgia and admiration for the ancient Greeks, though never so thoroughly or pathologically as his ill-fated best friend, who in 1804 literally went mad (see pp. 214, 218). Still, Hegel had given up classicism long before his first published writings—nearly a decade before it was given up by Schiller and Goethe. As for Schelling, he was a prodigy who became the leading disciple of the post-Kantian philosopher Fichte. The new star of the philosophy world, Schelling had published over six books before Hegel finished his first. He occupied a university chair at twenty-three, while Hegel was still making his way through tedious and isolating tutorships in Berne and Frankfurt. Personal envy can be a powerful philosophical motive: Hegel watched the meteoric success of his younger friend with jealousy, and it should not be surprising that this friendship ended badly and bitterly once the Hegelian comet had begun to move.[12]

In Tübingen and thereafter, the three friends greatly influenced each other, though Hegel was evidently the least giving of the three, contributing more by way of entertainment and wisecracks than intellectual substance.[13] He was a dull philosophy student, something of a moralist, and at twenty even his friends called him "the old man." Hölderlin greatly influenced Hegel's thinking about all matters cultural and religious, providing all institutions with a classical form. Schelling, on the other hand, eventually excited Hegel about Kantianism and Fichte, converted him to the Kantian revolution, and introduced him to most of the later themes of Hegel's own philosophy—the dialectic, the philosophical "system," the Absolute. As students, the three friends together enthusiastically read Rousseau, who was the most important modern influence on Hegel's younger days. Although enrolled in the theological seminary or *Stift,* neither Hegel nor his two friends had the slightest intention of entering the ministry. Each of them at some point considered a career in law. Hegel was a harsh critic of the theology he was being force-fed, and the three referred to their theology professor as "Old Sourdough." But Hegel's criticisms remained clandestine, and the first essays he wrote on religious topics—harsh condemnations of Christianity and modern culture in general—kept from public view, emerging only in the early years of this century. Nor did the Spartan environment and conservative attitudes of the Tübingen seminary correct the trio's lack of enthusiasm for the traditional Church. Hegel, Hölderlin, and Schelling were rebels—though comparatively timid ones who through casual conversation quietly conspired to bring the reforms in France inside the medieval walls of Germany.[14]

After graduating from Tübingen in 1793, Hegel used his ample spare time in Berne and Frankfurt to correspond with Hölderlin and Schelling, hike in the Alps, and read a new book by Immanuel Kant, *Religion within the Bounds of Reason Alone.* The main theme of this work provided the guideline for Hegel's career and the philosophical backbone of his youthful rebellion as well. This theme was the primacy of Reason, *practical* Reason, in all matters cultural and religious. Morality was the single most important human concern, and anything justifiable in religion and society had to serve morality. In one of his early essays from this period, Hegel echoed Kant by insisting that "the aim and essence of all true religion, and of our religion included, is human morality."[15] But Kant's harsh conception of morality had to be tempered with Hegel's admiration for the Greeks, their concept of "the good life," and their ideals of perfection and excellence. What began to emerge was a new paganism that was of the Enlightenment in principle, Christian in form, and deeply moral in content. "Let reason and freedom remain our watch word," he proposed in a letter to Schelling, "and the invisible church our point of union" (Kaufmann, p. 301).

Between 1793 and 1800 Hegel wrote a series of manuscripts in which he attempted to formulate his still crude dissatisfactions with contemporary German Christian life. Never intended for publication, these essays have been called Hegel's "early theological writings" and also—more appropriately—his "antitheological" writings. They are considered particularly important because they throw light on Hegel's concerns before he constructed the labyrinthian "system" associated with his name. (In fact, Hegel did not even consider a career in philosophy until he was almost thirty.)

The most revealing of the early manuscripts, which we know only in fragments, was written in 1793, when Hegel had just graduated from Tübingen. It is generally called "Folk Religion and Christianity," and this title captures both the conflict within Hegel and the impetus behind his life's work. The conflict, which Hegel presents by way of a historical-cultural contrast, is between simple "subjective" religion based on shared feelings and rituals, and authoritarian, dogmatic religion based on obscure theoretical precepts divorced from both concrete action and interpersonal community. For Hegel, "subjective" religion was epitomized by the ancient Greeks, the essence of whose religion was community feeling and morality in a broad sense that includes the good life. Christianity, on the other hand, represents "objective" religion, a term that Hegel, later the rationalist par excellence of "objective spirit," interprets negatively as depersonalized and without passion. Accordingly, Hegel emphasizes the need to reconceive Christianity in more "subjective" terms.[16]

The essay's comparison of Greek folk religion and Christian dogmatism is not altogether fair. Hegel contrasts Socrates and Christ, much to the advantage of Socrates: "The number of his closer friends was indeterminate . . . he had no mind to polish for himself a small corps that might be his bodyguard, with the same uniform, drill, passwords—a corps that would have one spirit and bear his name forever" (in Kaufmann, pp. 134–35). In general, in this early writing Hegel resembles no one so much as Nietzsche in his sarcasm and occasional virulence toward Christian theology and even toward Christ himself:

Not only does one train the Christian mob from childhood on to pray constantly; one also tries to persuade them of the supreme necessity of prayer by promising its sure fulfillment. And one has piled up such a heap of reasons for comfort in misfortune . . . that we might be sorry in the end that we cannot lose a father or a mother once a week. . . . It might be very interesting to compare all this with the faith of the Greeks. For them, misfortune was misfortune, pain was pain. (p. 134)

These harsh condemnations of Christianity, culminating in the charge that Christianity has provided modern humanity with "debasing monuments of human degradation," must give deep pause to those who believe that Hegel was one of the ultimate protectors of modern Christianity.

At the heart of his anti-Christian polemic, a straightforward moral doctrine begins to emerge. It is first of all based on Kant: the ultimate justification for any institution is practical reason, that is, whether or not that institution makes us better—more moral—as people. But it is also a move beyond Kant. First, Hegel sees Kant's distinction between reason and passion—between the universal principles of morality and the "subjective inclinations" of personal motivation—as a pathological condition. Hegel prefers a more "Greek" view[17] in which the good life consists of a total agreement, in fact an identity, of rational moral principles and personal passions and desires. Second, Hegel already sees that Kant's ethics of principles leaves out one of the most important ingredients in morality: the fact that moral rules are *social* principles derived from our existence in communities with different kinds of customs. Accordingly, Hegel replaces Kant's emphasis on moral principles with one on social participation and customs (in German, *Sitte*). The heart of practical reason, therefore, becomes what is called *Sittlichkeit,* membership in a community. In this concept the outlines of Hegel's later philosophy are already apparent.

In a subsequent essay Hegel tries one of the most outrageous conceptual moves of his career. (It is in fact much the same move that characterizes his later philosophy as well, but by then he has become much more subtle about it.) In his essay "The Life of Jesus" Hegel attempts what is today fairly common: a re-interpretation of Jesus as an ordinary human being, conceived in the usual manner. This in itself is not outrageous (though it would have been considered so in Germany at the time). What is outrageous is Hegel's reconstruction of Jesus' teachings so that they conform to—and even use the same language as—Kant's ethics. In other words, in 1795 Hegel is trying to "redo" Christianity, bring it up to date, make it less Christian and more secular. (God, for example, is defined simply as Reason, paralleling the recent Cult of Reason in revolutionary Paris.) Indeed, one way of understanding Hegel's philosophy as a whole is to think of it as trying to replace the Christian religion with a system that utilizes its superficial forms but is in fact wholly secular.[18]

One of Hegel's concerns, therefore, is the tendency of Christianity and religion in general to minimize humanity at the expense of something else; in Christianity and Judaism this "something else" is an all-powerful God "up there," in whose eternal shadow our lives are of no importance whatever. In philosophy and theology this "up there" concept is called "transcendence." In place of it, Hegel attempts to introduce the idea of an *immanent* God—a God "in here," in humanity itself. Consequently, the idea of "God as love" becomes of great importance to him even while he rejects most of what had been said of God in the past. God as the heart of community, and nothing more than that, becomes Hegel's way of integrating the folk religion he admired in the Greeks and the outward forms of Christianity.[19]

With his emphasis on "love" and community, Hegel is wholly repulsed by what he sees as the meaningless dogmatism of Christian authoritarianism. The Church, he charges, "is a system of contempt for human beings." The teachings of Christianity, he argues, have nothing "natural" about them—that is, to borrow a concept from Kant, they have nothing to do with practical, moral reason or with making us better, happier, or more sociable human beings. Instead of the "natural" religious feelings of the Greeks, Christianity is based upon *"positivity"*—ungrounded external authority. In another essay written in 1795, entitled "The Positivity of the Christian Religion," Hegel traces this authoritarianism back to Jesus himself ("I am the Way"). What replaces this religion, therefore, must be something wholly different, wholly reasonable, wholly "natural."

A final essay written in 1799—"The Spirit of Christianity and Its Fate" —is of particular interest because it introduces what will become three central concepts of Hegel's dialectic. First, Christianity may not be simply a "false" religion to be rejected altogether, but a stage in human development. This idea is not original with Hegel; he borrows it directly from Gotthold Lessing, who had published his pamphlet on "The Education of Man" in 1780:

Why shouldn't we see in all positive religions nothing but the way in which the human understanding everywhere could not but develop and shall continue to develop, instead of either smiling at one of them or getting wroth?[20]

Following Lessing, Hegel begins to soften his criticism of Christianity and to look for what is essential and humanistic in it, rather than what is dehumanizing. This involves a shift from a transcendent to an immanent God, a God within us, which Hegel takes to be the true meaning of Christ.

The second Hegelian concept introduced in the essay is "disharmony," or what Hegel will later call "alienation" and later still a "contradiction." A disharmony is an inconsistency—a conflict with our Enlightenment humanism in particular. The idea of a transcendent God, a God "up there," is a vast disharmony because in our own eyes it makes us seem small and insignificant. Similarly, the Kantian split between reason and passion, desire and "inclinations," is a disharmony, because it shatters our conception of ourselves as whole human beings, turning one part of our personalities against another. And so a third concept appears as Hegel begins to talk about the disharmony between people and the Law, between people and the State, and about how people can identify and become part of the powers that govern them, rather than seeing themselves as mere victims.[21] Here, slowly, begins Hegel's reworking of Rousseau, his insight into parallel problems in morality, religion, and politics, and his realization that what is needed most of all is not a critique of Christianity and German modernity, but rather a single grand, unifying conception that will bring the whole of our schizoid and disharmonious lives into unity and harmony.

The Urge to Synthesize

> Fichte has unquestionably opened the door with his *Critique of All Revelation*. He himself made moderate use; but once his principles are firmly accepted, it will be impossible to set up any end or dike for theological logic.
>
> Hegel, letter to Schelling, January 1795[22]

> From the Kantian system and its highest completion I expect a revolution in Germany.
>
> Hegel, letter to Schelling, April 1795[23]

In 1800 Hegel began an essay on a proposed constitution for Germany, starting with the observation that Germany was not then a state, though he hoped that it would soon become one. In 1802 Napoleon's invasion interrupted his work and—ironically—began to fulfill it. In a political sense, the real struggle for the unification of Germany had started. At the same time Hegel was turning from fragmentary criticisms and speculations on religion and society to an awareness of the global conceptual issues underlying those concerns. It was not until this time that he could seriously be called a philosopher.[24]

Rereading Kant, particularly his *Critique of Pure Reason,* Hegel gave him an attention and devotion that he had surely not given him in school. He also studied Gottlieb Fichte (1762–1814), who had been strongly influenced by Kant and had in turn strongly influenced Hegel's school friend Schelling. And of course he reread Schelling's already famous works and began to discuss serious philosophy with him, in place of the gossip, pranks, and practicalities exchanged over the past ten years of friendship. Together they edited a journal in Jena, while Hegel held a minor professional post and Schelling a professorship in the university. One of Hegel's first published essays was a comparison and criticism of the philosophies of Fichte and Schelling that showed a predictable preference for the latter.[25]

We shall have more to say about Fichte and Schelling in Chapter 14, for both were instrumental in establishing the intellectual foundations of German romanticism. Here we need be concerned only with their basic philosophical development, beginning with the revolutionary doctrines of Kant's *Critiques.* An enthusiastic follower of Kant, Fichte wrote a Kantian treatise called *A Critique of All Revelation* and sent it to the Great Philosopher, who so liked it that he secured Fichte a professorship in Jena. (A personal recommendation from Kant went very far in those days.) In his masterwork, *The Science of Knowledge,* Fichte developed what he believed to be the logical systematization of Kant's philosophy, turning Kant's "criticism" into metaphysics.[26] Simply stated, the basic project was to unite the first *Critique* on knowledge with the second *Critique* on morality, employing certain suggestions from the third *Critique*, in particular the idea of a teleological explanation.

A teleological explanation (see also p. 134) is an account in terms of inherent purposes. For example, one can give two very different accounts of why most higher animals have hearts. The casual account would describe the evolution of creatures with hearts, the genetic determination of certain organic structures, the development of the organs we call "hearts," and their composition and workings as innervated muscles, etc. In contrast, the teleological account would stress the function or purpose of hearts—to circulate the blood—taking the continued life and health of the organism as a goal to be attained, and the beating of the heart as its means. In Kant's third *Critique*, however, teleology provided an account of a phenomenon far more spectacular than such small biological conveniences: the very existence of the world had its ultimate function as a divine creation serving God's purposes. This was the grand metaphysical view developed by Fichte, but where Kant believed in a very traditional Christian God-Creator, Fichte developed the idea—soon to be taken over by Hegel—that the purpose of the universe is *intrinsic* to the universe itself, not imposed or created by a Being outside of it. (It is worth noting that Fichte was charged with atheism and fired from his university post on the basis of this view.) In terms of his neo-Kantian metaphysics, Fichte developed a philosophy in which *self-consciousness* is what develops teleologically and is primary, rather than either God or the material universe. In terms of his Kantian synthesis, Fichte's strategy was to collapse the opposed Kantian worlds of knowledge (nature, theory, and science) and freedom (morality, practice, and religion) into one single form of purposive self-consciousness. That single form, it turns out, is preeminently *practical*. In other words, Fichte rejects the opposition of Kant's first two *Critiques* and "reduces" Kant's philosophy to the second *Critique* in terms of the third. Kant called his philosophy a "transcendental idealism." Fichte calls his an *"ethical* idealism."

The basis of Fichte's philosophy is the Kantian concept of "constitution" or "synthesis." He utterly rejected the idea that the material world exists independently of our consciousness of it. In fact the first thing Fichte did, in order to "systematize" Kant, was to reject what he saw as an unfortunate remnant of pre-Kantian thinking: the Kantian notion of the thing-in-itself or noumenon. According to Fichte, there is *only* the world of our experience, nothing more. The basis of the world, for Fichte, is our consciousness of it. But where Kant had held that our knowledge of the world is based upon one kind of consciousness (in which we apply certain kinds of categories to experience), while our moral activities are based upon another kind of "practical" consciousness or *Will*, Fichte holds that all consciousness is essentially practical. There is no basic difference, in other words, between knowing something and willing something: both are matters of willful activity. Questions of knowledge, then, as well as questions about morality, are part of ethics. The question is always, "What will make us better human beings?" Fichte says, "The kind of philosophy a man chooses shows the kind of man he is."

Fichte, like many German intellectuals, did not share Kant's enthusiasm for the sciences and Newton. The spiritual-moral life was what concerned them, and in Fichte's philosophy this bias is reflected dramatically. The material world, he tells us, is nothing but a "posit," a stage upon which we can act out our moral principles and a system of obstacles to be overcome. (After all, what would it mean to talk of "morality," if there were no temptations to be overcome? And what would it mean to speak of "courage," if there were no dangers to be faced?) Kant's world of "Nature" was thus relegated to a strictly secondary place in Fichte's philosophy. Nature is merely a stage upon which we enact our moral struggles. It was in Fichte's philosophy that humanity's nearly complete domination and harnessing of natural forces received its most explicit philosophical statement.

Two further "extensions" of Kant's philosophy will complete our short sketch of Fichte. First, in his "Transcendental Deduction" Kant had argued that there could be but one set of categories through which we could experience and understand the world. Fichte, who saw the application of categories as an activity akin to—in fact part of—our acting upon moral principles, argued that there are several sets of categories through which we can constitute our world. In fact, Fichte's suggestion was rather impoverished: he named only two such sets—in effect, the "causal" categories of Kant's first *Critique* and the "moral" categories of the second (which obviously was the one he opted for). But the opening up of Kant's tight bureaucracy of the mind was the first stage in the radicalization of philosophy that began with Kant, blossomed in Hegel, and defined much of the thought of the rest of the nineteenth century.

But there is also another way in which Fichte extended Kant's thought. The self-consciousness that was the basis of Fichte's neo-Kantian metaphysics was not construed as a personal, individual self. Rather it was an "Absolute Self" lying behind our experiences and shared by all of us. Its conceptual antecedent was Kant's transcendental Ego, which Kant thought of sometimes as a personal and individual self and sometimes as "consciousness in general." The offspring of Fichte's concept, however, would be Hegel's concept of Spirit.

Hegel's debt to Schelling can be stated simply. First of all, Schelling took much more literally than Fichte the Kantian concept of teleology. Following Aristotle more than anyone, he conceived of a universe developing through time. The whole structure of his system was a demonstration of the growth and interplay of the concepts through which we are conscious of the world. Schelling's teleological demonstrations would directly inspire Hegel's use of "dialectic." Second, Schelling, who was more religious and conservative than Fichte, objected to Fichte's inordinate stress on ethics. To balance that stress, Schelling strongly emphasized the religious aspects of such a metaphysical system, using the notion of an immanent God, which he called *Weltgeist* or World Spirit. He also stressed the aesthetic priority of continuous creation. Simply put, God then is the self-conscious universe creating itself, its ultimate purpose being art. ("Purposeless purposiveness" Kant had said in his definition of beauty; the universe has no further purpose than to create itself as art.) Thus Schelling shared with Fichte the idea that the Absolute or *Weltgeist* was something other than individual self-consciousness.

Third and most important, Schelling found Fichte's complete neglect of science, and his relegation of nature to a mere instrument of morality, scandalous. So he supplemented Fichte with a philosophy of nature, concerning the need for which Hegel sided strongly with Schelling against Fichte. (Schelling's view of nature was far more aesthetic than Hegel's, but small matter.) Through Schelling, Hegel saw that the point of philosophy was above all else a grand *synthesis:* to bring together, without denying or minimizing any of them, philosophies of nature and ethics, religion and the new secularism; to show how our universal concepts of the world have evolved, and make clear the ultimate purpose of it all, which is ultimately *our* purpose. By 1804 Hegel was ready to combine his new philosophical sophistication and ambitions with the moral-cultural-religious "disharmonies" that he had begun to formulate a decade before, so as to produce a "system" in the new tradition of Kant, Fichte, and Schelling. Though no longer a young man, so far he had shown no great inventive abilities, was known already as a boring lecturer, and had produced nothing but a small number of articles which displayed no particular promise or excitement. No one could have predicted the explosive philosophical fusion that his thought would undergo in the next two years.

The Phenomenology of Spirit

In my *Phenomenology of Spirit,* which on that account was at its publication described as the first part of the "System of Philosophy," the method adopted was to begin with the first and simplest phase of mind, immediate consciousness, and to show how that stage gradually of necessity worked onward to the philosophical point of view, the necessity of that view being proved by the process. But in these circumstances it was impossible to restrict the quest to the mere form of consciousness. For the stage of philosophical knowledge is the richest in material and organization, and therefore, as it came before us in the shape of a result, it pre-supposed the existence of the concrete formations of consciousness, such as individual and social morality, art and religion.

Hegel, *Logic*[27]

Hegel considered his *Phenomenology* as merely the "introduction" to his philosophical system—a frightening thought. But we need not take this too seriously. It is a book that stands entirely on its own, which alone represents Hegel's great philosophical creation and which, it can be argued, is Hegel's most exciting, most significant, and certainly most inventive work. Hegel's later "system" can be seen as something of a stylized encore to the *Phenomenology.* To only slightly stretch a coincidence, one might say that, if Kant was the German equivalent of the French Revolution, then the publication of Hegel's *Phenomenology* corresponds to Napoleon's victory at Jena, which ended the age-old Holy Roman Empire and established the French Revolution as a worldwide or at least international movement. It can be seen as high irony, therefore, that Napoleon's victory immediately cost Hegel his job, and made it exceedingly difficult for him to deliver his manuscript to the publisher in Bamberg:

What worry I must feel about the former batches of manuscript, dispatched last Wednesday and Friday. . . . The Emperor—this world soul—I saw riding through the city to a review of his troops; it is indeed a wonderful feeling to see an individual who, here concentrated in a single point, sitting on a horse, reaches out over the world and dominates it. . . .[28]

The *Phenomenology* is the ultimate attempt at philosophical synthesis; in other words, it tries to do everything at once. It attacks traditional Christianity while defending spirituality and what can be called, in an extended sense, the religious attitude. It tries to come to terms with German nationalism, Napoleon, and the new internationalism. It attempts to defend and go beyond Kant, in the direction already charted by Fichte and Schelling. It seeks to outdo Hegel's colleague, friend, and arch-rival Schelling. It tries to reconstruct a Kantian theory of morality within the framework of a social theory—as *Sittlichkeit,* an ethics of community. It attempts to comprehend world history, and to understand the structure of the new world since the Enlightenment and the Revolution. It is a late start in philosophy: at thirty-six, for Hegel "it was now or never." It tries to complete and move beyond the French and German Enlightenments, to integrate classicism and Storm and Stress romanticism in a cosmic humanism. Above all, it is a neo-Fichtean attempt to merge philosophical theory and social practice or *praxis,* and to show how human knowledge is inseparable from human interests, how reason is empty unless viewed in a cultural and historical context.

The structure of the book reflects these multifarious aims. From the reader's point of view, the style is intentionally obscure, in that it often refers to many very different issues at once—metaphysical, religious, and political—and does so by eliminating nouns in favor of pronouns and by using inexplicit references in place of explicit ones. Then too, the array and organization of chapters is bewildering, and it is worth noting—by way of encouragement as well as warning—that there are some chapters whose very subject matter is still a matter of debate among scholars. The structure of the book is, to use an appropriate word, *dialectical:* one chapter grows from another, as if by way of reply, correcting it, adding to it, contradicting it. This means—again by way of warning to the reader— that the book does not begin with anything like a normal introduction and preface, in which the author states clearly what the problem is, what other authors have done with it, and how he intends to solve it. In fact, Hegel begins by stating arrogantly that there is no point in doing any such thing:

> In the case of a philosophical work it seems not only superfluous but, in view of the nature of philosophy, even inappropriate and misleading to begin, as writers usually do in a preface, by explaining the end the author had in mind, the circumstances which gave rise to the work, and the relation in which the writer takes it to stand to other treatises on the same subject. (*Phenomenology*, p. 67)

The terms of the book present another problem—again, one close to the heart of Hegel's inventions. One of the main themes of the book is the *change in concepts* through which we understand our world. Accordingly, certain basic terms actually change their meaning from chapter to chapter. Hegel is often accused of being a horrid philosophical jargonizer, but this is not true. The problem is in fact just the opposite: Hegel rejects the technical language of Kant and the Kantians in favor of everyday speech, whose terms change meaning according to context, without warning and without explanation. But this is perfectly in line with one of Hegel's most important philosophical doctrines—that the "same" words have very different meanings depending on the "form of consciousness" using them, and that these words change their meanings as these forms develop and become more sophisticated. (A simple example: consider how a child uses a word like the possessive pronoun "mine" while passing through the various stages of responsibility and possessiveness.)

The *Phenomenology* is Hegel's creative synthesis, his best attempt to begin the German revolution through philosophy: "Theoretical work, as I am becoming more convinced every day, accomplishes more in the world than practical work; once the realm [of concepts] is revolutionized, actuality does not hold out" (Kaufmann, p. 323). The book is divided into three unequal parts: (1) an introduction and three chapters called "Consciousness," in which Hegel rejects Hume's skepticism and defends Kant's conception of knowledge; (2) the section "Self-Consciousness," in which the practical dimensions of knowledge are defended (à la Fichte) and our most primitive encounters are examined, including the famous "master and slave" relation that was later adopted by Marx and Sartre; and (3) the much longer section on "Reason," in which Hegel brings together the new views of science, ethics, romanticism, the nature of the bourgeoisie and the Enlightenment, Kant's ethics, the primitive family and community, ancient tragedy, Napoleon and the French Revolution, a criticism of purely "negative" freedom (the Reign of Terror), the nature of religion in general, Greek art, Christianity, and finally "Absolute Knowledge" (which was no small philosophical conclusion). The first part of the book begins with "common sense" and shows—much as a philosophy professor might show a freshman class—how our everyday beliefs dissolve upon inspection, then discusses the development of transcendental idealism by Kant and Fichte. Kant's conception of "constitution" ("determination") is crucial, but so is Fichte's emphasis on the practical side of conceptualization. The first part ends and the second begins with Fichte's enthusiastic celebration of Life, which is prior to knowledge, again recalling those crucial lines from *Faust* (I, iv): "Grey are all theories,/And green the tree of life."

There is no need here to discuss the details of Hegel's arguments, but the progression between the three "forms of consciousness"—"sense certainty," "perception," and "Force and Understanding"—can be used to make a preliminary point about Hegel's famous dialectic. One might (badly) interpret these three in a "thesis-antithesis-synthesis" pattern (a triad introduced by Fichte and not Hegel, who never used it). But the logic is more subtle than this. The first step in dialectic is almost always some ordinary commonsense belief, which is seen to be inadequate as soon as one pursues it seriously. The next step attempts to resolve these inadequacies, not by rejecting commonsense beliefs but by correcting them. (It is often thought that Hegel is the ultimate rationalist, since he rejects sense experience in the very first chapter of his book and never talks about it again. But sense experience in fact constitutes the basis of his entire work. At the start he only corrects the ordinary view of what sense experience is, and in the following chapters adds further corrections, but never wholesale rejections.

The next step—in this case the final step, though Hegel's dialectic is only sometimes a triad—is a return to a view more like the commonsense view, but now reinterpreted with philosophical sophistication. (Thus "Force and Understanding" reinterprets "sense certainty" in precisely the way that Kant reinterprets and corrects Hume.) According to Hegel, this process of *thinking through* and correcting our conceptions is the essence of philosophy. But the same ideas that the philosopher pursues in his philosophy are embedded in the ideology of society, its politics, art, religion, and literature—in every human endeavor that can conceivably be said to "progress." One of the main arguments of the *Phenomenology* is exactly this: that all human experience is dialectical—it is a development through concepts rather than a mere "given" (data).

"Master," "Slave," and Spirit

> A self-consciousness has before it a self-consciousness. Only so and only then *is* it self-consciousness in actual fact. . . . With this we already have before us the notion of *Spirit*. What consciousness has further to become aware of, is the experience of what mind is—this absolute substance, which is . . . unity.
>
> Hegel, *Phenomenology*

The best known "form of consciousness" in Hegel's philosophy is the attitude of confrontation that he cites as the most elementary of human interrelationships. It is his version of that "state of nature" allegory which forms the basis of so many modern social philosophies—those of Hobbes, Locke, and Rousseau in particular. But when person meets person in Hegel's primitive parable ("self-consciousness has before it a self-consciousness"), their attitude is neither Rousseauan indifference nor Hobbesian greed, but rather a mutual demand for "recognition"—in other words, for status and respect. The Ego is always pervasive in German philosophy,[29] and for Hegel this primeval human encounter is fully self-conscious. According to him, it leads inevitably to a "fight to the death"— or at least, almost—the result of which is the submission of one side or the other. One becomes a slave in order to survive; the other becomes the master. Hegel's view of the beginnings of human society is nothing so civilized as the "social contract" that emerges from Hobbes, Locke, and Rousseau, and for the rest of his career Hegel rejects all such contract theories as a falsification of the true societal bonds.

In this master-slave relation, however, societal bonds are not yet in question. The question is personal identity and survival; the slave defines himself in terms of the master, while the master defines himself *as* master. But then a curious shift takes place—one which will influence generations of later thinkers. (Marx, for example, models his whole theory of class conflict on it, and Sartre makes it the basis of a theory of interpersonal development.) The master becomes dependent on the slave, first because he now needs the slave to take care of all those essential tasks that he used to see to himself, and second because his conception of himself as master depends on the slave's recognition of his mastery. But something strange is happening to the slave as well: he is beginning to appreciate his power over the master; he sees that, because of his abilities to take care of the essentials of life, he is in fact more independent than the master. And most important, he sees how his master's self-conception depends on his recognition, which he can now use as a subtle bargaining tool. The result is a bizarre "inversion" in which the master in fact becomes the slave and the slave, the master. Thus it is, Marx will say, in all competitive, exploitative systems.

In Hegel's philosophy, the point of the parable is much the same. So long as people face each other in a mutually competitive identity battle, rather than seeing themselves as a cooperative unity, this bizarre and mutually unsatisfying dialectic will keep repeating itself. Consequently, much of the rest of Hegel's philosophy is an attempt to trace the steps through which we can transcend this brutal relation. The ultimate step, of course, is Spirit. In the interim, he discusses various attempts to escape the master-slave dilemma, including the Roman escapist philosophies of stoicism and skepticism (essentially, the denial that anything matters), and the ultimate escape of Christianity, which he first introduces in the *Phenomenology* as "the Unhappy Consciousness"—"unhappy" because it seeks to escape the changing fleshliness of the world for pure soul and eternity, but always finds itself trapped in human, fleshly, transient form. Hegel discusses in detail the various forms of individualism, from short-run hedonism to Byronic romanticism, and the Kantian attempt to universalize morality, which Hegel sees as a major breakthrough in the realization of Spirit. He discusses the progress of the French Revolution in abstract terms as a move from Enlightenment to the Reign of Terror, the moral again being that individualism and an empty, "negative" concept of freedom—one which does not recognize the universality and unity of humanity—will only lead to disaster. Finally he discusses what he calls Spirit proper and its prototype the family: "implicit spirit," from which all human society is ultimately derived.

Hegel's Politics

> The state as a commonwealth is the transcendence not only of individual existence, but of existence itself and of the pure being in itself of the person. Man has his existence, his being and thought, only in the law.
>
> Hegel, "Jena Realphilosophie," 1805–6

Hegel has too often been represented as primarily a political philosopher when in his own mind he was without a doubt primarily a metaphysician and spokesman for human Spirit.[30] But among the penultimate manifestations of Spirit, political institutions rank relatively high—in fact, just below art and religion. There is virtually no politics as such in the

Phenomenology, but while writing that book Hegel was giving lectures at Jena on the nature of the State, defending the cause of German unity, and attacking individual as well as provincial isolationism. Anticipating the Wars of Liberation, he complained of the French conquest and domination of the lesser German states and prophetically, as in the *Phenomenology,* discussed the rise of a new political order. This was not the same Hegel who in 1821 would argue for the divine propriety of the Prussian government. In fact, the Hegel of 1806 was not unsympathetic to socialism, nor even to communism in the literal sense that sees the State as a "true community" and advocates the institutionalization of "the common interest."[31]

The main theme of 1806, however, would also be Hegel's main theme later on: the spiritual priority of the State, meaning priority over individuals and individual interests. The State, he would say in 1821, is "the March of God in the World"—something less, but only slightly so, than the divine right of kings.[32] Monarchy, which he defended on the grounds that the spiritual expression of the State needed a personal representative, was to be balanced by a constitution restricting the monarch—a concept he had been developing since 1800. He also believed in a balance of powers and a representative assembly of two houses (one upper and one lower), but he did not believe in popular suffrage, warning that "in a large state this would lead to mere 'electoral indifference.' " The State, he argued, represents the ultimate *real* interests of everyone, so that conflicts between it and private interests are unreal. Conflicts between states are unresolvable except through wars, which have nothing to do with which state is "right" (both must be, because they are states), but only with which right will prevail. In fact, wars are spiritually beneficial, Hegel argued, in that they remind us individuals of our petty, transient, and ultimately subservient status.

All politics, properly speaking, is an expansion of the family spirit, not a matter of a social contract.[33] Social contract theories assume that people are first of all individuals capable of entering into agreements before the existence of law. But, Hegel argues, laws are not "made"; they evolve through the organic relations of family, community, and the State, all of which exist prior to individuals and individual rights. What is common to these is the fact that they all are based on a concept of mutual identity, of organic unity. The State, for Hegel, is not a government which stands above its people. Rather it is the organic unity of the people themselves, much like Rousseau's General Will. Hegel's paradigm is the Greek city-state or *polis,* in which the unity of individual (citizen) interests and community interests was nearly perfect—or so the German classicists believed. Ideally, the modern state would be a modified and extended *polis.* Curious as it sounds to us today, one of the most important of these modifications would be the establishment of a *bureaucracy* of middle-class civil servants. Because they would be employees of the State, Hegel argues, they would constitute a "universal class"—a class whose interests coincide with the interests of the State. Since we usually view it as a paradigm of inefficiency and petty oppression, it is worth remembering that bureaucracy was Napoleon's solution to the far more absurd inefficiencies and inequities of the Old Regime, with its inherited positions and total disregard for merit. This aspect of bureaucracy is what Hegel also admires, while appreciating as well the elevation of the lost German middle class to a position of not only responsibility but "universality." Thus human society is "essentially" middle class.[34]

The State, from Hegel's first writings to his last, is something over and above not only individuals but even society (civil society) itself, insofar as society is conceived of individuals and groups in their separate commercial and social enterprises. It is in this context that Hegel's notion of *freedom* enters his political philosophy. We have seen that Hegel borrowed from Rousseau the paradoxical notion that an individual may well be "forced to be free" (pp. 67–70). Freedom, in Hegel's lexicon, is not primarily a property of individuals, but of Spirit itself. Spirit, he argues, is free— absolutely free. Its freedom consists in its spontaneous activities, and individuals are free insofar as they "participate" in this cosmic spiritual activity. Freedom is a property of the public world and of institutions; since there is no individual public or institution (though individuals may become institutions through public acclaim), there can be, strictly speaking, no individual freedom. Even the great "world historical individuals" like Napoleon are no more than *representations* of Spirit. Freedom, Hegel also argues, is equivalent to rationality—a notion he takes directly from Kant. Thus a criminal who is justly deprived of his freedom must nonetheless recognize the reason for this; so doing, in his rationality he is therefore also free. ("Forced to be free" in prison, in this case.) Freedom, then, as so often in German ideology, becomes a far more spiritual than political "organization of feeling." But if the feelings are personal, the organization is necessarily institutional and cultural. There is, strictly speaking, no such person as a "free individual."

In our liberal (mainly English) Enlightenment tradition, we are used to thinking of freedom as "freedom from constraint," freedom *from* unnecessary controls, rules, or limitations. In Hegel's terminology, however, freedom is opposed not to constraint, but to isolation. Freedom means participation—in families and tribes, in groups and communities, in society. Here he follows both Rousseau, who was working out his own personal problems, and also Fichte, who was beginning the fight for German nationalism. He is also following Kant, who emphasized the importance of "positive" freedom. We tend to think of this conception of freedom as a dangerous *mis*conception, as one that tramples human rights and the need to place these rights above the State. But to understand the course of

German history and ideology, including the nonpolitical metaphysics of romanticism as well as the very political ideology of Karl Marx, one must, if not accept this conception, at least appreciate it.

The Apotheosis of Spirit

> The goal, which is Absolute Knowledge or Spirit knowing itself as Spirit, finds its pathway in the recollection of spiritual forms as they are in themselves and as they accomplish the organization of their spiritual kingdom.
>
> Hegel, *Phenomenology*

By "religion" Hegel means a very general attitude of respect or even awe, and participation. The prototype of religion for him is the *cult,* a small community of worshippers or celebrants united by mutual beliefs and respect. Clearly, Hegel's earlier admiration for Greek folk religion has not been lost. (Even in his last lectures on the history of religion, this view is still prominent.) Christianity, then, is but one instance of religion, and as Hegel argued in "The Unhappy Consciousness," not a very satisfactory one. Religion, properly understood, does not turn on doctrines and the Church (again, some of the old themes are still central), but on a sense of respectful community. Thus in several long discussions of the Christian Holy Trinity, Hegel heretically minimizes the importance of the Father and the Son, while stressing the Holy Spirit and communion. Politically, the ideal is still the Greek *polis:* an ideal secular community with gods and goddesses who participated in community life much like superhumans. Christ, Hegel argues, is important only as an allegorical example of a fact that is true of all people—that they are in fact God incarnate. But Hegel robs this idea of its traditional mystical significance by rejecting the idea of any God other than Spirit—in other words, other than humanity itself.

Religion provides Hegel with his penultimate notion of Spirit because, unlike politics, religion has always had universalist pretensions of one kind or another; it is not limited by contingent natural boundaries. For Hegel, whose background was Lutheran, religion is a matter of pure consciousness rather than of institutions. And so it is religion—in Hegel's very general sense—that marks our recognition of Spirit, but so far only in truncated or perverted ways. In line with the mainstream of French and now German Enlightenment thinking, Hegel insists that all particular religions and sects have a far too limited vision of Spirit. The projection of our own spirituality into a transcendent God is a perversion of religion, a step toward self-denigration rather than toward ultimate self-respect. Hegel's language is very Christian, playing freely with the jargon he learned in the seminary, but his message is wholly anti-Christian. Its effect has been described by his student Heinrich Heine: "I was young and proud, and it pleased my vanity when I learned from Hegel that it was not the dear God who lived in Heaven that was God, as my grandmother supposed, but I myself here on earth" (Kaufmann, p. 359).

Hegel has often been interpreted as the last great rationalistic defender of Christianity,[35] whereas in fact he was one of the first great German thinkers to reject it in favor of an all-encompassing humanism. Hegel is often interpreted as defending the peculiar thesis that history has come to an end with his philosophy, but at least in the *Phenomenology* he clearly intends to signal a new beginning: the emergence of a concept of humanity which is not just a philosopher's dream but a concrete reality.

Dialectic and the Transcendental Pretense

> It is easier to see the faults of individuals, states and the governance of the world than to see what they all contain of the truth. . . . Thus the insight to which philosophy should help us is that the actual world is as it ought to be.
>
> Hegel, *Lectures on the Philosophy of History*

In ancient Greece "dialectic" meant "conversation": the truth was thought to emerge from the confrontation of opposing views. (Plato's Socratic dialogues are the classic example.) In Kant "dialectic" meant two opposed positions that were equally defensible, as for instance his famous "antinomies" (see pp. 126–27); but both positions were suspect. (Thus he called his Transcendental Dialectic a "logic of illusion.") Hegel, however, uses the concept of dialectic in a far more radical way: it is not only a method of argument, but the nature of reality. Hegel agrees with the ancients that truth emerges from the confrontation of opposed views, and with Kant that Reason may produce equally defensible philosophical positions. But he further argues that this should not induce suspicion but an insight, that reality itself is complex and paradoxical, even contradictory. This does *not* mean, however—as Hegel's logical critics have insisted—that the laws of logic have been brutally rejected; it rather points to Hegel's Kantian view that it is we who "constitute" reality, with the Fichtean addition that different people—or even the same people—may use different sets of concepts to carry out this constitution in different ways. Thus two opposed and equally "rational" views force us to deepen and expand our perspective, to see the common ground these contradictions share, and to correct our opinions on every side so as to achieve a more encompassing, more coherent, and less defensive position. The ultimate perspective, which Hegel calls "the Absolute" or "Absolute Knowledge," is that common ground presupposed in *all* such viewpoints: the "internal principle" that is in fact the essence of human nature, now raised to the level of cosmology. That internal principle, in a word, is *unity* or *totality*—*freedom* in history, *truth* in understanding, *participation* in politics, and *spirit* in all things human.

Hegel articulates and brings to fruition both the Enlightenment of Immanuel Kant and the *Bildungs* view of Goethe and Herder. He can still—for example, in his *Logic*—talk about Eternal Reason, but he clearly means the *process,* and not merely those principles expounded by Voltaire and his Enlightenment brethren. He can talk of "the realization of spirit," but within this secularized religious conception he clearly means to include the wide variety of human conceptions and forms of consciousness displayed in the *Phenomenology.* He can still talk in terms of "Truth," but he clearly means the truth that emerges and is created by human knowledge, not some external principle which philosophers since Hume had dismissed as unintelligible. Despite the fact that he openly rejected Newton, he called his own philosophy a "science," but in so doing he made it clear to every reader that he was giving them no less than universal truths, the essential principles of *all* human experience. And if it was Hegel who initiated that great nineteenth-century trend called "historicism," which taught that truth is relative to particular peoples at particular times and circumstances, he also leaves no doubt that he not only shares but carries to its "absolute" conclusion the transcendental pretense of his predecessors.

Hegel tried to have it both ways. Like Herder and Goethe before him and various German philosophers after him (for example, Marx and Heidegger), he never allowed himself to be clear about the lines that divide nationalism from internationalism, culture from human nature, and historicism from the transcendental pretense. He insisted that concepts are employed by different people in different ways, but also taught that there is an ultimate unified framework—Spirit—within which all these ways can be viewed as complementary. In other words, contradictions were not absolute after all, even if they appeared so from some limited perspective. Here was the hope of the Germans and of Europe, at the beginning of the traumatic new century. All men are essentially free: all contradictions and conflicts will dissolve into the Absolute. This is dialectic: the recognition of differences *and* the demonstration of their compatibility. But this underlying compatibility, it would seem, was nothing other than German idealism, projected as the foundation of all humanity. It was the Germanic nations who represented freedom, and an Enlightenment concept of freedom that was to be universalized for all humanity. The transcendental pretense, in other words, turns out to be the very heart of Hegel's dialectic, reinterpreted now in the dimension of *becoming.*

After the Absolute

> For the pensive God
> Hates
> Untimely Growth
>
>   Hölderlin

The *Phenomenology* was a timely act of creation. It summed up, in its obscure forms and transitions, the hopes and confusions of a frenzied age. But what could Hegel do as an encore? (Admittedly, Absolute Knowledge is a hard act to follow.) During the Napoleonic Wars, Hegel spent his time teaching high school and writing his ambitious *Science of Logic*.[36] When it was published at the end of the wars, he became the most famous philosopher in Germany. In 1816 he was offered professorial chairs in Berlin, Erlangen, and Heidelberg. He accepted Heidelberg, but moved to Berlin in 1818. He became *the* German philosopher, an "absolute" success, and during this time—in his famous but evidently boring lectures—prepared the "system" proper, which would rule philosophy for years in the same way that David's classical style dictated taste in French art during the same period. But the system was no longer the harbinger of great hope and change; it was the fossilization of a once vital and vibrant idea. Hegel had become a German institution, a public figure even in the Church, which he personally still despised. His student Heine complained that "the man who sailed around the world of spirit . . . intrepidly advanced to the north pole of thought where one's brain freezes in the abstract ice" (Kaufmann, p. 365). But in Hegel's system—in its failures as well as its success—we can finally appreciate the true motivating power of the transcendental pretense. Hegel did not believe that, in his philosophy, he gained actual control of the world. (Not even Napoleon, he argued, could have that.) And whether or not bourgeois ideology would be used to "humanize" the rest of the world in a European image, accompanied by imperialism and the "white man's burden," was not the motivation—even if it was the result—of that ideology. In his self-declared humility as "spokesman for the Absolute," Hegel was aware of something known to, but rarely admitted by, every philosopher, poet, priest, and politician: that seemingly selfless representation masks a tremendous sense of self-importance. The priest who represents God does not need to be a god; the philosopher who speaks of the Absolute does not have to speak for himself. "By naming a thing one possesses it," says Jean-Paul Sartre in his biography, *The Words;* the very idea of the Absolute in Hegel is such an appropriation—a making the universe one's own, and making all men brothers and all women sisters, whether they want to be or not. Thus even before the pretense is turned outward in the new form of "civilized" imperialism so familiar in this century, or in the new forms of authoritarianism, it has its intrinsic rewards. It allows us each to speak not only for ourselves and our peers but for humanity, even for the universe. It gives us a sense of solidarity and resolution, a sense of understanding, of belonging, and especially of *power*. And that is what the Enlightenment, and bourgeois ideology in general, had always been about.

After Hegel's death in a cholera epidemic in 1831, however, that sense of solidarity and resolution fell apart very quickly. The young leftists in Berlin were already revising Hegel by making explicit the revolutionary ideas and atheism implicit in his tongue-in-cheek theological language. Hegel's onetime friend (now enemy) Schelling was invited to Berlin by the government to combat what was now perceived as his pernicious influence. Scholars quickly turned the Hegelian enthusiasm of the *Phenomenology* into a dry, dead scholarship more appropriate to the System, while young Marx and his friends made the same works the foundation of a new kind of revolution. But what neither the scholars nor Marx and his friends seriously challenged was the transcendental pretense. Under the presumptuous name of "the Absolute"—or under a more modest title like "totality" or "the universal class"—it would remain the basis of bourgeois ideology for many years to come.

12 The Highest Wisdom, the Purest Speech: Beethoven

His talent amazed me; unfortunately he is an utterly untamed personality, not altogether in the wrong in holding the world to be detestable, but who does not make it any more enjoyable either for himself or for others by his attitude.

Goethe

Young Beethoven . . . he speaks the highest wisdom in a tongue his reason does not understand. . . . In this musician Beethoven, who spoke the purest speech of every nation, the German spirit redeemed the spirit of mankind from deep disgrace.

Richard Wagner

The realization of "spirit" had another form of expression which had no need of Hegelian articulation. In accordance with some of the dubious dichotomies of the times, one might say that Beethoven did for passion what Hegel had done with reason, or that Beethoven realized the spirit of the will as Hegel had the spirit of comprehension. Since Hegel himself ranked music among the "lower" arts precisely because of its inarticulateness, Beethoven and Hegel might seem to be in direct opposition. But in fact they were exactly complementary, each an expression of the *Zeitgeist* in his own way. As if to confirm its own existence, the "spirit of the times" manifested itself simultaneously in two very different geniuses, two very different media, and two very different life styles.[1]

"Dionysian" and "Apollonian" were the terms that Friedrich Nietzsche used in his *Birth of Tragedy* to characterize the lusty primitivism and the clear rationality, respectively, of the Greeks. They fit Beethoven and Hegel as well. The musician and the philosopher were exact contemporaries: Beethoven too was born in 1770, also in a provincial German town (Bonn). They never met or corresponded, and it is possible that they never even heard of each other. (Beethoven surely knew nothing of Hegel; Hegel was never very interested in music, and in any case never mentioned Beethoven even in his lectures on the arts.) Yet they expressed the new spirit of Europe as if in partnership, rising above their provincial bourgeois origins to become spokesmen for the age. Beethoven's explosive passions and "untamed personality" were brought under the most rigorous discipline when it came to the slow, cautious, repetitive process of composing, just as Hegel's dry, analytical professionalism was driven by the most furious flights of philosophical imagination. So it was with the age they lived in: "Dionysian" and "Apollonian" were but opposite sides of a very human spirituality, trying to get hold of itself.

In musicology even more than philosophy, historians tend to confine themselves to their medium, conscientiously neglecting external circumstances and relationships, including the "meaning" of a musical composition. A bit of biography, perhaps, but rarely an attempt at cross-cultural *Geisteswissenschaft* (literally, "the science of Spirit"). Just as Hegel is too often treated merely as the heir to Kant and the Kantians, so Beethoven is presented simply as the successor of Haydn and Mozart. But Beethoven was affected by the unsettled situation in Germany, the idealism of the French Revolution, and the promises and threats of Napoleon just as much as Hegel was. Both were enthusiasts of the new republican principles, and both were personally menaced by the wars. They shared the hopes that began the new century, and suffered from the same chaos and incessant trauma. They shared too in the reaction that accompanied the fall of Napoleon, and, most important, in the conflict and movement that we have been calling "dialectic."

It might seem odd to apply to music the concept of dialectic, which so far we have described primarily in terms of interaction between concepts, since in any but the broadest sense, music is nonconceptual. But "dialectic" refers primarily to a kind of structure, a nonstatic development driven on by internal principles, conflicts, and "disharmonies." (The concepts of "harmony" and "disharmony" are central to both Hegel and Beethoven.) Dialectic is opposed to static forms and structures—for example, the rigid categories attributed by Kant to human understanding, or the equally rigid sonata form that was handed down to Beethoven from Gluck, C. P. E. Bach, Haydn, and Mozart. Just as Hegel begins his dialectic with "common sense," rooting out its presuppositions and pushing its naive assurances to their logical extremes, so Beethoven begins with the most innocent phrasings and childlike melodies, not so much embellishing them (as later romantics would) as bringing out ominous echoes and undercurrents. And just as Hegel often finds a thesis best understood in confrontation with its opposite, so Beethoven finds his themes most powerfully presented when opposed to their dramatic counterparts: simplicity versus complexity, innocence versus ominousness, crescendo versus silence. It would not be farfetched to call them "contradictions." Beethoven's obsessive sense of resolution of opposites is identical to Hegel's equally obsessive sense of the Absolute. Central to both the composer and the philosopher is a Goethean awareness of growth and emergence, an unyielding sense of confusion and struggle, and a stubborn insistence on resolution. Finally, this sense of open structure allows both men to expand their compositions to lengths, complexities, and a grandeur (or arrogance) unprecedented in modern history. Both see themselves—if not always convincingly—as spokesmen for the human spirit in general. For both, their genius lay—as one musicologist has said of Beethoven—"in the ability to organize such a large amount of contrasting material into a unified harmonic whole."[2]

Overture

> The overture to Beethoven's opera *Fidelio* was performed recently, and all impartial musicians and music lovers were in complete agreement that never was anything written in music so incoherent, shrill, muddled, and ultimately shocking to the ear.
>
> A. von Kotzebue

It is common to divide Beethoven's life and work into three periods, a practice which is useful so long as one sees these periods as a process of development rather than, as in some authors, a sequence of three virtually distinct composers. The first period is one of development and mastery of a tradition. The second period, which begins with the new century, reflects the trauma of those years in both its structure and "content." (It is worth noting that Beethoven's *Eroica* Symphony shocked the musical world just as Hegel was putting together his *Phenomenology,* and that Napoleon played an important role in both.) The third period again reflects the times, being a period of reflection that follows the fall of Napoleon and accompanies the stasis of the Reaction. But where the Hegelian dialectic fossilized with the times, Beethoven's work developed in even bolder and more mysterious forms, as if in reaction against the Reaction. But as in the Hegelian dialectic, the last works of Beethoven absorb and transcend, rather than simply replace, the themes he developed even as a young prodigy.

Beethoven's father was a music teacher who resolved to make his son into another Mozart, and ruthlessly and sometimes cruelly pushed his young musical genius at the expense of his intellectual faculties, his social and emotional development, and surely his happiness. Beethoven wrote his first musical composition at ten, and he was a regular public performer at eleven (unlike Hegel, who showed little promise until his thirties; but this reflects the nature of philosophical versus musical talent, rather than the personalities themselves). Perhaps Beethoven did not at first prove to be another Mozart, but Mozart himself acknowledged his abilities when Beethoven briefly studied with him in Vienna in 1787. By the time Beethoven had moved to Vienna five years later to study composition with

Haydn, Mozart was dead, and Beethoven was eager to take his place.[3]

Beethoven was an arrogant and ungrateful pupil, convinced that he did not need rules or teachers; in fact, he learned quickly and well. Haydn acknowledged his student's genius with a grace as characteristic of the elder composer as it was unknown to the younger one. Although Beethoven by 1800 was one of the best-known pianists in Austria, performance was not his ambition. With Haydn's help and praise, it was already becoming clear that Beethoven would be the next great composer in Vienna and therefore in the world. Though it had original touches, his style was still very much that of his teacher, and in many ways more conservative. Meanwhile the Austrians were continuously at war with the French, and felt the threat of invasion. As an escape from fear, the hedonistic Viennese turned to music (as well as to food). Used to raise money for the war effort, concerts provided a ready source of income for performers. Beethoven took part, and through them earned a decent living, received many commissions for small pieces, and gained a substantial reputation.

About the turn of the century, Beethoven began sketches for his Third Symphony. Like Hegel, he had been and remained an enthusiast of the French Revolution, but Beethoven—at a safer distance, we should add—did not develop the reservations about it that Hegel did. And Beethoven, unlike Hegel, remained a radical democrat at least in theory. As the champion of the people and the defender of the Revolution, Napoleon was for him a personal hero. The Third or "Heroic" Symphony was, in a sense, "about" Napoleon and the ideals and tragedies of the Revolution. (Everyone knows the story—whether true or not—about Beethoven's reaction when he heard that Napoleon had made himself Emperor: he destroyed the dedication of the symphony.) With the "Heroic" Symphony, Beethoven anticipated and realized the same new spirit of Europe that Hegel was articulating in his philosophy. Having once entered this spiritual realm, Beethoven launched into the most prolific—perhaps even the happiest—period of his unhappy life, during which he wrote most of his symphonies, most of his best-known sonatas, concerti, and even an opera. But much of the energy that fueled his creativity was a reverberation of the excitement of the times.

Around 1815, when Europe entered a new, more inward phase, so did Beethoven. For a composer, he had been damned with the worst affliction imaginable: increasing deafness, which by this time was nearly total. His irascible personality turned to wholesale paranoia, and his last period was preoccupied with trivial domestic battles and lawsuits, poverty, loneliness, and long stretches of creative silence that, more than anything, drove him to despair. Yet in the midst of this seemingly impossible situation, he composed his most hopeful, even joyful, and many would say his greatest works. Furthermore, his life itself gave rise to a new cult of the struggling, suffering romantic artist. As he used his final period of reflection and suffering to achieve a deep and universal expression of the human spirit, other artists and admirers concluded that suffering and genius were one and the same. Over the next several decades—and even today—suffering alone could prove one's artistic credentials.[4]

The "Classical" Mood in Music

> Beethoven—that hideous counter-revolutionary petit bourgeois . . .
> Chiang Ching (the wife of Mao)

Music often seems to be a world of its own, aloof from the cares of the day and the traumas of the epoch. On the other hand, music "used" in anthems, battle songs, folk ballads, and musical comedies seem like music cheapened. But this impression is wrong not only for its snobbishness; it also errs in denying music its rightful place in human affairs, not just as escape but expression. However problematic the studies of "emotion in music" may be, they focus on the only possible explanation of the importance and meaning of music through history. Even that music which most emphatically declares its independence from history and human passion must by that very intention reveal itself as an expression of a certain historical epoch.

The "classical" mood in music was the mood of the Enlightenment. It claims a universal validity for a particular middle-class outlook. It turns its insistence on simplicity and clarity into a characterization of "reason" itself. It confers upon its own style the honor of being the *correct* style, and therefore beyond style and not a style at all. It was not haphazard when the word "classical" was generalized from its particular historical context to designate "good"—that is, sophisticated and enduring—music, whether traditional or contemporary. It was characteristic of classicism in music—as in the classicism of theater, art, and literature in Germany and France alike—to extol itself as basically and wholly human, "pure" and "simple," and as close as possible to the ideal. To be sure, classical music did not trace itself back to the music of the Greeks and Romans. In fact, the term "classical" was applied to this movement—to Haydn, Mozart, and the early Beethoven, in particular, with Gluck, C. P. E. Bach, and others as predecessors—only in retrospect by the romantic composers, as a way of distinguishing themselves from it. (But then again, the name "romanticism" was applied retrospectively, too.) The "classical movement," therefore, was not self-consciously a movement. Yet it did invoke a self-conscious ideology, albeit confined mainly to music, and in this respect can be viewed as another expression of a highly conscious, but not wholly *self*-conscious, age.

Neither Haydn nor Mozart displayed any noticeable interest in the events in France, or in the literary and cultural changes taking place in their own society; nor did these events and changes appear to have any significant effect on their music. They were "pure" musicians, apparently beyond the *Zeitgeist*. But their music was not free from the influences of humanity at large, however purely formal and "classical" a particular piece of music might appear.[5]

The spread of bourgeois culture in Europe made the music of Haydn and Mozart possible. Under the Old Regime, music had been private entertainment or accompaniment, commissioned for particular occasions and aimed at an exclusive audience. Baroque music, like rococo painting, flaunted its elaborate forms and techniques for those who could understand or afford them. Bach's later fugues were so complicated that at the time one had to be something of a scholar to follow them. Yet despite their complexity, these pieces were unabashedly emotional, in the service of our better passions. As all the arts gained an increasingly attentive and powerful middle-class audience, however, demands and expectations changed accordingly. Music now became a commodity, a public entertainment, and musicians had to become conscious of this naive new open market for their works. To appeal to this new source of patronage, new music was required—simple, thematic, memorable pieces that could be played often and without excessive difficulty. Music became more secular: welling devotional emotion, accordingly, was not considered one of its virtues. In addition to the new concert audience, there was a huge new class of private and family performers—housewives and eligible daughters, businessmen relaxing at home, and hopeful prodigies entertaining their relatives. The culturally aspiring bourgeoisie made the piano an almost required possession for even modest homes. The music to be played by and for such an amateurish audience had to develop accordingly.[6] And like the Enlightenment in general, this new movement encouraged geniuses. Two emerged above all the others—Haydn and Mozart.

Franz Joseph Haydn (1732–1809) was the first of the great musical entrepreneurs. He was indisputably a genius, but worked hard for his results. Although he often wrote mechanically and according to formula, to keep up his huge output of commissions (over one hundred symphonies alone), he proved his originality and genius in his technical innovations. He altered the nature of the orchestra, developed the sonata and symphonic form, and virtually created the string quartet. But Wolfgang Amadeus Mozart (1756–1791) was the superstar of this new musical business world. He had begun composing at four, and by the time he was independent from his overprotective father and self-supporting, he could turn out perfect pieces in Haydn-esque classical form virtually without effort. In his adolescence he developed a style of his own that would serve as the paradigm of classical composition forever. Unfortunately, having known great success as a child, he found himself a has-been at eighteen.

Not being the businessman that Haydn was, he proved incapable of managing his affairs, and despite his incredible output (over six hundred pieces), spent most of his short life in debt and penniless, and died a pauper.

Beethoven knew of Mozart's misfortunes, and no doubt turned away from public life partially as a result, preferring to develop his skills without depending on popular acclaim. But Beethoven was always part of that heritage, part of that businessman's musical world where the artist survived on commissions and public marketing. Though Beethoven sometimes appeared to be as incompetent in business and as "pure" in music as Mozart, he could sometimes be a shrewd entrepreneur and knew the worth of his wares. (Still, his brother handled most of his affairs.) In the last years of his life, he would know poverty, but never the utter desolation that killed Mozart. And where both Haydn and Mozart clearly served their patrons, Beethoven demanded a heroic status for himself, as if his patrons served and supported him. He would never allow his music to be simply a service to others, and would not accept many of those small commissions which obliged Haydn and Mozart to compose pieces for tea parties and incidental theater music. By insisting on absolute independence, he was able to carry his aristocratic and increasingly bourgeois audiences with him into uncharted realms of music and the human spirit. But the cultural basis of this feat was the ascendency of the middle class, its rigorous sense of enlightenment, its business sense, and its vehement insistence on independence in all human endeavors.

As the music of the Enlightenment, classical music is best characterized by its simplified style and formalized harmony, just as we have seen in classical art and literature. Emotion is to be controlled. (In Haydn and Mozart it is hard to find such emotional contrasts—joyful, somber, despairing, hopeful—as we are used to hearing in Beethoven.) One might say that Haydn played a role in the history of music parallel to—as well as contemporary with—that of David in French art. His music would have met with enthusiastic approval from the leaders of the French Enlightenment, Voltaire and Diderot in particular. It is worth noting that Rousseau, who had himself once been a composer and music critic, was among the first to encourage the new classical style of Gluck in Paris.[7] If we are willing to strain the parallel, we might also consider Mozart as being to music what Kant was to philosophy or what Goethe's classicism was to literature. Given the emphasis on the "purity" of forms, one might say that Mozart, like Kant and Goethe, so approached those formal ideals that their successors had to go beyond them.

The key to classical form is the sonata, the definitive component of the classical symphony and string quartet, the basic form of pieces for solo piano and for string and woodwind ensembles. This form reflects the sense of struggle and optimism of the Enlightenment in its mandatory sequence of fast movement–slow movement–gay movement–resolution, as well as in its sequence of prescribed key changes within movements, which also reflect this sense of tension followed by resolution. It is not surprising that the development of the sonata form corresponds in history precisely with the emergence of the Enlightenment. It had its origins in the aristocratic baroque, but emerged as the form par excellence for a musical composition only after 1750.[8]

Early Struggles

> Young Beethoven . . . we see daring the world from the first with that defiant temper which kept him in almost savage independence his whole life through: a stupendous sense-of-self, supported by the proudest spirit, armed him at every hour against the frivolous demands addressed to Music by a world of pleasure. . . . he is at all times like a man possessed.
>
> Richard Wagner

Even as a child Beethoven had been wild, rebellious, rude, a terrible snob, and emotionally unpredictable. He was neurotically antisocial at times, obnoxiously sociable at others. Perhaps it is the simplistic key to his development that he had no adequate outlet for the raging passions within him—defiance, anger, loneliness, and a general dislike of his fellow men. It is strange, for example, that despite volumes of testimony concerning the minutest details of Beethoven's life—how much he spent on which days for coffee, his taste for macaroni and cheese—we have virtually no idea whether he knew love or had a sex life, and if he did, whether it was satisfactory or frustrating. We have no records of grand affairs such as have been gleefully compiled regarding other composers (Mozart, Schubert, Wagner). It is true that Beethoven was virtually a prude when it came to talking about sexual matters (he was shocked by Mozart's "libertine" librettos), but it is also true that he was often obsessed with women, although he never married. (By contrast, Hegel married in 1811 and became something of a model husband. His mature system, accordingly, has a domestic tidiness, in stark contrast to the searching irresolution of Beethoven's late works.) Of Beethoven's romantic life, we know only a few love letters, addressee unknown, and the usual rumors of sexual prowess that are probably only the product of the nineteenth-century cult of the romantic artist. We know that in 1795 Beethoven proposed to a singer, Magdalena Willman, who turned him down because he was "ugly and half-crazy." We know of women friends, but not who was merely a friend, who an occasional lover, and perhaps a serious affair. A strange ignorance concerning the man most often chosen to represent the passions of the age! (It is sometimes suggested—as for so many great men before penicillin—that Beethoven's tragic illness was a late symptom of syphilis.) But the domestic mystery gives emphasis to an ideological platitude: Beethoven found within himself—in this new sense of "inner life" that joined the Enlightenment to romanticism in Germany—a sense of his own self-righteous worth and humanity. This awareness seems to have found no adequate expression anywhere else but his music.[9] And as in his music, Beethoven expressed contrary sides of the human personality in terrifyingly rapid succession, alternating charm and offensiveness, joking friendship and paranoid hostility, love of man and universal disgust.[10] The word "dialectic" is surely not inappropriate here, but like his genius and the times themselves, these neuroses and his righteous isolation needed time to develop.

Beethoven's exclusively musical education nearly crippled his intellect. He was poorly read, could not do the simplest problems in arithmetic, and borrowed uncritically the second-hand ideas he defended. Yet his few literary influences are revealing. He had read the Storm and Stress poets with some excitement and remained an enthusiast of Goethe and Schiller all his life. His temperament was irreducibly Faustian—struggling, defiant, greedily devouring everything that might be brought into his art, and ignoring all else. He was stubborn in the extreme and equally restless, grappling with fate and resigned to the destiny of his own achievements. Beethoven considered writing music for *Faust* almost from the moment Goethe's first fragment appeared. Schiller, the poet who so influenced Hegel, also influenced Beethoven, who learned from him the other side of *Faust*—his Kantian moralism and his ideological enthusiasm for the French Revolution and its liberty and equality (though for Beethoven, brotherhood remained a particularly distant third). He defended an abstract sensitivity to "poor suffering mankind," but worshipped individual heroism. In 1793 Beethoven had already considered setting Schiller's "Ode to Joy" to music, although this ambition would not be realized until the last of his symphonies. He also read Rousseau and, surprisingly, at least some Kant. (In his diary, he copied Kant's famous appreciation for "the heavens above and the moral law within.") To be sure, Beethoven was no philosopher. For that matter, he had surprisingly little to say even about music. Yet he is the most philosophical of all composers, at least until Wagner. His philosophy, taken from Rousseau and Kant, Goethe and Schiller, is expressed in his music just as surely as his attitudes about music are expressed in that music. (As Nietzsche said, "Beethoven's music is music about music.")

Beethoven composed with great difficulty. He typically carried a small sketchbook in his coat pocket and would jot down ideas as they came to him.

Unsummoned—I could seize them with my hands out in the open air; in the woods, while walking, in the silence of the night, early in the morning; assisted by moods which are translated by the poet into words, by me into tones, sounds that roar and storm about me until I have set them down in notes.

These little sketches would be transferred, painfully and often over a period of years, to larger sketchbooks at home, and developed. Familiar themes, like the opening measures of the Fifth Symphony, went through dozens of varying transformations before reaching the apparently spontaneous expression that we know so well.[11] Where Haydn wrote one hundred symphonies and Mozart fifty, Beethoven wrote "only" nine. But those nine were unheard-of in scope and ambition, developed over months or years with painstaking attention to structure, development, and detail. They were expressions of personality completely foreign to the earlier classicists, and like Beethoven's personality, were self-creations that broke the rules of all previous formulas.

Beethoven's first-period compositions were accomplished Haydn-esque works with touches of originality and a certain dynamism that Haydn himself lacked. The First Symphony (1800) displays certain peculiarly Beethovian mannerisms—for example, the use of a rising crescendo which climactically collapses into silence or whispering softness. But the symphony is important mainly because it happens to be Beethoven's, the beginning of a towering series of masterpieces that may never be equaled as the achievement of a single man. Similarly, the six quartets of Opus 18 (1800) are brilliantly delightful, with their sudden turns of phrase and development of simple themes, and their occasional brooding and violence, that already go beyond Haydn. One cannot describe these quartets in terms of deep passion and spiritual expression, perhaps, but the formal vehicle is already being made ready for later use. Beethoven had neither Haydn's flair for experimentation nor Mozart's spontaneous genius. Before he could move beyond his relatively less spirited predecessors, Beethoven would have to travel through hell. It may have been a very personal hell, but it coincided precisely with the inferno of the Napoleonic Wars that were about to engulf all Europe. Accordingly, Beethoven's very private expressions were to become the sounds of anguish and defiance of the whole of Europe.

Eroica

The Devil take you. I don't want to know anything about your whole system of ethics. *Power* is the morality of men who stand out from the rest, and it is also mine.

Beethoven, letter to von Zmeskall, late 1790s

> Being a really strong man, Beethoven could never have taken his morality of power with the seriousness of a Nietzsche. His ideal was the hero, not the strong man.
>
> J. W. F. Sullivan, *Beethoven*

As early as 1798, Beethoven experienced the symptoms of deafness, an affliction so singularly tragic for a musician that it could only seem like a diabolically conceived absurdity. But what is most deeply personal and isolating in a genius may turn out to be precisely what is most universal. Beethoven's struggle against the absurdity of his deafness, his defiance of "Fate," and his attempt to realize his salvation through achievement were precisely the experience of mankind at large. Without even knowing it—he attributed his success to his genius—Beethoven was developing his self-indulgent musical fantasies in accord with the hopes and worries of the times.

Beethoven's world was absolutely self-centered, however it might have been ideologized by his merely verbal universal humanism and liberalism. He was not writing for his patrons or his contemporaries, but for an ideal future audience. The particular people in his life were but accidents, not the universal mankind he sought. He had a truly Copernican attitude toward the world, and even if he had not read and quoted Kant, we could say that his personality was an example of the new attitudes wrought by Kantianism. He was on principle honest about his feelings, whatever the consequences, and therefore made many enemies. He saw his world, despite its absurdities, as an instrument of his own creativity. His deafness was a source of embarrassment to him, and so he withdrew ever deeper into himself and his music. In 1802 he made up a will of sorts (the Heiligenstadt Testament) in which he privately expressed the torment of his growing deafness. It was badly written, but nonetheless a classic document of despair and defiance.[12] He would live like an exile, resigned to his fate and dedicated to the realization of his genius. In retrospect, it is evident that this marked the transition in Beethoven's life from rebellious prodigy to spiritual genius. The now perfected classical sonata form was no absolute for him; it was an outline to be used as needed, a vehicle for expression. The violence only dimly apparent in the early sonatas, the melancholy and brooding barely discernible in the last of the early quartets, now became central to his music. The classical formulas had to become flexible, to fit the unruliness of Beethoven's emotional chaos.

The definitive act of this change of life was the Third Symphony (1804), the *Eroica,* a celebration—as the name suggests—of heroism. The original dedication to Napoleon has led some to see the piece as biography. Others have viewed it as an autobiography of Beethoven, the first movement representing his relatively happy and powerful younger days; the second movement (a funeral march), the times of despair; and the scherzo and conclusion, the new sense of resolution and defiance chronicled in the Testament of 1802. But no such interpretations do the work justice. Whatever he may or may not have had in mind during the months of composition, Beethoven was not writing a dramatic poem, but a spiritual odyssey that goes beyond any particular heroes, whether Napoleon or Beethoven himself. Like Hegel's *Phenomenology*, it conveys the education of the human spirit in general. It expresses happy times of innocence, the death of the old order and the birth of the new—a conception in which the development and not the formal outline is all important. This is not program music—music that tells a story—but the sensuous expression of a philosophical truth.

When the Third Symphony appeared, Beethoven was considered to be Haydn's rival as the most celebrated composer in Vienna. Yet he said of himself at that time that he had not yet started. (On his deathbed he would insist that he was "just beginning to compose.") While mapping out the *Eroica*, Beethoven had also been working on a ballet, *Prometheus*—a Goethean subject of defiance and Fate. He had only just completed his Second Symphony, a richly orchestrated and joyful piece which, like most of the even-numbered symphonies, appears to have been a lyrical distraction and experiment in gaiety written during a time of utter despair. This juxtaposition of personal despair and compositional joy is frequent in Beethoven, and should stand as a warning to those who take the idea of "music as personal expression" too simply. In fact, Beethoven's "expressions" often run counter to his feelings at any particular time. What are expressed are deep, conflicting emotional structures, not passing moods. In terms of the dynamics of composing, the idea that Beethoven worked on an adagio movement only when he felt relaxed or depressed, and on the scherzo only when in a prankish mood, reduces all such theories of creativity to nonsense.

The *Eroica* Symphony (E-flat major, op. 55) is of gigantic proportions and unprecedented complexity. Beethoven (like Hegel) had discovered that a piece must develop itself, and not be crammed into preordained lengths and sections. Accordingly, he allows himself the increased complexity and length needed for such organic development within and between movements. While the structure of the symphony's movements is in roughly traditional form—fast–slow–light–fast—the development is no longer only musical but expressive as well. There is an internal logic here of a kind never found in Haydn or Mozart. For example, the funeral march in C minor (the second movement of the work) begins with a ponderous but simple dirge that continues through the piece, soon becoming enmeshed in a complex fugue (which Coleridge described as "deep purple"), which becomes clarified once again with the help of the persistent march rhythm. An abrupt silence follows, then a bold finale borrowed from his ballet *Prometheus*.[13]

This symphony first reveals the dynamism and self-propulsion that characterize all of Beethoven's work. He is no longer dependent on conventional forms, though he stays within them when there is no need to do otherwise. Contemporary critics accused him of "trying to be original at any cost" (an accusation also leveled at Hegel). But it is a question not only of originality, but of an entirely new conception of the structure and function of music as a living organism, growing and developing under its own powers. What appeared as "lawlessness" and as "bizarre" was more often than not simply the failure of the critic to recognize dialectical logic as opposed to a logic of rigid forms and repetition.

Looking at the symphonies alone, one has the impression that Beethoven's *Eroica* emerges almost from nowhere, as if the Heiligenstadt Testament marked some possession by the devil, a Faustian pact of creativity. But if one looks at Beethoven's piano sonatas—the best place to study, not his spiritual evolution, but his musical education—one finds the dynamics of tension and suspension; the extended use of transition keys, and the adding of psychologically painful chords before resolution; and the stressing of off-beats and premature entries. All this developed gradually and studiously over a period of years. The *Pathétique* Sonata in C minor, op. 13 (1798), a first-period work, already demonstrates the manipulation of moods, the driving force of themes, and Beethoven's almost orchestral richness on the piano. He has already mastered a direct emotional appeal through simplicity of changing forms and sometimes violent rhythmic patterns (as if "to break the piano") that were unknown in formal music. The popular *Moonlight* Sonata (not Beethoven's title) in C-sharp minor (op. 27, no. 2) of 1801 already orders its movements according to its own needs, by beginning with the slow movement. Its deceptive simplicity makes it possible to play it either mechanically or spiritually, but never just "competently." The sonata affects a haunting mood, resolving uncomfortably with a favorite Beethoven device: a climactic coda, a pause as if to hold us at the peak of our passion, then a short cadenza that is slowed by another lull, then forced to an unprepared but not premature climax. With the *Tempest* Sonata of 1802 (D minor, op. 31, no. 2), Beethoven has already perfected the rhythmic drive and dramatic development of the simplest themes, coupled with dark passages that Beethoven marks "voice from the tomb." Thus the techniques of struggle and heroic determination, the driving turbulence and softly sustained melancholy of the first and second movements of the *Eroica,* have been developed to perfection over a period of years, and not all at once.

This traumatic period, 1803–1820, was rich in compositions—several of his best piano sonatas, including the *Waldstein* (in C, op. 53) and the *Appasionata* (in F minor, op. 57); the violin concerto; several piano concerti; five string quartets (the three *Rasoumovsky* Quartets and the Quartets in F minor, op. 95, and E-flat major, op. 74); three more symphonies: the Fourth, Fifth, and Sixth; incidental music to Goethe's play *Egmont*; and an opera with four separate overtures. These were surely not happy years for Beethoven, but perhaps even so his most fulfilling ones. His deafness was a constant source of despair and aggravation, and his doctors only vexed him further. Napoleon occupied Vienna in 1805, and again, after a heavy shelling, in 1809. Most of his friends left the city. His finances were desperate, inflation throughout Austria was horrendous, and food in the city was scarce. According to all reports, Beethoven had to live amid intolerable filth and poverty.

In the midst of this, he produced his most famous symphony, the Fifth (in C minor, op. 67, 1804–8), that miracle of Promethean defiance and conflict. The first movement is more single-mindedly rhythmical than almost any other in history, and has virtually no melody or lyricism whatever. (In spite of this, it became a major influence upon the extremely lyrical poets of the romantic generations.) By integrating and juxtaposing major and minor themes, by keeping the basic theme almost wholly rhythmical, this most celebrated of all symphonic movements affects us as pure determination, as unrelieved epic heroism and struggle. The weaker slow movement is followed by an allegro which repeats the rhythmic pattern of the first movement, embellishing it now with tone, color, and hesitant melodies, with galloping phrases halted by ripe suspensions, and so carries us exhausted into the perfect finale, where the themes of the earlier movements appear together in a rich orchestral triumph. This is surely the quintessential Beethoven of the second period. If the *Eroica* is the equivalent in sound of Hegel's *Phenomenology,* here perhaps is the *Logic,* the Absolute Truth, once sketchily realized, but now developed into a spiritual system that is pure and absolutely self-contained.

In 1805, while Vienna was occupied by Napoleon's troops, Beethoven with great difficulty composed his only opera, *Fidelio*. It is perhaps the weakest of Beethoven's major compositions, and the cause is not difficult to locate: by his own admission, he was never one for words; when called upon to write, he would "throw away the pen in disgust." The opera's various overtures and symphonic interludes are expectedly grand, and some of the more expressive passages are brilliant. But Beethoven's libretto is—in reaction to the "scandalous" librettos used by Mozart—a Kantian tale of morality and loyalty, as dry as the categorical imperative and as lacking in soul. It is Beethoven's music, therefore, which must carry the whole, and when not encumbered by dialogue it does so admirably. The weaknesses offer us a valuable diagnostic tool, a glimpse through the moral façade that so curiously masked this admittedly misanthropic and often crude recluse. Beethoven's "morality," like his politics, was wholly abstract, wholly Kantian. He loved "poor suffering mankind," but only from a distance. He detested them individually, and despite his recurrent evocation of French egalitarian themes, he considered the common people "scamps." Like most German and Austrian liberals, he looked to Napoleon for deliverance from the antiquated and crusty aristocracy (nowhere more antiquated or crustier than in the Austrian Empire). He tore up the projected dedication of the *Eroica* to Napoleon in rage: "Is he too nothing more than an ordinary human being?" But his rejection of Napoleon's "tyranny" clearly had far less to do with his sympathies for the French common people than with his own dashed hopes of liberation. He may have talked of equality, but he was a thoroughgoing Nietzschean elitist: "Our age needs powerful spirits to rule these wretched, small-minded perfidious scamps of men." Beethoven's spirituality, like Hegel's, was not on the level of everyday political realities. When Hegel finally wrote his book on politics, it had all the appearances of a totalitarian manifesto; and when Beethoven wrote an opera, even the genius of his music was incapable of giving life to the half-hearted heroism of his moral protagonists.

Finale

The last period of Beethoven's life was not a time of deserved success and contentment. He had created self-contained fragments of some great system, but it was not at all clear to him, as it had been to Hegel, how that system should be put together. Beethoven had not yet fully realized the Hegelian "yea-saying" that must accompany defiance and fate. Where Hegel's world had personally expanded, establishing him as the centerpiece of Berlin's cultural life, Beethoven's world had condensed into a silence of solitude and loneliness. Hegel's systematization had been the painless effort of a now glib and accomplished scholar to organize what he had long ago resolved for himself. Beethoven had yet to suffer more, so that he could give birth to his own absolute synthesis and joy. It is not surprising that Hegel's favorite author, Schiller, was also Beethoven's favorite. Just as the *Phenomenology* ends with two lines from Schiller—"The chalice of this realm of spirits,/Foams forth to God His own Infinitude"—so Beethoven's final symphony ends with the magnificent choral presentation of Schiller's "Ode to Joy":

> Joy, Divine spark of the Gods,
>   Daughter of Elysium.
> We enter your sanctuary,
>   Drunk with fire.
> Your magic reunites,
>   What custom has sternly parted.
> All men become brothers,
>   Where your gentle wings rest.

Following the rich period of productivity which lasted until 1810, Beethoven had fallen into a slump, tortured by what had now become total deafness, beset by his own poverty and a general financial crisis in Vienna. For a decade his productivity had been minimal. By 1812 he completed the Seventh and Eighth Symphonies (A major, op. 92, and F major, op. 93), both surprisingly jubilant expressions amid the unmatched despair of both Beethoven and his adopted city. What then followed was eight years of family quarrels and lawsuits, financial difficulties and ill health. Beginning in 1812, for several years Beethoven appears to have been obsessed with the idea of getting married and having a family. This impossible desire caused him only to feel his isolation even more. In a desperate attempt to fill the social and interpersonal abyss in his life, he made himself guardian of his nephew Karl at the death of his brother in 1815. Beyond dispute, he was an incompetent and disastrous guardian for a boy who had already manifested considerable emotional instability. With schizophrenic alternations between lack of concern and sternness, and then overindulgence and demands for affection, Beethoven must have emotionally crucified him. At the same time, Karl's mother appealed in court for custody of her son, and the legal battles between the two, in which Beethoven was considerably less than gallant, continued for over five years. While fighting his sister-in-law in court and grappling with his nephew's wounded soul at home, Beethoven was constantly battling his patrons and publishers, not to mention his total deafness and failing health. From all reports, his behavior toward everyone, even his most loyal friends, was utterly intolerable. His paranoia and rudeness had reached psychotic dimensions, and his pettiness could not have been endured by a saint.

It was a wonder, then, that Beethoven ever composed again at all. But in 1819 he completed his *Hammerklavier* Sonata (op. 106 in B-flat), perhaps the very greatest of his piano works. Here was proof that his mind had been not so much distracted by the sufferings of the preceding years as pushed to new depths. He needed time for the growth of what would be his most spectacular creations. Already comparable in its proportions to the still brewing Ninth Symphony, this titanic sonata is, as one reviewer has called it, Beethoven's conquest of Mount Everest.[14] The sonata begins with a melodic birthday greeting (to Archduke Rudolph, to whom it was dedicated), then presents a simple lyrical passage followed by a complex of emotions woven inextricably together, with the simple birthday greeting slipping through them like a single silver thread through a medieval tapestry. The energy and complexity of the scherzo, the grave tranquillity of the slow movement, and the technically improbable and superhuman joy of the final fugue are unmatched by anything preceding.

The two following years saw the completion of three more epic sonatas of similar complexity and then, in 1823, the *Missa Solemnis* and the Ninth Symphony. Both were performed the following year, the first in St. Petersburg and the second in Vienna. The symphony was enthusiastically received; Beethoven conducted, with the conclusion presenting the anecdotal but still heart-rending scene of the deaf composer being turned around to acknowledge the deafening ovation of his audience. Who would have thought that such suffering and psychotic pettiness could express such joy and celebration? It was as if Beethoven's spiritually crippled mind had been possessed by something much greater than himself, as if his petty jealousies and insecurities had become nothing less than tools of human destiny. Goethe's "daemon" had entered him also.

The Ninth Symphony (D minor, op. 125) probably appeared in a primitive form in Beethoven's sketchbooks as early as 1812, and his intention to set Schiller's ode to music dated from his first year in Vienna. At the risk of some controversy, it may be called Beethoven's greatest spiritual work.[15] If we want to *feel* Hegel's Absolute, we can best do so not by rereading the final chapter of his *Phenomenology* or the labyrinth of his *Logic,* but by letting ourselves be caught up in the dialectical complexities of this masterpiece.

Traditional symphonic and sonata form are utterly demolished in this final synthesis, as surely as the various distinctions of traditional thought had been crushed and assimilated into Hegel's Absolute Truth. (One critic has commented that in the wake of the Ninth, the classical landscape appears as if struck by an earthquake, with a few familiar landmarks scattered about in traumatically unfamiliar settings.) Virtually every musical form is incorporated here, every passion and every facet of human spirituality. The dramatic opening is Creation itself, the empty ether of a barely illuminated infinite expanse, disjointed phrases and scattered wastes, resolutely illuminated and synthesized by the booming D-minor theme. The following scherzo shows what has thus been created: a cosmic joke, inducing spasms of divine rhythmic belly laughs interspersed with fugal giggling and amusement. The adagio has been aptly compared to the adagio of the *Pathétique* Sonata of Beethoven's first period, just as various portions of the symphony have been compared with other works from the whole of Beethoven's career. It is hopefully not stretching our tonic comparison too much to say that this symphony unifies and synthesizes the whole of Western music, in the same way that Hegel's conception of Absolute Truth contains and synthesizes every stage in the development of human thought, through the direct confrontation and counterplay of every imaginable theme. The adagio is more melodic and lyrical than anything Beethoven had written in years. Its freshness recalls the spring-like pastoral simplicity of the Sixth Symphony. Here there can be no doubt: all is at peace in the world.

The choral finale is possibly, after the first movement of the Fifth

Symphony, the most popular of Beethoven's works. Though criticized by classical purists for its dependence upon a theme, Schiller's "Ode to Joy," the final movement is an ideal synthesis of the demands of that theme with the purely musical logic of the sonata form, considerably stretched and amended by Beethoven.

The last movement of the Ninth opens with a violence unusual even for Beethoven, shaking us from the peacefulness of the adagio. We are then in turn soothed paternally and rudely shaken. Returning to the first three movements, the orchestra briefly repeats the main theme of each in turn, until it finds the synthesis of all three—a simple lyrical theme almost religious in its seriousness, but with a levity unknown in truly religious hymns. It is variously rehearsed by the bass and then the strings, first solemnly, then gaily, and sung by a chorus of angels, then played by the whole orchestra as a triumphal march. There is a sudden softness, a sweetness of the adagio, and a return to the violence of the opening passages, then silence followed by the deep baritone proclaiming, as if in command, *"Freude"* (joy). The baritone is joined by other voices, then by the chorus, building to a choral climax. Then, as if for relief from this profundity, Beethoven introduces the tinkering of a little Turkish march, the sort of thing that one would expect more in Tchaikovsky. But the march develops with increasing solemnity and fuses with the chorale itself. With such reversals and changes in mood and intensity, Beethoven forces us through the remaining stages of his dialectic to lose ourselves in the increasingly rapid orchestral finale, leaving even the most casual listener disoriented and breathless at the end.

The final synthesis was not yet done, however, nor could it be, within the swollen grandeur of the symphony. The realization of universal brotherhood in his musical rendition of Schiller's "Ode" was not to be easily accomplished; as Hegel had also argued, this was the *beginning* of an era. Given the grand eloquence and spirituality of the last symphony, the next step required privacy and intimacy, a personal expression of the concrete loneliness which could not be forgotten in the vast expanses of Schiller and the chorale. The medium would be the string quartet, the most expressive and consequently most difficult of all musical forms. Here were laid bare the Platonic parts of the soul and the individual moments of universal spirit, struggling to unite themselves with the whole.

Beethoven had already written eleven quartets: the six Haydn-esque quartets of 1800; the three *Rasoumovsky* Quartets of 1806, which had been unappreciatively criticized for their technical difficulties and "perversities"; the comparatively classical tenth quartet of 1809; and the eleventh of 1810, which Robert Simpson has called a reflection of Beethoven's involvement with Goethe's *Egmont*—an expression of the concentration that he himself was no doubt desperately attempting to

muster in that time of peril when Vienna had been bombarded and occupied by the French. After that there were no more quartets until
Beethoven had completed all his other works—the last of the piano
sonatas, the *Missa Solemnis,* and the last symphony. In a sense, the last
quartets presupposed all these others. The last symphony was written for
his contemporaries and the last quartets—as he had once commented regarding the *Rasoumovsky* Quartets—"for another age."

With the possible exception of the first of these quartets (op. 127 in E-
flat major, of 1824), the technical difficulties and musical complexities of
these last works are such that musicians and audiences of Beethoven's
time found them utterly beyond their grasp. (No. 13, op. 130, in B-flat
major, for example, concludes with a grand fugue of such complexity that it
left its first audience in utter confusion; the publishers forced Beethoven to
delete it from the work, which he did with reluctance.) These quartets
have little respect for the conventions of the medium established by
Haydn. Opus 130 is in six movements, 131 in seven, 132 in five. Sobriety
and gloom interweave with gaiety and dance; there are heart throbbings,
and sobs with almost "mystical" scherzos.[16] A combination of tragedy
and mockery renders each quartet a living synthesis of the entire range of
human moods.

But the profundity or deep insight of these quartets must be interpreted
as far more than their capture and portrayal of human emotions and
loneliness, and they do far more than simply realize spirit in general, as the
last symphony had done. These quartets are the struggles of an individual
at the peak of his development who, with the ideal of universal humanity
already before him, must struggle with his own severe inadequacies. The
last symphony is Beethoven's grand expression of recognition and affiirma-
tion, while the last quartets are the brooding, painful struggles of a genius
thus enlightened to find that affirmation in himself. The last of the
quartets—in F major, op. 135, smaller in scope than the others—is the
lightness of resignation of a genius who realizes that he will never attain
his goal, that he is merely a man and a deeply flawed one, not the abstract
ideal of the German Enlightenment. The last of his works is the muttering
of a lost soul (the scherzo with its violent rhythmic interruptions), the
extreme tension of uncertain resignation (the slow movement), ending in
suspension without resolution—without the grand finale and conclusion so
familiar in Beethoven's earlier works. The stated theme of that last quartet
is simply "it must be," but as we listen to the final measures, we may well
feel that it is rather a question than an answer.[17]

13 The Classic/Romanticism Game: Ingres and Delacroix

> Ideal beauty—so ill-conceived in our time—designates only visible beauty, nature's beauty.
>
> Ingres

> Art is reason itself, adorned by genius, following a necessary course and controlled by higher laws.
>
> Delacroix

Kant once argued that beauty was the delicate synthesis of the ideals of nature and the free play of the imagination.[1] But in nineteenth-century France, where antitheses were more essential to bourgeois ideology than syntheses, the components of art were treated as antagonists, and the art of "ideal beauty" came to be *opposed* to art as imagination. There were ideological battles over the relative importance of line versus color, drawing versus painting, and a dozen other such implausible issues. By 1830 these "wars of the brush" had found two generals of genius, Jean Auguste Dominique Ingres (1780–1867) and Eugène Ferdinand Victor Delacroix (1798–1863). Of different generations and dissimilar in origin and temperament, they respectively represented—in their verbal diatribes as well as in their painting—the school of David's classicism and the new reaction to it that would soon be called romanticism. Their mutual but antagonistic emphasis on "correctness" showed that the transcendental pretense was alive and well after David: a plurality of styles would not be tolerated. Clearly, this was not the friendly complementary relation of neoclassicism and the late baroque of the preceding century. However unreal their distinctions, Ingres and Delacroix represented very real ideological as well as aesthetic hostilities.[2]

Presupposed in this seemingly silly battle (as Daumier, for example, depicted it later in the century)[3] were several revealing agreements. Both Ingres and Delacroix considered themselves to be expressing universal ideals and described their work as the representation of nature. Both insisted that their art was not mere personal expression, but obedience to universal principles of beauty. (If Ingres called Delacroix's work "ugly" and Delacroix called Ingres's work "false," this only underscored the implicit agreement.) It is within this recognizable ideological framework that the differences must be considered. It may well be, as Robert Rosenblum has convincingly argued, that the rigid black and white contrasts employed by historians and critics have formed a "semantic straitjacket" which has blocked rather than helped understanding of an extremely rich century of artistic production.[4] And it may be, as Walter Friedlander has complained, that the contrast itself betwen "classic" and "romantic" is ill conceived and false, since the first refers to a style based on antiquity, and the second to the mood and emotions expressed by the artist.[5] But even if the distinction is unhelpful or false, it is—to use the obvious pun—illustrative ideologically. The battle between Ingres and Delacroix is nothing less than the visual expression of the views so well articulated in Germany by Kant, Goethe, and Hegel. Ingres, following David but representing Kant, stressed ideal nature, the universality of its forms and the importance in art of "copying" eternal ideals.[6] Delacroix, who had seen Goya's etchings and read Goethe's *Faust*, expressed in his art the dramatic world view articulated by Hegel and scored by Beethoven. For him, nature was not form but vitality, life was spontaneous, and art the gift of genius and imagination "controlled by higher laws."

The outcome of my days is always the same: an infinite desire for what one never obtains, an emptiness one cannot fill, an intense longing to produce in all ways, to battle as much as possible against time that inexorably sweeps us along.[7]

"Official" Art and the Romantic Rebellion

> Copy, copy simply, wholeheartedly, abjectly that which you have before your eyes; art is never so perfect as when it resembles nature so closely that it might be mistaken for nature herself.
>
> Ingres

> Realism should be defined as the antithesis of art. The first of the arts—music—what does it imitate?

> All work in which imagination plays no part is impossible for me. What are most real to me are the illusions I create with my painting.
>
> Delacroix

When David snatched his classicist palette from Vien, so-called "neoclassical" painting had been established for a full century. But since Poussin, it had lacked not only genius but inspiration. In David's hands this formal and self-consciously simple style was enlisted in the service of the Revolution; long-dead heroes sprang to life as paragons of revolutionary virtue. The stiff, formal poses expressed universal ideals; the linear drawing conveyed the clarity of the Enlightenment; the subdued colors exemplified the dignity and restraint of the new bourgeois morality. An illiterate peasant could stand before David's *Brutus* in the Salon of 1789 and feel its significance, with the Revolution just outside the walls. The style as well as the subject expressed the new morality, and the "correctness" of the painting represented the rightness of the Revolution. But when the Revolution was over, the "correct" style survived its moral significance, and what remained were the formulas of a once inspired art. Even David's own brilliant technique lost its energy in exile, and the moral exuberance of his *Oath of the Horatii* gave way to the pretentious banality of reactionary classicism.[8]

Delacroix once wrote of Ingres, "There is nothing Homeric about him except his pretensions"; he also called him a "Chinese in Athens." Of himself, Ingres insisted, "I, I am a Greek." By 1824 Ingres was the representative of "official" art as defined by David. Even when he deplored the lack of "greatness" in the Salon, he approved of the idea of authority in art. The rules once used to murder artists with royalist sympathies were now used to dictate artistic style, though the ideological significance of those rules had long been forgotten. Appeal to the ancients was still compulsory, but the ideals they represented were more aesthetic than moral. "The ancients have seen all, understood all, felt all, depicted all," said Ingres, "and nature will always be beautiful when it resembles the beauties of antiquity" (Holt, p. 36). Linear form and drawing were emphasized above all else ("Drawing is everything," insisted Ingres), and restraint in the use of color remained as an aesthetic if no longer a moral principle—a matter of "good taste." But the idea of "correct" art was as uncompromising under Ingres as under David, and the new academic school of painting became as authoritarian as the old Royal Academy that David had been so instrumental in destroying.

If Ingres thrived on David's classicism, he did so only in the sense that Goethe too thrived on classicism—that is, in spite of it. He too used its discipline and limitations as a personal defense against the licentiousness of his passions. He was a "smoldering voluptuary," Mather suggests.[9] And then, the classicist style suited his remarkable talent for drawing as well as his temperament, while his long self-imposed exiles from Paris to Rome were motivated as much by his provincial distaste of sophisticated Paris as by sensitivity to the harsh criticism he sometimes received there. But if Rome and classicism suited Ingres, the same artistic mold was ill-suited to the personalities of other young artists, who were forced to adopt the official styles. One of David's best pupils, Baron Gros, found himself incapable of resolving the tension between his classicist training and his sentimental genius; in 1835 he drowned himself, allegedly in atonement for his infidelity to David's principles—an act whose moral nobility significantly suggested the self-sacrifice of the Roman heroes depicted in David's revolutionary allegories.[10]

Against the authority of official classical art, there had to be a rebellion. The spirit of revolution had not yet been defeated, least of all in the art world, and though David remained the guiding light, his most faithful pupils complained of his *Sabines,* for example, that it was "not Greek enough." Some of his followers, "the Primitifs," even looked at it with disgust as a return to the decadence of the rococo. Ingres went far beyond David when he told his students to "paint human legs like columns," and in place of David's practical rules he imposed a doctrine, declaring that "Poussin would never have been as great if he had not had a doctrine." Painting, in other words, had come to represent a theory of painting,[11] and it is not surprising that the paintings that most closely fit the theory were often far inferior to the paintings that fell short of it. This was certainly true of Ingres, and most dramatically true of David himself.

Even while David was leading the Academy, some of his favorite pupils like Gros, Gerard, and Girodet began expanding their repertoire to include medieval, gothic, and contemporary themes as well as classical allegories. The self-reflective clarity of David's *Horatii* began to be clouded in self-conscious mystery, as mystical, dreamy light replaced the clear luminescence of David's figures (e.g., Girodet's *Endymion* of 1793, and *The Entombment of Atala* of 1808). The strictures of Davidian space began to be relaxed; clouds and landscapes reappeared. Lines loosened, and the cold sculptural faces were invaded by psychology. (It is significant that Ingres is often praised for the psychology of his portraits.) And finally, the ultimate canon of "good taste" began to be challenged: colors became richer, more sensuous, finally breaking through the tyranny of line to become the defining property of painting.

The return of color in Prudhon, then Gros, then finally Théodore Géricault (1791–1824) more than coincidentally paralleled the changes in politics and philosophy in France as well as the rest of Europe. Napoleon's conception of the Revolution was not restraint but grandeur. As Emperor, he no longer had himself depicted in a simple colonel's uniform but in the grand robes of the Bourbon monarchs, and this could not help but affect the painters who depicted him. As the Wars of Liberation spread to more exotic lands—first Italy, then Egypt and the Levant, Spain, and finally Moscow—the simple moral and domestic subject matter of Enlightenment painting could not be sufficiently inspiring. Style as well as subject matter had to be more exotic, adventurous. And with the fall of Napoleon and the coming of the Reaction, the very function of painting in human life began to change. If Diderot and David had seen art as a didactic moral force, the artists who began their training after 1815 saw art as a source of excitement. This was a generation that as children had heard of the glorious Revolution and cheered Napoleon's troops through the streets of Paris.

They had lost brothers or fathers at Austerlitz or Borodino, and now knew the depression of defeat. Surely they were not going to be confined to the tedium of copying classical busts and representing no longer inspiring classical themes. Even Ingres, embittered by a rejection from the Salon in 1834, attacked the conformism of official art, which "stifles and corrupts the feeling for the great, the beautiful; artists are driven to exhibit there by the desire to get themselves noticed at any price. . . . Business rules instead of art." (He withdrew from the Academy for twenty years.)

"Romanticism is modern art, that is, intimacy, spirituality, color, aspiration towards the infinite." So wrote Baudelaire in 1846.[12] About Delacroix he added, "I do not know if he is proud of his title of 'romantic,' but his place is here, because a very long time ago—from his first work, in fact—the majority of the public placed him at the head of the *modern* school" (Holt, p. 79). The term "modern" had a double meaning—first of all as a term of praise, but also as a contrast to the antique and therefore to classicism.[13] Significantly, Baudelaire also cited Goya as a "modern"— in fact, "the first of the moderns"—and as a romantic. Goya, of course, would not have recognized the term. Delacroix rejected it, refusing to affiliate himself with any school or movement, all of which he considered "bastions of mediocrity." In fact, Delacroix often argued that he was the strict classicist, in contrast to the overidealized, desensualized figures of David and Ingres. But whatever he agreed to call himself, Delacroix clearly represented the antithesis of Ingres's classicism and the rebellion against the official art that then ruled Paris. His pride as well as his style assured that he would not receive his acclaim in the conservative art world, prompting Baudelaire's observation: "Up to the present, Eugène Delacroix has met with injustice. Criticism for him has been bitter and ignorant" (Holt, p. 79). Not that he was "ahead of his time"; rather, official art was behind, and its continued retreat to the classics only betrayed its unwillingness to recognize that the bourgeois ideals of the Enlightenment, so powerfully portrayed by David, had now been transformed into a very different set of concepts.

Portraits of the Artists

> Like Picasso in our century, Ingres can assume multiple historical guises and yet always remain himself.
>
> Robert Rosenblum, *Ingres*

> That bastard—he's really good!
> Picasso, on viewing Delacroix's *Death of Sardanapalus*

Ingres and Delacroix were not so different as David and Goya, contemporary geniuses whose development displayed the extreme differences between the cultures in which they lived and worked. Both Dominique Ingres and Eugène Delacroix were native-born Frenchmen, both educated under the postrevolutionary auspices of David's studios; they competed for the same commissions, the same awards, and were hung side by side in the same Salons in Paris. They were both children of a bourgeoisie already in power, and were trained in the arts as young children—both in music, and on the violin. Artists above all else, both determined the course of their days and lives for the sake of their painting, and neither allowed himself to be the least bit involved in the traumatic revolutions that shattered their mature lives twice. Ingres's contribution to the 1830 Revolution was to guard his treasured Italian masters in the Louvre and get into heated aesthetic disputes with other guards. Delacroix complained in 1848 that "this liberty gained by battles is no liberty at all." To Rousseau, for example, he objected, " 'Man is born free.' Never has a weightier piece of foolishness been uttered, no matter how great the philosopher who said it."[14]

But again, small differences may tell us as much as these gross similarities. Delacroix was born in Paris, into a family of some political prominence. (There are long-standing and substantial claims that his real father was none other than Talleyrand, Napoleon's onetime confidant turned royalist at the opportune moment.)[15] Ingres, on the other hand, was born into a provincial family of modest means (but considerable talent: his father too was an artist). The difference in circumstances is the same as between Voltaire and Rousseau, except that, in their subsequent development, it is the Parisian Delacroix who tends toward the visual philosophy of the heart (though he preferred Voltaire to Rousseau), and the provincial Ingres who is more often represented as the painter of "intellect." But then, the world into which these artists had been thrown was a very different world from the prerevolutionary and still "unenlightened" world of Voltaire and Rousseau. It is clear that neither Delacroix—even with his dandyism and aloof salon charm—nor Ingres, who remained somewhat of a bumpkin, ever approached the rapier wit and social grace of Voltaire, nor did either lead the "romantic" and isolated life so often associated with Rousseau. They were both great lovers of company and admirers, and while neither had a reputation as a bastion of tolerance and charm, both were free from that unpleasant paranoid temperament that fed Rousseau's personal revolution against society.

An artist's travels often indicate much about his temperament. David's and Goethe's trips to Italy tell us more about their artistic tendencies than any detailed biography of their early lives. Like David, Ingres was a winner of the *Prix de Rome,* but because of Napoleon's current campaigns in Italy he was not able to take the trip when he won the prize in 1801, therefore went instead in 1806. Significantly, without returning to France even once, he remained there eighteen years (1806–24), breaking his engagement and his old ties in order to stay. And many years later, discouraged by the less than total recognition he was obtaining in Paris, he returned to live in Rome once again (1834–40). Although Ingres often said, "I am a Greek," like Winckelmann and Goethe before him he never even made the attempt to go to Greece. The Renaissance Rome of Raphael was quite sufficient for him.[16]

Delacroix, on the other hand, never set foot in Italy, although it is evident that he would have welcomed such a trip. Instead, his travels took him to England, where a style of romanticism was already under way. But unlike Voltaire, Delacroix was less than fascinated by English life, and returned a more resigned but far from chauvinistic Frenchman. His main souvenir of England was in fact a discovery that he had made before he got there—the expansive and colorful rural landscapes of John Constable, whose paintings could be seen in the Paris Salon of 1824. But when Delacroix reached England in 1825, he had already assimilated Constable's technique to his own, and Constable the painter was not to be found in London. The outstanding adventure of Delacroix's life, however, was a trip to North Africa which was as well suited to his personal and artistic needs as Rome had been to David and Ingres. In 1832 he accompanied count de Mornay to Morocco on government business as official artist, expected to record the sights along the way. No government employee was ever better suited to his job: his restless "romantic" spirit ecstatically drank up the visual sights of the desert, and reveled timidly in the fierce Arab bands that, though unwelcome, accompanied the French and dangerously "entertained" them.[17] In Algiers Delacroix discovered what he argued to be the true classic spirit:

Imagine what it is to see, lying in the sun, walking the streets or mending shoes, men of consular type, each one a Cato or a Brutus, all in white like the senators of Rome and the Panathenaic procession of Athens. . . . The heroes of David and company would cut a poor figure here with their pink limbs.

In the hidden sensuality of the Arab harem he saw realized his own male-dominating fantasy of the place of women in a man's life. This wild and uninhibited yet elegant and luxurious life was well suited to Delacroix's imagination, though not to his Parisian personality, his physical well-being, or his urban terror of the wild and sensuous life depicted in his paintings.[18]

The differences in their life styles were striking. Ingres was a clumsy provincial gentleman who preferred the quiet of Rome and lived for his painting. He followed the advice of his friends in all other things, without a will of his own. He even followed their advice to get married, then deferred to his wife in all things practical after that. When his wife died, he was distraught for years; his friends advised him to marry again, which he did, and once again found himself in hands capable of managing the tedious affairs of everyday life far better than he. It seems that Ingres had no relations with any women other than his two wives. He was the ideal moral citizen, the pride of Kantian morality: a man of duty and principle even in and for—or rather *especially* in and for—his work. His diversion consisted of family dinner parties and light musical entertainment. He abstained from alcohol as much as possible. One cannot imagine that sober linear vision clouded by the pastel colors of intoxication.

Delacroix, on the other hand, was a self-styled aristocrat, a "dandy" of the times: too well dressed, a bit too elegant and aloof, but a great lover of parties and carousing, who developed a fondness for gin while in England and a fondness for women everywhere. He never considered marriage, which he saw as a prison, but fell sequentially in love with every variety of servant girl and with several elegant matrons. When he was in his prime, he found himself giddy over his sister's English maid. He had a thirty-year love affair with his own cousin (incest seems to have been an unspoken Enlightenment custom), and several other affairs of equal length, but he never allowed women to dominate him or interfere with his artistic efforts and energy. He avoided an available attachment with George Sand only because of her masculine toughness and his corresponding fears of domination. He had a far less professional relationship with his models than Ingres (who only painted them), filling his *Journals* with such entries as these:

Last Tuesday morning, a little baggage named Marie—19 years old—came to pose for me. I took a big chance of a disease with her.

A woman is a woman. . . . This delicious passion can destroy a man in the nicest possible way.

Delacroix had a close platoon of comrades with whom he would drink and party until morning, sometimes arguing about art and its principles, but more often indulging in gossip and boisterous camaraderie. Yet even this enjoyable party life was but a distraction to Delacroix. The first love of his life—"his one great mistress"—was his art, and his *Journals* are filled with frequent reminders of his need for healthy working time, from the confession that "he can only put in a good day's work when he knows the night holds in store for him some promise of enjoyment," to "early to bed, early to rise, makes a man healthy, wealthy and wise," coupled with a reminder to buy *Poor Richard's Almanac* as soon as possible. (If the coupling of Delacroix and Ben Franklin seems a bit surprising, one should remember that Franklin was also a great carouser and dandy in Paris—a far cry from the staid state portraits of him now found in Philadelphia.)

The feud between the two geniuses of the age had its origins early in their careers, long before they ever heard of each other. As a student of David, Ingres had come to consider himself a faithful copyist of the classics, and was wounded when his early entries in the Salon were attacked as "gothic." Faced with this accusation of infidelity, Ingres might have let himself out of his classical corset to explore and accept the potentialities that were his and his alone. Rosenblum, for example, sees in Ingres what Ingres himself could not see:

How can we reconcile this flexibility with Ingres's official position as the bigoted champion of Classical ideals throughout a long life-span that began in 1780 and ended in 1867, during which time he propagated the Classical faith both as a youth of twenty-four, fresh out of David's studio, and as an old man of seventy-eight, the venerated recipient of academic and official honors? And given Ingres's historical role as defender of the Classical tradition for two-thirds of the nineteenth century, how can we account for the fact that his art reveals startling heresies, that it could become the foundation not only for academic painting of the later nineteenth century but also for progressive currents in the modern tradition, from Degas, Renoir and Seurat to Matisse, Picasso and Gorky?

But Ingres did not accept himself; instead, he sucked in his pride and forced himself into a more rigid classical mold than before. Such servitude to an ideal could not but breed a certain self-righteousness and a corresponding resentment for all those who did not similarly conform. If Ingres turned against the schools and official art, it was only when they had turned against him. When the official critics were tormenting him with their justifiable dislike for his *Saint Symphorian* in 1834, Ingres would write terrible things about official art; but in 1855, when he was offered the presidency of the *Ecole,* the legion of honor, and other recognition, he voiced few anti-academic blasphemies. Long before Ingres returned from Rome to confront any of Delacroix's work, he was already embittered and paranoid in his self-righteous defense of the "true" principles of art, ready to attack any deviation from those principles (which after all were not his either) as a perversion of the arts and a worship of the "ugly" (see Holt, pp. 34 ff.).

Delacroix never had the chance to study with David, but in 1815, the year of Napoleon's defeat and David's exile, he entered the school of Pierre Guerin. He was an ambitious student, but without great expectations, when the drastic political change forced him to make an essential choice. Because his family had had strong Bonapartist and revolutionary attachments (his father had voted in the Assembly for the death of Louis XVI), Delacroix could expect little support for his modest artistic ambitions. He could either renounce art or fire up those ambitions to push his way through the State-supported *Ecole des Beaux-Arts* founded by David. The *Ecole* was run by Baron Gros, classicist and unfortunate future suicide. Gros, like Ingres, had strapped himself with an artistic ideal too restrictive for his genius, and likewise was all the more strict about that ideal and demanding of his students. Inevitably, Delacroix disliked this training, although his newly inspired ambition got him through. Even while a student he was bitterly opposed to academic painting, official rules, and schools of art in general. But Delacroix cannot be held up as a noble Socratic figure defying the prejudices of the time. He may never have accepted a position in a school, but he considered teaching to be a waste of his energies. And if he long stood on the outside of official art, it cannot be said that he did not desire an entrance: the long delay of his admission to the French Academy was not due to his unwillingness to join. And when the honor was finally offered to him only a few years before his death, he willingly accepted it without a show of bitterness.

Both artists, in fact, were as socially ambitious as they were dedicated to their unique styles of painting. In their very different temperaments they were both instances of the new bourgeois consciousness of social success that had replaced all vestiges of spirituality in Europe. Their ideals were secular, their inspiration "natural." (Even their angels were wholly "natural.")[19] The same mentality that would soon place a bourgeois king on the throne of France in 1830 was manifested in the vigorously ambitious art of Ingres and Delacroix. For all the excitement about "classicism" and "romanticism," escape to Arcady and escape to gothic horror, both Ingres and Delacroix were wholly geniuses of their time, painters of contemporary feeling, and men who lived for success and the esteem of their critics and colleagues. Behind them lay centuries of spiritual, majestic, and charming art; ahead of them lay entirely new conceptions. (From Ingres would emerge the abstract linearity of Picasso and Matisse; from Delacroix, the coloristic expressionism of Cézanne and Van Gogh.)[20] But their lives and their work are first and foremost the expression of that very special turning point in the bourgeois world view during the first half of the nineteenth century, when the Enlightenment and its seeming antithesis were in the midst of far more than an aesthetic battle.

The Classic/Romanticism Game

In art, as in history, the late Eighteenth Century created such profound breaches with the past that today, in the late twentieth century, we are still grappling with the problems that then announced the dawn of a new era. In histories of art, this period of unprecedented complexity has generally been divided into the two presumably antagonistic categories of Neoclassicism and Romanticism, a black-and-white polarity that, in more refined histories, also permits a single shade of gray called Romantic Classicism. Yet, indispensable as they seem, . . . these two unequal categories are pitifully inadequate in analyzing the bewildering new variety of emotions, styles, and iconography that emerged in the late Eighteenth Century.

Robert Rosenblum, *Transformations*

That Delacroix called himself a classicist shows how much the terms "classic" and "romantic"—like Baudelaire's term "modern"—were more polemical than descriptive. We have already seen how Goethe, the father of German romanticism, dismissed that movement as "sickly," and in Chapter 14 we shall see that Fichte, the philosophical pilot of the German *Romantik,* dismissed its claims as "unscientific." Romanticism has often been characterized, then as today, as oversentimentalization and bourgeois overdramatization, as imaginative escapism and unrealistic utopianism, sometimes leading (albeit unwittingly) to fascism. Yet Delacroix firmly believed that "art is reason" and that "feeling must not be expressed to the point of nausea." His few nudes are far less sentimentalized than those of Ingres. Against the charge of escapism, surely the romantic involvements in Greece and in the Paris Revolution of 1830 must count heavily, even if Delacroix himself did not take part. Against utopianism and fascism, the reformist sentiments of Shelley and George Sand, and the typical freedom-loving sentiments of the romantics as a whole, must make us pause, even when Delacroix says that freedom is "nonsense." But on the other hand, the too easy characterization of romanticism as revolutionary must take account of Delacroix's disgust with the 1848 Revolution and his general political apathy (see Chapter 14, pp. 291–98). It is easy enough, once we have thrown over our preconceptions and looked through the work of the romantics, or even through the work of Delacroix alone, to give up the name entirely and conclude that there is no possible characterization of a movement or of a genius so multifaceted and original. But this would be as serious a mistake as the dogmatic attempts to confine romanticism to a single idea of false sentimentality or escapism or revolutionism.

The problem of definition and classification is not much better on the classicist side. If we look closely at the classicism of David (or of Goethe), we must discern at least three distinct "classical" themes that fuse into a single definition only in a few questionable cases (see pp. 207–8). First, classicism is indeed an appeal to "the classics": the heroes and stories of the ancient Greeks and Romans, at least as envisioned by the eighteenth- and nineteenth-century Europeans. Second, classicism is a stylistic emphasis on form and structure. In painting, David insisted that painted figures be modeled after sculptures; that painted space resemble the narrow sculptural space of a Roman frieze; that color be secondary to form—an embellishment, but never overly sensuous or excessive; that outlines be distinguished sharply; that drawing and modeling be essential; that a painting should be "polished" and smoothed over, with its brushwork hidden, to give it that sense of hyper-real translucence and starkness that expressed his moral and political epigrams so effectively. Third, classicism may be no more than a term of high praise, independent of subject matter and style (as in the expression, "That has class"): the "classic" is the ideal, and whatever is not classic—however defined at any particular time—is therefore faulty, whatever its merits. (Thus Ingres would call Delacroix, without shame, an "apostle of the ugly.")

In David's work these three very different characterizations fit together as a family, the classical style serving the classical themes and the two together expressing the moral ideals that made it, politically as well as aesthetically, the "correct" art of the Revolution. In Ingres's work also, the three meanings are grouped together at least artificially, but Ingres's classicism, as Delacroix once commented, is largely pretension (which is not in the least to deny that he produced works of genius). Ingres often deviates from classical themes, and if he strictly adheres to the Davidian canon that "well drawn is well painted," he is simply canonizing his own particular talents—he was a genius at drawing—into an artificially "correct" conception of style. It is obvious that Ingres, painting after the Revolution had become but a memory to many and history to most of his own generation, employed Davidian schemes and techniques without any of the moral force that had animated them earlier. Because of his genius, classicism retained its place as "correct" and "official" art for years to come. But his own work is not by any means academic. Unlike Baron Gros, he was not forced to adapt his talents to rules for which he found himself unsuited. Yet even Ingres's work sometimes suffers from a rigid moralization of artistic techniques. And more insidiously, his sometimes tenuous use of "classical" in the third sense, as the official ideal, becomes a polemical term bandied about by inaesthetic political juries and the Academy—a tool for stifling and discouraging competition, and for saving the rich favors of patronage for "acceptable" students and supporters.

To understand the ideological significance of "classicism" and "romanticism," one must begin by recognizing that these terms are as much polemical as descriptive. This is not to deny certain differences, but if one focuses solely on style and subject matter, as so many critics of the time (and since) have done, one is inevitably outraged by the simplistic battles of line versus color, light versus shadow, antique versus modern, and who is the "true" classicist. The classic/romanticism game begins with a number of pieces—Ingres and his paintings—on the one side, graced with official recognition and thereby on the offensive. On the other side stands Delacroix, supported by Géricault and the praise of many artists, timidly reinforced by a half-hearted militia of disgruntled ex-Davidians and by the literary friends with whom he caroused in and around the salons of Paris. The opening moves are routine: classical subject matter is Greek and Roman allegory and history painting; romantic subject matter is medieval or occasionally contemporary (Géricault's *Raft of the Medusa,* Delacroix's *Massacre at Chios*), but still obsessed with the horrible and the grotesque, consumed with sentimentality and exoticism. Classical style is linear and shallow, color is secondary, drawing essential. The surface is polished, brushstrokes hidden. The aim is exact representation, "imitation of nature's beauty." Most important, all is subdued and in "the best of taste." On the other side, romanticism treats color as primary, drawing as secondary. Lines are often indistinguishable and outlines nonexistent. Brushstrokes stand baldly exposed, as if the artist intended us to see his own involvement in the work. Above all, beauty may be of little concern; feeling is primary, and the subject matter and the style, particularly the color, are obviously intended to evoke extreme reactions of discomfort and even fear and horror.[21]

The following set of countermoves is familiar to every student of art history (and in form, to every student of Introductory Philosophy). It is the counterexample subgame, in which each initial move is met with a specific counterinstance. Many—in fact most—of Ingres's paintings are not classical in their subject matter at all, being very contemporary portraits of very contemporary bourgeois gentlemen and their wives. His nudes are not Greek, but more likely Oriental harem girls, the supposed favorite subjects of the romantics. On occasion he will paint grotesque sphinxes and dragons (as in *Oedipus* and *Roger and Angelica*), and he is surely not above the portrayal of sensuous and even titillating scenes of women in their bath and caressing each other. It is Delacroix, in fact, from whom we expect the most representative classical allegories; his later murals are as reminiscent of Raphael's *stanza* in the Vatican as anything Ingres ever painted. Whatever his classical pretensions, Ingres's admiration went distinctly to Renaissance art; it was Raphael, not the Greeks, who held his attention. The critics were far from wrong when they labeled some of his earlier works "gothic." Delacroix, on the other hand, could rightfully claim to be as close to the ancients as Ingres; but where Ingres saw the ancients through Winckelmann's eyes as "calm and serene," Delacroix saw them through his travels in Morocco—vital and often terrifying, a tenuous synthesis of tense poise and wild uninhibitedness. Thus the figures in the game begin to switch identities.

In style, critics have asked, can we not compare Ingres's brilliant sensitivity to color with Vermeer? As we look at the bright colors on the pleats of skirts and shawls and headbands, we wonder where the suggestion that color is to be de-emphasized might have originated. And as we look at Delacroix's "revolutionary" *Dante and Vergil* or *Massacre at Chios,* is the color there really so rule-defying, so unconventional, or so brilliant? And as we look through Delacroix's notebooks, can there be any doubt that he valued drawing and preliminary studies as much as Ingres? Ingres, the most "intellectual" of painters, kept no journals, read little philosophy or literature, and developed no artistic theory apart from his canons of "good taste." Delacroix's *Journals* are a masterpiece of literature; he read widely and often used literature for his themes; and he was among the most important "scientists" of color in the history of painting. The most romantic of artists, Delacroix painted few nudes, for he considered them overly seductive. His naked, not nude, ladies are more often than not corpses or victims, and in his paintings there is little of the sentimentality and voluptuousness often found in Ingres's odalisques. And are not Ingres's portraits paradigms of the psychological (e.g., *M. Bertin*)? Are not his female figures grotesquely distorted for the sake of effect? Is not Delacroix a master of balance and form? And so the game climaxes in an ironic conclusion: *Ingres is the great romantic* (Wildenstein) and "in no sense a classic" (Gautier), while *Delacroix is the arch-classicist* (Pach).

The next move is a step to sanity: as a corrective to the above absurdity, it is denied that there is *any* ultimate difference between Ingres and Delacroix, between classical and romantic. This is the position of Clive Bell, who reduces the dispute to "the idiotic battle of line and color"; of Robert Rosenblum, who rejects the significance of the distinction as "a coloration, not a style or a movement"; and of Kenneth Clark, who holds that "every great classicist was a romantic at heart and vice versa," and that "the distinction is more convenient than real." And here the game would seem to end, or at least force one back to the beginning.

On the Metaphysics of Painting

> What do events matter to Ingres? He was a genius outside of time. . . . His figures are exempted from growing old, withdrawn from the realm of life and its predicaments, liberated from mutation by their inexpressiveness.
>
> Picon, *Ingres*

> In artistic matters, I am a supernaturalist. I believe that the artist cannot find all his form in nature, but that the most remarkable are revealed to him in his soul, like the innate symbolism of innate ideas.
>
> Heinrich Heine, discussing Delacroix

What are we to make of the bitter battle that raged between Ingres and Delacroix? Were they mere personality clashes, personal resentment? And what of the undeniable difference in their styles, both as men and as painters, that confronts us at every comparison? In the Metropolitan Museum in New York, for example, *J. A. Moltedo,* an Ingres portrait of the postmaster general of Rome, hangs near Delacroix's modest *Abduction of Rebecca,* based on an incident in Sir Walter Scott's *Ivanhoe.* The struggling Rebecca and her captors contort on horseback in a violent pyramid, projected against a distant exotic background of smoke and flames. Less than a yard away, the proper and prosperous M. Moltedo smiles contentedly, as indifferent to the violence on his right as he probably was to the state of the Italian mail service (no doubt the same then as now). He is elegantly dressed in luscious brown and starched white silk, his hand conspicuously raised within the frame of the picture in order to show us his bejeweled gold ring on a fat white sausage finger. Four hairs on his brow are conscientiously out of place. He fills the canvas with the bulk of his self-importance, standing against a possible canvas backdrop of pleasing blue and tranquil sky, while a quiet Colosseum peers pretentiously over his left shoulder. There is not a brushstroke to be seen, nothing to distract from that rich and formal pose of smugness and prosperity. Delacroix's *Rebecca,* on the other hand, consists of slashes of color and "good black," open gashes of bloody red and virgin white, as if the canvas itself had been wounded like living flesh. One might trace an outline of Ingres's portrait and its features, almost cut them into a stencil; but *Rebecca* has no outlines, only swirls and splashes of struggle and violence. Are we to say that these differences are inconsequential—mere matters of "coloration" or "convenience"?

Consider next two portraits by Ingres and Delacroix of a similar subject, the violinist Paganini.[22] Knowing what we do of the model—his brilliant and flamboyant showmanship, his reputation for mystery, and the legend that he was possessed by the devil—how surprised we must be by Ingres, who gives us what might easily be the official portrait of the first violinist of the local civic orchestra. The polished linearity reduces him to another prosperous bourgeois citizen, contributing to his community with musicianship as other Ingres subjects contribute with their business and administrative skills. The long nose is flattened, the sinister face rounded and smoothed, the typically disheveled foppish hair carefully assembled and orchestrated. It is without doubt a beautiful depiction, but it captures nothing of its devilish subject. How different is Delacroix's tiny portrait (17″ x 11″), which makes no attempt at flattery and but little even at representation. Here one finds a nose even longer than life; jagged features gashed by deft and violent strokes of pigment; and a mysterious inner light that Delacroix, like Rembrandt, introduces to capture the suffering of the genius within. Ingres's violinist stands attentive in formal pose; Delacroix's stands awkward and impassioned, violently caressing his instrument. Sparkles of gold lend the dark Delacroix portrait an eerie glow, and the twist of the body gives the same impression of struggle and violence as in Rebecca's abduction. Is there still no difference to be seen?

Similarly, compare any of Ingres's many official but often beautiful portraits to the two Delacroix portrayals of his friends Chopin and George Sand.[23] (Delacroix only painted his friends, refused portrait commissions as demeaning.) What a marked difference between the evident suffering of George Sand (so obvious that she found it embarrassing) and the haughty indifference of Ingres's *Mme Moitessier.* Compare even the black dresses on each. How much of a difference can there be between two black gowns? A great deal: observe that fine static lace that becomes part of a cold plaster body, and then that warm black blanket of security that covers up embarrassed suffering. Or compare Ingres's brilliant *M. Bertin,* famously the most "psychological" of his portraits, with Delacroix's *Chopin,* with its suppressed suffering and entranced rapture in his own creativity. Which is the more "psychological"? What does "psychology" mean here? M. Bertin makes us aware of his importance (he was one of the most influential journalists in Paris), of his toughness and his social position. But we see not his soul but his *role:* the mask which he presents to the society he serves, and which he wishes preserved for eternity. What we see in Chopin is something very different: not a mask or a position but a dissected personality, reduced to its basic elements of tragedy and weakness.

In the Salon of 1824 the two masters clashed openly for the first time. Ingres contributed his *Vow of Louis XIII,* Delacroix his *Massacre at Chios.* Despite his own insistence that historical painting was most important and portraiture a "distraction," Ingres was typically at his worst in his multifigured canvases and at his best in his "tedious" distractions. His *Vow* consists of an imitation Raphael madonna and child, robbed of their Raphael-esque sweetness by their corset of linearity, floating airily on two-dimensional cotton clouds over a meticulously painted royal blue silk cloak that almost completely covers a kneeling king. What a difference between this artificial triangle of devoted king, sweet virgin, and charming cherubs, and the two triangles of despair at *Chios.* In place of Ingres's smooth folds and contours, we find strangled and twisted lines of red and yellow, heavy bodies collapsed in death and despair.[24] Compare Ingres's Christ child, comfortably nestled in his mother's almost two-dimensional lap, with the twisted child to the lower left of the Delacroix, struggling to suckle his murdered mother (an almost trite appeal to sentimentality, as several contemporary critics pointed out).

Similarly, compare the fruits of their next confrontation in the Salon of 1827: Ingres's *Apotheosis of Homer,* a celebration of the classics modeled after Raphael, and Delacroix's *Death of Sardanapalus,*[25] a sensational and gruesome portrayal of the sadistic revelries of a dying and disgusted tyrant. Atop Ingres's pyramid of classical (and occasionally more modern) heroes, Homer awaits crowning by an airily suspended angel. As in the *Vow,* each figure is meticulously painted, but there is no discernible relationship between the figures; each might have been cut from a separate portrait and pasted in. But each of Delacroix's contorted figures—a harem being butchered, a war horse dragged in for the slaughter, the King himself twisted in disinterested yet tense repose on the bed of blood-red silks—supports the others, and not a form in the painting lacks an essential relationship with any other. As in his *Massacre,* the unity of writhing and tortured corpses and victims takes precedence over any attempt at individual portrayal. Each figure complements another, not as a matter of mere design, but as a balance of forces and tensions, a system of interrelated S-curves such that we find ourselves almost twisting with them, partly in horror and partly in rhythm.

Ingres's figures are frozen in time, or rather are indifferent to time, as if they need never have lived, so long as we have their formal essence before us now. But Delacroix catches hold of a piece of time for us, keeps it alive through eternity, creates momentarily all its original frenzy and terror. Compare the disgusted indifference of the expiring King with the lifeless inexpressiveness of Homer, or the faces of death at *Chios* with the plastic tranquillity of Ingres's virgin. Compare also the generous, well-tempered, and balanced greens, blues, and reds of Ingres's *Homer* with the single-minded tempest of Delacroix's blood-reds and tragic ochres of *Sardanapalus*. What scene in history is bloodier than Delacroix's *Sardanapalus*? But where are the blood, the wounds, the ceremonial gashes, and the red drippings that have adorned every crucifix and beheading since the Middle Ages? There is not a drop, not even a slight laceration. The very painting itself—not its individual figures—is gashed and bleeding; it is the scene, and not just its victims, that explodes for us in bloody color. Again we might say that the red is the lifeblood of the painting, and its fleshy whites and yellows its wounded flesh, as we recede from the painting, our aesthetic sensibilities raped by this intrusion of horror. We have long been inundated with violence and gore, but to the staid bourgeoisie of Paris in 1827, still trying to repress the memories of the preceding era, *Sardanapalus* must certainly have been "in bad taste."

One further comparison: consider any of Ingres's deservedly famous odalisques and bathers, for example, his *Grande Odalisque* (1814) in the Louvre. Now consider the nude figures in Delacroix's *Sardanapalus,* or one of his very rare nudes like *Mademoiselle Rose* (1824). For all their alleged sensuality and seductive glances and poses, Ingres's bodies are anything but sensuous or seductive. The slight blushes of carefully integrated pink fail to thaw the cold, polished marble thighs and flanks, while the formal poses of sexual modesty and the distant but surely not provocative stare in the eyes cannot possibly excite any but the most determinedly prurient of viewers. The beauty of Ingres's nudes is not a sensuous one, but a purely abstract rhythmic harmony controlled by the artificiality of the poses, and enhanced by the sometimes grotesquely extended arms and necks, while undistracted by the slightest hint of anatomical exactness or fleshy tangibility. Delacroix's nudes, on the other hand, are soft and pudgy, far more accurate in their presentation than Ingres's *Odalisque,* even when forced into the postures of corpses and victims. Where Ingres's figures appear in a pose of embarrassed surprise, Delacroix's nudes actually seem to be embarrassed; there are no frozen half-turns away from the viewer, only that glowing pudgy nakedness that betrays the imperfection and mortality that Ingres always denied his subjects. A Delacroix breast is a vulnerable mound of soft flesh; an Ingres breast is more like a muscle on the marble statue of an ancient warrior. Ingres's subjects have no stomachs, for what disrupts smooth linearity more than a bulging midriff? Delacroix's models, on the other hand, have soft, pliable bodies; they are not designs but *substances,* ready to be grappled, stabbed, thrown to the ground, or abducted struggling on horseback. Neither of these artists is particularly interested in sensuality, but what *does* interest them is significantly different. What are these differences? Surely not only matters of line and color, or personal incongruities, or differences in technique or subject matter. Something more is at stake here, something which the judges of the 1827 Salon surely caught when they warned Delacroix that he would soon starve if he did not "change his ways."

Let us return to an earlier comparison, made in passing, between Ingres's and Delacroix's very different conceptions of the classics. Ingres's vision of the Greeks was that of Winckelmann—a calm and noble ideal world, eternal in its values and free from the ravages of fashion and time. But Delacroix pictured the ancient Greeks after the model of contemporary Arab tribesmen, wild and sensuous, recklessly daredevilish, and in immediate contact with the dangers and sufferings of life. In other words, Ingres's Greece was the world of Parmenides and Plato, a world of fixed and static ideals and forms which were too easily hidden by the illusions of change. The role of art, in Greek society and in the modern world of Ingres, was to represent and free these eternal forms from the imperfect appearances that manifested them. Delacroix, on the other hand, saw the ancient world as a world of excitement and danger—unlike contemporary Paris, which he found boring. It was the world of Heraclitus and Aristotle, a world of spiritual conflict and growth. It was a difference not just of personality or painting techniques, but of ideology: a confrontation within the spirit of the times. It was a metaphysical or philosophical difference within which Ingres and Delacroix, and classical and romantic painting, were but the visual representatives of a deep structure of the human spirit that was manifesting itself similarly in every other human endeavor, in Goethe's poetry and Hegel's philosophy, in Beethoven's music, and in the political currents of revolution and reaction that would twice again rip Paris apart in the first half of the nineteenth century.

The deep structure of the difference between Ingres and Delacroix—between the classical and the romantic—is no less than that omnipresent contrast in metaphysics between the formal and static on the one side, conflict and dialectic on the other. It is the same difference that exists between Kant and Goethe, or Kant and Hegel, or Mozart and Beethoven. Here is the new dialectic of human growth, once again a conflict wholly *within* the bourgeoisie, this absolutely victorious middle class that had smashed its aristocratic opposition once and for all. If there was still a Bourbon king on the French throne in 1829, that would soon be ended; and if there were still vestiges of the old and often misunderstood conflicts between Voltaire and Rousseau, these were but dead metaphysical relics of a struggling and aspiring bourgeoisie. Voltaire and Rousseau had been fused by the Revolution—and by Kant—and now formed a common base: Reason and Passion, Egalitarianism and Elitism, Revolution and Reaction. The new problems just emerging were of a very different kind. The lower classes and the misfortunes of oppressed groups in the far corners of Europe now concerned and sometimes embarrassed the Parisians, while at the same time a new problem hitherto unheard of reared its head: *boredom,* that restless disease that comes only with victory and leisure.

As the businessman's ideal of prosperity and success replaced the old slogans of "liberty, equality, fraternity," the intellectually astute and self-proclaimed elitist circles of the fashionable salons took it upon themselves —or found it forced upon them—to combat the growing tedium of a vulgar and increasingly industrial society. Delacroix, for example, complained often, both in public and in the privacy of his *Journals,* that "this progress is making men go ever faster and faster—but what about boredom?" There was a continuing revolutionary spirit, now strangely merged with bourgeois complacency. It no longer manifested itself only within Paris (except for the few days required to oust Charles X from his throne), but was extended to the victims of tyranny in Greece and, more confusedly, to the victims of the industrial revolution—the working classes closer to home. Thus the problem facing Ingres and Delacroix, and every person of the age, was simply, What are we to do with humanity? The Enlightenment had triumphed with the ideal of the Revolution. It was now an indisputably human world, with little place for God or the powers of nature—regardless of English romanticism's attempt to recapture them.[26] What was one to make of this new bourgeois model? Was this humanity's final achievement? Or was this but one more stage in the historical dialectic, with the European bourgeoisie but a passing moment?

In one sense, both Ingres and Delacroix were the last great spiritual artists in our tradition, for they were the last to seriously see themselves as the expression of a universal human spirit—as in Kant, Goethe, Hegel, and Beethoven. They were the last of those many generations who, as Hegel predicted, could view their art as an expression of the Absolute, the ultimate nature of human reality. There would be other religious artists, of course—Rouault, for example—who would be powerfully spiritual and expressive. But individual religious passion and despair are very different from the universal life of the human spirit; before Ingres's and Delacroix's careers had ended, art had recognized this spiritual loss and turned to more limited areas of human endeavor. By 1850 Courbet and Daumier had already given art a new role in politics, but without any of that moral spirit and universality that shone through the glossy canvases of David. "Realism"—and how many artists have not claimed to be realists?—is not characterized by any increase in its sense of reality (what is reality, anyway?), but rather by its drastic decrease in spirituality. This spiritless albeit moving depiction of the times easily withdraws into itself, as if deprived of its living warmth and reason for being. No wonder the art of the later nineteenth century resembled pornography as often as Poussin. And no wonder that the best art to emerge from this spiritual abyss was an art totally absorbed in itself, without the slightest sense of obligation to religion or politics, or to the human spirit in general ("art for art's sake"). Manet could depict an execution as indifferently as Brueghel could depict a grapefruit. Monet could dissect the colors of a lily pad with as much fervor and intensity as Ingres and Delacroix would lay bare the visual essence of humanity, celebrate twenty generations of human genius, or depict several dozen bathing nymphs or a gruesome lion hunt.[27]

There is no easy summary of the metaphysical issues that separate Ingres and Delacroix, and the movements they led. We have not yet developed what I will call an "ideology of art" to the extent that recent historians, following the lead of Erwin Panofsky, have developed an "iconology" of art's particulars. But we can, in a fairly mechanical way, spell out the distinctions which might be used in such a differential ideology, always keeping in mind that there is a family of resemblances at stake, not a cut-and-dried formula, so as to avoid the popular but sophomoric counterexample phase of the classic/romanticism game. And of course we must not let this ideological analysis interfere with the art itself. However much art ultimately expresses philosophy, art is art, and the aesthetics of sensuous visual forms is irreducible to any claims of validity or viability in the unsensuous world of the Concept.

The Ideology of Art

An ideology of art is an archaeological "dig" for the metaphysical principles embedded in painting (and sculpture, music, poetry, etc.). It *presupposes* precisely the principle that we have been following all along: to see in every contemporary human endeavor a similar set of philosophical viewpoints. Yet we have also seen that this *Zeitgeist* rarely if ever contains a single coherent set of principles, but rather a series of oppositions and conflicts that battle against each other until resolution, giving rise to yet further conflicts and growth. In the art of Ingres and Delacroix we find manifested the same oppositions that we find elsewhere—a conflict between the complacent and the restless, the fixed and the fluid, between acquiescence and struggle. In terms of philosophy it is the conflict between Kant and Hegel: whether the categories of our understanding are fixed and exact, or change with experience and adapt themselves to it; whether laws (be they scientific or moral) are timeless and universally necessary, or evolve and serve in different ways at different times. It is the question whether passions are indeed, as Kant insisted, "pathological," or whether, as Hegel insisted, "nothing great has ever been accomplished without them."[28]

Ingres's is the art of the finite, of the understanding, of accurate "representation" of details and minutiae, of the engraving on a bracelet or the pleating on a skirt, the lashes of a matron's eyes or the lace on her shawl. Even Ingres's spaces are absolutely finite and limited, almost two-dimensional, his portrait subjects often filling the small corner spaces or the armchairs in which they pose. Delacroix has little patience for detail; he is a holist interested in a painting as a unity that evolves forms and shapes within itself, a self-enclosed infinity that reflects (not represents) the human cosmos as a whole. His spaces reach back to an infinity typically cast in smoke and mist or, in his portraits, in the infinite expanse of a Constable background.[29] Ingres's figures are transfixed beyond time, beings-in-themselves who do not change or feel, and cannot change us or invoke feelings in us except for the cool contemplation of the formal beauties they represent.[30]

Delacroix's subjects, on the other hand, are caught in time, a time which reaches infinitely back and infinitely forward, filled with moments of anguish and excitement such as this or that particular one, and forcing us to share that anguish and excitement *now*. Aesthetically, Ingres is the artist of *beauty*, that immediate and eternal harmony that he claims to find in nature. But Delacroix is the artist of the *sublime*, the mediated and tenuous balance of forces in the midst of conflict, the struggles of victims caught in traumatic change, horror, and death.[31] Ingres's linearity is the visual representation of Kant's distinct categories, organizing experience decisively and unambiguously into individual objects in finite space. Delacroix's apparent lack of clarity is no other than Hegel's Reason, that is, Reason as evolving experience, struggling to grasp at ultimate meanings in the confusion of change. For Ingres there is no change, so of course he could tell his students to simply "draw from Nature," the source of eternal verities. But for Delacroix Nature was like a "vocabulary," containing the elements of the cosmos but requiring our imagination to unify them meaningfully. For Delacroix there was no "imitation"—only lack of imagination. The choice of subject matter—so often overemphasized—is of the least importance for an ideology of art, though it is worth noting that Delacroix painted horses while Ingres idealized nudes, and that Delacroix depicted contemporary atrocities while Ingres chose allegories. But underlying the choice of subject matter—even where Ingres paints more contemporary events, or where Delacroix paints portraits or classical allegories—is the basic metaphysical difference which manifests itself in the very nature of their painting. A Delacroix portrait has a violence about it that Ingres's *Roger Attacking a Dragon* lacks, for the basic difference is always that between force and understanding, struggle and complacency, violent evolution and ever-present ideals.

The styles of painting provide just as valid a metaphysical medium as the opacities of German idealist philosophy. Ingres's representation of space is an argument equivalent to Kant's "Transcendental Aesthetic," and Delacroix's hierarchies of ambiguous S-curves are the visual equivalent of Hegel's dialectic. The battle between line and color, far from being pedantic or trivial, is nothing less than the battle of world views spelled out for us in philosophy. Ingres's modeled outlines are fixed and specific, walling off the enclosed figures from the infinity that surrounds them. Delacroix's painterly figures merge with that infinity, move with it, force our eye to move ambiguously from form to form. The multiplicity and disconnectedness of the portraits in Ingres's *Homer* are far more than an aesthetic failing; they are a metaphysical problem—the integration of the separate finitudes into a single world picture. Similarly, the emphasis on color betrays far more than a certain sensuousness on the part of Delacroix and other painters. Color integrates as line does not, colors are "complementary" in a way that forms are not, and where a line walls off its enclosure, color is always a linkage outside of itself, a "complement," not an edge.

It is worth noting that philosophers (Locke, for instance) have long distinguished form and shape as a "primary" property, as opposed to color as a "secondary" property. Primary properties inhered in the object itself; secondary properties were in some sense "in us." And it had long been argued—ever since the Greek philosophers—that forms appealed to the intellect as aspects of reality, while colors appealed to the emotions and had more to do with our passions than with the world "outside of us." This distinction is significant here, for Ingres always claimed a kind of "objectivity" for his paintings based largely upon the fact that what he copied were *forms,* while color was relegated to a secondary and decorative role. Delacroix, on the other hand, never tired of insisting that his paintings were directed at the passions and subjectivity. But it is also noteworthy that Kant, among his many other insights, proved that form and "quality" (including color) were equally categorical, existing equally both "in us" and "in the world"; though the old alignment between form and intellect, color and passion remained, the principles of our understanding were also the principles of reality. Thus Ingres could claim to be interested in ideal reality, regulated by the principles of his art. Similarly, Delacroix could claim that he was not dealing solely with the passions, as if to merely titillate us, but rather—after Hegel—with the human spirit as a whole, which includes all reality. But where Ingres's reality consisted of collections of idealized objects and persons, Delacroix's reality was a totality within which objects and particular persons were but parts of an organic whole, an organism which might crush a young woman as well as an insect in its struggling for spiritual growth.

About twenty years ago the art historian E. H. Gombrich developed a now famous argument concerning the "psychoanalytic" foundations of late nineteenth-century official art, which he saw as more often than not resembling skilled but slick pornography. His argument, in a sentence, was that we find ourselves offended by these explicitly seductive nudes because they are simply *given* to us; they make no appeal to our sophisticated abilities of interpretation.[32] Indeed, such a phenomenon could easily develop from Ingres's official classicism, though Ingres himself surely should not be included here. The idealization of the nude, the firm and explicit outlines, and polished superficial painting allow the viewer only the passive recognition of a form fully rendered. Delacroix, on the other hand, makes us *work* for our experience, suffer through ambiguities and the horrors of our imaginations, and search our own souls for the passions with which to empathize with his suffering subjects. Whether the subjects are nude or not is unimportant; what matters is whether the experience is truly *ours* or not. Ingres may have been rightfully termed the painter of the "intellect," but the intellect was all his—his own calculations and constructions. But there is a difference, as some recent philosophers have argued, between calculating and thinking, and here we must judge Delacroix, in the second sense, the far greater "intellect." He makes us think not of composition or technique, but about our life and experience, and this is the thinking that evidently went into the painting as well. Where Ingres is concerned with fidelity to his principles, Delacroix is interested in his painting's *effect*. Ingres gives us perfect paintings, but Delacroix gives us traumatic experiences and spiritual growth.

Ingres, then, gives us painting of Kant's world of understanding, in which the universal ideal is manifested in the particular—in which the world is there for us, even if the principles according to which we must represent it are our own. Delacroix, on the other hand, gives us a visual representation of Hegel's dialectic of the spirit: an interconnected series of particulars which catches us up in the universal movement of a world that is just now being created by us, but in which we find ourselves victims as much as creators.

14 Dull Times: The Romantic Reaction

I want a hero, an uncommon want,
When every year and month sends forth a new one.

Byron, *Don Juan*

Ten years now, I have dragged my college
Along by the nose through zig and zag
Through up and down and round and round
And this is all that I have found—
The impossibility of knowledge!

I cannot presume to make use of my learning
I cannot presume I could open my mind,
To proselytize and improve mankind.

Goethe, *Faust*

Romanticism is the turning point of our ideological drama, its midlife crisis, the beginning of the bourgeois ulcer which attacks and digests itself with its own principles and pretensions. Romanticism, Marxism, existentialism—each despised and sought to destroy the degenerate bulk of the bourgeoisie, yet each was itself just as thoroughly bourgeois and decadent. The Enlightenment had turned sour. Because it now lacked opposition in France, and because the opposition was overwhelming in Germany, the bourgeoisie turned on itself in disgust, self-righteously opposing its own self-righteousness, rejecting its own principles in the name of those same principles.[1] "Hypocrisy" had been the charge of the philosophers against the Old Regime; "hypocrisy" became the charge of the bourgeoisie against themselves. By 1830 the very word "bourgeois" had taken on its familiar sneer of revulsion, its suggestion of the odor of decay sprayed over with a sweet-smelling, equally foul disinfectant. The novelist Stendhal, for example, described the new middle-class hero in quiet terms of opprobrium:

At the sight of him every hat is quickly raised. His hair is turning grey, and he is dressed in grey. He is a Companion of several Orders, has a high forehead, an aquiline nose, and on the whole his face is not wanting in a certain regularity; indeed, the first impression formed of it may be that it combines with the dignity of a village mayor that sort of charm which may still be found in a man of forty-eight or fifty. But soon the visitor from Paris is annoyed by a certain air of self-satisfaction and self-sufficiency mingled with a suggestion of limitations and want of originality. One feels, finally, that this man's talent is confined to securing the exact payment of whatever is owed to him and to postponing payment till the last possible moment when he is the debtor.[2]

The bourgeois intellectual began in turn to take on the now familiar attitude of ruthless self-contempt, combined strangely with an inalienable sense of superiority.[3] Voltaire had his cynicism and Rousseau his sense of corruption, but neither doubted his own inner righteousness or integrity. The new intellectual, however, began to suspect a corruption at the very core of his bourgeois soul—or a fatal emptiness, the very lack of a "soul." The aim became, therefore, to fill that vacuum with explicit ideology, with religion, poetry, fanaticism, self-abuse—anything that might replace that emptiness which once, only a few years before, had been filled with passion and enthusiasm.

The Age of Enthusiasm

> For the classicists, the ideal was found in the perfection of our human nature. The ideal for romantic poets is to be found in our sorrows.
> Charles Nodier[4]

Romanticism is often described solely in terms of its opposition to classicism in the arts, but this is to miss its significance entirely.[5] Petty artistic squabbles, as we argued in the last chapter, may be the manifestations of profound ideological differences. Our interpretation of this movement, accordingly, must be primarily philosophical. Romanticism has been generally recognized as the nemesis of the Enlightenment, even as the "anti-Enlightenment," but this is illuminating only when we appreciate how much the romantics shared with the Enlightenment, how much they were part of it, and how much their reactions were but variations on the same bourgeois ideology. To see such dialectical relations instead of mere antagonism, in fact, was one of the great lessons of the romantic movement, a healthy corrective to the self-righteous Manicheanism of the Enlightenment. But self-righteousness itself was one feature of bourgeois ideology left wholly intact by the romantics.

The Enlightenment was nothing if not enthusiasm. Its philosophers spouted "reason" but expressed their passion for life, for justice, for humanity. It is said that they expressed hope or confidence or even faith in the future, but this view is as inaccurate as it is unnecessary: what they expressed was sheer *vitality*. Theirs was a youthful ideology of challenge and excitement which gave life meaning even in the face of overwhelming opposition and the *lack* of hope, confidence, and faith. Ironically, it was only when this vitality had died—when its ideology had grown old and jaded in an age described by Kierkegaard as one of "understanding and reflection without passion"—that there was talk of "the Age of Enthusiasm." The romantics talked "passion," but what they expressed was despair, boredom, ennui. Theirs was a world in repose, spouting platitudes and challenging nothing. Romanticism, first of all, was the need to *create* new passions.

As a reaction against stale principles, uninspired art, and the generally dull world of the post-Napoleonic Reaction, the romantic movement—the reaction against the Reaction—took many disparate and often desperate directions, giving rise to the impression that there was no single "movement" at all.[6] In Germany romanticism became nationalism, sentimentalism, abstruse philosophy, and bad poetry. In France romanticism became fashionable ostentatiousness, disruptiveness, living theater, and bourgeois adventurism. In fact, if we were to seek out a single image of the romantic rebellion in France, we should think of Théophile Gautier flaunting his flamboyant red smoking jacket, so markedly vulgar in the proper society of 1830 Paris, in order "to exasperate the Philistines." Accordingly, while romanticism promoted itself in the name of liberation and humanism— both good Enlightenment concepts—it established itself as pretentious, overly sentimental, escapist, insincere, artificial, and obnoxious—all charges that three generations before had been leveled at the Enlightenment philosophers. But where the Enlightenment philosophers had expressed their passions in confrontation, the romantics used their confrontations to bolster their passions.

The most enthusiastic spokesmen of romanticism had missed the bloody festivals of the turn of the century; they were too young or they were German. In either case, they had been raised on legends, on echoes of excitement from the past or from across the border. They could afford to despise peace and prosperity, the lack of excitement and inspiration, the ruling "fat brood of mediocrity,"[7] and the vulgar materialism that represented the drab new world. Their ideal was a bohemian ideal of rebellion against efficiency without emotion, against rigid forms and platitudes that still boasted of their revolutionary origins, against self-righteousness and complacency that left no room for their own self-righteousness and ambitions. Using ostentatiousness, pornography, dandyism, metaphysical obscurity, or mock heroism, the young romantics did what they could, in a world that had become frustratingly nonviolent, to "exasperate the Philistines."[8]

Because romanticism saw itself as opposing the Enlightenment, it had to simplify and falsify Enlightenment ideology as much as the Enlightenment had once simplified and falsified the complexities of the Middle Ages. The romantics ignored the similarities and stressed the differences—even if only differences in emphasis—between themselves and the Enlightenment. They exaggerated the distinction between reason and passion, which was never all that important to "the Age of Reason."[9] They contrasted their own renewed Christianity (converting to Catholicism was a popular ritual among German romantics) with the alleged atheism of the Enlightenment —another falsification.[10] They made it seem as if the Enlightenment, which included some of the best historians of the modern age, had wholly neglected tradition and history, obliterating the past in their obsession with the future. In point of fact, the romantics themselves distorted the past in their despair over the present. But if the battle lines were false and confusing—as in the artistic clash between romantic and classicist painters— the ideological conflict behind such clashes and their shared bourgeois pretensions had yet to be shown.

If the battles between the romantics and the classicists were often confused and confusing, it was because, whatever the superficial disagreements and vehement sloganeering, the underlying ideology was the same. Thus the best romantic painter, Delacroix, insisted that he was "the true classicist," and the most powerful romantic philosophers—Fichte and Hegel, for example—rejected "romanticism" and insisted on their commitment to "Reason." In a new age the thrust and polemics had to be different; the underlying pretensions, however, were distinctly bourgeois.

Above all, the bourgeois sense of self-importance and need for moral righteousness motivated the romantics as much as they had the Enlightenment. Romantics too called themselves "liberals," defined themselves in terms of abstract ideals, and ranged themselves as "moderns" against the old, outdated, often oppressive Enlightenment heroes. True, they had a heightened sense of history, and the concept of self had taken some new turns. For the philosophers of the Enlightenment, the self had been a given, autonomous, sensitive, rational individual, inspired by universal reason and universal human nature; for the romantics, it was more of an instantiation of the universal, a manifestation of a cosmic will. Yet the romantics celebrated national differences as the Enlightenment had not, and it was they who encouraged the cult of genius and the ideal of the hero.[11] ("I want a hero," insisted Byron, whereas Voltaire had complained, "I hate heroes; they are so noisy.")

These differences were indicative of very different struggles: the Enlightenment against aristocratic privileges, the romantics against bourgeois mediocrity and, in Germany, the suffocation of local identity from excess internationalism. In the Enlightenment the abstraction "human" had been used to deny privilege and prejudice, allowing the ambitious bourgeoisie to assert their new identities; for the romantics, however, abstract humanism had come to represent a denial of self-identity, the impossibility of heroism, the illegitimacy of "national character." Accordingly, the romantics altered the concept of self-identity in two ways: they broadened it to include not just humanity but the cosmos, thus arguing under a quasi-religious image (as in Hegel) for a far more arrogant humanism than even the Enlightenment had suggested; and they qualified it once again to make room for ethnic identity and especially the role of the hero and the genius. What is revealing, however, is that both the Enlightenment and romanticism used a combination of abstract universalism and particularism to undermine their immediate social circumstances, including the legitimacy of French internationalism in Germany and the power of the new bourgeoisie in France. Both Enlightenment and romantic philosophers held themselves up as champions of "humanity" and even "the common man." And this could be done by even the uncommonest of men, by paranoid Rousseau, by the Olympian Goethe and the obscurantist philosophers of Germany.

Universalism; the transcendental pretense; the concept of "human nature"; the sense of the bourgeois "absolute" and of nature as a tool, a source of inspiration; the unyielding emphasis on "freedom" and "liberation," whether from bad governments or oppressive rules; the self-righteous battle against stupidity or banality—all these were inherited from the Enlightenment by the romantics. Only within this family genealogy can we hope to understand their dramatic differences. And only by appreciating the power of boredom and frustration, the lack of engaging ideals in the spirit of the times, shall we understand why the bourgeois ideology should have manifested itself in such self-destructive, overly sentimental, and frequently obnoxious behavior.[12]

Romanticism and the Politics of Experience

> Though there is no such thing as Romanticism, there emphatically *was* something which—for lack of any other brief name—may still be called a Romantic period; . . . the half century 1780–1830.
>
> Now the German Romantics of the 1790s were in conscious and zealous—though not in consistent or unwavering—revolt against all assumptions, but first of all in the history of art. They conceived and proclaimed themselves to be the prophets of a new, a "modern" art—and "modern" is what *they* primarily meant by "Romantic."
>
> Arthur Lovejoy, "The Meaning of Romanticism"

The bitter conflict between the classical and the romantic, wrenched out of context, is particularly instructive. On the most superficial but by no means unimportant level of meaning, the terms were *political* weapons. The concept of classicism, with its built-in appeal to ancient ideals of perfection, was taken by its advocates to refer necessarily to what is best in both art and humanity. Consequently, its arguments became tautologies, and attacks against it became inconsistencies. Romanticism too received its persuasive definitions. The German critic Friedrich von Schlegel defined romantic poetry as "progressive universal poetry," and elsewhere as simply "modern," as opposed to out-of-date, literature.[13] In the same vein, the French romantic Stendhal characterized the difference between romanticism and classicism thus:

Romanticism is the art of presenting to people the literary works which, in the actual state of their habits and beliefs, are capable of giving them the greatest possible pleasure; Classicism, on the contrary, presents them with literature which gave the greatest possible pleasure to their great grandfathers.[14]

Stendhal wrapped up his argument by saying that "all great writers were romantics in their own day," thus creating a tautology of his own in defense of romanticism. Yet later, reacting against the dominating and, in his opinion, distasteful influence of Victor Hugo, Stendhal rejected the name "romantic" for himself, and even Victor Hugo later gave up the name, calling himself a "realist" when "romanticism" was no longer in fashion.

The glorification of romanticism repeated the idealism of classicism; in fact, its progenitors in Germany were the same figures who had dominated classicism—Schiller and Goethe in particular. In France, Racine and Corneille were resurrected as protoromantic authors, tempered necessarily by what Stendhal politely called "the extreme dignity then in fashion" in the court of Louis XIV. The German poet Novalis (Friedrich von Hardenberg) transported the classical ideal of human perfection into the romantic camp:

The world must be made romantic. Then once more we shall discover its original meaning. To make something romantic is nothing else but a qualitative potentialization. In such an operation, the lower self becomes identified with the higher self. We ourselves are this series of qualitative potentials.[15]

Similarly, Victor Hugo defined romanticism as "liberalism in literature": "It would be strange if, in this age, liberty, like light, should penetrate everywhere except to the one place where freedom is most natural—the domain of thought."[16] The argument continues to this day; Herbert Read, in his interpretation of surrealism as the ultimate victory of romanticism, bitterly insists that

Classicism represents for us now, and always has represented for us, the forces of oppression; Classicism is the intellectual counterpart of political tyranny. . . . Wherever the blood of martyrs stains the ground, there you will find a doric column or perhaps a statue of Minerva.[17]

Against the "tyranny" of classical canons of taste, the romantic artists indeed insisted on complete freedom and the "divine right" of genius. The

Schlegel brothers spoke for their generation when they argued that "the only law for the artist is that he accepts no laws outside of himself." So too, Hugo in France: "Let us take the hammer to theories and poetic systems. . . . There are neither rules nor models." Romanticism presented itself as the spirit of the modern age—and therefore a universally accessible populism—and as a cult of genius besides. The combination of defense of the common person with literary elitism is not unfamiliar, but it was awkward even then. Hugo announced that "the poets must walk before the people and show them the way." In tones much like the manifestos of the Schlegels, he insisted that "writers should be judged, not according to rules and species, which are contrary to nature and art, but according to the immutable principles of the art of composition, and the special laws of their individual temperaments."[18]

Unfortunately, the romantic movement produced very few geniuses, and those it did produce survived only because they transcended the apparent nihilism of such advice. They in fact followed Goethe's suggestions about "freedom within limitation," stretching rather than breaking the rules only after many years of development had carried them to an unnecessary canonical obstacle. They still believed in what Hugo called "the immutable principles of the art of composition." Furthermore, those who made the most noise about romanticism often contributed least to it. Hugo wrote his greatest works when the polemics of 1830 were well behind him; the later Beethoven could not have given a treble clef about the romantic rules or lack of them; Delacroix painted within a set of formal traditions just as much as Ingres, although he characterized those traditions differently. (Conversely, Ingres succeeded in spite of, and not because of, the classical canons he defended.) Romanticism is in fact best understood through some of its mediocrities, who had more time for manifestos and less reason for confusion in their style. But this does not mean that the movement itself is mediocre; the mediocrities define an essential thread of the ideology of the times, without which one cannot understand the geniuses who rise above it.

The attack on romanticism was as bitter as its defense. Goethe called romanticism "sickly" and "pathological." In our own time this diagnosis has been often repeated—for example, by Irving Babbitt, who sees his criticism of romanticism as "stripping idealistic disguises from egoism, exposing . . . sham spirituality."[19] Similarly Arnold Hauser, from a Marxist point of view, condemns romanticism as "irrational and escapist," as "a one-sidedness" and a "fear of the present," as "childish" and an

escape to Utopia and fairy tale, to the unconscious and the fantastic, the uncanny and mysterious, to childhood and nature, to dreams and madness, . . . all disguised and more or less sublimated forms of the same feeling, of the same yearning for irresponsibility and a life free from suffering and frustration.[20]

Politically, romanticism was the continuation of the French Revolution "by other means." In Germany, where revolutionary ideals were never given free expression, romanticism was a world view which allowed at least artistic and intellectual expression of freedom, however impossible such expression was in the political world. Romanticism also provided the psychological energy to unify an otherwise isolated and timid people into what would become, by the latter half of the century, the new gravitational center of European culture. In France, romanticism flowered after the fall of Napoleon. During the years of revolution and war, the French surely did not need an ideology to further excite them, but rather the soothing formalism of classical harmony. But one must not make the mistake, as many scholars have, of equating romanticism with reaction, just because the one typically accompanied the other. It is not romanticism that is responsible for reaction; on the contrary, romanticism may be the only possible means of keeping the spirit of rebellion alive in such times. Indeed, in the first half of the nineteenth century this was its primary function.[21]

Neither classicism nor romanticism was a political movement as such. Like all ideologies, they were spurred on by political considerations and called upon to serve political purposes. But the "revolutionary" spirit of romanticism was as much cultural and personal as political, just as the ideals of classicism were artistic and spiritual. Still, an ideology may outlive its cultural functions and become archaic or decadent. For David, classicism served a revolutionary function; with Ingres, it became reactionary and oppressive. For Victor Hugo and Heinrich Heine, romanticism served the causes of liberalism and was partially responsible for revolutions and the success of German nationalism. But some of the romantic poetry and painting in France and Germany was as sweetly sentimental and escapist as the harshest critics ever charged, rejecting all social and political responsibilities as if the present world did not exist at all.[22] It was against this cheapened form of romanticism, and against the archaic "ideals" of degenerate classicism, that the very powerful "realist" movements began in mid-century.

Neither classicism nor romanticism can be divorced from political realities; yet neither was a political movement as such. Both served to fill deficits in the human spirit. Classicism gave form to chaotic vitality; romanticism gave life to spiritual decadents. These functions were highlighted by the failures. Baron Gros drowned himself because he could not maintain his teacher David's already stale classical formulas in an age that was increasingly romantic.[23] He blamed himself for failing the ideals of his master, when he had only denied his own timely sentiments. Finding life's everyday disappointments not enough, the German poet Heinrich Kleist (1777–1811) linked up with a woman dying of cancer and killed himself with her, the victim of post-Kantian skepticism. In place of the

Kant of the Enlightenment, he had invented a Kant of despair and a world unknowable and uncaring, anticipating Schopenhauer.[24] In the years of peace, with battlefield slaughters no longer a daily statistic, the number of suicides soared astronomically. *Werther,* the champion of eighteenth-century sentimentalism, became the reality of the nineteenth-century newspapers. Romantic artists tended to burn out early—Schubert, Shelley, Géricault—often driving themselves mad in the process. The frenzy of self-motivation, unlike the worries of war, knows no respite. Schizophrenia became popular and heroic. So did philosophy. Revolutions produce few great thoughts, wars none; it is peace that leaves that void in human life which ceaselessly produces philosophy (whatever its quality), and so, despite their seeming antithesis, it is above all romanticism that produces philosophy.[25] The classical philosophers were analytical; they wanted to clarify. The romantic philosophers are typically speculative, inspiring, edifying, inventive. Thus Novalis: "Insofar as I render a higher meaning to what is ordinary, a mysterious appearance to what is customary, an infinite look to the finite, I am romanticizing" (*Reader,* p. 51). Novalis himself was one of the self-declared "beautiful souls" who defended the bloated sentimentality of early romanticism even during the terrors of the Napoleonic Wars. The banality and superfluousness of that form of German romanticism attests to the absurdity of an ideology that had not yet found its time. But if classicism tends to degenerate into empty formalism, and romanticism into sentimentality and bombast, that only proves that these movements must not be taken out of their spiritual context.

Romanticism as Metaphysics

> Romantic art dissolves the ideal of classical art, which is the latter's visible unity. Romantic art has acquired a content far richer. . . . In brief, the essence of Romantic art lies in the artistic object's being free, concrete, and the spiritual idea in its very essence—all this revealed to the inner rather than the outer eye.
>
> Hegel, Introduction to *Philosophy of Art*

If we are to appreciate romanticism as a living ideology, rather than a series of petty squabbles between adolescent artists and writers, it is absolutely essential that we understand it as a revolutionary *metaphysics,* as a profound revision of our beliefs about the structure of the world and human experience. The same, of course, must be said of classicism. It too reflects a profound metaphysical need, not simply the pretensions of a small group of poets and painters. Both movements have been damaged as much by their defenders as by their enemies. We have learned to see classicism and romanticism as warring camps in parochial disputes, rather than as complementary world views that between them define the ideology of a historical epoch.

In Chapter 10 we suggested that classicism might not be a "movement" at all, but one of the enduring threads in the fabric of Western culture. The same can now be said of romanticism. Classicism, however, by its very nature rejoices in the idea of its durability, whereas romanticism by *its* nature prefers to think of itself as movement; therefore we might consider the respective metaphors a matter of temperament rather than analysis. What is important is that classicism and romanticism are essentially a confrontation of not wholly distinct but easily identifiable differences within the bourgeois soul: the fever of the passions, the cool judgments of reason, the inevitability of growth and change, the absolute need for understanding and stability. Even Goethe had said, with reason, that "feeling is everything."[26]

Romanticism, like classicism, has been traced by some scholars all the way back to the Greeks. Its own advocates typically traced it to the Middle Ages, sometimes even by definition. In France, Mme de Staël spoke as an advocate and explicator of the new movement in Germany:

The word *romantic* has been lately introduced in Germany, to designate that kind of poetry which is derived from the songs of the Troubadours; that which owes its birth to the union of chivalry and Christianity. . . . The new school maintains the same system in the fine arts as in literature, and affirms that Christianity is the course of all modern genius. (*Reader*, pp. 65–66)

Heinrich Heine, performing the same ambassadorial function, later explained to the French: "What was the Romantic school in Germany? It was nothing else than the reawakening of the poetry of the middle ages" (*Reader*, p. 67).

For our purposes, however, we need to look for the origins of romanticism only as far back as Jean-Jacques Rousseau. He is, by virtually all accounts, the father of modern romanticism. But if this is so, the lineage traced to him is typically confused. It is a misunderstanding of Rousseau (as we argued in Chapter 3) to view him as the irrational sentimentalist. Yet it is just this misreading of Rousseau which provides the components of eighteenth-century European and English romanticism, in particular the soppy sentimentality of Goethe's *Werther* and the Storm and Stress period as a whole. For this reason, we might best refer to this pseudo-Rousseauan movement as a "preromanticism"[27]—at best, an unsophisticated precursor of the profound metaphysical theses of nineteenth-century romanticism.

The preromanticism of Rousseau had been given some semblance of philosophical form by Johann Herder (see p. 142). He replaced the individualistic "noble savage" image of Rousseau, as well as the sentimental hero of *Werther*, with a collective sense of "folk spirit" or *Volkgeist*.

Superimposed on the emphasis on passion, therefore, were the legends and traditions of a people. The Storm and Stress poets defined this people through their poetry as essentially sentimental and "gothic." It was a sentimentality that allowed for and even invited extended philosophical expression. And German romanticism would come to its maturity only through philosophy.

Like everything else in nineteenth-century Germany, romanticism was given its form and impetus by Kant's philosophy and of course Napoleon. Yet Kant himself was surely no romantic. He considered the passions "pathological," loathed obscurity, loved science, defended the Enlightenment without compromise, and would not tolerate the falsified version of Rousseau that then had such currency in Germany.[28] If anything, Kant represented the most sophisticated philosophical expression of classical ideals and universal, eternal Reason. Yet the deep structure of romanticism developed nonetheless through the language and from some of the germinal ideas of Kant's *Critiques*. Three avowed Kantians—Gottlieb Fichte, Friedrich Schelling, and Arthur Schopenhauer—turned the Kantian philosophy to very different purposes from those that Kant intended. Their philosophies provide the intellectual skeleton of what might otherwise have been the formless mush of German romanticism. Some of their friends— particularly the brothers Schlegel, Schiller, and the poet Novalis—turned this philosophy into inspiration. Meanwhile Coleridge and Heine, among others, spread the new romantic gospel among the curious and (at this point) philosophically bankrupt English and French.[29]

The Kant of romanticism, needless to say, was not the Kant of the *Critique of Pure Reason*, at least as he understood his own book. The shape of romanticism was to be found there, nonetheless, and it was not long before this shape had given form to the gothic sentiments of Storm and Stress. One proponent of mysticism, for example, Friedrich Jacobi (1743–1819), used Kant's arguments concerning the limits of knowledge to show that reality could only be *felt,* not known. Even more important, however, were the concepts of Kant's second and third *Critiques:* Fichte shifted the emphasis from knowledge to action, using Kant's *Critique of Practical Reason,* while Schelling used his *Critique of Judgment* to further shift the emphasis to aesthetics and teleology (see p. 235). The Kantian phrase "purposeless purposiveness" came to define the aesthetic theories and the lives of a great many romantic poets. The idea of a universal organic whole, in which certain figures emerged as divine spokesmen, was taken with liberties from Kant, and the idea of the "free play of the imagination," which formed the heart of the aesthetic theories of Schiller and Coleridge,[30] was likewise borrowed directly from Kant. And it was Kant, the avid Newtonian, who denied to anyone in the world of science the title "genius," reserving that honored term for the arts. It was from this claim that the romantics forged their most central and, in practice, most obnoxious thesis—the privileged nature of the artistic genius.

Fichte was discussed in Chapter 11 as an important transition figure from Kant to Hegel. Here he must be treated as the key transition figure from Kant to romanticism. (It is Fichte's misfortune, alas, to almost always mark a transition from Kant to something—a matter of the way he described himself.) The contrast between Fichte and Kant is itself dramatic. We have already commented on Kant's dry, moral bachelor existence, his never leaving his hometown, and, apart from a daily glass of sherry or two, his life wholly devoid of excitement outside the study. Unlike Kant and most of the Kantians, however, Fichte was not of an academic temperament at all. He was a young radical fired with enthusiasm for the French Revolution and willing, unlike Kant, to go out in the streets and talk about it. At considerable personal risk he formed one of the local Jacobin Clubs, and was active in German reform movements long before they had acquired popular support. He was interested in Kant's critical philosophy not so much for the sake of the future of philosophy, but as a means to a more exciting and dramatic way of life. His emphasis on the "systematization of Kant" was academic cosmetics, for he was not interested in the ponderous enterprise then being undertaken by the first generation of Kantian disciples. They wanted a "system of critical philosophy"; Fichte wanted "the vocation of man." He was a charismatic lecturer, an outspoken German chauvinist, a known heretic, and a personal force in German culture. He predicted that, in twenty or thirty years, there would be no more kings, and an entirely new kind of personal freedom. In his hands, the dry, academic principles of the new Kantian philosophy turned into a powerful inspiration for a new way of life.

Fichte became enthusiastic about Kant, just as he became enthusiastic about many things. In fact, his enthusiasm was such that, having once inspired the old philosopher to obtain for him a professorial chair, he later made Kant feel obliged to publicly disown his maverick philosophy.[31] For if Kant was the philosophical equivalent of the French Revolution, as Heine and Marx after him often insisted, then Fichte was its conceptual Reign of Terror—dogmatic, charismatic, and out of control all at once, desperately grasping for unity but only increasing confusion. In fact, with Heine's pardon, one might say that Fichte and not Kant became the intellectual equivalent of Robespierre in Germany (see p. 115).

Fichte became influential in the 1790s, when with the French Revolution across the border, and the beginnings of the new revolutionary French imperialism pushing across the Rhine, the isolated provinces of Germany were still immersed in feudalism and idealistic philosophy. In this ambiguous climate Fichte's academic attempt to "systematize" Kant was in fact a call to arms, a passionate plea for Germany to join the new world. Like many of his contemporaries, Fichte did not share Kant's enthusiasm for science, but he did share Kant's strong-willed moral views. Fichte's friends always referred to him as a staunch moralist, and his philosophy, accordingly, was not a "completion" of Kant's philosophy so much as its undoing. Fichte performed radical surgery on the whole Kantian world picture, wrenching the focus of human nature away from understanding and toward actions, changing our view of truth from an eternal set of given categories to an existential choice of life styles.[32] Nature, he insisted, is nothing more than a stage upon which we can act out our heroics and prove our moral natures. To see the world through the eyes of a scientist, he argued, is to be something less than human, a mere observer or what is worse, a mere object. Humanity *makes* its world, Fichte insisted, and that creative act was the heart of Kantian philosophy; the rest was just "scholasticism."

It has already been stated (Chapter 11) that the subject of Fichte's philosophy is an Absolute Self, a self "behind" every individual consciousness that is ultimately one, despite the apparent distinctness of individual people. This self is not a knowing but a *striving* self, and behind the obscurities of Fichte's metaphysical writings it takes little imagination to discern the call to nationalism. Like virtually everyone of his time, he was strongly influenced by Rousseau, from whom he borrowed the concepts of the General Will and the social contract, as well as the general theme (from *Emile*) of the role of the State in providing moral education for its citizens—its primary and ultimately sole function. Having completed this education, Fichte said, the State will "wither away"—a dubious promise that would reappear several times in nineteenth-century German politics, most notably in Marx.

The world was a testing ground for this absolute, infinitely striving Self, and we are its instruments, its agents, its manifestations. For us the ultimate truth lies in our spontaneous recognition of this mutual belonging, in obeying the voice of the Absolute in all of us, which Fichte called *conscience*. Whatever respect Fichte displayed for Kant's categorical imperatives, he far preferred the immediacy of the moral spirit, a difference which it is easy to find in their life styles as well as philosophies. And for Fichte this moral spirit had built into it a political turn. The circumstances of life, for one thing, had themselves become highly political, and much more so in Jena and Berlin than in Königsberg. The striving of the Absolute Self had its most immediate expression in the new German national striving. Kantian morality had become in Fichte a principle of the primacy of the State. Moral freedom had become, as in Rousseau, the freedom to participate and to *obey*. It was appropriate that in 1807–8 Fichte personally delivered the series of "Addresses to the German State," which are most often identified as the birth of explicit German nationalism, commencing the Wars of Liberation that would be Germany's first real struggle.

The call to action, the idea of a Self "behind" all selves, the concept of our ultimate creation of ourselves and even of the world itself—this was just the philosophy that the old Storm and Stress poets and the new romantics, tired of cold classicism, wanted to hear. Even Goethe was an admirer of Fichte, whose *Wissenschaftlehre* he summarized in a line: "In the beginning was the *Act*." The idea of the world as a stage appealed to these lovers of the "barbarian" Shakespeare.[33] The times were ripe for a new expression of the German folk spirit in absolutist terms, with the vision of a world mission as well as a common tradition and identity. As for the idea of the artist as a spokesman driven by conscience, by the voice of the Absolute within, and creating the universe according to dictates not known and rules not yet established—what could be more appealing? And so Novalis turned Fichte's "ethical idealism" into a "creative idealism." The brothers Schlegel quickly identified their own aesthetic ambitions with Fichte's subterranean moral Absolute, and declared their new aesthetic theories to be in fact the highest moral theories. Politics—an arena still devoid of serious radical action—became the province of the poets. Jacobi turned Kant into a defense of Christian mysticism, and then Friedrich Schleiermacher (1768–1834) argued that religion must dispense with conceptualization altogether and appeal to simple feeling—in particular, feelings of dependence (to which Hegel later rejoined that such a criterion would make a dog a far better Christian than the most pious among us).[34] Thus in only a few years, and even while Kant was still alive, the Kantian philosophy found its most powerful expression in a series of romantic philosophies that could not have been more diametrically opposed to the temperament of the old revolutionary himself. (But after all, Robespierre became the first dictator in the name of democracy, and Napoleon was the culmination of a revolution that strove to end all kings and absolute rulers.)

The philosophical abilities of Novalis and the Schlegels were such that romanticism would not have matured past Storm and Stress enthusiasm, if it had not found a philosophical friend. But Fichte, unfortunately, repudiated the romantic interpretation of his ideas explicitly and publicly. So the philosophical friend turned out to be Friedrich Schelling (1775–1854), a companion of Novalis and the Schlegels, but also one of the most talented young philosophers in Germany. We have already met Schelling as the younger friend and classmate of Hegel and Hölderlin at Tübingen. He was a precocious genius who had earned a chair in philosophy and the admiration of Goethe by the time he was twenty-three. Though a follower of Fichte, he balanced Fichte's limited conception of Nature as a moral stage with a picture of Nature as a self-creating organic system, ideal for the romantic image. He emphasized, even more than Fichte, the distinction between the individual and the Absolute Ego, pursuing the idea that we are all but agents of the Absolute World Soul (*Weltseele*), which turns out to be Nature also. Here was the combination of arrogant moral autonomy and humble participation in the whole of Nature that the romantics had been seeking ever since Rousseau. Moreover, this self-creating was ultimately an *aesthetic* act. Nature and the World Soul, ourselves writ large, were nothing less than God as a great artist, creating himself through Nature and through us. And that made us, through our participation, not only artists but absolute artists.

Besides anticipating the main theses of Hegel's philosophy, Schelling articulated the otherwise obscure sentiments of the dominant poetic spirit of the time. In fact, he did so even better than Hegel, who insisted more than Schelling on the importance of Enlightenment Reason and critical concepts. Schelling, on the other hand, preferred to talk about "intuition," a far more romantic notion perfectly fitted for the pretensions of undisciplined genius. (In fact, Hegel and Schelling were of a like mind, and Schelling was right to complain bitterly when Hegel accused him, in the *Phenomenology* and elsewhere, of "empty formalism" and obscure intuitionism.)[35] Schelling's system in fact provided the intellectual backbone for a movement that itself had no backbone, despite the fact that many of the romantics explicitly repudiated philosophy in general for its hyperrationality (Kierkegaard and Marx, two most important second-generation romantics, among them). Indeed, it is no small irony that Novalis and Friedrich Schlegel in particular should have attacked philosophy in the name of poetry, using the most sophisticated arguments based on the most modern of philosophical ideas.

Hegel transcends romanticism. Because of Schelling's close affiliation to it, he repudiated it publicly and sarcastically. But at the heart of Hegel's system one finds the best of romanticism: emphasis on the primacy of passion, which must never be lost sight of in the midst of Hegel's celebrations of reason and "the Concept"; rejection of Kantian *stasis* in favor of the "fluidity" of reason and the openness of human forms of life; and appreciation for not only morality but the preconscious foundations of morality in the family, the tribe, and the religious cult (which brings him closer to Herder and the romantics than even Fichte and Schelling).[36] But most of all it is Hegel's world view—his concept of Absolute Spirit acting through all of us in ceaseless striving to become ever more all-encompassing and meaningful—that makes Hegel, despite his disclaimers, the heart of romanticism. It is a mistake to think that despair, meaninglessness, and cynicism are essential to romanticism; they are but one of its expressions. Hegel's view of a swirling human universe in violent motion—with ourselves and our confused, tentative concepts and often ignorant actions caught up in and contributing to the core of it, for God (and Hegel) knows what purpose—that is the romantic vision at its finest. And it is Hegel's hard-headed political realism, not Fichte's charismatic polemics, which forms the philosophical foundation for the German State that eventually, for better or for worse, will emerge.

Yet despite his awareness of "the slaughter bench of history," Hegel remained an optimist. But optimism as such, no matter how qualified, was not the favorite attitude of the romantics. Furthermore, despite Hegel's emphasis on the primacy of the passions, he still argued for the rationality of those passions, their cooperation with reason, and the ultimate rationality of not only all human action but the universe itself. In 1806 such optimism and Enlightenment confidence in reason may still have been in tune with the *Zeitgeist,* but as the days of the Reaction grew increasingly hopeless, optimism and reason became out of date as well. Hegel continued to fortify his system, turning the enthusiasm of the *Phenomenology* into the logical apologetics of the 1820s, but philosophy was already moving elsewhere. Thus Schelling—more romantic, conservative, and Christian than ever—enjoyed a comeback after Hegel's death, and at the government's behest taught in Berlin to combat the atheistic and rebellious influence of the young Hegelians. The new romantic philosophy was despairingly pessimistic, and reason played a part only in its formulation, not in its content: that is, the universe was meaningless, but the idea that the universe was meaningless was not.

The romantics of the middle third of the century found an ideal exponent of these new sentiments in Arthur Schopenhauer (1788–1860), whose cynicism was and still is chilling, and whose view of the rationality of human action, as well as that of the universe, came close to Absolute *Ir*rationality. His writing seethed with wit and resentment. His diagnosis of the contemporary spirit could be summed up in one word: *absurd;* his prognosis, in another: *hopeless.* (His father, ironically, had been a devout admirer and advocate of Voltaire—but that was before the Revolution, the Reaction, and Hegel.) Schopenhauer too had been a student of Kant and Fichte, and prefaced his main work, *The World as Will and Idea* (1819), with the warning that he presupposed that anyone who bothered to read him would already know Kant thoroughly. Schopenhauer followed Fichte —and therefore Schelling and Hegel—in shifting the emphasis away from Kant's celebration of Newtonian science and toward the Will. Again like Fichte, even more than Kant he stressed the creative—and, he added, the "illusory"—status of our knowledge of the world. Furthermore, like Fichte, Schelling, and Hegel, Schopenhauer emphasized the idea that our concepts of individuality and individual self are somewhat of a sham; it is something else—something cosmic acting through us—that constitutes our real self-identity. For Schopenhauer this "something else" was the Will itself—not an individual will but, as for the other philosophers, an absolute and all-encompassing Will, acting through every thing and creature in Nature as well as through every human being.

Schopenhauer—like Kant, Fichte, Schelling, and Hegel—was an "idealist": he believed that the world is constituted by us. He was also a "transcendentalist," believing that the great force of the world—in his case Will, rather than Absolute Spirit—acted through us. But if Schopenhauer was part of the family of Kantians, that family was not a happy one. The differences between his philosophy and the others'—particularly Hegel's—overshadowed the affinities. Schopenhauer's Will—unlike Hegel's Spirit, Fichte's Absolute, and Schelling's World Soul—was neither moral nor creative nor rational, and the actions it prompted in us were not in any sense guided by "the cunning of reason." Our strivings were ultimately aimless and irrational. Schopenhauer told his contemporaries in no uncertain terms that a dog's life was better than theirs, and that their faculties of reason had doomed them to unhappiness. Accordingly, he loathed Hegel's optimism and rationalism, and slandered the Great Philosopher at every opportunity. Teaching in Berlin at the same university as Hegel, just when Hegel's reputation was at its peak, in the purest spite Schopenhauer scheduled his lectures at exactly the same time as his rival's, and when he got no students at all, had to leave his teaching position. It was an apt expression of a philosophy that was at once cosmically grand and utterly petty.

In some ways Schopenhauer remained closer to Kant than did the other Kantians. For example, he did not deny, as they did, the separation between theory and practice, between knowledge and reasons for action. But unlike Kant, Schopenhauer used this separation to defend two different kinds of *ir*rationality, distinguishing the illusion of knowledge from the irrationality of all human action. His philosophy, accordingly, was a curious combination of Kant's first *Critique* (taken *very* seriously), Fichte's arrogant idealism, Eastern mysticism (which he was among the first to bring into Western thought), and a biting pessimism that turned Hegel's dialectic of Spirit into the irrational and pointless striving of an impersonal and destructive cosmic Will. Following Kant again, Schopenhauer took the Will to be ultimate reality, more real than the world itself, which was mere "appearance." But this Will was not "our" will, and not within our control. It was a metaphysical force which consumed us and drove us senselessly onward, for no reason at all. Writing in the Reaction, and without the heroic nostalgia for Napoleon that many others felt, Schopenhauer saw even the most noble and courageous human actions as senseless gestures.

What is the "cure" for this hopeless situation? Schopenhauer rejects suicide: that would be "giving in." Resentment is the guiding passion of this romanticism—or, to be more charitable: resignation. Since reason is responsible for our pretentious foolishness, reason must provide the cure. With a strange combination of Buddhism, the rational resignation of Spinoza, and a perverse twist of the Christian concept of the same, Schopenhauer suggests that we abstain from participation in these senseless human follies. Instead, we should allow ourselves to be cynically entertained, withdrawn in a kind of aesthetic contemplation as we celebrate the purposelessness of the world instead of giving in to it.

Schopenhauer's name, book, and views did not become immediately prominent in German intellectual circles. He did not enjoy the youthful celebrity of Schelling òr the respectable solidarity of the mature Hegel. Yet despite his teachings, he vehemently wanted these things, and not getting them only made him more bitter, more cynical, and more ambitious. He received the recognition he deserved (if anyone deserved anything) only in the late 1840s, almost thirty years after the publication of his main work, and only some ten years before his death. Meanwhile, however, he ignored the ascetic suggestions of his philosophy, enjoyed many good dinners, boasted of his connoisseurship in wine and women, and lusted his way through affairs, even while writing notorious diatribes against love, women, and human relations in general. The combination of cynicism and the good life did not strike his mid-century contemporaries as the least bit inconsistent. To the contrary, for them this represented a kind of ideal which, together with the growing nationalistic fervor still generated by Fichte and given ideological support by Hegel, would breed a dangerously cruel attitude toward human life in general. It would first appear in the grandeur and pomposity of Wagnerian opera, on the basis of explicitly Schopenhauerian themes. A few years later it would manifest itself in the iron fist of Bismarck.

The Significance of Romanticism

> Romanticism, badly defined so many times, when all is said and done is only—and here is the real definition, if you view Romanticism from its militant side—liberalism in literature.
>
> Victor Hugo, "Preface to *Hernani*"[37]

It is easy to make fun of romanticism, to dismiss it as childish or warn against it as dangerous. It claimed so much, and in such extravagant terms; its spokesmen were often so obnoxious, and in the light of modern German aggression, so dangerous.[38] But romanticism signifies far more than its surface abuses would suggest. German nationalism and French internationalism—like the cults of genius and heroes, the grand philosophies and the diatribes against philosophy—were but expressions of a profound ideological need, the need for identity and involvement in the world. And this need, in turn, was basic to a very particular kind of ideology—bourgeois ideology, with its excessive emphasis on both the importance of the individual and the unity of "humanity," and its inadequate conception of concrete social relationships. Even in Germany, where the sense of local identity was increasingly powerful, this identity had to be subsumed under more cosmic concepts and rationalized (as in Hegel) by appeal to the grand abstractions of "Spirit." Whatever the differences between romanticism, classicism, and the Enlightenment, they shared the same cosmic demand for personal significance, for a passionate sense of themselves and their place in the universe. It may be, as Croce has argued, that this search was but compensation for the loss of religion brought about by the Enlightenment, and many of the romantics themselves, at least in Germany and Italy, would have agreed.[39] But one could just as well say that the Enlightenment and romanticism identified the quest that had been deceptively pursued by religion—which is essentially what Hegel, Heine, and many of the French romantics did believe. The search for personal significance is the key to romanticism.

Passion and personal significance are never far apart. Enlightenment thinkers, embattled against the Old Regime, never lacked passionate involvement; their ideas and sense of self thrust it upon them. But the romantics, deprived of that battleground, had to seek not only expression but the passions to express—something other than despair at lack of passion, and hopelessness. Ironically, their discontent was born of contentment and comfort as much as of bitterness. They were the first of many spoiled bourgeois generations who could afford what they called a "malaise of the spirit": an unhappiness resulting from too easy rather than too hard a life. The oppressiveness of the Bourbon Restoration was nothing compared to the oppressiveness of the boredom that it caused. The backwardness of Germany after the failure of the Wars of Liberation was nothing compared to the philistine banality with which the burghers adjusted to their new life. With romanticism the new generation of middle-class activists, poets, artists, and philosophers turned against their own ideology, in the name of the same principles they had learned from the Enlightenment, the Revolution, and Napoleon—dignity, freedom, self-importance, ambition, the importance of nature, the need to be "universal" in one's particularity.

Superficially, the behavior of the romantics might be dismissed as adolescent rebellion, but they were much older than adolescents—ideologically, at the prime of life, and increasingly successful, bored, and discontent. At a deeper level, they can be seen as a reaction against the now stale principles of the Enlightenment, expressing the need for a new ideology of movement, Will, and passion. But at a deeper level still, romanticism is less a reaction to the Enlightenment than a continuation of it—an expression of its most basic needs, including self-assertion against evil and corruption. But the source of this evil and corruption was now the bourgeoisie itself. With romanticism, therefore, this once unified class begins to devour itself. It begins to search for alternative models, the more exotic the better. Thus Delacroix turns to Morocco and other romantics look back to the Middle Ages.[40] Poets turn to Catholicism and philosophers to the East.

But these exotic alternatives to bourgeois life are too distant, too inaccessible, too exotic. So the next generation of bourgeois romantics will find the nemesis of the corrupted bourgeoisie closer to home. Marx finds it in an alternative class, more "universal" than the bourgeoisie, that had quietly participated in the Enlightenment and the Revolution just as much as the more articulate bourgeois spokesmen. And Kierkegaard finds it in the depths of his own "soul," that peculiar metaphysical-theological entity so despised and dismissed by Voltaire and the Enlightenment. Having begun as a progressive push for worldly status, bourgeois ideology now becomes the rejection of that same status as a mark of decadence; in fact, in the best tradition of the movement, it becomes self-denial, a kind of self-righteous individual defiance, and thus the most important development of that bourgeois way of thinking that it so passionately seeks to destroy.

15 From Poetry to Revolution: The Young Marx

> Man's self-esteem, his sense of freedom, must be reawakened in the breast of the German people. This sense vanished from the world with the Greeks, and with Christianity it took up residence in the blue mists of heaven, but only with its aid can society ever again become a community of men that can fulfill their highest needs, a democratic state.
>
> Marx, letter to Arnold Ruge, May 1843[1]

Karl Marx (1818–1883) was not thrust into the world with full beard and dogma, the self-appointed champion of the proletariat armed with the "iron laws of history." Whatever has been made of him, and whatever he later made of himself, in his youth he was a romantic poet, a punster and Shakespeare fan, an Enlightenment liberal and literary critic, and above all a humanist—the heir of Kant, Goethe, Schiller, and Hegel, rather than the precursor of Lenin, Stalin, and Mao. In 1841 Marx's friend Moses Hess called him "a fusion of Rousseau, Voltaire, D'Holbach, Lessing, Heine, and Hegel."

A Sentimental Journey

> Jenny! Do I dare avow
> That in love we have exchanged our souls.
> That as one they throb and glow,
> And that through their waves one current rolls?
>
> Then the gauntlet do I fling
> Scornful in the world's wide open face.
>
> Marx, to Jenny von Westphalen[2]

At seventeen Marx was a hard-drinking, dashing young law student in Bonn who fought duels and was madly in love with a baron's daughter, Jenny von Westphalen. He was sentimental, his head stuffed with aesthetic images, literary ambitions, borrowed phrases, and clumsy clichés. He disdained physical labor and avoided it successfully his entire life—even when his children were starving in London years later. He was impractical and impossible with money, which in any event he rarely had. A law student in name only, he took courses mostly in literature, classical mythology, and art history. Certainly he had nothing of the bureaucratic temperament required for the legal profession, being much better suited to the life of poetry and bohemian rebellion that he intended to live. In a poem entitled "Feelings" (1836) he declared:

> I am caught in endless strife,
> Endless ferment, endless dream;
> I cannot conform to life,
> Will not travel with the stream.
>
> Heaven I would comprehend,
> I would draw the world to me;
> Loving, hating, I intend
> That my star shine brilliantly.[3]

Above all he was passionate—a true romantic—about Jenny, about poetry and literature, about his own possibilities and a grand abstraction—*the perfectibility of man*. His ultimate inspiration was this singular ideal that in such different ways had fueled the French Enlightenment and German romanticism, and given modern content to nostalgic classicism and Storm and Stress gothicism. This idea—what humanity *could* be—was so much more exhilarating than the cool analysis of the dull and dreary workaday reality around him. To celebrate and inspire our sense of the possible—that was his task, like Goethe, like Schiller. When Marx left high school in Trier in 1835, he wrote of his goals in life as "the goal of perfection," "human dignity," and "working for humanity." How? As *Dichter*, poet, spokesman. Thus began the career of the most important poet *manqué* in recorded history.

The small town of Trier was practically on the border of France. Marx grew up a Francophile, however strong his German identity. His father had quoted Voltaire and Rousseau to him since childhood. Revolutionary France and its ideals were still alive, even if the Revolution and Napoleon had become history before Marx was born. When he was only twelve, the Revolution of 1830 fired his imagination and made the still feudal governments of Germany look like dinosaurs in contrast to the rapid changes and powerful ideologies to the West. The German burghers were philistines compared with the elegant French bourgeoisie, intolerably complacent where the French had long been radicalized.[4] The religious obsessions of Lutheran Germany seemed like wholesale absurdities compared to the Cult of Reason in Paris. Marx's father had nominally converted from Judaism, a religion that he had accepted only loosely anyway and that constituted an impossible social obstacle. Convinced that one religion was no more absurd than another, Heinrich Marx found the official religion at least much more convenient. That young Karl should have had similar attitudes about the irrelevance and foolishness of religion is therefore neither surprising nor debatable. It is, however, an open and too-often-asked question to what extent his Jewish background affected his outlook on life and ideologies in general—for example, his radical sympathies with the oppressed and the underdog, and his tendency to identify a "chosen people" and speak of "the redemption of humanity" as their task. Even his attention to political economy has been interpreted as a function of his Jewish heritage. Such questions seem fruitless, if only because their answers lead more often to abuse than understanding. Let it suffice to say that Marx was, in his origins, an *outsider,* a German with a largely French temperament, an atheist who was raised with both a Jewish heritage and a Protestant sanction. It was easier for him to identify with the whole of humanity than with any artificially circumscribed political, social, or religious group.

And yet, however strong his Francophilia and his French Enlightenment sympathies, as poet, *Dichter,* and spokesman Marx was by language and by Storm and Stress temperament a German. His idea of perfection derived from Schiller and Goethe as much as from Voltaire and Rousseau. "Emancipation" referred to the senses and sensitivity, not to governments. It was the development of human creativity, the education of the sentiments, the fulfillment of good living, and the creation of the *total person* that guided his rebellion.[5]

He had not yet developed, nor probably even sensed, the idea that economic pressures and inequities might be the source of the spiritual and aesthetic malaise he attacked. Yet following Schiller, he argued that the modern emphasis on specialization and anonymous production was dehumanizing and destructive of creativity, reducing human beings to mere cogs in a great machine. This was not a protoeconomic argument, but part and parcel of that curious amalgam of classical idealism and romantic holism—for example, after Fichte—that defined much of the German Enlightenment temperament. Marx was a naturalist, and he shared with Goethe and Schiller the idea that man was a part of nature and as such defined nature as well. The reigning philosophical metaphor of his youth was what, following Hegel, he would later call "objectification," though he learned the concept itself from Schiller:

Man is to turn everything which is mere form into world and make all his possibilities fully manifest. . . . he is to destroy everything in himself which is mere world, and bring harmony in all his changes. In other words, he is to externalize all that is within him, and give form to all that is outside him.[6]

Marx's concept of humanity was a concept of creativity, with freedom of expression and full sensitivity as its highest ideals. Accordingly, his heroes were the poets far more than the revolutionaries and socialists whom he occasionally met or heard about, and whom he considered "dogmatic" and "vulgar." In terms of contemporaries, his idol seemed to be Heinrich Heine, who would later become his good friend in Paris. Through Heine's writings Marx became further enthused about the possibilities of German poetry, about the power of ideas to shape the world. It was Heine, who had been a personal student of Hegel, who first suggested to Marx that German philosophy, obscure and abstract as it seemed, could be the spiritual equivalent of the French Revolution.[7]

Marx's ambition to perfect humanity through his own poetry was short-lived. His borrowed lines, excessive sentimentality, and derivative style betrayed a lack of originality if not of talent, too. He was discouraged from his enthusiasm by his father, who had a powerful influence on him, and—more effectively—by publishers who rejected his poems. By 1837 he would give up his ambitions as "delusions" and his work as "shot through with idealism" and "pure fantasy" (Prawer, p. 12). It was, in other words, too romantic. His French sense of concrete action was already winning against his German sense of fantasy:

> Let us not walk, in brooding anxiety,
> Under the yoke that weighs us down:
> For longing and desire
> And action—these remain to us in spite of all. (Prawer, p. 12)

The question for him now was how to bridge the gap between his youthful idealism and his gnawing but still ill-defined search for down-to-earth humanism. The first step toward an answer—after he had transferred from Bonn to Berlin in 1837—was an excruciating trip through the Hegelian dialectic.

Hegel and Prometheus

> From idealism, which I equated by the way with Kant and Fichte, I went on to seek the Idea in the real itself. . . . This work [reading Hegel], for the purposes of which I familiarized myself with natural science, Schelling and history . . . has caused me an endless headache.
>
> Marx, letter to his father, 1837

When Marx went to Berlin, Hegel had died only six years before and his influence, to put it mildly, still dominated the university. During those years, a student in Berlin found becoming a Hegelian as compelling as becoming a Marxist would be many years later. But the compulsory affiliation only rarely involved or provoked understanding. Marx was probably one of the few young Hegelians who made a serious study of Hegel while adopting the usual catchphrases. Turning to philosophy and history, he made friends with Bruno Bauer, whom he met that year, and became one of the young leftist Hegelians who saw through the official philosopher's conservativism to the radical humanism at its base. Even so, it is important to note that what excited Marx about Hegel was primarily his work on aesthetics, and hardly at all his writings on politics and the State. Marx had not yet given up his literary ambitions (though now despairing of them), and the Hegel that first inspired him was the defender of romanticism as the highest and last phase of art. "We have learnt our lesson of Hegel, and are not purged of his Aesthetic" (Prawer, p. 32).

During that spring and summer of 1837, Marx made a detailed study of Hegel's *Phenomenology of Spirit,* which he would always recognize as Hegel's most important and exciting work. He did not yet study (had he even read it?) Hegel's *Philosophy of Right,* the Prussian political apology which eventually would spark the apocalyptic disagreement between their two systems.[8] What impressed the young Hegelians most of all was Hegel's Enlightenment concept of Reason, combined with his German sense of history and his awareness of the impact of the French Revolution and its aftermath. They appreciated the tradition of "critique" that had been developing from Kant to Hegel, and they saw in the latter's concept of conflict and resolution a method of criticism far more powerful than anything produced by even the Enlightenment. However, at this point of their lives Marx and the other young Hegelians saw the task of philosophy, as Hegel defended it, as an attempt to *understand* the world and consequently to make it more rational. The idea of forcibly *changing* it, in contrast to understanding and "realizing" it, was not yet a part of their vocabulary. Above all, it was Hegel's enthusiasm that inspired the young Hegelians. The optimism built into the concept of "realizing the ideal" excited them enormously, and like Hegel they did not yet clearly distinguish between two kinds of "realizing": simply *recognizing,* and *making true* (see p. 224).

The one radical aspect of his view of Hegel was Marx's view of religion. The official view of Hegel, defended by the often well-positioned (in university chairs) Hegelian "right," was that Hegel had ably and absolutely defended Christianity for modern times. Marx and Bauer suspected otherwise. Beneath the nominal Christian coating of theological terminology and trinities, they saw—as Heine had seen and Kierkegaard would also see—the latent atheism of the whole project (see pp. 343–44). On the pretext of bringing God down to modern man, Hegel had in fact—or so the young leftists agreed—raised man up to God, in fact, identified man with God and so rejected God altogether. In the preface to his doctoral dissertation in philosophy, written from 1839 to 1841, Marx resembles no one so much as Heine in reducing Hegel's supposed apologetics to atheism:

Philosophy makes no secret of this. The confession of Prometheus: "In a word, I detest all gods" is her [philosophy's] own confession, her own watchword against all the gods of heaven and earth who do not recognize man's self-consciousness as the highest divinity. It will have none other besides.

The image of Prometheus with reference to Hegelianism might sound strange, but here Marx joins the two generations before him (including Hegel) in bemoaning the lost defiance and vitality of the ancient Greeks: "Prometheus is the foremost saint and martyr in the philosopher's calendar." So Hegel, the official philosopher of Christianity and the Prussian state, becomes Prometheus, the pagan demigod who stole fire from heaven: "So philosophy, having extended itself to comprehend the whole world, turns against the phenomenal world. So it is now with Hegelian philosophy."[9]

As for Marx's dissertation itself, *On the Difference between Democritus' and Epicurus' Philosophies of Nature,* there is one substantial point of interest: Marx, who would later discover "the iron laws of history," defended the Epicurean notion of human freedom against what he considered the too harsh determinism of Democritus. Later, when he came to appreciate Hegel's philosophy better, the idea of "freedom *from* necessity" (like Goethe's "freedom within limitation") provided him with a reconciliation. Meanwhile, far from being the harsh determinist-materialist he is often said to have become, Marx was more of a proto-existentialist and romantic, placing a strong emphasis on the importance of individual choice and the idea that "man makes himself."[10]

German poetry did not end with romanticism, as Hegel seemed to have suggested, but the end of youthful romanticism ended Marx's poetic career. First his own poetry turned against the romantics:

> He is a German,
> And he lavishly throws about,
> "melody" and "soul"
> At every opportunity.

Or:

> That *sounds* romantic
> But dear young Sir,
> It's *only* sound. (Prawer, p. 14)

Then his criticism turned harsh, especially against his own poetry. He tried to start a critical journal, but without success. He started a Platonic dialogue, a novel, and a farcical play—*Oulanem,* a takeoff of Goethe's *Faust*—but found his mind hurtling headlong into Hegelian philosophy. (He later said of the dialogue, "The last sentence was the beginning of

Hegel's system.") By 1841 the young poet had become a philosopher looking for a profession. The doctoral dissertation was his professional entrance fee, and he fully intended to enter upon an academic career. But then as now, radical young thinkers found no jobs in Germany, whatever their talent or achievements. A job looked promising in Bonn, but it fell through. (And what if he had got it and become Professor Marx? Whence then the October Revolution and Mao?) At the time Marx had not published or even uttered a single politically threatening word, but since mere spirit can alarm the backward and complacent, it became obvious that there would be no room for him in the universities or even in the high schools. As a matter of practical urgency, Marx turned his frustrated ambitions to journalism.

Marx's Hegelianism was still thin and superficial. The idea of "dialectic," to be so associated later with his name, had not yet excited him. Politics did not provoke him to comment, much less moral indignation and outrage. But a deep structure of epic historical conflict and change had impressed itself upon him, and within months he would discover the contents to fuel it, and to satisfy his youthful ambitions to serve the cause of human perfection.

Feuerbach, Materialism, and "Turning Hegel on His Head"

> The same spirit that constructs railways with the hands of workers, constructs philosophical systems in the brains of philosophers. Philosophy does not exist outside the world, any more than the brain exists outside of man because it is not situated in the stomach.
>
> The *positive* humanistic and naturalistic criticism begins with *Feuerbach*. The less blatant Feuerbach's writings, the more certain, profound, comprehensive and lasting is their influence; they are the only writings since Hegel's *Phenomenology* and *Logic* to contain a real theoretical revolution.
>
> Marx, early writings[11]

Ludwig Feuerbach (1804–1872) blasted into the idealistic world of German philosophy in 1841, as Marx was completing his dissertation and finding himself more and more drawn toward Hegel. Feuerbach had studied with the Great Philosopher himself. He had even taught philosophy for a few years, until it was discovered that he was the author of a scandalous anti-Christian pamphlet, for which he was fired. That ended his short academic career, but in the 1840s he became a cult hero and martyr for the new freethinking spirit in Germany. Feuerbach attacked Hegel, idealism in general, and above all the religious escapism that he saw as basic to all such philosophy. His book, *The Essence of Christianity* (1841), wrenched an entire generation of young Hegelians, including Marx, away from their master and back to the essentials of realistic criticism. For Marx—and simultaneously for Friedrich Engels, who had just arrived in Berlin to study with Schelling—Feuerbach's down-to-earth humanism was a welcome antidote for the obscurities of Hegelian rationalism. And even though Marx discerned—as Feuerbach did not—the atheistic underpinnings of Hegel's nominal theism, the explicit atheism of Feuerbach was a rallying point for those more concerned with attacking religion than defending Hegel.

Feuerbach was a self-styled *materialist,* but it is important that his position not be confused with the far more radical materialism of certain French Enlightenment thinkers, notably D'Holbach, who had argued that "only matter is real." Feuerbach, like most German intellectuals, found such neo-Newtonianism "vulgar," and scientific materialism "obtuse." His materialism was rather a rejection of the current "idealist" dogmas, which made ideas and thoughts more real than things, events, and actions. "I do not generate the object from the thought," he wrote in 1843, "but the thought from the object." (A few years later, in his *German Ideology,* Marx virtually paraphrased this line.) Like Schiller before him, Feuerbach celebrated "the natural man," the world of the body and the senses. But unlike Schiller and all the idealists—Kant, Fichte, Schelling, and Hegel— Feuerbach minimized the role of the imagination and thought, and maximized the role of simple perception. He denied what in one form or another they all maintained: that consciousness in some sense *produces* the world. Feuerbach was a simple commonsense *realist* who believed that the world is just *there,* as it is, before we ever get our conceptual or perceptual hooks on it. This was the essence of his materialism, which however did not in any way *deny* consciousness; rather it put it back in its proper, subordinate, and receptive (rather than creative) place. Exactly the same must be said of Marx's own much touted but so often exaggerated materialism.[12]

Feuerbach's attack on Hegel is based on the layman's view—so easily baffled by the twists of Hegelian dialectic—that what is most real is what can be seen and touched, what is "tangible." Feuerbach sees Hegel as presenting a perverse "inversion" of reality in which abstract ideas are most real, and flesh-and-blood people and the seemingly solid world of objects mere "instances" of these ideas; in effect, he sees him as a new Platonist. But this, Feuerbach asserts, is putting things upside down, like standing on one's head. The business of philosophy, accordingly, is to set us back on our feet again.[13] "Only a sensible being is a real true being," Feuerbach insists, and the only sensible philosophy is what we today would call anthropology—a concern with real, concrete individuals in their responses to the rest of the world, in which thoughts and ideas play only a small part. Furthermore, thoughts and ideas often as not play a pernicious escapist role in our experience, as for instance in religion. Feuerbach, a century before Jean-Paul Sartre, says that religion is man's desire to be God, and that such hopeless fantasies only make our lives unnecessarily frustrated and filled with illusion. Hegel's philosophy, according to Feuerbach, only reifies such fantasies and "alienates and expropriates from man his typical essence and activity." In reaction, Feuerbach urges philosophy away from heavenly ideas and back to mundane matters:

> The doctrine of food is of great ethical and political significance. Food becomes blood, blood becomes heart and brain, thoughts and mind-stuff. Human fare is the foundation of human culture and thought. Would you improve a nation? Give it, instead of declamations against sin, better food. Man is what he eats.

(The last sentence is a notorious pun: *"Man ist was er isst."*)[14]

When Marx read Feuerbach's attack on Christianity in 1841, he announced with a horrible pun of his own: "There is no other path to the truth except that through the fiery stream [*feuer-bach*]!" Immediately his attention shifted away from the ideas and thoughts of the philosophers to the material conditions of human life. It was from Feuerbach that he learned to see the whole of philosophy, religion, and abstract thought in general as a rationalization for unsatisfactory living—a rationalization that he would later call "ideology."[15]

Marx's own living conditions at this time were none too satisfactory: his academic ambitions had proved fruitless, he was poor and without a job. Still in love with Jenny, he lacked the means for marriage. He was a writer without a career, no longer able to enjoy the luxury of academic writing as when he had been a student. Accordingly, when Marx accepted a job with *Die Rheinische Zeitung,* it was not so much a matter of political militancy as need. In fact, Marx's first concern was still the business of writing itself, and his first forays into the political world were defenses of freedom of the press against the harsh censorship laws of Prussia. He was not yet a radical—at most, perhaps a good liberal.[16] His main objection to censorship was that mediocre bureaucratic minds were empowered to judge the writings of talented young authors. He was still the querulous young bohemian poet of Bonn, not yet the firebrand of history. When he broke with Bauer later that year, one of his main objections was Bauer's abuse of the German language.

But any incursion into politics becomes a lesson in power and its abuses. What began as a defense of writing—"Journalism is not just a trade," he argued—became a defense of truth itself: "Censorship infringes the rights of the object (truth) as well as of the subject." The censors attacked polemics and "tone." In a blast of Hegelianism, Marx responded that "truth is a matter of not only results, but of the way they are reached" (Prawer, pp. 34–35). And once the battle was joined between truth and the government, the Manichaean basis of political radicalism had been established. For his energetic liberalism, Marx became editor-in-chief of the newspaper and the *bête noire* of the Prussian censors.

At this point in his career, however, Marx's concern was hardly radical. His attack, ultimately, was just a defense of writing style ("Le style c'est l'homme," he says). He was still a good liberal, a writer defending his right to write as an advocate of "the open society." He turns back to Hegel, and with a critical eye begins to suspect just how much of Hegel's politics is a kind of mystifying defense of Prussian authoritarianism. And Feuerbach, too, he objects, was too concerned "with nature and not enough with truth" (Prawer, p. 57). Marx flirts with communism for the first time, after a superficial reading of some of the French socialists, but that too he rejects as a danger to an open society, as "a dogmatic abstraction," as insufficiently humanistic, and as too concerned about the idea of private property! All these philosophies were idealistic rationalizations—but of what? Marx was not yet a Marxist.

"Critique" and Poor Reason

> . . . we do not anticipate the world with our dogmas but instead attempt to discover the new world through the critique of the old. . . . There can still be no doubt about the task confronting us at present: *the ruthless criticism of the existing order,* ruthless in that it will shrink neither from its own discoveries nor from conflict with the powers that be.
>
> Marx, early writings[17]

Criticism was the spirit of the Enlightenment—uncompromising scrutiny of all existing institutions and ideas. In France the target was most often institutions; in Germany, ideas. Thus Kant's *Critiques* left political institutions and the Church wholly unscathed, while Hegel's critiques became virtually *post hoc* rationalizations of institutions, not only leaving them unchallenged but defending them as well. In Germany, in other words, "critique" was far from uncompromising, where power was concerned. Consequently, Marx preferred the French version, for he had come to see, via Feuerbach, that reason, ideas, and ideologies were most typically the masks of institutions and not, as Hegel had argued, their essence and reason for being. "Reason has always existed," Marx too insists, "but not always in a rational form" (Coletti, p. 208).

The year 1843 was crucial in Marx's turn to radicalism. The Prussian government suppressed his newspaper because of its stand against government censorship, making Marx an "undesirable" in Germany. On his part, Marx felt a combination of personal outrage and enthusiasm: disgust with the German "philistines" (he also calls them "toads" and "brainless creatures") and their archaic governments ("a ship of fools"), but at the same time a new sense of impending change (to what extent fueled by wishful thinking is beside the point). Consequently, this Schiller-style aesthete, who had been concerned almost wholly with the "emancipation of the senses" and the freedom to develop his own literary style, turned his skills to politics. Together with Arnold Ruge (a friend who was collaborating with Feuerbach), Marx planned a series of radical international yearbooks, in the belief that French-style critique would inspire a German revolution. As he wrote to Ruge: "When all the inner conditions are met, *the day of the German resurrection* will be heralded by the crowing of the Gallic cock" (Coletti, p. 257).

To gain the freedom to carry out such a project, Marx left Germany for Paris in October 1843. To clarify his personal life, he and Jenny had been married in June. In Paris he began a detailed study of the French Revolution, seeking a recipe rather than mere historical understanding. And he began the writing and editing of the yearbooks, to which he invited Feuerbach and Bauer to contribute. In fact, only the first (double) issue of the *German-French Yearbooks* would be published—which was enough, however, to make of Marx an international outlaw. "Nothing prevents us, therefore," he wrote Ruge, "from lining our criticism with a criticism of politics, from taking sides in politics, i.e. from entering into real struggles and identifying ourselves with them." The word "revolution" was now prominent in his writings, and he declared his hatred for not only the "philistine monarchy" but "for the whole system of industry and commerce, of property and the exploitation of man." His irritation with German backwardness became biting criticism, aimed in particular at complacency and lack of imagination: "The Germans are such prudent realists that not one of their wishes and their wildest fantasies ever extends beyond the bare actualities of life" (Coletti, p. 205).

On a trip with Ruge to Holland, Marx cried out against the image that the Prussian government presented to foreigners, and vowed to aid the cause of "the German resurrection" in the way that he could be most effective—as critic:

It is clear that the arm of criticism cannot replace the criticism of arms. Material force can only be overthrown by material force. But theory also becomes a material force once it has seized the masses.[18]

Our program must be: the reform of consciousness, obscure to itself, whether it appears in religious or political form. It will then become plain that the world has long since dreamed of something of which it needs only to become conscious for it to possess in reality. . . . We are therefore in a position to sum up the credo of our journals [the *German-French Yearbooks*] in a *single word:* the self-clarification (critical philosophy) of the struggles and wishes of the age.

With his now familiar pseudoreligious irony, Marx concluded: "To obtain forgiveness for its sins, mankind needs only to declare them for what they are" (Coletti, p. 209). In other words, "the truth shall set you free." The goal of Marx's new critical philosophy was exactly the same as that of the older Kantian-Hegelian criticism: *truth*. But where the truth of the old idealism simply allowed us to understand and accept (albeit on newly discovered rational grounds), the new criticism had as its explicit ambition the *rejection* of the ideas it criticized. Two years later, in his oft-quoted thesis on Feuerbach, Marx declared: "The philosophers have only *interpreted* the world, in various ways; the point is to *change* it."[19]

The search for truth is not always obvious in Marx's incendiary polemics, but it must be remembered that the truth alone, flatly stated in a factual way, will probably not incite to action. The difference between statistics and outrage, for example, will be in the presentation, not the facts. In his arguments against government censorship, Marx had insisted on the importance of *tone* for a critic, the "way to truth" as well as "the results." The censors, in turn, were explicitly on the lookout for "vehemence, overintensity and arrogance"—not a bad description of Marx's style. But style and flamboyance, even with an obvious polemical tone, do not mean lack of veracity. In any evaluation of Marx it must be remembered that his search was not, as in Hegel, a "voyage of discovery," but an incitement to upheaval. And if philosophy, religion, and what he (again, after Feuerbach) came to call "ideology" were in fact a series of illusions and masks for the powers that be, then critique must indeed be an act of intellectual violence, for it asks us to see through and reject platitudes that we previously accepted as obvious.

This radical conception of critique raises an important philosophical question: Marx wants to go beyond Kant and Hegel not only in identifying the presuppositions of our thinking, but in evaluating and rejecting them. This requires, however, a criterion according to which such presuppositions are to be weighed. (Kant and Hegel argued this in some detail.) But it is here that many accounts of Marx fall short, for it has too often been argued that Marxism is a philosophy with *no* presuppositions, which too easily comes to mean no such standards, as if Marxism itself could serve as the basis for all evaluation, including self-evaluation. Here a grasp of Marx's Enlightenment background is absolutely necessary, to understand not only his early writings but also the standard that lay, often unmentioned, at the basis of everything else he ever wrote. The standard against which he weighs all ideas, institutions, and ideologies is his humanism: his youthful concern for happiness, for a full life of the senses, for freedom of expression and human dignity. Divorced from his Enlightenment roots, as he has been by many recent communist "purists" (Althusser, for example), Marx loses not only the basis for his polemics—which degenerate into badly written "science" (and largely false science at that)—but also the intelligibility and appeal of his project: "To be radical is to grasp things by the root. But for man the root is man himself."[20]

Back to Hegel

> The criticism of the German philosophy of the right and of the state which was given its most logical, profound and complete expression by *Hegel*, is at once the critical analysis of the modern state and of the reality connected with it and a definitive negation of all past forms of political and juridical consciousness in Germany.
>
> Marx, *Contribution*

After resigning from *Die Rheinische Zeitung,* Marx used his ample free time to undertake an extensive review of Hegel's political theories, and of *The Philosophy of Right* in particular. The Hegelian method and a sense of dialectic were already very much a part of his thinking. (This is sometimes obscured by the fact that Marx attacks Hegel's particular *use* of dialectic as "the Hegelian dialectic" [Coletti, p. 385].) But Marx was now critical of Hegel's conservative results in a deep and perceptive way, seeing how easily the Hegelian theory justified the incompetent and inhumane totalitarianism of the Prussian monarchy. He even disagreed with Hegel's republicanism, for now, very much under the influence of Rousseau, he was beginning to formulate a view of government—that of a radical democrat.[21] "Democracy cannot be represented," he argued; laws and constitutions could never take the place of and must never be put above the General Will of the People. He also argued, anticipating one of his most famous prophesies, that true democracy would induce a "withering away of the state." Clearly, Marx was siding with the French radicals—with Rousseau in particular—against Hegel. The state, which held such a primary place in German ideology, was at most for him a secondary concern. The General Will and the People, usually treated so cautiously by German writers, were the central concepts of his new politics. However, these views were still strictly *political:* the basic—that is, economic—formulation of these views had not yet emerged.

Marx's study of Hegel begins with a detailed commentary on Hegel's theory of the modern state.[22] The basic disagreements had already been anticipated by Feuerbach, though not worked out. The main objection would be, as always, Hegel's insistence on making abstractions (e.g., the Idea of the State) into primary realities, and concrete particulars (e.g., the material needs of flesh-and-blood people) into derivatives of these abstractions. (All of this is horribly confused by the fact that Hegel refers to these abstractions as "concrete totality," and to the particulars as "abstractions"

—that is, as less than the whole.) The general complaint that Hegel abuses his radical method to obtain extremely conservative results is now developed in detail. In place of the vague complaints of his student days, Marx now shows *how* Hegel attempts to justify existing institutions (in the disguise of mere description) as "the realization of the Idea." Marx objects in particular to Hegel's justification of the State as "the Absolute Idea, which takes as its goal explicit realization as infinite real mind," completely ignoring people and their needs and thus "inverting" the State, a mere abstract idea, with human reality. Marx accuses Hegel of thus "mystifying" the basic question of politics, rather than asking straightforwardly what *in fact* makes people better off, freer and happier, and (a residual romantic commitment) more harmonious and creative. Mere description and obscure justifications, Marx concludes, must give way to criticism of things as they are, with a constant view to making them better.

Whatever their disagreements, however, Marx thinks the Hegelian analysis is important enough for him to base his whole philosophy on its examination. Moreover, it is necessary to always keep in mind how much he is in agreement with some of its basic principles. It is Hegel, Marx insists, who has captured the essence of the modern state, and thus he must be the point of departure for any philosophical critique: "Hegel should not be blamed for describing the essence of the modern state as it is, but for identifying what is with the *essence* of the state" (Coletti, p. 127). In other words, Marx disagrees not with Hegel's account of the world, but only with Hegel's insistence that things are as they *ought* to be, that the real is indeed "rational" (whereas, Marx insists, "irrational reality" shows itself at every turn). Most important, Marx and Hegel—despite all their obvious disagreements—share the same political ideal against which all institutions and theories are to be measured: society as an organic, living whole in which all individuals are completely "at home."

The more ideal and profound view of recent philosophy proceeds from the whole. It looks on the state as the great organism, in which legal, moral and political freedom must be realized and in which the individual citizen in obeying the laws of the state only obeys the natural laws of his own reason, of human reason. (*Works,* I, 202)

For both Marx and Hegel, this ideal is the classical ideal of the Greek *polis,* the city-state in which everyone speaks for himself or herself, and all personal interests ideally coincide with the general interest, as in an extended family. (Both Marx and Hegel explicitly use the family as prototype here, except that Hegel, as usual, sees the family as an instance of an abstract ideal rather than as a concrete model for the ideal.)

It is on the basis of their shared model of an organic society, with its coincidence of public and private interests, that Marx attacks Hegel—and through him the society he describes—as failing to approach this organic ideal. Yet even here disagreements are tempered by, as well as based upon, agreements. Thus both Marx and Hegel reject the Lockean concept of a social contract, which neither accepts from Rousseau. Such a contract, they argue, glorifies competitive egoism and personal interests in what they call "civil society," but renders impossible the integration and family-community feeling which they in turn idealize. And although they disagree sharply on the legitimacy of private property, Hegel and Marx both agree —again contrary to Locke—that property is not a human right as such but, at most, a means to self-realization. (Hegel argues that it is necessary as such a means; Marx argues that it is no means at all, but *destructive* of self-realization.) Moreover, they both agree on the concept of a "universal class" whose members' interests coincide with the public interest, and which therefore serves as the force of reconciliation between civil and political society. (But Hegel thinks this is the middle class, the State-employed bureaucracy; Marx rejects this class as not "disinterested" or "universal" at all, though in the spring of 1843 he had yet to develop his conception of such a class.) Finally, the persistent Marxian concepts of "emergence," "realization," and "self-creation" are all basic dialectical concepts à la Hegel. In fact, their agreement on this dialectical model is so complete that it never even needs to be stated. Marx will use it throughout his life's work.

Politically, Marx objects to Hegel's defense of monarchy as "the personality of the state."[23] "A beautiful piece of logic," Marx sarcastically quips, as if society needed to be instantiated in a particular person (especially the likes of Frederick Wilhelm IV!), and as if the myriad of other personalities in the society—the People—did not count at all. Regarding the People, Hegel's reaction to the later days of the French Revolution had been decisive:

The usual sense, however, in which men have recently begun to speak of the "sovereignty of the people" is that it is something *opposed to the sovereignty existent in the monarch.* So opposed to the sovereignty of the monarch, the sovereignty of the people is one of the confused notions based on the *wild* idea of the "people." (*Philosophy of Right,* para. 279)

"As if the people were not the real state," Marx comments, and accuses Hegel of deceitful "triviality":

The "confused notion" and the "wild idea" are to be found here solely in Hegel. It is of course true that if sovereignty *exists* in the monarch, then it is foolish to speak of an opposed sovereignty in the people. . . . But, the real question is whether the sovereignty enshrined in the monarch is not simply an illusion. Sovereignty of the monarch or of the people—that is the question. (Coletti, p. 86)

Marx's choice is clear: following Rousseau, he insists that sovereignty resides *only* in the people: "It goes without saying that all forms of the state have democracy for their truth and that they are untrue to the extent that they are not democracy" (Coletti, p. 89). And again the "inversion" argument: "Hegel proceeds from the state and conceives man as the subjectivized state: democracy proceeds from man and conceives of the state as objectified man" (p. 87).

Universal suffrage is the only possible meaning of democracy. Marx rejects the prominence of constitutions and laws, as well as the more ancient institution of oppression, on the grounds that it is always "the self-determination of the people" that counts. Constitutions and laws are legitimate insofar as they are popular expressions, but they have no "higher" status, as the "natural law" philosophers of the Enlightenment (e.g., Voltaire; see p. 44) had long argued. Marx is not, in this sense, a republican, and here, where Hegel and other former enthusiasts of the French Revolution turned to despair when such "higher laws" failed to calm the violent "law of the revolution" itself, Marx believes that the popular revolution did not go far enough! For one thing, the Third Estate retained its illusion as a single class, instead of betraying the very real differences within it and making these *politically* significant (Coletti, p. 146).

Therefore, Marx argues, Hegel's main claim to success—the reconciliation of civil society and the state—is an illusion obscured by his idealism. What has not yet been questioned is the legitimacy of both civil society— "competitive individualism, egoism held in check by universality"—and the state, which is, after all, "an abstraction."[24] Regarding the State, even in these early writings it is clear that Marx looks forward to its "withering away": "In modern times the French have understood this to mean that the *political state disappears* in a true democracy."[25] Regarding civil society, which Marx, following Hobbes and Hegel, describes as a "war of everyone against everyone else" (Coletti, p. 101), it is clear that no such society could ever hope to realize the ideal integration of the *polis*. The critique of Hegel shows that the roots of human society lie in a very different conception of society.

Paris, Engels, and British Economics

Marx arrived in Paris in October 1843. What he found was a city of conspiracy—a haven for romantics, anarchists, and assorted political and cultural exiles from every country in Europe. The Russian Bakunin was there, beginning his polemics on anarchism. Proudhon, Fourier, Saint-Simon, and other French utopians were already popular, and some of their ideas were even being tried on a small scale, as for example in Fourier-type communes on the outskirts of Paris. There were working-class radicals as well, already developing labor unions and learning the potential power of strikes and protests.[26] There was Heinrich Heine (whose poetry and essays Marx had admired as a student), using Paris as a base from which to launch his ironic attacks on Germany. And there was Friedrich Engels, whom Marx had met only briefly in Cologne the year before, now in Paris to write about the working class in England. Within weeks Marx had met and abstractly conspired with Bakunin, begun his attack on the French utopians, observed and met with the working radicals, become a good friend and personal critic to Heine,[27] and begun the discussions that would lead to a lifelong working partnership with Engels.

To understand Marx's shift toward communism and an economic approach in general, it is necessary to appreciate the impact of his most important intellectual discovery in Paris—more important even than Engels (who led him to it), or the socialists, or the workers, or even Heine. The books of the British political economists—Adam Smith, David Ricardo, and James Mill, among others—turned Marx onto the path he seems in retrospect to have been looking for all along. It was economics that would provide the driving force of the Hegelian dialectic, rather than the abstract implications of logic and ideas. It was economics that would fill in the gaps in his political theories, still too caught up in Rousseau-like allegories and Greek nostalgia.

With British economics, the mechanisms of change became evident to him. Money and wealth, which are products of work, provide the missing links to history and politics. The irony is that those who work are not those who enjoy its products; the history of the West is the inevitable struggle against this "contradiction." The basis of the true dialectic—henceforth the *material* dialectic—would be economics, and the new vocabulary would no longer be the civil-society language borrowed from Hegel, but the jargon of "wages" and "capital" drawn from the British.[28]

Of course economics was not an exclusively British discovery, but the industrial revolution had been going full steam in England for many years, while it was just maturing in France and had barely begun in "philistine" Germany. In France, however, the utopian socialists had also (after the English) "discovered" the working class. Marx had not—not yet, and his first serious contacts with economics came from the relatively naive French utopians. Claude Henri, comte de Saint-Simon (1760–1825), an impoverished noble who had renounced his title during the Revolution, had talked about the working class and impending class conflict (a century of "invention and destruction") before Marx was born. His more humbly born compatriot, Pierre Proudhon (1809–1865), a proto-anarchist from whom Bakunin would learn much ("he was the master of us all"), in 1840 had baldly announced, "Property is theft." In fact, however, he was not a communist, and advocated the elimination not of private property but of its flagrant abuses—the exploitation of labor, and the ownership of more property than one could work oneself. It was his humanistic axiom that no one should have a right to ownership without producing some "human," and not just personal, benefit. Proudhon even attacked communism as being necessarily authoritarian. He preferred a moderate socialist anarchism. Though in his *Poverty of Philosophy* (1847) Marx would break with him on this issue, even so he called Proudhon's work "the first decisive, vigorous and scientific examination" of property.

But Charles Fourier (1772–1837) was perhaps the most fascinating of the French utopians. He developed a theory of emotional and sexual repression a century before Freud, but emerged with a radical utopian solution in place of Freud's own later pessimism in *Civilization and Its Discontents*. Fourier blames capitalism, financial inequality and insecurity, and harsh, tedious working conditions for the poor state of psychological health. He suggested breaking up society into independent communes that would bring "the end of civilization" as we know it. Each commune or "phalanx" would be organized around common ownership and complete sexual and emotional freedom. Though Marx made fun of these idyllic suggestions, he also appreciated Fourier's experimenting with "alternative life styles," and the socialist's recognition, however un-Marxist, of the economic barbarism of modernity. (Fourier was also, one might add, a gourmet and an excellent chef—no beans and brown rice in *his* commune!)

It is a difficult and probably useless task to determine the influences on a thinker—who inspired him, who provided ideas, who just triggered off or clarified some concept already there, who supplied words or style, who merely made an impression. But it is important to realize that, in that crucial autumn in Paris, Marx was not alone in his radical thinking and his hopes. In the Paris circles he frequented, there was a veritable competition to diagnose the ills of society and offer promising alternatives—almost all of them socialist and/or anarchist in temperament. Marx's early writings, in which he was beginning to formulate his basic philosophy, were not unusual in either their radical tone or their politico-economic content. Such was the current fashion. Marx, one can say in retrospect, just did it better— in the end, more fashionably—than anyone else.

What Marx learned and borrowed from the British economists, and how he reacted against them, has filled books, but we can summarize a few basic points.[29] Adam Smith (1723–1790) was a moral philosopher whose *Wealth of Nations* (1776) virtually began the science of political economics. (Engels called him "the Luther of political economy.")[30] His basic principles are easily stated:

1. The source of all wealth is people's work, or *labor*.
2. Everyone in "civilized society" is a "merchant" of a kind—renting land, working for wages, or working for profits. Everyone too is a consumer.
3. Prices—whether rents, wages, or profits—depend on the "law of supply and demand."
4. If everyone follows his or her own personal interests, and tries to make the

most money from what he has—land, skills, luck, or ingenuity—the society in general will benefit. (Smith calls this "the invisible hand" of reason. "We address ourselves not to their [industrialist] *humanity* but to their *self-love*, and never talk to them of *our own necessities* but of their advantages.) [31]

5. Governments must allow total freedom of production and trade. There should be no laws or "shackles" to interfere with the operation of a free marketplace.

There is a bleaker side to these simple principles of "free enterprise" and "supply and demand," and their optimism. Smith sees that competition is possible only when capital is widely distributed, but he also sees that inherent in the free market system—because big industry has more buying power—is the tendency toward monopoly, which kills competition and free enterprise. He sees too that the natural result of maximizing profits is the *minimizing* of wages, and even suggests that the richer the country, the lower the wages. And since the general welfare of society can be measured only by the prosperity and welfare of its members, and since most of the members will be workers who are minimally paid and whose fortunes are totally at the mercy of forces beyond their control, a wealthy society will also tend to be a society governed by monopoly, with high prices, high unemployment, and low wages. Inevitably, the workers will suffer, and the whole society must therefore be called unhappy. Smith did not allow himself to draw out most of these conclusions,[32] but his successors, including Marx, did not hesitate to recognize the utter brutality inherent in such a system: "According to Smith, the normal wage is the lowest which is compatible with common humanity, i.e. with a bestial existence" (Bottomore, p. 69).

In historical perspective, it is a matter of ideology whether one sees Smith as the great liberal defender of free enterprise, or as an early diagnostician of the oppression that capitalism requires. It is clear that Marx chooses the second, complaining, while quoting Smith persistently, that "indolent landowners and busy capitalists" who operate in their own greedy self-interest find this interest not at all compatible with the needs and interests of the great majority of humanity—the workers—whether or not such egoism serves "the wealth of nations." Smith himself, one might argue, merely described as a scientist the laws he believed to operate in contemporary economics—with a certain optimism, to be sure, but not with any particular moral leanings. (For a professor of moral philosophy, it is remarkable that moral concepts—in particular the notion of "sympathy," about which he had written extensively—never enter his economic discourse.) But for Marx, Smith had done for economics what Hegel had done for politics: he had described the current state of affairs, with all its myths and illusions of beneficence, in such a way that a critic (Marx, for instance) could draw from it the hidden presuppositions responsible for the unhappiness and less than wholly human existence of the greater proportion of humanity.

Smith was just the beginning. The French economist Jean Baptiste Say (1767–1832) had read *The Wealth of Nations* before the turn of the century and had written his own *Treatise on Political Economy* (1803), in which he argued that basic value was determined not by labor, as Smith insisted, but by *utility*—how much things were desired and how hard they were to get. Thus Say shifted the primary emphasis from human activity to Smith's "supply and demand" of consumerism. Where Smith had glorified the division of labor for the good of the economy, Say recognized its debilitating effects on the individual worker—which Marx praised as "an advance." Say also saw that the emphasis on technology, while allowing for more production at less cost, created idleness, tedium, and unemployment. Furthermore, he stressed the advantages of an open market, but again, from the self-appointed position of "scientific objectivity," rather than out of moral advocacy.

Next on Marx's reading list was David Ricardo (1772–1823). More interested in the distribution of wealth than in the means of production, Ricardo developed the thoroughly pessimistic doctrine ("the law of rent") that economic systems will inevitably overpower human needs, and the worker will necessarily be reduced to bare subsistence support—just enough to keep him working. Ricardo agrees with Smith that work is the source of all value, but he sees that the worker inevitably gets the worst part of the deal. Ricardo borrows heavily from Thomas Malthus (1766–1834), who had earlier issued the dire prediction that, as people multiply much faster than food production, wars and famine are necessary to restrict the population. Ricardo, too, sees that human happiness has little place in the laws of economics, and Marx praises him for this perception:

Nations are merely workshops for production, and man is a machine for consuming and producing. Human life is a piece of capital. Economic laws rule the world blindly. For Ricardo men are nothing, the product everything.[33]

Marx complains: "The real aim of production is not how many workers a particular sum of capital can support, but how much interest it brings in and how much it *earns* each year" (Bottomore, p. 184). But again, Ricardo speaks with the detached voice of the scientist. Marx comments: "Ricardo lets political economy speak its own language. He is not to blame if this language is not that of morals" (p. 173). And again: "Political economy [has] become increasingly *cynical* from Smith through Say to Ricardo" (Coletti, p. 343). The main thing that Marx will add to these "increasingly cynical" theories is not itself theoretical: it is a sense of *outrage*.

In a personal commentary on James Mill's *Elements of Political Economy* (1826), which he read in Paris in 1844, Marx more and more sees the crucial problem of the whole of political economy as not just economic oppression of the worker, but the dehumanization of all work and of human life itself. According to political economy, he says, "our mutual value . . . is the *value* of our mutual objects. For me, therefore, man himself is *worthless*" (p. 277). Man's "soul" itself becomes a "money-soul" (p. 262), while "human individuality, human *morality,* have become both articles of commerce and the *material* which money inhabits. . . . Man is a being alienated from himself" (p. 265).

The Basic Formulation

> Where is there a *real* possibility of emancipation in Germany?
>
> This is our reply. A class must be formed which has *radical chains,* a class in civil society which is not a class of civil society, a class which is the dissolution of all classes, a sphere of society which has a *universal* character because its sufferings are universal and does not claim a *particular* redress because the wrong which is done to it is not a *particular wrong* but *wrong in general.*
>
> Marx, *Critique of Hegel*[34]

Marx did not invent "the working class"—Engels had come to Paris to write a book about it; Saint-Simon had talked about it many years before —nor was or is it clear that such a class exists as a concrete entity.[35] Notice, in Marx's first formulation just cited, that he speaks of "the *formation* of a class," not simply of its recognition. Nevertheless, two concerns now motivate Marx's philosophy and will continue to do so: the political and economic oppression of those who work for wages—despite the fact (invoked by Smith and Ricardo) that only human work is the ultimate source of worth; and the alienation of people from the products of their work, which ought to give them a sense of pride and self-esteem, but instead makes prostitutes of them.

Smith, Say, Ricardo, and the French socialists all recognized the plight of workers, but either without the moral indignation that Marx brings to the problem, or without a general, radical, revolutionary concept of *universal* emancipation that Marx now begins to demand. With indignation and a revolutionary posture, Marx touches the conscience and the pride of the nineteenth-century world. However much the later Marx may be "scientific," it is the continuing sense of outrage that explains his enormous influence. And despite his parochial hopes for the emancipation of Germany in particular—where even today Marxism exerts the least influence in Europe—it is the idea of universal emancipation that gives Marxism a sense of something more than mere self-interest.[36] And it is this same outrage that marks "the ideology of the proletariat" as a strictly *bourgeois* ideology!

The idea of a universal class was of course not new, being the heart of Hegel's theory of representative government. But, Marx argues against Hegel, the bureaucratic middle class is neither "disinterested" nor "universal." On the contrary, the middle class in France, although fighting under the banner of "universal rights," had clearly been struggling for its own interests. And yet, despite the familiar Marxist tirades against "the counter-revolutionary bourgeois," it is important to realize that Marx admires the revolutionary fervor and success of the French bourgeoisie (Coletti, pp. 200, 201, 413). (The German burgher, however, he still considers "philistinic"—"in its armchair, stupid and dumb.") But history has moved on in France, and it is no longer the middle class, with their illusion of unity in the Third Estate (see p. 88), that constitutes the oppressed class. At one time the bourgeoisie struggled against kings, aristocrats, *and bureaucrats,* but now, as the bourgeoisie takes their place, says Marx,

the proletariat is already beginning its struggle with the bourgeoisie. The middle class hardly dares to conceive of the idea of emancipation from its own point of view before the development of social conditions and the progress of political theory show that this point of view is already antiquated or at least disputable.[37]

The *personal* interests of the middle class are now primary, according to Marx. Gone are the slogans of "liberty and equality," replaced by the inhuman laws of political economy, benefiting some at the expense of others. So much for the middle-class claim to universality. But the workers, Marx says, reflect the *source* of the present problems as well as their own self-interests. Accordingly, he argues, they represent the emancipation and even "the total redemption of humanity" (p. 256). Marx emerges as the champion of the Enlightenment, now no longer serving the interests of the bourgeoisie.

A serious critical question emerges at this point: might not Marx be making the same error regarding the still unformed working class that he sees in Hegel's defense of the middle class? It is not clear that such oppression is all of a kind: for example, racism, sexism, and regional differences in educational opportunities must be distinguished among the inequities facing "the worker." Then too, the plight of the "lumpenproletariat," the desperately poor and unemployed, surely deserves more attention than Marx gives it. (The unfortunate Marxist tendency to criticize all such issues as "bourgeois narcissism" only glosses over the problems.) This is not the place to attack such a problem, but the extent to which Marx's theorizing is based on the same kind of abstraction that he criticized in Hegel, and driven by the same kind of wishful thinking, is surely an issue in understanding Marx himself. A perpetual exile and outsider, for the rest of his life Marx hoped for the radical changes that would let him return to Germany. Accordingly, he sought a force *within* Germany which might effect such changes—surely not the German burghers and bureaucrats, or the feudal aristocracy and monarchy. The working class was Marx's abstract hope, substantiated by experiences in Paris and by Engels's description of industrially advanced England.[38] It is partly a question of motivation, not only in Marx's recognition of the possibility of such a class, but in his *identification* with it. The question strikes a deep philosophical chord: why does anyone identify with a group of which he or she is not a member? It would be unfair to say that Marx's interests were based only on what he saw as the revolutionary potential of the working class. The moral concepts of "sympathy" and "compassion" will take us so far, but no farther. Otherwise, why the black-and-white, good-and-evil, oppressed-and-oppressor polarities, apart from their obvious polemical value?[39] It was not just a law of history that Marx claimed to have found, but a moral issue that demanded his lifelong dedication. The passion that produces such morally divisive issues is something much more than mere *com*-passion.

The concept of the "proletariat,"[40] or working class, appears for the first time in Marx's introduction to his projected *Contribution to the Critique of Hegel's Philosophy of Right,* written in Paris and published, without the *Contribution* itself, in the *German-French Yearbooks.* Clearly, he had not yet developed the concept even earlier that year, for in his *Critique of Hegel* he had said: "The only noteworthy feature is that the *absence of property* and the *class of immediate labor,* concrete labor, do not so much constitute a class of civil society as provide the ground on which the circles of civil society move and have their being" (Coletti, pp. 146–47). This makes our emphasis on the phrase "the *formation* of a class" (italics mine) all the more important. Marx further states: "The proletariat is only beginning to form itself in Germany as a result of the *industrial* movement. For what constitutes the proletariat is not naturally existing poverty but poverty artificially *produced*" (Bottomore, p. 58). It is the system of private property, as described by Smith and the other British economists, that in turn produces that poverty, so "when the proletariat demands the negation of *private property,* it is only elevating to a *principle for society* what society has already made a principle *for* the proletariat" (p. 59).[41]

Technical abstractions and problems aside, Marx recognizes and appreciates the reality of *poverty*—a new kind, not of circumstance or neglect but of *exploitation.* This poverty had been rationalized for centuries of Christian charity and compassion; had been neglected by the Enlightenment, which had its own middle-class interests in mind;[42] had been ignored even during the French Revolution, when the power of the poor first surfaced as a politically effective force, uncontrolled by abstract ideologies and libertarian niceties; and had been glossed over by the economic scientists, for whom poverty was merely one of the necessary ingredients in the capitalist cake. But Marx is outraged, and he becomes the modern prophet of poverty not as an abstraction (whether or not the concept of "class" or "proletariat" might be), but as a real source of indignation which should, and was beginning to, trouble all people with the slightest claim to the elevated principles of the modern age. And by 1840 poverty could no longer be attributed simply to circumstances, misfortune, God's will, or mere neglect. It was poverty *willfully produced* through the exploitation of the new commerce and industry. Because of this new *willful* factor, the working class was born from the ideology of the middle class.

The Problems of "Alienation"

> Man's own deed becomes an alien power opposed to him, which enslaves him instead of being controlled by him.
>
> Marx, *The German Ideology*[43]

In 1844 Marx began to integrate his studies of Hegel and economics, his humanism and his growing sense of "communism," into an original and self-consciously systematic form. His three "economic and philosophical manuscripts" center around one particular concept drawn from Hegel, "alienation,"[44] and its antithesis or antidote, "total man" (one could also say "the whole person"). Basic to the concept of "alienation," of course, is the system of capitalism and private property, but it is important to note that, in these manuscripts, Marx sees private property as a necessary consequence of "alienated labor," not the other way around (Coletti, p. 337). "Alienated labor," in turn, is "alienated life" (p. 332). This equation reveals the basic thesis of the whole of Marx's view—that man *is* his activity, his labor, properly understood. The view is at once very Hegelian and very much part of the Protestant Ethic that also forms the basis of capitalism.[45] But Marx is concerned with "total man," while Protestantism and capitalism are responsible for "alienated man" turned away from "human nature." Thus despite the preponderance of economics (discussed in the preceding section), the manuscripts of 1844 are essentially concerned with the philosophical problem of the nature of man.

Marx's concept of "total man" is the same concept he inherited from Schiller. Again, despite the economic concerns, total man is defined not in terms of production as such, but rather by the classical concepts of "the emancipation of the senses" (Coletti, p. 352), and "enjoyment of social existence" and "vital human expression" (p. 351), including especially works of art (p. 329) as well as material necessities. The key concept here, to be juxtaposed against the economic concept of production, is *expression*. One's work is an expression of more than one's personal needs and desires, for it is also an expression of one's humanity. This is the same "objectification" that Hegel had discussed as "spirit," though Marx criticizes Hegel for an entirely one-sided emphasis on thought, to the neglect of physical activity and the senses. It is the same too as Schiller's concept of "externalizing what is inner": in other words, for Marx, work is not merely a practical activity (in the narrow sense of satisfying material needs), but an *expression* that is humanly essential. Here Marx the young romantic is still very much alive, and nothing could be further from his thinking than the "crude" view of work as a distasteful *means* to sustain and enrich life that is to be avoided if at all possible (p. 326). In fact, the idea of work as a means lies at the basis of "alienated labor." Attacking this conception is the point of the whole argument of the manuscripts: "Labor itself—not only in present conditions but universally in so far as its purpose is merely the increase of wealth—is harmful and deleterious" (Bottomore, p. 76). Human activity, i.e. labor—if we can divorce that word from its nasty connotation of "work" as opposed to "pleasure"—is not a means but an end. It is what it is to be human (Coletti, pp. 326–34). "Man," says Marx, "produces when he is free from physical need and only produces in freedom from such need" (Bottomore, p. 128). And in the "Essay on James Mill" he observes: "My labor (unalienated) would be the *free expression* and hence the *enjoyment* of life. In the framework of private property it is the *alienation of life* since I work in order to live. . . . My labor is *not* life" (Coletti, p. 278).

The term Marx uses to describe the nature of man, which he took directly from Feuerbach, is "species-being" (*Gattungswesen*). Not a wholly fortunate choice of words, it means first of all that man is a *social* being, and that all production and expression are primarily a social act, not one in order to earn money: "My *own* existence *is* social activity. Therefore, what I create for myself I create for society, conscious of myself as a social being" (Bottomore, p. 138). In his commentary on Mill earlier that year Marx argued, as he argues here, that as a social being one enjoys another's use or enjoyment of one's own creations, and that it is in such reciprocal exchange—very different from barter or marketing or any other kind of "deal"—that human bonds are realized.

This sense of man as a social ("species") being is also, of course, very Hegelian, and the organic unity of humanity that is its basis, with man as part of nature and "nature [as] man's *inorganic body*" and "the object and the tool of his life activity" (Coletti, p. 328), is as Hegelian as could be. So too are the ideas that expression is human essence, that freedom is the expression of certain basic necessities (that is, man's social, creative nature), and that individual independence can make sense *only* within the context of harmonious social life (p. 328). Marx, like Hegel, takes the concept "fraternity" very seriously—much more than the bourgeois sloganeers of the French Revolution: "The brotherhood of man is not a hollow phrase, it is a reality, and the nobility of man shines forth upon us from their work-worn figures" (Bottomore, p. 143).

If "total man" is a creative, social being, what then is "alienated man," who Marx says is a regression from the cave man and wholly self-deprived (p. 366)? Alienation is (logically from the preceding) the stifling of one's creativity that results when one is forced to produce objects of no personal significance (e.g., on an assembly line), or to turn freely created objects into mere marketable merchandise (e.g., works of art bought from the artist, who loses not only possession and all rights to the work, but tends to become a conscious producer of marketable works, no longer expressive so much as sellable). Also, alienation is the breaking of our "natural" social bonds by the "unnatural" relations of competition.[46] These forms of alienation combine in a system that culminates, as the reader will have anticipated, in the institutions of private property and capitalism based on wage-labor. (Marx's causal relationships here tend to be inconsistent; see Coletti, pp. 332–34.) The arch-villain, however, is *money* itself, "the *pimp* between need and object, between life and man's means of life" (p. 375). (Marx often uses sexually tinged metaphors—Freudians take note.) It is money that is responsible for that alienating "inversion" that Marx (following Feuerbach) complained of in Hegel's philosophy:

Money, then, appears as a *disruptive* power for the individual and to those social and other bonds which claim to be self-subsistent entities. It transforms loyalty into treason, love into hate, hate into love, virtue into vice, vice into virtue, servant into master, master into servant, nonsense into reason and reason into nonsense. (Bottomore, p. 193)

Money makes "universal exploitation" into an inevitable abuse of "communal human nature"; because of it, "every need is an opportunity for stepping up to one's neighbor in sham friendship and saying to him: 'Dear friend, I can give you what you need, but you know the terms' " (Coletti, p. 359). And it is money, finally, that motivates the self-denial that makes us slaves of our own greed:

The less you eat, drink, buy books, go to the theater, go dancing, go drinking, think, love, theorize, sing, paint, fence, etc., the more you *save* and the greater will become that treasure which neither moths nor maggots can consume—your *capital.* The less you *are,* the less you give expression to your life, the more you *have,* the greater is your *alienated* life. . . . So all passions and all activity are submerged in *greed.* (Bottomore, pp. 171–72)

The basic thesis, therefore, is this: the more we *have,* the less we *are.* The details need some scrutinizing, but Marx's outlook is clear: it is not just the exploited worker who concerns him, but the crippled "money-soul" of mankind in general. It is not, then, just an argument about ownership (which he would dismiss as "crude"); the much-touted scare-phrase "the abolition of private property" is essentially a means to "restore man to himself as a *social*—i.e., human—being" (Coletti, p. 348). Finally, says Marx, "*Communism,* as fully developed naturalism, is humanism. . . . It is the resolution of the riddle of history and knows itself to be the solution" (Bottomore, p. 155).

"Praxis"

> The philosophers have *only* interpreted the world, in various ways; the point is to *change* it.
>
> Marx, *Theses on Feuerbach*

With the thesis that we *make* our world and ourselves, Marx brings to fruition the central ideas of the French and German Enlightenments, Hegel and romanticism. But in Marx this thesis is no longer an abstract view of reason or the power of intellectual categories; it is the down-to-earth and straightforward assertion that, for all *practical* purposes, the world that surrounds, threatens, and sustains us is a humanly created world. The much celebrated synthesis of "theory" and "practice" designated by the Greek word *praxis,* therefore, is already inherent in the very nature of human life. (Hegel had argued this, too.) For Marx, theorizing and changing the world are one and the same. Over two decades later, in 1867, when he had finished the first volume of *Kapital,* he wrote:

[For this work] I have sacrificed health, happiness and family . . . I laugh at so-called "practical" men and their wisdom. If one were willing to be an ox, one could naturally turn one's back on human suffering and look after one's own skin. But I would really have considered myself "unpractical" if I caved in before making my book, or at least my manuscript, quite ready.[47]

The seriousness of his endeavor cost not only his "health, happiness and family," but his friends as well. Marx did not take disagreement tolerantly; over the years he broke with Bauer, Ruge, Proudhon, and others, turning on them in always less than tactful public criticism. In 1845 he had turned against Feuerbach, his onetime hero, with eleven famous "theses," the best known of which is quoted above. He complained not only that Feuerbach was complacent, overly individualistic, and not sensuous enough (!), but —the unkindest cut of all—that he was still in essence a Hegelian. The break with Proudhon two years later was equally bitter, ignoring all that the two men had shared and agreed upon for so many years. Only Engels seems to have survived the personal-theoretical purges. By 1845 their lifelong friendship had solidified, mainly on the basis of what Marx perceived as their "complete agreement on all theoretical issues." When the

Prussian reaction against the *Yearbook* became so great that the French expelled Marx from Paris, he would eventually—after a three-year stay in Brussels and a brief return to Germany—end up in London, where he and his family were supported by Engels for the rest of his life. (After the publication of the first volume of *Kapital*, Marx wrote to Engels, "It is you alone that I have to thank for making this possible.")[48]

His life became his theoretical work, and his theoretical work became the practical guidelines for future generations of radicals. In 1848 events in Europe and Marx's increasingly radical views came together in a dramatic way. Riots erupted throughout Europe, first in Italy, then in Paris, resulting in the abdication of the French King, replaced by a new and more liberal government and in time by a new Napoleon. From Paris the revolts spread to Germany, initiating a brief period of confused liberalism that allowed Marx to return to his homeland for the last time. None of these revolutions had much lasting effect, if one looks at what soon followed: a new Emperor in France, and a return to the old "dinosaur" policies of Frederick Wilhelm IV in Prussia. But unlike the revolutions of the first half of the century, the new spirit of revolt had not only a large working-class participation, but a distinct and sometimes dominant working-class ideology as well. It is thus appropriate that Marx and Engels's most famous single collaboration, *The Communist Manifesto,* appeared at the very outset of these revolutions. In the strictest sense of the term, there was no causal relation between the two, but Marx and Engels's pamphlet was an apt expression of the working-class sentiment that erupted in revolt, and formulated—some would say once and for all—the hopes, conflicts, and theory of conflict that would define much of the workers' movement for many years to come.

The *Manifesto*'s beginning is famous:

A specter is haunting Europe—the specter of communism. All the powers of old Europe have entered into a holy alliance to exorcise this specter: Pope and Czar, Metternich and Guizot, French Radicals and German police spies.

Where is the party in opposition that has not been decried as communistic by its opponents in power? Where the opposition that has not hurled back the branding reproach of Communism . . . ?[49]

The pamphlet proceeds to declare that "Communism is already acknowledged by all European powers to be itself a power," and that "it is high time that Communists should openly, in the face of the whole world, publish their views, their aims, their tendencies and meet this nursery tale of the specter of communism with a Manifesto of the Communist Party." The body of the text opens with the thesis: "The history of all hitherto existing society is the history of class struggles" (p. 13). Later Marx would admit that the *Manifesto* oversimplified his views considerably, but that piece, even more than his other work, was explicitly and primarily polemical. Its brief history of the West is a caricature, but a powerful one. It follows Hegel (who followed Lessing) in separating the entire history of the world into simply defined epochs that in Marx, naturally, are classified by economic categories. The distinction between the business and management class or *bourgeoisie,* and the working class or *proletariat,* is now etched into the European mind as a fundamental distinction. If it was not wholly real before, it is now *made* real by theory. The bourgeoisie, Marx argues, has long been the revolutionary class, and through it the overthrow of feudalism was made possible and accomplished. But now the tables have turned, and the downfall of the middle class is imminent at the hands of its own creation, the working class, "like the sorcerer who is no longer able to control the powers he has created": "What the bourgeoisie, therefore, produces above all, is its own gravediggers. Its fall and the victory of the proletariat are equally inevitable" (p. 45).

The *Manifesto* goes on to call for an end to private property, the abolition of the traditional family, an end to nationalism and "nations," an increase in production through collective ownership of industry, and a series of programs—many of them not radical at all today—until "in place of the old bourgeois society, with its classes and class antagonisms, we shall have an association, in which the free development of each is the condition for the free development of all" (p. 54). That last sentence underscores the problem which has always bothered liberal sympathizers of Marxism—the questionable promise that collective priorities will make possible individual freedom and happiness as well. Whether this is possible is not for us to question here, nor shall we point to the many failures, abuses, and hypocrisies defended in the name of this belief. But it should be emphasized that this problem is not at all peculiar to Marxism, but is inherent in Hegel's philosophy, implicit in the philosophies of the French Enlightenment, and brutally manifest in all the politics of Europe from the French Revolution through Napoleon until the revolutions of 1848. Thus it is a question of open debate—and is still debated—whether the final call of the *Manifesto* is a declaration of violent emancipation, an end and culmination of the humanism of the Enlightenment, or to the contrary an open attack on all that the Enlightenment defended:

Let the ruling classes tremble at a communist revolution. The proletarians have nothing to lose but their chains. They have a world to win.

Working men of all countries, unite! (p. 82)

16 The Singular Universal:[1] Søren Kierkegaard

> Each age has its own characteristic depravity. Ours is perhaps not pleasure or indulgence or sensuality, but rather a dissolute, pantheistic contempt for the individual man.
>
> Kierkegaard, *Concluding Unscientific Postscript*[2]

> Our age is essentially one of understanding and reflection, without passion, momentarily bursting into enthusiasm, and shrewdly relapsing into repose.
>
> Kierkegaard, *The Present Age*[3]

The hundred-year epoch covered in this study has been characterized, from a cultural point of view, as a period of rapid secularization; from a social point of view, as one witnessing the dramatic rise of the middle class; and from a political point of view, as one of rapidly rising nationalism and international imperialism. But philosophically, the epoch was the victory of "humanism"—the conquest of gods and nature; the extension of the bourgeois ego to the whole of the Cosmos. The world of Western Europe had become thoroughly "humanized"—that is, thoroughly middle class. But the once idealistic and revolutionary bourgeoisie had now settled back on its haunches to become not only the dominant class, but in its own eyes the *only* class as well. This "fat brood of mediocrity," as Hesse would later call them, had few battles to fight, except to get richer and more comfortable, and consequently more self-satisfied and self-righteous. "Middle-class morality" was no longer the Roman patriotism depicted in David's paintings, but the day-to-day conventions of avoiding inconvenience, such as paying one's debts (at the last possible minute, as Stendhal observed). Troubles were brewing in the working class, but the new reactionary government could keep them in check without concern on the part of the good citizens. This was the world that had been fought for—the "realization of the human spirit," "the perfectibility of man."

Nowhere was the bourgeoisie more bourgeois than in Scandinavia, which, with Holland, had been made thoroughly bourgeois long before the Revolution in France. Even the working classes in those countries had the more or less comfortable life of the middle class. In fact, class distinctions were difficult to make: everyone looked and acted disturbingly—or comfortingly—the same. Without battles to fight, with profits to be made and everyday duties to be carried out efficiently, the gray army of citizens would march through Oslo, Amsterdam, Stockholm, and Copenhagen under gray skies with gray expressions of smug, if depressed, self-satisfaction. The Enlightenment and Kantian morality prevailed here; no battles were necessary to establish them. Even romanticism, or a gray version of it, was accepted in poetry, art, and theater as a matter of daily course. "Objectively," everything was perfect. There was peace and there was food. Everyone remembered when there had been neither. They were even used to the weather. Humanity had been perfected, it seemed, or at least it was well on its way. But there were those, naturally enough, who hated this new and nearly "perfect" world, not just in its most recent manifestations—vulgar, materialistic, and hypocritical—but down to its bourgeois roots in the Enlightenment, its secularization, its class consciousness, and the whole mass mentality that had become synonymous with modernity.[4]

Because life seemed to objectively perfect, the oppressiveness that isolated individuals felt so much more intensely than anyone else was extremely hard to rationalize. It was not so much a fact as a feeling, but a basic feeling—as if essential to the human condition itself. Peace and prosperity, by alleviating external threats and struggles, had made it possible for the "inner life" to emerge, and it turned out to be as full of turmoil, dangers, and confusions as anything from the perilous years before.

The First Existentialist

> What I really lack is to be clear in my mind *what I am to do, not* what I am to know, except insofar as a certain understanding must precede every action. The thing is to understand myself, to see what God really wishes *me* to do; the thing is to find a truth which is true *for me,* to find *the idea for which I can live and die.*
>
> Kierkegaard, *Journals,* 1835[5]

In the summer of 1841 Søren Kierkegaard completed his master's degree in Copenhagen with a dissertation entitled "The Concept of Irony." "Irony" would be the watchword of his life, and his method. He would never practice as a minister—would in fact reject all that the position offered and represented. He was engaged to an attractive young woman, Regina Olsen, with whom he had fallen in love when she was only fourteen, and who promised him his most likely chance for durable happiness.[6] But he broke the engagement without explanation, and fled for a while to Berlin. He hated the frivolity of parties and the banality of conventional conversation, but forced himself to be "the life of the party" of bourgeois Copenhagen—not out of sociability so much as desperation:

> I have just returned from a party of which I was the life and soul; wit poured from my lips, everyone laughed and admired me—but I went away—and the dash should be as long as the earth's orbit————————————and wanted to shoot myself. (*Journals,* 1834)

He despised "the Public," but spent his life in the public eye.[7] He defended spontaneity and passion, but a friend described him as "so unspontaneous that I don't know how he can eat or sleep." His life consisted of self-destructive opposites. He was heir to the romantics, in his soul a great adventurer. But the events of 1841—a graduation, a broken engagement, and a short trip to Berlin—were all that ever happened in the life of Søren Kierkegaard.[8]

He was ugly, misshapen, and neurotically shy and ill at ease, yet also a devastating wit and a notorious flirt. He attacked the age for its excessive reflection, but spent his entire life in the seclusion of his study—reflecting. He was a rebel and a tactless critic who insisted above all that he be allowed to think and act for himself; yet he defended a religious authoritarianism that would have made even Bismarck's Prussia look like a liberal state. He was self-consciously eccentric, but tended to project his misery as if it were "the human condition" as such. The most radical individualism, too, partakes in the transcendental pretense. Incapable of personal relationships, he defended a "personal relationship with God" as the most meaningful possible life. Having spurned marriage himself, he continued to glorify it as few ever had.[9] He used his wit as a weapon, as if to compensate for his painful sense of personal inadequacy:

> I was already an old man when I was born. . . . Delicate, slender, and weak, deprived of almost every condition for holding my own with other boys, or even for passing as a complete human being in comparison with the others; melancholy, sick in soul, in many ways profoundly unfortunate, one thing I had: an eminently shrewd wit, given me presumably in order that I might not be defenseless. (*Journals,* 1835)

Kierkegaard's life was a rationalization of his life. It was as though he had "already died." Just as Voltaire had used his sarcasm to point out the foolishness of his society, so Kierkegaard used irony to point out the hopelessness of his. But if his wit savored of Voltaire, his personality was pure Rousseau: isolated, paranoid, bitter, self-destructive, resentful, and defensive to the extreme. Above all—even while brutally demeaning himself—he was self-righteous, with that same familiar sense of "the integrity of one's inner self" and "noble sentiments" that defines Rousseau's defensive *Confessions.* Like Rousseau, Kierkegaard projected his own suffering and alienation as a blot against the whole of modern society, a "subjective truth" against which objective institutions became empty and meaningless.[10] Where Rousseau cried "corruption," Kierkegaard was revolted by "hypocrisy." He ridiculed those who did not share his unhappiness, his sense of religious guilt, his morbid view of life. But where Rousseau then proceeded to draw up the blueprints for revolution, Kierkegaard resigned himself to a life of melancholy, seeking through his writings to find others like him, and encourage them to quietly withdraw from the modern world and return to the more compassionate times that had preceded the Enlightenment, the Reformation, and everything that might conceivably be called the "progress" of humanity. He retreated into a singular personal example of the human—himself.

Irony implies its antithesis. Socratic irony is intellectual confidence parading as ignorance, or ignorance that knows itself to be the only knowledge. Kierkegaard's irony was self-righteousness parading as humility—or as he would prefer it, misery that knows itself as the end of all happiness. Kierkegaard lived a life that pointed to its opposites. He attacked hypocrisy through irony, when it is not at all easy to tell them apart. He accused the modern world of having "forgotten how to live"—this man who felt barely alive—leveling this charge in particular against Hegel, the now deceased champion of the Absolute who ruled intellectual life in Denmark. Hegel had lived in the thick of the Napoleonic Wars and the German Wars of Liberation. He had enjoyed an eminently successful career and an ostensibly happy marriage. He had seemed as intellectually and personally fulfilled as anyone in the modern age. Yet it was Kierkegaard—born too late for the wars, living alone and lonely, ridiculed by the local papers, and embroiled in petty battles with everyone—who complained that Hegel and the others did not know how to live:

Like Leporello, learned literary men keep a list, but the point is what they lack; while Don Juan seduces girls and enjoys himself—Leporello notes down the time, the place, and a description of the girl. (*Journals*, 1837)

What are we to make of this—the ultimate outsider attacking the modern world with his provincial wit and utter incapacity for contentment?[11] But this bitter irony is intended, and not just pathetic. Kierkegaard is quite aware that he is denying the significance of "great events" and living through them, rejecting the bourgeois trappings of success and respectability, and even happiness. When he broke his engagement with Regina, he noted in his *Journals:*

If I had not been . . . melancholy, my union with her would have made me happier than I had ever dreamed of being. But insofar as I was what, alas, I was, I had to say that I could be happier in my unhappiness without her than with her. (p. 171)

It is easy to see through Kierkegaard's complaints as ingenious cries of resentment against his own misery and isolation, against the success and apparent happiness of his contemporaries, against petty bourgeois standards and even the Danish weather. But it is necessary to see this miserable man, attacking the modern age in terms of the long-fought-against ideals of the Middle Ages, as the champion of a very different tradition: that of Augustine and Pascal, groping for something eternal behind the changes and comforts of modern secular life.[12] The transcendental pretense, we have acknowledged (p. xiv), did not originate with the Enlightenment, which only gave it its modern secular emphasis. Its roots were firmly planted in the Christian concept of man, and it is to that version of the pretense—the Christian picture of a world of individuals, universal in their quest for salvation—that Kierkegaard returned. The route we have followed, from the Enlightenment to the 1840s, has been the road of progress slowed by reaction, a public process of public figures with public ambitions and influence. Voltaire, Goethe, Kant, Hegel, Robespierre, Napoleon, Marx—these men had a vision of the future, a sense of the march of humanity. But something had been left out, something "spiritual" in the old—not the Hegelian—sense. And if, to find it, Kierkegaard had to reject the whole of the modern world and return to the Middle Ages, and prefer the most obstinate reaction to enlightened progress, he was more than willing to do so.

When he visited Berlin, Kierkegaard attended the "anti-Hegel" lectures being given by Hegel's school friend Schelling (see p. 305). (In that lecture hall with him were Friedrich Engels and Michael Bakunin.) From Schelling, Kierkegaard heard what he wanted to hear about the philosopher who ruled Danish theology: Hegel had "neglected existence" in favor of "the Concept," and therefore had defended a purely "negative" philosophy. No matter that this interpretation of Hegel was dubious and born of old quarrels and resentments. It was enough to establish, for Kierkegaard's purposes, the crowning failure of the modern age: the existing individual had been lost in "the Collective Idea."

Inspired by Schelling but driven by his own obsessions, Kierkegaard began to attack the atheistic, humanistic, and antireligious implications of Hegelianism, which by then were becoming so evident in the "young left" Hegelians (see pp. 313–14). And as he attacked Hegel, he attacked the "public" secularization of the modern world. To "really live," according to Kierkegaard, meant to be a Christian, and a Christian *first of all*. Religion could not be "synthesized" into a life of secular success, or tacked onto science as a "hypothesis," or "conceptualized" ("raised to the level of the concept") à la Hegel. It could not be squeezed into Sunday mornings, weddings, and funerals. It could not even be compromised with marriage:

She has not, after all, the first place in my life. No, no, humanly speaking certainly—and how willing would I not prove it, . . . but God has the first place. My engagement to her and the break are really my relation to God, they are, if I may say so, divinely speaking, my engagement to God. (*Journals*, p. 224)

Nothing in the modern world or the modern Church recognized the primacy of this "engagement," and nothing in this modern world or the Church, therefore, deserved to be called "Christian." Later in his career Kierkegaard would declare, "My task is a Socratic task, to revise the conception of what it means to be a Christian."

In fact, his task was to redefine what it means to be a human being. Against the Enlightenment he insisted that to be human is not to be reasonable or to define oneself in terms of "universal Reason." Against Marx he would have argued that it is not to be social or political, not to be part of a party or a class, not to labor, and not to produce. Against all forms of secularization he argued that this is not a human but an ultimately divine world. Against all forms of "collectivism" he argued that to be human is *not* to be part of "the spirit of the times" but to be an *individual*. And against humanism he argued that to be human is in fact to give up the primacy of the human for God. But this attack on secular humanism was itself a prime example of the humanistic thesis: the universality of the human spirit.

"Existentialism" is a twentieth-century conception, but its origins are in the nineteenth. Its central concepts—freedom, subjectivity, choice, and the isolated, crisis-ridden individual—are nowhere defended more poetically and passionately than in Søren Kierkegaard.[13] He was concerned with defending the religious way of life in an epoch that had tried to discard it completely. In reaction, Kierkegaard insisted on the rights of the individual to go against his times; to choose a way of life most fitting for oneself, no matter how "irrational"; to think as an individual rather than always as a spokesman for humanity. In this stance, however, Kierkegaard transcended his religious reactionism to initiate a very new, rebellious anti-Socratic attitude—a search not for objective but for "subjective" truth, based not on morality or success or the pursuit of happiness, but purely on a sense of individual autonomy far more radical than anything in the Enlightenment. His would be an extreme case of romantic heroism—in a hero who would do nothing but suffer and write about his suffering.

During the whole of bourgeois ("universal") history—and well before —it had been assumed in one form or another that truth was a function of the world, and that reason in some form would dictate universally the right course of action for everyone, even if, as in Schopenhauer, that course of action was total *in*action. But with Kierkegaard, the very idea of universal Reason and "the right" course of action begins to fall apart. There are no answers, no reasons. The religious life is "right" only as Kierkegaard's personal commitment. In itself it is absurd, and certainly not "true." In a sense, therefore, there can be no philosophy, no objective examination of "the good life." There is just life, the life of the individual, to be suffered through and coped with by the individual. And this condition is itself the human universal. Life consists of dilemmas, despair, and the desperate solutions of personal commitment—what Kierkegaard calls "subjective truth." Thus even the concept of "truth" takes an inward turn—in other words, away from science, reason, and public opinion, and toward the "truth" of personal feelings, decisions, and obsessions.

The Meaning of Existence

> It is impossible to exist wthout passion, unless we understand the word "exist" in the loose sense of a so-called existence. . . . Eternity is a winged horse, infinitely fast, and time is a worn out jade; the existing individual is the driver. That is to say, he is such a driver when his mode of existence is not an existence loosely so-called; for then he is no driver but a drunken peasant who lies asleep in the wagon and lets the horses take care of themselves. To be sure, he also drives and is a driver, and so there are many who—also exist.
>
> Kierkegaard, *Concluding Unscientific Postscript*

In 1842 Kierkegaard was completing an essay on "boredom," as appropriate to his times as Hegel's philosophy of history had been to his. It was to be part of a volume he was putting together with the provocative title *Either/Or:* a selection of philosophical voices and views left intentionally without a resolution. The device of writing under pseudonyms was one that Kierkegaard would employ for much of his career, not so as to hide his authorship (which everyone was aware of), but to distinguish the often contradictory opinions of his invented spokesmen from his own, if that was possible. His method, he often insisted, was "indirect": he would present but not actually defend alternative viewpoints, forcing the reader to make a choice. And the writing itself was typically tongue-in-cheek, ironic. For example:

Boredom is the root of all evil. Strange that boredom, in itself so staid and solid, should have such power to set in motion. The influence it exerts is altogether magical, except that it is not the influence of attraction, but of repulsion. (*Either/Or,* I, 281)

Boredom is a disease of the privileged and the otherwise comfortable, a sure symptom of decadence. It is not just emptiness, but frustration of an inner striving. It was a familiar mood during the Reaction, but Kierkegaard takes it to be more than "the spirit of the times"; it is rather the essence of the human condition and not only human:

The gods were bored, and so they created man. Adam was bored because he was alone, and so Eve was created. Thus boredom entered the world, and increased in proportion to the increase of population. Adam was bored alone; then Adam and Eve were bored together; then Adam and Eve and Cain and Abel were bored *en famille.* (p. 282)

But Kierkegaard was bored alone—and of course bored with his contemporaries. He was not conceptually alone, however, in that the spirit of romanticism had been born from boredom decades before, and in response had created a cosmic philosophy of eternal striving and frustration. Like Schopenhauer, for example, Kierkegaard envisioned a meaningless world constantly frustrating the ceaseless efforts of the human will. But unlike Schopenhauer, Kierkegaard took this will to be strictly individual, not "the world in itself." As in Goethe's *Faust,* Kierkegaard found the end of the struggle to be religious salvation, mysterious and unpredictable. But unlike Goethe, he took this salvation as something to be striven for throughout the whole of one's life and with the whole of one's being, and not just a gratuitous dramatic surprise (see p. 159). Kierkegaard was an heir to the romantics, not ahead of his times as he believed, but behind. Romanticism was already dead in France, England, and Germany, supplanted by realism, which was preparing further revolutions. What was new in Kierkegaard was that romanticism had now become a wholly *personal* matter, not a movement. His version of the "cult of genius" was to make himself into a subjective hero, entirely individual, and thereby the spokesman for *all,* albeit for himself as well.

The answer to boredom, according to Kierkegaard, was not action. The romantic emphasis on action—so common in later existentialism—is not to be found in Kierkegaard. His response to boredom was just the opposite —to *limit* one's field of action as much as possible, and to attack the problem purely through imagination:

My method does not consist in change of field, but resembles the true rotation method in changing the crop and the mode of cultivation. . . . The more you limit yourself, the more fertile you become in invention. A prisoner in solitary confinement for life becomes very inventive, and a spider may furnish him with much entertainment. (*Either/Or,* I, 288)

Byron had run off to fight for Greek liberation; Fichte had set in motion the wheels of German nationalism. But Kierkegaard condemned himself to "solitary confinement for life," intensifying his "inner" life by making his "outer" life as minimal as possible.[14] He would not, in fact, retreat to a monastery (an image he often used), but he made his outwardly routine life in Denmark no more than a façade, the wall of a private monastical order within which he privately set about inventing his world of choices and voices, expressing the hopes and the hopelessness that he knew he must face alone.

It was Fichte who had introduced the idea of alternatives, of either/or. It was Fichte who had said that the kind of philosophy one chooses depends upon the kind of man one is. The idea of a "synthesis," a "both/ and," was Hegel's addition, and Kierkegaard flatly rejected it. Life is a series of personal decisions, not so much between courses of action but between attitudes toward life, or "spheres of existence." *Either* one believes in salvation with "all of one's heart," *or* one does not. *Either* one chooses to recognize the moral law as ultimate, *or* one does not. All choices are fraught with uncertainty; there are no guarantees. There is no solution to boredom and frustration, but only different ways of living with them.

To be human, to really "exist," according to Kierkegaard, is to passionately commit oneself to a way of life, a "sphere of existence." The religious life is but one of a number of alternatives, and it would be meaningless to call it the "right" choice. The meaning of life is the meaning we choose. The life of "pleasure and excesses" is such a life, too, but for Kierkegaard—who had experimented with it, if only briefly—such a life meant unbearable guilt and meaningless repetition. The life of a moralist—Socrates, for example—would be another alternative, giving meaning to life not through good acts but through recognition of the meaning of good and evil:

> My either/or does not in the first instance denote the choice between good and evil; it denotes the choice whereby one chooses good *and* evil/or excludes them. Here the question is under what determinants one would contemplate the whole of existence and would himself live. (*Either/Or,* II, 171)

It might sound as if *any* way of life is as good as any other, and "objectively" this may be true. But in the face of such "objective uncertainty," it is solely one's *subjective* needs and willingness to commit oneself that count. When Kierkegaard recognizes that the life of pleasure is not for him, he does not say that it is "wrong." He does try to show that it will lead to either repetition or cynicism, but this too is a personal matter, not a matter of "right" and "wrong," nor a subject for philosophical self-righteousness and advice. What is essential is to choose: "In making a choice it is not so much a question of choosing the right as of the energy, the earnestness, the pathos with which one chooses" (II, 141). It is *how* one chooses (how much passion? how sincerely?) that matters, not *what* one chooses: "The objective accent falls on *what* is said, the subjective accent on *how* it is said" (*Postscript,* p. 181). Which "sphere of existence" is chosen is not particularly important, except for its "subjective" significance, since all "spheres" are equally unjustified. It is the choosing itself that makes one a human being, the need for choice that is universal, without regard for what is "right" and without any guarantees of psychological success: "The most tremendous thing which has been granted to man is: the choice of freedom" (*Journals,* 1850).

Most people, however, have not chosen at all. Accordingly, Kierkegaard complained, "there are no longer any human beings." Most people simply followed and accepted—accepted their parents, their church, their government, Hegel's philosophy. They flowed with the "Spirit of the Age": if

Christianity was "in," they were Christians; if atheism was the rage, they were atheists. If it was time for a "sexual revolution," everyone became a sensualist; when it was a time for moral seriousness, a moralist. It was against this passivity, against this conception of oneself as a "moment" of humanity rather than an integral human being, that Kierkegaard reacted. He defended at all costs the need to choose. The "perfection of humanity" through "enlightenment" would not, he insisted, give meaning to individual human lives. On the contrary, a society without struggle and without choices would provide its citizens with the most meaningless of lives, which was precisely what Kierkegaard saw happening in modern "enlightened" Europe. The triumph of the Enlightenment and Hegel's "realization of spirit" had been spiritual disasters:

In the midst of all our exultation over the achievements of the age and the nineteenth century, there sounds a note of poorly conceived contempt for the individual man; in the midst of the self-importance of the contemporary generation there is revealed a sense of despair over being human. (*Postscript*, p. 328)

Back to the Monastery

> Back into the monastery out of which Luther broke—that is the truth
> —that is what must be done.
> Kierkegaard, *Attack upon Christendom*, sect. III

One cannot say in the same breath and with the same meaning that Kierkegaard was a Christian, and that in Denmark virtually everyone was a Christian. Nothing was more routine than being Christian in Denmark; one was born of Christian parents, christened, baptized, educated, confirmed—all as a matter of course.

Thus it was established by the state as a kind of eternal principle that every child is naturally born a Christian. As the state obligated itself to furnish eternal bliss for all Christians, so, to make the whole complete, it took upon itself to produce Christians. . . . so the state delivered, generation after generation, an assortment of Christians; each bearing the manufacturer's trademark of the state, with perfect accuracy one Christian exactly like all the others. . . . the point of Christianity became: the greatest possible uniformity of a factory product.[15]

Hegel had brought together the spirit of Christianity and the spirit of the State; the result, said Kierkegaard, was still called "Christianity," but it was in effect the wholesale rejection of everything Christian. One had rendered unto Caesar what belonged exclusively to God. Kierkegaard saw through Hegel's conception of an "immanent God" as essentially no God at all.[16] The notion that God was to be found in Hegel's reflections, incarnated in "the public," was the very opposite of what it meant to be a Christian: " 'The individual': now that the world has gone so far along the road of reflection, Christianity stands and falls with that category" (*Journals,* 1847). Christianity is an individual *commitment*—not a birthright, not a community, not a philosophy. So the first thing to do to become a Christian, Kierkegaard argued, is to attack the very idea of public "Christendom"—Hegel's Christian community "spirit." In fact, rather than paving the way, the continued success of "Christendom" rendered Kierkegaard's Christian revival more difficult: "It is easier to become a Christian when I am not a Christian than to become a Christian when I am one" (*Postscript,* p. 327).

From his father, Kierkegaard had learned to despise the easy secular life of the bourgeois Bible-reading, church-going Christian community. "Christianity is suffering," he had been taught, a deeply personal private suffering. It is a one-to-one confrontation with an unresponsive God—the traditional Old Testament God who had once confronted Abraham. It is a profound sense of one's own inadequacy—"sin"—and a wholly unjustified hope for redemption. (How much he would despise the smiling "born again" Christians of today.) Christianity is faith; faith is passion. Accepting Christianity, in other words, is making a passionate commitment. Understanding is not necessary. In fact, it is not possible. Against the Enlightenment ideal of a "rational" religion, Kierkegaard insists that Christianity is intrinsically paradoxical, impossible to prove, and it is paradox that provokes our passion: "When faith . . . begins to lose its passion, when faith begins to cease to be faith, then a proof becomes necessary so as to command respect from the side of unbelief" (*Postscript,* p. 31). The whole tenor of the Enlightenment, from Kant to Hegel, had been to make Christianity *plausible,* to justify its doctrines and prescribe them on *rational* grounds. But "if this effort were to succeed, then would this effort have the ironical fate that on the day of its triumph it would have lost everything and entirely quashed Christianity" (p. 326). Insofar as Christianity involves doctrines at all, they are absurd doctrines. But this absurdity is precisely what makes Christianity so valuable to its true believers—and to real thinking as well: "the paradox is the source of a thinker's passion, and the thinker without a paradox is like a lover without a feeling; a paltry mediocrity."[17]

To be a Christian in Christendom was simply to be one of "the Crowd," another anonymous member of the "great gaggle of geese" waddling through the streets of Copenhagen every Sunday morning. To become a Christian in Kierkegaard's terms was to endure the terrible sense of inadequacy and guilt that came from a personal confrontation with God: "Christianity begins with the doctrine of Sin, and therefore with the individual."[18] It is "the way of fear and trembling, of infinite resignation." One might well say that Christianity was Kierkegaard's rationalization for his own neurotic suffering, nor would he disagree: "Christianity is not melancholy; it is, on the contrary, glad tidings—for the melancholy" (*Journals*). This suffering, however, was not unique to him: as he saw it, his "task" was to find others like him, "seduce" them, and make them realize their own feelings and the religious way to give them meaning, for "a man who cannot seduce men cannot save them either" (*Journals*).

Kierkegaard, in other words, rejected the notion of "the spirit of the times" and turned his attention instead to individual differences, to the eccentrics and neurotics, to the exceptions who represented the real essence of humanity. Thus it was not the progress of humanity as such that concerned him, but the psychic life of isolated individuals. It was not the fate of Christianity that drove him, but rather what it meant to be a Christian.

The fault with the monastery was not asceticism, celibacy, etc.; no, the fault was that Christianity had been moderated by making the admission that all this was considered to be extraordinarily Christian—and the purely secular nonsense to be considered ordinary Christianity.[19]

For the Enlightenment, the transcendental pretense had become the weapon of the many against the few; for Kierkegaard, it became a weapon of the few against the many.

The Spheres of Existence

> The only reality that exists for an existing individual is his own ethical reality.
>
> Kierkegaard, *Journals*, 1835

Choosing a way of life requires an understanding of the alternatives: either/or. Choosing to be a Christian presupposes understanding—that is, understanding that Christianity is a paradoxical, incomprehensible way of life that flies in the face of modernity, and that rejects the primacy of humanism so central to contemporary thinking. This is complicated, however, by the fact that one cannot really understand what is involved in a "sphere of existence" before entering into it and passionately embracing it. This too involves an "objective uncertainty." All one can be sure of is the commitment itself, and the basic structure of the world view chosen. In the religious life, according to Kierkegaard, this basic structure is the isolated individual standing before God. In the two other "spheres" he delineates, these structures are immediate personal desire in the *aesthetic* way of life, and the reflective principles of morality in the *ethical* way of life.

Sometimes Kierkegaard characterizes these other "spheres" or "stages on life's way" in terms of an attitude toward choice, rather than what is chosen. For example, he sometimes characterizes the aesthetic life as if it is not chosen at all, and ignores choice in general, but this is not consistent with the basic arguments of *Either/Or* and his other works. The aesthetic way of life, like the other two spheres of existence, is best interpreted as a way of life that can be chosen or rejected, and that is defined in terms of its own criteria for more specific choices—namely, individual desires. Don Juan is Kierkegaard's favorite example of the aesthetic, and the character of the seducer appears in several of his early works, perhaps reflecting the life of "pleasure and excess" that he himself had tried and rejected some years before.[20] In the aesthetic sphere, "everything is for the moment, and in the same moment everything is over, and the same thing repeats itself endlessly." The choice of Don Juan is obviously appropriate. There is no question of obligation, nor even of asking whether the union will be a happy one. There is no question of a "relationship," since Don Juan "makes short work of it, and must always be regarded as absolutely victorious." Every woman is essentially the same as every other—a means to satisfy his desire. What makes Don Juan the paragon of the aesthetic life is the fact that his own desires dominate him completely. Moral principles do not interfere, nor does a religious sense of guilt. Kierkegaard most often characterizes this attitude in terms of its sense of time: "Every moment is indistinguishable from all other moments."

Of course one may disagree with this characterization of Don Juan. Freud, for example, would argue that the man is terrified of impotence, or Camus that he is fighting against the absurd. But what is essential is the idea of life without principle, a life of desire, a life with no sense of the eternal, of immortality, of divine judgment—a life of pure "immediacy."[21] The aesthetic life is not confined to the sensuous life of a seducer, however, nor of course is it primarily a male form of life (although Kierkegaard, in his rationalized and exaggerated esteem for the purity of women, often talks as if it were). Health and public honors, beauty or talent of any sort, can also be central to the aesthetic life. Mozart, for example, counts as an example of the aesthetic life style, not only because of his behind-the-piano Don Juan-ing, but because of his personal obsession with music. Beethoven or Delacroix can be included, too. In other words, the aesthetic life may involve a set of standards which are more than merely individual—artistic standards, for example; but the ultimate criterion and the ultimate impetus are one's own tastes and desires.[22]

This seemingly attractive Dionysian life has its problems, however. It is not merely a matter of continuous pleasure and satisfaction; there is also pain and dissatisfaction. There is frustration, failure, and worst of all, *boredom*. Boredom is the hell of the aesthetic life. The result is either an escape from boredom through meaningless repetition—"each moment like every other," therefore signifying nothing other than the moment—or, if one recognizes this, cynicism. Within the aesthetic life, therefore, one faces a choice of sorts: to deny the meaninglessness of life by plunging into ever more intensive and perhaps desperate adventures, or to reflect on the meaninglessness of it all and live in the face of this absurdity. Kierkegaard, in other words, is arguing that this seemingly happy-go-lucky life style, despite its intentions, is as ultimately unhappy and filled with hopelessness as Kierkegaard's own pathos-ridden existence: "So it appears that every aesthetic view of life is in despair, and that everyone who lives aesthetically is in despair, whether he knows it or not."

Kierkegaard's aim here is transparent. He has already insisted that the choice of life styles is arbitrary, that there is no reason to choose one over another. Yet he wants to seduce us into the religious way of life so as to defend, in a psychological (not logical) way, the universality of his position. So he tries to show that the alternative styles of life, which ostensibly begin without the despair and sense of inadequacy so explicit in his version of Christianity, end in despair also. Don Juan soon ceases to act out of pleasure and begins to act from desperation, to avoid boredom and the recognition of meaninglessness. Faust is relevant as well, for in his wisdom he sees through the idea that one can gratify one's desires, and therefore denies them out of pride. Being still within the aesthetic sphere, however, this pride is shut off from salvation and becomes pure cynicism. And then, Kierkegaard adds, the aesthetic person is prone to the worst fate of all: the temptation, from sheer despair, to join the Crowd and by so doing obliterate both self-reflection and passion. (Ahasuerus, the Wandering Jew, is the example he cites.) So he says in effect, just you try to be happy, and when you fail, the apparent melancholy of the religious life will begin to seem attractive indeed.

The ethical life differs from the aesthetic primarily in its appeal to impersonal principles rather than personal desires and whims. It is, explicitly, the life of the universal. The model for the ethical life is Socrates, who publicly and courageously denied his own desires and pleasures on the basis of loyalty and justice, even when these had been turned against him. The spokesman for the ethical life, however, is Kant. His categorical imperative, the moral law that commands absolutely without reference to individual circumstances or inclinations, is precisely the law by which the ethical person lives: "The ethical as such is the universal; and as the universal it applies to everyone, which may be expressed from another point of view by saying that it applies every instant."[23] Again, the characterization in terms of time is essential; the ultimate comparison is between merely secular and therefore insignificant time, and eternity. But notice that eternity is here reduced to a bourgeois category—universality. Between the aesthetic and the ethical spheres, the comparison is between living for the moment and recognizing something that transcends the moment: duty and the moral law. The appeal to an "objective" law prevents that sense of meaninglessness that is the fate of the aesthetic life, for it does not concern itself with personal gratification or even success but only, in Kant's terms, with a "good will."

But the arrogance of this will, according to Kierkegaard, traps it in despair just as surely as demands for gratification trap the aesthetic life. Using one of Kant's key arguments against him, Kierkegaard insists that a will which is "autonomous"—that is, which "gives the moral law unto itself," as Kant demanded—has no ultimate justification or sanction; ultimately, such a will becomes mere "lawlessness and experimentation"—in other words, Kant's "negative freedom," which Hegel identified with the Terror of the French Revolution. This is irony indeed (as is the identification of the aesthetic life of self-gratification with ultimate frustration and despair, its opposite). Kant had wholly rejected such "negative freedom" on the basis of his belief that "autonomy" had significance only through the use of universal Reason, through which we dictate *the*—not *our*—moral law to ourselves. What Kierkegaard is suggesting here—and it had actually been argued by Hegel—is that any "autonomous" human law, even if universally applied and dictated by reason, will ultimately be arbitrary. This humanistic arrogance is precisely what the ethical sphere shares with the aesthetic. But unlike the aesthetic life, the ethical life is fully reflective and self-appraising. Deliberate decisions are its central practice, just as action on whim or intuition is the prototype of the aesthetic (which prompts Kierkegaard to sometimes argue that the aesthetic is not really a "choice" at all). The ethical life, therefore, cannot help but become aware of this absurd arrogance and the trivialization of its own "absolute" principles of reason. This is, of course, precisely the dialectic that had appeared ideologically from Kant through Fichte to Hegel. Kierkegaard despises that arrogance, hates the triviality, distrusts "Reason" and even "ideology." In the name of bourgeois individualism and its own arrogance, therefore, he rejects the bourgeois ideal of universality and even the concept of human nature. For him, this awareness of ultimate arbitrariness and lack of justification poisons the secular self-righteousness of the bourgeois ethical life, just as Hegel saw in the example of Antigone, for example, a split between the moral law and the divine law or, we might say, between two equally undeniable universal laws. And so the universal ethical life also ends in despair.[24]

The ethical life, it is important to realize, is also the social life, properly speaking. The aesthetic person may *use* other people for personal enjoyment or advantage, perhaps even on moral pretexts, but narcissistic manipulation (like Hegel's Master and Slave) is not yet "social." (Napoleon comes first to mind, but also Beethoven—and perhaps even Kierkegaard?) Marriage is the central institution of the ethical way of life, as definitive of the ethical attitude as the seducer is of the aesthetic. To understand Kierkegaard, one must grasp how different these two are. The idea of marriage as a "pleasure bond," as mutual gratification and satisfaction, is wholly foreign to him. His broken engagement was not a rejection of pleasure and happiness so much as the recognition that the obligations involved were too much for him, incompatible with his religious longings and his obsessive melancholy.[25] The decision to get married (as argued by a young seducer and the self-righteous pastor in *Either/Or,* for example) is the best possible focal point on the ultimate incompatibility of the aesthetic and ethical ways of life.[26]

The religious way of life is really the Christian way of life as defined by Kierkegaard. It is based upon an individual relationship to God, and since God—unlike desire and moral principles—makes few explicit demands of us, it is a life that is mostly empty of specific acts and decisions. It is defined, however, by one continuous overall decision: the commitment to believe. Outwardly, the "knight of resignation" acts more or less like everyone else. Inwardly, he is "infinitely interested in the reality of another," and the whole passion of his being must be directed toward this mystery. For Kierkegaard, the central concept of the religious life is *sin,* that nonspecific but overwhelming sense of guilt that attaches to the individual's very existence as shame before God. Religious guilt differs from ethical guilt precisely in this nonspecificity. The ethical person feels guilty because of some act committed or omitted; the religious person feels guilty just for being alive. But when the "arrogance" of the ethical life begins to become evident, that sense of guilt may well become generalized, and the person "seduced" into becoming a Christian. (Kierkegaard's equating of "religious" with "Christian," of course, represents the most unabashed version of the transcendental pretense.)[27]

Kierkegaard is not always clear about the delineation of the ethical and religious ways of life. It is clear to him that, in his obedience to God and scripture, a Christian must follow the principles of Christian morality. (In his time this was already reactionary; Kant and his followers had argued for the autonomy of the moral law, insisting that Christianity followed from morality, not the other way around.) Yet it is clearly possible, as in the case of Antigone, that the moral law and divine law may conflict. The Judaeo-Christian example that Kierkegaard uses is the Abraham story: what could be more immoral (to put it mildly) than murdering one's own son? But what would be more of a rejection of a personal relationship with God than not to obey one of his very rare more-or-less direct commands? In such a dilemma, the truly religious person will recognize a "teleological suspension of the ethical"—in other words, the need to carry out the heinous order with the absolute faith that it will somehow work out. Not even Kierkegaard thinks himself capable of becoming such a "knight of faith," but then, neither does he expect any such dilemma. But his "knight of resignation" is a sufficiently powerful ideal to keep the religious way of life full of passion and free from the hopeless despair that ultimately engulfs the other two ways of life. There is always the unflinching hope that God, at the end of the ordeal of life, will snatch up the "worm" of one's soul as in the last scene of Goethe's *Faust*. And it is this hope alone that makes life possible, and meaningful, for the likes of Søren Kierkegaard.

Against the Spirit of the Age

> In order that everything should be reduced to the same level, it is first of all necessary to procure a phantom, its spirit, a monstrous abstraction, an all-embracing something that is nothing, a mirage—and that phantom is the public. It is only in an age which is without passion, yet reflective, that such a phantom can develop itself.
>
> Kierkegaard, *The Present Age*

There is a paradox intrinsic to Kierkegaard's philosophy which he shares with most later existentialist authors: he insists, on the one hand, that no life style is the "right" one, that the choice is ultimately arbitrary and that there can be no progress or better-and-worse "dialectic" of life styles. On the other hand, he argues with great passion for one life style, the religious mode of existence, and seems to be saying that, given the despair at the end of the other spheres of existence, it is indeed universally the "best." To avoid this inconsistency, one must always remember Kierkegaard's own characterization of himself as a "seducer," rather than a philosopher properly speaking. He sees himself in a certain Socratic role, trying "to revise what it means to be a Christian"—a role that one cannot fulfill while being equally an advocate of the aesthetic and the ethical life. He has to make his own choice clear, if he is to make his point at all. This is the final message of his philosophy, whether or not we are seduced into becoming Christians in his harsh sense: the significance of life is to be found individually and in our passions, or not at all. Ideologically, Kierkegaard's Christian solution is not nearly so significant as his individualist and "inward" revolt—the final turn of the bourgeois mind on itself. No longer is the individual defined by the universal; the universal is now defined by the individual, and even denied by the individual as well.[28] But it is still the transcendental pretense, still the projection of the bourgeois ideology into "humanity" as a whole. Kierkegaard's Christianity is but a medieval disguise for a uniquely modern invention.

Hegel's "world historical individual" had come and gone. The middle class had established itself, and nowhere more than in Copenhagen, as absolute. The image of progress had become a backdrop for a situation comedy, and Fichtean heroism had become an empty pretense in a world where all the obstacles to self-realization had been internalized. The Revolution of 1848 in Copenhagen was a Sunday parade of citizens to the palace; consequently, the only rebellion that Kierkegaard could envision was a rebellion *against* "the public" and its revolutionary banalities. But the rebellion he advocated was itself an inward rebellion, a return to "subjectivity"; even his advocacy of it was masked with contradictory opinions of conflicting pseudonymous authors, and with an irony that typically said the very opposite of what it advocated. The absolute unity of the modern world—the cry that once embattled all Europe—had become a colossal bore. The new call issued by Kierkegaard was instead a plea for fragmentation, a turn to "the individual," a rejection of the Enlightenment, presupposing its successes.[29] Just when the world seemed to so many to have been, if not "perfected," at least advanced beyond the dreams of our ancestors, the emptiness of those dreams began to become apparent. In a world purged of superstition and myth, people started to feel the need for what they had so energetically attacked only a century before. In a world of comparative efficiency and rationality, they began to realize the need for passion and *ir*rationality. In a world where the "right" way to live was being written into new constitutions, people began to feel—as Hegel had said they ought to—that as individuals they counted all the less, and should expect less both from and for themselves.[30] Against this relatively happy, comfortable, comformist, and self-righteous life, the unhappy recluse Søren Kierkegaard took up his pen as a double-edged ironic sword, and attacked the public in general and the spirit of the age, as Voltaire had done a century before. But Voltaire had signaled the start of an epoch; Kierkegaard marked its conclusion. The pretension of "Universal History" was beginning to look ridiculous; the aspirations of "humanity" would soon be found elsewhere. The bourgeoisie had no more great hopes, no great passions, only the self-satisfied reflection and enjoyment of their achievements "on behalf of humanity"—in other words, themselves. They had created a new and thoroughly bourgeois individual—isolated, arrogant, and enormously unhappy, even while living an ideology of happiness. This new individual rejected his own origins—in history, society, and ideology—in the name of autonomy, freedom, and individuality. And in this respect Kierkegaard was not, as he thought, an exceptional and "untimely" individual, but a true example of his age. Even his retreat to Christianity was not particularly exceptional, but rather a predictable escape from the extreme individualism *cum* universal pretenses shared by the whole of the bourgeoisie. What had not yet been thoroughly challenged, even by Kierkegaard, was the underlying presumption of the overall ideology—namely, the right of any European personality or idea, however persuasive, to represent itself as the truth of humanity. In fact, "humanity" itself would eventually have to undergo a thorough ideological self-examination.

Concluding Post-Enlightenment Subscript: The Problem of "Humanity"and the "End of Man"

> ... *how transitory all human structures are, nay how oppressive the best institutions become in the course of a few generations.* The plant blossoms and fades; your fathers have died, and mouldered into dust: your temple is fallen: your tabernacle, the tables of your law are no more; language itself, that bond of mankind, becomes antiquated: and shall a political constitution, shall a system of government or religion, that can be erected solely on these, endure forever?
>
> Johann Gottfried von Herder, *Ideas towards a Philosophy of the History of Man*

Hegel viewed the whole of history, from the ancient despots to modern times, as the realization of the idea that every person, as a human being ("man as man"), is free. This, he said, was "the end of history," that is, both its goal and the beginning of its final chapter. But the story was far from finished. We now see through Hegel's transcendental pretense, the very idea of "man as man" read back into history and projected across all borders. It was a form of ideological imperialism that reached "absolute" proportions with Hegel, but it has been with us ever since, virtually unchallengeable, even "self-evident." The romantics, Marx, and Kierkegaard threw their weight against it, but even they in their very attacks presupposed the concept of a universal human nature that formed its basis. Toward the end of the nineteenth century Friedrich Nietzsche and Wilhelm Dilthey fought the pretense, but not with any significant success. As much as scholars have made of the "historicism" of that period, it too remained both timid and arrogant, and was unwilling to concede its own limitations.

At the beginning of this century, Edmund Husserl cultivated an army of "phenomenologists," armed with a Kantian concept of "transcendental subjectivity," to combat the historicism of Dilthey and Nietzsche and establish once and for all the universality of truth and the essence of *The*

357

Human Mind. In the middle of the century in France, Jean-Paul Sartre, also a phenomenologist, made his career as an existentialist by rejecting the concept of human nature, but only as a way of defending his own dogmatic humanism, in which he too assumed a universality of the human condition with freedom as its essence. Thus instead of viewing freedom as a curious local obsession—which it is—Sartre insisted on projecting it as the "being" of all being human, even applied to people who would not understand, much less be interested in, that concept. In his more recent work, Sartre's familiar French pretense becomes even more belligerent, as he once again defends the Enlightenment concepts of universal history and universal freedom, even to the extent of excluding certain "primitive" people, who recognize neither history nor freedom, from the realm of the human. Opposing Sartre on his home ground has been Claude Lévi-Strauss, an anthropologist who defends the "primitive" à la Rousseau as the paragon of human nature as such, of which we are a "corrupted" variation. But the differences between Sartre and Lévi-Strauss are superficial compared to the similarities, for both again are locked into a peculiarly bourgeois belief in the transcendental human mind—only the paradigms differ—and both are self-avowed Marxists, too.

In England and America, meanwhile, the Enlightenment still reigns; the sacred notions of individual autonomy and human rights still rule ethics and political philosophy. Philosophies such as logical positivism and even pragmatism openly avow their allegiance to the Enlightenment, Hume, and human rationality, presupposing universal post-Newtonian science as their paradigm and rejecting with extreme suspicion all talk of ideological, cultural, and conceptual determination of truth and human nature. Only recently—in the American pragmatism of William James and W. V. O. Quine, for example—has the pretense been seriously challenged at all, but still in the name of science and that peculiarly rigid form of logicizing that at most suggests, but rarely admits, its own pretensions. The transcendental pretense, in other words, is alive and well in Western (i.e., European and Anglo-American) thought.

Now I am certainly not denying nor even questioning the fact that we can clearly distinguish members of a certain biological species as "human" (perhaps allowing Nazis, fetuses, and gorillas as borderline cases). But the boundaries of the "human" shift so easily from biology to morality and so to absurd presumptions about universal motives, passions, duties, rights, sex roles, monogamy, the need for authority, the legitimacy of capitalism, and the inevitability of socialism. What is called "humanity" thus becomes a wholly *moral* term: a figment of our transcendental imaginations (or lack of imagination), and the projection of our own ideas onto some ill-defined and self-serving mythical universal class. At best, talk of the "human" is crude polemical generalization, an uncritical gloss of a million unknown cases based on a few casual experiences away from home. Talk about the "human" is like talk about "Orientals" or "Americans" or "Texans" or "New Yorkers"—indispensable for tourists and historicists, but never to be taken literally. If it is true that all generalizations are dangerous, then talk of the "human" is worse than dangerous. It is a pretentious fraud, a glib generalization parading as an essence. And if we still find it difficult to avoid the word, it must be "under erasure," as Jacques Derrida says, to be used as a tool of reference which probably has but minimal meaning. It is what seems beyond question that needs questioning.

If we reject the transcendental pretense, what is to be proposed in its place? But the denial of a thesis is not necessarily a thesis. To deny the ideological unity of "humanity" is not thereby to imply that there is some other a priori grouping—classes, cultures, or societies—defined on the basis of intelligence, history, language, dining-table manners, or the status of indoor plumbing, upon which to base our transcendental generalizations. It is rather to insist that "humanity" is based on a wholly implausible hypothesis and employed as a totally fraudulent excuse for not taking other people seriously. In place of our lazy and pretentious talk about the "human," we can say at most that we are generalizing about some people who lived in Europe at such and such a time, or about those people who have used syllogistic logic in their thinking, or about those who ascribe particular importance to their history or their freedom or their artistic geniuses. All philosophy is essentially plural and anonymous autobiography: vague first-person anthropology in which the scope of the particular tribe discussed is either ignored—or suppressed—in favor of the transcendental pretense.

One problem, however, persists: if we reject the transcendental pretense and the concept of "humanity," then what happens to *human rights, human dignity,* and other *humanitarian* advances that have in fact been made possible by the transcendental pretense? Does this entail a new provincialism, an indifference to torture and injustice in other lands or a principled lack of concern for the plight of peoples not ourselves? Not at all. What is essential is to admit how impoverished the justification of our noblest causes becomes, when based upon so frail an abstraction, and how arbitrary is our employment of those concerns, when based upon so indiscriminate a generalization. There is no reason why we cannot continue, as Ronald Dworkin insists, to "take rights seriously"; but the foundations of those rights need no longer be a fallacious inference from biology, a few myopic philosophical arguments, and the universal pretense of self-righteousness.

Once, to be sure, the pretense provided confidence, humanitarian ideals, and ideological support for movements and twists of history about which we can display only enthusiasm: the end of feudalism and its divine rights for well-born fools; the creation of our Bill of Rights and our enormous if excessive concern for self-realization; and our principled sense of the rights and well-being of others. But today we turn to "human rights" not so much from benevolence as arrogance, in order to assert once again our universal authority over the proper moral order for humanity. (Thus the inconsistency of bearing down on Rhodesia, while willfully ignoring the wholesale butchery in Cambodia during the 1970s.) Noble abstractions can be a cover for cowardice, a canopy for indecision, as well as a self-aggrandizing pretension.

I have not discussed the more insidious consequences of the pretense—racism, fascism, the "white man's burden," and the destruction of half the world's cultures in the name of "progress" (from savagery to our own bourgeois life)—nor have I mentioned our patronizing attitudes toward those cultures that we arrogantly call "developing" if they want to become like us, and "backward" if they do not. But as we sense that history is beginning to pass us by, shifting to what we call the Third World (which does not recognize the supposedly European essence of all things human), it is necessary to give up the once innocent pretense of the European Enlightenment, and with it the concepts of the "human," "humanity," and "mankind." This is not the end of history but only the end of what the bourgeois philosophers have presumptuously called "universal history." It is not the "end of ideology," as Daniel Bell wrote several years ago, but only the end of bourgeois ideologies—including Marxism—in which the transcendental pretense reigns supreme.

At the turn of the nineteenth century the French philosopher Charles Fourier announced "the end of civilization," and for the past few years in Paris Michel Foucault has been arguing "the end of Man." These are overly dramatic slogans, loaded down with misleading suggestions of apocalypse, but we know what they mean. It is time to become fully aware how much our history and our philosophy have been defined not by their universality but by their pretense of it. It is time for us to realize that our vacuous individualism can no longer be supported by our pretentious universalism, that we are but one peculiar culture among many, that we have underrated the importance of culture, that our history—or our rejection of history—and our concept of human nature are but one curious set of myths among many. Rousseau, Kant, Hegel, Marx, and the others were great storytellers, Homerids of a new and abstract odyssey. The hero was a fictional character called "humanity," ourselves writ large and glorified on the stage of the gods. But that story is, or ought to be, finished. It is time to begin listening seriously to others.

Notes

Preface

1. Karl Marx and Friedrich Engels, *The German Ideology*, trans. W. Lough, C. Dutt, and C. P. Magill, ed. C. J. Arthur (New York: International Publishers, 1970).
2. Throughout this book I will use the terms "bourgeois" and "middle class" more or less interchangeably, despite the fact that the first is a relatively precise European political-historical coinage, and the second, an extremely loose bit of American sociological jargon. In the Introduction I will define what I mean by these terms. For a good analysis of the differences between them, and much that is of interest regarding the bourgeois ideology in general, see John Lukacs, *The Passing of the Modern Age* (New York: Harper & Row, 1970).
3. David Hume, *Enquiry Concerning Human Nature*, ed. L. A. Selby-Bigge (Oxford: Oxford University Press, 1975), Book I, sect. viii.
4. This is not to say that the new ideology at any point launched an actual attack on family and community; to the contrary, most of the philosophers took them both for granted and, like Rousseau, assumed them to form the most "natural" of societies. But the struggle for "equal opportunity regardless of birth" had serious consequences for that "natural" sense of family and community, as the ideological focus was systematically shifted to the alleged primacy of the individual (*"I* think, therefore *I* exist"), and to the unity of "humanity" as a whole—or at least the State as a whole—as the only philosophically legitimate collective.
5. Two hundred years ago, at the dawn of "universal history," Voltaire tried to persuade his mistress, the Mme du Châtelet, that history could be something more than "an object of disgust," "the crowding into our heads the chronological list of all the dynasties, wars, and battles." But the fantasy lingers on. Thomas Hardy once championed Napoleon on the grounds that "war makes rattling good history, peace is a bore"; and an American journalist swore recently that "history means . . . wars." Since he then ended his piece with the comment that "wars are meaningless," the conclusion must be that history itself is meaningless (Geoffrey Norman, *Esquire,* November 28, 1978).

Introduction

1. Paul Ziff, in *The Owl of Minerva*, ed. Charles J. Bontempo and S. Jack Odell (New York: McGraw-Hill, 1975).

2. I will use the word "general" for noncommittal open-ended distribution, saving the technical word "universal" for claims which necessarily apply to every member of a class.

3. Michel Foucault describes this nicely in his *Archaeology of Knowledge*, trans. A. M. Sheridan Smith (New York: Harper & Row, 1972).

4. He uses the term in his *Elements of Ideology* (1801–1815). Tracy led a group of "ideologues" at the Institut National under Napoleon. A detailed discussion of the function of ideology in Enlightenment thought can be found in Hans Barth, *Truth and Ideology* (Berkeley: University of California Press, 1976), and in George Lichtheim, *The Concept of Ideology and Other Essays* (New York: Random House, 1967).

5. Marx himself so used it, for example, with Engels in *The German Ideology* (New York: International Publishers, 1970), p. 1: "The first volume of this present publication has the aim of uncloaking these sheep, who take themselves and are taken as wolves; of showing how their bleating merely imitates in a philosophical form the conceptions of the German middle class."

6. Notably, Raymond Williams in *Keywords: A Vocabulary of Culture and Society* (New York: Oxford University Press, 1976), pp. 126 ff.; and Clifford Geertz, "Ideology as a Cultural System," in his *The Interpretation of Cultures* (New York: Basic Books, 1973), pp. 193 ff.

7. For example, see Werner Stark, *The Sociology of Knowledge* (London: Humanities, 1958), p. 48: "Ideological thought is . . . shady, something that ought to be overcome and banished from our mind." The classic attack, even though it begins with an attempt to defend ideology, is Karl Mannheim, *Ideology and Utopia* (New York: Harcourt Brace Jovanovich, 1976), which follows Marx and Engels's general strategy in *The German Ideology* (while attacking them, too), classifying all ideology as "illusion."

8. For the first, see Daniel Bell, *The End of Ideology* (New York: Free Press, 1965); for the second, Marx and Engels: "The ideas of the ruling class are in every epoch the ruling ideas" (*German Ideology*, p. 59).

9. Douglas Kellner distinguishes between ideology as "-ism," consisting of revolutionary programs and polemics, and ideology as "hegemony," or ideology in the hands of established power; what they share in common, argues Kellner, is their essentially political nature and their tendency to be unself-critical ("Ideology and the Communication Revolution," an unpublished manuscript). See Williams, p. 117, for his important emphasis on the cultural aspects of hegemony as an alternative to Marxist materialism.

10. Mannheim, *Ideology and Utopia*, pp. 59 ff. See Geertz, *Interpretation of Cultures*, pp. 194 ff., on what he calls "Mannheim's Paradox."

11. The best such conception of "culture" is Clifford Geertz's *Interpretation of Cultures*, Chapter I. Geertz's often repeated emphasis on culture applies to ideology (which in his work might be interpreted as the semiotics of culture): "A cultureless human being would probably turn out to be not an intrinsically talented though unfulfilled ape, but a wholly mindless and consequently unworkable monstrosity" (p. 68 et passim). Following Gilbert Ryle's quasi-behaviorism too closely for comfort, Geertz tends to collapse culture and ideology, leaving insufficient room for a concept of ideology distinct from the concept of culture. But it is asking too much, and requires trivializing either the concept of ideology or the concept of behavior, to insist that an ideology—in particular an ideology that deals

in grand abstractions—must manifest itself in expressive behavior of the sort that Ryle continuously uses for his examples (winks, playing cricket, helping oneself to another piece of cake, etc.). The conflict of ideologies in the French Revolution, for example, would fare very poorly in such an analysis.

12. It is not in every society that a politician's mere *talk* about human rights in an indication of virtue. Voltaire made it very clear that he considered verbal ability a virtue so distinguished that it overrode most egalitarian demands, while Marxists (if not Marx himself) have often been curiously impressed with the right words, regardless of intentions, consequences, or actions.

13. To understand is not necessarily to explain; interpretation, for example, is understanding not necessarily accompanied by explanation. The frequent obsession with explaining ideologies is due largely to the mistaken idea that they are superficial epiphenomena ("superstructures," for example) whose presence is a symptom to be diagnosed. Thus Marxists developed an appealing conspiratorial-selfishness theory of ideology, according to which an ideology is always an expression of economic needs or a rationalization of economic interests. Against this narrow view, Parsons and others developed what Geertz has called "strain theory," which also sees ideology as a symptom, a pathological attempt to reconcile conflicts in society with a soothing if not distorting reinterpretation. But if an ideology is not a superficial symptom, as I have argued, but the "logic" of a culture, then explanation is hardly in order, unless one means, "Why do they believe this instead of that?" or "How could such a society originate?" What does not make sense is the question, "Why do they need an ideology?"

14. See Raymond Williams, *Keywords*, on "bourgeois"; John Lukacs, *The Passing of the Modern Age* (New York: Harper & Row, 1970), and "The Bourgeois Interior" in *American Scholar* (1970); and Jacques Ellul, *Métamorphose du bourgeois* (Paris, 1967).

15. See the Russian existentialist Nicolai Berdyaev, *The Bourgeois Mind* (1943).

16. For instance, Gustave Flaubert—"I call a bourgeois anyone who thinks *bassement*"—and of course Marx: ". . . the bleating of the bourgeois sheep." Marx often adopted the term made popular by the French romantics, for example Théophile Gautier, who announced his constant pleasure in "exacerbating the *Philistines*." Still today, to be "bourgeois" can mean anything negative, from aggressively powerful to impotently weak, from tasteless to overly concerned with *haute culture*, from materialistic to antimaterialistic, capitalist, or revolutionary. One gets the impression, at least at first, that the word comes to mean little more than "nasty." But certain ideological patterns emerge, and if the term is to have meaning, certain nonevaluative distinctions have to be recognized. And that means, above all, giving up the silly premise of so many modern authors that to identify something as "bourgeois" is *ipso pipso* to be forced to reject it.

17. The roots are *burger, burgher*. The old French *burgeis*, and Middle French *burgeis, burges, borges*, meaning "inhabitant of a borough," were first translated into English as "burgess." The French term *bourgeois*, however, remains the most familiar ideological category. See Raymond Williams, p. 37; also the *Oxford English Dictionary*, "bourgeois." In simple sociological terms, it is important that the American term "middle class" not be taken as an equivalent of "bourgeoisie." Thus Lukacs, *The Passing of the*

Modern Age: "Every society has a class that is situated in the middle, between the upper and the lower classes. Not every class had, or has, a bourgeoisie. The existence of a middle class is a universal, a sociological phenomenon. The existence of the bourgeois, on the other hand, has been a particular phenomenon, a historical reality" (pp. 616–17). We might quibble with the claim that "every society has a class . . . in the middle," but it is important that the bourgeoisie be identified in some far more historically specific way than its "middle" status. Similarly Williams (*Keywords*, p. 37) notes that because of Marxist usage, "bourgeois" is not merely "middle class," since it refers essentially to a role in a capitalist economy. But if we reject the narrow Marxist sense and remain wary of the too broad sociological sense, we can quite safely continue to move freely between the French and the American, since the bourgeoisie also played (and play) a function in modern society—communist even more than capitalist—which is distinctly a "middle" role.

18. An enormous population increase is but one of the socioeconomic factors that must be taken into account in trying to fit our ideological interpretation into a more general account of the period. The increase in population had the direct effect of making more bourgeois jobs and professions immediately required, as well as the equally direct effect of increasing their numbers. The shift to a market and money economy, and the sudden urbanization of Europe, had equally significant effects on the status of the middle class, the consequent growth of bureaucracy, the pressure for equal opportunity, and the possibility of rapid advancement and influence. See Eric Hobsbawm, *The Age of Capital* (New York: Scribners, 1975).

19. For example, the Enlightenment philosophers as well as later romantics appealed to exotic cultures (the Orient, the South Pacific, ancient Greece) not just to contrast themselves with others, but also to make a point of the underlying similarities and unity of human nature, sometimes more obvious in others than in ourselves.

20. Philosophers sometimes use the term "universal" to refer to any property which can be shared by any number of particulars (e.g., the color red), or to any concept that can be instantiated by any number of individuals (e.g., the concept of a dog). As I am using the term here, however, it is limited to claims and concepts which are assumed to apply to every human being.

21. Geertz, *Interpretation of Cultures:* "To be human is thus not to be Everyman; it is to be a particular kind of man, and of course, men differ" (p. 53). A far more complex example from what we have been taught to consider "our own" history is the Greek distinction between Greek (truly human) versus "bar-barian," with language as its primary basis. In Aristotle, for example, the ambiguity between tribalism and humanism is pronounced.

22. Michel Foucault's *The Archaeology of Knowledge* overstates this thesis, announcing the formidable-sounding phrase "end of Man." What he means, I take it, is what we also mean: that the presumptuous notion of universal humanity, ignoring differences and "discontinuities" in favor of unwarranted generalities and continuities, is near a historical end.

23. See Williams, *Keywords*, on "Humanity" (p. 122).

24. See Fawn Brodie's excellent biography, *Thomas Jefferson: An Intimate History* (New York: Norton, 1974), for an indelibly personal picture of how ideologically devious even the best humanists can be.

25. Aristotle set the pattern for such "functional" ethics, but it reappears in less obvious forms in Rousseau, Kant, and Hegel, and in the most perverse

form imaginable in the writing of the marquis de Sade (see Chapter 4), who does more than his share to discredit all such arguments.

26. See Peter Gay, *The Enlightenment: An Interpretation* (New York: Vintage, 1966), for an excellent bibliographical essay on the literature on this topic.

27. But perhaps it is time to take seriously Gore Vidal's recent lament: "With some pride, the inventor-owners of the United States announced that their republic would be 'a government of laws and not of men.' The world applauded. It never occurred to any Enlightenment figure in the eighteenth century that law was not preferable to man. The republic was then given to lawyers to govern. Predictably, lawyers make laws, giving work to other lawyers. As a result of two centuries of law-making, every aspect of man's life has either been prescribed for or proscribed by laws that even as they are promulgated split amoeba-like to create more laws. The end to this Malthusian nightmare of law metastasized is nowhere in sight" (*New York Review of Books*, June 29, 1978).

28. Arguing against the existence of miracles, David Hume said that they could be believed *if* they fit into the "natural" laws of normal human experience, which is precisely to rule them out beforehand.

29. The overemphasis on Reason as the key to the Enlightenment has caused more misunderstandings than understanding; the most serious, perhaps, is Carl Becker's *The Heavenly City of the Eighteenth Century Philosophers* (New Haven: Yale University Press, 1932).

30. The Catholic Church had always (as its name implies) commanded universal obedience, but during the Enlightenment religion suffered enormously from the attempt to save it from the new ideology by insisting that the truth was to be found in all religions (like contemporary "ecumenicalism"). But as the particular content of any religion is generalized, it loses precisely those features that make it religious. This is also true of the religion of humanism.

31. It is important to keep in mind that science was a model for the Enlightenment not just because of its own successes, but also because it was such an outstanding example of a kind of thinking which was being sought in every aspect of human life. On this point I differ in emphasis with Gary Wills, *The Invention of America* (New York: Doubleday, 1978), who gives too little appreciation to these abstract concerns and the *pretentiousness* of science.

32. By "resentment" I do not mean mere status conflict or competition for attention, wealth, or whatever, but that much more complex emotion that has built into it the language of rights, injustice, and principled malevolence. See my book *The Passions* (New York: Doubleday-Anchor, 1976), Chapter 11.

33. John Lukacs's *The Passing of the Modern Age* is particularly good on this aspect of bourgeois culture. He identifies "the bourgeois era" by what he calls "the internalization of the human condition" (p. 622), a period of increased awareness of "the interior landscape of our minds" (p. 623), and defends his thesis with examples drawn from everything from furniture to Christmas celebrations. Discounting the supposed inwardness of earlier times, he rightly says, "All of its spiritual aspirations notwithstanding, the Medieval civilization was strongly external, 'all good things in life were a proud or cruel publicity' (Huizinga)" (p. 622). Thus Kierkegaard's "inwardness," for example, was not at all medieval, as he claimed, but very modern and very bourgeois (see Chapter 16).

34. Peter Gay thus refers to the Enlightenment as "the rise of modern paganism." Given our preoccupation with happiness today, it is worth remembering that it is a surprisingly modern conception. The pagan conception before it, in fact, is strictly an objective notion, as in Aristotle's *Ethics*, in which happiness is no more than—and not merely brought about by—communal recognition and honor, wealth, health, etc. The assumption that both dignity and happiness were goals built into human nature was explicitly argued by Kant, and he makes it brutally clear that these were not to be confused with any outward facts about the situation of the individual. But in Kant's terms and in the general thinking of the period, subjectivity and objectivity were not antithetical (the way we often use those terms), but complementary.

1. *The Enlightenment in France and the Rise of the Bourgeoisie*

1. The French *philosophes* were often not philosophers in the standard sense of the word, being far more concerned with concrete cultural and social issues than with the abstractions and puzzles that constitute much of the history of philosophy. There is no reason, however, to withhold their title from them; to give it to them without implicit qualifications, I simply use the English in every case.
2. Elinor Barber, *The Bourgeoisie in Eighteenth Century France* (Princeton: Princeton University Press, 1965).
3. Denis Diderot, *Supplement to Bougainville's Voyage*, in Peter Gay, ed., *The Enlightenment: A Comprehensive Anthology* (New York: Simon and Schuster, 1973).
4. The single most powerful analysis of the Enlightenment, on which much of this chapter is based, is Volume I of Peter Gay's *The Enlightement: An Interpretation*, cited hereafter as Gay. Gay minimizes some of the underlying ideological issues, however, while concentrating on the explicit philosophy and sociology of the philosophers. He also minimizes the political ambitions of the philosophers, emphasizing their self-conscious role as critics and correctives. In stressing their antimetaphysical bias, he does not emphasize the extent to which they themselves were defending a new metaphysics, itself an ideological expression in the context of a grand political class battle. But however one may disagree regarding emphasis, Gay's book must be the absolute starting point for anyone pursuing an understanding of the Enlightenment. Also helpful within our perspective are Ernst Cassirer, *The Philosophy of the Enlightenment* (Princeton: Princeton University Press, 1951), with its strong Kantian flavor; and Lester Crocker, *An Age of Crisis: Man and World in Eighteenth Century Thought* (Baltimore: Johns Hopkins University Press, 1959), which emphasizes the "dark side" of the Enlightenment, the role of passions, and the psychological underpinnings of Enlightenment ideology (especially Chapter 9). See also George R. Havens, *The Age of Ideas: From Reaction to Revolution in Eighteenth Century France* (New York: Free Press, 1965). The background of the Enlightenment is discussed in Paul Hazard, *The European Mind: The Critical Years, 1680–1715* (New Haven: Yale University Press,

1953). For the English Enlightenment—a defense of its intellectual opposition—see R. R. Palmer, *Catholics and Unbelievers in Eighteenth Century France* (Princeton: Princeton University Press, 1939).

5. Gay, pp. 72 ff.: "The Greek Miracle."
6. Gay, Chapter 3, pp. 127 ff. and pp. 178 ff.
7. See, most famously, Carl Becker, *The Heavenly City of the Eighteenth Century Philosophers* (New Haven: Yale University Press, 1932), who argues perversely that the Enlightenment philosophers were actually intellectual holdovers from medieval scholasticism, whose concept of "reason" they could borrow uncritically. This assumes, of course, a monolithic and unproblematic concept of "reason," which the history of philosophy ought certainly to have dispelled. Becker writes as if he were wholly oblivious to the fact that the French philosophers were engaged in a social struggle, rather than merrily debating issues and predicting the future. His main thesis, however, that the Enlightenment philosophers should *not* be taken at face value, is an important insight, and a balance to Gay's enthusiastic appreciation, which most of the time takes the philosophers entirely at their word. As an antidote, see R. O. Rockwood, ed., *Carl Becker's Heavenly City Revisited* (Ithaca, N.Y.: Cornell University Press, 1958), cited hereafter as Rockwood.
8. See especially Gay, I, 8 ff., and II, Chapter 5, on the "paganism" of the Enlightenment.
9. See Charles Frankel, *Faith of Reason* (New York: King's Crown, 1948).
10. Descartes was a great mathematician and empirical scientist as well as a philosopher. He developed a mechanistic theory of the universe a half century before Newton, and argued extensively in favor of "the testimony of the senses." The Enlightenment criticism of Descartes as a metaphysician who despised the senses and science in favor of abstract speculation was based on an appalling misreading of his works. Voltaire should have known better, but so too should many commentators who, on Voltaire's testimony, have left Descartes out of the Enlightenment altogether. For a defense of Descartes's essential importance for the Enlightenment, see Henry Guerlac's article on Newton in Rockwood, pp. 3 ff. and especially p. 15. See also Aram Vartanian, *Diderot and Descartes: A Study of Scientific Naturalism in the Enlightenment* (Princeton: Princeton University Press, 1953), and Gay, II, 617–19.
11. See Becker, *Heavenly City*.
12. See Alvin Gouldner, *The Dialectic of Ideology and Technology* (New York: Seabury, 1976); Lucien Febvre and Henri-Jean Martin, *The Coming of the Book* (London: New Left Review, 1976); and of course Marshall McLuhan, *The Gutenberg Galaxy* (Toronto: Toronto University Press, 1962).
13. The *Encyclopédie* has since been made available in English in part (New York: Dover Books, 1959), 2 vols. The reprinting of the whole *Encyclopédie* is in process.
14. "In eighteenth-century France, abuses were glaring enough to invite the most scathing criticism, while the machinery of repression was inefficient enough to permit the critic adequate room for maneuvering" (Gay, I, 10).
15. Max Horkheimer and Theodor Adorno, *The Dialectics of Enlightenment* (New York: Seabury, 1972), a strangely frustrating book that emphasizes the "one-dimensional" myth of the Enlightenment attack on mythologizing.

See also A. N. Whitehead, *Science and the Modern World* (New York: Free Press, 1967), and the defense of the Enlightenment in Cassirer, *The Philosophy of the Enlightenment.*

16. In Patrick Gardner, *Theories of History* (New York: Free Press, 1959), and W. T. Jones, *A History of Western Philosophy*, 2nd ed. (New York: Harcourt Brace Jovanovich, 1975), Vol. 4, pp. 2–3.
17. See Gay, II, Chapter 4 and p. 489, where he emphasizes "the discontinuity rather than the continuity," with bibliographical correctives. See also his reply to Becker in Rockwood. For an unhelpful but *au courant* discussion of "discontinuities" in general, see Michel Foucault, *Archaeology of Knowledge.*
18. Voltaire rejected the medieval concept of "soul," supposedly using arguments from Locke, destroying this "false" abstract concept of human nature, in order to replace it with the equally universal—and some would say equally abstract and indefinable—concept of human reason.
19. Hume makes this argument again and again, despite his interest in human differences and "national character." The very title, "A Treatise on Human Nature," like most works of the period, displays this uncritical confidence in human nature and universality.
20. The *Persian Letters* (Indianapolis: Bobbs-Merrill, 1964) were the prototype of many of Voltaire's ironic parodies and criticisms; they are excerpted in Gay's anthology. Many historians such as Havens and Gay (cited above) see Montesquieu and his landmark book, *The Spirit of the Laws* (1748), as the true beginning of the Enlightenment. Perhaps, but ideologically he was always the pure aristocrat and defender of the aristocracy. He was indisputably an enlightened thinker, but hardly one of the Enlightenment bourgeois family.
21. Voltaire and Diderot both traveled extensively within Europe, to the courts of Prussia and Russia as well as to England. Rousseau covered as much ground, though usually on the run. But neither the courts of Europe nor the boardinghouses of the underground provided sufficient basis for their universal pronouncements about "humanity." Here we discern the a priori basis of the most empirical observations, the projection of one's own personality as the prototype of humanity.
22. But see Gore Vidal, cited in note 27 of the Introduction.
23. See Ernest Gellner, "Explanations in History," in Gardner, *Theories of History*, p. 48.
24. See Horkheimer and Adorno, *Dialectics of Enlightenment*, Chapter 1.
25. Quoted in Jones, *History of Western Philosophy*, p. 3.
26. See J. B. Bury, *Idea of Progress* (London: Macmillan, 1920).
27. More innocently, Gay uses the word "confidence" instead of "optimism," while Becker uses "faith," though both words seem more self-assured than the paranoia of the times would allow.
28. The figures are from Georges Lefebvre, *The Coming of the French Revolution*, trans. R. R. Palmer (Princeton: Princeton University Press, 1947).

2. *The Double-Edged Sword: Voltaire*

1. See Peter Gay, *The Party of Humanity* (New York: Norton, 1971), and *Voltaire's Politics: The Poet as Realist* (Princeton: Princeton University

Press, 1959). Also, Gustave Lanson, *Voltaire,* trans. Robert A. Wagner (New York: Wiley, 1966), and I. O. Wade, *The Search for a New Voltaire* (Philadelphia: American Philosophical Society, 1958).

2. Peter Gay, *The Enlightenment: An Interpretation* (New York: Vintage, 1966), I, 16.

3. Article I: "Men are born and remain free and equal before the law"; and Article III: "Sovereignty resides in the nation." It is important to remember that Voltaire, as well as Rousseau, employed the notion of "national sovereignty" and that this particular article lends itself to both radical republicanism and more conservative monarchism, and to a belief in social stratification. Locke and Voltaire, for example, both believed that sovereignty and sharp distinctions in social classes were wholly compatible. The declaration, as a matter of fact, also allows for class distinctions "in the good of the nation."

4. Gay, I, 16. But this applies only to his career before 1760, when he became a "defender of causes" and anything but "resigned."

5. See Theodore Besterman, ed., *Voltaire Studies* (Geneva: International Scholarly Book Service, 1954).

6. They were first published in England in translation in 1733 as the *Letters Concerning the English Nation.* They appeared the following year in France as the *Lettres philosophiques.* They are published in this country in translation by Ernest Dilworth as *Philosophical Letters* (New York: Bobbs-Merrill, 1961). All quotes are from this source; subsequent references appear in the text.

7. Locke did believe in the soul—and in other ideas not drawn from experience (see Chapter 1). Locke's own use of the concept of Reason, contrary to his ideological insistence on "empiricism," is only superficially an attack on "Reason" and its alleged ability to provide us with truths about the world. Despite his thematic insistence on the sensory basis of every proposition, every time he reached a philosophical impasse defending a concept he wanted to defend (e.g., God or soul), he immediately shifted his appeal to the Cartesian concepts of "reason" and "self-evidence." Politically, too, Locke was a great *post-hoc* rationalizer, however radical his ideal (already realized in England) might have seemed to the French philosophers.

8. See Gay, I, 11, 321, et passim.

9. But to attack pessimism is not yet to be an "optimist."

10. As early as 1844, Marx was complaining that the bourgeoisie used "Reason" as a way of viewing all human life through their own eyes and interests, as if their way of life were the only reasonable one. The Marxist term for this monopoly of vision is "hegemony" (see Introduction, note 9), and it is the hegemony of bourgeois reason that leads Marx and his followers to condemn generally the insidious notion of "ideology" as a fabric of illusions put forward universally to promote the interests of a particular class. See Max Horkheimer and Theodor Adorno, *The Dialectics of Enlightenment* (New York: Seabury, 1972), and Herbert Marcuse's contribution to *A Critique of Pure Tolerance* (Boston: Beacon, 1969). See also Jean-Paul Sartre, *Search for a Method* (New York: Vintage, 1968).

11. Voltaire had far more confidence in the rational abilities of the English and his fellow Frenchmen than he did in the comparatively "primitive" intellects of the European masses to the east. Thus he could abide Frederick's tyrannies in Prussia, though he would have found them intolerable in France. Similarly, there is a well-known exchange between Diderot and

Catherine of Russia in which she complains, though "enlightened" herself, that he, as philosopher, "need only engrave his thoughts on paper, while she, unfortunate princess, must work with human skin, a much frailer tissue." This would not have been a persuasive argument in France, but it seemed acceptable to Diderot where illiterate Russian peasants were concerned.

12. For a similar use of the concept of "natural rights" in support of current libertarian theory, see Robert Nozick, *Anarchy, State and Utopia* (New York: Basic Books, 1974). Nozick begins by defending (against anarchists) a "minimal state" whose power is restricted to enforcing contracts, protecting property, etc., and by defending an extremely "pure" notion of "natural rights," including the right to own property. A fine argument against his position, from which I have borrowed in this section, is Baruch Brody, "Natural Rights and Political Philosophy," in *Philosophica* (1979).

13. Quoted in Lester Crocker, *Nature and Culture* (Baltimore: Johns Hopkins University Press, 1963), p. 345.

14. Theodore Besterman, ed., *Voltaire's Correspondence* (Geneva: International Scholarly Book Service, 1974).

15. His most famous case, the defense of Jean Calas in 1762, involved saving a reputation rather than a life: Calas had been executed for heresy the year before, and Voltaire took up the tragedy as avenging angel, attacking the institutions that continued to make religious persecution and prejudice possible.

16. N. L. Torrey, *Voltaire and the English Deists* (New York: Russell & Russell, 1930), and *The Spirit of Voltaire* (New York: Russell & Russell, 1938).

17. Hume is the most famous exception; he maintained his atheism even on his deathbed. Diderot was a more problematic case; he espoused atheism, but with an obvious sense of hesitation—as if in a gamble.

18. The distance between Voltaire's Pangloss and the historical Leibniz can be measured not only by the omission of Leibniz's best arguments, but by the inclusion of themes that were not his at all. For example, one of Leibniz's chief doctrines, which he advanced against Newton, was a rejection of the mechanistic view of cause and effect; yet Pangloss bases the whole of his metaphysics (he is actually a teacher of "metaphysico-theologigo-cosmolonigology") on the Newtonian-Kantian principle that "there is no cause without an effect."

19. In an earlier satire, *Memnon,* he had similarly "demonstrated," by way of parody, the absurdities of pure rational thought.

20. *Candide,* trans. Richard Aldington, ed. N. L. Torrey (New York: Appleton-Century-Crofts, 1946), p. 54.

21. See Gay, I, 200–203, and I. O. Wade, *Voltaire and Candide* (Princeton: Princeton University Press, 1959).

3. *Paranoia to Politics: Rousseau*

1. It might be said that the ideology of the other philosophers was purely critical, not philosophical, while Rousseau was less a critical than a utopian philosopher; but the difference here must rather be one of explicitness of ideas. There is no such thing as a critical ideology without an implicit system of ideas which it uses as a standard; and there is no philosophy (as

opposed to mere description or parroting of catechisms) which is not in part criticism as well.

2. Just when D'Alembert and Diderot were besieged by official censors and the threat of imprisonment for their *Encyclopédie,* Rousseau publicly attacked D'Alembert's article on his hometown, Geneva. The basis of the attack—aimed largely at Voltaire, who had probably prompted D'Alembert's article—was the "degeneration of morals" and "incitement of dangerous passions" which would result from introducing classical theater into puritanical Geneva. For a general discussion of the philosophers' expulsion of Rousseau, see Peter Gay, *The Enlightenment,* Vol. I.

3. *Emile,* trans. B. Foxley (New York: Dutton, 1974), p. 253.

4. This is often ignored by Rousseau's harshest critics, notably Irving Babbitt, *Rousseau and Romanticism* (New York: AMS Press, 1976), who argues to absurd lengths against both Rousseau and romanticism, both dubiously interpreted. Rousseau emerges an irrational, irresponsible, and self-indulgent idealist (which he was), but not a philosopher at all. This charge is answered by Ernst Cassirer in *The Question of Jean-Jacques Rousseau* (Bloomington: Indiana University Press, 1963), although Cassirer perhaps errs in the other direction, making too complete a distinction between Rousseau's personality and his proto-Kantian philosophy. See also Peter Gay's introduction to Cassirer's study.

5. This is not just to say, however, that Rousseau was the ideologue behind the demogogue Robespierre, the architect of the Reign of Terror and the first dictator of modern Europe (see Chapter 5). If Rousseau laid the foundations for European totalitarianism, he equally set out the basis for republicanism and democracy. This is not the picture, however, that emerges from the one-sided portraits in Taine's *L'Ancien Régime* (New York, 1896); Sir Karl Popper's *The Open Society and Its Enemies* (London: Routledge and Kegan Paul, 1945); and of course Edmund Burke's *Reflections on the Revolution in France* (New York: Dutton, 1976). For a more balanced account, see Henri Peyre, "The Influence of Eighteenth Century Ideas on the French Revolution," in the book by the same title (New Haven: Yale University Press, 1941).

6. *Confessions,* trans. John M. Cohen (Harmondsworth: Penguin, 1954).

7. *Discourse on the Origins of Inequality among Men* (New York: E. P. Dutton, 1976), p. 275.

8. *Confessions,* pp. 166–67. This image of "freedom in prison" recurs throughout French literature—in Stendhal, Camus, and Sartre, to name only a few who have used it. But this shows that the "liberty" that concerns Rousseau is only tangentially political; first of all, it is a concept of the imagination.

9. The concept of childhood innocence can itself be traced back to Rousseau. Although we think of that concept as being as old as the Christian era, the radical emphasis on innocence originates with Rousseau. It can be contrasted, for example, with Hobbes's portrait of "natural" man as savage, selfish, and anything but innocent. This does not mean that we should make too much of the "noble savage" image that has emerged from Rousseau—a portrait that he did not intend as historical. But it is an attempt to spell out the "deeper" levels of human nature—that is, what Rousseau insisted on seeing in himself: a childhood innocence inhibited by a pathological adult cynicism. "For my part, I publicly and fearlessly declare that anyone, even if he has not read my writings, who will examine my nature, my character, my morals, my likings, my pleasures and my habits with his

own eyes and can still believe me a dishonorable man, is a man who deserves to be stifled" (*Confessions*, p. 606).

10. Voltaire, *Philosophical Dictionary*, trans. Peter Gay (New York: Basic Books, 1962), p. 245.

11. This is discussed in detail in Arthur O. Lovejoy, "The Supposed Primitivism of Rousseau's *Discourse on Inequality*," in *Essays in the History of Ideas* (Baltimore: Johns Hopkins University Press, 1948), pp. 14–37.

12. This confusion is at least as common as the "noble savage" bromide. E.g.: "The theory of Rousseau, that man is naturally a savage, perpetually at war with his followers, that society is an afterthought, something artificial and superfluous to his nature, is as opposed to historical facts as it is degrading to the human race" (John J. Ford, S.J.). A far more accurate portrait is in Woody Allen's *Getting Even* (New York: Random House, 1971): "Is it true, Doctor Helmholtz, that man is naturally savage, as Hobbes says, or naturally kind and gentle, as in Rousseau? Well, both. On weekdays, Hobbes is right. On weekends, Rousseau." Cf. Rousseau's popular novel *Julie:* "Which is more important to me, my happiness at the expense of mankind, or the happiness of others at my expense?"

13. Quoted in Cassirer, p. 18.

14. Rousseau's reply in his *Confessions* has no such wit or charm: "Though Voltaire has always appeared to believe in God, he has really only believed in the devil, because his so-called God is nothing but a malicious being who, according to his belief, only takes pleasure in doing harm. The absurdity of this doctrine leaps to the eye, and it is particularly revolting in a man loaded with every kind of blessing who, living in the lap of luxury, seeks to disillusion his fellow men by a frightening and cruel picture of all the calamities from which he himself is exempt" (p. 38). The gross inaccuracy of this characterization of Voltaire's deism should be obvious from Chapter 2.

15. See Lovejoy, especially pp. 15 ff.

16. The epigraph of the *Second Discourse* is a quote from Aristotle: "We should consider what is natural not in things which are depraved, but in those which are rightly ordered according to nature."

17. *The Social Contract*, ed. Charles M. Sherover (New York: New American Library, 1974); all quotations from *The Social Contract* from this edition.

18. "The social order is a sacred right which is the basis of other rights. Nevertheless, this right does not come from nature, and must therefore be founded on conventions" (p. 7).

19. Quoted from Roger D. Masters, *The Political Philosophy of Jean-Jacques Rousseau* (Princeton: Princeton University Press, 1968). I have benefited from Masters's discussions throughout this chapter.

20. Quoted from Masters.

21. See respectively Peyre, "Influence," and Charles E. Vaughn, *Studies in the History of Political Philosophy* (New York: Russell & Russell, 1960).

4. *Warning Signs: Hume and Sade*

1. *The Dialogues Concerning Natural Religion* were published posthumously (New York: Bobbs-Merrill, 1953). All quotations in the text are from this edition. The standard biography is E. C. Mossner, *The Life of David*

Hume (Oxford: Oxford University Press, 1960). The standard survey of his philosophy is N. Kemp Smith, *The Philosophy of David Hume* (London: Oxford University Press, 1941).

2. *Treatise of Human Nature,* ed. L. A. Selby-Bigge (Oxford: Oxford University Press, 1855); first published in 1739.

3. Hume's most accessible works are his two *Enquiries: Concerning Human Understanding* (1748) and *Concerning the Principles of Morals* (1751). They are available in a single edition—L. A. Selby-Bigge, ed. (Oxford: Oxford University Press, 1902)—and are intended for a more popular audience than his earlier *Treatise of Human Nature.*

4. See Boswell's conversation with the dying Hume in Gay, *The Enlightenment* (New York: Simon and Schuster, 1973), p. 263.

5. Sade's most widely read works are *Justine, Philosophy in the Bedroom, The New Justine, Cries of Love,* and *120 Days of Sodom.* Most of these are now available in English in paperback form. Recent years have seen a wealth of Sade defenses, most impressively by Simone de Beauvoir, "Must We Burn de Sade?" in *The Marquis de Sade* (New York: Grove Press, 1953); Maurice Blanchot, in *The Marquis de Sade* (New York: Grove Press, 1965); and Roland Barthes, *Loyola, Fourier and de Sade* (New York: Hill & Wang, 1976). Quotations are from Beauvoir's *The Marquis de Sade* and Richard Seaver and Austryn Wainhouse, trans., *The Marquis de Sade* (New York: Grove Press, 1965). William Gass has credited the philosopher marquis with a new form of argument—sexual arousal itself as a proof of human nature (in "Philosophy and Fiction," a lecture given at the University of Texas at Austin, Austin, Texas, October 13, 1978).

6. *Juliette,* trans. A. Wainhouse, in *The Marquis de Sade.*

7. *Dialogue between a Priest and a Dying Man,* trans. Paul Dinnage, in *The Marquis de Sade.*

8. *Justine,* trans. R. Seaver and A. Wainhouse, in *The Marquis de Sade.*

9. "In the solitude of his prison cells, Sade lived through an ethical darkness similar to the intellectual light in which Descartes wrapped himself" (Simone de Beauvoir, p. 82).

10. *Philosophy in the Bedroom,* in *The Marquis de Sade,* trans. R. Seaver and A. Wainhouse, pp. 273–74.

11. *The New Justine,* trans. Paul Dinnage.

12. "Neither as an author nor as sexual pervert does Sade compel our attention. . . . Sade's aberrations begin to acquire value when, instead of enduring them as his fixed nature, he elaborates an immense system in order to justify them" (Simone de Beauvoir, p. 12).

13. Peter Weiss, *The Persecution and Assassination of Jean-Paul Marat as Performed by the Inmates of the Asylum at Charenton under the Direction of the Marquis de Sade* (London: Calder, 1965).

5. In the Name of Humanity: The French Revolution

1. In 1789 "the People" referred to the entire Third Estate, peasants, workers, small shopkeepers, and general riffraff, and their representatives in Paris, the merchants, lawyers, professors, and other professionals. Yet many of the peasants owned their own land and were not the suffering serfs that some accounts made them out to be. Nor were the "mobs" of the city so

mindless or crude as conservative commentators like Burke and Taine would have us believe. Of particular importance was that group of workers and shopkeepers called the *sans-culottes*, defined by the working-class clothing they wore but best characterized, not by the fictional accounts of their vengeance (like Dickens's *Tale of Two Cities*), but by their strong if not always well-informed *moral* stance toward the Revolution. Richard Cobb, for example, describes them as "puritans, for whom vice went hand in hand with counterrevolution. They therefore condemned celibacy, gastronomy, gambling, prostitution, obscenity, finery, and luxury; but on the other hand, they showed a marked indulgence for drunkenness." In F. A. Kafker and J. M. Laux, eds., *The French Revolution: Conflicts of Interpretation*, 2nd ed. (New York: Random House, 1968), pp. 157 f. The *sans-culottes* are generally given credit as the heart of the popular revolution, but it is equally important to include the petty bourgeoisie, property owners, merchants, civil servants, and professional people as well as servants, peasants, and workers. See for example George Rudé, "The Crowd in the French Revolution," in Kafker and Laux, pp. 180–81. See also Crane Brinton, *A Decade of Revolution, 1789–1799* (New York: Harper & Row, 1934), pp. 22–24; and Albert Soboul, "The French Revolution, 1787–99," in Kafker and Laux, pp. 187 f. Important background can be found in Louis Chevalier, *Laboring Classes and Dangerous Classes in Paris during the First Half of the Nineteenth Century* (New York: Fertig, 1973); Jeff Kaplow, *France on the Eve of the Revolution* (New York: Wiley, 1971); O. Hufton, *The Poor of Eighteenth Century France* (Oxford: Oxford University Press, 1975); and R. Darnton, "Poverty, Crime and Revolution," *New York Review of Books* (October 2, 1975).

2. Carlyle, half tongue in cheek, comments that "all things are in revolution; in change from moment to moment. Revolution, you answer, means *speedier* change. For ourselves, we answer that French revolution means here the open violent rebellion and victory of disimprisoned Anarchy against corrupt worn-out Authority." From *The French Revolution*, 2 vols. (New York: Dutton, 1955), I, 182.

3. The role of Enlightenment ideology in the French Revolution is debated in Kafker and Laux and in Henri Peyre, "The Influence of Eighteenth Century Ideas on the French Revolution," in Franklin L. Baumer, ed., *Intellectual Movements in Modern European History* (London: Macmillan, 1965), pp. 63–84. Our sympathies, however, are clearly with Alexis de Tocqueville, *The Old Regime and the French Revolution* (New York: Doubleday, 1955): "These doctrines [of natural equality, popular sovereignty, uniformity of rules, abolition of caste] are not only the causes of the revolution; they are its substance; they constitute the most fundamental, the most durable, the truest portion of its work" (p. 19).

4. Hippolyte A. Taine reports the comment of a peasant girl to an American observer: "Something was to be done by some great folks for the poor folks, but she didn't know who or how." *The French Revolution*, 3 vols., trans. J. Durand (New York: Holt, 1885), I, 8.

5. Tocqueville (*Old Regime*, pp. 179–80): "When the time for action came, men dealt with political questions on literary principles . . . but what is a merit in an author is a defect in a statesman, and characteristics which improve a book may be fatal to a revolution."

6. When the Americans gained their independence, they had long adopted English Enlightenment principles and practices. They had a tradition of

government, they knew how to run a representative state. There were few established and unearned interests to cope with, and millions of square miles of uncultivated land to be developed. In France there was no tradition of representative government, no traditions that would help them through the vacuum left by the crumbling of the old order. And America had no starving masses, no resentful aristocrats, no single powerful church that functioned as a second national government, and no armies on the border, ready to invade. One foreign observer in Paris described the debates there as a people "wanting an American constitution but ignoring the fact that there were no American citizens to make it work."

7. Tocqueville, *Old Regime:* "The most critical moment for bad governments is the one which witnesses their first steps toward reform." See also Georges Lefebvre, *The Coming of the French Revolution,* trans. R. R. Palmer (Princeton: Princeton University Press, 1947); and R. R. Palmer, *The World of the French Revolution* (New York: Harper & Row, 1972) and *The Age of Democratic Revolution,* 2 vols. (Princeton: Princeton University Press, 1969–70).

8. "It was the aristocracy that precipitated the revolution by forcing the king to call the Estates General" (Lefebvre, p. 210).

9. Abbé Sieyès, "What Is the Third Estate?"

10. Burke's *Reflections on the Revolution in France* (New York: Dutton, 1976) is the classic statement of the "conservative" (i.e., disapproving) view of the occurrences in France. His rejection, like that of Taine years later, was based on the belief—certainly confirmed during the subsequent years, but by no means thereby justifying his general dismissal of the revolutionary ideals—that only tradition could prevent a people from going to the abyss of anarchy. (Taine: "It's as if they were trying to build an *old* house.") Curiously, the English tended to be hard on the revolution that was, at least at first, imitative of their own. Burke, like Hume before him, was torn between aristocratic and bourgeois pretensions, between respect for authority and rebellion. Given the fact that England had well survived its own revolution of 1688, this tension is instructive. The Germans on the other hand, being years behind, looked on with enthusiasm (see Chapter 6).

11. Thus Taine: "It is the boldest and least scrupulous who march ahead and set the example in destruction. The example is contagious; the beginning was the craving for bread, the end is murder and incendiarism; the savagery which is unchained adding its unlimited violence to the limited revolt of necessity" (I, 14). But cf. Carlyle's enthusiasm: "Yes, Reader, here is the miracle. Out of that putrescent rubbish of Scepticism, Sensualism, Sentimentalism, hollow Machiavelism, such a Faith has verily risen; flaming in the heart of a People. A whole People, awakening as it were to consciousness in deep misery, believes that it is within reach of a Fraternal Heaven-on-Earth" (II, 203).

12. See Lefebvre; but cf. Tocqueville: "The condition of the French peasantry was worse in some respects in the eighteenth century than it had been in the thirteenth" (p. 151). Of the bourgeoisie, Tocqueville says, "While the citizen and the noble had grown more like each other, the distance between them had increased; their mutual resemblance had rather alienated than united them" (p. 109). See also R. R. Palmer, *The World of the French Revolution,* p. 160. Cf. Darton: "The revolution was a luxury that only the bourgeoisie could afford" (p. 23).

13. See Lefebvre, especially pp. 184–87.

14. Letter to Comte Jean Diodati, August 3, 1789.
15. See R. R. Palmer, *Twelve Who Ruled: The Year of the Terror in the French Revolution* (Princeton: Princeton University Press, 1941), and J. M. Thompson, *The Leaders of the French Revolution* (New York: Harper & Row, 1967). There are also admirable and differing portraits in H. G. Wells, *Outline of History* (New York: Doubleday, 1971), and Crane Brinton, *A Decade of Revolution* (New York: Harper & Row, 1934). For a distinctly nasty set of portraits (as one would expect), but with hundreds of anecdotes and a virtual catalogue of atrocities, see Taine, especially Vol. II.
16. Quoted in Thompson, p. 25.
17. Thompson, p. 25.
18. B. Whitlock, *Lafayette* (New York: Appleton, 1929).
19. Quoted in Taine, *The French Revolution*, II, 26.
20. From a contemporary, in 1794: "Danton always believed, and, what is worse as to himself at least, always maintained, that a popular system of government for this country was absurd; that the people were too ignorant, too inconstant, and too corrupt to support a legal administration; that, habituated to obey, they required a master. . . . He was too voluptuous for his ambition, too indolent to acquire supreme power. Moreover, his object seems rather to have been great wealth, than great fame" (Brinton, *A Decade of Revolution*, pp. 105–6). See also H. G. Wells, *Outline of History*, p. 900, and A. Souboul, "Danton," in the *Encyclopaedia Britannica*, Vol. 7, pp. 64–66.
21. Not surprisingly, historians of a conservative temperament reserve their worst abuse for Marat. Thus Taine: "Three men among the Jacobins, Marat, Danton, and Robespierre, merited distinction and possessed authority. . . . Of the three, Marat is the most monstrous: he borders on the lunatic, of which he displays the chief characteristics" (*The French Revolution*, III, 138). Even Carlyle, generally a sympathizer of the Revolution, calls Marat "squalid" and a "dog-leech." H. G. Wells, on the other hand, envisions him as a true hero of the Revolution: "Throughout Marat played a bitter and yet often a just part; he was a great man, a fine intelligence, in a skin of fire [an allusion to his skin disease], wrung with that organic hate in the blood that is not a product of the mind but of the body." Crane Brinton gives him a qualified defense: "Only as the militant professional radical is Marat to be understood. To condemn him utterly requires a somewhat robust faith in the finalities of this everyday world" (*Outline of History*, p. 899).
22. "Let us not be afraid to repeat it, we are farther from liberty than ever: for not only are we slaves, but we are slaves legally, as a consequence of the perfidy of our legislators, who have become the accomplices of a rehabilitated despotism. . . . The objectives of the revolution have been missed completely." From *Amis du peuple*, July 7, 1792.
23. "We desire to substitute in our country, morality for egoism, honesty for mere honor, principle for habit, duty for decorum, the empire of reason for the tyranny of fashion, contempt of vice for scorn of misfortune, pride for insolence, large-mindedness for vanity. . . .

"We wish in short to fulfill the course of nature, to accomplish the destiny of mankind, to make good the promises of philosophy, to absolve Providence from the long reign of tyranny and crime." From "Definition of the Goals of the Revolution," February 5, 1794. See T. M. Thompson,

Robespierre (Oxford: Oxford University Press, 1953); Jean Matat, *Robespierre* (New York: Scribners, 1971); and G. Rude, ed., *Robespierre* (Englewood Cliffs, N.J.: Prentice-Hall, 1976).

24. Brinton (*A Decade of Revolution,* pp. 108–9): "Robespierre survived because the Terror was in large part a religious movement, and Robespierre had many of the ·qualities of a second-rate religious leader. His speeches were sermons, edifying to the faithful, quite empty to the unbeliever. . . . His churches were the Jacobin clubs, his congregations the few who were 'at the height of revolutionary circumstances.' . . . Intolerant of opponents, very sure of his own righteousness, his own prescience, relishing the forms of ritual, neat, precise, ascetic, wrapped always in the soothing warmth of words that evade definition, partially, and therefore fatally, insulated by these words from the outside world, Robespierre in the end exhibited that extreme inconsistency between thought and action which, in men forced to act, is the mark either of the conscious hypocrite or of the religious fanatic. There is no evidence that Robespierre possessed either the intelligence or the courage necessary for such persistent and large-scale hypocrisy."

25. H. G. Wells, *Outline of History,* p. 897: " 'Well,' said the king, 'here you have me!' Also he remarked that he was hungry. At dinner he commended the wine, 'quite excellent wine.' What the queen said is not recorded."

26. A letter was found, from Marie Antoinette to her brother, Leopold II of Austria: "It is not a question only of the safety of France; it is a question of the tranquillity of Europe. . . . It was not a simple revolt against the government of France; it was an insurrection against all established governments. Its principles tended to arouse all nations against all sovereigns" (September 8, 1791).

27. The change in the calendar was as instructive as it was poetic: the months were renamed Vendémiaire, Brumaire, Frimaire, Nivôse, Pluviôse, Ventôse, Germinal, Floréal, Prairial, Messidor, Thermidor, Fructidor—to which the British quickly replied, "Wheezy, Sneezy, Freezy, Slippy, Drippy, Nippy, Showery, Flowery, Bowery, Wheaty, Heaty, Sweety."

28. *The Law of Suspects* (September 17, 1793):

"1. Immediately after the publication of the present decree all the suspect-persons who are in the territory of the Republic and who are still at liberty shall be placed under arrest.

"2. These are accounted suspect-persons: 1st, those who by their conduct, their connections, their remarks or their writings show themselves the partisans of tyranny or federalism and the enemies of liberty; 2d, those who cannot, in the manner prescribed by the decree of March 21st last, justify their means of existence and the performance of their civic duties; 3d, those who have been refused certificates of civism; 4th, public functionaries suspended or removed from their functions by the National Convention or its commissioners and not reinstated, especially those who have been or shall be removed in virtue of the decree of August 14th last; 5th, those of the former nobles, all of the husbands, wives, fathers, mothers, sons or daughters, brothers or sisters, and agents of the Émigrés who have not constantly manifested their attachment to the revolution; 6th, those who have emigrated from France in the interval from July 1, 1789, to the publication of the decree of March 30–April 8, 1792, although they may have returned to France within the period fixed by that decree or earlier."

29. "How we judge the 'second' revolution in France depends entirely on our judgment of the strength and chances in 1792, of a counter-revolt aiming at integral restoration, with an accompanying repression and punishment of those implicated in the subversion of the old order" (Palmer, *The Age of Democratic Revolution*, II, 36).

30. *Decree for Establishing the Worship of the Supreme Being* (May 7, 1794):

    "1. The French people recognize the existence of the Supreme Being and the immortality of the soul.

    "2. They recognize that the worship worthy of the Supreme Being is the practice of the duties of man.

    "3. They place in the first rank of these duties, to detest bad faith and tyranny, to punish tyrants and traitors, to relieve the unfortunate, to respect the weak, to defend the oppressed, to do to others all the good that is possible and not to be unjust to anyone.

    "4. Festivals shall be instituted to remind man of the thought of the Divinity and of the dignity of his being."

31. But not "till it destroyed civil as well as political institutions, manners, customs, laws, and even the mother tongue; till having dashed in pieces the machinery of government, it shook the foundations of society, and seemed anxious to assail even God himself; till it overflowed the frontier and, by dint of method unknown before, by new systems of tactics, by murderous maxims, and 'armed opinions' (to use the language of Pitt), overthrew the landmarks of empires, broke crowns, and crushed subjects, while strange to say, it won them over to its side" (Tocqueville, *Old Regime*, p. 16).

6. *The Enlightenment in Germany: Kant's Transcendental Revolution*

1. For a good history of Germany during this period, see R. R. Palmer and Joel Colton, *A History of the Modern World* (New York: Knopf, 1965), Chapter 10; for a more intellectual but fragmented treatment see Hans Kohn, *The Mind of Germany* (New York: Scribners, 1960).

2. Perhaps *Verklärung*, a confused transfiguration, would be a more accurate title for the Enlightenment in Germany, torn as it was between romanticism, French rationalism, British empiricism, and political anti-Enlightenment reactions.

3. R. R. Palmer, *The World of the French Revolution* (New York: Harper & Row, 1971), p. 236.

4. *The German Ideology*, p. 206. Similarly, Arnold Hauser describes the German bourgeoisie: "These people retired to what they called the level of the 'universally human,' a level above all classes, ranks and groups, made a virtue out of their lack of practical mindedness and called it 'idealism,' let 'inwardness' triumph over the limitations of time and space. Out of their involuntary passivity, they developed an ideal of the idyllic private life, and out of their lack of external freedom, the idea of inward freedom and of the sovereignty of the spirit over common empirical reality." From *A Social History of Art* (New York: Vintage, 1958), Vol. III, p. 106.

5. Leibniz (1646–1716) anticipated the German Enlightenment by well over

a hundred years, but his was an international life and career. He spent several years in Paris, where he knew some of the proto-Enlightenment French philosophers. Much of his career he spent in protracted debate with the two intellectual giants of the British Enlightenment, Newton and Locke. He was, indirectly, the main influence on Kant's overall philosophy via Kant's teacher Christian Wolff, an orthodox Leibnizian. When Kant came to challenge Leibniz, it was by way of compromise with the more empirical elements in the British Enlightenment, particularly after his initial confrontation with the works of Hume.

6. Years later Hegel distinguished between the "subjective idealism" of the British epistemologists ("All that we can know are our own experiences"), the "transcendental idealism" of Kant ("We know the world because we supply its essential categories"), Fichte's "ethical idealism" ("The world is a stage for our moral activities"), and his own "absolute idealism" ("The world is determined both in terms of knowledge and morals by our concepts"). Despite Kant's own radical sympathies, and despite the explicit political philosophies of Fichte and Hegel, politics never plays a central role in any of these idealisms. How different from the "philosophies" of Voltaire and Rousseau!

7. *Reason and Revolution* (Boston: Beacon, 1960), p. 3.

8. For Rousseau, "freedom" came to mean "obedience"—even to the point of "forcing a man to be free" (see Chapter 3, pp. 64–68). It is therefore significant that Rousseau, more than any other French Enlightenment author, had a profound influence on the whole of the German *Aufklärung* and on Kant in particular.

9. Heine, *Germany, Works*, V, 136.

10. Nietzsche, "Untimely Meditations," III, quoted in Walter Kaufmann, *Nietzsche* (New York: Meridian, 1956), p. 88.

11. Ernst Cassirer, in *Rousseau, Kant and Goethe* (Princeton: Princeton University Press, 1970), tells us that Kant's almost empty study contained a single adornment, a portrait of Rousseau. Cassirer also says that Kant's famous daily walks were interrupted only once, when he discovered Rousseau's *Emile* and could not put it down.

12. Both requirements are needed. A principle might apply to all conscious creatures (i.e., be universal), but only *happen* to so apply—in other words, not necessarily; for example, it may be a true principle that all conscious creatures are larger than a cashew nut, but there is nothing necessary about this.

13. *Critique of Pure Reason,* trans. N. Kemp Smith (New York: Macmillan, 1958), B 29. All translations are from this source, hereafter cited as *CPR*. Page numbers are those of the original German texts: *A* for the first edition (1781) and *B* for the second edition (1787); these appear as marginal references in Kemp Smith.

14. See W. H. Walsh on Kant's "Categories" in R. P. Wolff, ed., *Kant* (New York: Doubleday-Anchor, 1967), pp. 67 ff.; and Jonathan Bennett, *Kant's Analytic* (Cambridge: Cambridge University Press, 1966).

15. See John Silber, "The Copernican Revolution in Ethics," in Wolff, pp. 266–90.

16. See Kohn, Chapter 3.

17. *CPR* B xv. Which recalls a Russian proverb: "Philosophy is like pouring from one empty vessel into another."

18. *Prolegomena to Any Future Metaphysics,* trans. L. W. Beck (New York: Bobbs-Merrill, 1956), p. 116. The quote at the head of this section is from p. 67.
19. The word "metaphysics" is ambiguous in Kant: sometimes it means "ultimate principles," sometimes "nonempirical principles," and sometimes only this triad of problems: God, Freedom, and the Immortality of the Soul.
20. This had been attempted half-heartedly by Locke and disastrously by Hume, both of whom nevertheless continued to hold on to their substance. Kant too can be accused of less than a no-holds-barred investigation; only the philosophers who follow him, already turning against the Enlightenment, will carry out this "critique" in earnest.
21. A more complete account of Kant's terminology can be given. Statements that are true by virtue of logic or language are called *analytic;* in such statements, the second concept is "contained in" the first. Thus "a horse is an animal" is analytic because "animal" is part of the meaning of the word "horse." Statements that are not analytic are synthetic: for example, "there are no rabbits in New Zealand" is synthetic, while "a rabbit is a rabbit" is trivially analytic. We have already said that "a priori" means universal and necessary. The contrast to a priori knowledge is empirical knowledge—knowledge that can be gained only through particular experiences or information, and that is not necessary. (Kant sometimes uses the more metaphysical word "contingent" for "not necessary," and the phrase "a posteriori" for "empirical.") Hume's two categories would then be (1) analytic and a priori (that is, logically true and necessary), and (2) synthetic and empirical (that is, not logically true but based on experience and not necessary). Kant's new category of synthetic a priori principles consists of principles that are not logically true yet necessary. There can be no analytic empirical statements, because a statement cannot be true *both* on the basis of logic and experience alone.
22. Kant's own list of categories and corresponding principles is twelve in number—four groups of three each. It is generally agreed that the list is arbitrary and borrowed uncritically from the academic psychologists of the day, but this in no way undermines the persuasiveness of Kant's arguments for the necessity of *some* such set of categories, whether corresponding to his list or not.
23. *Foundations of the Metaphysics of Morals,* trans. L. W. Beck (New York: Bobbs-Merrill, 1953), p. 107.
24. Ogden Nash, *Verses from 1929 On* (New York: Random House, 1959).
25. Kant, a fragment quoted in Cassirer, *Rousseau, Kant, and Goethe,* p. 22.
26. *Critique of Practical Reason,* trans. L. W. Beck (New York: Bobbs-Merrill, 1956). The passages quoted here, however, are from Kant's smaller work, *Foundations of the Metaphysics of Morals* (see note 23).
27. Cf. the fragment quoted by Cassirer: "Newton was the first to discern order and regularity in combination with great simplicity, where before him men had encountered disorder and unrelated diversity. Since Newton the comets follow geometrical orbits. Rousseau was the first to discover beneath the varying forms human nature assumes, the deeply concealed essence of man. . . . After Newton and Rousseau, the ways of God are justified."
28. *Critique of Judgment,* trans. J. C. Meredith (Oxford: Oxford University Press, 1928). The quote at the head of this section is from p. 413.

29. Cf. Voltaire's deism, which accepted this stronger sense of purpose that Kant refuted in his rejection of "the cosmological argument" in *CPR*.
30. See, for example, his reply to Voltaire, in Chapter 3, p. 70.
31. Kant's own view of history was an impetus to this move. See his "History from a Cosmopolitan Point of View," reprinted in Gardner, *Theories of History*, and quoted in our Introduction, p. 7.
32. *Perpetual Peace*, trans. L. W. Beck (New York: Bobbs-Merrill, 1939).
33. Among the more accessible secondary sources for study of Kant, for those with little background, are S. Körner, *Kant* (London: Penguin, 1967), and H. J. Paton, *The Categorical Imperative* (Chicago: University of Chicago Press, 1948). For a modest bibliography, see R. P. Wolff, ed., *Kant*, pp. 409 ff.

7. *The Poetry of Self-Realization: Goethe and His* Faust

1. Most German intellectuals, unlike Kant, did not particularly admire Newton, and even found his cosmology in bad taste.
2. The contrast between Goethe and Kant, here as elsewhere, is more a matter of emphasis than of contradiction. In his third *Critique*, which Goethe greatly admired, Kant too defends the concept of genius as the expression of humanity. He did not apply that concept to his own role, but certainly held an extremely proud and even arrogant view of his own importance. See for example Chapter 14, note 31.
3. Goethe's appreciation of Kant's *Critique of Judgment*, however, specifically included praise for Kant's notion of "teleology," which Goethe used in his own work. Kant's concept of Reason was not wholly static and fixed, but his concept of the understanding and its categories was, and his conception of rational growth was surely overshadowed by his Newtonian arguments.
4. Hamann was not just Kant's contemporary in Königsberg; surprisingly, they were good friends. Despite their obvious disagreements, Kant was even willing to listen to and correspond with Hamann, and some of Kant's very last works show the imprint of these conversations, including a mystical interpretation of the moral law that is wholly foreign to Kant's well-known ethical works.
5. My translations of Goethe's notes, comments, and conversations are taken from *Truth and Poetry*, trans. Rev. A. J. W. Morrison (London: H. G. Bohn, 1848–49); *Conversations and Encounters*, trans. and ed. David Luke and Robert Pick (Chicago: H. Regnery, 1966); and *Criticisms, Reflections and Maxims of Goethe*, trans. W. B. Rönnfeldt (London: Scott, 1897).
6. For example, one of Goethe's more celebrated plays in Germany is a celebration of an ordinary German stumblebum named "Hermann," who is dull, unattractive, uninterestingly hard-working, and routinely moral. The play, *Hermann and Dorothea*, is set during the latter days of the French Revolution, and the moral contrast between dull but peaceful Hermann and radical, exciting Dorothea is anything but subtle.
7. E.g., Walter Kaufmann in his preface to *Faust* (New York: Doubleday, 1961).
8. John Barth in his *End of the Road* asks, "Who is more free, the rebel who

flaunts all authority and must pay for it, or the man who sees that all rules are arbitrary, and so makes its rules his own?" (New York: Doubleday, 1958).

9. Heine, for example, dismissed him: "Goethe has never conceived his 'ideal life' deeply, much less lived it" (*Germany*).

10. Nietzsche too had a change of mind. Having once dismissed Goethe as "the sage of Weimar," he later adopted him as one of his few examples of the *Ubermensch* (a concept that originates in *Faust*). Similarly, Hermann Hesse introduces Goethe as the exemplary "immortal" in his Goethe-esque novel *Steppenwolf*. In fact, Hesse's "magic theater" in that novel is an apt adoption of Goethe's own view of life as a multiplicity of forms which *together* constitute human nature.

11. Schiller tells Goethe that his biography "is a book that greatly helps our culture," to which Goethe in his modest fashion replies, "Those are merely the results from my life, and the particular facts related serve only to confirm a general reflection—a higher truth." But then, as a young man, he had argued that "one should say a great deal in a few words" (*Sorrows of Young Werther*).

12. While there were translations and international exchanges of books (Shakespeare and Voltaire, for example), it was not until the end of the eighteenth century that readers began to *identify* with the literature and characters of other nations. (Except the classics, of course, and the Bible, which were considered part of everyone's home literature.)

13. In his later "Reflections" he complains, "Instead of saying something nice about the book, all of them wanted to know how much of it was true!" (*Werther*, p. 151).

14. On Winckelmann, see Chapter 10, pp. 212–18.

15. Henry Hatfield, *Goethe: A Critical Introduction* (Norfolk, Conn.: J. Laughlin, 1963), p. 72. Hatfield's book is of enormous help in deciphering the many turns of Goethe's life.

16. *Travels in Italy*, in L. Lewisohn, *Goethe* (New York: Farrar, Straus, 1949).

17. *Roman Elegies*, trans. L. R. Lind (Lawrence, Kans.: University of Kansas Press, 1974).

18. *Roman Elegies*. This period of Goethe's life will be discussed in more detail in Chapter 10, pp. 212–18.

19. See quote, Introduction, p. 7.

20. Unlike Rousseau, Goethe did not see society as such as a "corruption" or a hindrance to virtue; like the later Rousseau and most Germans, he viewed it as the context within which the individual could realize his natural potential.

21. *Conversations of Goethe and Eckermann*, trans. John Oxenford (London: J. M. Dent, 1930).

22. The terms are from Schiller, *Naive and Sentimental Poetry*.

23. In Kant the word "aesthetic" means "sensuous," with no particular reference to art. The latter meaning comes from the philosopher Baumgarten (*Aesthetica*, 1750)—a new usage that Kant protested.

24. Schiller, *Letters on Aesthetic Education*, trans. R. Snell (New York: Ungar, 1965).

25. "Gifts of Fortune," in *Poems of Schiller, Complete*, "attempted in English" by Edgar Alfred Bowring (London: J. W. Parker, 1851).

26. "Ode to Joy," in *Poems of Schiller*.

27. *Wallenstein*, trans. C. G. N. Lockhart (Edinburgh: W. Blackwood, 1887).

28. *Letters on Aesthetic Education*, third letter.
29. Snell lists no fewer than eight different meanings of "nature" in one letter alone, in his introduction to the Ungar edition.
30. *Genealogy of Morals*, trans. Walter Kaufmann (New York: Random House, 1966), III, 4.
31. *Faust*, I, iv. Most of the passages cited are from the Walter Kaufmann translation, but I have also benefited from Harry Levine, "Faust: Still Striving and Struggling," *New York Review of Books* (November 25, 1976); and Randall Jarrell, *Faust*, Parts I and II.
32. Hatfield, *Goethe*, p. 143.
33. Faust can be read as a dramatic and wildly imaginative Rousseauan *Confessions;* but Goethe, unlike Rousseau, knows how to laugh at himself, after a fashion. Rousseau, however, might well have approved of Goethe's "daemon" theory: what would be more convenient than to say "the devil made me do it" after every transgression?

8. *"The Finest Man since Caesar": Napoleon and Revolutionary Despotism*

1. Felix Markham, in *Napoleon and the Awakening of Europe* (London: English University Press, 1954), gives a good brief account of Napoleon's "liberation" movements throughout Europe and the way they turned against him. He argues that Napoleon failed to see the danger of nationalism in Germany, Spain, and elsewhere precisely because he was so much a man of the Enlightenment, assumed the cosmopolitan nature of the Revolution, and failed to appreciate the extent to which French internationalism and local nationalism did not always seek the same ends (p. 116 et passim).
2. This is not to say that Napoleon used the principles of Enlightenment cynically and merely as propaganda tools; he demonstrably believed in them at least to some extent. That is, he accepted the general spirit of reform and toleration, but of "freedom" he often had little to say. But then again, one finds in his letters an illiberal sprinkling of ideological manipulation, such as his comment on German liberation: "In Germany the common people want to be protected against the great ones. . . . I desire nothing from our Compact but food and money, and it is the great ones, not the common people, who can supply me with those. I let the great ones alone and the others will have to manage the best they can." Quoted by A. Sorel in Pieter Geyl, ed., *Napoleon: For and Against* (New Haven: Yale University Press, 1945), p. 262.
3. Quoted in Albert Carr, *Napoleon Speaks* (New York: Viking, 1941), p. 370.
4. *War and Peace*, trans. Ann Dunnigan (New York: New American Library, 1968), especially pp. 1412 ff.
5. *A Life of Napoleon* (London: Rodale Press, 1956), p. 181. Stendhal (Henri Beyle) wrote his *Life* while Napoleon was still alive, but he revised it several times, and it was not in fact published until after the author's death. The representation of Napoleonic heroism became a persistent theme in Stendhal's novels: for example, the liberation of Italy that forms the background for *The Charterhouse of Parma*, and the clandestine worship of the Emperor by young Julien Sorel in *The Red and the Black*. The same ro-

mantic nostalgia can be found in Alexander Dumas's *Napoleon* (New York: Putnam's, 1894); his *Count of Monte Cristo* begins with an ill-fated visit to the Emperor in exile at Elba. If these two accounts are sometimes embarrassingly sympathetic, they nevertheless balance the slanderous abuse which Stendhal describes in France after Napoleon's fall (p. 7).

6. It is not coincidental that the "great man" phenomenon appeared simultaneously in other realms of life: David became the unchallenged dictator of French art following the Revolution; in Austria, Beethoven rose to equal pre-eminence in music; and in Prussia, Hegel established himself as the "absolute" philosopher following the reign of Kant, who had held that status for years after his death. Goethe, of course, had already established himself as the master of German letters.

7. Sidney Hook, *The Hero in History* (Boston: Beacon, 1943), discusses the general problem of the "great man" phenomenon, especially in Chapter 3 and his well-known section on "The Eventful Man and the Event-Making Man" (pp. 151–83). Hegel's views, which are summarized in the introduction to his lectures on the *Philosophy of History*, are discussed by Hook in some detail (Chapter 4). In many ways Hook provides the philosophical groundwork of the view argued by Tolstoy in *War and Peace*. This connection is brilliantly examined in Isaiah Berlin's *The Hedgehog and the Fox* (New York: Simon and Schuster, 1953).

8. Tolstoy makes a major point about the *illusion* of control, but again this leaves open (or out) the problem of representation. One who has the appearance of representation may, within limits, act on behalf of everyone else, and if that is not power, one would be hard pressed to provide a better instance.

9. Albert Guerard, *Napoleon I* (New York: Knopf, 1956). For an account of Napoleon's years in exile, see Gil Martineau, *Napoleon's St. Helena*, trans. F. Partridge (London: Rand McNally, 1969). Napoleon's letters and documents are found in many collections in English; I have used John Howard, trans. and ed., *Letters and Documents of Napoleon* (New York: Oxford University Press, 1961); also Albert Carr, *Napoleon Speaks*. On Napoleon's life and personality, I have used John Holland Rose, *The Life of Napoleon*, 2 vols. (New York: Macmillan, 1902); *The Personality of Napoleon* (New York: Putnam's, 1912); Andre Castelot, *Napoleon* (New York: Harper & Row, 1967); and, especially, Herbert Butterfield's invaluable *Napoleon* (New York: Collier, 1962).

10. On Napoleon's military and political career, see J. M. Thompson, *Napoleon Bonaparte: His Rise and Fall* (Oxford: Blackwell, 1958), and Castelot, *Napoleon*. A good short treatment is Felix Markham, *Napoleon*.

11. Anthony Burgess has created a modern masterpiece of this scene: *Napoleon Symphony* (New York: Knopf, 1974).

12. Palmer and Cotton, *A History of the Modern World* (New York: Knopf, 1965), p. 410.

9. *The Good, the Beautiful, and the Ugly: David and Goya*

1. This was even truer, however, of the new Academy under David's direction *after* the Revolution. More interesting still, but beyond the scope of our study, was the later politics of "art for art's sake," which despite its explicit

rejection of social relevance is extremely revealing about a concept of society in which at least one essential activity is self-consciously and self-righteously alienated from the rest.

2. A classic treatment of art in its social context is Arnold Hauser's *Social History of Art* (New York: Vintage, 1951), especially Vol. III (including rococo, classicism, and nineteenth-century art). It is a mode of treatment not in favor with many art historians, not because of its Marxist bias but its extrinsic ideological analyses. Even Sir Herbert Read, an art critic with unusual social concern, makes what for us must be the worst error when, in *Goya in the Democratic Tradition* (New York: Schocken, 1968), he objects to Klingender's treatment of Goya: "Such achievements, though 'fused in the crucible of life,' have little or no relevance to an artist's inner consciousness, a stage illuminated from the front by lights reflected from 'the clash of material forces,' but receding in the background into the darkness of unconscious motives and archetypal myths" (p. xi). The inadequate dichotomy between "material forces" and the "unconscious motives" of the artist, which leads Klingender to overemphasize the first and Sir Herbert to overemphasize the second, must be filled in with the conceptual linkage between the individual artist and his social context—that is, with ideology. And an ideology is much more, as we have continually argued, than merely an attitude toward social conditions or one caused by them.

3. *Critique of Judgment,* trans. J. C. Meredith (Oxford: Oxford University Press, 1952), para. 59.

4. On Poussin, see Anthony Blunt, *Nicolas Poussin* (New York: Bollingen/Pantheon, 1967), and Walter Friedlander, *Nicolas Poussin: A New Approach* (New York: Abrams, 1966).

5. See also André Malraux's lyrical tribute to Goya in his *Saturn: An Essay on Goya* (New York: Phaidon, 1957), which emphasizes Goya's "modernism" and "romanticism" for its freedom of expression and fantasy, at the expense of reality. He too sees Goya's art as primarily a reaction against and a rejection of his "circumstances," as protosurrealism with a penchant for fantasy and the "Absurd." Despite the dubiousness of these distinctions, Malraux surely gives us the most readable treatment. For a good but fair criticism, see Nigel Glendinning, *Goya and His Critics* (New Haven: Yale University Press, 1977). For an interpretation much more supportive of my own, see Sylvia Horwitz, *Francisco Goya: Painter of Kings and Demons* (New York: Harper & Row, 1974).

6. "Divina Razó—No dejes ninguno." Drawing title no. 122, Prado Museum, Madrid.

7. David was sent to Boucher as a student, who in turn introduced him to Vien, one of the leading classical painters in Paris. Goya was influenced most powerfully by Tiepolo, in the flamboyant rococo style, but actually studied with Anton Raphael Mengs, an influential German classicist and good friend of Johann Winckelmann (see Chapter 10).

8. John Canaday, *Mainstreams of Modern Art* (New York: Holt, Rinehart and Winston, 1959); also Walter Friedlander, *David to Delacroix* (Cambridge, Mass.: Harvard University Press, 1952); Malraux, *Saturn.*

9. *Letters on Aesthetic Education,* trans. Reginald Snell (New York: Ungar, 1965).

10. On Boucher, see C. M. Bearne, *A Court Painter and His Circle* (New York: McBride, Nast, 1914). On Fragonard, see G. Wildenstein, *Paintings of Fragonard* (London: Phaidon, 1960).

11. An excellent account of the overall artistic temperament of the period is P. Schneider, *The World of Watteau* (New York: Time-Life, 1967).
12. See Hauser, Vol. III, especially Chapters 1 and 5.
13. See Friedlander, *David to Delacroix*, p. 9. Also Robert Rosenblum, *The International Style of 1800* (New York: Garland, 1976), note 24.
14. Both David and Goya went to Rome, but the differences are revealing. David applied for a prestigious *Prix de Rome* and was so disappointed when he failed to win twice that he attempted to starve himself to death. He finally won the prize in 1774 and it changed his life. Goya, on the other hand, traveled to Italy as a young *majo,* bullfighting and carousing, and the classical wonders of antiquity seemed not to affect him in the slightest.
15. See Friedlander, *David to Delacroix*, p. 12. Having advised young David to study under Vien, "of course Boucher added that Vien's art was perhaps a little cold, and that should David find the atelier down there too boring, he had only to drop in from time to time and he would make good Vien's shortcomings, *en vous apprenant à mettre de la chaleur et casser un bras avec grâce.* . . . He learned quite a bit from Boucher, as his early works show, and he was never to become an outspoken anticolorist."
16. On "nature" and "naturalism" in Greuze, see Friedlander, *David to Delacroix*, p. 9; and Anita Brookner, *Greuze* (New York: Graphics Society, 1972), Chapter 1.
17. But it has often been said that Greuze used rococo eroticism even as he criticized it. Brookner comments that some of his paintings of "adolescent girls on the verge of orgasm" seem "tawdry, if not obscene" (p. 154).
18. This term comes from Rosenblum, *International Style.* Brookner adds "shabby" and "muddled," as well as "tawdry" and "obscene" (*Greuze,* p. 155).
19. Brookner is particularly good in emphasizing the cult of *sensibilité,* although her ideological characterizations are insufficient for the period as a whole ("an age of reason and an age of emotion," for example). She insists throughout that his is "middle or lower class art," that he ignores in fact the true lessons of classic (i.e., Renaissance) Italian painting, and that "he is as representative of the 18th Century in France as the art of Boucher and Fragonard" (*Greuze,* pp. 37–38).
20. Cf. Malraux, *Saturn,* who also depicts Goya as in some sense primarily a "religious" artist.
21. D. L. Dowd, *Pageant Master of the Republic* (New York: Arno, 1948), p. 22.
22. Ironically, Friedlander uses this false dichotomy to replace what he considers the falser dichotomy of "classic" and "romantic" (see Chapter 13): "Two main currents appear in French painting after the sixteenth century: the rational and the irrational. The first is apt to be moral and didactic; the second is free of such ethical tendencies . . ." (p. 1). "Though the discussions were apparently concerned with the technical and the visual— drawing versus color, calm versus movement . . . the real battle was between discipline and morality on one side and amoral slackening of rules and subjective irrationality on the other" (p. 4). See also R. Rosenblum, *Transformations in Late Eighteenth-Century Art* (Princeton: Princeton University Press, 1967).
23. In Elizabeth Holt, ed., *From the Classicists to the Impressionists,* Vol. III

of *A Documentary History of Art* (New York: Doubleday, 1966), pp. 4 ff., Catalogue of the Salon, year VIII.

24. The phrase is from M. W. Brown, *The Painting of the French Revolution* (New York: Critics Group, 1938), p. 17. Quoted in Dowd, *Pageant Master*, p. 4: "Philosophy was the fire in which art was forged as a sword of the revolution."

25. David's revolutionary world was a distinctively masculine world; it is only men who have heroic roles. The women, when there are women, represent the unheroic and sentimental. The wives and daughters of Brutus cry in the corner while he sits stoically in the forward shadows. The wives and sisters of the Horatii cry in another corner as their husbands take the oath of heroism. It is therefore worth noting that his later work becomes more "feminine" not only in style but in theme. The Sabine women, for example, dominate the action of his painting of 1799, and the flat, more curvaceous drawing becomes far more appropriate to the softness of David's portraits than to the hard, marble surfaces of his early heroes' muscles. See Rosenblum, *International Style*, p. 81.

26. Livy, writing eighteen hundred years before, used the same story to the same end in Rome itself.

27. See André Maurois's *J. L. David* (Paris: Dimanche, 1948); also Edmund Lucie-Smith, *French Painting* (London: Thames and Hudson, 1971), Chapter 8.

28. Dowd, *Pageant Master*, p. 18.

29. Quoted in Friedlander, *David to Delacroix*, p. 19.

30. F. Klingender, *Goya in the Democratic Tradition* (New York: Schocken, 1968).

31. Klingender, pp. 13 f. and 17 f. Cf. Horwitz, p. 7: "They hoped Ferdinand IV would bring better times, but in the same way they hoped for good weather." And the contemporary philosopher de Azara, representing the spirit of Voltaire and Rousseau in Spain: "Only Spain sleeps, or better yet, is dead."

32. The Aragon oath of allegiance to the king went, "We who are as good as you swear to you who are no better than we, to accept you as our king, provided you observe all our liberties and laws, but if not, not." A social contract, yes, but hardly a universal and "democratic" one. Quoted in Klingender, p. 18.

33. Goya's well-known unmatched pair of portraits, one of Godoy—smug, comfortable, banal, dangerous—and the other of his wife—timid, wretched, silently suffering—is illustrative. See Pierre Gassier and Juliet Wilson, *Goya: His Life and Work* (London: Thames and Hudson, 1971). And then there is the rightly famous royal family portrait that Gautier later described as "the corner baker and his wife after they won the lottery" (Horwitz, *Francisco Goya*, p. 118).

34. The Romans kidnapped the Sabine women, married them, had families by them. The Sabines retaliated, but in the midst of the battle, the women themselves forced a halt to the mutual slaughter. Loosely modeled after one of a pair by Poussin, David's painting depicts the women's intervention.

35. Rosenblum, *International Style*, pp. 135 ff., summarizes the transformation to the "archaic" as "purity of outline and two dimensional organization." The *Horatii*, David complained, was "too realistic" (p. 136). The *Sabines* is even "antirealism," devoid of the staged spatial framework of the

Horatii, without the "sweeping" energy of will" (p. 74) of the earlier painting and far more intellectual and abstract; style had replaced the "manifesto" of the *Horatii*.

36. *Los Caprichos* (New York: Dover, 1970).
37. Charles Baudelaire, *The Salon of 1846*, reprinted in part in Holt, *From the Classicists to the Impressionists*, p. 171.
38. See F. Markham, *Napoleon and the Awakening of Europe* (London: English University Press, 1954), pp. 115 ff. Klingender describes this as the democratic uprising, and Goya's depiction of it as his dedication to radicalism. It was in fact a popular guerrilla war—a "war of monks," as Napoleon sneeringly described it. But it was also a battle for the corrupt and far-from-democratic Ferdinand, as the symbol of Spain versus foreign intrusions—a patriotic battle, but the very opposite of a democratic struggle. Cf. Horwitz, *Francisco Goya*, pp. 137 f.
39. Goya, *The Disasters of War* (New York: Dover, 1968).
40. The literary analogue would certainly be Tolstoy's description of the Battle of Austerlitz in *War and Peace*.

10. *The Romance of Classicism: The Phantom of the Ancients*

1. For an extensive treatment of these themes, see Jon D. Solomon, *The Ancient World in the Cinema* (Cranbury, N.J.: A. S. Barnes, 1978).
2. See especially E. Butler, *The Tyranny of Greece over Germany* (Boston: Beacon, 1958).
3. In France the fantasy turned on reasonably concrete political and social hopes and expectations; in Germany the fantasies tend rather to reflect despair and hopelessness, or at least the absence of hope. Kant applauded the French Revolution, but certainly expected no repetition of it in East Prussia.
4. Both Goethe and Winckelmann visited Rome. Winckelmann was killed before he reached Greece; Goethe never even tried.
5. For an interesting if sometimes tedious modern rehearsal of these same models, see Robert Pirsig, *Zen and the Art of Motorcycle Maintenance* (New York: Morrow, 1974).
6. These differences are spelled out extensively in Butler, *Tyranny*.
7. See Paul Woodruff, "Rousseau, Molière, and the Ethics of Laughter," *Philosophy and Literature*, Vol. 1 (Fall 1977), pp. 325–36.
8. *Faust*, Part II, is translated only in part by Walter Kaufmann (New York: Doubleday, 1961) and by Louis MacNeice (Oxford: Oxford University Press, 1960).
9. See Butler, *Tyranny*.
10. On Gottsched and the Storm and Stress poets, see Henri Braunschweig, *Enlightenment and Romanticism in Eighteenth Century Prussia*, trans. F. Jellinek (Chicago: University of Chicago Press, 1974).
11. See Butler, *Tyranny*.
12. All these quotations are from the Kaufmann translation.
13. Particularly Nietzsche, *Birth of Tragedy*.
14. Winckelmann, quoted in Butler, *Tyranny*.
15. Winckelmann, quoted in Butler, *Tyranny*.

16. Goethe's sexual mythology of the Greeks and Romans might be profitably compared with the more recent sexual fantasies of German scholars regarding their less inhibited contemporaries—for example, Wilhelm Reich's lusty fantasies concerning South Sea islanders at the beginning of this century.
17. Hölderlin, *Hyperion*, trans. W. Trask (New York: Ungar, 1965).

11. *The Universal in Action: G. W. F. Hegel*

1. G. W. F. Hegel, *The Philosophy of Right*, trans. Sir Malcolm Knox, (Oxford: Oxford University Press, 1967), p. 13. The reference to "grey on grey" (see also the lead quote in our Preface) is from Goethe's *Faust*, I, iv: "Grey are all theories."
2. G. W. F. Hegel, *The Phenomenology of Mind*, trans. J. B. Baillie (New York: Harper & Row, 1966), cited hereafter as *Phenomenology*. Another translation is *The Phenomenology of Spirit*, trans. A. V. Miller (Oxford: Oxford University Press, 1977). All quotes are from Baillie.
3. Part III, "Philosophy of Spirit," para. 377; trans. W. Wallace (Oxford: Clarendon, 1971), p. 1.
4. See J. N. Findlay, *Hegel: A Reexamination* (Oxford: Oxford University Press, 1977), especially Chapter 2; and Charles Taylor, *Hegel* (Cambridge: Cambridge University Press, 1976), especially Chapter 3.
5. See Herbert Marcuse, *Reason and Revolution* (Boston: Beacon, 1960); George Armstrong Kelly, *Idealism, Politics and History* (Cambridge: Cambridge University Press, 1969); and Shlomo Avineri, *Hegel's Theory of the Modern State* (Cambridge: Cambridge University Press, 1973).
6. For a discussion of Hegel's alleged conservatism versus Enlightenment liberalism, see Marcuse and Avineri respectively. Also see Raymond Plant, *Hegel* (Bloomington, Ind.: Indiana University Press, 1969).
7. Hegel compared himself to the Dutch philosopher Spinoza in this regard, but protects himself against charges of atheism by emphasizing the "spiritual" side of the Absolute.
8. G. W. F. Hegel, *Philosophy of History*, Introduction, translated by R. S. Hartman as *Reason in History* (New York: Bobbs-Merrill, 1953), p. 1. On the notion "universal history," see also Burleigh Wilkins, *Hegel's Philosophy of History* (Ithaca, N.Y.: Cornell University Press, 1974), and George D. O'Brien, *Hegel on Reason and History* (Chicago: University of Chicago Press, 1975).
9. Max Horkheimer and Theodor Adorno, *The Dialectics of Enlightenment*, Chapter 1.
10. See Charles Taylor's moving plea for a renewed Hegelianism in his *Hegel*. Also, E. Gellner's review of Taylor in *Encounter* (1976).
11. From Walter Kaufmann, *Hegel: A Reinterpretation; Texts and Commentary* (New York: Doubleday, 1965), p. 301. Kaufmann's translations of some of Hegel's letters are the most accessible in English, and I have used them here. His book also provides excellent biographical material.
12. See Kaufmann for a good discussion of this.
13. H. S. Harris, *Hegel's Development: Towards the Sunlight* (Oxford: Oxford University Press, 1972). This is a remarkably complete account of Hegel's education and early influences, particularly his years at the seminary with

Schelling and Hölderlin. It was Hölderlin who taught Hegel "the fluidity of the concept" and "the awareness of being at one with all that lives," and Schelling who provided Hegel with the skeleton of his system.

14. See Harris and Kaufmann for contrasting views of Hegel's early attitudes toward politics and religion.

15. *Hegel's Early Theological Writings,* trans. Sir Malcolm Knox (Philadelphia: University of Pennsylvania Press, 1961), p. 58.

16. Ironically, this is just the view argued by Kierkegaard *against* Hegel a half century later (see Chapter 16).

17. Aristotle's *Nichomachean Ethics* would be the beginnings of a model, rather than Kant's *Critique of Practical Reason.*

18. I have defended this unorthodox view at length in "The Secret Hegel (and Kierkegaard's Complaint)," *Philosophical Forum* (1979).

19. Paul Tillich has argued that Hegel's whole philosophy is based upon the attempt to project love into a metaphysical principle. See his *Love, Power, and Justice* (New York: Oxford University Press, 1954).

20. Quoted in Kaufmann, *Hegel,* pp. 41–42.

21. In *Reason and Revolution,* Marcuse takes the unusual view that these early essays are *primarily* motivated by political and social interests.

22. In Kaufmann, *Hegel,* p. 301.

23. In Kaufmann, *Hegel,* p. 303.

24. See, however, Harris, *Hegel's Development,* for the long preliminaries to this decision.

25. "The Difference between the Systems of Fichte and Schelling," trans. W. Cerf and H. S. Harris (New York: SUNY Press, 1976).

26. Fichte, *Wissenschaftlehre* (*Science of Knowledge*), trans. Peter Heath and John Lachs (New York: Appleton-Century-Crofts, 1970).

27. *Logic* (Part I of the *Encyclopedia*), trans. William Wallace (Oxford: Clarendon, 1975), p. 58.

28. Letter of October 13, 1806, in Jena.

29. George Santayana, in *The Ego in German Philosophy,* exaggerates the case against Germany, perhaps, but the Ego plays a central role throughout the whole of bourgeois ideology. Thus Marx rightly takes cosmic egomania to be the core of "the German (bourgeois) ideology."

30. The worst offender is Karl Popper, in *The Open Society and Its Enemies,* a book that is mentioned in connection with Hegel mainly to be refuted. See, for example, Walter Kaufmann's "The Hegel Myth and Its Method" in *From Shakespeare to Existentialism* (New York: Doubleday, 1960).

31. See Avineri, *Hegel's Theory,* for the strong statement of Hegel's liberalism.

32. *Philosophy of Right,* p. 258.

33. The difference with Rousseau here is revealing: both philosophers accept the family as the basic model for the ideal society, but Hegel wholly rejects Rousseau's supposition that members of the family are significant and autonomous independently of the family. And it is worth noting that neither philosopher retains the "naturalness" of the family as the structure of society itself.

34. See Marcuse, *Reason and Revolution,* especially pp. 183 ff.

35. For example, J. M. McTaggart, *Studies in the Hegelian Dialectic* (New York: Russell & Russell, 1964). See my reply in "The Secret of Hegel (and Kierkegaard's Complaint)," *Philosophical Forum* (1979).

36. *Science of Logic,* trans A. V. Miller (Atlantic Highlands, N.J.: Humanities, 1969). Dieter Heinrich of the University of Heidelberg has defended the

claim that, in fact, the preliminary ideas of the *Logic* were antecedent to the *Phenomenology* (*Hegel in Context*).

12. *The Highest Wisdom, the Purest Speech: Beethoven*

1. It was the philosopher Schopenhauer (Chapter 14) from whom Wagner borrowed the phrase, "he speaks with the highest wisdom in a tongue his reason does not understand." Hegel ranked music among the lower arts precisely because of its inarticulateness, the same reason the romantics, including Schopenhauer, considered it to be the highest of the arts.
2. See J. W. F. Sullivan, *Beethoven: His Spiritual Development* (New York: Vintage, 1944). My discussion in this chapter has been heavily influenced —even "inspired"—by Sullivan's *Beethoven*. I have tried to avoid technical discussions of the music, but have benefited enormously from Charles Rosen, *The Classical Style* (New York: Viking, 1971), and its brilliant analysis of the music referred to in this chapter. After the final draft of this chapter was finished, Maynard Solomon's *Beethoven* (New York: Schirmer, 1977) appeared, which I also recommend, particularly regarding the connections between Beethoven's music and ideology.
3. For a good biography from original sources, see L. Nohl, *Life of Beethoven*, trans. J. Lalor (Chicago: McClurg, 1902). Also Emile Ludwig's *Beethoven: Life of a Conqueror*, trans. George Stewart McManus (New York: Putnam's, 1943) and A. W. Thayer, *Life of Beethoven*, 2 vols. (Princeton: Princeton University Press, 1964). For a different viewpoint, see D. F. Tovey, *Beethoven* (London: Oxford University Press, 1945).
4. Sullivan, *Beethoven*, especially pp. 79 ff.
5. For a good argument against the notion of Beethoven's bourgeois ideology, see Maynard Solomon, "Beethoven, Sonata and Utopia," *Telos*, Vol. 6 (Fall 1971), and the reply by this author and Maynard Solomon's rebuttal in *Telos*, Vol. 7 (Winter 1972).
6. Donald J. Grout, *A History of Western Music* (New York: Norton, 1973).
7. Rousseau also approved pure sentimentality in music, the way it dispensed with convention and was more "human." Schopenhauer and Nietzsche also praised music as the highest of arts—against Hegel—because of its inarticulate expression of "will."
8. Maynard Solomon, *Telos*.
9. Maynard Solomon, *Telos*, especially pp. 41 ff.
10. In 1799 Beethoven wrote two letters to Hummell: first he wrote, "You are a false dog . . . go to Hell." Days later, "You are a good friend."
11. Leonard Bernstein has illustrated this in his discussion of the Fifth Symphony in his Charles Eliot Norton Lectures at Harvard, published by the Harvard University Press in 1976. For a more classical discussion, see Romaine Rolland, *Beethoven, the Creator*, trans. E. Newman (New York: Dover, 1929).
12. Quoted in full in Sullivan, pp. 73–77. See also pp. 109 ff. and George R. Marek, *Beethoven* (New York: Funk & Wagnalls, 1969), pp. 325 ff.
13. For an excellent, not too technical companion for this and Beethoven's other works, see D. Arnold and N. Fortune, eds., *The Beethoven Companion* (London: Faber & Faber, 1971).
14. Denis Matthews, *Beethoven Piano Sonatas* (Seattle: University of Washington Press, 1967), p. 48.

15. Stravinsky, however, considered it a "failure": *Dialogues and a Diary* (with Robert Craft) (New York: Doubleday, 1963), pp. 112 f.
16. P. Radcliffe, *Beethoven's String Quartets* (New York: Dutton, 1968), especially pp. 109 ff.
17. Radcliffe, p. 174.

13. *The Classic/Romanticism Game: Ingres and Delacroix*

1. *Critique of Judgment,* trans. J. C. Meredith (London: Oxford University Press, 1952).
2. Vien and Boucher had been friends. David made "correctness" in art a life-and-death affair; his absolutism is behind the antagonism between Ingres and Delacroix as well. Walter Friedlander, in his *David to Delacroix* (Cambridge, Mass.: Harvard University Press, 1952), argues that Delacroix emerges as a champion of the "high baroque," and that his conflict with Ingres is a resurrection of the seventeenth-century conflict between Poussin and Rubens (p. 106). But this ignores the ideological impotence of classicism under Poussin, as well as the violent hostilities that marked the nineteenth-century battles.
3. Honoré Daumier's cartoon "The Wars of the Brush" summarizes the skeptical attitude of the times.
4. Robert Rosenblum, *Transformations in Late 18th Century Art* (Princeton: Princeton University Press, 1967).
5. Friedlander, *David to Delacroix.*
6. Ingres's "doctrine" consists of notes from his students, reprinted in part in Elizabeth Holt, *Classicism to Impressionism,* Vol. III of *A Documentary History of Art* (New York: Doubleday-Anchor, 1966), p. 34. Cited hereafter as Holt.
7. *Journals,* trans. and ed. Walter Pach (New York: Viking, 1972). One must, however, keep in mind the warning that Delacroix himself gives us at the beginning of his entries: "If a man of talent would set down his thoughts on the arts, let him express them as they occur to him; let him not fear to contradict himself; there will be more fruit for his harvest amid the profusion of his ideas, even if contradictory, than in the skein of a work which has been combed, squeezed, and cut up, for the sake of concentrating on its form." Thus we should not work too hard to square his medieval fictional fantasies, for example, with his insistence, "I paint what I see."
8. Robert Rosenblum, *The International Style of 1800* (New York: Garland, 1976).
9. F. Mather, *Western Painting since the Renaissance* (New York: Cooper, 1939).
10. On Antoine (Baron) Gros, see, e.g., Chapter 2 of John Canaday, *Mainstreams of Modern Art* (New York: Holt, Rinehart and Winston, 1959), and William Vaughan, *Romantic Art* (New York: Oxford University Press, 1978).
11. Cf. Tom Wolfe's *The Painted Word* (New York: Farrar, Straus & Giroux, 1976), which argues that modern art is largely an illustration of critical theory, rather than theory's subject matter.

12. Baudelaire was one of the first champions of Delacroix's art and romantic painting in general. See Holt.
13. The "modernist" term of praise continues, as for example in Robert Motherwell's introduction to Delacroix's *Journals* (pp. 7–8): "*l'art moderne,* an art made by self-chosen individuals rather than the tribal artists of the past."
14. Delacroix makes repeated references to Rousseau in his *Journals,* but even more to Voltaire. Just as Delacroix and Ingres force us to have serious doubts about their "classic/romanticism" antagonism, so the usual references to Rousseau as the originator of romanticism, rather than the Enlightenment and bourgeois ideology as a whole, must give us pause.
15. See Tom Prideaux's enjoyable book *The World of Delacroix* (New York: Time-Life, 1966), pp. 17 ff.
16. On Ingres and Raphael, see especially Robert Rosenblum, *Ingres* (New York: Abrams, 1968); also Walter Pach, *Ingres* (New York: Hacker, 1939).
17. See Prideaux, *Delacroix,* pp. 101–20, and the rich illustrations in René Huyghe's *Delacroix,* trans. Jonathan Griffin (New York: Abrams, 1963), and *Delacroix au Maroc* (Rabat: Mission Universitaire et Culturelle Française, 1963). See too *Delacroix* (Paris: Flammarion, 1975/Milan: Rizzoli, 1972).
18. "From the start, the fighting horses stood up and fought with a fierceness which made me tremble . . . but it was really admirable for a painting" (*Journals*).
19. See Delacroix's *Jacob Wrestling with the Angel.*
20. Prideaux, *Delacroix,* pp. 188–89.
21. One set of categories that might be systematically adopted for a relevant ideological analysis is in H. Wölfflin, *Principles of Art History,* trans. M. D. Hottinger (New York: Dover, 1946). For example, "the linear vs. the painterly," "plane vs. recession," "closed vs. open" space, "multiplicity vs. unity," "clear vs. unclear," "imitative vs. decorative" (pp. 14 f.). The underlying assumption, with which we must wholly agree, is that there is no such thing as "mere" representation in painting. *Style,* the term so overused by the classicists, is utterly inseparable from representation.
22. Both portraits are reproduced, with a photograph of Paganini, in Prideaux, pp. 136–37.
23. The portraits are in Prideaux, *Delacroix,* pp. 138–39. Originally they were one, but the double portrait was cut in half.
24. "His pale blue citron, luminously asleep against that patch of dramatic violet, somber blue, blood red . . . terrible emerald, a regular metaphysical philosophy of color." So remarked Vincent van Gogh, looking at *Chios;* quoted in *Van Gogh,* Museum of Modern Art show, 1973.
25. *Sardanapalus* is in the Louvre, and is reproduced in Prideaux, p. 76. An excellent analysis of the painting and its sources and studies is Jack J. Spector, *Delacroix: The Death of Sardanapalus* (New York: Viking, 1974).
26. The relation of English (and German) romanticism to the French is a matter of considerable disagreement. It is often said, and correctly, that French romanticism was a relatively late movement, borrowing heavily from the English in particular. English romanticism, however, is temperamentally a very different movement, and one would have trouble making an ideological match of any plausibility between Delacroix and, for example, Constable, who influenced his use of color considerably. English

romanticism—technical innovations and colorism aside—was far more defined by its rural naturalism than the violence and emotion of the French movement. See Robert Rosenblum, *The Northern Romantic Tradition* (New York: Harper & Row, 1975), and Hubert Schrade, *German Romantic Painting* (New York: Abrams, 1967).

27. For Ingres's *Turkish Bath*, see Rosenblum, *Ingres*, p. 171. One version of Delacroix's *Lion Hunt* is in the Art Institute of Chicago; it is reproduced in Prideaux, pp. 182–83.

28. Kant, *Foundations of the Metaphysics of Morals*, Chapter 2. Hegel, *Reason in History*, trans. R. S. Hartman (New York: Bobbs-Merrill, 1953).

29. A brief comparison of Constable and Delacroix is in Prideaux, pp. 54–55, with a (too small) reproduction of the former's *Hay Wain*, which was displayed in Paris in the Salon of 1824. On Constable, see Basil Taylor, *Constable* (London: Phaidon, 1973), and Karl Kroeber, *Romantic Landscape Vision* (Madison: University of Wisconsin Press, 1975), on Wordsworth and Constable.

30. See Rosenblum on *Turkish Bath*, *Ingres*, pp. 169–72. One might argue, however, that what Ingres proves is precisely the *falseness* of geometry, at least where human form is concerned.

31. The distinction between beauty and the sublime is best known from Kant's *Critique of Judgment* and from Edmund Burke's *Inquiry into the Origin of Our Ideas of the Sublime and Beautiful* (Notre Dame, Ind.: University of Notre Dame Press, 1968).

32. "It is in my opinion, at least, a very dry work, and what is more, a patchwork of borrowing from the Italian masters. The Madonna is doubtlessly beautiful, but it is a sort of *material* beauty, which excludes the impression of divinity." Stendhal on Ingres's *Vow of Louis XIII*, in the Salon of 1824. Reprinted in Holt, p. 45.

14. *Dull Times: The Romantic Reaction*

1. Schopenhauer told an already bored world that nothing is less moving than an idea "whose time has already come." The once revolutionary convictions of the Enlightenment in France had become the platitudes of an empty way of life. See especially F. Artz, *Reaction and Revolution, 1814–1832* (New York: Harper, 1934). In Germany the Enlightenment did not so much fail as become perverted; if Frederick the Great could pretend to be the champion of Enlightenment, then national liberation must surely lie elsewhere. In fact, the Storm and Stress movement in poetry claimed recognition as the true expression of the new bourgeois ambitions. Accordingly, "Old Fritz" quashed the movement—ironically, in terms of "Enlightenment"—defending his own interests in internationalism against the local interests of his citizens.

2. *The Red and the Black*, trans. Lloyd C. Parks (New York: Signet, 1970). Stendhal rejected the name "romantic," despite the fact that he was the most articulate and insightful of the new critics, and the best possible example in France of the continuity between Enlightenment criticism and romantic frustration. But this rejection of a name is itself a significant ideological symbol of the bourgeois insistence on individual representation and uniqueness. One sees it again when Albert Camus refuses to call him-

self an "existentialist" (because of the identity with Sartre), or more recently when Michel Foucault accused his critics of "idiocy" for aligning him with the structuralism of Lévi-Strauss.

3. Max Horkheimer and Theodor Adorno, in *The Dialectics of Enlightenment* (New York: Seabury, 1972), Chapter 1, argue, from an embarrassingly romantic point of view, that this self-destruction is inherent in the very conception of Enlightenment itself. This is, however, to wrench its ideals out of their historical context, and to confuse the self-destructive potential of a movement with its vicissitudes in a very special set of conditions.

4. Charles Nodier, from *A Report on Byron's Vampire*, reprinted in H. E. Hugo, *The Romantic Reader* (New York: Viking, 1957), p. 59. Cited hereafter as *Reader*.

5. E.g., Mario Praz, *The Romantic Agony* (London: Oxford, 1933). But often romanticism in the arts serves at least as the paradigm of analysis, even when a more general view is intended. For example, René Wellek, " 'The Concept of Romanticism' in Literary History," *Comparative Literature* (1949), reprinted in part in John Halsted, ed., *Romanticism* (Lexington, Mass.: Heath, 1965), pp. 45–52. Art historians typically define or reject definitions of romanticism on the basis of exclusively historical artistic evidence, paying some attention perhaps to literature, but rarely to ideology as such. A notable exception, important mainly for its excesses, is Sir Herbert Read's damnation of classicism as fascism in *Surrealism* (New York: Praeger, 1972). A good general collection of original works is Eugen Weber, *Paths to the Present* (New York: Harper & Row, 1960).

6. A. O. Lovejoy, "On the Discrimination of Romanticisms," in *Essays in the History of Ideas* (Baltimore: Johns Hopkins University Press, 1948), pp. 228 ff. See also the rebuttal by Wellek, " 'The Concept of Romanticism.' "

7. The phrase is from Hermann Hesse, *Steppenwolf*, trans. Joseph Mileck (New York: Holt, Rinehart and Winston, 1955).

8. The role of violence in romanticism is worth a book, particularly regarding the romantic middle-class terrorists of today. In nineteenth-century romanticism, however, violence was remarkably contained, and far more like the shouting matches of the Enlightenment than the bomb-throwing anarchism that would later become its offspring. See P. Viereck, *Metapolitics: From the Romantics to Hitler* (New York: Capricorn, 1961); also H. S. Reiss, ed., *Political Thought of the German Romantics, 1793–1815* (Oxford: Blackwell, 1955).

9. See Chapter 1, pp. 21–22. See also Lester Crocker, *Age of Crisis* (Baltimore: Johns Hopkins University Press, 1959), and *Nature and Culture* (Baltimore: Johns Hopkins University Press, 1963).

10. See Chapter 1, pp. 24–26. The case of Newton, above all, refutes the glib equation of Enlightenment materialism and atheism. But see also M. H. Abrams, *Natural Supernaturalism* (New York: Norton, 1973).

11. See E. Bentley, *A Century of Hero Worship* (New York: Lippincott, 1944).

12. Again, these same charges were often leveled against the Enlightenment philosophers, too. But forced passions and historionics always tend to be overdisplayed, as if to prove the point, so the romantics inevitably emerged with that display of self-indulgence that has so often been criticized by sympathizers like Heinrich Heine, as well as severe critics like Babbitt and Hauser, and at the time even Goethe.

13. See A. O. Lovejoy, "The Meaning of 'Romantic' in Early German Romanticism," in *Essays in the History of Ideas*, pp. 183 ff.

14. From *Racine and Shakespeare*, reprinted in *Reader*, p. 59.
15. *Fragments*, reprinted in *Reader*, p. 51.
16. "Preface to *Cromwell*," reprinted in *Reader,* p. 63.
17. Herbert Read, *Surrealism* (New York: Praeger, 1971).
18. "Preface to *Cromwell*," in *Reader*, p. 63.
19. *Rousseau and Romanticism* (Boston: Houghton-Mifflin, 1919).
20. *A Social History of Art*, Vol. III (New York: Vintage, 1951).
21. This insistence also turns against those who defend the romantics, as for example Jacques Barzun in *Romanticism and the Modern Ego* (Boston: Little, Brown, 1943): "In the Romantic period, this problem was to create a new world on the ruins of the old." To make romanticism intrinsically revolutionary and constructive is to miss the crisis of the spirit that was its motivation.
22. Cf. Heine in *Germany:* "Had you been acquainted in 1830 with the German philosophy of nature, you could not have produced the revolution of July [1830, in France]. . . . Perverse philosophical ideas would have dampened your enthusiasm, would have paralyzed your courage." But see Hans Kohn, *The Idea of Nationalism* (New York: Macmillan, 1946).
23. See Chapter 13, pp. 267–71, and Canaday's brief account in *Mainstreams of Modern Art* (New York: Holt, Rinehart and Winston, 1959). Also Walter Friedlander, *David to Delacroix* (Cambridge, Mass.: Harvard University Press, 1952), and Marcel Brion, *Art in the Romantic Era* (New York: Praeger, 1950).
24. On Kleist see Walter Silz, *Early German Romanticism* (Cambridge, Mass.: Harvard University Press, 1929), and D. Hentschel, *The Byronic Teuton* (London: Methuen, 1940).
25. See Sigmund Freud, *Civilization and Its Discontents,* trans. J. Strachey (New York: Norton, 1962). For a less sensible view, see Babbitt, *Rousseau and Romanticism.*
26. See my *Passions* (New York: Doubleday-Anchor, 1976), Chapter 6; also Crocker, *Man and Nature.*
27. Lovejoy, "On the Discrimination of Romanticisms," in *Essays in the History of Ideas,* pp. 228 ff.
28. Kant's own view of Rousseau almost wholly neglected the psychological aspects of sentimentality and focused wholly on the "rational" aspects of Rousseau's conception of "inner virtue." If this is an inaccurate representation of Rousseau, it is not more so than the romantic depiction of him as the enemy of reason and the champion of pure passion. See Ernst Cassirer, *Rousseau, Kant, and Goethe* (New York: Harper & Row, 1970).
29. Curiously, the one French philosopher of note during this entire period was Auguste Comte, the first positivist and a sworn enemy of the ideals of the romantic age.
30. English romanticism requires a wholly different treatment, even if some of the sources might remain the same. In England, even more than in France and Germany, the romantic movement is demonstrably continuous with the Enlightenment, its basic motivation similar, but the circumstances of its appearance sufficiently different so that simple generalizations should be avoided. See H. A. Beer, *History of English Romanticism in the Eighteenth Century* (New York: Holt, 1948), and Crane Brinton, *The Political Ideas of the English Romanticists* (Oxford: Milford, 1926). Also F. W. Stokoe, *German Influence on the English Romantic Movement* (Cambridge: Cambridge University Press, 1926).

31. "I hereby declare that I regard Fichte's *Theory of Science* as a totally indefensible system. . . . I am so opposed to metaphysics, as defined according to Fichtean principles, that I have advised him, in a letter, to turn his fine literary gifts to the problem of applying the *Critique of Pure Reason* rather than squandering them in cultivating fruitless sophistries. . . . There is an Italian proverb: May God protect us from our friends, and we shall watch out for our enemies ourselves." Quoted from A. Zweig, ed., *Kant's Philosophical Correspondence* (Chicago: University of Chicago Press, 1967), published August 7, 1799.

32. Fichte, *Wissenschaftlehre (Science of Knowledge)*, trans. Peter Heath and John Lachs (New York: Appleton-Century-Crofts, 1970).

33. Herder and Heine were both champions of Shakespeare. Herder used him as a conscientiously vulgar foil against French classicism, which represented the Enlightenment of Frederick the Great. Heine used him as a foil against Goethe and the sentimental poetry of the German Storm and Sress movement, as well as against the stale classicism of the 1790s.

34. On Schleiermacher, see R. Brandt, *The Philosophy of Schleiermacher* (Westport, Conn.: Greenwood, 1968).

35. Letter to Hegel, November 2, 1807, reprinted in Walter Kaufmann, *Hegel* (New York: Doubleday, 1965), p. 321.

36. See Richard Kroner's introduction to Hegel's *Early Theological Writings* (Philadelphia: University of Pennsylvania Press, 1971).

37. In *Reader*, p. 57. Yet for all of his talk about "political realism" and "liberation," Hugo stayed in bed with a friend for the duration of the Revolution of 1830.

38. See Viereck, *Metapolitics*.

39. Benedetto Croce, *History of Europe in the Nineteenth Century*, trans. Furst (London: Allen & Unwin, 1934).

40. See J. J. Saunders, *The Age of Revolution* (New York: Hoyt, 1949).

15. *From Poetry to Revolution: The Young Marx*

1. In *Karl Marx: Early Writings*, ed. Lucio Coletti (London: Penguin, 1974), p. 281. Cited hereafter as Coletti.

2. Karl Marx and Friedrich Engels, *Collected Works* (New York: International Publishers, 1976), I, 586. Cited hereafter as *Works*.

3. *Works*, I, 585. Reprinted and discussed in S. Prawer, *Karl Marx and World Literature* (Oxford: Oxford University Press, 1976), pp. 10 f.

4. See the letter to Ruge in Coletti, p. 281.

5. See Prawer, p. 15. For an excellent account of Marx's early enthusiasm, see David McClellan, *Karl Marx: His Life and Thought* (New York: Harper & Row, 1973), pp. 1–61.

6. Schiller, *Letters on the Aesthetic Education of Man* (Oxford: Oxford University Press, 1977), Letter XI.

7. David McClellan, *The Thought of Karl Marx* (New York: Harper & Row, 1971). Marx says this in *German Ideology* as well as in his early works. It has been recently repeated by Herbert Marcuse in *Reason and Revolution* (Boston: Beacon, 1960).

8. McClellan, *The Thought of Karl Marx;* McClellan, *Karl Marx*.

9. Berlin, March 1841. *Works*, I, 262–63, quoted in Prawer, p. 34.

10. McClellan, *Karl Marx*. Also Marcuse, *Reason and Revolution*.

11. *Works*, I, 206; *Early Writings*, trans. T. Bottomore (New York: McGraw-Hill, 1964), p. 64.

12. See Shlomo Avineri, *The Social and Political Thought of Karl Marx* (Cambridge: Cambridge University Press, 1970). Also Robert Tucker, *Philosophy and Myth in Karl Marx* (Cambridge: Cambridge University Press, 1972). And see Marx's own attack on Feuerbach's "contemplative materialism" in *Theses on Feuerbach*.

13. This image was used by Hegel. Feuerbach inverted it in *Groundwork for a Philosophy of the Future*, 1843, and later Marx used it in *German Ideology*.

14. Quoted in Harald Hoffding, *History of Modern Philosophy*, trans. B. E. Meyer (New York: Humanities Press, 1950), II, 281.

15. This term, which Marx and his followers used abusively against their opponents, has ironically been turned against them in this century. See Introduction, p. 7.

16. See Avineri, *The Social and Political Thought of Karl Marx*, p. 183; and Tucker, *Philosophy and Myth in Karl Marx*, pp. 218 ff.

17. Coletti, p. 207.

18. *Contribution to the Critique of Hegel's Doctrine of the State*. In Coletti, p. 251. Cited hereafter as *Contribution*.

19. *Theses on Feuerbach*, in Coletti, p. 423.

20. Bottomore, p. 52. "Root" is another of Marx's puns: *radix,* which gives the adjective *radicus,* is Latin for "root."

21. See McClellan, *Karl Marx*, pp. 67–75, and Avineri, pp. 31 f.

22. *Contribution*, in Coletti, pp. 57–198, based on that part of Hegel's *Philosophy of Right*, trans. Sir Malcolm Knox (Oxford: Oxford University Press, 1967), entitled "The State" (paras. 261–313).

23. Coletti, p. 84, referring to Hegel, para. 279.

24. Coletti, p. 101, referring to Hegel, para. 289; Coletti, pp. 66 ff.

25. Coletti, p. 88. Cf. p. 152 (Schelling) and p. 302 (Fichte).

26. McClellan, *Karl Marx*, especially on Marx in Brussels and Cologne, pp. 137 ff. and 189 ff.

27. When Marx was forced to leave Paris in 1845, pressured by the Prussian government, he would claim that it was Heine he would "miss the most."

28. It was Engels, never Marx, who developed the unintelligible philosophy of "dialectical materialism." In Marx as in Hegel, dialectic is a product of human activity, not just a part of nature.

29. One such book is E. Mandel, *The Formation of Marx's Economic Thought* (London, 1971).

30. Quoted by Marx in Coletti, p. 342.

31. Coletti, p. 369. The italics are Marx's.

32. See Robert Heilbroner, *The Worldly Philosophers* (New York: Simon and Schuster, 1972), pp. 38–67.

33. Bottomore, p. 98. Marx is paraphrasing Chapter 26 in Ricardo's *On the Principles of Political Economy and Taxation* (New York: Dutton, 1933).

34. Bottomore, p. 58.

35. We are leaving aside the sophistry that all *classes,* as opposed to individuals, are *ipso facto* abstractions—an ontological issue that we certainly need not touch here. See Chapter 11, p. 221.

36. Marx rejects what he calls "crude" communism, which depends on the *envy* of the workers. Envy is not an emotion of emancipation but an ex-

pression of the same sickness and greed of which they are but the most obvious victims. Hence, the familiar slogan, "No one is free until everyone is free."

37. Coletti, p. 255. In France in 1844, even the King was bourgeois: Louis-Philippe, who had been installed by the Revolution of 1830. In Germany the oppressive—but, vis à vis the King, powerless—bureaucracy, so glorified by Hegel, was a primary source of day-to-day irritation and an instrument of the new industrialists.

38. Consider Marx's notes on the Silesian weaver's rebellion (Coletti, pp. 401 ff.), in which he argues that this small workers' protest is the first fully theoretically conscious proletarian uprising, more advanced even than any so far in England or France. See Coletti, p. 451.

39. "No one ever died on the barricades for a few more dollars of credit," says one commentator (Munro).

40. The origin of the word is unclear. See Raymond Williams, *Keywords* (Oxford: Oxford University Press, 1976), and Avineri, *Social and Political Thought of Karl Marx*, pp. 41 f.

41. The dangerous flirtation here with the vengeance principles of "crude" communism is an endemic temptation of the whole argument, undercutting, whenever it appears, the "universal class" argument.

42. Cf. Jefferson, Adams, and others, as discussed in Hannah Arendt, *On Revolution* (New York: Viking, 1965). Voltaire talked of "the rabble," and even Rousseau was far more interested in "moral corruption" than physical needs.

43. *Works*, III, 33.

44. Three different words—*Entfremdung, Entäusserung, Veräusserung*—all translate as "alienation" or "estrangement."

45. See Max Weber's classic, *The Protestant Ethic and the Spirit of Capitalism* (New York: Scribners, 1930).

46. The Marxist catechism distinguishes four forms of alienation:
   (a) alienation from the product of one's activity, which belongs to another;
   (b) alienation from the product of the activity itself;
   (c) alienation from self;
   (d) alienation from other men (Coletti, pp. 429–30).

47. Quoted in McClellan, *The Thought of Karl Marx*, p. 83.

48. Quoted in McClellan, *The Thought of Karl Marx*, p. 84.

49. *Communist Manifesto* (New York: International Publishers, 1970), p. 11.

16. *The Singular Universal: Søren Kierkegaard*

1. I have taken this title directly from Jean-Paul Sartre's essay on Kierkegaard.

2. Trans. D. Swenson and W. Lowrie (Princeton: Princeton University Press, 1944), p. 33. Cited hereafter as *Postscript*. Kierkegaard wrote the work under the pseudonym "Johannes Climacus."

3. Trans. W. Lowrie (New York: Harper, 1940), p. 50.

4. "In order that everything should be reduced to the same level, it is first necessary to procure a phantom, its spirit, a monstrous abstraction, an all-embracing something that is nothing, a mirage—and that phantom is

the public. It is only in an age which is without passion, yet reflective, that such a phantom can develop itself" (*The Present Age,* p. 59). Note the equation between passion and individuality, an important ingredient in Kierkegaard's rejection of "reason."

5. *Journals* (1834–54), trans. and ed. A. Dru (London: Oxford University Press, 1938).

6. See W. Lowrie, *A Short Life of Kierkegaard* (Princeton: Princeton University Press, 1942), and J. Thompson, *The Lonely Labyrinth* (Carbondale, Ill.: University of Southern Illinois Press, 1967). In this regard, Kierkegaard's own *Journal* entries of 1834–35 are revealing and touching, if pathetic (e.g., p. 71).

7. His tactless polemics against the Church and its ministers (particularly his less than tasteful attack on a powerful bishop just after his death), and his attacks on the press—particularly his criticism of the sensationalist *Corsair,* which retaliated by making him a cartoonist's delight and joke throughout Copenhagen—combined to make him a public spectacle who could not even walk along the street without being abused by children and smirked at by the public he scorned.

8. An excellent account of Kierkegaard's life and the dramatic contrast between his inward passion and outward banality is Thompson's *Lonely Labyrinth.* The most sensitive treatment of Kierkegaard's philosophy, with reference to both his life and his method, is Louis Mackey, *Kierkegaard: A Kind of Poet* (Philadelphia: University of Pennsylvania Press, 1972).

9. Kierkegaard, *Either/Or,* 2 vols., trans. David Swenson, Walter Lowrie, and Howard Johnston (Princeton: Princeton University Press, 1959). Kierkegaard "edited" it under the pseudonym "Victor Eremita." Vol. 2 is Kierkegaard's defense of marriage, in the form of letters from a pastor to a young libertine.

10. The concept of "subjective truth" is a central philosophical problem in Kierkegaard's writings—and a polemical and paradoxical phrase. I have tried to analyze it in *From Rationalism to Existentialism* (Atlantic Highlands, N.J.: Humanities Press, 1972), and "Kierkegaard and 'Subjective Truth,' " in *Philosophy Today* (1977). See also Mackey, *Kierkegaard.*

11. Woody Allen refers to himself as "anhedonic" in this regard, and not incidentally once named an imaginary rock music group "The Concluding Unscientific Postscript."

12. This tradition, including Kierkegaard, is sympathetically presented by Malcolm Muggeridge in his recent "The Third Testament," a BBC television presentation in six parts, published under the same title (Boston: Little, Brown, 1976).

13. See especially Mackey; also H. Diem, *Kierkegaard's Dialectic of Existence* (Edinburgh: University of Edinburgh Press, 1959), and J. Collins, *The Mind of Kierkegaard* (Chicago: Gateway, 1953).

14. This theme had occupied the romantics before him and would preoccupy the existentialists who followed him, e.g., Stendhal's Julien (*The Red and the Black*) and Fabrizio (*The Charterhouse of Parma*), Sartre's short story "The Wall," large segments of his *Being and Nothingness,* and Camus's *The Stranger.*

15. *Papirer,* XI, A 12, quoted in A. MacIntyre, "Kierkegaard," in P. Edwards, ed., *The Encyclopedia of Philosophy* (New York: Macmillan, 1967).

16. See Chapter 11, p. 243. Kierkegaard's main attack is in *Concluding Unscientific Postscript.*

17. *Philosophical Fragments,* trans. D. Swenson and H. Hong (Princeton: Princeton University Press, 1962), p. 46. Published under the pseudonym "Johannes Climacus."

18. *Sickness unto Death,* trans. W. Lowrie (New York: Oxford University Press, 1954), p. 197. Published under the pseudonym "Anticlimacus."

19. *Attack upon Christendom,* trans. W. Lowrie (Princeton: Princeton University Press, 1946), sect. III.

20. *Either/Or,* Vol. I, contains both a long discussion of Mozart's opera *Don Giovanni* and its leading character, and a "Diary of a Seducer" (pp. 297–440) which, fictional or not, is as revealing of Kierkegaard's naiveté about the world as it is demonstrative of his keen psychological insights.

21. The emphasis on "immediacy" loads the argument heavily against the aesthetic sphere, particularly since Kierkegaard characterizes "the immediate" in such terms that it is logically impossible. But Don Juan, it can be argued, is not concerned with "the immediate" in this sense at all, but to the contrary lives as he does just because he knows the power of delayed gratification and challenge.

22. The role of the artist forces Kierkegaard to modify his strict characterization of the aesthetic life as "immediacy," but as he does so, many of his arguments against this life style are seriously weakened.

23. *Fear and Trembling,* trans. Walter Lowrie (New York: Oxford University Press, 1954), p. 64. Published under the pseudonym "Johannes de Silentio."

24. Kierkegaard's attitude toward the ethical life varies considerably, however. This conclusion is not at all evident in *Either/Or,* Vol. II, for there as elsewhere Kierkegaard tends to merge the ethical with the religious, and to characterize what would seem to be an ethical commitment in quasi-religious terms. It makes all the difference in the world, for example, whether marriage is characterized as a holy sacrament and a duty to God, or a strictly human contractual agreement and interpersonal obligation. Kierkegaard, it can be argued, never allows himself to appreciate the force of this distinction.

25. Again, one may suspect a degree of rationalization. But what Kierkegaard was arguing is what many people in the wake of the "sexual revolution" of the 1960s are starting to accept: that marriage is much more than a "relationship"; it is an institutional, legal, and moral bond at least, perhaps a religious bond as well, beyond not only the realm of personal desire and satisfaction, but mere "mutual" agreement as well. In fact, the general withdrawal and excessive legalism of the 1970s can be compared on many accounts with Kierkegaard's own reactions against the Reaction and the empty revolutions of the early nineteenth century.

26. I have discussed this at length in *From Rationalism to Existentialism,* Chapter 3.

27. One should also note, however, the arrogance of the religious life: the concept of "salvation," the absolute sense of self-righteousness that prevails in spite of—or because of—the emphasis on self-demeaning humility and the elevation of one's *Self* ("the individual") above the lot of humanity and into a "higher" realm. Once again, a bourgeois rejection or bourgeois arrogance and self-righteousness turns out to be founded on even more arrogance and self-righteousness. But in Kierkegaard's case it is an arrogance that has its ideological roots in the Middle Ages as well as—in its individualism—in the Enlightenment.

28. Friedrich Nietzsche—who never had the opportunity to read Kierkegaard—

continues this existentialist tradition of individualism and passionate revolt even in vigorous opposition to Kierkegaard's religious piety. Nietzsche
himself was a good bourgeois gentleman—see for example the description
by Lou Andreas Salomé reprinted in my *Nietzsche* (New York: Doubleday-
Anchor, 1973)—but also perhaps the harshest single critic the bourgeoisie
ever had, Marx and Marxists included.

29. "Presupposing its successes" is essential. As in the ideology of so many in-
dividualists—existentialists, libertarians, and anarchists—a certain stability
of society and faith in "human nature" is utterly indispensable, which
once again is a certain sign of bourgeois presuppositions. This is not
necessarily to dismiss such views, but it does require that they give up what
is often taken as their first premise—the primordial status of the "individual." It can be said that Kierkegaard—and bourgeois ideology in general
—not so much defend or discover as create "the individual."

30. *Phenomenology*, Preface, p. 131, quoted on p. 223, Chapter 11.

Index

Death of Lepeletier, The (David), 195
Death of Marat, The (David), 195, 209
Death of Sardanapalus (Delacroix), 271, 282–84
Death of Socrates (David), 191, 195
Declaration of Independence, American, 43, 95
Declaration of the Rights of Man and Citizen, 36, 92, 95–96
Deism, 50–51, 53, 79
Delacroix, Victor Eugène, 203, 209, 267–89, 293, 296, 308, 351. *See also titles of paintings*
Journals, 274, 279, 285
De Launay, Charles, 82, 94
Democracy, 28, 322, 325
Derrida, Jacques, 359
Descartes, René, 12, 15, 31, 43, 52, 115, 211
Discourse on Method, 25, 42
Meditations, 24–25
Voltaire on, 40–41
Determinism, 133
Dialectic, 17–19, 285
Beethoven and, 249, 264
Hegel and, 238–39, 244–45, 250, 322
Marx and, 316, 322, 326
Dialogues on Natural Religion (Hume), 75
Dickens, Charles, 87, 106
Diderot, Denis, 6, 30, 54, 59, 182, 183, 187, 188, 254
Encyclopédie, 26, 49, 66
new morality and, 21–22
Tahitian dialogues, 21–22, 29
Die Rheinische Zeitung, 318–19, 322
Dignity, 14, 15, 222
Dilthey, Wilhelm, 357
Disasters of War (Goya), 202
Discourse on Method (Descartes), 25, 42
Disharmony. *See* Alienation
Distribution of Eagles, The (David), 198
"Divine right of kings," 27, 28, 45, 46
Dworkin, Ronald, 359

Education of Mankind (Lessing), 147
Education through Art (Read), 182
Either/Or (Kierkegaard), 345, 346, 347, 351, 354
Elements of Political Economy (Mill), 329–30
Eliot, T. S., 140
Emile (Rousseau), 54–55, 62, 64–65, 66, 67, 71, 75, 147, 222, 302
Empiricism, 12, 40, 42, 52, 115, 118
Hume and, 75–78, 119
Voltaire and, 40, 41
Encyclopedia of the Philosophical Sciences (Hegel), 220

Encyclopédie (Diderot), 26, 49, 66
Engels, Friedrich, xii, 326, 327, 330, 336–37, 343
Communist Manifesto, The, 337–38
English Letters (Voltaire), 35, 37–41, 49, 75
Enlightenment, the, xvi, 6, 11–14, 16–18, 19, 24, 55, 78, 117, 141, 221, 351. *See also names of Enlightenment philosophers*
art and, 183–204 *passim*
classicism and. *See* Classicism and neoclassicism
dark side of, 33–34, 185
end of, in France, 109
in France, and rise of bourgeoisie, 20–34, 35, 253
French Revolution and ideology of, 66, 70, 84, 88–89, 92, 95–108 *passim*
in Germany, 110–36, 150, 152, 157, 186, 222–23
Goethe and, 137, 157
humanism of, 28–30, 31, 224
inconsistencies in ideology of, 33–34, 55, 73, 88, 97
music and, 248–66 *passim*
Napoleon and, 160, 161, 162, 164, 167, 168–69, 176
optimism and, 32–33, 55
progress and, 32, 55
reason and. *See* Reason
as revolution in print, 25–26
romanticism and. *See* Romanticism
Enquiry Concerning Human Understanding (Hume), 75–78, 205
Enquiry Concerning Human Morals, An (Hume), 73
"Essay on James Mill" (Marx), 334
Essence of Christianity, The (Feuerbach), 316–17
Executions of the Third of May, The (Goya), 202
Existentialism, 83, 290, 339–56
Experience, 12, 15, 120, 123, 127

Faith, Kant and, 118
Family, 15–16, 17, 60, 63, 240
Fascism, 67, 277
Faust (Goethe), 138, 140, 142, 146, 149–50, 154–59, 183, 210, 211–17 *passim*, 218, 256, 290, 346
"Feelings" (Marx), 311
Ferdinand VII, 177, 201, 203
Feudalism, 95, 192
Feuerbach, Paul von, 133, 316–19, 320, 321, 334, 336
Essence of Christianity, The, 316–17
Fichte, Johann Gottlieb, 3, 133, 293, 346
Critique of All Revelation, A, 232